C000111613

# Vermont

**A guide to the Green Mountain state**

Unknown

# Alpha Editions

This edition published in 2020

ISBN : 9789354013485

Design and Setting By
**Alpha Editions**
email - alphaedis@gmail.com

As per information held with us this book is in Public Domain.
This book is a reproduction of an important historical work. Alpha Editions
uses the best technology to reproduce historical work in the same manner
it was first published to preserve its original nature. Any marks or number
seen are left intentionally to preserve its true form.

# VERMONT

A GUIDE TO THE GREEN MOUNTAIN STATE

# WORKS PROGRESS ADMINISTRATION

### WALKER-JOHNSON BUILDING
### 1734 NEW YORK AVENUE NW.
### WASHINGTON, D. C.

**HARRY L. HOPKINS**
ADMINISTRATOR

Vermont: A Guide to the Green Mountain State is, in order of publication, the second volume in the New England group of the American Guide Series, written by members of the Federal Writers' Project of the Works Progress Administration. Though the project was originally designed to give useful employment to needy writers and research workers it has gradually developed the more ambitious objective of utilizing the talent among the unemployed writers to create and present a comprehensive portrait of America. Since such a task has never been undertaken before it was necessary to design new methods as well as to prepare new tools. The result is a collective work to which all the writers and research workers contributed according to their talents, and the final collation of facts and the rewriting and editing of the material was done by a few experienced authors and editors in central offices. This book, therefore, represents a blend of the work of the entire personnel, aided by consultants who have volunteered their services most generously.

Though compiled as an independent unit "Vermont: A Guide to the Green Mountain State" gains in significance when recognized as part of a series of fifty-five volumes that, when completed, will cover the entire United States, Alaska, and Puerto Rico.

In addition to this large integrated set of guides many books of historical or interpretative nature are being written by the Federal Writers' Project. As they appear in increasing numbers, the American public, we hope, will come to appreciate more fully not only the unusual scope of this undertaking, but also the excellence aimed at in this work. The Federal Writers' Project, directed by Henry G. Alsberg, is in the Division of Women's and Professional Projects under Ellen S. Woodward, Assistant Administrator.

Harry L. Hopkins
Administrator

# PREFACE

THE first Community Church in America was built a century and a quarter ago in a small Vermont village. The fact has gone little-noted by commentators zealous to preserve the over-simplified concept of Vermont as the epitome of individualism. Yet it was no historical inadvertence, for surely the Green Mountain Boys themselves attest co-operation to be one of the valid and basic traditions of the State. A co-operative book, therefore, on Vermont by Vermonters, no more offends propriety than a co-operative creamery, or the house-raising of earlier days, or any other community enterprise. New Englanders have always had to work together. And if writers are to be induced to work together (that slightly staggering postulate upon which the American Guide series of publications is based), New England writers might be expected to bring it off with somewhat less than the normal anguish. It is not, then, so unusual that Vermont should be represented fairly early in the list of State guide-books created by the Federal Writers' Project of the Works Progress Administration. Perhaps that skepticism, ostensibly joyless but actually one of the few secret delights of the Puritan soul, which one finds so common north of Boston, was a help. No Vermont farmer will admit until after the hay is in the barn that he really expects a catch in any given season. No Vermonter is old enough to remember a season when crops really *did* fail.

This is a new kind of book. It was written in a new way. Time will judge the quality of both innovations, but each at least adds a little to the immemorially tenuous excuse for a Preface. Under the circumstances something may usefully be said here as to what the volume aims at and how it was put together.

The newness of the book consists primarily of its tours. Twenty-five hundred miles of road, paralleling and crossing and curling around the countless ridges of the Green Mountains, have been described, in a way which, it is hoped, will not merely facilitate but also suggest and stimulate travel. The statistical staunchness of the indispensable old bluebook (with its junctions at helpful red barns, just 1.3 miles from its essential watering-troughs) has been retained to the fullest feasible extent. But further than this there has been an effort to interweave the background of a State — the scenery, the history, the society and the culture of Vermont — so that the visitor may become conscious of our landscape in a genuine, a three-dimensional fashion.

Yet even the most ardent advocate of decimal mileages will acknowledge the need for a wider orientation, if one is to make progress toward understanding a region. We have, therefore, opened the book with a series of brief introductory essays, calculated not to provide definitive studies of agriculture, ethnology, industry, architecture, or meteorology, but aimed rather at giving the reader a succinct yet adequate outline of the society and the corner of the earth which he will find more specifically commented upon as he pursues the tours.

To avoid interrupting the continuity of the tour descriptions, we have lifted out the portions dealing with the larger towns and given them an independent section in the volume. There is a selective bibliography for those who may wish to dig a little deeper beneath the surface; there are maps for the cartographically minded who enjoy the surface for its own sake.

None of this is individual procedure; it is laid out according to the standard plan for all State guide-books in the American Guide Series. Standard likewise have been the organization and carrying out of the work.

Nobody in his senses would attempt to explain how writers work. But some light can be thrown upon the way in which the material for this volume was assembled so that it could be worked upon. A score or more of research workers scattered throughout the State were engaged for over a year in gathering data and in forwarding it to Montpelier. A handful of editors in the central office sifted and checked and revised this accumulation. A still smaller group took the results in hand and in mind and went out on the road, covering every foot of the tours (in some cases driving over sections three or four times), and returned to piece together the mosaic of the tour descriptions. A great amount of independent research by the editors was, of course, also required before any final copy could be produced. And the contributions of voluntary assistants and consultants (of which, fortunately, almost every town furnished generous examples) had to be incorporated. But even then it sounds simpler than it was. It remains only to note the rôle of that parvenu in literary nomenclature, and still slightly anomalous individual — the State Director. A State Director functions as an absorbent of worries and an occasional suggester of similes. His job, being a baffling combination of midwifery and the assembly line, can scarcely be expected to attain the dignity of a profession. He is mentioned only because so many people will ask why he exists.

If a book cannot stand on its own feet, it is certainly not to be justified for its by-products. At the same time, no volume like the present can come into being without a variety of corollary results. And of the many such, I believe two definitely significant. One is the indication, which strengthens with each new publication of the American Guide Series, that writing can be nationally fostered, that literature will ultimately repay, as other arts have for centuries, what governments choose to expend upon it. The other result likewise is to be thought of as applying nationally. It lies in the impact which this work has inevitably made upon the minds of the writers themselves. If great writing must be rooted in the soil, if genuine creation must grow out of the artist's intense identification with his background, is it too optimistic to expect that these forty-eight State books will help to prepare at least a few writers who, in the years to come, can write more deeply of America through knowing their parts of America deeply?

At the risk of redundance (since all this book is Vermont), one word more may be spared about the State itself, about its rôle in the country today. No Vermonter would wish to deny that the State has, from the outset, carried particularism to the verge of intransigence; the motives only are in dispute. Vermont apologists have defended this attitude as the very essence of liberty. Outside observers have considered it as a consistent manifestation of unenlightened perversity.

Both assumptions are misleading. For Vermont's early attitude of defiance resulted from the radicalism of hard-pressed frontiersmen; in recent years ultra-conservatism has distinguished this region from other parts of the country where progressive tendencies have been, for a generation, on the increase. The decade from 1850 to 1860 was a pivotal one here. Then it was that the population curve for a hundred hill towns turned downward. If 'Yankee Doodle' was literally the overture to the exciting era of Vermont history, 'Susannah' was as clearly the recessional. The people, the wealth, the energy that had built the State were from then on either drained westward or gradually hardened into a more restricted pattern. Lacking large cities and the consequent opportunities for successful careers, Vermont has for three generations exported its most promising young people to urban centers outside its borders. The resultant population has an abnormally high proportion of elderly people.

Vermont is to be thought of, then, as that quite natural phenomenon — the young, rash idealist who has been tamed, mellowed, and reconciled with the years. Youth often succeeds through violence to the *status quo,* only to turn in the sequel as ardently to its defense.

In such a new land as America this cycle should not be too readily condemned; it not only suggests a capacity for growth, but provides a situation which can be at once a yardstick and a balance wheel for progress in the country as a whole.

In a volume of this nature it is impossible to acknowledge adequately the total amount of assistance which has been received. Literally hundreds of Vermonters, in every corner of the State, have contributed generously. Scores of volunteer consultants have checked the local copy. The Guide has thus been more truly a cooperative and representative undertaking than any Vermont book in generations. Our appreciation is sincere, though it cannot be individually expressed.

In the same way we must make composite acknowledgment of the sympathetic and valuable aid given by State departments, by Federal agencies, by historical societies, colleges, and libraries, all of whose research facilities have been made available to the project.

We are under personal obligation to those whose connection with the work has been an especially intimate one. Among them are Mr. Charles Crane, of Montpelier; Professor Hugh S. Morrison, of Dartmouth College; Mr. Dorman B. E. Kent, of Montpelier; Mr. Vrest Orton, of Weston; Mr. Harrison J. Conant, State Librarian; Professor Arthur Wallace Peach and Professor K. R. B. Flint, of Norwich University; and Mrs. Mabel W. Mayforth of Barre.

Several of the essays have been in whole or in part contributed by consultants. The essay on agriculture was almost entirely the work of Dr. John A. Hitchcock of the Vermont Experiment Station; the natural setting essay was written by Dr. Robert K. Doten, formerly of the Geology faculty of the Massachusetts Institute of Technology. Mr. Raymond E. Bassett, of Burlington, supplied valuable material for the transportation article, and Miss Elin Anderson, formerly of the Eugenics Survey in Vermont, provided a summary of several years of research for the essay on racial elements. Finally, the share which Mrs. Dorothy Canfield Fisher, of Arlington, has had in the Guide is only partially indicated by her own essay, 'Vermonters.' She has taken an active interest in the work through all its stages, has been a steady friend and perceptive critic. This volume was prepared under the editorial supervision of Joseph Gaer, Editor-in-Chief of the New England Guides and Chief Field Supervisor of the Federal Writers' Project.

DANA DOTEN, *State Director*

# CONTENTS

FOREWORD: Federal Administrator, Works Progress Administration     v

PREFACE: State Director, Federal Writers' Project     vii

HOW TO USE THE GUIDE     xvii

GENERAL INFORMATION     xix

CALENDAR OF EVENTS     xxiii

## I. VERMONT: THE GENERAL BACKGROUND

VERMONTERS: *Dorothy Canfield Fisher*     3

NATURAL SETTING     10

FLORA AND FAUNA     18

HISTORY     21

AGRICULTURE     38

INDUSTRY AND COMMERCE     43

TRANSPORTATION     46

RACIAL ELEMENTS     51

EDUCATION     53

RECREATION     58

ARCHITECTURE     64

LITERATURE     70

## II. MAIN STREET AND VILLAGE GREEN
### (*City and Town Descriptions*)

Barre     77

Bellows Falls     81

Bennington     85

Brattleboro     95

Burlington                                              101
Middlebury                                              111
Montpelier                                              115
Newport                                                 123
Rutland                                                 126
St. Albans                                              133
St. Johnsbury                                           138
Springfield                                             142
Windsor                                                 146
Woodstock                                               151

## III. HIGH ROADS AND LOW ROADS (TOURS)

*(Mile-by-Mile Description of the State's Highways)*

TOUR 1  Massachusetts (Greenfield) to Canada (Sherbrooke).
        US 5                                            159

     1A Brattleboro to Junction with State 11. State 30    186

     1B Enosburg Falls to Jeffersonville. State 108     191

     1C Bloomfield to Junction with US 7. State 105     193

     1D Derby to West Burke. State 105, 5A              200

     1E Canada (Sherbrooke) to Junction with US 5.
        State 114                                       204

     1F Canada (Sherbrooke) to Junction with US 2. State
        114 and 102                                     207

     2  Connecticut River to Junction with US 5. State 11,
        10, 106, 12, 12A, and 12B                       211

     2A Barre to White River Junction. State 14         227

     2B East Barre to Junction with State 14. State 110  235

     2C Barton to Hardwick. State 12                    238

     3  Junction of State 105 and State 100 to Junction with
        US 5. State 100, US 2, State 100B, 107, 103     243

     3A Lowell to East Berkshire. State 58, 118         258

     3B Stowe to St. Albans. State 108, 15, 104         260

3C  Warren to Lake Champlain Bridge (Chimney Point).
     State 17                                                   265

3D  Hancock to East Middlebury.  State 125                      271

4   Canada (Montreal) to Massachusetts (Williamstown).
     US 7                                                       275

4A  Windmill Point (Lake Champlain) to Junction with
     US 7 (near Burlington).  US 2                              302

4B  Vergennes to Fair Haven.  State 30A                        308

4C  Middlebury to Manchester Center.  State 30                 315

4D  Pierce's Corner (Clarendon) to Junction with State
     100.    State 103                                          324

4E  Manchester Center to Chester.  State 11                    328

5   New Hampshire (Lancaster) to Burlington.  US 2             332

5A  West Danville to Winooski.  State 15                       342

5B  Wells River to Montpelier.  US 302                         350

5C  Richmond to Ackworth.  State 116                           354

6   New Hampshire (Lebanon) to New York (White-
     hall).  US 4                                               357

7   New Hampshire (Keene) to New York (Troy).
     State  9                                                   365

CHRONOLOGY                                                      371

BIBLIOGRAPHY                                                    373

INDEX                                                           381

# ILLUSTRATIONS

TO ACCOMPANY THE INTRODUCTORY SECTION  *between* 38 *and* 39

Vermont's Cows  *Highton*  A Civic Center, Dorset  *Highton*
Summer  *Lee*  Filling Silo  *Lee*
Winter  *Lee*  Granite Quarry  *Highton*
Ski Tow  *State Publicity Service*  An Old College Building, Middlebury
Making Maple Syrup  *Highton*
  *Rutland Herald*

TO ACCOMPANY TOURS 1, 1A, 1B, 1C, 1D, 1E, 1F  *between* 82 *and* 83

Windham County Courthouse at  Original Fireplace with Crane, Isaac
  Newfane  *Highton*  Bayley House  *Highton*
Covered Bridge over West River,  Brunswick Mineral Springs  *Derrick*
  near Brattleboro  *Highton*  Old Stone House, Brownington
Sawmill, near Newfane  *Highton*  *Derrick*
Estey Organ Works, Brattleboro  Island Pond  *Richardson*
  *Highton*  Willoughby Lake  *Derrick*
Living Room of the Isaac Bayley  Burke Hollow  *Highton*
  House, Newbury  *Highton*  Averill Lake  *Richardson*
  Lake Memphremagog  *Richardson*

TO ACCOMPANY TOURS 2, 2A, 2B, 2C  *between* 112 *and* 113

Mt. Ascutney  *Richardson*  Granite Quarry, Barre  *Highton*
Hutchinson House (1793), Wood-  State House, Montpelier  *Highton*
  stock  *Highton*  Interior of Old West Church, Calais
Windsor County Homestead Ex-  *Houston*
  ample of 'Continuous Architec-  Woodbury Pond, Woodbury
  ture'  *Lee*  *Chandler*
Brookfield Floating Bridge  Interior of Simpson Memorial Library,
  *Rutland Herald*  East Craftsbury  *Highton*
Covered Bridge, near East Corinth  Craftsbury Common  *Highton*
  *Highton*

TO ACCOMPANY TOURS 3, 3A, 3B, 3C, 3D  *between* 142 *and* 143

Jay Peak  *Richardson*  Meeting House, with Horse Shed, near
Hazens Notch  *Derrick*  Waterbury Center  *Lee*
Asbestos Mine, Belvidere Mountain  Range Road, between Lincoln and
  *Derrick*  Ripton  *Lee*
Power Plant at Fairfax Falls  Seven Gables, between Lincoln and
  *Highton*  Ripton  *Lee*
Looking South from the Chin, Mt.  Buttermilk Falls, Granville Gulf  *Lee*
  Mansfield  *Richardson*  'Potato Hill,' Lincoln  *Lee*
Smuggler's Notch, Mt. Mansfield  Typical Marker where Long Trail
  *Richardson*  Crosses Highway  *Highton*

TO ACCOMPANY TOURS 4, 4A, 4B, 4C          *between* 202 *and* 203

Grand Isle County Scene near
    Starksboro          *Highton*
Champlain Valley near St. Albans
                        *Chandler*
Town Hall Originally Built as a
    Church              *Highton*
View from Battery Park, Burling-
    ton                 *Highton*
Grassemount, University of Ver-
    mont Dormitory, Burlington
                        *Stevens*

Otter Creek                   *Lee*
Stump Fence, near Vergennes
                        *Highton*
Harvest Time in Addison County
                            *Lee*
First Congregational Church, Middle-
    bury                *Highton*
Old College Row, Middlebury   *Lee*
Lake Dunmore                  *Lee*
Vermont's Deepest Marble Quarry,
    near Pittsford
                *Vermont Marble Company*

TO ACCOMPANY TOURS 4, 4C, 4D, 4E          *between* 248 *and* 249

Proctor Marble Sheds
        *Vermont Marble Company*
Village Street, Pawlet  *Highton*
The Old Stone Shop, Wallingford
                        *Highton*
Hoyt House, Manchester  *Highton*
Gardens in Dorset       *Highton*
County Store, Dorset    *Highton*

St. James' Church and Cemetery,
    Arlington           *Highton*
Congregational Church, Old Benning-
    ton                 *Highton*
Bennington College, North Benning-
    ton                 *Highton*
Bennington Battle Monument, Old
    Bennington          *Highton*

TO ACCOMPANY TOURS 5, 5A, 5B, 5C          *between* 292 *and* 293

Modern Sap Lines, St. Johnsbury
                *Rutland Herald*
Plowing — Caledonia County
                        *Highton*
State House Portico, Montpelier
                        *Highton*
Camel's Hump (Lion Couchant),
    from Bolton Gorge        *Lee*
Autumn in Smuggler's Notch
                    *Richardson*
Lamoille River, near Johnson
                    *Richardson*

Old Stone House in the Shadow of
    Mt. Mansfield, near Underhill
                        *Chandler*
Hanksville, South of Huntington *Lee*
Winooski Valley and Camel's Hump,
    from French Hill    *Chandler*
Dairy Region, Chittenden County
                        *Highton*
Unitarian Church, Burlington
                        *Highton*

TO ACCOMPANY TOURS 6 AND 7          *between* 338 *and* 339

Quechee Gorge          *Coleman*
Marble, West Rutland    *Highton*
Pulpit in Federated Church, Castle-
    ton                 *Chandler*
Turkey Farm, Rutland County
                *Rutland Herald*
Historic Hayes Tavern, West Brat-
    tleboro             *Highton*

View North from Molly Stark Trail,
    near Marlboro       *Highton*
Highest Church in Vermont, Wood-
    ford                *Highton*
Spring Orchard along Molly Stark
    Trail, near Woodford    *Highton*
Parson Dewey House (1763), Old
    Bennington          *Highton*

LARGE MAP OF VERMONT                              Back Pocket
Reverse side: Recreation Map          Winter Sports Map

# HOW TO USE THE GUIDE

*General Information on the State* contains practical information for the State as a whole; the introduction to each city and tour description also contains specific information of a practical sort.

The *Essay Section* of the Guide is designed to give a reasonably comprehensive survey of the State's natural setting, history, and social, economic, and cultural development. Limitations of space forbid elaborately detailed treatments of these subjects, but a classified bibliography is included in the book. A great many persons, places, events, etc., mentioned in the essays are treated at some length in the city and tour descriptions; these are found by reference to the index. The 'Vermont Guide' is not only a practical travel book; it will also serve as a valuable reference work.

The Guide is built on a framework of Tour Descriptions, written, with a few exceptions, to follow the principal highways from south to north or from east to west. This orientation will not, of course, always coincide with the direction in which the tourist travels through the State. Since most visitors plan their trips as loop tours, it is clearly impossible to accommodate a standard pattern to individual desires, and, for the sake of uniformity, some more or less arbitrary procedure must be adopted. The descriptions are, however, written and printed in such a style that they may be followed in the reverse direction. In many cases the highway descriptions are useful to travelers on railroads. Whenever railroads parallel the described highway the fact is stated in the tour heading.

As a matter of convenience, lengthy *Descriptions of Cities and Towns* are removed from the tour sections of the book and separately grouped in alphabetical order.

Each tour description contains cross-references to other tours crossing or branching from the route described; it also contains cross-references to all descriptions of cities and towns removed from the tour descriptions.

Readers can find the descriptions of important routes by examining the tour index or the tour key map. As far as possible, each tour description follows a single main route; descriptions of minor routes branching from, or crossing, the main routes are in smaller type. The long route descriptions are divided into sections at important junctions.

Cumulative mileage is used on main and side tours, the mileage being counted from the beginning of each section or, on side tours, from the junction with the main route. The mileage notations are at best relative, since totals depend to some extent on the manner in which cars are driven — whether they cut around other cars, round curves on the inside or outside of the road, and so forth. Then, too, the totals will in the future vary from those in this book because of road-building in which curves will be eliminated and routes will be carried around cities and villages formerly on the routes.

Inter-State routes are described from and to the State Lines; in the *Index to Tours* and in the tour headings the names of the nearest out-of-State cities of importance on the routes are listed in parentheses to enable travelers readily to identify the routes.

Descriptions of points of interest in the larger towns and cities are numbered and arranged in the order in which they can conveniently be visited.

Points of interest in cities, towns, and villages have been indexed separately rather than under the names of such communities, because many persons know the name of a point of interest, but are doubtful as to the name of the community in which it is situated.

# GENERAL INFORMATION

(State map, showing highways, topography, recreational areas, and points of interest, in pocket, inside of back cover. See List of Illustrations for Key Map to Tours, and Transportation Map, showing airlines, railroads, and bus lines.)

*Railroads:* Central Vermont Ry. (CVR), Rutland R.R. (RR), Boston & Maine R.R. (B&M), Canadian Pacific R.R. (CPR), Delaware and Hudson R.R. (D&H), Maine Central R.R. (MCR), Canadian National Grand Trunk R.R. (CNGT), St. Johnsbury & Lake Champlain Ry. (St. J&LC), Montpelier & Wells River R.R. (M&WR), West River R.R. (WRR), Hoosac Tunnel & Wilmington R.R. (HT&W). On account of the State's topography most of the railroads run north to south; rail connections east to west are scanty and poor. St.J&LC and M&WR are primarily freight lines. CVR is a subsidiary of Canadian National. (*See Transportation Map.*)

*Highways:* Two Federal highways run north and south (US 5, US 7), and two Federal highways run east to west (US 2, US 4). Inspection only at the international boundary. Gasoline stations are plentiful throughout the State. The State Highway Patrol covers the main thoroughfares. Gasoline tax, 4¢. (For highway routes *see State Map.*)

*Bus Lines:* Interstate bus lines: Vermont Transit Co. (-V-), Champlain Coach Lines (-C-), Frontier Coach Lines (-F-), Rutland Bus Co. (-R-), Bee Line Inc. (-B-), Keene-Brattleboro Trans. (-K-), Boston & Maine Transp. Co. (-B-). Local bus routes: Greenwood Bus Co. (-G-), Rutland & White River Jct. (-RW-), White R., Wells R. & St. J. (-W-), Burlington & Cambridge Jct. (-BC-), Mower Bus Line (-M-), Rutland & Montpelier (-RM-), Grande Isle Motor Bus Co. (-GI-), Montpelier & St. Johnsbury (-MS-), Waterbury & Morrisville (-WM-). (*See Transportation Map* for interstate bus lines.)

*Airlines:* Boston & Maine Airline (Boston to Burlington) stops at Barre–Montpelier and Burlington. Other airports at Bennington, Bristol, Fair Haven, Manchester, Rutland, St. Johnsbury, Springfield, and White River Junction (not on regular passenger line). (*See Transportation Map.*)

*Motor Vehicle Laws (Digest):* Maximum speed for pleasure cars, 50 *m.*; pleasure cars with trailers or semi-trailers, 40 *m.*; motor busses with 12 passengers or more, 40 *m.*; trucks under 2 ton, 35 *m.*; trucks over 2 ton, 30 *m.* Full reciprocity granted to non-residents except when their vehicles are operated for hire between points within the State. Minimum age for drivers; junior operator, 16; senior operator, 18. Hand signals are prescribed, or approved type of mechanical signal. Spotlights are permitted under certain conditions. Personal injury or property damage (over $25) must be reported to the Motor Vehicle Department without delay.

*Prohibited:* Parking on highways, use of stickers, except in lower right-hand corner of windshield and not to exceed 4 in. in width and 12 in. in length.

*Accommodations:* First-class hotel accommodations in cities; resorts during season. Tourist homes and inns outside urban centers are numerous and generally satisfactory. Tourist camps are somewhat scattered and usually confined to the less populated areas and lake districts. With the exception of winter sports centers, rural sections offer limited accommodations during the winter months.

*Climate and Equipment:* Temperature subject to abrupt and drastic changes in any season. Summer nights are invariably cool, sometimes quite cold, and topcoats are often required. In spring and fall the days are apt to be intermittently cool and warm, with topcoats a necessity. The highways are kept open throughout the winter, but sudden storms may cause temporary blockades, and winter travelers should note weather reports. Equipment for trails, hiking or other forms of recreation can be procured in almost any sizable village.

*State Fish and Game Laws (Digest):* For hunting and fishing areas and laws see accompanying chart.

*Liquor Regulations:*

### CLASS OF LICENSES

First Class — Beer and wine on premises.
Second Class — Beer and wine off premises.
Third Class — Spirituous liquors on premises.
State Stores — Spirituous liquors off premises.
Beer to 6 per cent and wines to 14 per cent sold by privately owned package stores and on premise licensees. Fortified wines over 14 per cent and spirituous liquors sold by State-owned package stores and third-class licensees for on-premise consumption.

### HOURS OF SALE

State Stores — 10 A.M. to 6 P.M. Eastern Standard Time, or Daylight Saving Time if prevailing. Saturdays — 10 A.M. to 8 P.M. Closed on Holidays.

On and off premise licensees — 8 A.M. to 12 P.M. Eastern Standard Time except Sundays. Hours on Sundays — 12 noon to 3 P.M. and 6 P.M. to 8 P.M. Eastern Standard Time with regular meals by third-class licensees.

*Picking of Wild Flowers:* In State Forests and State Forest Parks flowers may be picked in reasonable quantities for non-commercial purposes at a distance of 50 feet from any road or trail. Certain restrictions on rare plants in these areas and other public lands are contained in the general laws relating to forestry which may be procured from the State Forestry Service, Montpelier, Vermont.

*Cutting or Marking of Trees:* The cutting or marking of trees except where permission is indicated is strictly forbidden.

*Building of Campfires:* In State Forests and State Forest Parks this practice is allowed only in designated areas.

# CALENDAR OF EVENTS

*Only events of general interest are listed. Many opening dates vary with the years, and are placed in the week in which they usually occur. The abbreviation 'nfd' signifies event occurs during the month but has no fixed date.*

| Jan. Feb. nfd March | Brattleboro and Woodstock | Winter Sports and Carnivals. |
|---|---|---|
| Feb. 2 | Barton | Winter Circus. |
| Feb. 12 | State Wide | Maple Festival. |
| Feb. 3d wk | Middlebury | Intercollegiate Carnival. |
| Feb. 3d wk | Stowe | Winter Carnival. |
| Feb. 22 | Burlington | Kake Walk (Univ. of Vermont). |
| Feb. March nfd | Announced | State Basketball Tourneys. |
| May 1 | Burlington | Founders' Day (Univ. of Vermont). |
| May 16–20 | State Wide | Apple Blossom Week. |
| May 31 | Brandon | May Celebration and Pageant. |
| May nfd | Burlington | Music Festival. |
| May nfd | Announced | Vermont Choral Society and State Federation Concert. |
| June nfd | Burlington | Northern Artists' Exhibition. |
| June nfd | Announced | Vermont State Shoot. |
| Summer | Woodstock | String Quartet Concerts. |
| July 4 wks | Bread Loaf | School of Writers. |
| July nfd | Dorset | Little Theater Tournament. |
| July nfd | Announced | Amateur State Golf Tournament. |
| July 3d wk | Announced | Green Mt. Horse Association Trail Ride. |
| Aug. 1st 2 wks | Bread Loaf | Writers' Conference. |
| Aug. 16 | State Wide | Bennington Battle Day. |
| Aug. nfd | Manchester | Southern Artists' Exhibition. |
| Aug. nfd | Manchester | Manchester Flower Show. |
| Aug. nfd | Announced | Horse Shows. |
| Aug. nfd | Announced | Amateur State Tennis Tournament. |
| Aug. nfd | Lake Bomoseen Lake Champlain Lake Dunmore Lake St. Catherine | Regattas. |
| Aug. nfd | Barton | Sugaring Off. |
| Aug. nfd Sept. Oct. | Rutland Essex Tunbridge Barton Morrisville | Fairs. |
| Sept. 20– Oct. 16 | State Wide | Fall Foliage Festival. |

# I. VERMONT: THE GENERAL BACKGROUND

# VERMONTERS

## BY DOROTHY CANFIELD FISHER

A GUIDE–BOOK exists only, of course, for people who do not live in the region described. Presumably nobody who reads this book knows Vermonters. Are there, we wonder, as the volume goes to press, any general remarks about Vermont which might help visitors to understand, and hence better to enjoy their stay in our midst?

It is only honest to say that a great many sensible Vermonters think generalizations of this kind all nonsense. 'We're just like any other Americans,' they say impatiently. 'All this quaint old-time stuff is the bunk.' And perhaps it is. How can anybody tell? To know your own home country intimately enough to speak about its ways with authority, you must have lived there so continuously as not to have had time to learn — really learn — the ways of another region well enough to make a comparison. No law of physics is more immutable. So all I can do is to quote a few comments from observers of our ways, and hazard a few guesses of my own.

My first commentator is my godfather. His life was laid out according to a geographical pattern very familiar to us here in Vermont. He was born in Morrisville, one of our finest old small towns. When he was small the family moved to Kansas. There he became, after education at the State University, a very successful corporation lawyer, who earned, I make the guess, every year of his life an income seven or eight times the salary of the Governor of Vermont. He had been moved away from Vermont when he was too young to remember it; he lived continuously in Kansas for all of a long and unusually successful life. But he never got over the feeling that he was in essence a Vermonter. I set down this brief account of him as a framework for the remark he often made. We did not altogether like it, and usually protested, but as I grow older I understand more of the truth behind his fanciful notion. 'What ought to be done with the old State,' he would say meditatively, 'is to turn it into a National Park of a new kind — keep it just as it is, with Vermonters managing just as they do — so the rest of the country could come in to see how their grandparents lived.'

Now let me put with that remark, before I comment on it myself, another one, frequently made by a French friend of mine, who for many years spent her vacations (her work was in New York) in a small boarding-house in our Vermont village frequented by local people. 'It's so like France!' she often said relishingly. Americans to whom she made this remark always exclaimed wonderingly, 'What *do* you *mean*?' and she explained: 'Well, when my fellow boarders, chatting about Arlington happenings, speak of somebody they always mention "who he is," and by that they mean who his parents and perhaps his grandparents were, who his brothers and sisters are. "He's Lottie Roberts's son. Don't you remember, she married Joel Lane's youngest boy?" That is, like the French people they instinctively and invariably think of the individual in the frame of his family, not isolated from his past. Of course newcomers and tramps, whose families they don't know, are disconcerting to them, like silhouettes, only two-dimensional, not to be counted on for lack of knowledge of them. And that's the way we French feel about strangers and newcomers. And then' — she spoke with Gallic seriousness on this next point — 'Vermont is the only place in America where I ever hear *thrift* spoken of with respect.'

Yes, I think it is nearly safe, by and large, in spite of many exceptions, in spite of the snappy, up-and-coming young Vermonters you meet all over the State, who pooh-pooh the idea that they are in any way different from snappy, up-and-coming young Iowans or Californians, to say that Vermont represents the past, is a piece of the past in the midst of the present and future.

Now there are, of course, both advantages and disadvantages in everything. Until the depression, America, living lavishly in what it thought was the future, looked down with amused scorn on people so backward as to go on adding up the figures of their columns and putting down the accurate total, rather than a bigger one that would look prettier. Before President Coolidge made the name of our State known to modern people, we were so far in the past as to be practically invisible. Those were the days when you gave your address to a saleswoman in New York as 'Arlington, Vermont,' and she asked, her pencil hovering over the page, 'Yes — and what State, please?' (thinking 'Vermont,' we used wrathfully to imagine, was some fancy name for a new 'development' in the suburbs). Nowadays when you tell New York saleswomen that you live in Vermont they say, 'Oh, how nice! I envy you!' This change is not due to any sudden discovery of our virtues. It is caused by (*a*) the advent into fashionable favor of winter sports, Vermont sounding like a place where you can wear ski pants, and (*b*) the depression. The shock of that last event made a good many Americans turn, disillusioned, away from the future that wasn't so near as they thought and perhaps was going to be very different from what they hoped, back towards the past still jogging with slow steadiness on its horse-and-buggy back-road way. Not to be disagreeable, just to be frank, some of these yearners after the past rub us the wrong way with their praise of what we ruefully know to be mere narrowness and stagnation, qualities from which we struggle hard to escape, they being (like bragging to a Californian, and real estate inflation to Florida people) the special temptation of our especial way of life.

But these varying opinions, going up and down apparently as money is easy or hard to get in the big world, are only what other people think of us. There are real and actual disadvantages in being the past that have nothing to do with what people think of you. For one thing Vermont belongs to the Federated States of North America as firmly as any rich, industrialized New York or Illinois, and must try to pull its weight honestly in the nation, as well as making both the ends of its own small budget meet. Our opinion on American problems is seriously asked (for instance, on election day and when Amendments to the Constitution are proposed) by the nation. Well, it puts us in a difficult position. We have, firmly fixed in our minds, a mental habit on which we base all our judgments, the conviction that no opinion is any good unless it is founded on first-hand knowledge of the facts. Our ideal is not to take other people's say-so as to what the facts are, but to make our decisions out of our own personal experience and observation.

That is sound. That is according to the best principles of sacred scientific procedure. The hitch comes in the fact that we have had too little first-hand experience of many of the problems of modern American life to serve as premises for all the conclusions needed. How can we, still 'living fifty years ago' as my godfather used to say, have that 'hunch' for sound decisions in industrial conditions which can only come from long personal experience and observation? We still live in small units where personal relations are the almost invariable rule of daily life, not the exception. On our streets it is the sight of a totally unknown face or figure which arrests the attention, rather than, as in big cities, the strangeness of occasionally seeing somebody you know. How can we form valid judgments on ways to manage a life so different from ours, on expedients for handling great masses of people who never laid eyes on each other before? For instance, how do we know what is fairness and right treatment for vast armies of working men who have literally only their wages to live on? How can we help it, if forming our conceptions from our own observation of life — we really don't know what you are talking about when you speak of 'the proletariat' and explain that it means people with no possessions? With us (of course all these statements are true only in a general way) a man who by the time he is middle-aged has *no* possessions, is either unlucky far beyond the usual chances of life, or cranky and hard to get along with, or sick, or weak, or has a plague of a wife, or is unnaturally passive in mind or body — or lazy. Yes, we still use that antique word, obsolescent elsewhere. That is, if a Vermonter has no possessions of any sort after a fair number of years of mature life, his lack is apt to be caused more by some individual idiosyncrasy or personal misfortune of his than by an organization of society which dooms him to extreme poverty, no matter how great his industry, conscientiousness, and good character. Do not misunderstand me. A great many Vermonters have so little cash every year that it would scare you if you knew the sum. Our 'working people' are paid much less than they should be, to be comfortable, to have what they really need. They and their wives do not go to the dentist as often as they should, and a serious illness in the family is a major economic catastrophe (although, still having a 'family' in the old sense of a fairly numerous clan, they are helped through such calamities by everybody in the connection putting his shoulder to the wheel). But relatively to the rest of the community there is no such contrast between their life and that of other people as that we find described in many modern novels and magazines; and there is still the old American open door of material opportunity for anybody who cares enough about money to buy it with perseverance, hard work, reliable character, and moderate efficiency in some useful occupation.

Everybody in Vermont is still in a situation close enough to the primitive and natural to be not wholly conditioned by the amount of cash in his pockets. Our life, it is true, bears hardly on the sick, the old, and on widows and orphans. We sometimes feel sadly that those who for one reason or another have not their full share of vitality and vigor have a harder time in Vermont than in richer States. The help given them from town or State is perhaps less well organized, less well implemented with personnel and money than in States with larger budgets. But still the tradition among us of indefatigable neighborliness and personal responsibility for help to the needy who are personally known to us may to some extent make up for this. At any rate, it is true that people in normal health can, *by their own efforts without cash*, to some extent make their environment and daily life more to their taste. If a man wants more vegetables, he can raise them in his garden and with his wife can or dry or put away in his cellar what they do not use in summer. If he wants more heat in the winter, it is never hard for a man known to be honest and reliable to make an arrangement with a neighbor who owns a woodlot, so that swinging his own axe he can add to his fuel. If he wants more fruit in his diet, he and his wife and the children can pick, on Sundays and holidays, raspberries and blueberries by the bushel, and there are always apples to be had for the taking away, plenty good enough to make canned applesauce out of. If he wants an extra room or a porch added to his house, lumber is cheap, all his neighbors understand raising a frame and are willing to help him do this, so that (within moderate limits) he can build on what he likes. He is not, that is, no matter how poor, in the nightmare helplessness of the modern urban wage-earner, gripped fast (so we understand) in the rigid, impersonal framework of a society organized uniquely around money, who when he loses his job can do nothing but sit in his tenement-house room staring at the wall and dreading the appearance of the rent collector. That condition, rather than poverty and hardship (of which we have a great plenty in our poor State), would seem to us the really stultifying and unendurable position into which to force self-respecting able-bodied human beings.

We gather from what we read in books and newspapers and liberal magazines that life in intensively industrialized States is very different from ours, and we realize that our opinion on many modern problems can't be of much more value than the opinions of some city people who come for vacations to the midst of a remote, specially poor low-quality group of Vermonters, and who, after a summer or two of misunderstanding everything they see, tell us what is the matter with Vermont. We do not in the least claim to know what is the matter with the roaring, money-making industrialized world, or with the share-cropping misery of rural life in one-crop regions. We realize that we are laggards from the past century, still living in what Marx kindly calls 'the idiocy of rural life,' and we know that our rural life is like that of the past, not like that of much of the present. We know that our ignorance of, our lack of instinctive 'feeling' for those modern industrial and mass-life problems make us seem to you like your great-aunt in curl papers, but we are helpless before our tradition of not pretending to know more than we do, of not being other than what we are. Our restricted observation of human life leads us to these conclusions. So all we can do, when our opinion is called for, is to remind the rest of you of the standards, ideals, judgments, and decisions that were the rules when your father was a little boy. And since it was on those standards, ideals, judgments, and decisions that America

got to where she is (for good and bad), we may possibly be performing
a small useful function in the national economy by this reminder.

Of advantages in living thus more or less in the past there are many.
A typical example is our one-room district school. About forty years ago
— roughly speaking — the prosperous part of America, the part that lives
in the present with one foot in the future, turned against the district
school with impatient distaste. It was dreary, it was poor; a graded school
where the children could be separated according to age and degree of
learning was obviously better; there was no janitor; the curriculum was
meager; it looked like yesterday — away with it! Putting their hands into
their pockets, well garnished with money made in industrialism, the well-
to-do States began building fine consolidated schools, big three-story
brick edifices that were the pride of the country. They looked like today
all right, like tomorrow indeed, almost as up-to-date as factories or office
buildings, with janitors and furnaces and basements, and everything in
the way of running them on too large a scale for children to meddle with,
and lots of corridors, up and down which children in great masses could
be marched. To these modern emporiums of learning the children of
richer States than Vermont were taken in fine big shining school busses
over good level roads. The one-room 'deestrick skule' looked beside
those resplendent buildings like the poor country cousin from the farm.
Vermonters looked wistful about the 'advantages' other people's children
were getting, but the one-room district school was all most Vermont communities could afford, and in our State, when you can't afford something,
your tradition calls upon you to go without it. So the State did the best
it could with its outmoded small old schools, making them more comfortable in a plain country way with jacketed stoves, and better floors,
and more window space and movable desks, and offering special salary
inducements to persuade teachers to stay in them.

Not at all through superior wisdom or prescience did Vermont communities not bond themselves heavily to wipe out all district schools.
Like many things supposed to spring from Vermont 'character,' the policy
towards the district school was closely connected with our economic
situation. It came from plain material necessity and the habit of recogniz-
ing material necessity when you see it, and not pretending it doesn't
exist. We couldn't afford those massive great schools. So we got along
without them, like older people getting along with their battered furniture, instead of getting a lot of new pieces on the installment plan.

And exactly as happens sometimes in the case of the older furniture
thus kept and used, some pieces of it turned out to be fine authentic

antiques, of considerably greater value than the modern things which re-placed it. After a generation of the big barrack-like primary schools, the wise, deeper-natured among the educators, both here and in Europe, began to say, 'But the big modern school separates the child too much from natural ways of living. It would be better to break up those great masses, with the deadening effect masses always have on human imagina-tions, into small units where the relations between the children and be-tween the class and teacher are more family-like and personal. It would be better to have small schools in the country close to nature, so that the children could learn as they live about natural processes. It would be better to keep the school equipment and outfit and administration very simple, so that the children could genuinely help in keeping its necessary processes going.'

To our astonishment the wisest of the world's educators began ex-pensively to re-create the kind of education our country children have always had, and reversing the direction taken by those long shiny modern school busses, began to carry city children out to country day schools. It was exactly like having the grandchildren come back on a visit to the old back-road farm home, and admire the plain ladder-back chairs and ancient cherry tables, scorning the overstuffed suites which their parents had worked so hard to buy.

So yes, on the whole, taken with many reservations and much caution, it is perhaps safe to tell you visitors to our State that if you will think of us as representing the American past, you may have a better understand-ing of what you see in Vermont. We warn you that we shall probably object (and perhaps with asperity) to this generalization in almost every single concrete case in which you try to apply it. And we probably can find valid reasons for our every objection. But there is a sort of floating pervasive truth in a sound generalization, that colors the atmosphere all around, behind, and in front of concrete exceptions. So I think on the whole that it will be safe for you to take as a sort of master key to Vermont life the hypothesis that, in a manner of speaking and in some respects, we represent the past — it will be safe, that is, if you don't say too much to us about it.

# NATURAL SETTING

## GEOGRAPHY AND TOPOGRAPHY

ALTHOUGH it has an area of only 9564 square miles and hence ranks forty-second in size among the States, Vermont contains a much more diversified range of scenic interest than many a much larger State. Notwithstanding the presence of broad valleys, such as that of the Connecticut River on the east and of Lake Champlain on the west, the State as a whole is essentially a mountainous area. Elevations range from 95 feet at the surface of Lake Champlain to 4393 feet at the summit of Mount Mansfield, while the average for the State as a whole is 1000 feet — equal to that of New Hampshire and greater than that of the four other New England States. There are twenty-one peaks with an altitude of more than 3500 feet and six of more than 4000 feet. While in general the mountains show the smoothly rounded outlines typical of geologically old ranges, there are areas of rugged topography and strong relief. In the town of Bolton there is a difference in elevation of nearly 4000 feet between the Winooski River and the summit of Camel's Hump only four miles to the south.

*Mountains.* The mountains of the State, although often spoken of collectively as the Green Mountains, actually consist of at least four distinct groups, which form more or less continuous ranges traversing the State with a general parallelism in a north-south direction. Of these the Green Mountains proper are the largest and in many ways the most important. They extend from Massachusetts to the Canadian line through the center of the State, and thus divide it into an eastern and a western portion with a high mountain mass between. This division has played an important part in the development of the State, and is a factor even today. The Green Mountains form a practically continuous range, varying in width and height, as far north as Mount Pico, from which point north they split into two slightly diverging ranges, the eastern one developing into the Worcester Range. The Green Mountain range includes the highest peaks in the State, culminating in such elevations as Mount Mansfield (4393 ft.), Killington (4241 ft.), Mount Ellen (4135 ft.), and

Camel's Hump (4083 ft.). The important talc, asbestos, and verde antique deposits of the State are found along the eastern slopes of the range.

Scenically, the Taconic Mountains are next in importance. They occupy the southwestern portion of the State, beginning in Massachusetts and extending along the western border of Vermont as far north as Sudbury. Considerably lower and less extensive than the Green Mountains, they still contribute greatly to the beauty of the State. The principal peaks include: Equinox (3816 ft.) in Manchester, Green Peak (3185 ft.) in Dorset, Herrick Mountain (2727 ft.) in Ira, and Bird Mountain (2210 ft.) in West Rutland. The Taconic range contains the important marble deposits of the State.

The third group, called the Granite Hills, lies east of the Green Mountains and extends from somewhat below the middle of the State to the Canadian line. Though not conspicuous objects on the landscape, Millstone Hill (1700 ft.) in Barre being the highest elevation in the group, they are important in that they contain the valuable granite resources of the State.

The final group, called the Red Sandrock Hills, extends along the edge of Lake Champlain from Addison on the south to St. Albans. Starting with Snake Mountain (1271 ft.), they form a series of long ridges with occasional higher hills — such as Mount Philo (968 ft.) and Pease Mountain (740 ft.) in Charlotte — which grow progressively lower northward. The hills form a conspicuous part of the scenery of the Champlain Valley. The beauty of such shore points as Red Rocks, Rock Point, and Mallett's Bay is due to them. The handsome Mallett's Bay 'marble' (really a dolomite), as well as the red building stone so much used in the city of Burlington, are obtained from the rocks of these hills.

In addition to the four more or less well-defined ranges just mentioned, there are a number of isolated peaks in the eastern part of the State — such as Mount Ascutney (3114 ft.) in Windsor and Mount Monadnock (3200 ft.) in Lemington — which owe their elevation to the fact that they are composed of harder rocks than those of the surrounding country and hence have been left as erosion remnants.

*Rivers.* The rivers of the State, besides adding greatly to its scenic beauty, are important as sources of hydro-electric power and because of the fact that, aside from the Champlain Valley, their valleys contain the bulk of the arable lands of the State.

The Connecticut River, forming the entire eastern border, is the largest and most important, but is actually under the control of New Hampshire

since the boundary line follows the low-water mark on the stream's
western side. Otter Creek, rising in the town of Dorset and flowing ninety
miles northward to empty into Lake Champlain about eight miles west
of Vergennes, is the longest river within the State. The Batten Kill, also
rising in Dorset but flowing southward, and the Walloomsac south of it,
occupy the remainder of the great valley between the Taconic and the
Green Mountains. In general, because of the central mass of the Green
Mountains, the rivers of the State either flow down that range's eastern
slopes into the Connecticut or down the western into Lake Champlain.
There are, however, three streams which are interesting exceptions to
this general rule, in that they rise to the east of and flow directly through
the mass of the Green Mountains to enter Lake Champlain. These three
streams, the Missisquoi, the Lamoille, and the Winooski, are apparently
'antecedent' rivers — that is, they ran in their present courses before
the Green Mountains were formed, and were able to cut down their
valleys rapidly enough to maintain them against the rising mountains.
The great valley of the Winooski where it cuts through the main range of
the mountains is nearly four thousand feet deep, and equals in scenic
grandeur many of the canyons of the West.

*Lakes and Ponds.* Lake Champlain, one hundred and twenty miles
long and constituting for nearly one hundred miles the western boundary
of Vermont, is jointly owned by the States of Vermont and New York
and the Province of Quebec. Lake Memphremagog, the second largest
lake in which Vermont has an interest, forms part of the northern
boundary of the State; about one-quarter of its sixty square miles of
area is in Vermont, and the rest in Quebec. The largest natural body of
water entirely within the State is Lake Bomoseen in Castleton, with an
area of eight square miles. The highest considerable body of water is
Sterling Pond in Stowe, lying at an elevation of 3200 feet.

Most of Vermont's more than one hundred lakes and ponds owe their
origin to the great ice-sheet which once covered the State, and which
formed them by scouring out hollows in the rocks and damming up
stream valleys with rock waste (glacial drift). A number, however, have
an origin independent of any glacial action. Thus, Lake Champlain
occupies the western portion of the great Champlain Valley, a structural
feature formed in early geological times by the down-faulting of its western margin. Picturesque Lake Willoughby rests in a U-shaped trough
formed by the down-faulting of a block of the earth's crust between
Mounts Hor and Pisgah; the ice-sheet somewhat modified the form of
this trough and, by damming up the southern end, gave rise to the lake

in its present form. Lake Dunmore and Silver Lake occupy synclinal folds in rocks, and are retained by glacial gravels.

## GEOLOGY

The scenery of any area, as well as the economic life of its inhabitants, is in the last analysis dependent upon its geological history. Hence it is felt that the following sketch of the geology of the State will help the visitor in understanding the Vermont of today.[1]

Although representatives of the three great rock types (igneous, sedimentary, and metamorphic) occur in the State, the metamorphic (schists, slates, gneisses) are the most common, forming the bedrock of most of the State, with the exception of the Champlain Valley and the Granite Hills. The rocks of the Champlain Valley are almost entirely sedimentary, largely limestones and shales with some sandstones and conglomerates. The Granite Hills, together with certain mountains such as Ascutney and Monadnock, are the principal examples of igneous rocks to be found in the State.

In general, the various rock formations of the State may be considered as occurring in a series of north-south trending belts of differing widths. Each band may consist of several more or less closely related rock types, and individual bands may not continue the entire length of the State; but the following generalizations are useful in outlining the distribution of rocks in the State. Beginning at the Connecticut River in the east and proceeding westward, the rocks encountered are as follows:

1. A belt of schist of variable width from the Canadian line south to Bellows Falls. In this are found the copper deposits of Strafford and Vershire.

2. A narrow belt of slate, not more than a mile or two wide, extending from Burke to the Massachusetts line.

3. A wide belt, up to twenty miles or more across, consisting of a number of types of schists, extending the length of the State. The granite batholith of the Granite Hills has been intruded into this formation.

4. A second narrow belt of dark slate, up to three miles wide, from Lake Memphremagog through Bethel.

5. A wide belt of schists and gneisses forming the main chain of the

---

[1] Those interested in more detailed accounts of the geology and natural resources of Vermont are advised to consult the volumes of the biennial 'Reports of the State Geologist on the Mineral Industries and Geology of Vermont,' which may be found in most of the larger libraries.

Green Mountains and extending the length of the State. Some thirty miles wide in the north, it gradually narrows to eighteen in the south. It consists of a number of types of metamorphic rocks, including much chlorite and mica schist highly contorted, and encloses the lenses of altered intrusives forming the talc, verde antique, and asbestos deposits of the State.

6. West of the mountains, and in part forming their western foothills, is a belt of sedimentary rocks, strongly folded near the mountains, which underlies much of the Champlain Valley. It is composed of an eastern conglomerate and a western silicious limestone member in the northern half of the State. These die out in the south, and are replaced by a variety of sedimentary beds.

7. West of the last belt and following rather closely the eastern shore of the lake is a belt of red sandstones, shales, and dolomites, forming the Red Sandrock Hills.

8. Finally, forming the islands in Lake Champlain and in places its eastern shore, is a series of flat-lying shales and limestones. The forces forming the Taconic Mountains to the south of the valley changed (metamorphosed) these rocks into slates and marbles.

In addition very extensive deposits of sands and gravels are scattered everywhere throughout the State, representing the material left on the retreat of the great ice sheet of the Glacial Period.

No rocks as old as the ancient Archean formations of the Adirondack Mountains of New York State are definitely known in Vermont, though it is possible that some of the intensely metamorphosed schists and gneisses of the Green Mountain core may be of this age. The known geological history of the Vermont area began in early Paleozoic times with the invasion of the Lower Cambrian sea into the area now forming the Champlain Valley. This was probably the result of the down-faulting of a crustal block along the eastern margin of the Adirondack Massif initiating the structural lowland of the Champlain Valley, which has continued in existence in one form or another to the present. Sands, clays, and dolomitic muds washed from the adjacent land areas accumulated to the depth of several thousand feet in the sea thus formed, and later became the rocks whose remnants now form the red sandrock and other Cambrian formations of the valley.

Toward the close of the Cambrian there was some uplift and consequent erosion, but in early Ordovician times there was again subsidence and a renewal of sedimentation. The Ordovician seas appear to have covered at one time or another nearly the entire area now included within the

State of Vermont, for rocks carrying fossils of that age are found in both the eastern and western sides of the State and it seems probable that some of the schists of the Green Mountain core are their metamorphic equivalents, as are the slates and marbles of the Taconic area. The limestones of this age in the northern part of the Champlain Valley carry in places an abundant fossil fauna. Thus, some of the beaches on Grand Isle are covered with fossil brachiopods which have weathered out of the limestone outcrops, while a fossil coral reef on Isle La Motte furnishes one of the earliest examples of Colonial corals.

The close of the Ordovician marked the end of any important sedimentation in the Vermont area, as far as is now known. At that time strong compressive forces, apparently acting from the east, produced sharp folds in the sediments of the Taconic area, giving birth to the Taconic Mountains and at the same time causing some folding and uplift along the Green Mountain axis. In the Champlain Valley area these crustal forces found relief through the development of the Champlain overthrust rather than through folding of the rocks. This overthrust extends from Canada along the eastern shore of the lake nearly to the New York line, and brought Cambrian rocks over the younger Ordovician. During this overthrusting, cubic miles of rock were moved bodily westward for miles. The thrust plane is beautifully exposed at Rock Point just north of Burlington, where the red Cambrian formations may be seen resting on black Ordovician shale. '

In late Paleozoic times, probably in connection with renewed mountain-building activity at the close of the Devonian, came the implacement of granitic batholiths whose exposed upper portions now form the Granite Hills. Other bodies of igneous rocks, such as the syenitic intrusive stocks of Mounts Monadnock and Ascutney, were presumably formed at about the same time.

At the close of the Paleozoic came the great mountain-building period known as the Appalachian Revolution, which affected the entire Appalachian region of North America and in the Vermont area raised the Green Mountain region into a lofty mountain range and produced the very intense crushing and metamorphism of its rocks.

An interesting illustration of the tremendous stresses to which the rocks involved in these mountain-building movements were subjected may be seen in the spontaneous explosive splitting of quarry blocks at some of the marble quarries. In spite of the immense period of time which has elapsed since the stresses were imposed, enough residual strain remains to cause these great solid blocks of rock to split asunder. A somewhat similar case is a common experience in the granite quarries, where great blocks freed except on the under side suddenly snap loose with a sharp report.

No Mesozoic history is recorded in the Vermont area, but in the early Tertiary (Eocene) deposits of clays of various types, including small bodies of bog iron and manganese, ores and beds of lignite were formed. These are now found along the Champlain Valley from Colchester south to Bennington. The lignite beds, known as the Brandon lignites, though actually occurring at Forestdale three miles north, were discovered while digging for clay and were at one time exploited as a substitute for coal. The lignites are of interest in that they contain a rich fossil flora consisting of several hundred species of fruits and nuts of tropical and subtropical plants. It thus appears that a warm climate prevailed at that time, in this part of the State at least.

Sometime between the formation of the Brandon lignite and the Pleistocene a revolutionary change in climate occurred, bringing on the great Pleistocene Glacial Age with conditions similar to those in the Antarctic today. The changes produced in the scenery of Vermont during the Glacial Period were probably greater than during any other period of similar length. A great ice-sheet advancing southward from Labrador covered the country with thousands of feet of ice, overriding even the highest mountains. This mass of slowly moving ice carried away the soil and loosened rock and gouged out the solid rocks, rounding off the hills and widening and deepening the valleys. Its great weight caused a subsidence of the land, so that at the close of the period the Vermont area was five hundred or six hundred feet lower than it is today and the waters of the melting ice, augmented by an invasion of the sea, covered much of the State, leaving the mountains standing as islands. Relieved of its ice load, the land gradually rose until the present level was reached, while the flood waters drained off and the streams re-established themselves. During a long period the Champlain Valley was filled by a sea hundreds of feet deep, which reached well up on the western foothills of the mountains and formed arms running far up the river valleys. Incoming streams built extensive deltas where they entered this sea, and as it gradually receded successive deltas were formed, each farther out from the mountain front, until at the present day they are being formed in Lake Champlain. Remnants of these ancient deltas, forming level sand and gravel plains and flat-topped terraces, may be seen today at many places along the Champlain Valley and the valleys entering it. Marine fossils have been found on many of them, sometimes several hundred feet above present sea level. They are found at various elevations, as can be seen by anyone traveling up the Winooski Valley, particularly in the vicinity of Richmond. The Burlington Airport and the village of Bristol are built on such plains. Similar formations exist in the eastern part of the State, where several large glacial lakes were formed with the melting of the ice.

Rounded and grooved ledges, polished rock surfaces, ice-born boulders (erratics), and great deposits of unsorted sands, clays, and gravels (glacial till) throughout the State are further evidences of the former presence of the ice. The steep escarpment on the southern end of the summit of Camel's Hump is the result of the 'plucking' action of the ice. The damming of the normal drainage by glacial drift, and the floods of water resulting from the melting of the ice, caused the erosion of deep gashes in the rocks — as at Williamstown and Northfield Gulfs — and produced the pot-holes and water-worn forms of the rocks on the sides of many of the valleys high above even the flood stages of the present.

## CLIMATE

Vermont's climate is, in general, the varied one of the north temperate zone, yet there are distinct differences between the climates of various sections of the State's relatively small area. The average annual temperature ranges from 38° to 46°. The U.S. Weather Bureau Station at Northfield gives the highest temperature as 98°, the lowest as − 41°. The average growing season of the Connecticut Valley is thirty days shorter than that of the Champlain Valley (120 as opposed to 150). The central part of the State, comprising the Green Mountain range and its foothills, has an even shorter season; but because of the scarcity of arable land there, this fact has little bearing upon agriculture. This same central strip has also the heaviest snow cover — ten feet on an average. The sections east and west of the center have an average snow cover of from eight to ten feet, the Champlain Valley and the east central section an average of from four to eight feet. The average annual rainfall varies from thirty-four inches in the Champlain Valley and east central section to forty inches in the northern and central parts. A small strip in the extreme south receives fifty inches.

# FLORA AND FAUNA

THE flora of Vermont, like that of the north temperate zone in general, is extensive and varied. There is no period between April and November when the Vermont countryside does not provide a seasonal display of floral beauty — the first tender grays of the pussy-willow; the anemones, arbutus, and violets in April; the lilacs and apple-blossoms in May; the daisies, buttercups, and red-clover blooms (the red clover is the State flower) of summer; the goldenrod and gentians of early autumn; and the ultimate hectic spectacle of the dying foliage of all the deciduous trees in October.

Trees are scenically the most important of Vermont plants. Most ancient in this group are the conifers, of which fifteen varieties are found in the State. Of these, the most valuable commercially is the white pine, which is depicted on the State seal. Of the three species of spruce, the red spruce is most abundant and valuable, and is largely responsible for the dark green of Vermont's wooded mountains. The most common deciduous trees found in the State include several varieties of maple, elm, birch, beech, oak, hickory, ash, cherry, and butternut.

Of ferns, the highest class of flowerless plants, there are eighty-one distinct species in Vermont. Mount Mansfield and near-by Smuggler's Notch are the best territory for these plants. Here, as early as 1807, Pursh discovered the graceful shield fern called Braun's holly fern (*aspidium aculeatum Braunii*); and about seventy years later the botanist Pringle, in an intensive survey of the region, discovered three other species of fern not previously found in this country. Many interesting varieties of fern also grow on the limestone cliffs in the Western part of the State. In the southern part of Rutland County, ferns are gathered on a commercial scale and stored in refrigeration for winter use.

There are 130 species of the grass family and 192 of the sedge family in Vermont. The former group is valuable for fodder; the latter, in general, is not. Both groups include many remarkably graceful varieties that approach the beauty of ferns.

Of the flower-producing plants found in the State, no enumeration can be attempted here, though careful botanical studies of Vermont's flora may be consulted in any good Vermont library. There are 1482 species, classified under 481 genera and 101 families. More than half the species are included in a relatively few families: the conifers, grasses, and sedges, already mentioned; the orchid family, whose 43 species include the beautiful lady's-slipper; the rose family, of which there are more than 80 species; the pea family, whose 46 species include the various types of clover; the heath family, which includes the arbutus and several of our edible berries; and the buttercup family, which includes the springtime anemone and the marsh marigold or cowslip.

Many of the floral species of Vermont have a State-wide distribution; others are found only in limited areas. About thirty species grow only on the summits of mountains; about fifty only in swampy bogs. There is in general a considerable difference between the flora of eastern and western Vermont, due to the lower altitude and clay and calcareous soils of the Champlain Valley and to the fact that many species have apparently been unable to cross the barrier of the central range of the Green Mountains.

Some of the animals that were most plentiful in Vermont when its settlement by white men was begun have now become extinct here — as, for example, the wolf, foraging from Canada for Vermont sheep; the fierce panther, or catamount, that would attack a man on horseback; the lordly moose and caribou; the trout-loving otter; and the beaver. Early Vermont local history is rich in anecdotes about these animals, and some of them still haunt the Vermont imagination. Each year, in various localities, the scream of the 'painter' is heard again, or a moose is seen crashing through the underbrush; but the fact remains that no panther or moose has been killed in the State for many years.

Chief of Vermont's game animals is the deer. Indiscriminately slaughtered for more than a century, these animals became almost extinct in the 1870's. Seventeen of them, purchased with private funds, were set free in Rutland County in 1878, and the Legislature declared a continuous closed season on the whole breed until 1896. They have become fairly numerous since that time, the number of bucks killed during the annual ten-day open season having averaged about two thousand in recent years.       •

Large numbers of various fur-bearing animals that are trapped for their pelts still abound in Vermont. According to figures reported to the Fish and Game Department by licensed fur-buyers, the number taken in 1936 was as follows: muskrats, 72,726; skunks, nearly 30,000; raccoons, 15,000; foxes, 11,076; mink, 6500. Twenty-six bears and twenty lynxes, or wildcats, were also killed in that year. (Neither the wildcats nor the relatively small bears found in this State ever attack a human being.) Rabbits, squirrels, woodchucks, and hedgehogs are plentiful throughout most of the State, and are killed in large numbers for sport, for food, and for the protection of crops.

Nearly all kinds of fresh-water fish, except some that are native only to tropical waters, are found in Vermont's lakes and streams. Chief of these from the sportsman's viewpoint are the several varieties of trout: speckled (brook), lake (longe), golden (indigenous to Lake Averill), and three introduced varieties — rainbow, steelhead, and landlocked salmon. It is to the propagation and protection of the trout, or *salmonidae*, that the Fish and Game Service, through its hatcheries and rearing pools, has devoted its chief energies for several years. Other important game and food fishes in Vermont waters include the wall-eyed pike, the pickerel, the catfish (bullpout), and the perch.

# HISTORY

SO FAR as is known, there was never any permanent Indian settlement of Vermont comparable to the Iroquois occupation of parts of what is now New York. Vermont was popular, however, as a hunting ground; parts of it were periodically subjected to such crude cultivation as the tribes knew; and during the seventeenth and eighteenth centuries it was a thoroughfare for the Canadian Indians who raided settlements to the south. Vermont had also been the scene of bitter Indian warfare before the advent of the white man. The Iroquois Nations, superior in intelligence and organization, had driven out the Algonquins who originally claimed this territory and would doubtless have maintained and extended their domination had not their old enemies secured the aid of the French early in the seventeenth century. There are few townships in which scattered traces of at least temporary Indian occupation have not been found. The largest and most important settlements, however, appear to have been at Vernon, Newbury, Swanton, and Orwell. The Indian remains at these places, and others but slightly less significant, are suggestive and illuminating, but sometimes conflicting, and it is not likely that the story of the Indian in Vermont will ever emerge complete and coherent from unrecorded antiquity.

Samuel Champlain, the French explorer, was the first white man known to have seen any part of the country that now comprises the State of Vermont. This was in 1609, when, coming from Canada, he went up the long lake that now bears his name and with his Algonquin allies engaged in successful battle with the Iroquois. By incurring then the undying enmity of the latter tribe, Champlain paradoxically laid the basis for the ultimate loss of French control of the region at the same time that he temporarily established it. For the proud Iroquois never forgave the nation that first humiliated them with 'white man's lightning,' and they relentlessly pursued the French along the 'Great Warpath' — between the Hudson and the St. Lawrence — until the latter bowed in ultimate defeat to the British a century and a half later.

The first attempted settlement within the limits of the present State was also French and of a military nature, though motivated in part by religious zeal. In 1666, Captain La Mothe built a fort and a shrine to

Sainte Anne on Isle La Motte in Lake Champlain, but the settlement was short-lived. In 1690, Captain Jacobus de Warm and a party from Albany, New York, established an outpost at what is now Chimney Point, in Addison Township, but this settlement ended with the military emergency that had brought it into being. Throughout the seventeenth and well into the eighteenth century, Vermont was a no-man's land, a passageway for French and Indian raiding parties seeking to harass the English settlements to the south and east. Furthermore, lying as it did between the two great natural water routes of the northeast, the Connecticut River and Lake Champlain, the territory possessed a strategic importance that was early recognized.

To protect its western settlements, Massachusetts, in 1724, established Fort Dummer, near present Brattleboro, the site being a part of the 'Equivalent Lands,' the soil but not the jurisdiction of which Massachusetts had ceded to Connecticut in 1715 in return for lands already settled by Massachusetts that a new survey had located in Connecticut. This is accepted as the first permanent settlement on Vermont soil; the first one in or near which white men have lived continuously from its founding to the present day. In 1731, France built a fort at Crown Point and a small village opposite on the Vermont side, but though extensive grants were allotted, the French made little attempt at the actual settlement of the region, all claims to which they formally relinquished to Great Britain by treaty in 1763.

The British monarchs, however, did not await this formality before granting with royal largesse the land that is now Vermont. In fact, the clouded and turbulent early history of this State and the very methods by which it became an independent territorial unit and then a State were dependent, not upon the fact that the land had not been granted, but rather upon the fact that it had been granted too many times; in terms of maddening ambiguity; by kings and governors who knew not what they were giving; and often to land speculators who cared little under whose jurisdiction their grants lay. In the commission which King George issued to Benning Wentworth as governor of New Hampshire on July 3, 1741, the New Hampshire territory was defined as extending 'due West Cross the said River [Merrimack] till it meets with our other governments.' But the eastern limits of the Province of New York had never been publicly proclaimed by the King. As Timothy Walker said in 1778: 'The King had never told his Governor of New Hampshire, in express terms, how far west he should go, and there stop, nor his Governor of New York how far east he should go and then cease.' But Governor Benning Wentworth was a shrewd, aggressive man, whose policy was always to go as far as possible in any direction in the interests of himself and his province. On September 6, 1744, the Crown, acting upon a report of the Privy Council that 'the same is now within the District of New Hampshire,' had ordered the Governor of New Hampshire to move the Assembly to provide for the maintenance of Fort Dummer, which was west of the Connecticut River. He therefore assumed — not without expectations of being challenged — that the province of New Hampshire extended as far westward as did Massachusetts and Connecticut. On that assumption he granted on January 3, 1749 (O.S.), to himself and several of his Portsmouth neighbors, the township of Bennington, the western border of which was an extension north of the line between Massachusetts and New York. Governor George Clinton of New York soon informed Governor Wentworth that he was making grants outside his jurisdiction, since the great grant made in 1664 by Charles II to his brother James, Duke of York, expressly included 'all the land from the west side of the Conectecutte River to the East side of De la Ware Bay.' He added that Connecticut's western border had been fixed where it was long ago to the satisfaction of both parties, but that Massachusetts' claims, like New Hampshire's, rested on 'intrusion.' Governor Wentworth, in reply, suggested that the matter be referred to the Crown, His Majesty's decision to be final for both parties, and Governor Clinton agreed. Wentworth continued, however, to make grants in what is now Vermont to the number of sixteen before 1754, though none so far west as Bennington. In 1754, war with France broke out; the Vermont territory was again open to invasion from the north and was not in demand; and the whole matter rested.

After the capture of Ticonderoga and Crown Point by the British in 1759, Governor Wentworth continued his grants, making as many as sixty in one year, until he had ultimately portioned out a very large part of what is now Vermont, then known as the New Hampshire Grants. The King and his Council were slow to act, though frequently besought by clever New York spokesmen; but at last, in his famous order of July 20, 1764, His Majesty declared 'the Western Banks of the River Connecticut to be the Boundary Line between the said two Provinces of New Hampshire and New York.' Thereupon New York immediately assumed that 'to be' was retroactive, declared all of Wentworth's grants to be null and void, and began to make new grants to new grantees of lands already held under the New Hampshire title. The dynamite, fifteen years in the mixing, was now ready.

The news of the King's decision was not known in the disputed territory until the summer of 1765. From that time until the battle of Lexington, the future State of Vermont was the scene of an important part of Colonial history that has been much romanticized and much misunderstood, especially in its motives. The settlers on the New Hampshire Grants were fearful for their land titles and in most instances unable to repurchase them by payment of additional fees to New York. Many of them were deeply in debt and about to lose their hard-won possessions by legal processes anyway. For this reason the first outbreaks of actual violence against New York consisted of the breaking up of the Cumberland County Court at Windsor in 1770, and armed resistance to a sheriff's posse at Bennington in 1771. The seizure of the courthouse at Westminster by one hundred armed men on March 13, 1775, resulting in the death of two of the rebels, has been extravagantly called the Westminster Massacre. It has also been designated the first engagement of the American Revolution by persons who failed to understand that the insurrection was against the authority and practice of the Province of New York, not against the British Crown, to which, as a matter of fact, the insurgents were in the very process of making a direct appeal. On the western side of the State, resistance to New York authority was more widespread, better organized, and even bolder. Here the 'Green Mountain Boys,' organized by Ethan Allen in 1770–71, persistently harassed and persecuted grantees of land in Vermont under New York title and even carried their depredations into the Province of New York itself. There was little of the heroic in these attacks, usually rendered safe by surprise and numbers. That most of the men in these groups thought themselves wronged is understandable, but they were aggressive outlaws from the only duly constituted government in the Colonies at that time. Nevertheless, the fact that there was a closely knit fighting group in this region, ready to respond at a minute's notice to the call of rousing if not always disinterested leaders, was one so fortuitously auspicious to the Colonial cause in the immediately ensuing struggle that posterity has not been entirely wrong in glossing over the real reasons for its being there.

Between 1765 and 1775 there had been, on both sides of the State, several conventions, the records of which are unfortunately incomplete, made up of delegates chosen from the Committees of Safety in the various towns. The most significant of these conventions was the so-called fourth Cumberland County Convention at Westminster on April 11, 1775; for it was there that the delegates voted to petition the Crown of England for a new and separate province and designated a committee to prepare the petition. The fact that this committee never functioned was due to the receipt of some startling news from a little place called Lexington, Massachusetts.

The American Revolution had begun. Upon receipt of that news, the inhabitants of the New Hampshire Grants ceased their hostile actions against New York and, for a time at least, lost most of their hostile feeling. Not to have done so would have considerably retarded the Colonial cause and might have altered the whole subsequent history of the State.

On May 10, 1775, less than a month after Lexington and Concord, Ethan Allen, who had been joined by Benedict Arnold, crossed Lake Champlain with eighty-three followers and captured Fort Ticonderoga, at that time the largest and most impregnable fortification in this country, without resistance from a sleeping British force of not more than fifty men. (Seventeen years earlier four thousand Frenchmen under Montcalm had successfully repelled sixteen thousand British assailants.) It was utterly in keeping with the man — and the most zealous debunkers have not been able to establish proof to the contrary — that Allen should have demanded the fort's surrender 'In the name of the Great Jehovah and the Continental Congress' — 'in spite of the fact,' as a later critic has said, 'that he held a commission from neither source.' The capture of Ticonderoga, followed on the 12th by the taking of the fort at Crown Point by Seth Warner, deprived the British of what, properly garrisoned, might have been an important northern base during the ensuing struggle; and it supplied Washington with nearly one hundred and fifty cannons by means of which he was able to drive the British from Boston the next winter; but its most important result was the thrill that ran through all the Colonies at the news of it and that made it one of the major factors in turning a local Massachusetts affray into a united American cause.

The idea of making a separate State of the New Hampshire Grants occurred to many individuals long before it was mentioned in any official document. But it was certain to gain wider favor when the national Declaration of Independence, of July 4, 1776, abrogated all allegiance to Great Britain. The New Hampshire Grants were no longer a part of New York, many of their inhabitants argued, since the grant of 1664 by Charles II was now nullified. A continuation of this line of reasoning would also have rendered null the township grants under Benning Wentworth and left the territory, governmentally speaking, in that 'state of nature' in which one of its spokesmen maintained it actually to be. There were many, however, and among them some of the ablest men in

the Grants, especially in the eastern townships, who sincerely believed
that it was both unfair and unwise to wage a separate fight for independence from New York at a time when all the Colonies were engaged —
or should have been — in winning their common independence from a
common enemy. But the aggressive faction prevailed and, as when any
bold venture meets with lasting success, made heroes of its leaders.

In treating this early period of Vermont history, it is often impossible
to learn the absolute truth, for the truth rests, not in documents and records, but in the collective mental and emotional reactions of the men
and women of Vermont at that time. These reactions were never completely unified, were frequently the result of misunderstanding and personal motives, and can never be entirely recaptured. History can be too
realistically as well as too romantically written. Most histories of Vermont have erred, not in making its founders and early leaders heroes —
that they surely were — but in making them perfect ones. Vermont's
early history, in the form familiar to 'every schoolboy,' consists of a small
group of glamorous incidents including the Green Mountain Boys' defense of their land titles against the threat of the Yorkers, the indomitable
Ethan Allen's capture of Ticonderoga, and the crucial battle of Bennington, which affected Saratoga, which in turn determined the fate of the
nation. If these passages of Vermont history appear to some to be under-
stressed in this brief account, it is not because their importance is not
recognized, but rather because that importance is so universally known
and accepted that it has seemed wiser to attempt to delineate broadly
the background and moving causes than merely to assert it again.

In a series of conventions (none of them wholly representative) the
ideas of independence were gradually articulated. Of great importance
was the encouragement of Dr. Thomas Young, then of Philadelphia, a
shrewd, learned, and liberal man, who convinced those interested in
forming a new State that they would be admitted to representation in
the general Congress as soon as they had done so. It was Young also who
by addressing these men as 'the inhabitants of Vermont' caused that name
to be adopted, in June, 1777, though Verd-Mont had been suggested
several years before as a suitable name for the region. A final impetus
to secession was given by the publication, on April 22, 1777, of the new
Constitution of New York State, which, in a number of ways, was extremely distasteful to an overwhelmingly large majority of the men on
the New Hampshire Grants, including many who up to that time had
been stubbornly loyal.

At last, in Windsor, in a convention that lasted six days, July 2–8,

1777, seventy-odd delegates asserted again the independence of Vermont (the State had declared its independence the previous January at Westminster) and unanimously adopted a Constitution for the State's government. It is unlikely that this task would have been completed had not a violent thunderstorm, following close upon the receipt of the news on July 8 of the evacuation of Ticonderoga, forced the convention to remain in Windsor long enough for a final reading and acceptance of the draft of the constitution. It is even less likely that the work of this convention would have been accomplished, in the face of danger from Burgoyne's rapidly approaching army, had its delegates known that on June 30 the petition and aspirations to statehood of the New Hampshire Grants had been peremptorily if not contemptuously rejected by the Continental Congress.

The first Constitution of Vermont, which has inevitably undergone revision since, was modeled closely upon that of Pennsylvania and was thus the result of the political philosophies of Benjamin Franklin and William Penn, based upon English common law. There were, however, several differences and additions. The Bill of Rights stated that no person of legal age 'ought to be holden by law to serve any person as a servant, slave, or apprentice.' This is the first express constitutional prohibition of all human slavery in history, but the importance of its priority can easily be — and has been — exaggerated. The Constitution of Delaware, a year earlier, had undoubtedly carried the same intention, though it expressly prohibited the sale or enslaving of only Negroes, Indians, and mulattoes. The Vermont clause was locally effective mainly against the bondage of apprenticeship, since there were never any Negro slaves in Vermont. The 1790 census report, which attributed sixteen colored slaves to this State, was in error; in 1870 an examination of the original manuscript returns showed that a careless compiler had transferred the numeral '16' from the foot of the 'free colored' column to that of the adjacent 'slaves' column.

In forming the actual frame of government the chief features of the Vermont plan were these: the change of right of suffrage from a taxpaying to a manhood basis; the provision for a unicameral legislature; and the diminution of executive power in the form of the governor's council. Of these changes the first is by far the most notable. *Vermont was the first State in this country to provide universal manhood suffrage.* Every other State Constitution — despite the proclamations of equality in the preambles — made the right to vote dependent upon property, owned or rented, or a specified yearly income.

The first general election in the new State was held on March 3, 1778; the General Assembly convened on March 12 to count the votes for State officers; and the next day — despite the fact that it was Friday the 13th — the government was inaugurated, with Governor Chittenden at its head. Ethan Allen was not more perfectly suited to lead the men of Vermont under arms than was Thomas Chittenden to be the head of its body politic. For eighteen years this unlearned, uneloquent, informal one-eyed giant of a man governed the people of this State, most of whom felt, with Ethan Allen, that Tom Chittenden was bound to be right even when he couldn't tell why.

From July 8, 1777, to March 4, 1791, Vermont was a completely independent republic, but it was also a tottering one. There were many within the confines of the new State, especially in the southeastern part, who refused to recognize its authority and remained stubbornly loyal to and in communication with New York. Another cause of dissension and ill feeling was the proposed annexation of sixteen towns in western New Hampshire whose inhabitants desired them to become a part of Vermont. The annexation actually did take place, but was not permanent.

The idea of ultimately joining the union of the other thirteen States was in the mind of most Vermonters from the time when statehood was first achieved. Those States, however, had more urgent matters to consider, and were, furthermore, antagonized by Vermont's revolt from New York authority during such crucial times and by the fact that, valuable as its services had been at Ticonderoga, Crown Point, Hubbardton, and Bennington, the State had taken almost no aggressive part in the later stages of the Revolution, although it maintained and garrisoned a series of forts within its own borders as a northern line of defense. So withdrawn was Vermont from the struggle — and the struggle from Vermont — that the British actually approached some of its leaders in an attempt to align the State with their cause and make it a Crown dependency. But while there were many Tories in Vermont, as elsewhere, they certainly never constituted a majority of the population; and later historians have seen in its passive and ambiguous attitude a conscious and extremely strategic policy by which the British were restrained from launching through its territory an offensive against the Colonies to the south. Vermont maintained its independence for nearly fourteen years, longer, in fact, than it desired to, and during that time it performed almost all of the acts of a sovereign government, including issuing bills of credit, coining money, regulating weights and measures, establishing post offices, naturalizing citizens of other States and countries, and corresponding with foreign governments.

The story of the admission of Vermont into the Union is one of long delays and mutual misunderstandings. Vermont was led to believe that it would be admitted long before it was, and each disappointment strengthened its feeling of independence and endangered the balance of the chip on its shoulder. George Washington seriously believed that it would be necessary to subdue Vermont with arms, as his long and justly famous letter of February 11, 1783, to the President of Congress makes clear. Happily Washington was for once wrong. Vermont steadily gained the friendly confidence of neighboring States. The ancient dispute with New York over land grants was settled forever in 1790 for $30,000. Vermont ratified and adopted the Constitution of the United States at Bennington in January, 1791. And on March 4 of the same year, Congress unanimously passed an act for the admission of Vermont into the Union as the fourteenth State and the first one to be added to the original thirteen. Vermont's little home-built ship of State — buffeted by storms beyond its control, endangered by dissension and even mutiny among the crew, sometimes unwisely but always daringly manned — was safe in harbor at last. Vermont has retained and maintained in significant ways its own inviolable identity, but the most distinctive as well as the most tempestuous period of its history ended when it became one of the United States of America.

In the thirty years since 1760, Vermont had developed from a wilderness inhabited by 300 people to a sovereign State with a population of 85,-425. The two decades following its admission to the Union brought the greatest increase in population that the State has ever known: from 85,-425 in 1790 to 154,465 in 1800 to 217,895 in 1810. No other northern or eastern State showed so large an increase by percentage during this period. Many of the new immigrants came, as in the earliest days, from southern New England. The country was still largely agricultural, and Vermont seemed to offer an opportunity somewhat similar to that presented by the West at a later period. For this reason many of the newcomers settled in the relatively undeveloped northern sections of the State.

During the same two decades six new counties and fifty-one townships were settled. By 1810 the State had assumed very much the geographical division that obtains today, with the exception of a few townships and Lamoille County, which was created in 1835. The Constitution underwent its last general revision in 1793, the permanent capital was established at Montpelier in 1805, and a State House was built there in 1808. The University of Vermont was opened in 1800, and the first bank was chartered in 1806.

In this period of general stabilization and creation of institutions necessary for a socially as well as a politically independent State, Vermont
also achieved the highest degree of economic self-sufficiency that it has
ever known. The Embargo Act that preceded the War of 1812 stimulated
the establishment of more small factories, mills, and forges than can ever
exist here again under modern methods of production and distribution.
In 1810, for example, there were one hundred and twenty-five distilleries
in the State; in 1850 there was not one.

With the declaration of war against Great Britain in 1812, Vermont
again became a frontier State to a hostile country. An invasion of this
country from Canada — and one seemed inevitable — was to be anti-
cipated through Vermont. Panic seized the inhabitants of the northern
part of the State, and frenzied preparations were made to resist an attack. In this crisis Vermonters reverted more or less to the attitude that
had been forced upon them during the Revolution. Late in 1813, Governor
Martin Chittenden, son of the first governor, issued a proclamation ordering the Vermont Militia stationed at Plattsburgh to return home, de-
claring: 'the military strength and resources of this State must be reserved for its own defence and protection exclusively excepting in cases
provided for by the Constitution of the U. States; and then under orders
only from the Commander-in-chief.' As a result of this proclamation,
resolutions were introduced into the National Congress requesting the
Attorney General of the United States to institute prosecution against
Governor Chittenden, but they were tabled.

Much less easy to condone than an imperfect conception of the respon-
sibilities of union was the wholesale smuggling which was carried on between Vermont and Canada and which Federal officers, despite several
violent affrays, were unable to halt. In 1814, Sir George Prevost, Governor General of Canada, reported: 'two-thirds of the army in Canada are
at this moment eating beef provided by American contractors, drawn
principally from the States of Vermont and New York.' And General
Izard of the American army reported to the Secretary of War: 'were it not
for these supplies [Vermont cattle] the British forces in Canada would
soon be suffering from famine.'

Oddly enough, however, it was as the base of the naval activities of
Macdonough's fleet on Lake Champlain that Vermont was most vitally
involved in this struggle. The 'poor forlorn looking squadron' chose
Shelburne as winter quarters in 1812–13. After an unsuccessful engage-
ment the next June and two British raids by water on Burlington and
Swanton in August, Macdonough chose the small city of Vergennes, on

the navigable Otter Creek, as the place in which to winter (1813-14), and above all to add to, his fleet. In the yards at Vergennes new ships, of Vermont timber, were constructed in record time: ships without which the decisive battle of Plattsburgh, which gave America control of Lake Champlain as completely as Perry's victory had given it control of Lake Erie, could not have been won in the following September. This battle saved Vermont from immediate British occupation, and Vermonters appropriately played an important part in the land engagement that accompanied the naval victory. The State had redeemed itself — if it can be called redemption to have rendered, however tardily, whole-hearted support to what Woodrow Wilson termed a 'clumsy, foolhardy, haphazard war.'

The year 1816, 'the famine year,' or 'eighteen hundred and froze to death,' brought the greatest physical hardships that the inhabitants of this State as a whole have ever known. On June 8 a foot of snow fell and blew into drifts two and three feet high. There was a little snow in July and August and a heavy frost on September 10. Almost no crops were harvested that fall. Much of the livestock in the State perished, the hay crop having failed. Nettles, wild turnips, hedgehogs, and other crude substitutes for ordinary fare kept all but a few of the human inhabitants from starvation, but the suffering was so intense that the year proved a vital factor in greatly increasing the emigration from Vermont to the lands of promise in the West, particularly Ohio — an exodus that was duplicated in all the New England States.

Beginning in the 1820's, though there had been previous rumblings, and reaching its greatest intensity about 1835, the Anti-Masonic movement colored and disturbed the political and emotional life of Vermont to an almost incredible extent. Not limited to this State, it was more dominant here than anywhere else in this part of the country, and Caledonia County was the acknowledged center of the movement in New England. Masons were excluded from jury service and town offices, Masonic clergymen were driven from their pulpits, and members of families were irrevocably alienated from one another. In 1831 Governor Palmer was elected on an Anti-Masonic ticket and was re-elected in the three succeeding years. In the election of 1832, Vermont was the only State in the Union to cast its votes for the Anti-Masonic presidential candidate, William Wirt. Many Masons withdrew from the order, and in 1834 all the lodges in Washington and Windham Counties were voluntarily dissolved by their members. The Burlington *Sentinel* (1835) charged that, Anti-Masonry being about to expire, its supporters were preparing to leap upon 'the hobby of anti-slavery.' Again in 1837, Senator Wright of New York, a former Vermonter, in a long letter addressed to the people of this State, expressed apprehension that the distraction of Anti-Masonry would be succeeded 'by some other exciting topic or political hobby, like Anti-Slavery or modern Abolitionism.' It may be true that the training in agitation afforded by this earlier fury contributed appreciably to the persistence and effectiveness of the later crusade. But the hatred of slavery in Vermont, which never ceased to grow in intensity during the next twenty-five years, was not bounded by party lines and sprang from a belief too deep-rooted and long-cherished to be rightly called a hobby.

It was, however, the desire of the people of Vermont during the earliest years of this period to check the further growth of slavery rather than to abolish it where it already existed. In 1837, resolutions by the Vermont Legislature were presented to the National Senate protesting against the annexation of Texas and, further, 'against the admission into the Union of any State whose Constitution tolerates domestic slavery.' Senator King of Alabama called these resolutions 'an infamous libel on, and an insult to, the South.' Calhoun, in a personal letter, referred to the Vermont Resolutions as 'the first move from a State' and 'a new and bold move from a higher quarter.' Congress responded to these and similar resolutions by passing the famous 'Gag Laws,' which seemed to Vermonters to violate the sacred right of petition. In his opening address to the Legislature of 1844 Governor Slade maintained that the annexation of Texas would constitute 'a new Union' and one with which Vermont should 'have no connection.'

Vermonters had, therefore, little enthusiasm for the Mexican War, feeling as they did that it was being fought to add slave territory to the country. On June 1, 1846, Governor Slade proclaimed, 'the voluntary service of those who may be disposed to engage in this war will be accepted to an extent sufficient to form one battalion of five companies of infantry,' which must certainly be one of the faintest calls to arms ever officially issued. Not all Vermonters were so lukewarm, however. Truman Ransom resigned the presidency of Norwich University to become a major in, and later lieutenant colonel in command of, the Ninth Regiment. He was killed at Chapultepec, at the capture of which two members of the single Vermont company, Sergeant-Major Fairbanks and Captain Kimball, were the first to reach the roof of the Bishop's Palace and lower the Mexican colors.

The Vermont Legislature continued to make annual resolutions protesting against the practice of slavery and to send copies of them to the legislatures of all the other States. Almost every Southern State at one time or another returned equally dogmatic replies, some of which violated dignity if not sobriety. A resolution offered in the Georgia Legislature in 1856 proposed to transmit to the Governor of Vermont a former pro-slavery resolution enclosed in a leaden bullet, the addition of gunpowder and a coil of rope being later suggested. Another Georgia resolution requested President Pierce to employ enough able-bodied Irishmen to dig a ditch around Vermont and float 'the thing' into the Atlantic Ocean. The *Richmond* (Va.) *Enquirer* in 1856 spoke of Vermont as 'Always foremost in the path of infamy.' Throughout the nation Vermont became the variously regarded symbol of an unyielding determination that slavery must be abolished forever from all parts of the United States.

The abrogation of the Missouri Compromise relative to Nebraska ruined the Whig Party in the nation, and in 1856 gave control of Vermont to the new anti-slavery Republican Party, which has dominated it ever since. In the election of 1860 Lincoln received four times as many votes in Vermont as did Stephen A. Douglas, despite the fact that the latter was the first native-born Vermonter ever to be nominated for the presidency and campaigned in this State in person. Thus ruthlessly did the people of Vermont subjugate all other emotions and considerations to upholding what they believed to be the right side of the cause that was about to disrupt the nation.

Of all the wars waged by this country, the Civil War was the one that Vermonters entered most willingly and wholeheartedly and the one that cost them the heaviest toll. The State furnished 34,328 men (not counting large numbers who had emigrated westward from Vermont to such States as Ohio and Michigan), more than 91 per cent of whom were enlisted men. Five thousand one hundred and twenty-eight Vermonters died in service, and the State contributed $9,323,407 to war funds, including town bounties.

Though no actual battle took place on Vermont soil, the State was the scene of a Confederate raid, which took place at St. Albans in October, 1864, and threatened to precipitate an international crisis. As a result of the Canadian Courts' decisions in favor of the Confederate raiders, Congress abrogated the Canadian reciprocity treaty and both nations guarded the frontier for some time afterward. (*See ST. ALBANS.*)

Between 1866 and 1870, Vermont was in turn the base of operations against Canada by the Fenians, the Irish enthusiasts who aimed to take Canada away from the British Empire. Although there was some private sympathy with these ill-organized and abortive Fenian raids, they were, of course, not publicly countenanced or officially approved. (*See Tour 1D*, *FRANKLIN*.)

Between the Civil and Spanish-American Wars, Vermont remained in a condition that must be called relatively static, if not sluggish. The war between the States had taken a heavy toll from farms, hamlets, and cities of the men who would have been most energetic in all kinds of private and civic enterprises. The desertion of the hill farms, one of the State's most vital problems until the recent reclamation of many of them as summer homes, was well under way. Sheep-raising had ceased to be of real importance in the State's agriculture, and the transition to dairying was progressing slowly. There was no appreciable growth in population.

Still there did occur in this period some important changes and innovations in the governmental and State departments. Biennial sessions of the Legislature, which body had become bicameral in 1836, were begun in 1870. The next year the State Constitution underwent extensive amendment. The office of State Superintendent of Education was created in 1874, the State Board of Health was organized in 1886, and the State Highway Commission was established in 1898.

Throughout these years native sons of Vermont were making history outside the State. Senator Justin S. Morrill, whose record of almost forty-four continuous years of service in the House and Senate has never been equaled, conceived and brought to passage the Morrill Act, which through governmental aid led directly to the establishment of our entire present system of State-supported agricultural, scientific, and industrial schools of college rank. Senator George F. Edmunds was the author of the Electoral Commission Bill and the Senate member of the commission established by it that averted what at least threatened to be another civil upheaval over the Hayes-Tilden (1876) election. He was the author of the vital parts of the Sherman Anti-Trust Bill, and his name was twice (1880 and 1884) placed in nomination for the presidency. Judge Luke Poland, who served at various times as a member of both National Houses, rendered a great and unique service to his country by making the first revision of the laws of the United States ever attempted. In 1874, Congress accepted without a single amendment or reservation his decisions as to the incompatibility of some of its own enactments that had successively overlapped one another for nearly a century.

In 1880, Chester A. Arthur was elected Vice-President, and upon President Garfield's death in September, 1881, he succeeded to the presidency. He was the first native Vermonter to hold either office. (*See Tour 1E, FAIRFIELD*.)

In 1888, Levi P. Morton, a native Vermonter who had been United States Minister to France under Garfield, was elected Vice-President, with President Benjamin Harrison, in securing whose nomination the Republican delegation from Vermont had taken the lead.

Redfield Proctor, ex-Governor of Vermont and Secretary of War under Harrison, was United States Senator from Vermont from 1891 until his death in 1908. His speech in 1898 depicting conditions in Cuba as he had found them on a personal visit was an immediate factor in precipitating the Spanish-American War: 'one of those rare utterances which have really shaped public policies.'

The brief war with Spain brought such glory to George Dewey, who was born in Montpelier, and to Charles Clark, who, though born in Bradford, called the State Capital his home in later life, that it was facetiously referred to as 'the conflict between the town of Montpelier and the Kingdom of Spain.'

Backed by Senator Proctor and by Theodore Roosevelt, then Assistant Secretary of the Navy, Commodore Dewey, though ranked by seven superior officers, was given command of the Asiatic station in November, 1897. On the first day of May, 1898, he annihilated the Spanish fleet in Manila Bay. In a short morning's fighting, in which not a single American was killed, Spain's power in the Pacific was destroyed and the Philippine Islands were acquired by this country.

Scarcely less important and even more dramatic was the sixty-six day trip of Captain Clark from San Francisco to Santiago with the 'Oregon,' the pride of the American fleet, by way of the Straits of Magellan, which no modern battleship had previously navigated. He arrived at Santiago just in time to take the lead in the destruction of the Spanish fleet as it attempted to escape from Santiago harbor. The fifteen-thousand-mile race of the 'Oregon' did much to prove the efficiency of the battleship as an instrument of modern warfare and to impress upon the consciousness of America the desirability of the Panama Canal.

That the entrance of this country into the World War which so grimly climaxed the peaceful opening years of the century was favored by Vermonters in general is certain. In the spring of 1917, but *before* the declaration of war, the Vermont Legislature appropriated one million dollars for war purposes, an act that not only won wide acclaim, but also spared Vermont the financial embarrassment in which so many other States found themselves soon afterward. In the actual warfare nearly two thousand men and officers of the First Vermont Regiment, as a part of the Twenty-Sixth Division, were a part of the first United States Division in

France and the first National Guard troops to engage in actual combat. The refusal of the War Department to keep the Vermont regiment intact, however, deprived the State of the individuality its soldiers achieved in the Civil War. Exact statistics regarding Vermonters in the World War are difficult to obtain because there was no distinctive State organization and many Vermont men enlisted in other States and in Canada. According to the report of the Adjutant General, approximately 16,000 men were in service, more than half of them overseas, among whom the deaths from all causes totaled 642. The Commander-in-Chief of the Atlantic fleet during the World War was Admiral Henry T. Mayo, of Burlington, the fourth officer of his rank that this little inland State has given to the nation.

In 1920, Calvin Coolidge, a native Vermonter, was nominated and elected Vice-President of the United States on the Republican ticket with Warren G. Harding. In August, 1923, President Harding died after a short illness, and Coolidge succeeded to the presidency. He was visiting his aged father at his home in Plymouth, Vermont, when the news of Harding's death reached him, and he was sworn into the presidency by his father that night by the light of a kerosene lamp. This scene, so homely and so typically democratic, captured the imagination of the American people as no other connected with the presidency had since the days of Abraham Lincoln. Not since Lincoln, in fact, had there been a President so essentially homespun as Coolidge was. Those commentators who have expressed the belief that Calvin Coolidge's Yankee terseness, simple ways, and oft-repeated love of both the rigors and the beauties of his native State were a part of a sustained political pose are deluded by their own sophistication. In 1924, Coolidge was elected President, the first Vermonter ever to achieve that honor, though Chester A. Arthur, like Coolidge himself, had succeeded to the presidency.

The first week of November, 1927, brought the worst flood that Vermont has ever known, not even excepting that of 1830. Whole sections of towns and villages were swept away, sixty lives were lost, roads and railroads were in places obliterated, and millions of dollars' worth of damage was done. To help prevent a recurrence of this catastrophe, the Federal Government has built three large flood-control dams in strategic areas, and several others are proposed.

In 1936, Vermont gained national notice by declining the Green Mountain Parkway, which the Federal Government at an expense of $18,000,-000 proposed to establish as a National Park running the whole length of the State, with a motor highway, a bridle path, and a foot trail. The creation of the Parkway was contingent upon the conveying by Vermont to the United States of approximately 35,000 acres of land, to be governed and administered by Congress. The Parkway was defeated by a popular referendum.

In the presidential election of 1936, Vermont was one of only two States that returned a Republican plurality, adding its three electoral votes for Alfred M. Landon to the five from Maine. The parallel with 1912, when Vermont and Utah stood alone for Taft, and with 1832, when Vermont was the only State to support the Anti-Masonic candidates, is notable and gives evidence that in recent times as in its earliest days Vermont has retained that spirit of independence which has brought it both great praise and great obloquy, but which has always, whatever the issue, been the dominating force behind its history.

# AGRICULTURE

THE early settlement of Vermont was attended by dissension, controversy, and confusion that were scarcely favorable to even such a stable husbandry as the rugged and undeveloped land itself would have permitted. But in 1790 the State was for the first time politically unified and at peace (*see History*). There followed a decade of intensive settlement and development in which the population of Vermont nearly doubled. (In 1790 the population was 85,425; by 1800 it had risen to 154,465.) A century was to pass before it doubled again. The period of a strictly pioneer economy in which each household was sufficient unto itself had ended by 1790. An extensive trade with Boston, Hartford, and other southern New England cities had already begun to develop. Troy and New York City were also important markets, and northwestern Vermont carried on a considerable commerce with Montreal and Quebec.

The earliest item of export was pot and pearl ash, a by-product of land-clearing operations. Potash manufacture continued as late as 1840, but long before that date it had been relegated to a place of minor importance by the development of a highly diversified agriculture. Potatoes were grown for sale to starch factories. Wheat and rye were shipped to some extent, and some grain was sold to distilleries, but livestock, especially beef cattle, formed the real basis of the agriculture of the region.

*Grain and Meat Farming.* Beef, pork, mutton, butter, cheese, and grain were freighted out in winter on sleds drawn by four- to eight-horse teams. Large numbers of cattle were driven overland to Boston, New York, and other markets. A gazetteer of the State published in 1808 estimated the annual deliveries of Vermont cattle on the hoof in the Boston market at from twelve to fifteen thousand head.

Lake Champlain on the western and the Connecticut River on the eastern border of the State were highways for a large water-borne commerce. Trade on the Connecticut was facilitated by the completion of the Bellows Falls Canal in 1802. The Whitehall Canal connecting the lower end of Lake Champlain with the Hudson River was opened in 1819.

At no time has Vermont agriculture remained in a stable condition over an extended period of time. Hardly has one system of farming become generally established before it has begun to give way to another.

# ILLUSTRATIONS

The General Background

OF FIRST IMPORTANCE
Vermont's cows (which outnumber her people) are the main support of
agriculture and a prominent feature of the landscape

SUMMER

WINTER

SKI TOW

MAKING MAPLE SYRUP

**A CIVIC CENTER**
As found in a hundred Vermont towns

FILLING SILO

GRANITE QUARRY

AN OLD COLLEGE BUILDING, MIDDLEBURY

The process has been one of continual change, and each generation has seen a different type of farming prevail. The self-sufficing agriculture of the pioneers gave way to a mixed grain and livestock farming in the hands of their sons. The next generation saw the merino sheep dominate the agriculture of the State.

*Sheep Farming.* The shift of emphasis to sheep farming was due in part to sharper competition from other regions in the grain and meat markets of the cities of the Atlantic seaboard and in the foreign markets to which they were the door. Western New York and Ohio were occupied nearly as early as was Vermont, and produce from these regions soon found its way into Eastern markets. This movement was greatly accelerated by the opening of the Erie Canal in 1825.

On the other hand, the rapid expansion of the textile industry of southern New England opened an eager market for wool within easy reach of Vermont's pastures and meadows. As early as 1798 sheep were described as 'universally acknowledged to be the most useful' domestic animal. In 1824 it was predicted that 'the raising of wool [would] probably at no distant period constitute a principal branch of agricultural employment.'

Sheep-raising reached its peak in the decade from 1830 to 1840, but it continued to dominate the agriculture of the State until after the Civil War. The causes of the decline in the sheep industry and the substitution of a different type of agriculture were essentially the same as those which had, a generation before, led to the shift from grain and beef cattle to wool-growing. The era of railroad-building, beginning in earnest about 1850, gave Vermont readier access to its markets, but it also took away most of the advantage which, prior to the coming of the railroad, a proximity to these markets had provided. The extension of railroads into the West brought vast areas of free grazing land within reach of Eastern markets, and wool from Montana and Wyoming largely displaced that from Ohio and Vermont.

The twenty years following the Civil War constituted another period of profound change, this time from sheep to dairy cattle. It is not meant to suggest that the decline in sheep-raising had not begun at the beginning of this period or that the change to dairying was complete at its close, but this was the period of most rapid transition and it was one of severe depression in Vermont agriculture.

Two factors had an important bearing on the situation. One was the invention of horse-drawn harvesting machinery; the other was the industrial growth of the Northeast. Grain-growing was relatively unimportant in Vermont agriculture, but the invention of grain-harvesting machinery was an important factor in the rapid exploitation of the Mississippi Valley which loosed a flood of agricultural products on the world's markets. More immediate in its effect was the introduction of hay-making tools. Scattered boulders, steep hillsides, and small irregular fields were not serious obstacles when the scythe and the bull rake were the tools used. The mowing machine, industrial competition in the labor market, and the call of the West resulted in the transfer of considerable areas from tillage to pasture and in a large reduction in the farm labor force. These changes led to the combination of farms into larger units and, in some cases, to the entire abandonment of farms. Such a process is necessarily slow and painful, and it is by no means yet complete.

*Dairy Cattle.* As competition rendered sheep-raising less and less profitable, Vermont turned to the manufacture of butter and cheese, especially the former, finding a market in the rapidly increasing population of the cities lying to the south of the State. Vermont already had a considerable number of dairy cows, but the change from sheep-raising to dairying involved more than a simple increase in the number of cattle and a decrease in the number of sheep. Previous to the middle of the nineteenth century such dairy products as were made were primarily for home use, and although some were sold, their production was merely incidental to the raising of beef. The cattle were partly 'black cattle' descended from stock brought in by the first settlers, and partly Durhams (Shorthorns). There were also a few Devons, but the Durham was the principal breed.

Breeding stock of the dairy breeds (Ayrshire, Holstein, and Jersey) was introduced during the decade from 1860 to 1870, and from then on their development was rapid. The Jersey breed soon established itself in a position of leadership; indeed, it is hardly too much to say that the Jersey cow transformed Vermont into a dairy State.

Butter shipments to city markets increased rapidly. From St. Albans in Franklin County they tripled during the twenty years from 1852 to 1871, rising from 1,149,225 pounds to 3,270,182 pounds annually. During the same period cheese shipments from the same point rose from approximately 600,000 to 2,000,000 pounds and then declined to 400,000 pounds annually.

This was all dairy butter and cheese, delivered weekly to buyers at the railroad. The milk was set in shallow pans, skimmed, and the butter made in hand churns. The decade from 1870 to 1880 saw the quite general adoption of the deep, cold-setting method and the introduction and steady growth of a system of creameries. These latter were mostly gathered-cream factories, payment being made on the basis of the number of 'spaces' of cream in the creamer. Cheese factories were built in considerable numbers during the same period, but at no time have they approached the creameries in importance.

The centrifugal separator, introduced into Vermont in 1884, gave a further stimulus to the development of the butter factory system. The earlier separators were suitable only for creamery use, and for a few years there was a tendency to shift from cream gathering to the delivery of whole milk. The production of dairy-size separators swung the balance again the other way, and during the decade from 1900 to 1910 by far the greater part of Vermont milk was separated on the farm and the cream sold to butter factories. The advent of the separator also opened up a new market for butterfat in the form of sweet cream.

Vermont had seen grain, meat, and wool from Western points one after the other dominating the markets which it had once claimed as its own. As early as 1870, when the shift to dairying in Vermont was no more than well under way, the presence of Midwestern butter in Eastern markets again raised the specter of Western competition. As the dairy regions of Ohio, Wisconsin, Michigan, and Minnesota developed, the struggle for the market became more and more acute.

Again Vermont farmers found their most profitable course to be a shifting of ground, and again a major factor in the situation was the growth of population along the Atlantic seaboard.

*Milk.* This time the change was from the sale of cream to the butter factory to the sale of milk for consumption in fluid form. The change, though not so difficult as the one which a former generation had to make from sheep to dairy cattle, has nevertheless necessitated many adjustments in farm economy. It has been in process approximately thirty years and the State is now entirely within the boundaries of the New York and Boston milk sheds. During recent years approximately eighty per cent of the deliveries at dairy plants has been in the form of fluid milk, and of this, not quite two-thirds has been reshipped in the same form.

Boston receives more than fifty per cent of its milk supply from Vermont. In 1935 nearly 270,000,000 pounds of fluid milk were shipped to Boston and 125,500,000 pounds to New York.

The other important agricultural products of Vermont include forage, corn for grain, potatoes, apples, and poultry, Vermont turkeys being especially prized in the Boston and New York markets.

Vermont also leads all other States in the production of maple sugar and is primarily associated in the minds of many persons with this product, yet the value of the sugar crop in 1935, when the yield was greater and the prices were higher than they had been for several years, was only three per cent of the total value of the State's agricultural products. The most significant development in the maple-sugar industry in recent years has been the swing from sugar to fluid syrup. As late as the beginning of the present century most of the maple sap gathered was converted into solid sugar; in 1935 only seven per cent of the total output in pounds was in that form. This amazing change is due in part to the extensive use of fluid syrup in the manufacture of cigarettes and in part, apparently, to a change in taste, for the solid sugar form continued to be popular long after it had ceased to be widely used as a substitute for refined cane or beet sugar.

The Morgan horse, which was developed as a distinct breed in this State, has been important for more than a century and a quarter in the agriculture of Vermont, on whose hill farms horses can never be entirely supplanted by machinery. The preservation and stabilization of the pure Morgan strain has been the province of the horse-breeder rather than of the dirt farmer. But the farmers of Vermont have reason to be grateful for the Morgan's stamina and will-to-work, which have proved to be prepotent attributes even when the blood was crossed with that of heavier breeds.

The constant succession of changes in the agriculture of the State in the past suggests that still others may be in store for the future, but prophecy is too hazardous to venture. Three things in the main have been the impelling and guiding forces in past changes. These are the opening-up of new agricultural lands, the development of new transportation facilities, and the growth of population in near-by market centers. Students of population trends do not foresee a continued increase in the number of people in this area comparable to the increase in the past. Changes in food habits, however, may affect the agriculture of Vermont significantly. There are no new agricultural lands within the boundaries of the United States which are open to settlement, but developments in the markets, foreign and domestic, in which their products are sold may cause changes in the agriculture of Midwestern States which will affect the competitive situation in Eastern markets. Furthermore, it is at least possible that developments are impending in transportation comparable in their significance to the building of the Erie Canal or to the railroad construction program of the nineteenth century.

# INDUSTRY AND COMMERCE

VERMONT'S industrial development began almost simultaneously with its first settlement. The enterprising pioneers were quick to take advantage of the water-power, the availability of which was in many cases the reason for their choice of location. Just as much of the early agriculture was merely for domestic and neighborhood use, so individual industries were small and served only their immediate vicinities.

Lumber was the State's earliest export, soon complemented by considerable amounts of pot and pearl ash. The ash was obtained by the burning, not only of wood waste, but also of fine timber cut from the heavily wooded areas where settlements were established. If this seems to have been a wasteful procedure, it should be remembered that the pioneer, eager to get his crops started, cleared his land as rapidly as possible, that he had no time to dress the logs, and that there was no market for the timber he soon saw piled around him. Moreover, the manufacture of pot and pearl ash, to be exported to Canada and thence to Europe, provided him with almost the only cash money he had, for most business was conducted by barter.

Wider areas were cleared as settlements grew into towns, and the possibilities of Lake Champlain and its tributaries for transportation were soon more fully realized. Lumbering was the first large industry to be solidly established in Vermont. From the mouth of the Winooski River, and from other parts of the State lying in the Champlain Valley, great rafts of logs, and later of roughly dressed lumber, were floated to Quebec for the English market. In the late 1840's the tide of shipping reversed, and the products of the great Canadian forests came over the lake to Vermont. In the 1880's only two cities in the country surpassed Burlington in the amount of lumber worked and sold. By the latest census figures the yearly value of Vermont's lumber and lumber products is slightly less than $7,300,000; that of wood turned and shaped and other wooden goods, $2,700,000; and that of furniture upwards of $3,600,000. The saw logs, veneer wood, firewood, pulpwood, railroad ties, poles, and piling cut yearly in Vermont have an aggregate value of more than $4,900,000. The annual yield of the State's forests is about 425,000,000 feet.

With the need for warm clothing to withstand the rigorous winter climate, it was natural that wool production should have been an early industry. Before the Revolution a woolen mill had been established at Bennington. By 1810, according to the first dependable records, there were 166 fulling mills manufacturing woolen goods to the yearly value of nearly $1,500,000. Ten years later the value of woolens had fallen to less than $200,000, because of the stagnation of business and the national embargo accompanying the War of 1812. It was many years before the industry recovered; even in 1840 it had not regained its 1810 level, but by 1870 it had risen to more than $3,500,000. By then, however, lower-priced wool from the West was coming to the Eastern markets, farmers were selling their sheep, and again there was a slump. By the 1930's, however, the value of woolen cloth, knit goods, and clothing was nearly $7,500,000.

Paper-making was another early Vermont industry, a mill having been established at Bennington in 1784. Much of its product was sent through the forests on horseback to New York State, previous to the building of a paper mill at Troy, New York. Ten years later Colonel Matthew Lyon, son-in-law of Governor Chittenden, was manufacturing wrapping paper and newsprint at Fair Haven, and by 1810 there were eleven mills in the State with an output valued at more than $70,000 annually. This early product was, of course, chiefly rag paper, the first successful pulp-wood process not being evolved until the 1860's. This was at Bellows Falls, the principal center of paper-making in the State at present. By 1910 the paper industry ranked sixth in importance in Vermont, and by the 1930's it stood third, with a yearly production of paper, paper goods, wood pulp, and fiber valued at about $8,000,000.

In the development of its mineral resources Vermont holds a prominent place among the States of the Union. It ranks second in the production of marble, granite, and slate. Vermont marble, ranging in color from Parian white to jet black, and comprising about one hundred varieties, has been chosen for more than seventy per cent of the monuments and statuary in the country (see RUTLAND). Vermont granite is for the most part of high quality, fine-grained, and attractively shaded. Like the marble it is particularly well suited for ornamental and monumental purposes and, carved and polished for building trim, it supplies about half the nation's demand in this field (see BARRE). Quarries of both stones are seemingly inexhaustible. Extensive granite deposits are on the eastern side of the State, principally near Barre, Woodbury, Bethel, and Dummerston. The long marble area on the western side begins in Bennington County and stretches northward into Chittenden County, the principal quarries being near West Rutland, Proctor, Dorset, Middlebury, and at Isle La Motte and Fisk in Grand Isle County.

Of the State's four distinct slate regions, the principal one, and one of the most remarkable slate areas in the country, is in the western part of Rutland County, lying between the Taconic Mountains and Lake Champlain. It is about twenty-six miles in length and varies in width from five to ten miles. Quarries about Fair Haven produce unfading varieties of green, purple, and mottled slate; these varieties are said to be found nowhere else in the United States and are in great demand for decorative roofing. Other quarries produce black slate, also for roofing; while a few confine themselves to mill stock, which is sawed into slabs for billiard-table tops, electric switchboards, and similar products. In all, Vermont produces about forty-five per cent of the slate used in the United States.

The best asbestos deposits in the State are in the vicinity of Belvidere Mountain, though there are numerous outcroppings elsewhere. Apparently the deposits are related to those in Canada, the most extensive known in the world. The rock is of short fiber and has come into considerable use for brake linings and insulating material.

Lime, to the value of $500,000 yearly, talc, soapstone, kaolin, and ocher are other minerals that are mined in Vermont in considerable quantities. Talc — about one-fourth of all produced in the United States at present — promises to assume increasing importance with the greater demand for it by manufacturers of such diverse commodities as paper, rubber, waterproof paint, gypsum wall plasters, shade-cloth and curtains, and, of course, toilet powders and soaps.

Among the minor products of Vermont industry — no complete enumeration of which can be attempted here — several are of interest because of their unusual or historic nature: organs, manufactured at Brattleboro since 1835; scythe handles, from a plant at Bellows Falls that survives despite the machine reaper; scales, of many types and degrees of precision, manufactured at Rutland and St. Johnsbury; turret lathes, identified since their inception with a Springfield factory; and steel squares, supplied by a factory at South Shaftsbury, the town where they were invented.

# TRANSPORTATION

VERMONT'S relatively small area; its recent conscious and intensive campaign to attract tourists; its geographical location, which makes it a thoroughfare between the eastern United States and eastern Canada, including Montreal; and the extensive rehabilitation of railroads, highways, and bridges damaged by the great flood of 1927: all these factors have resulted in a network of highways and trunk lines that makes travel within or through the State both expeditious and comfortable.

It was not ever thus. In the early days Vermont's mountains and sparsely populated rural districts were all but inaccessible and remained rural and sparsely populated because they were so. Much travel was on foot or horseback, unless goods or produce were being arduously transported in ox-carts. Such roads as did exist were not only rough, but were tortuous, following brooks and rivers through wasteful miles of curves and windings because bridges could not be built and maintained, but seldom swerving for mountains.

Early Vermonters were well aware of the need for adequate routes of travel and commercial transport long before they acquired them. As early as 1763, Jacob Bayley, one of the most judicious settlers on the Grants, petitioned the General Court of New Hampshire for aid in building a road from Dover to the newly opened territory around Newbury. More ambitious was the projected water-route from Vermont to the sea to be made by cutting a canal from Lake Champlain to the St. Lawrence River. Actively agitated during the 1780's, the project was dropped after Vermont's entrance into the Union, though it has proponents even today.

The first real roads in Vermont were of military origin. The earliest was the Crown Point Military Road, built in 1759-60, which entered the State at Springfield, crossed it on a northwestern slant, and left it at Chimney Point, just across from its terminus at Crown Point, New York. It was of the old 'corduroy' type, consisting of the trunks of small trees laid transversely in the path cleared by felling them. Similarly constructed was General Moses Hazen's military road, built in the summer of 1779 for a proposed second invasion of Canada. Beginning at Newbury, it extended north of northwest through the sections that are now Caledonia and Orleans Counties, ending near the scenic mountain cut now called Hazen's Notch in the township of Westfield. Neither of these roads fulfilled the important military purposes for which they were built, but both remained the chief routes of travel in their respective sections for many years and aided materially in the settlement and development of the State.

The next roads of importance were the turnpikes, which under private or corporate ownership often made highways possible in places where the towns could not have afforded to build them, and facilitated the early (1801) establishment of stagecoach lines. Beginning at the very end of the eighteenth century, these roads were maintained on a toll basis for forty years, a very few of them much longer than that. When popular rebellion forced abandonment of the toll charges, many of these roads were purchased by towns and incorporated into the general highway system.

It was in the utilization of the natural water-routes on both sides of the State that early Vermonters showed the most interest and initiative. Captain Samuel Morey of Fairlee, whose work was antedated by that of John Fitch, operated a steam-driven boat on the Connecticut River as early as 1793 (see Tour 1, FAIRLEE). In 1808, less than a year after the success of Fulton's 'Clermont,' the steamer 'Vermont' was launched on Lake Champlain, the second steamship in the world to be put into regular commercial operation. Other steamships soon followed, and in 1826 the Champlain Transportation Company was formed and incorporated by the State Legislature. Still in operation, it is today the oldest active commercial steamship company in the world.

Burlington remained a busy shipping port until the late years of the nineteenth century. A considerable fleet of sailing vessels engaged in the lumber trade with Canada operated from there, in addition to freight and passenger steamers. The water-route formed by the Hudson River, Champlain Canal, and Lake Champlain is still extensively used for transporting such freight as petroleum products, coal, and fertilizer from New York. The automobile ferries at frequent intervals are important links in the routes connecting summer resort sections of the Adirondacks and the Green and the White Mountains.

During the 1830's steamers operated on the Connecticut River between Hartford, Connecticut, and White River Junction, and one boat — which, according to a local commentator, was constructed 'for the navigation of heavy dew' — even plowed as far north as Wells River. There has been at least one steamship operating regularly since 1854 on Lake Memphremagog.

The competition between Boston and New York for trade with the newly opened West was the immediate motivating force behind the building of the first railroad in Vermont, the Vermont Central. This competition dated from the opening of the Erie Canal in 1825. At first, capitalists of northern New York, Vermont, and Boston sought to fight the Erie with another canal route between Boston and Ogdensburg, New York. The coming of the railroads put an end to this plan, but a part of the canal survey, made in 1824, was utilized in choosing the route of the Vermont Central, which was regarded by its builders, not as a Vermont line, but primarily as a link in a trunk route between Boston and the Great Lakes. Ground was broken at Northfield in January, 1846, for the building of the Vermont Central, and the first passenger train was run, between White River Junction and Bethel, on June 26, 1848. Less than two years later the company went into a receivership, as a result of which it became united with the Vermont and Canada Railroad for many years. At present, as the Central Vermont Railways, Inc., it is a subsidiary of Canadian National Railways, Inc., and serves as an important connection between transcontinental lines of the parent corporation and the cities of the Atlantic seaboard of the United States.

The route of the Vermont Central is illustrative of the fact that personalities, local pride, and executive willfulness sometimes supplanted logic and the ideal of service in laying out the early railroads. Montpelier and Barre, for instance, were both left off the main line of the Central largely because of Governor Paine's determination to include his home town, Northfield, where he also established the company's head offices and built the most elaborate depot. Burlington, too, the largest city in the State, was left off the main line because the men there engaged in shipping on Lake Champlain had opposed the railroad from the first. They quite accurately foresaw that the products of farms and small industries throughout northern Vermont, which they had been shipping by water to Albany and New York, would be diverted by the railroad to Boston.

The second railroad in the State, however, the Lake Champlain and Connecticut River Railroad, now the Rutland, received the support of the Burlington shipping interests because it did not tap their trading area and it did open up new territory to the south. The road was begun a short time after the Central and was its bitter rival for many years, at one time nearly gaining stock control of it.

The third line to be opened in Vermont was the Passumpsic and Connecticut Rivers Railroad, roughly paralleling the Rutland on the east side of the State. Governor Fairbanks of St. Johnsbury was one of the chief financial backers of this line, which was more successful in avoiding financial difficulties than either of its two slightly earlier competitors.

Today the chief railway systems of Vermont are composed of these three pioneer roads, under different ownership and with some extensions: the Rutland on the west side, the Central Vermont in the central part, and the Boston and Maine and the Canadian Pacific on the east side of the State. There are, of course, other connecting lines and freight lines that are of local importance.

The electric railroad has come and gone in Vermont within a lifetime. The first one, which began operations in 1893, ran between Burlington and Winooski, replacing an earlier horse-car line. Today only one electric line remains: that connecting Springfield with its nearest steam railroad station at Charlestown, New Hampshire. In Burlington, Rutland, Montpelier, Barre, and other towns and cities where street-cars handled local traffic twenty years ago, they have today been supplanted by busses and trucks. Thomas Davenport, who was born in Williamstown, Vermont, and did his great work in Brandon, not only invented and obtained a patent for the first electric motor in history (1837), but also made a model of the first street-car, which actually ran on a small circular track and is now preserved at the Smithsonian Institution in Washington.

Vermont's progress in building hard-surface roads was slow until the flood of 1927 destroyed many bridges and miles of highways. This disaster served to arouse the State to a planned, progressive highway-building policy that has resulted in superior-to-gravel roads on most of the main-traveled routes (*see General Information*).

The rural nature of Vermont and the adequate coverage of the greater part of it by steam and electric railroads retarded the development of bus lines within and through the State. The highway improvements made since 1927, the increased facilities for keeping the main routes open for winter travel, and Vermont's ever-growing popularity both as a summer and a winter resort have made possible a network of bus lines covering the whole State except for a few areas in the extreme northern and northeastern sections.

Because it lacks large centers of population, Vermont was later than some States in the development of aviation and flying facilities. Private and municipal initiative, however, has led to the establishment of twelve airports, six of them with storage hangars, and one (Burlington) radio-equipped. The only regular commercial air line through the State is that between Boston and Montreal. Daily planes stop on schedule at Barre and Montpelier (one stop) and Burlington, where the customs are cleared.

It seems highly probable that in the near future air travel will play an increasingly important rôle in bringing from metropolitan areas visitors who wish to spend a brief vacation in Vermont and to consume as little of it as possible in transit.

# RACIAL ELEMENTS

THE people of Vermont are, and always have been, predominantly of English stock. The State was settled during the latter half of the eighteenth century by colonists from Massachusetts, New Hampshire, New York, and, above all, Connecticut, who were mainly of English extraction. The lack of new lands to develop and the absence of large manufacturing centers have left the State relatively unaffected by the waves of foreign immigration that have swept over almost every settled section of the country since 1830. During the past hundred years foreign-born persons have constituted, on an average, from ten to thirteen per cent of the total population of the State. The considerable variation over different periods of the ethnic origin of this foreign element can be explained partly, if not chiefly, by the affinity that undoubtedly exists between certain racial groups and certain types of labor.

In 1850, there were approximately fifteen thousand Irish in Vermont, this number constituting nearly half of the foreign-born and five per cent of the total population. They outnumbered all other groups among the laborers who built the first railroads in the State and operated the mills and quarries of that period. In these occupations, however, they have for the most part long since been replaced by other peoples. More thoroughly than any other race, the Irish have become assimilated and now occupy many positions of executive responsibility.

Since 1900 the largest single immigrant group has been the French-Canadian. As early as the 1830's this element began replacing the Yankee farmers in the northernmost tier of counties; today they constitute approximately one-quarter of the population there (including second generation) as compared with thirteen per cent of the State's total. In some towns they outnumber the inhabitants of English stock, and in several the parts of the Roman Catholic service that are not in Latin are conducted in French as well as in English. Since 1860 this group has also come in increasing numbers to the larger towns and cities of northern Vermont, in particular to the textile centers of Burlington and Winooski.

Recent immigrants are for the most part concentrated in the manufacturing and quarry towns. In the mills and machine shops of Windsor County — in Windsor, Springfield, Cavendish, Proctorsville, and Ludlow

— there is a considerable foreign element that is predominantly Slavic. In the Rutland County quarry towns — Proctor, West Rutland, and Poultney — the Poles, Czechs, and Russians have been joined by numbers of Austrians and Swedes. In Poultney, Castleton, and Fair Haven, settlements of Welsh keep alive their own traditions and maintain their racial customs as strictly as the Welsh always do, wherever they settle. Beautiful music, for instance, is still heard in half a dozen Welsh churches in this section.

In Barre, the heart of the granite quarry region in Washington County, Scots and Italians predominate over other immigrant groups. The Scots in Barre are largely from Aberdeen, itself an important granite district. The Italians, many of whom are highly skilled stonecutters, are mostly from the quarry areas of north central Italy.

Forming a thin crescent from Andover on the eastern side of the State to Sandgate on the western, is a sprinkling of Finns who have eagerly bought farms, many of them abandoned, in this area. It is interesting to note that a large percentage of them have come from the manufacturing cities of New Hampshire to which they, or their parents, originally immigrated. Their settling in Vermont constitutes a real reversion to the soil.

To summarize: The largest foreign-born group in Vermont is the French-Canadians, who constitute five per cent of the State's total population. The next largest is the non-French-Canadians, with slightly less than three per cent. No other foreign-born group constitutes so much as one per cent of the total. When the classification is broadened to include persons of foreign or mixed parentage, the percentages are as follows: French-Canadian, thirteen per cent; non-French-Canadian, seven per cent; Irish, slightly less than three per cent; Italian, two per cent; and English, slightly less than two per cent.

The concentration of these foreign-born groups in a relatively few towns, cities, and localities has undoubtedly retarded their assimilation. It is also partly responsible, no doubt, for the fact that the foreign elements in Vermont have made no appreciable contribution to arts or manners and no changes in the ways of living — or of thinking — of Vermonters. Still the members of the second generation, those of mixed or foreign parentage, through education and imitation have in most instances become scarcely distinguishable from their companions whose forebears for many generations have lived in the State.

# EDUCATION

IN THE very earliest days of the New Hampshire Grants, reading and sums, at least, were taught in the home by parents who had received some education in the Colonies to the south from which most of the early settlers were drawn. There was never a law in the Grants, however, as there was in Massachusetts, compelling 'All Parents to teach their children to read... on penalty of 20s and to catechise them once a week.'

The earliest known public provision for education in Vermont was made on December 23, 1761, when the town of Guilford voted that land be set aside for a school. Bennington, however, was the first town to use public funds to build a schoolhouse.

The first general provision for education in the State occurs in the original (1777) constitution, Section 40 of which reads: 'A School or Schools shall be established in each town by the Legislature, for the convenient instruction of Youth, with such Salaries to the masters, paid by each town, making proper Use of School-lands in each town, thereby to enable them to instruct Youth at low Prices: One Grammar School in each County, and one University in this State ought to be established by Direction of the General Assembly.' By this passage, knotty in syntax, but clear in intent, Vermont became the first State to provide through the fundamental law of its constitution for a clearly articulated system of education beginning with primary schools and concluding with a university.

The fact that this liberal conception was truncated in the 1786 revision of the constitution to omit all mention of a State University was due in part to the fact that Vermont had, in the interval, more or less 'adopted' Dartmouth College. In 1785 that institution, toward which New Hampshire had, in the words of its first president, 'shown a very cool disposition,' had been given a land grant of twenty-three thousand acres by the Vermont General Assembly. This tract, later surveyed as the entire township of Wheelock, the college still owns. As a result of this grant, Vermont stands alone as the only State ever to have come, as a State, to the relief of an educational institution outside its own borders.

Vermont's first School Law, enacted in 1782, provided for the division of towns into independently administered *districts*, a wasteful and decentralized system that was not wholly abolished until 1892, when the town system was made compulsory. The general trend in Vermont toward fewer and better schools has been hastened by the depopulation of many rural districts and the introduction of an extensive system of transportation of pupils.

The maintenance of the first schools was mainly by voluntary subscription or taxation by the inhabitants of the various districts. Not until 1826 was authorization given by law to tax the grand list a definite percentage — pitifully small at first — for school revenue. Nevertheless the acceptance of the idea of elementary education supported wholly by public funds had been achieved.

Publicly maintained schools of secondary rank, however, were not yet deemed necessary. This fact was chiefly due to the academies, or grammar schools, which had already been established and which continued to increase in number for more than three decades. The first secondary school in Vermont was Clio Hall, founded in 1780 at Bennington. Nine others were founded before the close of the eighteenth century, sixty-five more were added before 1850, and by the beginning of the Civil War the number had reached the amazing total of one hundred and nine. Several of these schools, especially among those founded before 1840, were denominational institutions, established, controlled, and, in part at least, supported by the churches. The rise of the public high school, beginning in the 1840's and gathering great impetus toward the end of the century, decreased the number and lessened the importance of the academies, though twenty-one of them are operating today. But it should never be forgotten that for nearly a century — a formative century — they provided respectable training for rural youth and constituted the essential link between the district school and the university.

It is possible that in a democracy, especially in a young democracy, there is danger of placing too much emphasis on the universality and availability of educational institutions and too little on the quality of the instruction they provide. No reproach should be given to those earliest school-teachers who in crude one-room buildings, with pebbles for counters, ink made from maple bark, and a handful of books — the Bible and whatever else they could get — taught the fundamentals of literacy to such children as could be spared from work to learn them. But on the other hand much honor should be accorded to the leaders who, as time and growth permitted, raised teaching from a primitive level to that of a scientifically trained profession. It is Vermont's good fortune that the pioneer in this field happened to choose this State as his work-

shop. This man, the Reverend Samuel Read Hall (1795-1876), opened
at Concord Corner, Vermont, on March 11, 1823, a 'teachers seminary'
which is now recognizable — and recognized — as the first normal school
in America. He conducted this school until 1830, when he left Vermont
for seven years to teach at Andover, Massachusetts, but before leaving
he wrote and published the first pedagogical textbook written or printed
in America, his 'Lectures on School-Keeping' (1829). Not even the material tools of teaching were untouched by Mr. Hall's innovations, for
he was the first person to introduce the blackboard into the schoolroom,
in the form of pine boards planed smooth and painted black. Everyone
who reads — who can read — these words will have been indirectly subjected to the influence of this man, who was a leader in introducing or suggesting so many of the changes that most clearly distinguish recent schooling from that of an earlier day.

There are at present three normal schools in the State, at Johnson,
Lyndon Center, and Castleton. The Department of Education at the
University of Vermont, which specializes in teacher training, is also under
the supervision of the State Board of Education and is State-supported.
What was formerly another normal school at Randolph Center is now the
Vermont State School of Agriculture.

Vermont also possesses institutions of higher learning, each of which
has a distinctive educational emphasis and its own composite personality.

On November 3, 1791, a bill passed the Vermont Legislature entitled
'An Act for the purpose of founding a University at Burlington.' Among
the earliest agitators for and the heaviest subscribers in support of this
university were the Allens, especially Ira. The institution began its active
career in 1801, ten years after its establishment. Not even a condensed
history of this school, or any other, can be given here, but mention must
be made of a noble experiment by the University of Vermont under its
most famous president, the Reverend James Marsh, who headed it from
1826 to 1833, when he resigned the presidency for the more congenial
professorship of intellectual and moral philosophy. President Marsh, influenced mainly by the prose writings of S. T. Coleridge, enlarged and
revised the curriculum to make philosophy 'the oscillating nerve that
should connect the various studies together,' a philosophy, different from
any previously taught in this country, that had extricated itself from
Locke. The influence of President Marsh and his system is reflected in
American Transcendentalism, of which a prominent research scholar has
recently pronounced him to be the true progenitor. In addition to its
departments of arts and sciences the present university includes the only

medical college in the State and the Vermont State Agricultural College.

Although not incorporated until 1800, Middlebury College has as long a history of actual service as has the University. It has been asserted that Middlebury was founded, in part at least, under the influence of Yale to counteract the alleged irreligion of the Allen influence at the University. If this is true, it is a striking example of a noble conclusion arrived at by faulty premises, for the Allens had no connection with, or influence upon, the University by the time it began actually to function, though they had been prominent in its conception. Never a large school, Middlebury has always maintained high scholastic standards which are reflected in the unusually large number of its graduates who have become well known as academic scholars. In recent years Middlebury has become most widely known for its summer school, which specializes in modern languages. The English School and School of Creative Writing, held at near-by Bread Loaf, has become a kind of national seminar in creative and critical writing.

Norwich University is the only military college in the State and among the leading ones of the country. It was founded in 1819 at Norwich by Captain Alden Partridge, a former superintendent of West Point, moved to Connecticut in 1824, and returned to Norwich in 1829. In 1866, after a disastrous fire, the university was removed to Northfield, its present and presumably permanent home. In an address delivered in 1820, Captain Partridge expressed the belief that the system of education in the United States was 'defective' in that: 'First: It is not sufficiently practical nor properly adapted to the duties an American citizen may be called upon to Discharge. Second: Another defect is the entire neglect in all our principal seminaries of physical education, of the cultivation and improvement of the physical powers of the student.' The routine and training of Norwich have consistently tried to remedy these 'defects' ever since.

St. Michael's College, in Winooski, was established in 1904 by the Fathers of St. Edmund, who had suffered confiscation of their schools in France. During its early years, made difficult by the lack of funds, the school was of the Continental preparatory school type. In 1913 it was incorporated as St. Michael's College. Trinity College, established in 1925 by the Catholic Sisters of Mercy, in Burlington, is the only Catholic College for women in the State.

The youngest of Vermont's institutions of higher learning is Bennington College, for girls, which after many years of preliminary planning began actual instruction in 1932. The aims of the college, explicitly stated and dominating its whole system of operation, are to encourage voluntary

self-dependent education throughout life; to develop permanent intellectual interests; to train students for social co-operation and responsibility;
and, finally, to fit each student's course of study as far as possible to her
individual tastes, talents, and needs. The academic year is divided into
two parts by a winter recess of two months which students are urged to
treat as a field period for observation and investigation correlated with
their work on the campus.

There are also in Vermont three junior colleges: Goddard Junior College, at Barre; Green Mountain Junior College, at Poultney; and Vermont
Junior College, at Montpelier.

Vermont has several educational 'firsts' other than those mentioned
which would be fitted into their proper places in a comprehensive history
of education in the State. All of these pioneer distinctions, however, might
in themselves add up to comparatively little. Their vital significance lies
in the fact that they are but manifestations of a spirit that has pervaded
Vermont from its earliest days: an innate and unshakable belief that it is
better to know than not to know.

# RECREATION

NEW ENGLAND as a whole is becoming more and more conscious of the value of recreation in its economy. Both the New England Council and the New England Regional Planning Commission are placing emphasis upon summer and winter sports developments, the first from a promotional, the second from a planning point of view. For Vermont in particular the nationwide increase in interest in recreation is significant. Although the undesirable types of exploitation common to some areas have been minimized here (so that the slogan of 'Unspoiled Vermont' is not yet hyperbole), nevertheless the State has seen its income from recreation rise in recent years to levels rivaling such traditional industries as milk production and quarrying.

From the Vermont Publicity Service in Montpelier may be secured publications describing in detail recreational advantages and facilities — booklets on hunting and fishing, on golf, on summer homes for sale, a directory of hotels and tourist resorts, and the like. Here no detailed prospectus can be attempted, but merely a brief account of the scope and variety of recreation in Vermont, together with some description of several of the more important recreational developments.

The primary appeal of Vermont for the visitor lies in its natural beauty. From the week-end tourist to the owner of a summer home people are drawn here by the charm and relative remoteness from modern life of Vermont's mountains, lakes, and streams. It is, therefore, to the hiker, the equestrian, the camper, the nature-lover that the State has most to offer. It is not, however, deficient in other facilities. Boating is enjoyed on the larger lakes, with Champlain naturally the leader in this respect. Canoeing is possible on many of the larger streams, such as Otter Creek, West River, and White River. There is an adequate supply of golf courses, though few are as elaborate as those in neighboring States. Opportunities for tennis are more limited, but the courts at Brattleboro and Middlebury, for example, are of tournament quality. Bathing is as common as are the scores of lakes and ponds, with every year more beaches being improved and rendered accessible by the State Forestry Service and the National Forest Service.

In winter sports facilities Vermont has made rapid progress in the past

few years. Ski trails, ski jumps, and ski tows are liberally distributed
throughout the State, and are now brought closer to large urban districts by an improved schedule of snow trains. The Mount Mansfield region is considered one of the leading winter sports areas in the East.

A descriptive summary of four important recreational developments in
Vermont, all of which are more completely discussed elsewhere in this
volume or in available publications, follows:


1. *The Long Trail*

The treatment of the Long Trail in this book is necessarily suggestive
and incomplete. Its course is indicated on the tour map, and cross-references are made to it at the more important points at which it crosses the
routes of the tours. Persons planning to hike the Long Trail, or any part
of it, should communicate with the Green Mountain Club, Rutland, Vermont. Their Guide Book (50¢) not only gives detailed descriptions of the
route, including shelters and stopping places, but contains valuable sug-
gestions as to equipment, food, and rules of the Trail.

On March 11, 1910, twenty-three hiking enthusiasts, headed by James
P. Taylor, then principal of Vermont Academy at Saxtons River, met at
Burlington and formed the Green Mountain Club, the purpose of which
was to build a foot-trail over the main range of the Green Mountains from
Massachusetts to the Canadian Line. Small at first, and financially handicapped, the group gradually acquired a larger membership, including
many persons outside the State. Those who were unable to contribute
money gave of their time, the actual construction of the Trail being done
largely by volunteer labor. Early progress was impeded by the necessity
of clearing away each year's undergrowth from the completed parts of the
Trail. In several places completed stretches were abandoned for a higher
location, a discouraging process at the time, but one that resulted in a
scenic gain. The 261-mile 'Footpath in the Wilderness' was finished in
1928, and the Green Mountain Club, which maintains and publicizes it,
is now on a solid financial basis, with more than 1500 paid memberships.

The Trail is divided into four main sections. The northernmost division, from the Canadian Line to Johnson, was the last to be built. This is
probably the wildest part of the route and is distinguished by the view from
Jay Peak, the highest mountain in northern Vermont, and the crossing
of Hazens Notch.

The second section, from Johnson to Camel's Hump, is the most strenuous, crossing six major mountains, including Mansfield, the highest moun-

tain in the State, which, with a hotel, a clubhouse, and camps, is a favorite stopping place.

The section from Camel's Hump to Killington Peak is called the Monroe Skyline Trail, in honor of Professor Will Monroe, of Montclair, New Jersey, one of the most ardent early supporters of the project. On this division, at Sherburne Pass, is the Long Trail Lodge, a commodious rustic building given to the club by the widow and son of ex-Governor Proctor.

The southernmost division, extending from Killington Peak to the Massachusetts Line, zigzags to cross the peaks of the southern range of the Green Mountains, including Stratton Mountain, the highest eminence in southern Vermont.

The Trail is more often taken from south to north. By traveling in this direction, hikers achieve a kind of scenic climax in the vistas of the Adirondacks, Lake Champlain, and the White Mountains that occur throughout the northern sections, though the smooth timbered hills of the southern end and the prospects of the Taconics to the west have their own distinctive, if less spectacular, beauty.

2. *Bridle Paths of the Green Mountain Horse Association*

The intricate and comprehensive network of bridle paths mapped and marked by the Green Mountain Horse Association lies mainly on dirt roads not covered by the tours in this book. Persons planning riding trips in the State should write to the Secretary of the Association, at Rutland, Vermont. The Guide (50¢) of the Association gives detailed directions for all bridle routes and lists overnight accommodations.

Until recently the saddle horse has played a minor rôle in this State. The choice of Vermont as a testing ground for United States Cavalry mounts first called attention to the unlimited possibilities here for civilian riding. In 1926 a group of horse-lovers organized the Green Mountain Horse Association, the purposes of which were to promote the breeding and use of good horses in this State and to develop a State-wide bridle-trail system. Much of the success of the organization was due to the enthusiasm and ability of the late Ethel Clement Field, of Mendon.

The Association has drawn up a list of recommended overnight stops where riders and their mounts can be accommodated at a uniform and moderate cost. In January, 1937, it began the publication, in addition to its annual Guide, of *The Vermont Horse and Bridle Trail Bulletin*, a well-edited quarterly devoted to informative articles and notices regarding horses and horsemen in this State.

Though not directly sponsored by it, the increase in the number and size of horse shows in Vermont in recent years is undoubtedly due in part to the stimulus given by the Association. Another factor is the considerable number of fine saddle horses brought here each year by summer residents and by the managements of the various summer camps that make riding a major attraction. Most of the cities and larger towns have riding clubs supported by local people.

With more than a thousand miles of marked bridle paths that run through some of the most scenic and unspoiled sections of the State, Vermont has become in a remarkably short time one of the real riding centers of the East.

### 3. *State Forests and State Forest Parks*

Vermont has 19 State Forests, containing 43,288 acres, and 14 State Forest Parks, containing 9519 acres. Battell Park, 10,000 acres, at Ripton, is controlled by Middlebury College but is open to the public. Included in these reserve areas are several of the highest and most commanding mountains in the State, such as Mansfield, Camel's Hump, and Ascutney. Most of the parks lie on or near the main highways and are noted in the tours, where detailed descriptions of the facilities will be found.

The lands are administered by the Vermont Forest Service in collaboration with the United States Forest Service. The chief functions of these organizations are the prevention and detection of fires, the protection of white pine against blister rust, and the furnishing of advice and guidance to owners of private woodlands. A nursery is maintained at Essex Junction in which millions of forest transplants are raised for sale at production cost.

These reserve areas serve several practical purposes. They afford large game refuges. They help in the regulation of stream flow by preventing the denuding of several important watersheds. And they are performing an essential service in rehabilitating the forests which the extensive lumbering operations in Vermont during the last century depleted or abandoned to inferior growths.

Their chief appeal to the traveler, however, lies in their scenic beauty and recreational opportunities. The numerous lakes and streams afford excellent facilities for swimming, fishing, and boating. During the winter months the forest lands constitute some of the best terrain in the State for winter sports. The Proctor-Piper State Forest, in Cavendish, has a mile-long bobsled run, the only one of its kind in New England, and the Mount Mansfield State Forest contains forty miles of ski trails and runs that are among the most popular in the East. There are numerous summer picnic and camping sites. The transformation of State Forests into State Parks has been brought about in the last five years, largely through the work of the Civilian Conservation Corps, and the co-operation of the National Park Service.

A network of motor roads, bridle paths, and foot-trails penetrates the forests and parks. The Long Trail also runs through several of them, with feeder trails connecting it with areas lying off the main range. The Youth Hostel Movement, recently introduced into this country from Europe, provides a chain of inexpensive overnight accommodations for hikers and cyclists over a 500-mile circuit through the White and the Green Mountains. This route, which avoids heavily traveled highways when possible, passes through several of the parks.

With the exception of certain plainly posted areas, the forests and parks are open to the public for all legitimate uses. The building of camp-fires, except where permission is indicated, and the cutting and marking of trees are strictly forbidden. Flowers may be picked in reasonable quantities for non-commercial purposes at a distance of fifty feet from any road or trail. Toll charges are made for the maintenance of some of the mountain motor roads, and nominal fees are charged for firewood and the use of lockers and tent-floors by overnight campers.

4. *The Green Mountain National Forest*

The Green Mountain National Forest, one of the most recently established of national forests, is a large public estate managed by the United States Forest Service. It extends in a strip ten to twenty miles wide along the Green Mountains from the township of Winhall to a point near the southeast corner of Washington County, with the exception of a fourteen-mile gap between Mendon and Wallingford. Its area is 162,000 acres, which ultimately, according to present plans, will be increased to 485,000 acres. Expansion is slow, because no land is acquired by direct condemnation, and areas better suited to agricultural purposes or for summer home developments are not considered.

The major activities of the Forest Service include timber management, acquisition and surveys, engineering, management of wild life, and recreation.

The main objectives of timber management are the stabilizing of those industries and communities that are dependent upon it for materials; the thinning out of dense young stands growing up in areas that were completely cut over during private ownership; the weeding out of diseased and unproductive trees; and the practice of other sound principles of timber management: all designed to restore to usefulness and productivity large areas of timberland that were formerly unmanaged.

The surveying of lands acquired is necessarily very thorough and accurate. Forest base maps are prepared from aerial surveys.

The engineering branch superintends the construction of truck trails, hiking trails, bridges, telephone lines, and all other structural improvements. Truck trails are open to public travel except during short periods of extreme fire hazards when the forest is closed to visitors.

The management of wild life includes the conducting of surveys and research and the making of plans for improving the environment of fish and game. Nearly two hundred stream-improvement devices have been installed by this department.

Opportunities for outdoor recreation in this area are varied. Hapgood Pond, in Peru township, has a fine sand beach and has been developed for picnicking, camping, and swimming. There are several mountain streams and forests that offer excellent fishing and hunting, subject to the laws of the Vermont Fish & Game Service. A ski trail of the cross-country type has been developed in the vicinity of Bread Loaf Mountain, and others are projected. The Forest is traversed for sixty-five miles by the Long Trail, on which the Forest Service has built five log Adirondack shelters. Many miles of the bridle-trail network planned and maintained by the Green Mountain Horse Association lie within this scenic area.

Recently four units of the Civilian Conservation Corps located in the Forest have given valuable assistance in the development and maintenance of all branches of Forest improvements.

Main highways which give access to the Forest are US 4 and 7 and State 8, 11, 30, 100, and 103A. Many secondary improved and unimproved gravel roads penetrate or skirt the Forest boundaries.

Not yet a reality, but approved by the National Park Service and likely to become one, is the Green Mountain National Park. This reserve of 124,000 acres would extend from Mount Ellen to the Lamoille Valley and would include Mount Mansfield and Camel's Hump. The realization of this project would assure the preservation of a section of the State that is unsurpassed in scenic beauty, in geological interest, and in the variety of its flora.

| FISH: | JAN. | FEB. | MAR. | APR. | MAY. | JUNE | JULY | AU |
|---|---|---|---|---|---|---|---|---|
| X BROOK TROUT-BROWN, LOCH LEVEN, STEELHEAD, RAINBOW, GREYLING OR BLACK SPOTTED TROUT | | | | | | | | |
| X GOLDEN B LAKE TROUT, LANDLOCKED SALMON | | | | | | | | |
| X BLACK BASS | | | | | | | | |
| X MUSKALLONGE | | | | 14 | | 15 | | |
| X PIKE PERCH (WALL EYED PIKE) | | | | | | | | |
| X PICKEREL | | | 14 | | | | | |
| " (SHOOTING 3 SPEARING) (IN CERTAIN WATERS) | | | 15 | | 14 | | | |

| GAME: | | | | | | | | |
|---|---|---|---|---|---|---|---|---|
| BEAR (NOT PROTECTED) | | | | | | | | |
| DEER WITH HORNS NOT LESS THAN THREE INCHES (SUNDAYS EXCEPTED) | | | | | | | | |
| MOOSE, CARIBOU, ELK | | | | | | | | |
| X RABBITS OR HARES | | | | | | | | |
| GRAY SQUIRREL | | | | | | | | |
| COTTONTAIL RABBIT (NOT PROTECTED) | | | | | | | | |

| FUR BEARING ANIMALS: | | | | | | | | |
|---|---|---|---|---|---|---|---|---|
| X MUSKRAT (TRAPPING) | | | | | 19 | | | |
| " (SHOOTING) | | | | | 20 | | | |
| X MINK, OTTER, MARTEN | | | 14 | | | | | |
| X FOX, SKUNK | | | 14 | | | | | |
| FISHERCAT 8 BEAVER | | | | | | | | |
| RACCOON | | | | | | | | |

| GAME BIRDS: | | | | | | | | |
|---|---|---|---|---|---|---|---|---|
| PHEASANT (COCK BIRDS ONLY) | | | | | | | | |
| QUAIL | | | | | | | | |
| PARTRIDGE (RUFFED GROUSE) | | | | | | | | |
| WOODCOCK | | | | | | | | |
| EUROPEAN PARTRIDGE, UPLAND PLOVER | | | | | | | | |
| WOOD DUCK | | | | | | | | |
| ENGLISH SNIPE, PLOVER (OTHER THAN UPLAND PLOVER) AND SHORE BIRDS | SEE FEDERAL LAWS | | | | | | | |
| WILD DUCKS (OTHER THAN WOOD DUCKS) | " " " | | | | | | | |
| WILD GEESE | " " " | | | | | | | |

LICENSES: RESIDENT HUNTING                                          $ 1.25
         NON RESIDENT HUNTING                                        10.50
         RESIDENT COMBINATION HUNTING AND FISHING                     2.00
         RESIDENT TRAPPING                                            1.25
         NON RESIDENT TRAPPING                                       50.00
X NOTE: SEE GENERAL LAWS FOR EXCEPTIONS AND SPECIAL PROVISIONS

FISH & GAME SERVICE
R. P. HUNTER, DIRECTOR

| ⅁. | SEPT. | OCT. | NOV. | DEC. | DAILY LIMIT | SEASON LIMIT | LENGTH LIMIT | METHOD OF TAKING | HOUR LIMIT |
|---|---|---|---|---|---|---|---|---|---|
| 14 | | | | | 5 LBS. OR 20 FISH | | 6 IN | ANGLING | ONE HOUR BEFORE |
| | | | | | GOLDEN 5 LBS OR 20 FISH. LK TR & SALMON 10 LBS. | | GOLDEN 6 IN, LK TR & SALM. 15 IN | | SUNRISE |
| | | | | | 10 FISH | | 10 IN. | | TO TWO |
| | | | | | 25 LBS | | 12 IN. | | HOURS |
| | | | | | 25 LBS | | 10 IN. | | AFTER |
| | | | | | 25 LBS. | | 10 IN. | | SUNSET |
| | | | | | 25 LBS. | | 12 IN. | | |
| | | | | | | | | | |
| | | | | | NO LIMITS | | | | |
| | | 21-30 | | | | | | SHOOTING | 9 A.M. TO 5 P.M. |
| | | | | | NO OPEN SEASON | | | | SUNRISE |
| | | | | | 3 | | | " | TO |
| | | | | | 4 | | | " | SUNSET |
| | | | | | NO LIMITS | | | " | |
| | | | | | | | | | |
| | | 25 | | | NO LIMITS | | | TRAPPING | |
| | | | | | | | | SHOOTING | NO |
| | | 25 | | | " " | | | TRAPPING | |
| | | 25 | | | | | | TRAP OR DOG & GUN | LIMITS |
| | | 25 | | | NO OPEN SEASON | | | | |
| | | 25 | | | | 15 | | TRAP OR DOG & GUN | |
| | WEDNESDAYS & SATURDAYS | | | | | | | | |
| | | | | | 2 | 4 | | SHOOTING | |
| | 15 | | | | 4 | | | " | SUNRISE |
| | | | | | 4 | 25 | | " | TO |
| | | | | | 4 | 25 | | " | SUNSET |
| | | | | | NO OPEN SEASON | | | | |
| | | | | | " " " | | | | |
| | | | | | 10 | | | SEE FED. LAW | |
| | | | | | 10 | 40 | | " " " | |
| | | | | | 4 | 5 | | SEE EXCEPTION ON HRS FOR GUN USE | |

RESIDENT FISHING     $1.25
NON RESIDENT FISHING   5.15 FOR SEASON
"    "        2.35   "   14 DAYS
            1.65   "   3 DAYS

# ARCHITECTURE

IN THE history of American architecture the Vermont chapter is the story of an area that was settled much later than the seaboard colonies, and then only sparsely. It is an area that imposed on its early settlers and their descendants a stern economy induced by a topography that restricted transportation, communication, and commerce. The varied developments in early American architecture made a belated appearance in a region as remote from fashionable centers as Vermont was. At a time when the seacoast towns were well settled and displaying developed styles of architecture, Vermont was still a frontier State. However, it was not a too-distant frontier and the first frame structures were based on examples of well-developed styles in the near-by coastal areas. For the most part its buildings are variants on the purest types of the styles they represent, and it is in these variations that we discern the ingenuity, individuality and general good taste of the designers, builders, and original owners.

In a sense Vermont may be said to have leaped the usual transitional stages, and elements characteristic of very primitive New England Colonial work are rarely found here. There are no second-story overhangs, and a gambrel roof is very exceptional. The first buildings among the heavily forested hills of Vermont were naturally of rough-hewn logs. None of these shelters, forts or houses remains, and it is not recorded where or when the first frame structure in the area was built. Probably it did not antedate by many years the Henry House, in North Bennington, which is said to date from 1763. The Old Constitution House in Windsor, 1772, is an early example of frame construction, a long, narrow two-story building with a steeply pitched gable roof. The Congregational Church at Chester dates from 1773, while the Rockingham Meeting House, built in 1787, is a landmark in the history of the architecture of the State. It also is a two-story frame clapboard structure, having seven bays, a modillioned cornice, and a gable roof. The simplicity of the building emphasizes the decorative note in the cornice — undoubtedly Vermont's conservative acknowledgment of the greater elegancies that were flowering elsewhere in late eighteenth-century New England Colonial work. In 1784, the Old Center Meeting House was built in Hartford, while the Old South Church in Windsor dates from 1798. Both are frame structures.

Early Vermont farmhouses, invariably of wood, were built primarily to meet utilitarian requirements. The great body of this work consisted of simple buildings, adapted to rural purposes, and displaying little or no influence of any formal style. The older houses are plain story-and-a-half structures of wood with rough pine floor boards, crude fireplaces, usually closed up now, handwrought iron hinges, and worn flagstone entrance steps. Many of those built later, between 1800 and 1825, are of a more spacious type, comfortable and attractive. The earlier practice of connecting house, barns, and shed — a concession to the rigors of winter — was later abandoned in the interests of sanitation, but many examples of this 'continuous architecture' remain.

The type of house found near Bennington is similar to that built in great numbers in the North Connecticut Valley. They are narrow and rectangular in plan but well proportioned. An early and interesting, though not a typical, example is the Colonel Johnson House built in 1775 in Newbury. Considering the date, it is surprising to find quoined corners, a modillioned cornice, and a paneled entrance doorway, refinements customary in the earlier New England settlements, but not widely used in Vermont until about 1800.

Excellent examples of early, more typical houses are the Richardson House built in 1787, the Hutchinson House, now the White Cupboard Inn, dating from 1794, and the Benjamin Swan House, 1801, all in Woodstock. In general they combine spaciousness with simplicity, although in the Hutchinson House there are a few sophisticated touches such as the pillared side porch and the circular louvered openings in the gable end.

With the admission of the State to the Union in 1791, there began a period of prosperity which was reflected in architecture. It was also a time coincidental with the maturing of the first native architects, for Charles Bulfinch in Boston, Samuel McIntire in Salem, and Asher Benjamin in Greenfield were consolidating the New England tradition at the high point of its development. No buildings in their entirety in Vermont are attributed to Bulfinch or McIntire, but it is certain that their influence was vital. In connection with the Unitarian Church (1816), Burlington, it is recorded that Bulfinch and Peter Banner, architect of the Park Street Church, Boston, both received fees for professional services. Benjamin lived for several years in Windsor and did considerable work there (see WINDSOR). His influence is further reflected in the Congregational churches in Bennington and Middlebury, the designer of both, Lavius Fillmore, having obviously studied Benjamin's celebrated handbooks. It was shortly before 1800 that the publications issued by the

Adam brothers began to circulate among the architects on this side of the Atlantic. Benjamin, a skillful carpenter, drew freely from these publications for the details in his books, such as 'Country Builder's Assistant, Fully Explaining the Best Methods for Striking Regular and Quirked Mouldings' (1805).

In listing names that influenced the course of architecture in Vermont we must include that of Thomas Royal Dake, who went to Castleton about 1807 and worked there for nearly half a century (*see Tour* 6, *CASTLETON*). Though he was entirely original at times, as in the Cole House (1833), Dake showed the influence of Bulfinch and McIntire and, like them, of the Adam brothers. The Ransom House (1840) in Castleton, a favorite photographic subject today, is one of his late experiments, an adaptation of the temple façade to residential purposes. It is more or less duplicated in the Ebenezer Wilcox House at Orwell. Both houses display the architectural oddity of five Ionic columns on the entrance façade. This results in a column in the center — a free interpretation indeed of the classic formula.

Characteristic details that are found in Vermont work previous to the Greek Revival of 1820, include beaded corner boards as well as beaded corners on columns, wood quoins, small triglyphs in the frieze, and modillioned and dentiled cornices. The more elaborate houses of this period show the Adam influence in the use of delicately carved festoons, urns, and rosettes. There are many examples of the triple-arched window, as well as the Palladian motif, on houses and churches. Graceful adaptations of the motif to house entrances were made, the Palladian side windows forming the side lights for the arched doorway. Interiors received their share of attention as good details of wood mantels and wall paneling indicate.

'Maple Grove' (1804) in Randolph Center is a graceful example of the work at this time. The detail of the cornices, the delicate fanlight and nice disposition of carved ornament on the white exterior are matched by the elaborate ceiling-high paneled mantels within. The Isaac Bayley House (1800) in Newbury is a good example of the almost flat roof, circled by a white balustrade with finial posts. The parlor interior is distinguished by arched alcoves at the sides of the fireplace.

With Vermont notable as a source of such staple building materials as marble, granite, and slate, it is natural to look for evidence of their use. Wood, of course, was plentiful and was the most widely employed of the native materials. Mainly in modern work, however, is marble or granite used and only in the southwest part of the State, adjacent to the quarries, is slate freely used for roofs. Here most roofs are slate, the use of the material extending even to the covering of such a utilitarian structure as an ice house. Clay for brick was not plentiful and its use in consequence was somewhat restricted. Some of the old taverns, however, of one hundred years ago were built of brick, and there are outstanding examples of more formal work such as the church at Weathersfield Center (1821) that indicate the skill and taste governing the use of this material.

Grassemount (1804) in Burlington, now a women's dormitory at the University of Vermont, is a fine, well-known example. Though marred by later additions, the charm of its detail remains in the arched insets of pink brick around the windows, the second-story pilasters, and the columned cupola encircled by a white balustrade. The Bailey House (1823), in Woodstock, illustrates how the well-balanced proportions of the Georgian house is often nicely accented by the pattern of the fenestration. In Norwich is the Constant Murdock House, dating from 1788 and probably the earliest preserved example of the pure Georgian mode in the State.

Vermont, as has been said, reflected the trends in the neighboring States in her own way. The Greek Revival did not flourish in Vermont in the sense of a frequent and complete use of the forms of the style. It left its mark in a general way in its effect on details and general proportions used on houses whose essential form belonged to an earlier period. In many of the churches the classic flavor did not extend beyond the Greek Doric columns of the portico. In the State Capitol building in Montpelier an effort was made to extend the idiom to the entire building (*see MONT-PELIER*). The work of Dake in Castleton in the Greek Revival style has been discussed above.

Domestic architecture in this State since 1850 has followed no very set pattern. There were fewer great private fortunes amassed here during the latter half of the nineteenth century than in most northern and eastern States, and consequently fewer baroque mansions in the General Grant 'gingerbread' manner. Occasionally one may be seen, however, with wide lawns and a weather-vaned coach-house, dominating a village in ornate ugliness. The preservation and restoration, during recent years, of the earlier and simpler houses of Vermont have exerted an appreciable influence on suburban building, much of which has followed the Colonial or Dutch Colonial style of small, neat, unpretentious houses.

The chief public buildings of Vermont other than the churches are the town halls and the county courthouses. In several instances one structure first served the community as a church and then as a town hall, or *vice*

*versa (see GEORGIA, LOWELL, RICHMOND, ROCKINGHAM).*
The predominant style of Vermont courthouses is either semi-ecclesiastical or, in a few counties, that of the Greek Revival. Of the latter type the Windham County Courthouse, at Newfane, is the most representative example, an almost pure expression of the Doric mode except for the domed cupola.

Between the rolling hills that characterize the State are numerous valleys and little rivers that accompany the roads. This frequent association of river and highway is symbolized in the Vermont picture by the covered wooden bridge — a functional picturesque, and thoroughly characteristic item in the State's construction work. About two hundred of these structures still dot the highways in spite of the great number that were destroyed in the floods of 1927. Many theories are advanced as to the original reason for covering these structures, but time has proved none better than the protection of the bridge's own structural elements. Some of these essential links in transportation have been in use over a hundred years. Some authorities consider the bridge at Cambridge across the Lamoille River on Route 5 the best example of a covered bridge in the State.

The great variety of treatment of church towers and spires is a characteristic element of the Vermont scene. In contrast with the rolling green and blue of the Vermont hills these white sentinels provide the needed accent to the serenity of the landscape. A square tower rising from the front of the church, terminating in a belfry surmounted by a spire was the most common form. The First Congregational Church (1806) in Bennington and the Old South Church (1798) in Windsor are excellent examples. The cone-shaped spire is used with good effect on the Congregational Church, Middlebury (1806–09). Very occasionally a drastic departure from the form was ventured as in the Old Round Church, actually sixteen-sided, built in Richmond in 1813. It is a two-story frame structure surmounted at its center by an open octagonal belfry and lantern, with bell-shaped roof. The interiors of the churches were for the most part plain to the point of severity, and the infrequent original pulpit compositions as in the Federated Church (1833) in Castleton were limited by an aestheticism rooted in a moral distrust of the ornate. Fortunately the basement vestry, which despite its varied functional value has marred the lines of so many later churches, occurred very seldom in the earlier ones.

For the formal student of American architecture, therefore, Vermont is not the happy hunting ground that States settled and built up earlier can justly claim to be. For the informal observer, however, almost every section of the State preserves at least a few old houses and churches in the building of which individuality and ingenuity combined to produce something of lasting beauty.

# LITERATURE

IT WOULD be strange indeed if a State as small, as self-conscious, as isolated from cultural centers during its early days, and as homogeneous racially as Vermont should not have produced at least a small body of writing that is indigenous and distinctive. When that writing celebrates events important in Vermont history, is colored with something of the beauty of the Vermont hills, and is salty with traces of the Vermont character, personality, and ways of speech, it may assume a certain importance that transcends its frequently doubtful value as pure literature. Those who love Vermont and those who wish to know it better may, therefore, study and even cherish this body of prose and verse without evoking the suspicion that their enthusiasm has clouded their judgment.

Vermont's first poet was Thomas Rowley (1721–96), who came to Danby from Connecticut in 1789 and played an important part in the turbulent history of the New Hampshire Grants and their struggle for independence and statehood. Rowley's verses — almost wholly on contemporary political themes — may not, as has often been said, have 'set the mountains on fire,' but it is beyond dispute that their rugged swing did help to fire the hearts of the Green Mountain Boys in their heavy moments.

Royall Tyler (1757–1826), born in Boston, but a resident of Vermont for most of his adult life, Chief Justice of the Vermont Supreme Court, and professor of jurisprudence at the University of Vermont, has a real significance in the history of early American literature. He wrote the first American comedy ('The Contrast,' 1786) to be regularly acted on a professional stage; he wrote the first American novel ('The Algerine Captive,' 1797) to be republished in England; and in Jonathan, in the play, and Updike Underhill, in the novel, he created the first real Yankee type in literature: an achievement of far-reaching effects, though of dubious glory.

Ethan Allen, Vermont's most famous hero of Revolutionary days, was the author of two books, 'A Narrative of Ethan Allen's Captivity' and 'Reason the Only Oracle of Man.' The first is revelatory of the audacity and reckless courage that made Allen one of the most colorful and most successful of patriot leaders. The second, though not wholly his own work, is compact of the deistic skepticism that made his name a very symbol for godlessness among the godly; so much so that under entry of February 28, 1789, President Ezra Stiles of Yale recorded in his diary with pious certainty: 'Feb. 13 — Genl. Ethan Allen of Vermont died & went to hell this day.'

During the nineteenth century Vermont, like the rest of the country, produced too many versifiers who published in newspaper columns and cheaply printed volumes their sentimental, moral, and religious effusions, imitative and uninspired. Among the Vermont poets who rose several cubits above the general level, at least four deserve mention: Anne C. Lynch Botta (1815–91); Julia C. Dorr (1825–1913); Charles Gamage Eastman (1813–60), uncritically dubbed 'The Burns of New England'; and John Godfrey Saxe (1816–87) — all of whom left a few poems worthy of a place in representative anthologies of nineteenth-century American verse.

The outstanding Vermont writer of the last century, however, was a prose writer, Rowland E. Robinson (1833–1900). Born and brought up in rural Vermont, Robinson spent a lifetime observing the manners and habits and listening to the speech of Vermonters. His books of loosely connected sketches, anecdotes, and essays re-create authentically a way of living and a way of speaking that have disappeared forever even from the fastnesses of the Green Mountains. Not in the first flight of creative artists, Robinson nevertheless left us books that are always readable and frequently re-readable because of the warm humanity of the characterizations, the pervading love of nature expressing itself with careful accuracy, and the vanished rhythms of true Yankee speech. Those who believe that uniformity in national life and language is achieved only at the heavy cost of the charm that lies in differences should read at least one of Rowland Robinson's books. They will find there the completest record we shall ever have of a little corner of American civilization that was both colorful and unique.

Even more popular than Robinson's books in their day were the historical romances of Daniel P. Thompson (1797–1868), of which 'The Green Mountain Boys' is by far the best. Unreliable in the factual details of their historical background, they were emotionally accurate, and their honest native melodrama served to keep alive in the Vermont consciousness a number of Vermont heroes whose exploits have proved much less exciting material in the hands of later and more scholarly historians. Van Wyck Brooks has said of 'The Green Mountain Boys': 'It was a home-grown product, if ever literature saw one, as unpretentious as a log-cabin, but it was built on such a good model that no faults of style or execution counted in the final result. . . . This was a Yankee tale as brisk and wholesome as any mountain ballad. It was a border-song in prose.'

Among later works of fiction whose scenes are laid against a Vermont background, the best known are 'Hester of the Grants,' by Theodora Peck; 'The Greater Glory,' by William Dudley Pelley; and 'The Wood-Carver of 'Lympus,' by Mary Waller.

The most popular Vermont poet of the present century was Daniel Cady (1861–1934). Although Mr. Cady was a man of considerable scholarship and in his later years wrote much verse of a more serious nature, his ultimate fame will probably rest, as does his present one, on the four volumes of his 'Rhymes of Rural Vermont.' It is easy to speak patronizingly of these poems. It is also very foolish to do so. They are the equal of any dialect verse written in America with the exception of some of the works of James Russell Lowell. As regards subject matter and diction, they have as much right to critical consideration as have many of the most popular poems of Rudyard Kipling (who married a Vermont girl and lived in the State from 1892 to 1896). The technique of Dan Cady's poetry is flawless. The factual details are photographically remembered. And the comprehensiveness with which they cover the homely aspects of country life in Vermont during the latter half of the nineteenth century makes them the poetic counterpart of Robinson's works, with much of the same sort of value.

Walter Hard's books, 'Salt of Vermont' and 'Some Vermonters,' preserve in free-verse form something of the same tradition. Hard's major emphasis, however, is upon the collective Vermont personality and quirks of Yankee character. If his work has less appeal, to Vermonters themselves at least, than that of Cady, it is because it is less affectionately written and more obviously conscious of preserving something unique for the rest of the world to see.

In recent years a growing number of well-known writers have made Vermont their permanent home. Though not native sons and daughters, if these people choose Vermont as their inspiration and workshop, they belong — in a sense — to this State in a more significant way than they could be said to do from the mere accident of birth here. On a farm at South Shaftsbury lives Robert Frost, one of the greatest of American poets. The traits that most clearly distinguish Frost's verse: his terseness, his dry, piercing wit, his oblique approach to a moral conclusion, his fusion into poetry of the tempi and inflections of living speech, his unshakable sanity — all mark him as the heir to an intellectual and spiritual heritage that is utterly Yankee, if not exclusively Vermont.

Unrelated to Robert Frost by family or style of verse, Frances Frost, of Saint Albans, has shown in half a dozen volumes that her rank among the important young American poets of today is secure and valid. Articulate and explicitly intense, her verse is nevertheless often akin to that of Emily Dickinson in its concentration and economy.

In Bennington County live three women writers of distinction whom Robert Frost himself has called Vermont's 'three verities': Dorothy Canfield (Fisher), 'wise and a novelist'; Zephine Humphrey (Fahnestock), 'mystic and an essayist'; and Sarah Cleghorn, 'saintly and a poet.' The profound social sympathy that permeates the work of these women is proof that Vermont is not an artist's ivory tower, not a 'colony,' but a vantage-point of quietude from which the world's injustices are to be battled, not ignored. This is the very theme, indeed, that underlies much of the work of the young novelist Elliot Merrick, of Craftsbury, whose early books are of such splendid promise as to be already a kind of fulfillment.

There are, of course, other authors, an ever-increasing number of them, who spend a part of the year in Vermont, like Sinclair Lewis and his wife, Dorothy Thompson, whose summer home is in Barnard. And there is the Writers' Summer School and Conference at Breadloaf, near Middlebury College, at which a score of well-known creative writers, critics, and teachers of literature meet annually to exchange ideas and to absorb something of the serenity of the school's setting. Vermont does not claim these; she has no need to. The most important spot in an artist's geography is not necessarily the place where he pays his taxes. The impact of Vermont upon American letters is ultimately perhaps to be measured, not in writers-per-square-mile, but in terms of influence; in a suggestion of artistry, not a congestion of artists.

# II. MAIN STREET AND VILLAGE GREEN

# BARRE

*City:* Alt. 609, pop. 11,307.

*Railroad Station:* Central Vermont Ry., Montpelier & Wells River R.R., Depot Square, N. Main St.

*Bus Station:* Vermont Transit Co., Frontier Coach Line, Rutland-Montpelier Bus, N. Main St.

*Airport:* Central Vermont Airways (B. & M. Trans. Co.), Berlin, 4 *m.* from city, taxi fare 50¢, time 10 min.

*Accommodations:* Two hotels; tourist homes and camps.

*Information:* City Park, Main St., booth during summer months. Chamber of Commerce, Woman's Club Bldg., City Park.

*Annual Events:* Sportsmen's Show, Barre Fish and Game Club, last week in Sept.

BARRE, the Granite Center, is so charged with aggressive activity as to seem curiously misplaced in its setting of green hills moulded roughly around the valley of the Stevens and Jail Branches of the Winooski. This aliveness is without question due to the granite industry, which dominates Barre from the stark gray quarries on Millstone Hill to the long, somber sheds on the river flats. Something of this aggressive spirit, however, came with the first settlers. In March, 1793, the town was organized under the charter name of Wildersburgh, but the pioneers held that name to be too 'uncouth,' and in September a town meeting was held to choose another. It is legendary that this meeting reached a white heat. Two Massachusetts men, Thompson of Holden and Sherman of Barre, stood out for the names of their respective home towns until words were no longer strong enough. Thompson knocked his opponent down with a solid smash, and jumped on him to finish the bout. But as they thrashed and plunged about, collecting slivers from the barn floor, Sherman slugged Thompson until the latter rolled away groaning, and lay still. Sherman then sprang to his feet and panted: 'There, by God, the name is Barre!' And Barre the name has been ever since.

From the air (the city is on the main route of the Central Vermont Airway) Barre appears as a cluster of dwellings and long sheds by the railroad, with the shattered mass of Millstone Hill, great slices of which have been devoured by fifty years of quarrying, completely dominating the settlements along the river banks.

Main Street, an extremely long thoroughfare, is paved with granite blocks and lined on either side with close-set places of business, dingy buildings masked by colored fronts, gilt signs, and show-windows. To enter this long narrow stretch from the open countryside is to come suddenly upon a virile little city transplanted from some busier section to the heart of rural Vermont. Here and there grave century-old brick houses of Georgian Colonial style overlook the noisy flow of traffic. The green triangle of City Park, ranged around with the granite and brick of public buildings, churches, and school, is a brief respite from undiluted commercialism. The statue of Robert Burns, which looks down upon the park from the High School grounds, is effective symbolism for a city where Scotch granite-workers form a strong element. The survival of the philosophy of 'a man's a man for a' that' is evidenced by Barre's election and re-election of a Socialist mayor, the only one in Vermont. Rising southeast from this central plaza is the Trow Hill section, where attractive homes rest comfortably on terraced streets and lawns. Architecturally the city is conspicuous for the absence of granite buildings, being thus in contrast to the towns in Vermont's marble belt where local stone has served excellently for civic construction. Also notable is the fact that, though the Italian and Scotch races here predominate, neither Catholic nor Presbyterian churches are prominent.

Granite-cutters are well paid for their work, which requires extreme skill, and is also hazardous. Notoriously a free-spending and pleasure-seeking people, the stoneworkers are largely responsible for the vigor of Barre life. The swift circulation of money, the swarming streets and stores, the whole fast and lusty tempo that sets Barre apart from the rest of Vermont, is created by the hard-working, hard-playing stonecutters. It is characteristic of many busier towns in the State to relapse into quiet with nightfall, but not so Barre. Darkness falling from the hills is defied by the lighted length of Main Street; cars and people moving ceaselessly under the blaze of neon signs; restaurants, shops, and beer taverns bright and crowded; and the counterpoint of cash-register bells against the music of radio and phonograph.

Situated close together near the geographical center of the State, Vermont's twin cities, Barre and Montpelier, are natural and inevitable rivals, and offer a striking study of contrasts in appearance, character, and tone. Barre, forceful and arrogant, displays the haste and tension of a modern industrial community; Montpelier, serenely indifferent, is a true Vermont town, sleeping in the shadow of the hills. Barre may mock the Capital for being backward; Montpelier may scorn the Granite City as crude; but both are satisfied that in their very difference lies superiority.

In early times, three straggling villages grew up in Barre. Twingville, at the northern end, was built around the foundry of Joshua Twing, established in 1833. Gospel Village clustered about the first Congregational Church erected in 1808. Jockey Hollow, a flat section at the southern end of town, was used by pioneer sportsmen for the training of racehorses, and here began the sporting and gaming so prevalent in present-day Barre. As the town grew, the three villages merged.

The granite industry was started soon after the War of 1812 by two returned soldiers, Robert Parker and Thomas Courser, who opened the first quarry on Cobble Hill. The stone from early quarries was used for millstones, doorsteps, posts, and window-lintels. A finer grade of granite was found on Millstone Hill, to which quarrying activities were transferred and where they remain today (*see Tour 2C, WEBSTERVILLE, GRANITEVILLE*). From the quarries on Millstone, granite for the construction of the State Capitol was hauled to Montpelier by ox-team (1833–37). It is in the field of monumental stone, however, that Barre granite excels, because of its beauty and flawless texture. The granite comes in two principal shades, with many variations: the 'light' is nearly white, and the 'dark' is a soft blue-gray that takes a high polish. The Joseph Smith Monument (*see Tour 2C, SHARON*), a shaft 38½ feet in height, dedicated to the founder of Mormonism, is an example of the unblemished monoliths taken from the quarries on Millstone Hill.

From 1880 to 1890 the population of Barre jumped from 2060 to 6812, the most rapid advance ever made by a Vermont town in a decade, and directly traceable to the granite quarries, which brought an influx of Italian, Scotch, and some Scandinavian stoneworkers. The extension of the Central Vermont Railway from Montpelier to Barre in 1875 aided this boom in granite. A natural resultant was the flourishing of all other branches of business and trade. In 1894 Barre was chartered as a city.


## POINTS OF INTEREST


1. The *Granite Sheds*, stretched gaunt and grim on the valley bottom, are the major points of interest. Outstanding among scores of granite finishing plants are: Jones Bros. Co.; Marr & Gordon; Rock of Ages; Comolli & Co.; and Cook, Watkins & Patch. From the vast open quarries on Millstone Hill (alt. 1700) huge blocks of stone are freighted down a steep winding track by way of switch-backs, to these plants, and here the processes of sawing, polishing, and carving may be observed. Massive gang-saws are employed in the first process, with long multiple blades adjusted to cut the desired sizes. It takes an hour to saw four inches into a granite block. Streams of chilled shot are fed under the notched blades, and a constant flow of water is required to prevent both the shot and the saw from melting in the intense heat of friction. Then pneumatic hammers with a number of steel striking blades (chisels) work across the block, producing a rough but even surface called a hammered finish. For a polished finish the operation is conducted in four stages: steel shot, coarse emery, and fine emery are used successively as abrasives under the polish wheel; the final gloss is attained with polishing putty (oxide of tin) under a felt disk, which gives the granite a rich blue-gray sheen, permanently lustrous. Much of the carving and lettering is now done with pneumatic sandblast machines, but skilled stone-carvers are still found in all the finishing plants.

2. The *Robert Burns Memorial Statue* faces the central plaza from the Spaulding High School grounds, a graceful and dignified figure on a beautiful base, considered a notably fine example of granite carving. J. Massey Rhind of Edinburgh, Scotland, designed the statue, and Samuel Novelli, Barre craftsman, did the carving. Rhind, disappointed in not doing the actual carving himself, died in 1936 without ever seeing the finished piece. The panels in the base, depicting scenes from Burns's poetry, were modeled by James King and cut by a Barre artisan, Eli Corti. The memorial, presented by the Scotsmen of the city, was unveiled in 1899.

3. *Youth Victorious*, City Park. was carved by Gino Tosi, local stonecutter, from the design made by H. P. Jennewein. The central figure and entire motif is a kneeling male figure, representing youth victorious, but supplicating even in victory. A granite exedra forms a semi-circular background. The symbolism is unusual in the treatment of a war memorial.

4. *Aldrich Public Library*, City Park (*open weekdays 1 to 8*), a square brick building with large windows and ornamental entrance portico, was dedicated in 1908 and contains 20,000 volumes.

5. *Episcopal Church*, City Park. Of all the Barre churches, this modest little structure, vaguely reminiscent of a small English abbey, is, oddly enough, the only one constructed of granite.

6. The *Twing House*, 431 N. Main St. (*private*), a red-brick Georgian style house with granite sills and lintels, was built in 1834 for Joshua Twing, the machinist who fathered industrial Barre. The handsome central porch has four Ionic columns, and is flanked on both sides by wings with Doric porticoes. Imposing cornices and windows, and the frieze, are a gesture toward elegance. Once aloof, the Twing House now is elbowed by a beer tavern and a gasoline station.

7. The *Twing Foundry*, N. Main St., a long red-brick structure on the flats across from the house, was established in 1833. Granite-working tools and machinery are made here by Smith, Whitcomb & Cook.

8. The *Wheelock House*, 145 N. Main St. (*private*), 1823-25, a red-brick house of the Georgian type with granite trim and four high chimneys, stands with gable end and arched sentinel window facing the street. The entrance is beautifully detailed; delicate leaded glass fanlight and sidelights frame the door, and mouldings harmonize with the slender Ionic columns. The granite arch and monolithic pilasters reveal sensitive hand-tooling. The structure maintains its dignity in the midst of the commercial hurly-burly that surrounds it.

9. The *Paddock House*, 188 S. Main St. (*private*), red-brick on a granite foundation, was built in 1814 for Robert Paddock, the farmer-doctor who was Barre's first physician (an early job was removing the splinters from the combatants in the memorable fist fight). This is the best of the Georgian houses; the lines are right, and the white trim is in pleasing contrast with the red brick. The entrance has four graceful pilasters and an attractive

fanlight. Dr. Paddock charged from 25¢ to $1 for making calls, depending on the case and the distance traveled.

10. *Goddard Junior College* (girls), Seminary Hill, is housed in two high brick structures displaying characteristics associated with the General Grant period, above Summer St. on the eastern side of town. The school was chartered in 1863 as the Green Mountain Central Institute under the Universalist Church, largely through the efforts of William R. Shipman. The main building was completed in 1870 and the name of the school was changed to Goddard Seminary, in honor of Mary Goddard whose philanthropy made the building possible. The Thompson Memorial dormitory was added later. Goddard was coeducational until 1929, when it became a girls' school. In 1936 it achieved the rank of junior college. Outstanding among the educators associated with Goddard were Arthur W. Peirce, who later became headmaster of Dean Academy; Orlando K. Hollister; and Persis A. Thompson, known as 'the mother of Goddard.' Perhaps the best known graduates of the school are Miriam Hopkins (1919), stage and screen actress, and Allene Corliss (1918), fiction writer.

11. *Elmwood Cemetery*, Washington St., and *Hope Cemetery*, Merchant St., contain exceptionally fine granite memorials.

# BELLOWS FALLS

*Village:* Alt. 309, pop. 3930.
*Railroad Station:* B. & M. R.R. and Rutland R.R., Union Station.
*Bus Stations:* Wright Bus Line, Rutland and points N.; Bee Line, through N. & S., Fletcher News Shop; stage line to Alstead, N.H., and points E.; Hemenway Bus Line to Saxtons River and points W., Post Office.
*Accommodations:* Four hotels; several tourist homes.

BELLOWS FALLS lies on one of the most sharply defined series of terraces that the Connecticut River has cut throughout its long course. On the New Hampshire side towers Mount Kilburn, stark and craggy; to the west rise the green hills of Vermont. Bellows Falls is definitely divided into three levels; the bottom lands, shaped into an island by a canal, are occupied by industry and a railroad; the middle level is the business mart; the upper sections are residential. The main thoroughfare, Westminster Street, is hemmed in by the bluff covered by homes and the industrial flats along the river. The height of the two- and three-story brick buildings packed on either side is accentuated by the extreme narrowness of the street. The tall brick tower of the Town Hall overshadows

69370

this canyon; projecting signs hang over narrow sidewalks, and store-windows reflect the jam of pedestrians and automobiles. Compressed between the walls of vari-shaded brick, the small central square makes a peaceful oasis in the most crowded business district of the State. A concrete stairway, an unusual device for Vermont, climbs from Westminster to the level of School Street. From the flats below, the smoke of factories and locomotives rises to shroud the defile made by the river and hangs in a gray pall over the dark bulk of Mount Kilburn, standing grimly like a backdrop for the Bellows Falls drama of concentrated industrialism and commercialism. The scene has a strong similarity to that of Brattleboro, and, less marked, to that of Windsor.

The town's most distinctive scenic feature is the falls, originally called Great Falls and named, like the town itself, for Colonel Benjamin Bellows, of Walpole, an early proprietor. The falls are divided at their verge by a large rock, which at low water diverts the whole flow into the sixteen-foot western channel below, the narrowest point in the river's entire length. During a freshet the waters dash against the rock, rise high into the air, and fall in smashing sheets fifty feet below to drive through both channels with a violence that has altered the near-by landscape several times. Usually destructive, these freshets have occasionally been beneficial, as when the one of 1797 created the river-bank sites of several of the town's present factories by filling a worthless swamp-hole with alluvial deposits.

At least a dozen persons have gone over these falls and lived. The first of whom there is any record was an Abnaki squaw, whose adventure was celebrated in print as early as 1781. Carelessly allowing her canoe to be drawn to a point where she could not paddle against the current, the squaw drank a bottle of rum that she was taking to her brave and lay down in the canoe to await her fate. She was fished out below the falls, quite safe and quite drunk. The latest person known to have made the brief but perilous trip was Captain Paul Boyton, who passed over the falls in a rubber suit in 1879 before a crowd of two thousand people.

The falls occasioned the construction here, between 1792 and 1802, of the first canal in America upon which work was actually begun, though not the first completed for navigation. Built by John Atkinson of London, it was retained until 1858, though little used after 1840. Nine locks were necessary to lift the barges, rafts, and small steamers over the falls. In the early 1830's the 'William Hall' made a trial trip up the river. The trip ended at Hartland and was never repeated, for the 'William Hall,' a side-wheeler, was bigger than any boat the canal-builders had visioned and had to be drawn past the falls by means of ox-power, via the village street. After the late 1840's the railroads soon destroyed all commercial navigation on the northern Connecticut, and the shrill blasts of their locomotives, instead of the merry, rowdy songs of the boatmen, were flung against the gaunt sides of Mount Kilburn to reverberate with piercing intensity over the town.

# ILLUSTRATIONS
*to accompany*
Tours 1, 1A, 1B, 1C, 1D, 1E, 1F

WINDHAM COUNTY COURTHOUSE AT NEWFANE

COVERED BRIDGE OVER WEST RIVER, NEAR BRATTLEBORO

SAWMILL, NEAR NEWFANE

ESTEY ORGAN WORKS, BRATTLEBORO

ISAAC BAYLEY HOUSE, NEWBURY
Living room, with 'Courting Alcove' (R) and 'Marriage Arch' (L)

ISAAC BAYLEY HOUSE, NEWBURY
Original fireplace with crane

BRUNSWICK MINERAL SPRINGS

OLD STONE HOUSE, BROWNINGTON
Now occupied by Orleans County Historical Society

ISLAND POND

WILLOUGHBY LAKE

BURKE HOLLOW

AVERILL LAKE

LAKE MEMPHREMAGOG

The first bridge across the Connecticut River, and for eleven years the only one, was built here in 1785 by Colonel Enoch Hale, and was conducted as a toll bridge until 1840. It stood very near the site of the present concrete bridge south of the falls. In 1912 this bridge, a painting of which is fortunately preserved in Rockingham Library, was chosen by an executive committee of the American Society of Mechanical Engineers as one of the eight best and most important wooden bridges ever built in this country. The steel bridge north of the falls was built in 1904–05. Its 540-foot eastern span is one of the longest highway arch spans in the east and one of the few that have a suspended floor. The double-arch stone bridge of the Fitchburg division of the Boston & Maine Railroad has a notably low rise in proportion to the length of its span: twenty feet to one hundred and forty, for each arch.

The same natural spectacle that has given the town its name, an amusing store of anecdotes, and a minor distinction in the history of American transportation has, more significantly, furnished the water privilege that chiefly accounts for its industrial development and well-being. From the earliest days, the power of the falls has been utilized for a multitude of manufactures, beginning with the inevitable saw- and grist-mill. In 1802, Bill Blake moved here from Alstead, New Hampshire, and established one of the first paper mills in Vermont. The stock was rags, which were sorted at tables by girls and cut up on discarded scythes set into the tables. This early venture lasted until 1846. In 1869, William A. Russell, of Lawrence, Massachusetts, later first president of the International Paper Company, established a mill here where was conducted one of the first successful attempts to manufacture paper from pulp. Since that time Bellows Falls has been one of the largest paper-producing towns in the country. It is also an important producer of farm machinery and maple-sugar-making equipment, and the largest shipping center for fluid milk in southern Vermont. A curious deviation from the stable and suitable industrial development of the town occurred between 1835 and 1845, when a number of local business and professional men undertook the production of silk. The exotic industry prospered for a time, and the company refused an offer of $20,000 for its mulberry groves, which were shortly afterwards killed by a severe winter. There are still preserved in town a number of articles made from Bellows Falls silk.

Bellows Falls, though not a permanent settlement, was a favorite camping ground of the Abnaki Indians, many of whose relics and implements have been uncovered here. Near the foot of the falls was formerly one of the two most interesting series of Indian rock carvings in the State, the figures of which have become almost entirely covered or obliterated. One reason for the popularity of the spot was the great number of shad and salmon that were to be found at the foot of the falls. Another was the commanding view of the surrounding country from Mount Kilburn. During the French and Indian Wars both the English Colonies and the French in Canada offered bounties for the scalps of their enemies, and many Colonial scalping parties foraged through this section in search of

Indian scalps, for which the Governor of Massachusetts paid bounties up to £100. Extant records show that Mount Kilburn here, Mount Wantastiquet at Brattleboro, and Mount Ascutney at Windsor were among the eminences where the scouts 'lodged on ye top and viewed for smoaks' of Indian fires. The last Abnaki Indian seen in Bellows Falls was an aged chieftain who came here to die in 1856 and lies in an unmarked grave in Restland Cemetery. The 'smokes' viewed from Mount Kilburn now are chiefly those of the mills where millions of pounds of paper have been produced, enabling another generation to indulge in such scalpings as are done with printer's ink.

## POINTS OF INTEREST

1. The *Bellows Falls High School* (1927), School St., is a commodious modern building of gray brick and concrete. On the ground floor, just inside the entrance, is a fine mural painting by Steven Belaski, a local artist, commemorating the encampment north of town near the mouth of the Williams River of a large party of Indians and 112 white captives taken in a raid on Greenfield, Mass., in 1704. The day was Sunday, and the Rev. John Williams, for whom the river was later named, preached what is thought to have been the first Protestant sermon ever delivered on Vermont soil (*see Tour 3, Sec. b*).

2. The *Immanuel Church* (Episcopal), Church St., was founded by John Atkinson, builder of the Bellows Falls Canal. The present church building, in a modified Gothic style, dates from 1867. The bell, which was part of the first church built in Bellows Falls, was cast in the Paul Revere foundry. Hung in 1819, it was for 30 years the only church bell in town and was used as a fire alarm, for curfew at 9 P.M., and to announce the death of any resident within the village limits. The death knell was three strokes for a man, two for a woman, followed by strokes to the number of the dead person's years. One Sunday morning in the 1830's pious worshipers were outraged to find that a sign from the entrance to the river canal had been nailed firm and high over the door of the Immanuel Church reading, 'All Enter Stern Foremost.'

3. The *Rockingham Public Hospital*, Westminster St., is pleasantly situated on the shady brow of a hill. The main building is a large pillared structure in the style of the Greek Revival. It is one of a pair of twin houses built in 1829 by Colonel Alexander Fleming and Captain Henry Green, both sons-in-law of John Atkinson the canal-builder. Not until they were completed did the men decide which should have his choice. The question was settled by a game of whist. Captain Green won, and chose the building now occupied by the hospital.

4. The *Bellows Falls Hydro-Electric Corp.* (*open to inspection*), Bridge St., a subsidiary of the New England Power Co., is housed in a large modern (1928) brick structure, its bright and spotless interior matched by neat

terraced lawns outside. The three large generators of the plant have a capacity of 60,000 kilowatt-hours. The use of natural water-power for the development of electrical energy, for consumption here or transmission elsewhere, was made possible by the reconstruction of the dam and canal in 1926–28 at a cost of more than $4,000,000.

5. The *Former Home of Hetty Green*, School St., at junction with Westminster St., is a dingy house of faded yellow brick, more interesting for its associations than for its architecture. It was at one time the home of Edwin H. Stoughton and Charles B. Stoughton, two brothers who came here from Chester in 1853 and both of whom became brigadier generals in the Civil War. The house is primarily noted, however, as the home for many years of Henrietta Howland Robinson Green (1834–1916), who married Edward H. Green, a successful Bellows Falls business man, in 1867. Hetty Green personally managed and greatly increased the large fortune and world-wide enterprises that she inherited from her father, a prominent figure in nineteenth-century whaling and China trade. She was long known as the richest woman in America and was probably the most astute woman financier who has ever lived. She was almost the only great financier who foresaw the panic of 1907 in time to convert most of her investments into cash, by means of which she increased her own wealth at the same time that she saved many others from ruin. She was undoubtedly somewhat penurious personally — partly as a result of the countless importunings that disturbed the quiet, simple life she desired; but local tales, such as that of her storming out of a milliner's shop in a fury because she couldn't find a becoming hat for less than three dollars, should be taken, if at all, with several grains of salt.

6. The *Rockingham Free Public Library* (*open* 1–8; *Sat.* 1–9), 65 Westminster St., is of yellow brick with granite trim. In addition to its book collection of 27,000 volumes, there is a small museum of relics, oddities, and a few paintings on the second floor. One of the paintings shows the original toll bridge built in 1785 by Colonel Enoch Hale.

# BENNINGTON

*Village:* Alt. 672, pop. 7390.

*Railroad Stations:* Rutland R.R., North Bennington, 5.4 *m.* west on State 67A.
*Bus Station:* Bennington Bus Co., Vermont Transit, Wager Bus Line, Berkshire Bus Line, Brattleboro and Keene (N.H.) Transit; Bus Terminal, 101 North St.
*Airport:* Bennington Airport, 3½ *m.* west of village, taxi fare 50¢, time 10 min., no regular passenger service.

*Accommodations:* Three downtown hotels, open all year; three summer hotels in Old Bennington; usual tourist homes and camps.

*Information:* Information Booth, 207 South St.

*Annual Events:* Golf Tournament, Mt. Anthony Country Club (Aug.); Elks Ball, Elks Club (March); Easter Ball, President's Birthday Ball, St. Patrick's Day Ball, Elks Carnival, New Year's Ball, State Armory.

BENNINGTON, the first town chartered west of the Connecticut River by New Hampshire (1749), took the Christian name of Governor Benning Wentworth, who subsequently issued charters covering most of the territory now included in Vermont. Situated on the New York frontier, Bennington naturally became the focal point in the strife between the New Hampshire Grants and the 'Yorkers,' and was the background against which the opening scenes of Vermont history were enacted. The name of the town is most widely known in connection with the battle of Bennington (1777), which did much toward breaking Burgoyne's dominance in the northern theater of the Revolutionary War.

Present-day Bennington, the southwestern gateway of the State opening on both New York and Massachusetts, is composed of two distinct and contrasting sections. Old Bennington, the site of the original settlement on a broad sloping rise west of the village center, is a veritable outdoor museum of historic landmarks compactly grouped along Monument Avenue. Old Bennington is now an exclusive summer resort, after the manner of Manchester and Dorset. Grand new mansions are interspersed with the eighteenth-century homes built by the founders of the town, and the Colonial tradition is preserved by the new as well as the old. High over the scene of white summer homes, inns, Colonial houses, church and graveyard in a green setting, the clean stone thrust of Bennington Monument cuts the sky.

Bennington proper is a modern manufacturing town sprawled on the wide flats of the Walloomsac River. Motivated by southern New England industrialism, the village lacks beauty, in spite of the handsome public buildings that endeavor to alleviate the dullness of brick and wood blocks in the business area. Red factories and smokestacks mark the bottomlands, north and west of the center, where textile plants and paper mills form the industrial core of the town. Bennington is important commercially as well as industrially, serving as a trading center for the entire southwestern corner of Vermont. To the heavy summer tourist traffic, the village offers accommodations, trading, and recreational facilities.

The natural background of Bennington is more level and open than the usual Vermont countryside, although low hills slouch away from the undulant plains in long easy rises, and *Mt. Anthony* (alt. 2345) stands stately guard on the southwest. Northward the ridges close in to narrow and deepen the valley; southward lie the sharply cupped farmlands of Pownal; and to the east is upfolded the wilderness barrier of the Green Mountains. But opening and spreading west and northwest is a clear expanse of softly

rolling country, serene and graceful in contour and threaded by the Walloomsac.

The settlement of the town was begun by Captain Samuel Robinson of
Hardwick, Massachusetts, who was attracted by the site when he camped
here on his return from the French and Indian War (1755–56). In 1761,
Robinson led a half-dozen families back to settle along the broad terrace
of the slope now known as Monument Avenue. When New York surveyors came trespassing on Robinson's land, he immediately chopped
their surveying-chain in two with his hoe; but when the 'Yorkers' de-
sisted in a decent manner, Robinson graciously offered them the hospitality of his log house. In 1766, Samuel Robinson represented the New
Hampshire Grants in the Court of the King of England, and the following year he died in London. His descendants have been prominent in the
town and the State.

Throughout the controversy with New York, Bennington was the headquarters of the New Hampshire faction, and the band of men who became
the 'Green Mountain Boys' was known in York State as the 'Bennington
Mob.' The Green Mountain Boys were organized in 1770, with Seth
Warner as captain of the Bennington company, and Ethan Allen as
colonel in command of all the companies in the Grants. Their meeting-
place was the Green Mountain Tavern kept by Stephen Fay, and over
the sign they placed a stuffed catamount with bared teeth, snarling defiance toward the New York border. The most historic Vermont inn, it
came to be known as the Catamount Tavern (see below). When the Attorney General in Albany warned Allen that his followers had better
yield to the York proprietors, for 'Might often prevails against right,'
Ethan replied, 'The gods of the valleys are not the gods of the hills.'
The York lawyer asked what he meant; Allen said, 'Come up to Bennington and we'll show you.'

In 1771, New York decided to test by force her case against the 'outlaw
mobsters' of Bennington, and Sheriff Ten Eyck with three hundred
armed men moved to seize the Breakenridge farm. The news spread
swiftly and the men of Bennington snatched up muskets and pistols,
swords and scythes, clubs and pitchforks to rally to the aid of Breakenridge. They met the Yorkers at the covered bridge beyond the threatened farm, and before their menace Ten Eyck and his posse fell back toward Albany. The old covered bridge is still standing (see below). There
were many other skirmishes between the Yorkers and the Green Mountain Boys. When Tory John Munro's crew captured Remember Baker
of Arlington, ten Bennington horsemen pounded after in mad pursuit
and rescued Baker before the Yorkmen could get him over the border.
Munro was lashed into an unconscious state for his activities against the
Grants.

From Bennington to Burlington the rough-and-ready Green Mountain
Boys ranged, dealing out drumhead justice to all New York sympathizers
and Tories. Chieftain Ethan Allen won the name, among less compli-

mentary ones, of the 'Robin Hood of Vermont,' and had a price placed on his head, as did his lieutenants Warner, Baker, and Robert Cochran. Their lusty efforts, however justly they may be criticized and condemned, were the means of breaking New York's claims on the territory, and were the first steps toward statehood. With the approach of the Revolution, the Council of Safety, meeting at the Catamount Tavern, turned its attention to the imminence of a new and greater struggle. In 1775, at the Catamount, Ethan Allen conferred with agents from Massachusetts and Connecticut on the plan of capturing Fort Ticonderoga. A short time later, a stone storehouse for Continental military supplies and provisions was established on the summit, just northwest of where the monument now stands.

In the summer of 1777, General Burgoyne pushed down the Champlain Valley, taking Ticonderoga and Mount Independence without a struggle. Seth Warner's stubborn rear guard at Hubbardton protected the flight of the main army under St. Clair, but the British drive seemed irresistible and the whole country was alarmed. On July 30, Burgoyne tardily reached Fort Edward on the Hudson, after some days spent in dalliance with his mistress at Skenesboro. It appeared merely a question of time before he would join the British forces at Albany. But Burgoyne needed supplies badly, wanted horses to mount his dragoons, and was fatally overconfident. Learning of a storehouse in Bennington guarded only by militia, he dispatched Colonel Baum, with Riedesel and Fraser, under the following cocksure instructions, ' . . . Mount your dragoons . . . send me 1300 horses . . . seize Bennington . . . cross mountains to Rockingham and Brattleborough . . . try affections of country . . . take hostages . . . meet me a fortnight hence in Albany.' He expected little or no opposition from the people of the New Hampshire Grants, but he sent Breymann's German regulars to support Baum in case of unexpected developments.

Meanwhile the fear-stricken Colonies were striving to raise volunteers for defense against Burgoyne's advance. Colonel John Stark, veteran of the French War, Bunker Hill, Trenton, and Princeton, had retired to his New Hampshire farm in disgust when Congress promoted undeserving junior officers over his head. He was called back into service and given command of the forces gathered by New Hampshire. On his withdrawal from service, writers of the day had referred to him as 'a rustic Achilles sulking in his tent.' Now the promise of leadership filled him with eager activity, and he marched his men over the mountains to Bennington, arriving on August 9. On the 12th, Baum started his eastward march, unaware of the increased strength at Bennington. His detachment of eight hundred included musicians, officers' servants, and women camp-followers; his main strength was three hundred and seventy-five dismounted German dragoons, fifty British infantrymen, and some three hundred Indians, Tories, and Canadians.

By the 14th, Stark knew definitely of Baum's advance and moved his militiamen up to meet them, strengthened by volunteers from Bennington and other towns in the Grants and Massachusetts, a total force of eighteen hundred. At Sancoick Mills a vanguard of American riflemen fired on Baum's ranks from the brush, and retreated before the enemy, sniping at uniforms as they fell back. Eleazer Edgerton had stayed behind to burn St. Luke's Bridge over the Walloomsac, and Baum, forced to halt and restore the bridge, took his position on the hill over the river. After some skirmishing, Stark withdrew to plan the attack. On the 15th, it rained hard all day, and fighting was out of the question; sharp-shooting American scouts managed to keep enough powder dry to harass the enemy and pick off some outpost victims. Baum's position, naturally strong, was weakened by his deploying troops to defend the bridgeheads. On the steep hill-shoulder three hundred feet above the Walloomsac River, he built a breastwork of felled trees to bolster his main defense. But the wide scattering of his four detachments was poor strategy.

August 16 was bright and clear after the storm. Wet leaves glistened and the green earth steamed in the sultry sunshine. It is legendary that the lean, grim-mouthed Stark said, 'We beat them today, or Molly Stark's a widow.' At three o'clock in the hot afternoon, the attack started, with Nichols and Herrick carrying the left and right flanks respectively, the Indians and Canadians fleeing after but little show of opposition. The enemy's front outpost, manned by Tories behind a flimsy barrier of fence-rails and loose earth, fell before Hubbard and Stickney. The Tories fled across the river and up the hill, and Stark and Warner launched the big drive at Baum's main defense on the hill crest. Swarming across the bridgeways or splashing through the stream, the Americans clambered up the blazing hillside, a motley army in tattered shirt-sleeves and sweaty jackets. Stark and Warner were greeted by a ball from the Hessian four-pounder. 'The rascals know we're officers, all right,' cried Stark. 'They salute us with big guns.' A powder explosion threw the poorly manned English redoubt into confusion, and the charge of ragged farmers and tough woodsmen cleared the barricade. Deserted by their allies and hopelessly outnumbered, Baum and his Germans stood firm until their ammunition gave out; then, drawing their great broadswords and led by Baum, they tried to cut their way out. Baum fell, shot in the belly, and the rest, who were still alive and unwounded, either fled or surrendered. By five o'clock the Hessian forces were smashed and broken, and the Americans were scattered in pursuit, in the gathering of plunder, or the herding of prisoners.

In the meantime Breymann, notorious as a brutal drillmaster, was marching five hundred and fifty Germans to the aid of Baum at the rate of only one-half mile per hour, dragging his cannon through the mud, and halting ten times to the mile to dress and re-dress his ranks with eighteenth-century Prussian precision. But for these foolhardy parade-ground tactics, Breymann could have been there a day earlier and the issue might have been entirely changed. Instead of meeting Baum's detachment, Breymann ran into a scene of utter confusion and rifle-fire that raked his lines from rail-fences and wooded ridges; but he marched doggedly on.

The Americans, scattered and disorganized now, were wearied from their exertions in the August heat, wilted by the scorching sun. It has been said that Stark was in favor of falling back to re-form his ranks and prepare to meet the German reinforcements, but Seth Warner persuaded him to stay and fight it out on the spot. When the tired volunteers turned Baum's cannon on Breymann, Stark had to dismount and show his inexperienced men how to load and fire the guns. The Hessians were fatigued from marching through mud in their heavy equipment, but they were forcing the farmers back when, just before sunset, Warner's company of three hundred and fifty arrived from Manchester. The only fresh men on the field, they again turned the tide of battle and the Continentals surged forward. The German ammunition was running low, and Breymann's retreat in the fading light of day was turned into a rout. At dusk the Colonial victory was complete.

Stark took about six hundred prisoners, and over two hundred of the enemy were left dead on the field. The American losses were small, thirty killed and forty wounded. Baum and Tory Colonel Pfister were carried to a farmhouse, where both died of wounds, and were buried on the bank of the Walloomsac. The prisoners, many of them wounded, were paraded along the street between the log huts, of Old Bennington, before being lodged in the original Meeting House, the schoolhouse, and other houses and barns. 'With such a base show of rustic contempt was celebrated the turning of the tide against Burgoyne.' ('The Turning Point of the Revolution,' by Hoffman Nickerson, 1928.) The dead soldiers of both sides were interred in the Old Burying Ground.

Bennington was a crushing blow to the British, the beginning of the end for Burgoyne, and it made possible the later decisive victory of Gates and Arnold at Saratoga, which was the true turning-point of the Revolutionary War. Bennington is one of the few cases in history of improvised troops beating regular trained soldiers. The following excerpt from a letter of Burgoyne's to England, written after the battle of Bennington, reveals how his confidence was shaken by the totally unexpected and stunning blow: 'The Hampshire Grants in particular — a country unpeopled and almost unknown in the last war — now abounds with the most active and rebellious race on the continent, and hangs, like a gathering storm, on my left.'

During 1828–29, William Lloyd Garrison lived in Bennington and established one of his papers, *The Journal of the Times*. A great deal of his first interest in Abolition was developed here, with the motivations that directed his later life and relentless campaign against slavery and the South.


POINTS OF INTEREST (*Bennington proper*)


1. The *Post Office*, South and Union Sts., a long low modern structure of Vermont marble, has a classic severity of line and a portico with six fluted columns.

2. The *Courthouse*, South St., a handsome new brick building with marble trim and a white-pillared façade, is the fifth Bennington courthouse. The county has two shire towns: Manchester in the north, and Bennington in the south.

3. The *Bennington Free Library*, Silver St. (*Mon., Th., Sat.*, 10 *to* 9; *Tu., Wed., Fri.*, 10 *to* 12; 2 *to* 5.30), contains about 30,000 volumes. This is another of the attractive modern structures that dignify downtown Bennington, of brick trimmed with marble and graced with a rounded white entrance portico and white tower. The reading-room windows are modeled after those of the General Robinson House in Old Bennington, and the lantern over the entrance is a copy of the old courthouse lantern.

4. The *Norton-Fenton House*, 208 Pleasant St., a large two-family brick house built by Judge Luman Norton in 1838, is of interest for the specimen of Bennington pottery that rests on its porch, and for its history which links the two great names of Bennington pottery. As early as 1793, Captain John Norton and his sons manufactured pottery, plain and useful articles in stoneware and in a mottled brown and yellow ware known as Rockingham. Under the influence of Christopher Fenton, son-in-law of Judge Luman Norton, more delicate and elaborate types were produced. From 1850 to 1858, independent of the Nortons, Fenton turned out specimens of the potter's art now highly prized by collectors, including 'Parian,' a porcelain that resembled marble, and Fenton's 'Flint Enamel.' After a century of pottery-making, the enterprise was given up in 1894.

5. The *Vermont Soldiers' Home* (*open to visitors*), NE. of US 7, at the northern edge of the village, occupies the former estate of Seth B. Hunt, pioneer textile manufacturer, and is maintained by the State with some aid from the Federal Government. Equipped to house 84 residents, it serves as a home for disabled and homeless veterans. The long yellow building is set back in spacious pine-shaded grounds, which include a farm of 350 acres, a fine maple grove and a great fountain.

### POINTS OF INTEREST (*Old Bennington*)

1. The *Historical Museum* (*adm.* 15¢), Main St., originally the Church of St. Francis de Sales, was acquired by the Bennington Historical Society and converted to its present use in 1927. Built of native field-stone, with an iron-fenced courtyard opening between it and the smaller building, formerly the priest's house, the structure has an Old World aspect. The museum contains a wide variety of military relics and historical documents, including Stark's flag carried at the battle of Bennington, and a brass cannon captured from the Hessians. There is also an exhibit of Bennington pottery, and of utensils typical of early Vermont days.

2. The *Old Burying Ground*, Monument Ave., faces the Green where the original Meeting House stood. Here were buried the British and American

dead from the battle of Bennington, and here lie the fathers of Bennington who laid the foundations of Vermont — the Robinsons, the Fays, the Harwoods, the Deweys, the Fassetts, the Hubbells, and all the rest. Five Vermont governors rest here: Moses Robinson (1789–90); Isaac Tichenor (1797–1807; 1808–09); John S. Robinson (1853–54); Hiland Hall (1858–60); and John McCullough (1902–04). Many of the headstones are ornamented with pop-eyed, round-headed angels characteristic of the more elaborate Colonial memorials.

3. The *First Congregational Church*, Monument Ave., raises its gracefully graduated tower over the southern edge of the graveyard. The architect was Lavius Fillmore, a close student of the architectural handbooks of Asher Benjamin. It is considered, with Fillmore's Middlebury church, one of the most beautiful in the State. Of white-painted clapboards, with wood quoins, the structure has a Palladian window above the three entrance doors, and Palladian windows in three sides of the square tower, which supports an open belfry. The belfry is surmounted by a 'lantern' with oval windows, capped by a weathervane. The church was built in 1806. Services are held here from May to January.

4. The *Jedediah Dewey House*, Monument Ave. (second south of the church), a solid, square-built house painted white, with a huge central chimney, was built in 1763 by the Reverend Mr. Dewey, and is said to be the oldest frame house in the State. Parson Dewey was Bennington's first minister, and an accomplished carpenter as well, a fact attested by the strength and beauty of his home. On the Sabbath before the battle of Bennington, Parson Dewey delivered a rousing war sermon, invoking his people to take up arms and fight. That he was a man of willful purpose was shown one Sunday when Ethan Allen, disliking some remark from the pulpit, rose and started to stalk out. Dewey transfixed the bold Allen with a pointed forefinger and shouted: 'Sit down, thou blasphemer, and listen to the Word of God!' And Ethan Allen sat down. At another time Allen gained some measure of jocular revenge. Dewey was preaching a thanksgiving service for the capture of Ticonderoga, and giving rather more credit to God than to Allen for the victory. In the midst of the prayer, Allen interrupted with a voice full of mock pleading: 'Parson Dewey, Parson Dewey — please mention to the Lord about my being there!'

5. The *Walloomsac Inn*, Monument Ave., was founded in 1766 by Captain Elijah Dewey, son of the parson. Elijah commonly remarked that 'no one lost anything by going to church,' and he donated generously to its support. But he did not unite with the church until his last sickness. He served at Ticonderoga, Bennington, and Saratoga during the Revolution.

6. The *Site of Catamount Tavern*, Monument Ave., is marked by the figure of a lithe bronze catamount standing high on a granite base. This inn was founded as the Green Mountain House by Stephen Fay, and was often referred to as Landlord Fay's. Here the Green Mountain Boys gathered

over their rum, the Council of Safety laid the groundwork for the future
State of Vermont, Allen plotted the move against Ticonderoga, and Stark
and Warner planned the defense of Bennington. Before the battle of Bennington, British officers sent a haughty message to the Catamount Tavern, ordering dinner made ready for their triumphal entry. That August
evening, when British prisoners, their splendid uniforms torn, dirty,
and blood-smirched, shuffled wearily down the street between the ragged
and powder-stained backwoodsmen who had beaten them, Landlord Fay
stepped forward with a gallant bow and said: 'Gentlemen, the dinner
that you ordered is ready.' Stephen Fay had five sons fighting on Walloomsac Heights that day, and one of them, John, was killed. He was a
popular fellow and his death fired the Bennington volunteers with fury.
In the assault that followed they swept aside Baum's barricade. Another
son, Jonas, was secretary of the Council of Safety and surgeon of the
Green Mountain Boys. Benjamin Fay, still another son of the landlord,
was the first sheriff in the State.

7. The *Isaac Tichenor Mansion*, west of (behind) the Walloomsac Inn on
State 9, is set proudly back on a knoll fenced with white pickets to match
the white house. The latter was built prior to 1790 for the handsome
Princeton graduate who served as Governor of Vermont for eleven years,
and had a brilliant career as a Federalist statesman. Fond of hunting
and fishing, Tichenor was as much at home in the woods as in the draw-
ing-rooms of Washington. One day, while dining at home with friends,
he called suddenly for his fowling-piece, pointed to a bird in a tree outside
the open windows, and from his chair at table brought the bird down
with a shot.

8. The *Old Academy Library*, Monument Ave. (*open Thurs., 2 to 5; two
additional afternoons during summer*). Situated near the top of the grade
of Vermont's most historic avenue, this small red-brick building, with
recessed double doors and an open bell-tower, was erected in 1821 as an
academy, to be 'the finest building in the State.' It served as a secondary
school for three-quarters of a century, since which time (1897) it has been
used as a library, and now contains 8000 volumes.

9. The *Site of Samuel Robinson's Cabin*, Monument Ave., is plainly
marked just north of the Old Academy near the summit. Here the founder
of Bennington erected his log cabin in 1761. One night while Captain
Robinson was in London as agent of the New Hampshire Grants, 1767,
Mrs. Robinson chased wolves away from the cabin door, by dashing out
and waving glowing brands. The Friday prayer meetings of the primitive settlement were held in the Robinson home.

10. The *General David Robinson House*, Monument Ave., opposite the
Robinson marker, was built by the eighth son of Captain Samuel in 1795.
This beautiful Georgian Colonial structure, facing a wide picket-fenced
lawn, is framed by giant shade trees. The two-story dwelling is narrow
and rectangular, typical of the eighteenth-century houses found in the
State and also in the northern Connecticut Valley. Its delicate pedimented

entrance portico is painted white in pleasing contrast to the soft gray of the clapboarded siding and the dark green of the shutters. Attenuated Ionic pilasters form the most interesting feature of the exterior. Appearing at the corners of the façade and on either side of the portico, they rise in support of a bracketed cornice and central pediment. The distinctive triple-arched window above the entrance, though cramped and ill-placed, is in itself charming.

David Robinson fought as a private at Walloomsac Heights and later became major-general of militia. He was a man of great physical strength and courage, once going alone into a hayloft to drag forth a desperate outlaw whom no one else dared approach. The Robinsons were a husky, high-spirited clan, especially given to wrestling, in which they employed a hold that came to be known as the Robinson Lock. One day Governor Moses Robinson (1789–90) was riding through the mountains and stopped by chance at a house-raising. After the raising, the men began to wrestle, and the Governor watched quietly for a while, until the local bully had thrown all comers. Moses then stepped forward with a challenge, and threw the bully quickly and hard. The furious man leaped up for another try, raging at the 'spindle-shanked stranger' who had humbled him. They tangled and again Moses slammed the brawny fellow's shoulders to the sod. It was an added shock to the bully when he learned that the talented grappler was Governor of the State.

11. *Betsy Robinson's Tomb*, behind the General David Robinson House, is a rude but substantial arch of field-stones on a little knoll over the open field, built by David Robinson, Jr., son of the general, to receive the coffin of his beloved wife, Betsy. Here young David spent long hours of mourning, but his grief was finally terminated by the advent of a comely widow, who became his second wife.

12. The *Statue of Seth Warner* stands at the head of Monument Ave., in the shadow of the Battle Monument. The figure is in the uniform of a Continental Colonel. Less fiery and colorful than Ethan Allen, Warner was perhaps even more respected and trusted by his contemporaries, who often preferred his calm, steady competence to the arrogant swagger of Ethan. Warner's rear-guard action at Hubbardton made it possible for the main body of the retreating American army to escape, and his support of Stark at Bennington was invaluable.

13. The *Bennington Battle Monument* (*adm.* 15¢) towers 306 feet above the broad summit of the hill, where stood the storehouse which Burgoyne detailed Baum to capture. The highest battle monument in the world, it was dedicated in 1891 on the centennial of Vermont's admission to the Union. Within the great symmetrical spire of granite, 412 steps zigzag up past 34 landings to a lookout that commands marvelous vistas over Bennington and the serene contours of the green landscape.

## TOUR TO THE BATTLEFIELD (*cumulative mileage*)

Left (west) from the *Seth Warner Statue*, 0 *m.*, the road leads westward to a junction at 0.7 *m.* Left from this junction the road leads to another junction at 1.3 *m.*, from which the route is left. At 2 *m.* the road swings sharply right, and at 2.8 *m.* is a white farmhouse.

Left from this farmhouse the route leads to the *Site of the Breakenridge Farm* (R), 3.1 *m.*, which Sheriff Ten Eyck of Albany with 300 heavily armed henchmen set out to seize, only to be forestalled by the quick gathering of the Bennington mob.

Beyond the Breakenridge marker is the *Site of Seth Warner's House* (L), 3.3 *m.* Shortly beyond this site, at 3.5 *m.*, is the old *Henry House* (1769). This gray clapboarded house with its asymmetrical plan, sweeping shed roof, and wide front porch, is a notable departure from the usual regional type. The tall square columns of the porch with their interesting but crudely molded caps, the casual treatment of trim and detail, the long raked lines of the downspouts, and the generous proportions of the whole produce an effect of charming informality. It is said that Warner's house was identical in design with this one and that both were raised on the same day at a bee attended by most of the prominent figures in early Vermont history. Just beyond the Henry House is the *Old Covered Bridge*, said to be the strongest of its type in the world, and seemingly as staunch and sturdy today as it was when the Green Mountain Boys swarmed here to meet Sheriff Ten Eyck's Yorkers and turn them back toward Albany.

Left from the bridge, the road leads over a hillock to *Stark's Camping Ground* (R), 4.7 *m.* Here, on August 14, 15, and 16, 1777, were the headquarters of John Stark's militiamen and volunteers, before and during the action at the Battle of Bennington.

At 5.6 *m.* the route is left on a blacktop road, and at 5.7 *m.* (R) is the *Site of the House Where Baum and Pfister Died* of wounds on the day following their defeat. Both officers were buried on the bank of the Walloomsac in unmarked graves.

At 6.1 *m.* is the *New York Line.* Beyond the line at 8 *m.* the route swings (R) up the slope of *Baum's Hill*, or *Walloomsac Heights*, the scene of the battle.

# B R A T T L E B O R O

*Village:* Alt. 260, pop. 8709.

*Railroad Station:* B. & M. R.R. and Central Vermont Ry., S.E. side of town, near interstate bridge.

*Bus Stations:* Bee Line (through N. and S. connections); Brattleboro-to-Keene Trans. Co.; Brattleboro-to-Bennington Trans. Co.; West River Bus Co. (Rutland); depots near R.R. station.

*Accommodations:* Three hotels; many tourist homes.

*Information:* Booth on Main St. at junction with State 9 during summer months.

*Annual Events:* Horse Show, August; State Tennis Tournament, June or July; winter sports competitions, dates partly dependent on snow conditions.

BRATTLEBORO is the largest town in Vermont in population and is exceeded in this respect by only three cities. The southernmost sizable town on the eastern side of the State, it has adopted the publicity slogan 'Where Vermont Begins.' The phrase might equally well read, 'Where Vermont Began,' for the first permanent white settlement in Vermont was made in this township, about a mile and a half from the business district. Present Brattleboro, however, is one of a small number of Connecticut Valley towns whose varied commercial and industrial activities, while they have brought prosperity and steady growth, are by no means typical of Vermont as a whole.

Brattleboro spreads along the Connecticut from its junction with the West River south to Whetstone Brook, and climbs an irregular chain of plateaus to the west. The rocky wooded height of Wantastiquet Mountain on the New Hampshire shore of the Connecticut presses down upon the town from the east. Main Street passes from the brief charm of the Common into one of the most crowded business sections in Vermont, winds steeply down between darkened brick buildings to the native stone railroad station, south of which lie the yards and factories of the industrial flats along the river. The two islands at this point that formerly afforded sites for a dance hall and baseball park have been reduced to negligible shoals by the backed-up waters of the Vernon Dam, six miles below. From the semi-circle of terraces that rise west of Main Street houses look down upon the jumble of shed roofs and smokestacks. One of the plateaus is commanded by the handsomely landscaped Estey estate, with its mansion looking across to the opposite heights where the family fortune was made. With something of the loud, unlovely industrial atmosphere of Bellows Falls, where the Connecticut is even more sharply walled-in by hills, Brattleboro nevertheless possesses a greater variety than any of the other busy valley towns. West on State 9 lies a pleasant residential section, while to the north along US 5, from where the Common stands above the sweeping lawns of the Retreat, is a wealthy suburban district with some of the finest domestic architecture in the State.

Brattleboro was part of the land sold to private citizens by Connecticut in 1716, for about a farthing an acre. These lands, ceded to the State by Massachusetts in return for some settled territory that Massachusetts had granted, but which a new survey showed actually to be in Connecticut, were known as the 'Equivalent Lands.' Massachusetts obtained permission to establish an outpost here, mainly for the protection of the settlement at Northfield, and work was begun under the direction of Lieutenant-Governor Sir William Dummer, for whom the fort, completed in 1724, was named (see below).

In 1753 the town was granted by New Hampshire, within whose jurisdiction Fort Dummer had been declared to be, to the original proprietors, and was named for one of them, Colonel William Brattle, a land speculator who never set foot in the town. The first settlers under this grant chose the present site for their cabins because the hill served as a natural watchtower to guard against surprise attacks by the Indians. One such attack occurred, however, in 1758, in which Captain Fairbank Moor(e) and his son were slain and his wife and a four-weeks-old infant made captive and taken to Montreal, where they were later ransomed for seventy-four dollars. During the three decades prior to Vermont's admission to the Union, Brattleboro, like the majority of towns in this section, was a Tory stronghold.

In 1771, Stephen Greenleaf, from Boston, opened what is believed to have been the first store in the present State. Not of much significance in itself, the fact exemplifies the zeal for trade and industry that Brattleboro has always manifested to a degree equaled by few other Vermont towns. Of the many manufacturing firms that came into being during the last century, the most widely known was the Estey Organ Company. This business was begun in 1846, but did not develop until 1855, when it became the sole property of Jacob Estey. It was Estey's perseverance that triumphed over adversities — his factory was twice destroyed by fire and once devastated by flood — to win pre-eminence for his product in its field. During the latter half of the nineteenth century thousands of American women sewed till the small hours, picked berries under a blazing sun or rented the spare room, and saved their egg money in a cracked teapot on the top shelf with just one goal in mind: a black walnut Estey organ in the parlor. The 'parlor organ' is almost as obsolete as the top buggy, but the Estey Organ Company now leads in the manufacture of multi-manual pipe organs for churches and private homes.

Other commercial products of Brattleboro include cotton goods, penholders, brush handles, lacquer, heels, bathroom accessories, finished woods, toys, overalls, paper, soft drinks, and granite monuments and memorials. The printing establishments here are outstanding in the State.

But Brattleboro has not been wholly a mart of material things. Royall Tyler, Vermont's earliest man of letters, lived here for many years and wrote, under the pseudonym of 'Spondee,' his witty contributions to *The Farmer's Museum*, published at Walpole, New Hampshire, a periodical which, chiefly due to 'Spondee,' had a larger circulation than any other village paper in the country. Rudyard Kipling, who married a Brattleboro girl, lived a few miles north of the village for several years in the 1890's and did some of his best work here (*see Tour 1, Sec. c*).

But it is to the arts of painting, sculpture, and architecture that Brattleboro, through its native sons, has made the most distinguished contributions.

In Brattleboro was born, and here, in the Prospect Hill Cemetery overlooking the town, is buried, William Morris Hunt (1824–79), who, though not one of the few greatest American painters, was one of the most influential. It was Hunt who rescued from discouragement and an obscurity broken only by the critics who had ridiculed his 'clodhoppers,' Jean François Millet, the French artist, whose paintings ('The Angelus,' 'The Sower,' 'The Reaper') have in recent decades been almost too popular in this country. Hunt owned many of Millet's original canvases, including 'The Sower,' for which Millet unwillingly accepted sixty dollars. After helping Millet to establish the Barbizon school of painting, Hunt returned to this country and opened his own school of painting in Boston, where for a time he occupied much the same position in American portraiture as Sargent held later. In 1875 he executed two large murals for the Assembly chamber of the Capitol at Albany, New York, considered the most important American murals until they were surpassed by Sargent's in the Boston Public Library. They have unfortunately been quite ruined by the dampness of the walls upon which, unlike Sargent's work, they were directly painted.

Richard Morris Hunt (1827–95), William's younger brother, was the most fashionable of American architects. He did the Newport residences of Cornelius Vanderbilt, Mrs. William K. Vanderbilt, and Oliver Belmont. In New York City he did the town houses of Elbridge T. Gerry, John Jacob Astor, and William K. Vanderbilt, the latter, at Fifth Avenue and Fifty-Second Street, being generally regarded as the apogee of the architectural exhibitionism of nineteenth-century multi-millionaires. Hunt's public works include the Tribune Building (1873), among the first of the elevator office buildings; the Administration Building of the Columbian Exposition; the central portion of the Metropolitan Museum of Art; the National Observatory, in Washington; and the base of the Statue of Liberty.

Larkin Mead (1835–1910), the sculptor, though born across the river, grew up in Brattleboro and considered it his home. He first came to public notice through the 'Recording Angel,' which he sculptured in snow on New Year's Eve, 1856, at the junction of Linden and Main Streets. Rain and cold preserved the iced statue for several days, and — snow sculpture not being the common thing it now is — newspaper reporters came from Boston and other cities to see and write about it. James Russell Lowell celebrated it in a poem, 'A Good Word for Winter.' Mead later did several replicas in marble of what was originally a mere artistic prank. His best known work in this State is his colossal statue of Ethan Allen (1861), in the portico of the Capitol at Montpelier, which he duplicated for the Hall of Statuary in Washington. He also did the figure of Ceres (1857) on the Vermont Capitol dome. After the Civil War, during which he was staff artist for *Harper's Weekly*, he lived for several years in Italy, where he married — despite the Pope's disapproval and refusal of dispensation — a celebrated Italian beauty, Marietta di Benvenuti. In Italy he did most of the actual work on his most ambitious piece, the Lincoln Memorial at Springfield, Illinois, completed in 1883.

William Rutherford Mead (1846–1928), Larkin's younger brother, was one of the most distinguished of modern American architects. As a member of the firm of McKim, Mead, and White, he made the basic designs for a score of important public buildings, including the Capitol at Providence, Rhode Island, and the Boston Public Library. He became president of the American Academy at Rome in 1909 and was its guiding spirit for eighteen years. Elinor Mead, a sister of Larkin and William, was an artist of some reputation and wife of William Dean Howells, the novelist and editor of *The Atlantic Monthly*.

Brattleboro was the early home of James Fisk (1834–72), the jovial, impudent voluptuary and stock manipulator, whose unscrupulous method of making a fortune and spectacular manner of dissipating it outraged and amused the American public. It is just possible that Fisk's disregard of business ethics was partly due to a Brattleboro venture of his father, who opened a temperance hotel here in 1849, but was forced to close the idealistic establishment the following year for lack of patrons.

Water, however, contributed to Brattleboro's fame and prosperity during the years between 1845 and 1870, when the Brattleboro Hydropathic Establishment, utilizing the mineral springs here, became one of the most fashionable cures in the country, with an elaborate plant accommodating three hundred guests. Under the leadership of Dr. Robert Wesselhoeft, a German political refugee of high intelligence, the institution attracted many persons of literary and artistic talent as well as wealthy neurasthenics.

At Brattleboro are the national headquarters of the Holstein-Friesian Breeders' Association.

## POINTS OF INTEREST

1. The *Brattleboro Public Library* (Brooks Memorial Bldg.), 200 Main St. (*open weekdays* 10–9), of red brick with an arched portico, contains several collections of interest. The main library has about 25,000 volumes. The museum upstairs includes early American pioneer utensils, implements, relics, and several items of historical association, among them a suit of armor worn by the Mexican General Santa Ana. A small art collection is headed by a large original canvas of William Morris Hunt. This work, 'The Prodigal Son,' is an early example of Hunt's narrative painting and is inferior to much of his later and simpler work in portraiture. In separate rooms are the Loud collection of porcelains and paintings and the Phelps collection on 3000 rare books, documents, and broadsides donated by James H. Phelps in 1888.

2. The *Center Congregational Church*, Main St., the oldest in town (1842), is a white wooden structure, with decorative quoins and a tall graduated tower rising into a spire.

3. The *All Souls Church*, Main St., constructed of stone, is designed in a modified version of Gothic architecture. A marble copy of Mead's 'Recording Angel,' originally modeled in snow, was placed in this church as a memorial to the sculptor.

4. The *Estey Estate and Brattleboro Summer Theater*, School St. The mansion built by Jacob Estey is an ornate brown-brick structure, typical

of the grandiose monuments in the form of houses that American capitalists in the latter half of the nineteenth century erected to their own
success. It is now the summer residence of members of the theater group.
The theater itself (150 capacity) has been thoroughly remodeled from the
old red-brick Estey coach house, and stands at the end of an inviting
aisle of huge elms. Here during the summer months a repertory of recent plays is professionally produced at popular prices. The advisory
committee consisted in 1937 of Jane Cowl, Thornton Wilder, Claude
Rains, and Paul Osborn.

5. The *Estey Organ Works*, Birge St. (*open to inspection*), occupy half a
dozen slate-shingled buildings on a commanding plateau, the central
elevation of three that rise up west of the main business district. The
buildings to the rear of, and at right angles to, the main plant are the
'dry-houses,' where wood for the cases and inner parts of the organs is
thoroughly dried by a patented process. The plant has a capacity of
1800 organs a month.

6. The *Brattleboro Retreat*, Linden St. (1836), is a partially State-supported hospital for the insane. The brick buildings of the large plant,
some of recent construction, others dating from the earlier years of the
institution, are set in the quiet seclusion of spacious landscaped grounds.
There were about 700 patients in residence in 1937.

7. The *Brattleboro Outing Club and Ski Jump*, west of Cedar St., northwest part of town, are evidence of Brattleboro's intense interest in outdoor sports. The tennis courts here are the best in the State. The
bungalow clubhouse, while not suitable for large indoor gatherings,
serves to dispense hot refreshments to winter sport fans. The huge ski
jump has been a major factor in making the town one of the leaders in
winter sports in Vermont.

8. The *Austine School for the Deaf*, Maple St., overlooks the town from
a hill that rises in the western part of Brattleboro. Founded in 1912, the
school is privately endowed but receives State charges from both New
Hampshire and Vermont, some 40 Vermont children being enrolled. The
pupils, boys and girls from four to eighteen, receive the advantages of
the latest developments in both educational technique and equipment,
the latter including electrical apparatus.

9. The *Site of Fort Dummer*, 1.4 m. south of town on State 30. The actual
site of Fort Dummer (dismantled in 1763) is covered by the backed-up
waters of the Vernon Dam. The granite marker, beside the highway,
was moved 2200 feet northwest of its original site in 1928. Fort Dummer,
of which contemporary drawings are extant, was approximately 180 feet
square, of yellow pine timber. The wall of the fort was the back wall
of all the houses inside it, the roofs sloping up to the top of the fort.
Garrisoned by 55 men, including a dozen friendly Indians, the fort was
for its first two years in command of Captain Timothy Dwight, whose
son was the first white child born in Vermont, and was to be further
distinguished as the father of a President of Yale College.

# BURLINGTON

*City:* Alt. 100 to 489, pop. 24,789.

*Railroad Station:* Union Station, foot of Main St., Rutland R.R. and Central Vermont Railways. Most C.V. passenger traffic handled through Essex Junction, to which passengers are transferred from Bus Terminal, 137 St. Paul St. or Union Station.

*Bus Stations:* Terminal, 137 St. Paul St., Vermont Transit Co., Inc. (Interstate); Burlington Rapid Transit Co. (Interurban and City); Sherwood Hotel, Church St., Frontier-Champlain Coach Lines; Van Ness Hotel, Main St., Intrastate busses and liveries.

*Airport:* Municipal Airport, 3.1 *m.* east of city on US 2. Passenger service to Boston by Central Vermont–Boston & Maine Airways, Inc. Busses from Terminal, 137 St. Paul St., fare 50¢.

*Ferries:* Foot of King St., Port Kent, N.Y. Ferry; foot of College St., Port Douglas, N.Y. Ferry.

*Accommodations:* Three hotels, many boarding-houses and tourist inns; also several summer hotels in vicinity of city. Municipal Tourist Camp on Institute Rd., 2.5 *m.* north of city.

*Information:* Chamber of Commerce Tourist and Industrial Information Bureau, 194 Main St.

*Annual Events:* Vermont Union Agricultural Meeting and Vermont Farm Products Show, January; 'Kake Walk,' fraternity feature at University of Vermont, February; Sportsmen's Show, late winter; Maple Festival, spring; District Basketball Tournament, March; Lenten-Easter Concert by University Choir; University Glee Clubs' Opera, April; Music Festival, U. of V. 'Junior Week,' May; Green Mountain Playhouse, Inc., during ten weeks in summer presents outstanding plays; 2-day regatta on Lake Champlain for American and Canadian yacht clubs, early August; Christmas Concert, University Choir, December. The Community Concert Association gives three concerts during the October–April season.

BURLINGTON, the 'Queen City of Vermont,' is beautifully situated on a three-terraced slope rising from the broadest expanse of Lake Champlain. The waterway at its feet, which has contributed so great a part to its commercial prosperity, is one of America's loveliest lakes, stretching far away to the west to the Adirondacks, while on the east, extending north and south, are the Green Mountains.

On the tree-covered summit of the city, flanked by residential districts, stand the buildings of the University of Vermont; the business section occupies the middle terrace, and below are the railroad yards and shops, the docks and warehouses. With its broad streets and avenues regularly laid out, Burlington has the appearance of a modern city, but it is also old and, never having suffered from a great fire, it has preserved many of the gracious structures of an earlier day. So it is, that even in the business district, at the end of a modern vista, the eye is frequently greeted with the fair dignity of a columned portico or the grace of an exquisitely proportioned spire.

From the deck of a lake steamer Burlington appears as a wooded slope at the crest of which the University's spires emerge; from the tower of the Old Mill, the oldest college building, the city is a folding carpet of elms reaching down to the broad lake and pierced only by church steeples. The affinity between the college and the lake is typified in the University of Vermont song 'Champlain,' perhaps the only alma mater song which is entirely an anthem of praise to the beauty of natural setting. Possibly it was the willful provincialism of William Dean Howells which caused him to declare sunset over the Bay of Naples as second only to a Champlain sunset seen from Burlington, but July evenings here tend to exonerate him from that charge.

With the atmosphere of an educational center, with more than its share of libraries, museums, art galleries, and schools; with the added advantage of open country and the lake at its very doors, Burlington nevertheless has maintained its commercial importance. Threescore manufacturing establishments with good railroad and water transportational facilities send Burlington products out over the world.

In the first constitution of the Independent State of Vermont it was set forth that a State University should be established, and hardly had the little town of Burlington begun to recognize the commercial possibilities of lake navigation, when the University of Vermont was chartered in November, 1791, one of the first State colleges in the country. That was the year of Vermont's admission to the Union, and, with little else to give it, the State endowed its university with 29,000 acres of wild, forest-covered land, scattered through 120 townships.

Soon Burlington began to win a place as the most important of Champlain ports. Thereafter, through an era of more than fifty years, as grew the city, so grew the University. With the coming of the railroads in 1849 there was a pause for adjustment, but the opening of new markets and speedier transportation brought renewed prosperity both to the city and the college.

Burlington was chartered in 1763 by the Province of New Hampshire and settled in 1773. The name derives from the Burling family, large landholders in this region. The astute Ira Allen, whose family name is written large in the annals of Vermont, had established a shipyard, building the first local vessel, the schooner 'Liberty,' on the Winooski River in 1772.

In the spring of 1775, with the outbreak of the Revolution, most of the settlers left to join Ethan Allen at Bennington. From then on practically all activity ceased, particularly after 1776, when nearly all who had not answered the first call went south with the retreat of American forces from Canada.

It was not until the close of the war in 1783 that the pioneers returned, their company augmented by the lure of a veritable promised land, with every possibility of a fine fur trade, with vast supplies of standing timber and ample water-power — and always the lake for a waterway. Clearing the land, working from the lake front up the hill, was the first necessary task. In 1797, the town of Burlington was organized. Ethan Allen himself came back to the Onion River and passed the last years of his life in lord-of-the-manor fashion on his handsome farm north of town.

A road was put through to Winooski Falls. Pearl Street and Colchester Avenue combine to follow the route of this early thoroughfare, but it is King Street that those interested in the beginning of commercial Burlington will seek out. At the foot of this street, where there were three or four houses comprising the village of Burlington, a rude wharf of logs was chained together and moored. Gideon King (familiarly 'Old Gid King'), in whose honor the street was named, was probably the first to grasp the great possibilities of commercial navigation on Lake Champlain. He urged it, he initiated it, he prospered at it, until he was known in all the lake ports and far into Canada as 'Admiral of the Lake.' John Jacob Astor, at this time founding the Astor fortune in the fur trade, met King, appreciated him as a man of foresight, and chose him to look after his interests.

Also, it was in a room in the sizable home King had built on Battery Street that the law was administered in the early 1790's, but the lumbermen were clearing up the middle area of the town, so that in 1798 what is now City Hall Park was dedicated to the public and the first courthouse was erected.

Meanwhile the 'Admiral of the Lake' and those whom he had converted to his enthusiasm were flourishing. With Montreal and Quebec there was already a fine trade. Down the Winooski and Lamoille Rivers floated seemingly endless supplies of logs to be formed into crude rafts and towed, or sometimes sailed, to Canadian destinations. The ever-enterprising Ira Allen had built a sawmill at Winooski Falls and handier rafts of dressed lumber began to appear. Many of these carried cargoes of potash, made from the ashes of wood waste.

Near the foot of King Street was built in 1808 the steamboat 'Vermont,' which inaugurated steam navigation on Lake Champlain the following year, and was the second steamboat successfully operated commercially in this country. One hundred and twenty feet over all, of twenty-foot beam and of 167 tons burden, 'built and fitted up at great expense for the convenient accommodation of ladies and gentlemen who wish to pass Lake Champlain with safety and dispatch,' the 'Vermont' set out on her first voyage from Burlington in June, 1809, John Winans in command, scheduled 'to make the passage of the lake, 150 miles (to Whitehall), in the short time of twenty-four hours.'

Then occurred the outbreak of hostilities with England, and in 1812 Burlington became the Vermont center of military activity.

Some four thousand troups were quartered on what is now Battery Park.

From here a raiding party went out to attack St. Armand, Quebec, where twenty-five of the enemy were killed or wounded, and one hundred others captured and brought back to Burlington.

The remains of a parapet can be traced along the western border of Battery Park, directly commanding the lake. Here thirteen guns had been set up, and when, on June 13, 1813, three British war vessels appeared in the bay and started offensive operations, they were beaten off. After the victory at Plattsburg, naval operations on the lake were discontinued and eighteen months later a treaty of peace was signed between the United States and England. Burlington's merchants resumed trade negotiations with Canada and began to develop the commerce already built up to the south. Steamboats, growing constantly more dependable, appeared in increasing numbers.

In 1823 the opening of the Champlain Canal connected the lake with the Hudson River. Almost at once the course of a large part of Champlain Valley commerce was changed from Canada to New York. With a way open to tidewater from Canada and the lake ports to the Atlantic Ocean, well-financed companies became interested. They built steamers, and not content with single-ship capacity, sent them out at the head of long tows of canal boats which were soon a common sight going up and down the lake.

The canal was a door opening outward for the distribution of products, and swinging inward to admit cheaply, and expeditiously, what was desired. The harbor was busy with craft discharging and loading their cargoes, and shipyards hummed as they labored to supply the demand for more steamboats, more canal-boats, more sailing vessels — anything that could bear merchandise over the water. And not only the water was utilized. Enterprising companies or individuals built so-called 'landships' — great covered wagons which, laden with diverse commodities and drawn by as many teams of horses as the load required, traded to the east and north, bringing to Burlington the produce of all this section of the State.

An increasing demand for passenger accommodations created lively competition among the steamboat lines. In 1826 the Champlain Transportation Company was chartered and by 1848 it had absorbed all its rivals and was triumphantly running four steamers between St. Johns and Whitehall, two for day and two for night travel (*see Transportation*). Lake travel attained its peak during the forties, for in the last year of that decade came the railroads and a swift decline in business on the water. Boston, the nearest great city, now accessible by rail, attracted by far the larger part of the commercial trade, and Burlington, recognized as a desirable shipping point, got two railroads almost simultaneously.

The question of the route of the proposed Boston–Burlington railway aroused tremendous feeling. One group of enthusiastic promoters was all for routing it via Rutland; another group held out just as strongly to include Concord, N.H., and Montpelier. Neither side being willing to concede anything, and both having capital, construction of both roads was begun and soon developed into a race to be first to enter Burlington. The Rutland road reached its goal December 18, 1849, and a week later on Christmas Day, its rival, the Central Vermont, was in Winooski.

By this time the once vast timber supply in the vicinity of Burlington was no longer equal to the market demand. But the lumbermen had become busy in Canada, and with great barges of lumber coming in across the lake, with the railroads ready to transport the finished product south, the city became the greatest lumber port in New England and third in the United States.

The Burlington *Free Press*, the oldest daily in the State, was founded April 1, 1848, by De Witt Clinton Clarke, as both a morning and evening paper.

Far to the north of the fighting lines though it was, Burlington's part in the Civil War was an active one. The city sent full quotas in answer to the Government's repeated calls for men; merchants and banks contributed generously; large hospital camps were established for the sick and wounded sent North, and training camps prepared recruits to go to the front. One of these camps was notable as that of the Second Vermont Regiment, which later lost in killed and wounded some forty per cent of its men, several times the general ratio of the Northern forces.

Two months before Appomattox, a new era of enterprise and prosperity had begun with a division of the territory of the old town of Burlington, the larger section forming South Burlington while the smaller was incorporated as a city (February 21, 1865). A new unity of civic effort was at once noticeable, and Burlington began to lose the appearance of an overgrown country town and to assume an urban aspect.

Changes since the Civil War have been evolutionary rather than radical. The Canadian lumber business, hard hit by the depression of the seventies, recovered for one final period of prosperity before the high-tariff laws of the nineties cut it off permanently. Since the turn of the century, though wood products are still turned out in several plants, the dominance of lumber has been replaced by a diversity of industries, among which textiles and the processing of maple syrup are prominent.

The population, doubling in the last sixty years, has gradually lost its homogeneous nature through the influx of French-Canadians, Germans, Italians, and other races, until Burlington is the most cosmopolitan of Vermont cities.

Outstanding in the State also are the municipal services, including a highly profitable city-owned electric light plant, efficient street, fire, and police departments, and an extensive park system.

The many handsome estates on the higher hill streets, only recently beginning to yield to subdivision, are evidence of the prosperity of fifty years ago, and of the attractions of Burlington for retired wealth.

The University of Vermont, which was united with the State Agricultural

College in 1865, has grown steadily if slowly to its present enrollment of some 1300 men and women. It includes faculties of Engineering, Medicine, and Education; as well as Agriculture and Arts and Sciences (*see Education*). The physical plant, first greatly expanded under Vermont's great President Matthew Henry Buckham in the eighties and nineties, has developed rapidly in the last ten years (*see below, Points of Interest*). Of the many prominent men born in Burlington perhaps the best-known is John Dewey (1859), philosopher and educator.

Burlington has always faced the sunset. The charm and repose of the city today betoken an economic condition which, if not static, is certainly far removed from the bustling times of the past. Champlain is given over almost completely to the yachtsman and the fisherman.

But the lake may once again come to Burlington's rescue. For a hundred years local imagination has been periodically fired by dreams of a canal system that would link Champlain with the St. Lawrence and the Great Lakes. If the Champlain Seaway project, now being debated in Congress as a portion of the gigantic St. Lawrence Waterway proposal, should eventually become a reality, enthusiasts foresee Burlington as a world port, conveniently placed between New York and Montreal, safe harbor for the 'Queen Mary' and the 'Normandie.'

## POINTS OF INTEREST

1. *City Hall*, Main and Church Sts. This large modern Georgian structure, one of the most impressive municipal buildings in New England among cities of comparable size, was built in 1926 at a cost of more than $600,000. McKim, Mead and White were the architects. An attractive park lies behind the hall, and a fountain plays near the spot where in the early days a tall pine served as a town whipping post.

2. The *Van Ness Hotel* (1870), Main and St. Paul Sts., occupies the site of the Howard House, burned in 1867. Here were entertained Presidents Garfield and Theodore Roosevelt.

3. The *Champlain Transportation Co.*, Lakefront, foot of King St. This is the oldest steamship company in the country, having received its charter to operate passenger steamers on Lake Champlain from the Vermont Legislature October 26, 1826. A year later the steamboat 'Franklin' was launched. For 110 years the Champlain Transportation Co. has operated on the lake. The records show that 29 steamships have sailed under its charter.

4. *Battery Park*, Battery and Pearl Sts., has one of the most beautiful views of harbor and lake, with the Adirondacks in the distant background. It was used by the Government during the War of 1812 as a camp ground with some 4000 men quartered in temporary barracks to the north of the park. In 1813 a battery of 13 guns, firing from behind

a parapet erected where the lakeward sidewalk now runs, repulsed an attack of three British war vessels. The cannon in the park, presented to the city by the government in 1895, did service in the War of the Rebellion on the U.S. ships 'Constellation,' 'Monongahela,' 'Saratoga,' 'Savannah,' and 'Shamrock.'

5. The *Cathedral of the Immaculate Conception (St. Mary's)*, St. Paul and Cherry Sts., a Victorian Gothic structure of purple stone, the towers of which were not completed until 1904, was consecrated in December, 1867, though the corner-stone was laid four years prior to this. Surmounting the main tower is a gilded copper statue of the Virgin, inspired by the lines in the Apocalypse: 'And there appeared a great wonder in Heaven; a woman clothed with the sun and the moon under her feet, and upon her head a crown of twelve stars.' During the Feast of the Blessed Virgin the moon and halo of stars are lighted.

6. *St. Joseph's Church*, Allen St., two blocks north of Pearl St., of blended Romanesque and Renaissance architecture in light red sandstone, has the largest seating capacity of any ecclesiastical structure in Vermont. The corner-stone of the present edifice was laid in 1884 and the building was consecrated in 1901. A cock surmounts the cross atop the church — a weather-vane symbolic of the denial of St. Peter. Though rare in the United States, this symbol is not uncommon in Canada. It came from the provinces in France from which the ancestors of the present French-Canadians migrated.

7. The *Unitarian Church*, Pearl St. and Elmwood Ave., facing the north end of Church St., charmingly closes the vista through the main business district. Erected in 1816 by the First Congregational Society, this massive red-brick structure with its lofty clock-tower and crowning steeple is one of the most impressive ecclesiastical buildings in the State. The design of the church has been ascribed to Peter Banner, architect of the Park St. Church (1809) in Boston, but it is likely that Bulfinch passed on the plans. The detail of the arched entrance motif at the base of the tower recalls that of Park St. Church. The generous proportions of the body of the church and the almost archaic simplicity of its white trim are pleasing variations from the more elaborate and delicately carved white frame structures usually found in Vermont.

8. *Elmwood Avenue Cemetery*, Elmwood Ave., two blocks north of Pearl St. Here are buried Ethan Allen's wife, Zadock Thompson, Joseph Barron, pilot of Macdonough's flagship, the 'Saratoga,' at the battle of Plattsburg, Revolutionary War soldiers, and many early residents of the town of Burlington.

9. The *First Calvinistic Congregational Church*, S. Winooski Ave. and Buell St., dedicated in 1842, occupies the site of the first building (1812), which was burned in 1839. A brick structure of classic form, designed in Greek Revival style, with hexastyle portico and Ionic columns, it is surmounted by a belfry, or 'lantern,' which is a nearly exact copy of the choragic monument of Lysicrates in Athens. Napoleon so admired the

original monument as a splendid example of Greek art that he commanded that a copy of it be made in terra-cotta to be placed on his palace grounds at St. Cloud.

10. *Mount St. Mary's Academy*, Mansfield Ave., is a boarding and day school for young women. Designed as a central structure with wings extending north and south, four stories in height, it occupies a picturesque site overlooking the Winooski River and the lake. It was opened in 1889 and is conducted by the Sisters of Mercy, who came to Burlington from Manchester, New Hampshire, in 1874. Since 1925 it has included an advanced course known as Trinity College.

11. *Greenmount Cemetery*, Colchester Ave., contains the graves of Ethan Allen and many Revolutionary War soldiers, as well as many early residents of the town. Over Ethan Allen's grave rises a Tuscan shaft, 42 feet in height, topped by a spirited eight-foot statue of Allen, modeled by Peter Stephenson and cut in Carrara, Italy. The hero is represented as in the act of demanding the surrender of Fort Ticonderoga. The monument, unveiled July 4, 1873, is surrounded by a paling of muskets between posts of cannon.

12. The *College Green*, University of Vermont. Surrounded and enclosed by the University buildings and the residences of the faculty, the old College Green comprises a part of the fifty-acre lot originally deeded by Ira Allen as a site for the University. The first clearing was, however, not made there until 1799, several years after building operations had begun, and then the builders found it a convenient source for timber. A statue of General Lafayette, in bronze, of heroic size, stands in front of the College of Medicine, and commemorates the fact that Lafayette in 1825 laid the corner-stone of the Old Mill (see below). In the center of the campus is a statue of Ira Allen, founder of the University, the gift of the Hon. James B. Wilbur, and executed by Sherry Fry.

13. The *College of Medicine* is housed in a three-story brick building, erected 1905, at the north end of the College Green. Besides the laboratories, lecture halls, and recitation rooms used by the classes of the Medical College, it contains the Medical Library and the Pathological and Anatomical Museums. The administrative offices of the President, Comptroller, Registrar, Dean of the Medical College, and the Alumni Council are also here.

14. The *Robert Hull Fleming Museum*, Colchester Ave. (*open to public daily* 2–5, *adm. free*), was erected in 1931 by the University through the generosity of the late James B. Wilbur of Manchester, Vt., Miss Katherine Wolcott of Chicago, Ill., and six other friends of the University. Messrs. McKim, Mead and White were the architects. In this building, which covers 10,450 square feet, in addition to 13 exhibition rooms, there are offices, laboratory, storage-rooms, shops, and an auditorium. The museum houses much valuable and interesting material in art, archaeology, ethnology, geology, natural science, and Vermont history, the latter comprising the finest collection of Vermont Indian relics extant, and other material pertaining to early life in the State. The Cannon Oriental collection is a notable one; the Wilbur Room contains a personal library of Vermontiana; and the Geological Room in the basement shows, among other objects, a relief model of the State. A seismograph has been recently installed beneath the museum. In the Art Gallery there are exhibitions throughout the year, including classical and contemporary paintings.

15. The *Ira Allen Chapel*, University Place, dedicated in 1927, is also the gift of James B. Wilbur, and was also designed by McKim, Mead and White. Of red brick, the chapel is built in the form of a Latin cross. A campanile, 20 feet square and 170 feet high, has four clock faces and is topped by a powerful electric beacon, visible at night for many miles.

16. *Billings Library* (*open, college year*, 8.15–9, *Sun.* 2–6), University Place, gift of the late Hon. Frederick Billings of Woodstock, and erected in 1885, is a Romanesque structure of Longmeadow sandstone, a beautiful example of the work of the famous architect H. H. Richardson, who himself said of it, 'It's the best thing that I have yet done.' Beautifully grained Georgia pine is used for the interior finish and both interior and exterior of the building are rich in ornament. The library contains 145,000 volumes, the largest collection in the State, including the famous Marsh collection of 13,000 books dealing mainly with philology and European history and literature, the gift of George Perkins Marsh (*see WOODSTOCK*).

17. The *Williams Science Hall* (1896), University Place, contains the Pringle Herbarium, an outstanding collection of North American and European flowering plants and ferns, including nearly 150,000 specimens.

18. The *Old Mill*, University Place, dates from 1825 and is the principal recitation building of the University. This was the site of the first college building, begun in the spring of 1801. About 1850, three separate original buildings were joined into the present single structure, and in 1883 the Old Mill assumed its present form through the generosity of John P. Howard. It is of red brick, 250 feet long, 60 feet deep, and four stories in height. From the tower is the finest view in the city of the Champlain Valley and the Green and Adirondack Mountains.

19. The *Gymnasium*, south of the Old Mill, is a substantial brick structure, completed in 1901. It is provided with all modern apparatus for physical development, a running track of 396 feet, an armory and a shooting-gallery.

20. *Morrill Hall*, University Place, is a memorial to Senator Justin Smith Morrill of Vermont, father of the land-grant colleges and universities of the United States. The building was erected in 1907 for the College of Agriculture. A three-story edifice of buff brick, it contains class and laboratory rooms.

21. *Redstone*, S. Prospect St., *Robinson Hall*, and *Slade Hall*, comprise a group of dormitories for young women of the University. A. A. Buel, a wealthy resident of Burlington, built Redstone as a private residence in 1890, quarrying the red stone from his own estate and from the near-by Willard Ledge quarry. When the University acquired the property, the handsome stables were converted into the present Robinson Hall, and Slade Hall was added in 1929.

22. The *Mabel Louise Southwick Memorial* is the new Center for Women at the University, and is the fourth building on the so-called 'Redstone Campus.' It was begun in the fall of 1935 with an original bequest of $65,000 from the Southwick family and a PWA grant was added to complete the $225,000 project, which was opened in November, 1936. McKim, Mead and White were the architects. Two large lounge rooms flank the entrance, and there are two large halls, one a gymnasium, the other an entertainment hall providing for about 750 persons. The exterior design is modern Colonial in red brick with eight white front columns.

23. *Grassemount*, 411 Main St., was built by Thaddeus Tuttle in 1804 and was the home of Cornelius P. Van Ness, Governor of Vermont (1823–26), U.S. Minister to Spain (1829–30). It was also the home of Brigadier-General Heman Allen, U.S. Minister to Chili (1823–28). Lafayette was entertained here in 1825. The residence was acquired by the University in 1895 for a women's dormitory. Grassemount is perhaps the finest example in Vermont of the American Georgian style of architecture (*see Architecture*), notable for its grace of detail (as in the arched insets around the windows), and the cupola surrounded by a balustrade. The setting is appropriate — wide lawns, tall elms, and a sweeping lake view.

24. The *Church of Christ Scientist*, S. Union and Bay View Sts., is in the American Georgian style, with Ionic portico and a large oval window in

the pediment. It was built in 1927, and is distinguished, as are many Christian Science churches, by the absence of a belfry or spire.

25. The *Fletcher Free Library* (*open Mon., Wed., and Sat.* 9–6, 7–9; *Tues. and Fri.* 9–6; *Thurs.* 9–1), College St. and S. Winooski Ave., founded (1873) by Mrs. Mary L. Fletcher and her daughter Miss Mary M. Fletcher, is housed in a building given to the city by Andrew Carnegie (1904). Opened to the public in 1875 with 9000 volumes, in the old Courthouse on City Hall Park, the library had far outgrown its quarters by the turn of the century when Mr. Carnegie offered $50,000 for a new building on condition that the city supply $5000 for maintenance. Of red brick relieved with white terra-cotta, on a granite base, the structure has a most attractive setting, and is fully equipped. It contains 65,000 volumes.

26. The *Site of the First Jail* (S.W. corner College and Church Sts.). In the log structure built here in 1796, Ethan Allen's brother, Levi, a Tory, was imprisoned for debt and died (1801). Later the site was occupied by Lyman King's Hotel, a noted hostelry, till 1823.

27. *St. Paul's Episcopal Church*, St. Paul St., a beautiful square-towered Gothic edifice of blue limestone in the Victorian Gothic style, was erected in 1832. It has been several times enlarged and improved, the transepts dating from 1867.

28. At Rock Point, 2 *m.* north of City Hall, off North Ave., is *Bishop Hopkins Hall*, founded by the Rev. John Henry Hopkins, first Episcopalian Bishop of Vermont. This institution, incorporated in 1854 and opened in 1860, was, until 1899, a school for boys and numbered among its pupils Frederick Remington, famous painter of spirited Western scenes. In 1899, it became a school for girls, and some years ago had Helen Wills Moody, tennis champion, as a pupil. It is still under the auspices of the Episcopalian Church.

29. *Ethan Allen Park*, 2.5 *m.* north of City Hall, east of North Ave., is part of what was Ethan Allen's farm, his home at the time of his death. It had belonged to a Tory before the Revolution, was confiscated by the State of Vermont and later sold to Allen. The land was acquired (1902) by the Hon. W. J. Van Patten, Mayor of Burlington (1894–96), who sold most of it to the city for $10,000, donating the proceeds of the sale to the local branch of the Y.M.C.A. Reserved by Van Patten were about 12 acres between the road and the Winooski River, including a rocky cliff some 200 feet in height, known as Indian Rock from the legend that raiding Indians coming down the Winooski Valley spied upon their enemies from here. This tract the Mayor offered to the Society of the Sons of the American Revolution on condition that a substantial stone tower, a memorial to Ethan Allen, be erected on the cliff with a road to give access to it. The tower was built and was dedicated in 1905. From its summit there is an extensive view of country, from Split Rock on the south to Mount Royal on the north; the lake and Adirondacks on the west and to the east the Winooski River and the Green Mountains.

# MIDDLEBURY

*Village:* Alt. 366, pop. 2006.
*Railroad Station:* Rutland R.R., Seymour St.
*Bus Station:* Vermont Transit Co.; Champlain Coach Line, Middlebury Inn.
*Accommodations:* Two hotels; numerous tourist homes and cabins.
*Information:* Hotels.
*Annual Events:* College events (athletic contests, dances, commencement).

MIDDLEBURY is a charming college town. To its natural beauties and the appeal inherent in its relics and buildings expressive of the more gracious aspects of early Vermont, the presence of Middlebury College here for more than a century and a quarter has added a patina of intellectualism.

The town lies on both sides of Otter Creek, in the friendly shelter of Chipman Hill on the northeast, and spreads to the gentle slopes that border the valley. The village is centered by the park-like Common, west of which, on narrow Main Street, is the compact business district, where stores of the type common to a village of this size alternate with shops that cater to the more sophisticated tastes of town and gown.

Middlebury was granted in 1761, together with Salisbury and New Haven, and received its name from the fact that it lay midway between the other two. Benjamin Smalley was the first settler who came with his family and the first to build a log house, near the southern limit of the township, in 1773. The several families who had joined him by 1778 were in that year forced to evacuate their homes before a raiding party of Indians and Tories. Burying their pewter and all but a few provisions, and bidding farewell to their unharvested crops, the pioneers fled south to Pittsford, then a military post. Not until the spring of 1783 did they begin to return to Middlebury, which during the interval was a Colonial ghost town.

Middlebury College was chartered in 1800, on the foundation of the Addison County Grammar School (1797). The desire for an institution of higher learning among the early settlers, led by Gamaliel Painter, was quickened into decisive action by a visit here in 1800 of Timothy Dwight, president of Yale College and son of the first white child born on Vermont soil. Seldom has an educational institution come into being with such wholehearted support of the community. There was less unanimity, however, on the matter of a choice of location, one faction wanting it east of the river, another, west. The question was settled by competitive bidding in the form of contributions to the college, those who could not make cash offerings giving building materials and labor.

The history of Middlebury College has been one of many vicissitudes occasioned by lack of funds, an inadequate plant, and subsequent small enrollment. Today the college is on a sounder financial basis, and has a more efficient plant and a larger student body than at any time in its previous history. This is due partly to private benefactors, headed by Joseph Battell, and partly to the widespread reputation of its English and foreign language summer schools: Romance languages on the campus; the English School and Writers' Conference at Bread Loaf; and the German School at Bristol (*see Tours* 3C *and* 3D).

In Middlebury, Emma Hart, one of the foremost pioneers in American education, began her work when she came here from Connecticut in 1807 to take charge of the Middlebury Female Academy. She married Dr. Willard in 1809 and gave up the school, but in 1814, her husband having suffered financial reverses, she opened the Middlebury Female Seminary as a private institution. Her most famous school, at Troy, New York, was begun in 1821. Emma Hart Willard did more than any other one person to demonstrate that women were capable of mastering the subjects studied by men in schools of higher learning and to secure the establishment of institutions wherein they might study them. Her verse, though mediocre, includes one poem that is still remembered: 'Rocked in the Cradle of the Deep.'

Middlebury Village might almost be said to rest on a marble foundation, and it was here, in 1803, that the first extensive marble quarrying was begun in the State, by Eben Judd, who had discovered the deposits the year before and obtained a lease to 'dig' in them for 999 years. The quarries cannot be profitably operated by modern methods, however, and the present mill of the Vermont Marble Company, situated here, uses stone from the quarries of Rutland and Orange Counties.

In connection with the early marble industry, Isaac Markham discovered, or rediscovered, the method of sawing marble with sand and water and toothless saws that Pliny says was practiced by the ancient Ethiopians and that is still in use today. In 1799–1800, Josiah Nichols, Daniel Pettibone, and Ezekiel Chapman, working together in Nichols's blacksmith shop, discovered a practical method of welding cast steel. Norman Tupper and his associate mechanics, of East Middlebury, evolved the first machinery for the manufacture of doors and window sashes. In the number and scope of its inventions, Middlebury probably ranks second only to Windsor in this State.

Prominent native sons of Middlebury include William Slade, governor of Vermont (1844–46) and one of its ablest historical scholars; John W. Stewart, governor of Vermont (1870–72); and Edward J. Phelps. Educated at Middlebury and the Yale Law School, Phelps began his first practice of the law here. His many honors, among them the presidency of the American Bar Association, culminated in Cleveland's appointing him to be James Russell Lowell's successor as United States Minister to Great Britain, where he remained four years. His diplomatic achieve-

# ILLUSTRATIONS

*to accompany*

Tours 2, 2A, 2B, 2C

MT. ASCUTNEY

HUTCHINSON HOUSE (1793), WOODSTOCK

WINDSOR COUNTY HOMESTEAD
Example of 'Continuous Architecture

BROOKFIELD FLOATING BRIDGE
With inset showing detail of construction

COVERED BRIDGE, NEAR EAST CORINTH

GRANITE QUARRY, BARRE

STATE HOUSE, MONTPELIER

INTERIOR OF OLD WEST CHURCH, CALAIS

WOODBURY POND, WOODBURY

INTERIOR OF SIMPSON MEMORIAL LIBRARY, EAST CRAFTSBURY

CRAFTSBURY COMMON

ments there included the settlement of American fishing rights in Canadian North Atlantic waters; the resolution of the Bering Sea fur-seal question; the settlement of the boundary dispute between Great Britain and Venezuela; and the negotiation of an extradition treaty (*see Side Tour 5A, ESSEX JUNCTION*).

## POINTS OF INTEREST

1. The *Middlebury College Campus*, west of the business section, is a charming park-like area, with many trees shading its rolling surface. The well-spaced buildings are not so homogeneous architecturally as those of some modern campi, because Middlebury has never had huge sums with which to build a new plant all at once. Its buildings suggest, rather, the history of the enthusiasm with which it was supported in its early years, the depressions through which it subsequently passed, and its recent expansion. Dominant on the western crest of the main slope is *Mead Memorial Chapel* (1917), which translates the lines of a Colonial church into white marble, bulwarking the simple beauty of the design with lasting and almost symbolical strength. *Hepburn Hall* (1916), a men's dormitory in buff tapestry brick, stands beside it. At the eastern edge of the campus are three older buildings, all of limestone. *Painter Hall* (1816), the oldest, is in the tradition of dormitory architecture established by Harvard's 'Old Massachusetts.' It was given by, and named for, Gamaliel Painter, who has more right than anyone else to be called the father of Middlebury College, and of whom its students sing,

'He left us Painter Hall,
Noblest monument of all.'

The *Old Chapel* (1836) is a sturdy example of functional truth in architecture, now used as an administration building. *Starr Hall* (1861), a dormitory, completes this harmonious group. The *Egbert Starr Library* (1900, additions 1928) is built in a simple classic style of six varieties of Vermont marble. The pleasant, well-appointed interior is conducive to random browsing or scholarly research. The main library contains more than 65,000 volumes. The Julian W. Abernathy Library of American Literature, in the east wing, is a growing special collection of some 7000 volumes. The many first editions of American authors include one of the best collections anywhere of Thoreauiana: manuscripts, letters, relics, and first editions of Henry D. Thoreau. The *McCullough Gymnasium* (1910), no longer adequate to the needs of the college, the *Chemistry Building* (1913), and the *Warner Science Hall* (1901), which contains a museum of natural history, are all of marble. North of the older part of the campus is the women's campus, or 'the other side of the hill.' The two main buildings here are *Forest Hall* (1936), a handsome new sandstone dormitory for women, and the *Château* (1925), a large brick and stucco building in the French château style of architecture. Much less elaborate than most examples and copies of this mode, the Château escapes being anomalous by being architecturally appropriate to its function. During the college year it is used for all French classes and as a women's dormitory. In the summer it houses the French School. In both long session and summer school, only French is spoken inside the building, the girls who live here being bound by a pledge to speak no other language except when receiving off-campus visitors. Ultimately the women's campus will be developed into a quadrangle, which will make it a more distinct and closely knit unit.

2. The *Congregational Church*, facing the Common from the north, was built in 1806–09. In its main lines this impressive building resembles the First Congregational Church in Bennington, but the 136-foot tower is more elaborate and graceful in design. The broad façade consists of a central projecting bay with pediment. Over the well-proportioned entrance is a Palladian window typical of much Post-Colonial architecture in Vermont. Two arched doorways flank the main entrance. The tower rises in four stages to a delicately detailed eight-sided belfry surmounted by a short spire. Among the finest churches in Vermont, the building is an excellent example of early nineteenth-century architecture. It is based upon a design by Asher Benjamin published in his famous book, 'The Country Builder's Assistant.' The interior has a large central dome supported by four Ionic columns. The original plan of the auditorium had the pulpit in the center, surrounded by circular pews.

3. The *Sheldon Art Museum*, Main St. (*9–12, 2–5 weekdays except Tues.; 2–5 Sun.; adm. 25¢*). This varied collection of curios, relics, and pictures is housed in a three-story brick building dating from 1829, the gift of Henry J. Sheldon. The interior is furnished with early American furniture, china, glass, and utensils. There are also exhibits of old maps and newspapers, firearms, Indian relics, and early portraits. On the third story is an authentic restoration, even to a rum bottle, of the room of a Middlebury College student in the opening years of the nineteenth century. In an adjacent building is a collection of old tools and vehicles, including the two-seated surrey used by President Monroe during his visit to Middlebury.

4. The *Wainwright House*, Court St., was built by Gamaliel Painter in 1807. It is an excellent example of Federal architecture, its simple, strong main lines relieved by detailed decorations. The roof balustrade is typical. Especially noteworthy is the intricate interlacing of the carved frieze, a striking addition to a classic background of a motif, in the Adam tradition, that could be properly executed only in wood.

5. The *Community House* (*open to inspection*), corner of Main and Seymour Sts., was built in 1816 by Horatio Seymour, United States Senator from Vermont, 1821–33. It is of yellow-painted brick, with a hooded entrance, roof balustrade, and gable ends projecting above the roof incorporating the four end chimneys.

6. The *Exhibition Hall* of the now defunct Addison County Fair, east off Court St., was built in part in 1796 as the first courthouse of Addison County. The present form represents several later additions, including two-story columned porches on the front and rear and two-story pilaster treatment that give it a pseudo-classic appearance. The original building had a domed cupola.

7. The *Old Jail*, Washington St., was built in 1810 of native field-stone. It is now used as a private dwelling, porches and a wooden ell having been added. The unusual width of the entrance, evidenced by the gap in the masonry that is partly closed by fanlights, the resultant massive lintel over the doorway, and the thickness of the walls ($2\frac{1}{2}$ feet) are tangible reminders of the original purpose of the building.

# MONTPELIER

*City:* Alt. 523, pop. 7837.

*Railroad Stations:* Central Vermont Ry., State St., Montpelier & Wells River R.R., Main St.

*Bus Station:* Vermont Transit Co., Frontier Coach Line, Champlain Coach Line, B. & M. Transportation Co., Greenwood Bus Line, and all busses, Central Vermont depot, State St.

*Airport:* Central Vermont (B. & M. Transportation Co.), Berlin, 5 *m.* from city, taxi fare 50¢, time 10 min.

*Accommodations:* Three hotels, tourist homes, etc. Rates higher during sessions of legislature, Jan.–April, in odd years.

*Information:* State House lobby, State St., during summer months.

*Annual Events:* Horse Show, about Aug. 1, Montpelier Riding Club; High School Basketball Tournament (Junior Division), Feb. or March, Community Hall; Nurses' Ball, Jan., Armory, Barre St.; Governor's Reception and Ball, Jan. in odd years, City Hall; Women's Club Ball, Feb., City Hall.

MONTPELIER, the State Capital, was established as such in 1805, when the Legislature probably had in mind merely a convenient valley site near the geographical center of the State. The choice was happy in an accidental respect, for this small gap city on the main pass through the Green Mountains is cupped in wooded hills and lines the banks of peaceful streams, thus properly representing the State of valley towns. The granite State House stands dominantly above State Street, squarely backed by one wooded hillside and facing another across the narrow valley. Thus, close-guarded and confined, its clean Doric simplicity emphasized in native stone, this Capitol has for Vermont something of the symbolic character which Edinburgh Castle holds for Scotland. From near-by hill roads in summer, the gold dome, gleaming through thick greenery, alone reveals the presence of a city.

Three principal streets follow the Winooski River and its tributary, North Branch. Generations of school children were taught to chant the name of the Vermont Capital as 'Montpelier on the Onion River,' by which name the watercourse was known until Vermonters reverted to the Indian word for onion, Winooski. Main, State, and Elm Streets are the arteries from which unplanned side streets diverge to climb the hillsides banking the valley. The shopping section of Main Street, with its crowded brick and wooden buildings, a grain elevator towering over Clothespin Bridge, and the buff bulk of City Hall reared above the squat brick fire station, is much like the business district in any town of comparable size. The upper reaches of Main Street, however, have the dignity and charm of gracious homes set back under great elms in the best residential tradition, enhanced by the graceful ascendancy of church spires.

State Street, heterogeneously lined with old and modern structures, marked by the three imposing edifices of Capitol Square, is the heart of Montpelier. Here the life-insurance offices lie in the shadow of the State House, embodying the two fundamental forces that have built the city. The smooth sweep of terraced lawns rising to the elm-shaded dignity of the Capitol is flanked on one side by the severely simple Supreme Court Building and on the other by the handsome home office of the National Life. High on the hilltop back of the State House, the skyline is sentineled by the picturesque watch-tower of Hubbard Park.

Elm Street, the third main thoroughfare, slants off State and runs parallel to the North (Worcester) Branch, progressing from a row of shabby wooden houses, set on stonewall foundations built directly up from the water's edge, to a more pleasant residential section. Tree-lined streets branch irregularly to slant along hillsides and spread on summits, with homes set at all levels. In general the domestic architecture of the city is mixed and unrelated, with little Colonial color, yet many of the homes have dignity, and a certain unpretentious charm.

Closely interwoven in Montpelier's financial, economic, and social pattern are two prime strands — State affairs and the life-insurance business. At noontime and at four o'clock when the State offices and the insurance offices turn a flood of humanity into State Street, the city fairly swarms with a brief punctual life, that swiftly subsides to leave the streets quiet and empty.

There is an aloof, independent spirit about Montpelier and its people, a coldness bordering on indifference. While the town displays an interest in the cultural phases of life, it remains backward in several respects. Such an attitude, transcending normal Vermont conservatism, is perhaps traceable to the predominance of two bureaucracies, with the inertia and complacence inseparable from such a *milieu*. A community of 'white-collar workers,' in part transient, lacks the social vitality which a more balanced economy supplies.

Colonel Jacob Davis, Revolutionary veteran and leader among the pioneer settlers, named the town after the French city, Montpellier (*mont* — hill; *peller* — bare or shorn). It is sometimes thought that the presence of a bare hill looming over the site inspired this choice of name, but it is doubtful if the translation figured in Davis's selection, for he elsewhere demonstrated his fondness for French names (*see Tour 2, CALAIS*). In 1788, with ringing axe-blade, Colonel Davis cleared land along the North Branch and down the Onion River. Court Street, which today leads to the east portal of the State House, was the first road laid out by Davis and his followers. In the fall of 1807, two years after Montpelier had been named capital, State Street was opened between fields of waving corn, and the foundation of the original Pavilion Hotel was laid to house members of the Legislature. The first State House was occupied in 1809. As some old historian has said: 'There was manifested some degree of hope and courage by the people of Vermont, when they named this spot in the heart of the hills and depths of the forest as the place of making laws.'

The situation of Montpelier, on converging main roads at a junction of watercourses, made the town an important trading center from the start.

In 1827, a number of enterprising citizens started drilling for salt, a project tenaciously maintained for a number of years until, after penetrating through layers of slate-limestone to a depth of eight hundred and fifty feet, the drill stuck and the venture was abandoned, a failure. The development of the granite industry proved a very important factor in the city's growth, and brought in a large foreign element of stone-workers, who live chiefly in the Barre Street district, adjacent to the long gray granite sheds on the flats of the Winooski at the eastern edge of Montpelier.

In November, 1927, flood waters roared in yellow torrents through Montpelier streets, sweeping to second-story heights in ravaging progress. The city was shut off from the outside world and suffered immense property losses and damages. Recurrence of this disaster in 1936 was prevented by the Federal dams at Wrightsville and East Barre.

## POINTS OF INTEREST

1. *The Capitol* (*open weekdays* 8 *to* 4, *Sat.* 8 *to* 12), State St. The first State House, designed by Sylvanus Baldwin, was an odd three-storied wooden structure and served its first session of the Legislature in 1809. This crude building sufficed until 1836, when it was replaced by a beautiful Capitol of Barre granite, designed by Ammi B. Young. The magnificent Doric portico, modeled after the Temple of Theseus in Athens,

is retained in the third and present structure and remains the most striking architectural feature. Constructed of native Vermont granite, its design exemplifies the simplicity of the Greek revival mode. Its solemn dignity lightened by the gilt dome, its clear lines etched against the green curtain of a hillside, the Capitol rises above State Street, a fitting embodiment of the solid strength of a rugged State and its people. The interior of the second building was destroyed by fire in 1857, but the portico and granite walls withstood the flames. Renovations on the present State House were completed in 1859 by J. R. Richards. The edifice follows the general style and proportions of its predecessor, but stands larger and higher, a central structure with two wings, in the form of a Greek cross. The gleaming dome, visible for miles around, is leafed with pure gold and surmounted by a statue of Ceres, Goddess of Agriculture, the work of Larkin Goldsmith Mead (*see BRATTLEBORO*). This same Vermont sculptor made the marble statue of Ethan Allen, which stands within the portico and represents Allen demanding the surrender of Ticonderoga. On the other side of the portico is a brass cannon captured from the Hessians in the battle of Bennington.

The colonnaded façade is fronted by tall elms shading the broad smooth lawns that descend to State Street. Flanking the third terrace are two steel Krupp guns taken from the Spanish cruiser, 'Castilla,' sunk in Manila Bay, May 1, 1898, by the guns of Dewey's fleet. The lobby of the Capitol is stately and serene, with tessellated marble floor, Ionic columns, ornate hand-carved woodwork, and coffered panels in the ceiling. The walls are hung with portraits of Coolidge, Admirals Clark and Dewey, and memorials to other famous sons of Vermont. Mead's bust of Lincoln occupies a central place facing the main entrance. Along with Representatives' Hall and the Senate Chamber, the usual State offices are housed in the building. The Hall, treated in the Corinthian order, is semi-circular in plan with the rear wall serving as a background for the dais of the Speaker's chair. The Chamber, the finest room in the building, and in the State, is graced by a gallery supported by classic columns. In the Reception Room to the Governor's Suite, a large painting by Julian Scott depicts the Old Vermont Brigade in action at Cedar Creek (Civil War). An ancient carved English clock (*c.* 1720) stands in an opposite corner, and portraits of former governors line the walls. The second-floor lobby contains the battle flags of Vermont regiments in the Civil, Spanish, and World Wars, with silver plaques listing the engagements in which they were carried. Here also is a portrait of Judge Daniel P. Thompson, author of the 'Green Mountain Boys,' painted by Thomas Waterman Wood, Montpelier artist.

2. *Supreme Court Building (open weekdays 8–4, Sat. 8–12)*, State St. This severe gray structure of Barre granite stands at the eastern edge of the Capitol lawn, its clear plain lines at once harmonizing with and accentuating the eminence of the State House. In this building are the Supreme Court, Historical Society Museum, Vermont State Library, Free Public Library, and other State departments.

*Vermont Historical Society Museum*, main floor of the Supreme Court Building (*admission free*). The Vermont Historical and Antiquarian Society was incorporated at Barnet in 1838, through the efforts of Henry Stevens, and moved to Montpelier in 1851, where it occupied a room in the Capitol for many years. The modern name was adopted in 1857, and in 1918 the society moved to its present home. The museum contains an unusually fine genealogical and town history library, an excellent collection of geological specimens, exhibits of stuffed animals and birds, fascinating displays of old historic weapons, uniforms, tools, coins, relics, and manuscripts.

Unusual items include the following: the Bennington Declaration; the works of Royall Tyler, author of 'The Contrast,' the first professionally staged comedy written in America; the sword used by Lord Byron in Greece; a full-length portrait of Washington, a rather remarkable copy of a Stuart; the first geographical globes made in America, by James Wilson of Bradford in 1812; Sinclair Lewis's Nobel Prize Medal; the first Vermont newspaper; the skeleton of a whale that was unearthed in the State; first State coinage. The *Stephen Daye Press*, the first printing press in what is now the United States, is one of the features of the museum. It was sent to this country in 1638, accompanied by a printer named Stephen Daye, who operated it in Cambridge until 1649. The Greens and Spooners, famous early printers, came into possession of the press, eventually bringing it to Westminster, and then to Windsor, Vermont. Subsequently it was rescued from the dust and cobwebs of a Windsor barn, carefully restored, and brought to Montpelier for the museum.

The *Vermont State Library*, second floor. Although primarily a reference library, withdrawal privileges have been extended to all citizens of the State. The contents are devoted mainly to law, legislation, and the history and activities of Vermont.

The *Free Public Library*, basement floor. Conducted under the State Board of Education, this library mails books all over the State, for the cost of postage only. During the summer a book-wagon carries reading material into the remote rural sections.

3. The *National Life Building* (*open weekdays 8 to 4, visited by arrangement*), State St. This home office of the National Life Insurance Co., the largest office building in Vermont, is a dignified and impressive six-story structure of gray Rock of Ages Memorial granite, with an interior finished in Vermont marble. This is the only instance in which Rock of Ages monumental stone has been utilized in building construction.

National Life was founded in 1848, with Julius Y. Dewey, father of Admiral George Dewey, the leading promoter of the enterprise. Now Montpelier is the third largest insurance center in New England, with the headquarters of five prominent companies situated here, of which National Life is the largest and most outstanding. Three hundred persons are employed here.

4. *Pavilion Hotel*, State St. The original hotel, which entertained Lafayette in 1825, was built (about 1807–08) to accommodate the Legislature, and the present Pavilion, constructed in 1876, still furnishes quarters for the members and remains practically a State institution. The present hotel occupies the same site, and is roughly modeled after the original, although a great deal larger. The appearance and atmosphere of the huge rambling red-brick structure, with its white double porches and mansard roof, are reminiscent of the taste and politics of the General Grant era. Radio station WDEV has a broadcasting studio in the hotel.

5. The *American Fidelity Building*, 89 State St., a handsome homestead built by Hezekiah Reed in 1825, is one of the finest examples of Georgian architecture existing in the city, its purity of line clearly retained in the clean white-painted brick, with blinds in fresh green. There is an elliptical arch and fanlight over the entrance; cornice moldings add an ornamental touch; and iron stoop railings flank the steps.

6. The *Wood Gallery of Art* (*open* 2–5, 7–8.30 *daily*), 94 State St., was established in 1895 by Thomas Waterman Wood (1823–1903), the best of nineteenth-century Vermont painters, in co-operation with Professor John W. Burgess of Columbia.

The spacious main gallery is, rightly, above all else a memorial to the talent of Wood himself, and is dominated by his self-portraits and his *genre* paintings of nineteenth-century American — sometimes specifically Vermont — life. In addition, Wood was one of the greatest of modern copyists, and his many copies (one critic has called them 'translations') of the great painters of the past, particularly of Rembrandt van Rijn, are done with a distinction and a reverence that capture much of the beauty as well as the inner meaning of the originals. Wood became President of the American Water Color Society in 1878 and President of the National Academy of Design in 1891. His well-known Negro painting 'The Contraband, Recruit and Veteran,' is hung in the Metropolitan Museum.

The Wood Gallery is more than a memorial to one man, however. In recent years the trustees have purchased, as extensively as their funds permitted, representative canvases of the best contemporary Vermont painters, including Lillie, Schnakenberg, Lucioni, and Meyer. In time this section of the gallery should become the best permanent collection of paintings, water colors, and etchings executed by Vermont artists, and interpretive, in part at least, of the scenic and social background of the State.

7. *Athenwood* (*private; visitors welcome*), Northfield St., a brown churchlike structure of the Swiss chalet type, the summer home of Thomas Waterman Wood, stands high on a ledge on the southern outskirts of the city, overlooking the Winooski River. The unusual lines of the building and the eminence of its position make it an outstanding landmark. The name Athenwood, engraved on the front door, was given in honor of Mr.

Wood's wife, whose name, Minerva, suggested the Greek synonym, Athena. Built before 1850, the peak-roofed house was designed by Mr. Wood himself and contains six rooms of odd and angular shape. Close by, the artist erected a small studio in the same style of architecture, and there some of his best painting was done.

8. *Washington County Court House*, State St., erected in 1832, is a long red-brick structure with a white-pillared portico and clock-tower, in the Post-Colonial tradition of public-building architecture. The clean contrast of red and white and the trimness of line add much to the character of State Street. The old courtroom retains its original design, and the fireplaces, which once heated the building, remain as ornamental features in every room. The original Bulfinch-style tower, destroyed by fire in 1879, was replaced by the present one, which is bulky and decidedly inferior.

9. *Christ's Church*, State St. (1867), across from the courthouse, built of granite in the Victorian Gothic style, tempers the complex nature of State Street with a religious note.

10. The *Chester Wright House* (*private*), 159 State St., built in 1809 by Montpelier's first minister, has been carefully restored and stands on an elevation over the western end of State Street, facing the Winooski River. A large white house topped by a huge central chimney and surrounded by great elm trees, its modern additions conform to the original lines, so that the whole structure is a pleasing architectural unit.

11. The *Dewey House* (*private*), State St., birthplace of Admiral George Dewey, the hero of Manila, is a simple wooden house of a story-and-a-half with a steep-pitched roof. In this modest home, originally standing almost in the shadow of the Capitol but since moved westward on State St., Dewey was born in 1837. After graduating from Norwich and Annapolis, he served with Farragut's fleet at the capture of New Orleans (Civil War), and later distinguished himself in the attack on Fort Fisher. In 1897, when trouble with Spain became imminent, Dewey was given command of the Asiatic squadron and eventually dispatched to Manila. On April 30, 1898, Dewey steamed his flagship 'Olympia' into Manila Bay at the head of the American squadron and proceeded to wreck the Spanish fleet anchored there, without loss of a single American life. The Spanish boats were all sunk, burned, or deserted, and the shore batteries were silenced. Almost overnight George Dewey became a great national hero.

12. *Bethany Congregational Church*, Main and School Sts., built in 1867 of reddish-brown sandstone, is said to be one of the finest examples of Gothic architecture in the State, and a direct copy of an English original.

13. The *Kellogg-Hubbard Library* (*open weekdays 12 to 9*), Main St., a square solid building of rough-surfaced granite with superimposed loggias in the entrance pavilion, contains 22,289 volumes and periodicals, keeping well abreast of the literary trends of the times.

14. The *Davis House* (*private*), 91–93 Elm St., the first frame house in

Montpelier, was built by Colonel Jacob Davis and bears the date of its erection in 1790. This large plain frame structure is of interest for its historical significance and antiquity. In this house Colonel and Mrs. Davis entertained H.R.H. Prince Edward, Duke of Kent, the son of George III (and later the father of Queen Victoria). The royal guest was en route from Montreal to Boston with an entourage of some twenty armed attendants, who protected Edward to the extent of tasting his food as a safeguard against poison. It is said that the Davis hospitality soon set at rest any fears the British company may have held.

15. *Vermont Junior College* (formerly Montpelier Seminary), Seminary Hill, occupies a square open campus on a high plateau overlooking the city, on the site of the Civil War Sloan Hospital. The *Dormitories* were evolved from the hospital barracks. The red-brick *Administration Building* faces the broad campus, built in the ugly angular style of 1872, with a blunt tower, mansard roof, and arched windows, which contrive to give a Civil War Period flavor to the scene. The institution was founded in Newbury, 1834, under the auspices of the Methodist Episcopal Church, and removed to Montpelier in 1868, taking the name of Montpelier Seminary. The *Gary Library* (1935) is a modern red-brick structure with white-columned portico, and the *Gymnasium* is another recent red-brick addition in similar style. The campus, fringed by maples, is used as an athletic field. The name, Vermont Junior College, was adopted in 1936.

16. *Hubbard Park*, main entrance, Spring and Winter Sts., west entrance, Jordan St. These 134 acres of natural woodland on the heights that rise behind the Capitol were presented in 1900 by John E. Hubbard. The rock tower (designed by H. M. Cutler), left with incompleted turret to achieve a picturesque medieval aspect, looks down upon the treetops and housetops of Montpelier, and commands a broad panorama over the narrow Winooski Valley and the mountain ranges that march along the horizon on every side. Five miles of graveled road wind through the park, with delightful picnic spots along the way, equipped with outdoor fireplaces, lunch tables, and spring water. Norway and white pine and spruce, newly planted, grow beside fine stands of old hemlock and native maples. The park on its wild unspoiled hilltop is popular with picnic parties and sightseekers, as well as with lovers on spring and summer evenings.

17. The *Old Burying Ground*, Elm St., lies along the bank of the North Branch of the Winooski, with plain old headstones dating back to the early 1800's. The first Montpelier cemetery is no longer in existence.

*Points of Interest in the Environs:*

The *Wrightsville Dam* (3 m. north of city proper, but within city limits, on the road to Worcester) was started in 1933 and completed in 1935, a mammoth earthen dam exemplifying the flood-control projects carried out in Vermont by the Federal Government. The labor was provided by the Civilian Conservation Corps, with some 3600 ex-service men working under the direction of U.S. Army Engineers. The dam, finished in time to perform signal duty in protecting the Capital during the floods of 1936, extends 1500 feet across the valley of the North (Worcester) Branch, standing 90 feet high with a maximum top width of 165 feet. On March 20, 1936, the water behind the Wrightsville Dam rose to a height of 61 feet, within 11 feet of the spillway. While Montpelier merchants, remembering the ravages and destruction of 1927, hastened to move their goods upstairs, this mighty dam was retaining approximately 700 million cubic feet of water charged with churning ice cakes. Beyond doubt, the Wrightsville Dam was the vital factor in averting the disaster which threatened the entire Winooski Valley.

# NEWPORT

*City:* Alt. 723, pop. 5094.

*Railroad Station:* Canadian Pacific R.R. and Quebec Central R.R., Main St.

*Bus Station:* Greenwood Bus, Hurst's Hotel, Main St.

*Steamer:* The 'Anthemis' (150 pass.) docks near station, daily summer trips between Newport and Magog, P.Q.

*Accommodations:* Three centrally located hotels, tourist homes and camps; near-by summer hotels.

*Information:* Chamber of Commerce, Main St.

NEWPORT lies on a sloping promontory that juts across the southern end of Lake Memphremagog, with its outer fringes spread along the irregular hilly shoreline. The only incorporated city in northeastern Vermont, Newport is known as the Border City, and is one of the most popular gateways between Canada and New England. Memphremagog (Indian, 'Beautiful Waters') was a fishing ground and avenue of travel for the Indians, whose birch canoes skirted the wild, ragged shores long before the white settlers came. In the nineteenth century Newport was the base of operations for a big lumber business, but this fell off with the general slump in lumbering, and today the little city is a vacation resort and trading center. During the summer months heavy traffic between the eastern United States and Montreal flows unceasingly through Newport, impregnating the town with changing life and color. Many travelers, impressed by the cleanliness and beautiful setting of Vermont's northernmost city, stop over here to enjoy the freshness of lake and mountain vistas opening directly from the streets of this modern community.

The sloping breadth of Main Street is lined with up-to-date stores, which serve patrons from all the outlying towns. Residential sections stretch along the waterfront and ascend quiet, shady streets to the hills overlooking the lake. There is a marked contrast between the busy confusion of Main Street and the serene northward sweep of Memphremagog's waters between woodland shores and jagged mountains overshadowed by the rugged bulk of *Owl's Head* (alt. 3360), named for an Indian chief. The lake is thirty miles long, from one to four miles wide, and its surface is picturesquely broken by forested islands and headlands.

The railroad played a prominent part in the development of the town. A railway junction near the international border; the southern terminus of the Quebec Central Railroad; a Canadian Pacific station on the main line between Montreal and Boston; and an important customs port of entry, Newport is naturally a railroad center. The large yards near the depot, while less active than in the past, are still a busy scene, and ruddy-faced railroad men in blue overalls are familiar figures around the foot of Main Street. Much of the city's industry still hinges upon the waning lumber business, led by the old firm of Prouty and Miller, which once was among the biggest lumber companies east of the Mississippi (headquarters, Taunton, Massachusetts). When lumbering was at its peak, the bay was choked with logs rafted up the lake to the humming saws of the Prouty and Miller plant. The decline in the lumber trade and the railroad business left Newport faced with the necessity of developing its natural advantages as a summer resort. A fashionable colony has grown up around Camp Elizabeth at the pine-shaded Bluffs, north of the city on the eastern lakeshore.

Lake Memphremagog has a charm for sportsmen devoted to boating, swimming, and fishing. Each spring scores of fishermen and spectators crowd the railway platform, and lines are dropped into the bay a scant hundred feet from the traffic of Main Street. Ragged boys with makeshift poles rub shoulders with expensively outfitted anglers from the metropolitan districts, and the spectators cheer when some tousle-headed urchin hauls in the best catch of the day. Summer train passengers may see on one side a car-crammed concrete street, and on the other skilled diving exhibitions by tanned youngsters plunging from the cinder-blackened platform rail into the cool calm water of 'Magog. This contrast is the secret of Newport's charm.

The first known white visitors here were Rogers' Rangers, returning from a daring and successful offensive against St. Francis village in Canada, in 1759. Major Robert Rogers left Crown Point on September 13 with two hundred riflemen in green buckskin, sailing down to the north end of Lake Champlain, and from there marching through the wilderness. Messengers came to tell him that his boats and supplies, left in Missisquoi Bay, had been taken by the enemy, and that a powerful body was in pursuit of his Rangers. He kept this alarming information from his men, however, and pushed on toward the objective, sending scouts back to Crown Point with the word that his retreat would be down the Connecticut and that he must be met there with provisions. On the night of October 4 they reached St. Francis, where the Indians were holding a great ceremonial dance. Lord Jeffrey Amherst had given orders to fight Indian fashion and show no mercy to the tribe that had so long terrorized the white settlers. At four in the morning, the Rangers attacked the sleeping village. Rogers ordered that women and children be spared, but when the pale morning light fell on hundreds of white scalps hanging from poles above the houses, there was no restraining the inflamed Rangers, who slaughtered men, women, and children indiscriminately and burned the entire village. Two hundred Indians were killed and twenty taken prisoners. The Rangers lost but one man, and had six slightly wounded.

Rogers's plan was to follow the St. Francis and Magog Rivers to Lake Memphremagog, and thence cross to the Connecticut. On the march they were repeatedly harassed by pursuing Indians, but in ten days they reached the southern end of Memphremagog. Here it was voted that they split up into smaller parties, against Rogers's inclination. This was done, and here on the eastern side of the lake one squad was overtaken and wiped out by the enemy. The other parties, suffering from hunger, exposure, and constant strain, made for the Connecticut. Their foraging route through a dense wilderness is paralleled almost exactly by the modern automobile route, US 5 (*see Tour* 1). A good description of this expedition is in 'Northwest Passage,' by Kenneth Roberts (1937).

The first house in Newport was built by Deacon Martin Adams, who came north from St. Johnsbury in 1793, and by 1800 there were eleven families in the settlement. The charter was granted under the name of Duncansboro, for the chief proprietor, and the present name was adopted in 1816. Two prominent brothers were born here: Charles A. Prouty, longtime member of the Interstate Commerce Commission; and George H. Prouty, Governor of Vermont (1908–10).

## POINTS OF INTEREST

1. The *Federal Building*, Main St., stands at the crest of the sloping thoroughfare with other public buildings. Constructed of granite and brick, it houses the post office, and others, the most important of which is the U.S. Immigration Headquarters Office for District No. 1, including Maine, New Hampshire, Vermont, and New York border territory as far west as the Oswego County Line.

2. *Orleans County Court House*, Main St., in somber red brick, has been the center of judiciary life since the county seat was shifted from Irasburg to Newport.

3. *Goodrich Memorial Library*, Main St. (*open daily* 10.30 *to* 5; *Mon., Wed., Sat. evenings*), dedicated in 1899, is a baroque structure in red brick

with granite base and trim. Here are over 13,000 volumes, an excellent coin collection, and exhibits of stuffed animals and birds.

4. The *Catholic Church* (Ave Maris Stella), Prospect Hill, with twin granite towers flanking an arched portico, stands proudly above the city and lake. The view of Memphremagog from here is one of the finest obtainable, sweeping northward over the far reaches and islands of the long narrow lake with its broken shoreline and mountain background.

# RUTLAND

*City:* Alt. 560, pop. 17,315.

*Railroad Station:* Rutland R.R.; Delaware & Hudson R.R. (freight service only), Union Station, Merchants Row.

*Bus Station:* Rutland Bus Co., Vermont Transit Co., Champlain Frontier Coach Lines, Chamberlin & Burk, Crandall's: 114 Merchants Row, opposite railroad station.

*Airport:* one mile and a half south of city, on US 7 (no regular passenger service), taxi fare, 50¢.

*Accommodations:* Five hotels; tourist homes and camps.

*Information:* Chamber of Commerce, Mead Building, Merchants Row; Chamber of Commerce information booth, Main and West Sts., during summer months.

*Annual Events:* Masquerade Ball, Italo-American Society, February, Rutland Armory; Skating Carnival, February, Rotary Skating Rink; Maple Festival, March, Rutland Armory; District Basketball Tournament, March, Rutland Armory; Vermont Symphony Concerts, winter, Rutland Armory; Rutland Community Concerts, October–April season, High School Auditorium; Rutland Fair, one week, beginning Labor Day, Fair Grounds.

RUTLAND is set in the lovely widened valley of Otter Creek. Although second to Burlington in size, Rutland is eminently a city, with the spirit and inspiration of a city: railroad center, nucleus of trade highways, independent and individual. Hub for a trading population of 75,000 people, the city maintains a retail activity which has been consistent and vigorous. Manufactured products carry its name all over the world. It is, however, as the Marble City that Rutland has been primarily known for more than half a century.

The natural setting is relatively unaffected by industrial progress. The tree-bordered streets of the residential district blend into the meadows of the fertile valley. Pico, Killington, and Shrewsbury, three of the most striking Green Mountain peaks, rise sharply to the east, while the Taconic Range is thrown against the western sky.

There is no marble in the Marble City now. The old township of Rutland was subdivided in the eighties, the marble region being set apart as the townships of Proctor and West Rutland, so that politically the present city is separated from its source of power. But governmental makeup does not alter the fact that Rutland was built on marble and by the railroad which bears its name.

The visitor entering the city along US 7 drives through a residential district flanking the long, attractive Common, now known as Main Street Park, but called in early days 'Federal Square,' a well-preserved survival of eighteenth-century Rutland. Side streets dip westward down the hill to the business section, and beyond to the factories and the railroad yards. To the north lies another residential development near the country club.

Proximity to New York State, strategic railroad and highway location, and industrial activity have given Rutland an atmosphere of urban complexity more common to southern New England communities than to Vermont. But the transition, which came so quickly, after the Civil War, when the railroad and the marble business joined hands to build the modern city, has nevertheless not obliterated the old town. Colonial and Revolutionary Rutland are still visible despite the prominence of the shopping district and the presence of the big manufacturing plants.

Otter Creek had always been a favorite route for Indian travel, and was known as rich beaver country. A fur trader, James Cross, on an expedition from Fort Dummer in 1730, gives in his journal the first recorded description of the falls on the Otter at this point and the fertile adjacent territory. During the French and Indian War travel through here must have been considerable, for the site of the present city was a junction on the Crown Point Military Road which General Amherst ordered built across the mountains to connect the Champlain forts with the Connecticut Valley. Rutland was chartered in 1761 by Governor Benning Wentworth of New Hampshire. The first grantee, John Murray, of Rutland, Massachusetts, was responsible for the name of the township. Actual settlement was begun by James Mead, who brought his wife and ten children up over the mountains from Manchester in 1770 and established them in a log house near the falls which now bear his name. He was able shortly to build here a gristmill and sawmill, and in a few years Rutland was an active frontier community.

> 'West of the Mountains Green
>   Lies Rutland fair;
> The best that e'er was seen
>   For soil and air.
>
> .    .    .    .    .
>
> 'We value not New York,
>   With all their powers;
> For here we'll stay and work,
>   The land is ours.'

In such verse, appropriately crude, Thomas Rowley of Danby, who was the minstrel of the Green Mountain Boys, celebrated the fierce resistance to New York authority which the inhabitants of the New Hampshire Grants were making in the early years of Rutland's existence. Into the midst of this land controversy was thrust the graver issue of the dispute with Great Britain; and Rutland became a northern outpost of the Revolutionary War in Vermont. Fort Rutland was built in 1775, Fort Ranger (at Mead's Falls) in 1778, and in the latter year the town was made the headquarters for State troops. The cycle of early Vermont history — settlement, the building of a primitive self-sufficient economy, the struggles over title to land, the warfare with England — all this, in the case of Rutland, was telescoped into less than a decade.

In 1784 the county seat was moved from Tinmouth to Rutland, one of the five post offices of the independent Republic of Vermont was established here the same year, and from 1784 to 1804 various sessions of the legislature were held in Rutland. Vermont's admission to the Union in 1791 was enthusiastically greeted by an all-day celebration in Federal Square. In that era of innumerable and eloquent toasts, this occasion supplied a memorable one — 'The Union of Vermont with the United States: May it Flourish like our Pines and Continue as unshaken as our Mountains.'

Among the early notables of Rutland the Reverend Samuel Williams, author of the first history of the State ('Natural and Civil History of Vermont,' 1794), is perhaps the most impressive figure   A brilliant member of the Harvard faculty, honored both here and abroad for his scholarship, he resigned from his college position under a cloud and left Cambridge at the age of forty-five for what was then the frontier of New England, becoming in 1789 the minister of the Rutland Congregational Church. In 1794 he was one of the founders of the *Rutland Herald* which, becoming a daily in 1861, has had a continuous record of publication for almost a century and a half. Williams was active in promoting the University of Vermont, and, although disappointed at its final location in Burlington rather than Rutland, he lectured for two years, 1807 to 1808, on natural philosophy and astronomy.

Between 1800 and 1850, the town of Rutland grew from 2124 to 3715, an increase of 75 per cent; in the next thirty years the population more than tripled, reaching 12,149 in 1880, passing Burlington (which in 1850 had been twice the size of Rutland), and becoming, for the first and only time, the largest community in Vermont. The sudden shift in the fifties from a long period of normal growth to one of quick expansion was a result of two things — the arrival of the railroad and the subsequent boom in the marble business. The Rutland and Burlington Railroad, the first line to connect western Vermont and Boston, was completed in 1849 (*see Transportation*). Later known as the Rutland Railroad, it has been extended several times, has changed hands frequently, but has always maintained its headquarters here.

After the Civil War, Colonel Redfield Proctor returned to Rutland and set about transforming the marble business, which had been operating on a small scale for a generation, into one of the Nation's great industries. The marble deposits in the western part of the township were among the richest in the world, and their efficient exploitation soon brought prosperity to Rutland and power to the Proctor family. The Vermont Marble Company continued to expand until it controlled a major portion of the marble business in the country (see *Tour* 4, *PROCTOR*).

By 1886, the Proctor influence in Vermont had reached a point which made possible the partitioning of the old township of Rutland. Strongly urged by Redfield Proctor (who had been Governor from 1878 to 1880), bills were put through the State Legislature creating two new townships, Proctor and West Rutland, out of the marble district. Public opinion in Rutland was aroused against the change, the opponents protesting that 97 per cent of the property in Proctor was owned or controlled by the Proctor family. In 1892, a further partition took place, when the city of Rutland was organized, making four subdivisions of the original township.

The homogeneous nature of the population in the early days was of course definitely altered by Rutland's growth. With the building of the railroad came a large Irish group, and the marble business brought in new racial strains, including Italian, Polish, and Swedish.

Modern Rutland is prominent in the State as a retail trading center and an industrial community. Next to the marble business the most important manufacturing interest in Rutland's history has been that of the Howe Scales, which rank with the Fairbanks Scales of St. Johnsbury in national reputation. Moving to Rutland from Brandon in 1877, the company has operated here continuously since that time.

Rutland has contributed more than its share of leaders in the public life of the State and Nation. To mention but one group, seven Governors of Vermont were residents of Rutland: Israel Smith (1807–08), Charles K. Williams (1850–52), John B. Page (1867–69), Redfield Proctor (1878–80), John A. Mead (1910–12), Percival W. Clement (1919–21), and Charles M. Smith (1935–37). To this list might justly be added Fletcher D. Proctor (1906–08), and the younger Redfield Proctor (1923–25), although both were residents of Proctor.

There are only three places in Vermont which a visitor will feel to be cities; and whereas Barre remains a mining town tempered and restrained by its Vermont matrix and Burlington, with all its air of a great port and a university seat, still wears her queenliness with a sunset charm, Rutland alone maintains the vigor which her railroad gave. Rutland, more typically than either of her rivals, is the small American city — her roots sunk deep in the land and in her history, she yet has a keen eye on the main chance. Whatever the future of the State, business will be done in Rutland. And her traditional hold on Green Mountain politics appears unshakable.

## POINTS OF INTEREST

1. *Temple House*, 64 N. Main St., is a dignified, white-painted brick strúcture, backed by terraced gardens and topped with huge chimneys. Its graceful entrance motif definitely marks it as Georgian. Built in 1812, and known as Windyledge, it was the home of several generations of the Temple family.

2. *Aiken House*, 1 Aiken Place. At the end of an elm-shaded avenue stands the *First Congregational Parsonage*, built in 1849. A plain white wooden frame house, with rambling ells, it retains the old brick oven, Christian doors, and other interesting details of the period.

3. *Main St. Park*, now a quiet green playground, was in the early days the site of the courthouse, jail, pillory, and whipping-post. Here the hastily recruited troops drilled in Revolutionary days. Here, in 1791, was staged the all-day celebration when news came of Vermont's admission into the Union. The *Statue of the Green Mountain Boy*, with musket and powder horn, alert on a pinnacle of natural rocks, poised as if watching for attack, and a large *Boulder*, with bronze inset bearing the names of 'the men and women of Rutland who served in the World War,' were both placed here by Ann Story Chapter, D.A.R. Between Center and Washington Sts., the park widens to form the old parade ground. Here a white *Marble Bench* with tall entablature has been placed as a memorial to General Clarence Edwards, by the Yankee Division, A.E.F., on the occasion of their Third National Reunion, June 24, 1934.

4. *Sycamore Lodge*, Main St. near Park, was the home of Governor John B. Page, prominent in banking and railroad affairs and State Treasurer during the Civil War. President Rutherford Hayes and party were among the distinguished visitors at the Page home.

5. *Pond House*, 27 S. Main St., is a mellow buff-painted brick house with gabled façade. The small-paned windows are framed by brick arches painted white, and the wide marble sills accent the design. This was the home of Solomon Foot, president of the monster Whig Convention of 1840, later Congressman, and President of the Senate during the 36th and 37th Congresses. Associate and adviser of President Lincoln, he was outstanding among the great war senators.

6. *Kilburn House*, Main St. near Park. A swinging tavern sign, dated 1794, marks the home of the Rev. Samuel Williams, historian and scholar. This simple frame homestead, white clapboarded, with chimneys abutting the side elevations, has lost some of its characteristic beauty through alteration. The house was originally gambrel-roofed, with large central chimney.

7. *Morse House*, cor. Main and Madison Sts., was the home of Moses Strong, one of the great landholders of early Rutland. The large, square

house, painted white and set in spacious grounds, surmounted by a captain's walk, still retains the charm of the Georgian style, although the classic simplicity of the entrance and the delicacy of the cornices have been destroyed somewhat by the addition of a veranda.

8. *Church of Christ the King*, Main St., is a native white marble structure of English Gothic design. The statue of Christ, the King, placed above the entrance under a window of delicate tracery, the heavy wooden doors with their massive hinges, the restrained ornamentation and superb craftsmanship of the interior, all reflect modern rendering of the early Gothic tone. The sanctuary contains three marble altars and is separated from the nave by a finely carved marble rail, extending from the north to the south transept. The stained-glass windows are of excellent design and coloring. Above the main altar are represented the four Evangelists, while the windows in the north and south transepts portray the Transfiguration and the Childhood of Christ. The Stations of the Cross are cloisonné work in warm subdued colors. The grave simplicity of beams and columns, the carved oak organ loft, unite the entire structure into one homogeneous design, unsurpassed in the State. The church was completed in 1929.

9. *Pioneer Home*, 23 West St., is the oldest house in the city, and is still in use as a residence. The exact date of building is not known, but its weather-worn clapboards, never painted, and tiny window-panes, show the marks of age. The first recorded deed of the property is from Elias Buell to William Jenkins in 1793.

10. The *Congregational Church*, Court St., is a large cream-painted brick structure with an impressive spire, built in 1860. Set on an elevation, with pleasant greensward broken by flagged walks, it is a dominant feature of the hill section.

11. *Rutland Free Public Library* (*open daily* 10-6; 7-9 *Tuesdays and Saturdays*), Court St. The old Federal Building designed by Ammi B. Young, and recently restored with Civil Works Administration funds, is built of pressed brick, and painted buff. Its arched windows and doorways lend distinction, and the interior, with all the appurtenances of a modern library, is handsomely decorated. It contains 31,000 volumes and a notable collection of Vermontiana.

12. *Trinity Church*, West St., with its encircling green lawn, its square tower and gray walls shaded by elms, its adjoining chapel, its parish house and rectory, preserves a dignified contrast to the surrounding business section.

13. The *Federal Building*, West St., follows the modified classical style typical of the more recent Government construction. Native white marble forms the first story, while the upper three stories are of brick with marble trimmings and quoins. The central pedimented pavilion is in the Corinthian order. Six murals, done by Stephen Belaski, under the Federal Art Project, Works Progress Administration, portray outstanding events in the history of Vermont. The building was completed and

presented to the city in July, 1933. In addition to the Post Office Department, the courtroom and offices of the U.S. District Court, the U.S. Navy Recruiting Station, and other Federal agencies are located here.

14. *The Synagogue*, Grove St., was originally the Baxter Memorial Library, erected in 1889 as a memorial to General H. H. Baxter. It is built of rock-faced gray marble from the West Rutland quarries, in the Romanesque style of architecture.

15. *Riverside*, the State Reformatory for Women, State St., is a group of red-brick buildings, situated on the green terraces which rise from East Creek. Here a unique experiment in correctional methods has been conducted, and has attracted wide attention among penologists. The absence of bars, the homelike atmosphere of the living quarters, the quiet and beauty of the chapel, and the freedom of the open grounds surrounding the buildings, through which the inmates go about their tasks unguarded, are the subject of an article written by Dorothy Canfield Fisher and Sarah Cleghorn, entitled 'Miss Ross's Girls.' The system, inaugurated by the superintendent, the late Lena Ross, is founded upon her philosophy: 'The prison should be a hospital for body, mind, and soul, a place where one can return when out of a job or needing advice.' Visitors are welcomed to Riverside and every part of the institution is open to them.

16. The *Ripley Mill*, West St., is a 21-gang sawmill. Marble from the Danby, West Rutland, and other quarries of the Vermont Marble Company is sawed here. The business was started by William Ripley in 1844 and was carried on by his sons until 1869, when it was taken over by the Vermont Marble Company. An intimate story of these founders of the marble industry in Rutland is told by Thomas Emerson Ripley, grandson of William Ripley, in his book 'A Vermont Boyhood.'

17. *The Maples*, Dorr Road. Built on a high knoll overlooking Otter Creek this is one of the notable residences of Rutland. A large, plain, roomy house, enclosed by a stone wall, backed by wooded hills, and reached by a winding driveway, it was the home of Julia C. R. Dorr, poet. Here she was frequently hostess to Emerson, Longfellow, Lowell, Holmes, and other New England literary figures. *Fern Cottage*, a modern villa built on the estate, was the home of her artist daughter, Zulma DeLacy Steele, and her grandson, Frederick Dorr Steele, illustrator.

18. *Evergreen Cemetery*, West St., was part of a pine forest and retains much of the beauty of a grove. Enclosed by a wall of varying heights, built of massive blocks of marble, surmounted with flowering shrubs, and covered with vines, it is approached through a broad arch between the stone chapel and office at the entrance. Winding roads climb a succession of knolls. Among the graves is that of Colonel James Mead, first settler of Old Rutland.

19. *Gookin House*, west of the cemetery, built in 1781, on the site of the log church of the first settlers, is an old house in excellent preservation. The French wallpaper in the front hall, imported from England soon after 1812, is of Oriental design.

20. *Site of Fort Ranger*, Center Rutland. On the high bluff directly opposite the site of the marker, Fort Ranger was built in 1778 as headquarters for the State troops under the command of Captain Gideon Brownson. In 1781 the garrison was moved to Castleton, and the fort was used as a gathering-place for the people of the settlement.

21. *Center Rutland Falls*, US 4. This is locally known as Mead's Falls, after the first settler, who built his gristmill on the banks of the Otter, and his log house within a half-mile of the stream to the west. During the flood of 1927, Otter Creek swept away the railroad bridge which crosses the stream at this point, undermined the highway bridge, and carried near-by houses down the stream.

# ST. ALBANS

*City:* Alt. 409, pop. 8020.

*Railroad Station:* Central Vermont Ry., Lake and Federal Sts.

*Bus Stations:* Champlain Coach Line and Frontier Coach Line, Spencer Hotel, S. Main St.; Northern Bus Line, New American House, N. Main St.

*Accommodations:* Four hotels, boarding-houses, tourist homes, and camps.

*Information:* Spencer Hotel, S. Main St.

*Annual Events:* Child Health Day, May 1; Maple Festival, spring; ski meet with Montreal Ski Club, date dependent upon snow conditions; 3 Dramatic Club performances annually.

ST. ALBANS, the shire town of Franklin County, is rightly known as 'The Railroad City.' Containing the office headquarters, yards, and shops of the Central Vermont Railway (now a subsidiary of the Canadian National), it owes much of its vigorous growth to its excellent transportation facilities and its steady prosperity to the employment of large numbers of its residents by the railroad.

Yet St. Albans is largely free from the clamor, smoke, and smudge that more often than not detract from the physical appearance of railroad centers. This fact is partly due to the discreet location of the railroad yards and shops somewhat below and apart from the main business and residential sections, and partly to the almost inviolable beauty of the natural setting. The city stands on the gentle slope of an amphitheater formed by Green Mountain foothills. Its floor stretches over wide meadows to island-dotted Lake Champlain, behind which bulks the immutable purple of the northern Adirondacks. From the high eastern residential districts, or from near-by hills, St. Albans seems to rest submerged beneath a green sea of elms, from which rise only the slender spires of churches, like constant periscopes. This view caused Henry Ward Beecher to write that St. Albans was 'a place in the midst of a greater variety of scenic beauty than any other I can remember in America.'

In 1664, the territory that includes St. Albans was part of a French seigniory known as La Douville, so remaining until the accession of British rule in 1763. It was then included in one of the New Hampshire Grants. Eleven years later, the first settler, Jesse Welden, a half-breed Indian, came pioneering from Connecticut. He made an extensive clearing on Ball Island, in what is now St. Albans Bay, but disappeared during the Revolution, not to return till 1785. By this time the St. Francis Indians were friendly, and Welden ventured to clear and cultivate a tract of seventy acres near the center of the site of the present city. He was soon joined by other settlers, largely from the lower Connecticut Valley region of present Vermont, and in 1788 a town was formally organized. Among the early-comers was Levi Allen (brother of the famous Ethan), who laid claims, later invalidated, to so great a part of the town that he addressed his wife, in a letter, as 'Duchess of St. Albans.'

Chiefly because it was the northernmost sizable community in western Vermont, St. Albans has been the scene of a succession of violent happenings. During the years between 1807 and the War of 1812, it was probably the largest base of smuggling operations on Lake Champlain. The most active, notorious, and elusive of the smuggling craft, the aptly named 'Black Snake,' was employed by a St. Albans merchant to transport potash into Canada. The 'Black Snake' was finally captured after an encounter in which three Federal officers lost their lives. So bitter was the resentment of Vermonters against Jefferson's embargo — which prevented the disposal of what was often their only salable product (potash) at the only profitable market (Montreal) — that only one of the smugglers involved in the affray was hanged and those imprisoned were all subsequently pardoned.

In 1814, when Governor Martin Chittenden declined to call out the State militia to resist the imminent invasion of upper New York, eighty volunteers from St. Albans made up their own company and proceeded to Plattsburg, where they took active part in the land engagement of the decisive battle of September 11. Most of the population of St. Albans gathered on the hills east of town from which the smoke of the naval engagement was visible. Upon the sudden cessation of cannonading, they returned sadly home, convinced that Macdonough's Vermont-built fleet, smaller than that of the enemy, had been defeated. Not until sunset did a galloping horseman bring news of the complete victory that had been won when

'The Vermontese
As thick as bees
Came swarming o'er the lake, Sirs.'

St. Albans, with Swanton, was one of two Vermont towns seriously affected by the backwash of the rebellion of the Canadian-French population against British rule in the 'Papineau War' of 1837. Many of the rebels found sympathetic haven here, and feeling ran dangerously high. At a mass meeting of two thousand people held in St. Albans on December 19, 1837, supposedly reputable witnesses gave affidavits that public threats had been made by men of southern Canada to burn both St. Albans and Swanton to the ground. Fortunately, no outbreaks of any magnitude occurred before Generals Wood and Scott, of the United States Army, arrived to clear up the situation.

The most memorable day in the history of the city was October 19, 1864, the day of the St. Albans Raid, the most northerly engagement — if it can be called that — of the Civil War. Twenty-two Confederate soldiers, in small groups and dressed in civilian clothes, had insinuated themselves into the city over a period of several days. At three o'clock in the afternoon of the 19th, working with speed and precision, they entered all the banks in town simultaneously, killed one man and wounded others, and fled northward with more than $200,000, firing Sheldon Bridge behind them. The leaders were caught and tried in Canada, but acquitted on the ground that the raid was a legitimate act of formal warfare. This verdict caused so much international ill feeling that the Canadian Parliament appropriated $50,000 in gold to help defray the financial loss. The whole State of Vermont became taut with excitement upon receipt by telegraph of news of the raid, the extent of which was at first greatly exaggerated; its effect was, in fact, more important than the money involved.

In June, 1866, large numbers of Fenians, an Irish organization dedicated to the capture of Canada by arms and the establishment of an independent Irish State there, arrived in St. Albans by rail on their way north, as many as three hundred coming in on one train. Many of them slept on the St. Albans Common and in unoccupied buildings. Most of the Irish troops returned through this city after their ineffectual advance some six miles into Canada. The Green was then occupied by United States troops under General Meade, sent there by President Johnson to preserve neutrality. The soldiers remained for two weeks, escorting tired and disillusioned Irishmen to the special trains the Government provided for them, and delighting St. Albans with open-air band concerts in the evening.

The establishment of direct connection by rail with the outside world through the Central Vermont Railway was the turning-point in the industrial history of St. Albans, which had almost no importance as a shipping point during the heyday of water commerce on Lake Champlain. Construction of the road was begun in 1848 at Essex Junction, but was suspended when about half completed because of lack of funds. President Smith and other incorporators borrowed the needed money on their personal credit and saved the project from failure. The first train entered St. Albans on October 18, 1850, a diminutive wood-burning locomotive named 'Abigail Adams' having pulled it all the way from Montpelier.

With some of the bitter opposition that had marked the development of
the new project withdrawn, the Central Vermont grew rapidly and the
growth of the city coincided with it. In 1860, the general offices, originally at Northfield, were removed to St. Albans, and the machine and car
shops soon followed. Today, with buildings and yards covering an area of
135 acres, the Central Vermont employs nearly two thousand towns-
people.

In conjunction with its facilities for transportation, St. Albans has
developed a number of thriving industries, including the manufacture of
poultry and cattle feeds, maple sugar and sugar-making equipment,
canned goods, and lime. It is also an important production and distribution center for dairy products.

That neither border complications and surprise attacks nor a heady
industrial growth misled St. Albans into slighting its social and intellectual development is shown by its hospitals and clinics, its varied athletic
facilities, its many churches, its well-used library, and its remarkably
fine school system. During the nineteenth century a considerable number
of women poets resided here. In contemporary letters St. Albans is
represented by Frances Frost, one of the most sensitive younger poets, and
Allene Corliss, writer of popular novels and short stories.


POINTS OF INTEREST


1. *Taylor Park*, the city's large central Common, was named in honor
of its donor, Colonel Halloway Taylor, who deeded it to public use in
1799. Its shaded lawns and paths offer a restful contrast to the busy
streets which surround it. At the northern end is a handsome bronze
fountain, the gift of the late Governor John Gregory Smith. On the
southern lawn stands a World War memorial statue. A grim reminder of
another time and another manner of administering justice is the still
visible foundation of the old town whipping-post.

2. The *Railroad Station*, Lake and Federal Sts., built in 1866-67, is the
oldest in the State, and at the time of its erection was the largest and
most elaborate in New England. The 300-foot trainshed, partly closed at
the southern end, daringly swings its arch over the platform and four
tracks. It is said to be the last example extant of this earliest type of railway architecture.

3. *Bellows Free Academy*, S. Main St., is St Albans' most recent and most
important addition to its educational facilities. Erected in 1930, it was the
gift of Hiram Bellows (1876), who left to the city property, the proceeds
of which, after fifty years, were to be used for the building, equipment,
and support of a public academy. The Georgian-style building is one
of the most completely equipped secondary school structures in New
England. In addition to the commodious lecture rooms, laboratories,

and gymnasium, it has an auditorium with a seating capacity of more than 700.

4. The *Elizabeth Fisk Looms*, S. Main St. Housed in a picturesque cottage are two large hand-looms operated by women who have successfully revived the technique of weaving intricate designs into linen and of making vegetable dyes. A widely known example of their work is the woven coat of arms of Vermont in the State House at Montpelier, a duplicate of which is in the headquarters of the Federation of Women's Clubs in Washington.

5. The *St. Albans Free Library*, Maiden Lane (*open weekdays 2–6 and 7–9 P.M.*), occupies the lower floor of a handsome brick and Longmeadow sandstone structure that was one of Governor Smith's many gifts to the city. Among the 12,000 volumes is the Frank L. Greene Collection of Vermontiana, containing some 300 books and pamphlets, many of them exceedingly rare, relative to the history and literature of this State.

6. The *Hoyt House*, N. Main St., dating 1793, is the oldest in St. Albans. It was built by Silas Hathaway, who, though he died poor, at one time owned so much land that he was generally known as Baron Hathaway. Though of sturdy utilitarian plan, the house exhibits the instinctive feeling for symmetry possessed by so many early builders. The chief ornamental detail is a pleasing four-pillared entrance portico. During the early nineteenth century the building was used for a time as the Franklin County Courthouse.

7. The *Scoffield House*, N. Main and Hoyt Sts., erected in 1798, is another eighteenth-century dwelling of almost boxlike plainness except for its pillared entrance.

8. The *Campbell House*, Congress St., built in 1830, is a satisfying example of late Federal architecture, its brick sturdiness set off by a delicate Ionic portico.

9. The *Brigham House*, N. Main St., built in 1830, of brick, is distinguished by the delicate detail of its fanlight.

10. The *Hyde House*, Bank St. and Lincoln Ave., is an interesting specimen of a later style of architecture no longer generally admired. Built about 1845, it has the vertical and lapped siding, elaborate window frames, and crocketed gables once widely employed to produce 'elegance.'

# ST.  JOHNSBURY

*Village:* Alt. 655, pop. 7920.

*Railroad Station:* Canadian Pacific R.R., Maine Central R.R., St. Johnsbury &
Lake Champlain R.R., Depot Park, Railroad St.

*Bus Stations:* Grey Line (summer service), Avenue Hotel, Railroad St.; Goss
Bus and Greenwood Bus, Railroad St. Service Station; Montpelier Bus, St.
Johnsbury House, Main St.

*Airport:* 6 *m.* north on US 5 (no regular passenger line).

*Accommodations:* Four hotels, tourist homes and camps. Rates uniform the year
round.

*Information:* Court House Sq., Main St. at Eastern Ave. (summer months);
Chamber of Commerce office, 59 Main St.

*Annual Events:* Band Carnival, July; Junior Choir Festival, Spring; Kiwanis
Charity Ball, April; UCT Ball, May.

ST. JOHNSBURY, the shire town of Caledonia County, is the home of
the Fairbanks Scales and Cary Maple Sugar, and a gateway between the
Green Mountains of Vermont and the White Mountains of New Hampshire. Although in recent years it has assumed national leadership in the
maple-sugar industry, St. Johnsbury has been as clearly a one-family
town as any in the State. Physically the scales business and the Fairbanks
family have left their stamp on St. Johnsbury more conspicuously than
has the railroad in the case of St. Albans, and the great rambling factory
dominates the western entrance to town. The two finest public buildings
on Main Street were given by the Fairbanks family.

Situated at the confluence of three rivers, the Passumpsic, Moose, and
Sleeper's, St. Johnsbury stretches along the three valleys and surmounts
the dividing hills, having an exceptionally broken terrain. The two main
divisions in the central section of this vigorous village are marked by a
sharp difference in elevation. The principal business district is concentrated along Railroad Street in the central (Passumpsic) valley, typical
of active shopping sections in a trading center, with close-set buildings
of brick and stone fronted by signs and show-windows. On a broad
plateau known as the Plain, high above that level, the wide shaded Main
Street runs roughly parallel to Railroad Street. Main Street and environs
on the Plain constitute the most attractive part of St. Johnsbury, with
fine homes set back on shaded lawns, and the outstanding landmarks
arrayed here in gracious setting. The two main thoroughfares are connected by steep, winding Eastern Avenue, which is also lined with business places. Across the valley from Depot Park at the foot of Eastern
Avenue, a stern wooded bluff overlooks the Passumpsic and the lower
parts of town.

The largest town in northeastern Vermont, St. Johnsbury exhibits a broader scope of interests than is common to communities in this section of the State. Devotion to athletics is balanced by an appreciation of the arts and sciences traceable to the presence of an exceptional museum and attractive art gallery. The dominance of relatively stable industries over a long period has had its effect upon the social life as well as the physical appearance of the town. Interest in all branches of athletic sport is keen: the usual clubs are socially active; bowling alleys boom until closing time; the many dances are well attended; restaurants, beer taverns, and theaters are adequately patronized.

The territory was first granted by King George in 1770, under the name of Bessborough, and later Dunmore, but no settlement was made until 1786, when Jonathan Arnold and associates of Rhode Island received a charter from Governor Chittenden. Named in honor of Saint-Jean de Crèvecœur, French Consul at New York, author of 'Letters of an American Farmer,' and friend of Ethan Allen, it is the only town in the world bearing this name. In 1792, St. Johnsbury and other towns were set off from Orange County to form the new county of Caledonia, which took its name from the ancient Roman term for Scotland, out of deference to the Scottish colonies in Barnet and Ryegate (see Tour 1, Sec. b). In 1856 the county seat was transferred from Danville to St. Johnsbury.

Much of the history of St. Johnsbury is coincident with the history and munificence of the Fairbanks family. In 1830, Thaddeus Fairbanks, inventor of the first lever scale, took out his initial patent, and from that time the town dates its material growth and prosperity. Between 1830 and 1870, St. Johnsbury tripled in population, its growth during this period accounting almost entirely for the increase registered by Caledonia County as a whole. For his invention, Thaddeus Fairbanks was knighted by the Emperor of Austria, and to the Fairbanks dynasty, whose members were always philanthropic, St. Johnsbury owes much of its present beauty. Today Fairbanks Scales are shipped to all parts of the world.

The first airplane flight in Vermont was made in 1910 at the Caledonia County Fair in St. Johnsbury.


## POINTS OF INTEREST

1. *Arnold Park*, Main St., a shaded green at the head of Main, faces the length of the broad beautiful street along which church spires rise above the treetops of the Plain. A bronze tablet on a granite boulder here serves as a memorial to Dr. Jonathan Arnold, the Providence, R.I., surgeon who founded St. Johnsbury, and was principal proprietor of Lyndon and Sutton. Arnold's home, the first frame house in town, stood near the park.

2. The *Paddock Mansion*, Main St. (*private*), is set back sedately on a

smooth lawn. Built in 1820 by Judge Ephraim Paddock, the square frame house has an ornamental portico, balustraded roof, large white-capped windows, and doors handmade by Thaddeus Fairbanks. The landscape wallpaper in the parlor depicts Mt. Vesuvius and the Bay of Naples.

3. *North Congregational Church*, Main St., Gothic in style, is built of Isle La Motte stone, with ornamental red-granite pillars, interior woodwork of native cherry, and artistic window and wall decorations.

4. *Museum of Natural Science*, 81–85 Main St., presented by Colonel Franklin Fairbanks in 1891, is the best architectural work in town. Constructed of Longmeadow red sandstone in the Richardson Romanesque style, it is modeled somewhat after the Billings Library at the University of Vermont (*see BURLINGTON*), which Richardson considered representative of his finest work. The guardian lions by the entrance are strikingly rendered. The extensive variety of exhibits includes a complete collection of Vermont flora; a large bird collection; exhibits of mammals, reptiles, fish, and insects, shells, minerals, fossils, and ethnological specimens from abroad; relics from early history and various wars; a collection of old china, pewter, and glassware. The history of Vermont agriculture is illustrated by the array of agricultural implements. The museum, in co-operation with the public schools, sponsors an educational program. Such a museum is unusual for a town the size of St. Johnsbury, its only competitor in the State being the Fleming Museum at the University of Vermont (*see BURLINGTON*).

5. *Civil War Statue*, Main St., stands in Court House Square over the junction of Eastern Ave. with Main, a figure representing *America*, carved from Carrara marble by the Vermont sculptor, Larkin Goldsmith Mead (*see BRATTLEBORO*). Near the statue is an old hitching-rail still frequently used by farmers driving in to the county seat on legal or shopping errands.

6. The *Athenæum*, 30 Main St., dedicated in 1871 by Horace Fairbanks (Governor of Vermont, 1876–78), houses a public library and museum in a building designed by J. D. Hatch of New York. W. F. Poole, bibliographer, supervised the selection of books, which now number approximately 28,000 volumes. The Art Gallery, featured by Bierstadt's 'The Domes of the Yosemite,' has 56 other paintings and several pieces of statuary. Each New Year's Eve when Horace Fairbanks was alive, the Athenæum was opened for a general reception, the social event of the year. Among the guests of honor at receptions here have been Commander Peary and Henry M. Stanley. From the east balcony, President Harrison in 1891, and President Taft in 1912, addressed thousands of Vermonters.

7. *South Congregational Church*, Main St., constructed of wood painted white, is the most pleasing of the churches. A conical spire rises from the open bell-tower, which rests on a square base with clock faces. Three tall entrance doors open from the severe façade. In the interior broad-backed pews and the wide mahogany pulpit are reminiscent of early houses of worship.

8. *St. Johnsbury Academy*, Main St., founded in 1842 by Sir Thaddeus Fairbanks and brothers, Erastus and Joseph, is a private and endowed school, serving as a high school for local students through special tuition arrangements with the town. The trim red-brick buildings form an imposing group near the southern end of Main Street. *Fuller Hall*, the latest addition, is an excellent auditorium, a long brick structure with white-columned portico and a belfry.

9. The *Fairbanks Scale Works*, Western Ave., is the outgrowth of Thaddeus Fairbanks's invention of a device for weighing hemp in a factory where the fiber was cleaned and prepared for market. Investigation and experimenting with the principle of levers in a weighing-machine resulted ultimately in the development of the platform scale in 1830. Now all types and sizes are produced here, from the delicate apothecary's scale to enormous ship and railroad scales. The red-brick factory buildings are neat and clean. *St. Johnsbury Vocational School* is operated in connection with the plant, high-school curricula being combined with practical training.

10. The *Methodist Episcopal Church*, Central St., has a beautiful memorial window, 'Annunciation to the Shepherds,' by Tiffany.

11. The *Octagon House*, Eastern Ave. (*private*), was built of brick in 1852, and has on its estate two subsidiary houses of the same peculiar shape, one of brick and one of wood, forming a triumvirate of eight-sided structures on shady landscaped grounds near the heart of the business district.

12. The *Century House*, at the Four Corners (*private*), was erected in 1798 by William C. Arnold, much of the interior finish being hauled by ox-team from Connecticut. The handmade clapboards are fastened with old hammered nails. On the second floor is one remaining corner of the original ballroom, the floor marked in gray and yellow diamonds, which knew the stately grace of many a minuet.

13. The *Cary Maple Sugar Co.*, Portland St. (*visitors welcome*), had a modest start fifty years ago as a pioneer in the maple industry, and is now the largest maple-sugar plant in the country. The brick plant and storehouses occupy five acres, and every department is well-equipped. Each spring several million pounds of syrup are purchased and shipped here for processing and packing. *Maple Grove, Inc.*, a subsidiary of Cary, manufactures a wide variety of maple candies, and its attractive candy kitchen here is open for inspection.

14. *Government Fishery Station* is west of the village at Emerson Falls, where Sleeper's River comes foaming down a long rock ledge. Two million brook trout are raised here annually, and other varieties include landlocked salmon and small-mouthed bass. Distributions are made throughout Vermont, New Hampshire, and parts of New York. Sleeper's River was named by Jonathan Arnold, in ironic rebuke to the man who, left to guard the camp while Arnold and James Whitelaw (*see Tour 1, RYEGATE*) were surveying land, went to sleep on the bank of this river.

# SPRINGFIELD

*Village:* Alt. 410, pop. 4943.

*Railroad Station:* Nearest station, B. & M. R.R., Charlestown, N.H., 6 *m.* Electric car line connects with all trains in Charlestown, fare 25¢; 9 trips daily except Sunday (4).

*Bus Station:* Also in Charlestown at B. & M. Station for B. & M. Transportation Co. and Bee Line.

*Accommodations:* One hotel; tourist homes and rooming-houses.

*Information:* Gasoline Station, Main St., during summer months.

*Annual Events:* Amateur Astronomers' Meet at Stellafane; Air Meet, North Springfield; July Fourth Celebration; Elks Carnival and Ball; American Legion Ball; Knights of Columbus Ball.

SPRINGFIELD, the first of many towns to be named for Springfield, Massachusetts, has attained high rank in the field of machine-tool-making and a general industrial prominence not usually looked for in Vermont towns. Notable as this industrial development is, still more notable is the manner in which resultant prosperity has been directed into the proper channels. Industrial leaders and business men have made it possible for Springfield to ride the crest of large-scale manufacturing without creating the sooty slough that submerges so many factory towns. Inventive ability of employees has been fostered with unselfish care by employers who give their subordinates full credit, and even go to the extent of helping set them up in business. Keen minds and cultural tastes have left their mark on the life of the community.

The hills on which Springfield is built rise sharply on both sides of a narrow valley; residential sections overlook the strong-flowing Black River and the large plants along its banks. From the brick-built business center, crowded compactly about a small open square, streets diverge steeply, curving erratically up the hillsides between trim stone walls, with houses set at all levels along the slopes, looking down over roofs and treetops to the machine shops and mills on the valley bottom. Pleasant homes, lawns, and shade trees along the tranquil streets balance the compressed bleakness of the central square and the vibrant hum of manufacturing.

About 1750, a tribe of Abnaki Indians lived on French Meadows, near the mouth of the Black River. In 1752 they were joined by an outcast white man named John Nott, who was accepted because of his half-breed Indian wife. Other white squatters came later. The eastern end of the Crown Point Military Road was started on the Springfield side of the Connecticut, and a blockhouse was erected (1 mile north of Cheshire Toll Bridge) for the protection of the soldiers working on this strategic high-

# ILLUSTRATIONS
*to accompany*
Tours 3, 3A, 3B, 3C, 3D

JAY PEAK

HAZENS NOTCH

ASBESTOS MINE, BELVIDERE MOUNTAIN

POWER PLANT AT FAIRFAX FALLS

LOOKING SOUTH FROM THE CHIN, MT. MANSFIELD

SMUGGLER'S NOTCH, MT. MANSFIELD

MEETING HOUSE, WITH HORSE SHED, NEAR WATERBURY CENTER

RANGE ROAD, BETWEEN LINCOLN AND RIPTON

SEVEN GABLES, BETWEEN LINCOLN AND RIPTON

BUTTERMILK FALLS, GRANVILLE GULF

'POTATO HILL,' LINCOLN

TYPICAL MARKER WHERE LONG TRAIL CROSSES HIGHWAY

way, which linked the waterways of the Connecticut River, and Lake Champlain, and outpost Number Four at Charlestown, New Hampshire, with Crown Point, New York. The first real white settlement was begun in 1772 at Eureka, a hilltop site on the Crown Point Road, the pioneers avoiding the marshy lowlands of the Black River to break the soil back in the hills.

It was in 1774 that William Lockwood turned a farsighted eye to the valley, bought the land around the falls in the Black River, dammed the west branch stream, and put up a sawmill. Others followed the call of water-power in the churning roar of Lockwood Falls, and the inevitable trend of population from the hills to the valleys was under way. In 1808, Isaac Fisher came from Charlestown, New Hampshire, and secured most of the rights along the river, utilizing the water-power to operate a cotton mill, an oil mill, a carding shop, a foundry, and a woolen mill, thus establishing himself as the father of industrial Springfield. Fisher's primitive machine shop was a forerunner of the great plants that now stretch along the river flats.

The nineteenth century was drawing to a close when Springfield inventiveness burst upon the machine-tool world with new processes and vastly improved machines that were transmitted over America and Europe to the Far East. Among the mechanical geniuses who made these contributions were: Amasa Woolson, Adna Brown, James Hartness, E. R. Fellows, W. LeRoy Bryant, Fred Lovejoy, and Ralph E. Flanders.

Springfield has also been a leader in amateur astronomy, and here again James Hartness (Governor of Vermont, 1921–23) played a part. Hartness already had a private observatory on his estate, when he came in contact with Russell W. Porter, who possessed an intense interest in astronomy and telescope-making, but no funds for experimentation. There followed a notable instance of a rich man's hobby and a poor man's ardor uniting in a scientific contribution. The Springfield Telescope Makers' organization, founded by Porter in 1923, maintains a fine observatory, Stellafane (3 miles west, off State 11), where amateur astronomers and telescope-makers convene. In aviation Hartness was also a pioneer, soloing at fifty-five years of age as Vermont's first licensed pilot.

A strong foreign element has left its imprint on the community, bringing the color and flavor of eastern Europe. People of Polish and Russian extraction comprise nearly one-third of the population, and of no small importance have been their offerings to industry, music, art, and athletics. A good sporting town, Springfield's athletic teams are made up largely of Poles and Russians, and when men gather in the Community House lounge, drugstores, or beer gardens, talk of touchdowns and base hits is likely to prevail with that of the machine shops.

The Springfield Terminal Railway Company, the only electric railroad in northern New England, has been instrumental in the town's industrial rise. Conceived because of the manifold obstacles in the way of building a railway along the narrow Black River Valley and across the Connecticut, this electric car line furnishes fast, efficient passenger and freight service between Springfield and Charlestown, New Hampshire.

## POINTS OF INTEREST

1. The *Parks and Woolson Machine Co.*, Park St. (*visitors welcome*), the oldest shop in town, was founded in 1839 by Davidson and Parks, and has operated consistently since then, making cloth-finishing machinery. Amasa Woolson joined the firm in 1846, and with his chief assistant, Adna Brown, soon set their product ahead of all competitors, by inventing a broadcloth shearing machine that preserves the selvage (*listing*) of the cloth. Woolson and Brown were largely responsible for bringing Jones and Lamson Co. to Springfield from Windsor.

2. The *Jones and Lamson Machine Co.*, Clinton St. (*visitors welcome*), occupies immense factory sheds on the river flats at the eastern edge of the village, a plant so huge as to seem misplaced in Vermont. James Hartness, superintendent in 1889, became part owner, and under the impetus of his inventive genius, 'J and L' rode to the forefront in American machine-tool-making, and developed a large foreign business as well. Before the turn of the century the Hartness Flat Turret Lathe and the Fay Automatic had spread over America and Europe to remote China and India. The later growth of J and L has been steady but less spectacular. It has always been a training school for inventors, from which talented young men branch out to establish firms of their own, on the strength of innovations made in the J and L shops, and with the backing of J and L owners — a series of story-book careers in the Horatio Alger vein.

3. The *Fellows Gear Shaper Co.*, River St. (*visitors welcome*). The head of this big plant, E. R. Fellows, was chief draftsman for Jones and Lamson when he discovered a new and superior process for cutting gear teeth. As the merits of his process came to be recognized, the automobile industry began its expansion, and quiet gears were in great demand. Fellows's gear shaper shot to prominence, and now the machines which cut the majority of automobile gears, and gears for other machinery, come from this factory.

4. The *Bryant Chucking Grinder Co.*, Clinton St. (*visitors welcome*), was founded by W. LeRoy Bryant, who made his invention while working as chief draftsman under Mr. Hartness at Jones and Lamson, and then organized his own business.

5. The *Lovejoy Tool Co.*, Main St., is a late outgrowth from the parent company, J and L, with chief draftsman Fred Lovejoy perfecting an inserted bit tool-holder of simple design and superior solid construction.

6. The *John T. Slack Corp.*, Mineral St. (*visitors welcome*), operates shoddy mills producing 800 different grades of reworked wool. Among

the pioneers in wool reclamation, Slack began in 1871 to meet the clothing shortage prevalent after the Civil War. At the present time Slack is one of the largest shoddy plants in the world.

7. The *Community House*, S. Main St., originally a Jones and Lamson factory building, is now a spacious and well-equipped club, founded in 1919 by civic-minded industrialists to serve the diversified interests of the community. The first, and by far the most successful, venture of its kind in the State, it is the center of social and recreational life in the village, and an excellent example of social planning. Here in a friendly, informal atmosphere, Springfield youth finds a place to pass the time, away from the influences of the street corner, pool hall, and drinking-place. The exterior of the old machine shop still wears traces of its origin, but the interior has been completely remodeled and fitted with facilities for bowling, billiards, badminton, indoor tennis, volley ball, and shower baths. There are reading-rooms, lounges, pianos; the local dramatic club stages frequent plays; basketball games, banquets, dances, and bridge parties are held here. The building is owned by J and L, but the Manufacturers' Association operates the club.

8. The high *Falls Bridge* (1917) spans the chasm into which the Black River drops. The Indians used to fish for salmon in this deep pocket in the rocks. The first bridge was built in 1774 by William Lockwood, who felled hemlock trees across the gap. It is legendary that a blind man, when the rude bridge was being rebuilt, crossed unknowingly on a single stringer, while onlookers held their breath. Another story is that the town's first doctor rode up to the dismantled bridge one dark night, urged his horse forward and made the crossing on one strand in the jet blackness, blithely unaware of his peril until it was too late to turn back. In 1836 a sixteen-year-old girl deliberately emulated blind man and horse, walking one stringer over the gorge to settle a dare.

9. The *Chimney Corner Tea House*, Summer Hill Ave., is the best Colonial type structure within the village limits, with clear simple lines and balancing end chimneys. It occupies a beautiful site above the valley.

10. The *Old House*, Park St., a former tavern, was built in 1802, and is one of the oldest houses in the village proper. Most of the older homes were built back in the hills or near the Connecticut.

11. *Radio Station WNBX*, Bank Building, is the most powerful and one of the oldest of Vermont broadcasting stations.

12. The *Spafford Library*, Main St., with the Barnard Juvenile Annex, contains 19,000 volumes.

13. The *Congregational Church*, Main St., a red-brick structure with white-columned portico and high white spire, was erected in 1833 and remodeled in 1927.

14. The *Catholic Church*, Mansion Hill, completed in 1930, is constructed of Vermont marble in the Italian Romanesque style of architecture.

15. *St. Trinity Greek Orthodox Church*, Park St:, at the top of Seminary

Hill, was erected in 1909, high above the valley. Its architecture is undistinguished, but it is interesting for the picturesque and symbolic rites of pre-revolutionary Russia, preserved by the Russian families of Springfield. The Christmas and Easter ceremonies are particularly impressive. At Midnight Mass on Easter, the congregation light candles at the altar and bear them around the church in a stately procession.

# W I N D S O R

*Village:* Alt. 354, pop. 3680.

*Railroad Station:* Central Vermont Ry.

*Busses:* Bee Line; Vermont Transit Co.; stage lines to Plainfield, N.H., Meriden, N.H., and Cornish, N.H., and Reading and Cavendish.

*Accommodations:* One large hotel, three smaller inns, several tourist homes.

*Information:* Hotels and garages.

*Annual Events:* Armistice Day Ball; summer horse show: prison minstrels, early spring.

WINDSOR, the birthplace of Vermont, is in some ways an incongruous combination of the historic and antique with the industrial and modern; of the placidly reminiscent with the nervously aggressive. There is something about the town that remains static and indigenous in the face of all external influences toward change, yet the successive impacts of industrial developments and foreign influxes have left permanent marks, inwardly and outwardly.

Windsor is admirably situated on a terrace of the Connecticut River, with the green hills of Cornish to the east and dark Ascutney (*see Tour 1, Sec. a*) filling the western horizon. Without being crowded, the village is unusually compact. Main Street, with residential sections at both ends and the business district in the middle, runs north and south. State Street, the other leading artery, runs due west from the business section. Machine shops and uniform frame houses lie unobtrusively on lower ground between Main St. and the river.

Windsor was granted on July 6, 1761, by Governor Wentworth, of New Hampshire. A second grant was finally allowed by New York on March 28, 1772, to Colonel Nathan Stone, who for several years had been legally the sole owner of the township, having been deeded all lands by the other proprietors and settlers that he might more easily and effectively represent the town's interests before the New York court.

Settlement began in 1764, and by the close of the following year there were sixteen families here; in 1791 the population was 1542; and according to the official census of 1820, Windsor, with 2956 inhabitants, was the most populous town in the State.

The significance of Windsor, however, does not depend upon mere numbers. On July 2, 1777, a convention of delegates from the New Hampshire Grants met here to discuss and adopt a constitution erecting those grants into an independent State, their address to the Continental Congress of 1776 having been unfavorably regarded. The convention remained in session seven days. On July 8, the new constitution was adopted and a Council of Safety of twelve members was appointed to conduct the affairs of the new State until the first legislature should convene. The tale of the dramatic crisis in the State's history on July 8, 1777, has never ceased to be told. On that day a messenger from Colonel Seth Warner appeared before the convention with the disquieting news of the southern advance of General Burgoyne's army on the western side of the State. The constitution was undergoing a final reading, yet so great was the excitement and general alarm, especially among the delegates from the invaded territory, that the meeting was on the point of breaking up with its work unfinished. But suddenly a terrific thunderstorm broke; 'the road became a river, the yard became a strand.' The storm, whether a token of divine intervention, as many have believed, or merely a fortunate coincidence, compelled the men at Windsor to remain, to reconsider, and to complete the reading and adoption of the document that continues to serve as the bulwark of Vermont government a century and a half after Burgoyne and his eight thousand men were last seen here.

Following the creation of the new State, the General Assembly frequently convened here until Montpelier became the permanent capital in 1805. Between 1781 and 1794, Windsor was the shire or half-shire town of the county that had been given its name.

Since 1800, when Asahel Hubbard came to Windsor from Connecticut and built his experimental pump, the town has been the scene of more inventions and the home of more inventors than any other in the State. Hubbard's hydraulic pump was patented in 1828. In 1829, the National Hydraulic Company was organized and its shop installed at the State Prison here, of which Hubbard had conveniently been made warden through the political influence of his partner, Jabez Proctor, father of Senator Redfield Proctor. Agencies were established throughout the settled parts of the country and in Mexico. An early order was for a twenty-horsepower pump for the first city waterworks of St. Louis, Missouri. Hubbard delivered the pump personally and installed it. But the St. Louis aqueduct company did not, he found, have enough money to pay for it. Eager to return home, he accepted as part payment a pure white saddle horse, upon which he rode into Windsor several months after his departure and which was long known to the old inhabitants as 'the St. Louis horse.' In 1833, Hubbard sold the right to manufacture his pump in the State of Rhode Island to David Fales and Alvin Jenks, and today, more than a century later, the Fales and Jenks Machine Company of Pawtucket makes Hubbard pumps, unchanged in principle, with a capacity up to one thousand gallons per minute. George Hubbard, Asahel's nephew, invented the coffee percolator in 1876, and four years later patented a glazier's point and driver, which revolutionized the setting of window glass. In 1858, the manufacture was begun here of a sewing machine, locally designed, the business being sold after a few years to Thomas White, founder of the White Sewing Machine Company.

More than to any other goal, however, the ingenuity of Windsor men has been directed toward improvements in firearms. In 1835, Asahel Hubbard began the manufacture of the underhammer rifle invented by his gunsmith son-in-law, Nicanor Kendall. This weapon was the safest sporting arm that had been devised up to that time. Kendall designed it after he had wounded himself in the hand and put a bullet through the top-hair of his betrothed wife, one cold day when they were out riding, as he drew his rifle from under the fur laprobe to shoot at a squirrel. One of the first large orders for the Kendall rifles came in 1836 from the Republic of Texas, payment being two thousand acres of Texas land. In 1838, Richard Smith Lawrence, perhaps the greatest of the inventors who have worked here, moved to Windsor. Here he designed and constructed machinery which, for the first time, largely eliminated hand work in the manufacture of firearms. He later invented the lubricated bullet, which made breech-loading wholly practical for the first time, and in 1850 he began the first successful development and improvement of the repeating rifle, though he did not actually invent it. In 1866, Lawrence and Governor Oliver Winchester, of Connecticut, founded the Winchester Repeating Arms Company and developed the Winchester repeater, the importance of which in the history of the West is well known.

The industrial history of Windsor is vitally concerned with the inventive genius of a few men who have lived here. Early industries included several woolen mills that naturally followed the intensive breeding of merino sheep in this section; but Windsor's first real boom period occurred in the middle decades of the nineteenth century as a result of contracts for the manufacture of firearms during the Mexican, Crimean, and Civil Wars. The second such period, dependent upon the production of automatic machinery, occurred during and after the World War.

The Vermont *Journal and Advertiser*, published at Windsor, was the third newspaper in the State and is now the oldest, having appeared continuously since 1783. During the last years of the eighteenth and first quarter of the nineteenth century, Windsor was one of the leading towns in the State in the number of books and pamphlets issued from its presses. Here was printed in 1812, on the Stephen Daye press, the first Vermont Bible, now a bibliographical rarity, which included seven elaborate copper-plate engravings by Isaac Eddy, Vermont's earliest engraver (*see Tour 1, WEATHERSFIELD*).

There has long been in Windsor a greater percentage of foreign population than is found in most Vermont towns. The cotton mills that superseded the firearms factories in the 1870's brought considerable numbers of French-Canadians, most of whose descendants have departed or become assimilated. Among the present shop-workers the foreign-born are predominantly Slavic.

Prominent native sons of Windsor include Vietts Rice, inventor of the roller process for the manufacture of flour; Carlos Coolidge, Governor of Vermont (1848–50); Jonathan Hubbard, Congressman from Vermont (1809–11); James Whitcomb, Senator from, and Governor of, Indiana; and William H. H. Stowell, three times Congressman from Virginia.


## POINTS OF INTEREST


1. The *Old Constitution House*, North Main St. (*open as a tea house; admission free*), is the building in which the Constitution of Vermont was framed and adopted. It was then (1777) a public tavern and had probably been built about five years earlier, though the date is uncertain. It originally stood a short distance west of the site of the present railroad station. The building is owned and maintained by the Old Constitution House Association, to which it was presented on July 10, 1914, by Mrs. Caroline S. Fay and her children with the provision that it be 'restored, maintained, and preserved as an historic relic and be devoted to historical, literary, and social usages.' Every room in the building contains relics and documents significant to its own history or that of the State. The long and harmless controversy as to just which room was occupied by the Constitutional Convention is not likely ever to be settled beyond dispute, though present opinion favors the north upstairs room now used by the Windsor chapter of the D.A.R.

2. The *Vermont State Prison and House of Correction*, State St. (*open to visitors 9–11, 1–4, except Sat. aft., Sun., and holidays*). Windsor has been the seat of the Vermont State Prison since its inception in 1807. There is no adequate history of the penal institutions of this State, but the first five years of the prison's history are well covered in 'An Authentic History of the Vermont State Prison,' by John Russell, Jun., Windsor, 1812. Russell was nineteen years old when he wrote this work, and his only motive, he admits, was 'the aid that the sale of the copyright would afford the author in obtaining a collegial education.' Imprisonment during those early years was usually for one of three crimes: counterfeiting, horse-stealing, and highway robbery. As early as 1809 the labor of prisoners was employed by the State in the manufacture of articles such as shoes for marketing on a commercial scale. This practice has only recently been discontinued. The prison population, which for the last ten years has averaged around 350 men, is now employed only in the work of maintaining the prison plant and farm and in labor of a non-competitive

nature, such as State printing and the manufacture of number plates and highway signs. Every spring the prisoners stage a minstrel show in the chapel auditorium. So popular has this annual event become in recent years that it is repeated to full houses on four successive evenings.

3. The *Covered Toll Bridge*, 0.1 *m.* east of the four-corner intersection on South Main St., built in 1866, is the longest covered bridge in, or partly in, Vermont and the only one that retains the toll gate. The first bridge on this site was built in 1796, replacing a ferry. It was at this point that Lafayette entered Vermont, on June 28, 1825, for his brief tour of the State. The records (1811–40) of the earlier toll bridge here have been preserved, though in private hands, and make suggestive reading. On November 12, 1837, for instance, there passed 'Gen'l Lyman Mower' with '1 wagon, 1 sulky, 1 horse & rider, 600 sheep, 127 cattle.' The only possible conclusion is that there passed also, toll-free, some dogs.

4. The *Old South Church* (Congregational), Main St., was built in 1798, presumably after a design by Asher Benjamin (*see below*). It is a graceful white wooden structure, and its spacious lawns, unusual for a church centrally located in a busy commercial community, enhance its beauty. For years before this church was built, the Calvinistic Congregationalists of Windsor held Sunday meetings in one another's houses. From 1768 to 1774 they listened every third Sunday to the Reverend James Wellman, a Harvard graduate, who preached two out of three Sundays at Cornish, his home, across the river. It is told how, after fording the Connecticut on horseback, he would enter his 'pulpit' in some private home dripping wet, a sight that must have made some of his congregation stir uneasily, although it was some few years later that the Congregational minister in a neighboring town definitely stated that 'the same spirit which drove the herd of swine into the sea drove the Baptists into the water, and that they were hurried along by the devil until the rite was performed.'

5. The *Harriet Lane House* (1804), North Main St., is now an automobile show-room, though much of the exterior detail is intact. The attenuated Ionic pilasters, the delicately carved festoons on the friezes of the window heads, and the graceful Palladian window, are executed in striking simi-larity to the decorative patterns of the Adam brothers. This house was designed by Asher Benjamin, who lived and worked in Windsor for five years (1800–04). Even at that time he was the best-known architect in the Connecticut Valley, and later, after he established himself in Boston, his reputation, enhanced by his popular books on architectural design, became even greater. His work, like that of McIntire, was a variation, an elaboration, upon the style developed by the Adam brothers. His use of miniature fluted columns, Ionic pilasters, festooned carvings over windows and beside doors, and his repetition of entrance details in the second story resulted in houses that are, at their worst, slightly florid, at their best, superlatively handsome. Windsor's industrial growth has prevented the preservation of several of these houses. The Fullerton House (1800), the finest of all Benjamin houses, which stood just north of the post office, was razed in 1935 to make room for a filling station, its

interior and exterior decorative details being incorporated in a house of similar design in New Canaan, Connecticut.

6. The *Sherman Evarts House*, North Main St., is a narrow two-story dwelling with a low hipped roof and an extended ell in the rear. The façade is distinguished for its finer elements of mass and proportion. The classic detail, executed strictly in the Adam mode of the period, conveys a sense of restrained sophistication. Conspicuous features are the urns and festoons carved on the door and window headings, the delicately paneled pilasters, and the exceptionally fine cornice with its slender triglyphs.

7. The *William M. Evarts House*, North Main St., with its numerous wings and varying roof lines, is an interesting example of early utilitarian building and of the manner in which houses 'grew.'

8. The *Green House* (1791), Main St., now owned by the local Masonic Lodge, overlooks the heart of Windsor's business district from the brow of a hill. It is a plain two-story frame structure, somewhat marred by a later porch. The north front room downstairs preserves the original eighteenth-century wallpaper, probably of French origin. Early in the nineteenth century this house was a school for girls. Salmon P. Chase, later Chief Justice of the United States, who was born across the river in Cornish, obtained special permission as a very little boy to attend it in company with his older sisters.

---

# WOODSTOCK

---

*Village:* Alt. 705, pop. 1312.

*Railroad Station:* Nearest station, B. & M. R.R. and Central Vermont Ry., White River Junction, 15 *m.* Bus fare 75¢.

*Busses:* Three daily (except Sunday) to and from White River Junction; two daily to and from Rutland.

*Accommodations:* Three hotels (two open year round, one from June to November); many tourist homes; several small inns and tourist homes within 5-mile radius.

*Information:* Garages and hotels. See or write to Winter Sports Director, Woodstock, for winter sports information.

*Annual Events:* Field Day and parade, July 4; American Legion Ball, Nov. 11; Firemen's Ball, Dec. 31; Woodstock Ski Runners Club meet and other ski meets, winter, dependent on snow conditions.

WOODSTOCK is the village which probably more than any other in Vermont has reverently preserved both the physical setting and the

spiritual flavor of an earlier day. Long one of the favorite summer resorts in the State and recently a center of winter sports development,
Woodstock has nevertheless retained the somewhat astringent quality
of its native personality. Its instinctive reaction to change is negative:
it has no factories and wants none; it saw its railroad discontinued without regret; it tenaciously cherishes its old covered bridge, picturesque
but hazardous, at the west end of the village. If Woodstock sometimes
places sentiment above progress, if it is — as its rustic neighbors say —
too smug in its own well-being, it is perhaps by these very tokens a
microcosm of the State to which, culturally, intellectually, and politically,
it has contributed so much.

Visually Woodstock is one of the most charming villages in northern
New England, not only in itself, but on any one of its four main ap-
proaches. Lying on the banks of the Ottauquechee, most *rubato* of Vermont rivers, it is overlooked from the north by Mount Tom, on other
sides by lesser hills, some of which include parts of the residential sections.
Its broad streets are lined with houses and public buildings, beautiful
not merely because they are old, but because they were built in a tradition
of grace and beauty. The business square, neat and compact, centers
the village. Immediately west of the square is the long slender oval of
the Green, probably the most widely known village common in Vermont.
Throughout two-thirds of the last century — and to this very day by
some of the oldest inhabitants of near-by towns — the village was called
Woodstock Green, or simply 'the Green.' One of the first lots to be
cleared in the village, the Green assumed its present shape in 1830, about
seventy years too early to justify the harmless legend sometimes told to
visitors that it was laid out in the shape of the flagship of Admiral Dewey,
who spent his summers here during the latter part of his life.

The town was granted in 1761 and settled four years later by Timothy
Knox, a Harvard graduate. The first clergyman here was another Harvard man, Aaron Hutchinson, one of the best Biblical and classical
scholars in eighteenth-century New England and the man whose preaching at Bennington had such a powerful effect on Ethan Allen, who was
not notably susceptible to the clergy. It was men like these who from
the very beginning sounded an intellectual pitch that has never ceased
to vibrate.

In 1786, Woodstock became, with Windsor, half-shire town of Windsor
County, and in 1794 shire town, which it has remained ever since and for
which its central location in the county well qualifies it.

Woodstock was one of the leading publishing centers of the State prior
to 1850. The famous Stephen Daye press, the first press operative on
this continent north of Mexico (*see MONTPELIER*), was in use here
for a time, subsequent to its ownership by the Spooners and Isaac Eddy
in Windsor. The large bibliography of Woodstock presses includes
broadsides, verse, hymns, sermons, children's chap-books (the rigidity
of the moral instructions matched by the stiffness of the woodcut figures),

and the first Greek lexicon printed in North America. Since 1805 Woodstock has always had at least one newspaper, and at one time (1830) as
many as five were published here contemporaneously.

The best-known medical school in Vermont of its time was established
here in 1827 and operated until 1856. A schism in the faculty led to two
separate advertisements in the local papers, one by each faction, which
caused someone to remark that Woodstock was the only place in the
country except Philadelphia with two medical schools.

From 1846 to 1932, Woodstock was the seat of the Windsor County
Fair, which was at the time of its discontinuance the oldest county fair
in New England.

It has been claimed that the first express line in this country was that
established between Woodstock and Windsor in the 1820's by Alvin
Adams, who came here as a hostler's assistant at the old Bowker Tavern.
It is certain that Adams here began on a small scale the practice of the
business which he later developed into the world-wide enterprise of the
Adams Express Company.

The list of prominent men who have been closely associated with Woodstock either as native sons or through long residence is a proud one.

Jacob Collamer (1791–1865), born in Troy, New York, was graduated
from the University of Vermont in 1810 and made Woodstock his permanent home after 1836. He was Representative in Congress (1842–49),
Postmaster General (1849–50), and United States Senator (1855–65).
During the Civil War, Collamer was a close friend and personal adviser
of Lincoln, and it was he who drafted the bill, enacted July 13, 1861,
which gave the war its first Congressional sanction and invested the
President with new and necessary powers.

George P. Marsh (1801–82) was one of the most distinguished scholars
and most accomplished diplomats ever produced by this State. From
1844 to 1849 he was one of Vermont's Representatives in Congress.
After serving (1849–54) as United States Minister to Turkey, he delivered
a series of lecture courses at Columbia University and Lowell Institute
that established him as one of the leading philologians of the country.
In 1860, Lincoln appointed him first United States Minister to the new
kingdom of Italy, where for twenty-one years he remained the close
friend and consultant of King Victor Emmanuel and a beacon light of
American culture. Matthew Arnold said, after meeting him, that he
had found a man whose culture was so deep and so universal that it made
him forget about Yankeeism and rejoice only in the bond of race. Marsh
was a lifelong collector in diverse fields. Two of his collections (reptiles
and engravings) are in the Smithsonian Institution, in Washington, and
another is in the Billings Library at the University of Vermont (*see*
*BURLINGTON*). Of his twenty books, ranging in subject from philology
and zoology to art and philosophy, the greatest is 'Man and Nature,'
1864, revised in 1874 as 'The Earth as Modified by Human Action.'
This book is the fountainhead of the conservation movement; it first

suggested 'the possibility and the importance of the restoration of disturbed harmonies and the material improvement of waste and exhausted
regions.' A great many of the conservation and restoration programs in
which the National Government has interested itself most actively in
recent years were advanced by George P. Marsh almost seventy-five
years ago.

Hiram Powers (1805–73), born on a hill farm near Woodstock, became
in the middle decades of the last century the most famous of American
sculptors. His 'Greek Slave' (1843) engaged the attention of the American public as no other statue ever has done before or since. The original
was sold in England, but Powers made eight marble copies of it, one of
which is now in the Corcoran Gallery, in Washington. His one hundred
and fifty busts included characters famous in earlier history as well as
the great personages of his own day. The National Capitol has three of
his historical pieces: the bust of Marshall and the statues of Franklin
and Jefferson. The latter part of his life was spent in Florence, where
Nathaniel Hawthorne said the life of two continents flowed through his
studio. One of Powers's sons, Preston, was also a sculptor of considerable
skill and executed the statue of Jacob Collamer, now in the Capitol at
Washington.

Other famous residents of Woodstock include Frederick Billings, president of the Northern Pacific Railroad and the man who saved it in the
panic of 1873 and secured its extension beyond Dakota; James A. Mower,
major general in the Mexican and Civil Wars; Peter T. Washburne,
Julius Converse, and Franklin S. Billings, all governors of Vermont;
Charles L. Dana, president of the New York Academy of Medicine and
one of America's greatest neurologists; and John Cotton Dana, the man
who did more than anyone else to expand the function of the public
libraries of America and to educate the public to take advantage of them.
Despite the year-round stream of guests, Woodstock has completely
avoided the brazenness of much resort appeal. Even transient visitors
recognize this as the town's most potent charm. The grace of Woodstock's heritage, scenically, architecturally, and culturally, and the
ceaseless care with which it has been preserved leave little cause to wonder
why the Vermont poet, Daniel L. Cady, in his oft-quoted line, 'It beats
a day on Woodstock Green,' made a visit to this place the very yardstick
of human felicity.

POINTS OF INTEREST

1. The *Norman Williams Public Library*, facing the east end of the
Green from the south (8–12, 1–6 *daily;* 7–9 *Sat.*). This fine Richardsonian,
Romanesque building was completed in 1885, the gift of E. H. Williams
in memory of his father, Norman Williams, Secretary of State in Vermont
and one of the most civic-minded of men. The book collection here of

30,000 volumes is surpassed only by those of Burlington and Brattleboro among the public libraries of this State. The early and rare items, several of which are always on display, include one of the largest files of eighteenth and early nineteenth century newspapers in Vermont.

2. The *Williams Collection of Japanese Art*, in the Norman Williams Library, comprises choice examples of ceramics, ivories, bronzes, and prints, with a particularly beautiful group of netsukes. Though there are some items of considerable antiquity, the collection is more notable for showing the wide range and infinite finesse of modern Oriental craftsmanship.

3. The *Windsor County Courthouse*, first building west of the Library, is as good an example as there is in Vermont of a courthouse in the Georgian Colonial tradition: red brick, with white trim, quoined corners, and an arch-supported domed belfry. It was built in 1855 to replace an earlier courthouse that burned on the same site.

4. The *Old White Meeting House* (Congregational), Elm St., the oldest church in town (1808), was renovated in 1859 and 1890. The restoration is not perfect, since the original front entrance was eliminated, but the present balance of porticoed entrance and porte-cochère is not unpleasing. The graceful Bulfinch tower, white against the surrounding elms, houses a bell cast by Paul Revere and Sons. The *Christian* (1816) and *Universalist* (1835) Churches have bells by the same patriot and bell-founder, as does also the modern *Episcopal Church*.

5. The *Hutchinson House* (1794), across from the savings bank on the business square, is now a part of the White Cupboard Inn. Its outline is relieved by the ample-pillared side porch on the east. The end façade facing the bank has a fine third-story pediment whose arrangement of windows and shuttered openings, asymmetrical from that of the first two stories, makes a happy architectural climax to what might have been mere bulk.

6. The *Johnson House* (1809), the third house north of the Elm Tree Press on Elm St., is the best example of the late Georgian Colonial or Federal style of architecture in town. It has a distinguished Ionic-pillared portico, a roof balustrade, and four assertive end chimneys. The yew hedge surrounding the large lawns and gardens is matchless within the limits of this State.

7. The *Bailey House* (1823), west across the street from the Woodstock Inn, is an excellent example of the architectural solidity combined with grace that could be fashioned in the Georgian mode from brick and wood. It is notable for its fenestration and the square ends incorporating the four end chimneys.

The examples mentioned above are chosen arbitrarily from the many beautiful old houses lining the streets of Woodstock of which interested visitors will want to make a more comprehensive examination.

# III. HIGH ROADS AND LOW ROADS

TOUR 1: *From* MASSACHUSETTS LINE (*Greenfield*) *to* CANADIAN LINE (*Sherbrooke*), 197.2 *m.*, US 5.

Via (*sec. a*) Guilford, Brattleboro, Dummerston, Putney, Westminster, Bellows Falls, Weathersfield, Windsor, White River Junction; (*sec. b*) Norwich, Fairlee, Bradford, Newbury, Wells River, Barnet; (*sec. c*) St. Johnsbury, Lyndonville, Barton, Orleans, Coventry, Newport, Derby Line.

The Canadian Pacific R.R. and B. & M. R.R. parallel this route throughout.

Road is hard-surfaced except for a few short sections.

ONE of the main arteries of travel between New England and Eastern Canada, US 5 is an important thoroughfare along the lovely Connecticut Valley. The route follows closely the wilderness trail blazed by the Indians and taken up by the pioneers, and is the identical route used by one party of Rogers' Rangers in their southward flight to Charlestown, New Hampshire (Old Number Four), after raiding and burning the Indian village of St. Francis in 1759. In foraging through an unbroken wilderness, it was customary to follow the waterways, which in this case parallel US 5 — from Lake Memphremagog up the Barton River to Crystal Lake, along the Passumpsic River to the Connecticut, and down the Connecticut to Charlestown. Where now the sleek, powerful automobiles of a great nation race smoothly along winding ribbons of cement, less than two centuries ago a band of fighting woodsmen, facing death from wounds, starvation, and exposure, struggled through a dense wilderness.

*Sec. a. Massachusetts Line to White River Junction, 76.9 m.*

This southern section of the route lies mostly through the fertile Connecticut Valley. In general the country is more populous and less rural in aspect than most parts of the State, though many of the towns have been declining in population for more than a century, and Windsor County as a whole reached its peak of population in 1830. The southern end of the route passes through some of the earliest settled and consequently most historically interesting towns in the State.

The MASSACHUSETTS LINE, 0 *m.*

North of the State Line, US 5 runs through a diversified countryside, with the long hill of East Mountain (L) relieved by low valley lands.

GUILFORD (alt. 400, pop. township 663), 7.5 *m.*, is a small triangular village on Broad Brook in the township of the same name. Though no formal pitched battle was ever fought here, the town has probably been the scene of more internal strife and violence than any other in the State. It was granted by New Hampshire in 1754 and governed by committees of its own choosing until May 19, 1772, when its inhabitants voted of their own will that Guilford was in the County of Cumberland, Province

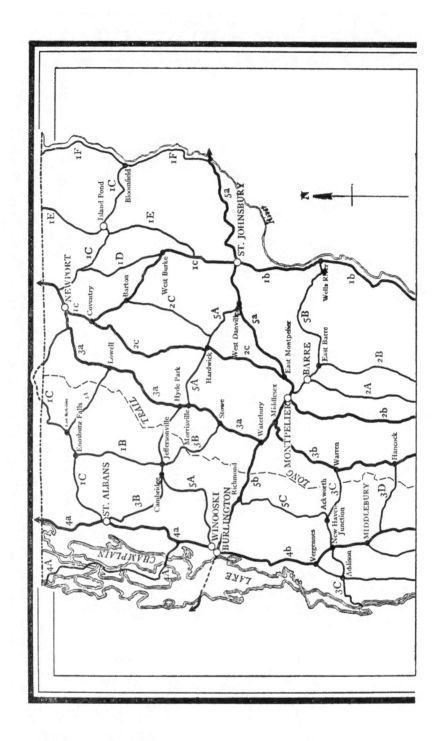

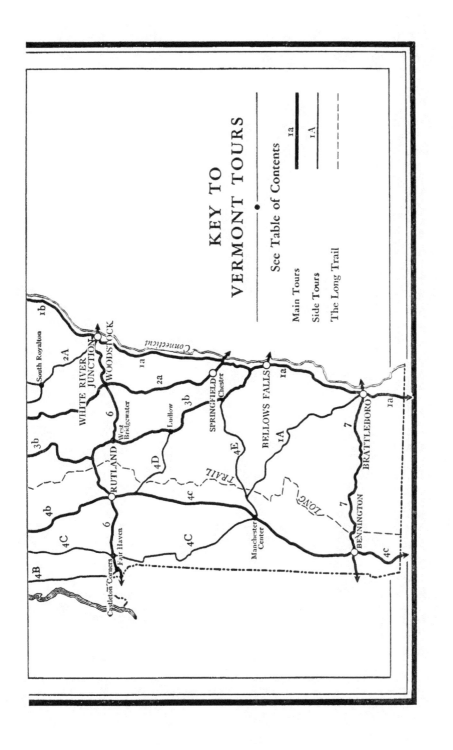

KEY TO
VERMONT TOURS

•

See Table of Contents

Main Tours          1a

Side Tours          1A

The Long Trail

of New York, and chose officers agreeable to the laws of that province. Beginning in 1776, however, an increasing number of residents began to question this jurisdiction, and there followed a period of fifteen years — until Vermont's admission into the Union in 1791 — during which the town was literally in a state of continuous civil war, with intermittent manifestations of physical violence. There were two sets of town officers and two town meetings, both heavily armed and augmented by armed sympathizers from neighboring towns, especially Brattleboro. The record for the May town meeting of 1782 reads in one place: 'Then the people met in general and voted to stand against the pretended State of Vermont.' That, of course, is from the records of the 'Yorker' faction. The Patriots' records no one can quote. They were stolen by the Yorkers and buried under the earth in the town pound for stray animals. When finally recovered, they were in an almost complete state of disintegration, barely recognizable for what they were. In the summer of 1783, Ethan Allen arrived in Guilford with 100 Green Mountain Boys and issued a proclamation whose language makes the phraseology he used at Ticonderoga seem almost equivocal: 'I, Ethan Allen, declare that unless the people of Guilford peaceably submit to the authority of Vermont, the town shall be made as desolate as were the cities of Sodom and Gomorrah, by God.' (There is a school of historians that prefers to omit the last comma in the quotation, but they are a minority.) He then established martial law, and the Vermont constable, for the first time, collected taxes from everyone who was supposed to pay them. But Ethan Allen had larger matters in hand than the proctoring of Guilford, and from 1784 to 1791 the town continued in a state that can only be called anarchy. When the authority of Vermont could no longer be questioned or resisted, a large majority of the Yorkers fled to the State to which they had been loyal. Bainbridge, in Chenango County, New York, was settled almost wholly by emigrants from Guilford.

Guilford's early growth was, relatively judged, meteoric, and in 1790, despite the loss of many Yorkers, it was, with 2432 inhabitants, the most populous town in the State. This was partly due to immigration and partly to the large families, exceeding even the norm of that time, that were the rule here. A detailed local census taken in 1772 shows that of the 84 married men living here then, only one, Captain William Bullock, was without issue, a distinction that he later removed. Not even in Vermont is Ethan Allen regarded as a divinely inspired prophet; and Guilford today, with its tea houses, tourist homes, summer residences, and fertile farms, is far removed yet from the ashes of desolation; still, remembering Ethan's unheeded threat, it is perhaps just worth noting that Guilford is the *only* town in Vermont whose population has shown a decrease in *every* census since 1790.

The name of *Governor's Mountain*, in the extreme northwestern part of town, is an example of Colonial irony. Governor Wentworth, in the original charter of Guilford, stipulated that 500 acres of land be reserved for him; and so it was — on the only considerable peak in the township, 1823 feet above sea level.

In 1791, Royall Tyler settled in Guilford and began the legal practice that culminated in his becoming, in 1807, Chief Justice of Vermont. Here he probably studied from life models the prototypes of Updyke Underhill, the first true Yankee character in literature and the narrator of Tyler's novel, 'The Algerine Captive,' 1797 (*see Literature*). Another pioneer settler who played an important rôle in shaping the early history of Vermont was Benjamin Carpenter. His large marble tombstone, in the western section of town, has a long inscription, listing his many services to the State, which concludes: 'Left this world and 146 persons of lineal posterity, March 29, 1804, aged 78 years, 10 months and 12 days, with a strong mind and full faith of a more glorious state hereafter. Stature about six feet — weight 200. Death had no terror.' A real Guilford man.

North of Guilford, US 5 runs through pleasant woodland before entering the Connecticut Valley at Brattleboro.

> BRATTLEBORO (alt. 300, pop. 9816) (*see BRATTLEBORO*), 9.9 *m.* Site of Fort Dummer, first permanent white settlement in the State; home of Estey organs; Estey Estate and summer theater; Center Congregational Church; All Souls Church; public library; Brattleboro Retreat; Austine School for Deaf; Brattleboro Outing Club and ski jump.

At 10.7 *m.*, US 5 crosses West River near its junction with the Connecticut.

At 12.6 *m.* is the junction with a country road.

> Left on this road and right from the next junction is *Naulahka* (*private*), 2 *m.*, the former home of Rudyard Kipling, who married Caroline Balestier of Brattleboro in 1892 and made his home here until late in 1896. Here he wrote the two 'Jungle Books,' 'The Seven Seas,' 'The Day's Work,' 'Captains Courageous,' and two short pieces that are included in 'Notes of Travel.' The house was designed by Kipling, and built by Jean Pigeon and nine assistants from Quebec on a rocky hillside looking across the huge Connecticut Valley to the grim bulk of Wantastiquet on the New Hampshire side of the river. The long bungalow type of structure, 90 × 30 feet, is of wood, the roof and sides shingled with dull green shingles, and rests on a high solid foundation of stone. Naulahka still retains the air of planned seclusion that Kipling found conducive to the creation of some of his best work. While Kipling may have loved the house and its setting, he had little fondness for the people of the neighborhood, as he makes plainly apparent in his posthumous autobiography, 'Something of Myself' (1937): '... so they watched as secretively as the New England or British peasant can, and what toleration they extended to the "Britisher" was solely for the sake of "the Balestier girl."'

North of this point, the route continues through the township of DUMMERSTON (pop. 604). Granted in 1753 as Fullam, the town assumed the name of Dummerston in very early days, but the charter was never changed or regranted. Not until 1937 did the Legislature confirm the name under which Dummerston had been conducting its affairs for more than a century and a half. The town reached its peak of population in 1810, when it had nearly three times as many people as it has today. From here the father of Rutherford B. Hayes emigrated to Ohio in 1817, five years before the birth of the future president.

PUTNEY (alt. 580, pop. township 835), 19.4 *m.*, is a quiet village with an antique flavor, the chief settlement in the township of the same name.

Putney was settled by white men in 1740, and a garrison was erected in the center of the fertile Great Meadow that lies in a bend of the Connecticut in the northeastern part of town. The fort was evacuated at the outbreak of the Cape Breton War in 1744. Settlement began again in 1753, and in 1755 a second fort was built, within which fifteen dwellings were erected, the main wall of the fort forming the back wall of the houses. In the fourth and fifth decades of the 19th century, Putney was for a number of years the scene of activity of one of the most magnetic, elusive, and provocative of the many American religious fanatics of that time whose bands of converted followers were convinced beyond logic and beyond the persuasion of persecution that the particular aberrations from Christianity of their particular Messiah were based 'upon the immutable basis of an apodictical principle.' This man was John Humphrey Noyes, son of a Vermont Congressman, and first cousin, on his mother's side, of President Rutherford B. Hayes. Born in Brattleboro in 1811, Noyes was 'converted' to the Congregational Church in Putney, after being graduated from Dartmouth at the age of nineteen, and continued his studies at the theological schools at Andover, Massachusetts, and Yale College. While at New Haven, Noyes became interested in the doctrine of the Perfectionists, a sect which he influenced so vitally that he is often erroneously stated to have founded it. In January, 1837, after the woman he wished to marry had married another man, Noyes wrote his famous 'Battle-Axe Letter,' so-called because the man he wrote it to caused it to be published in the same year in the 'Battle-Axe and Weapons of War,' a Philadelphia publication whose editor agreed with Noyes's ideas. Among other things this letter stated: 'In a holy community there is no more reason why sexual intercourse should be restrained by law, than why eating and drinking should be — and there is as little occasion for shame in one case as in the other.' Noyes came to Putney in 1838 and soon collected a band of followers here. Despite the unequivocality of the passage quoted above, it was nearly a decade before the citizens of Putney realized that he had led his followers from communism of property, through communism of households, to communism of love, or, as he called it, Complex Marriage. He was arrested on October 25, 1847, gave bond for his appearance for trial, and then with irreligious haste fled to Oneida, New York, where he was later followed by a considerable number of his group. There his influence ultimately resulted in much good. He agreed, in his own words, to 'give up the practice of Complex Marriage, not as renouncing belief in principles and prospective finality of that institution, but in deference to public sentiment.' The Oneida Community was reorganized on January 1, 1881, as a joint-stock company, and 'Bible Communism' came to an end. The admirable subsequent history of the Community as a social and economic experiment is well known. But Putney, subconsciously, perhaps, has never quite recovered from the thunderbolt of horror that hit it in 1847 when it learned what it had been harboring. As recently as 1935, a summer dramatic school that had been conducted here was forced to move because its members persisted in wearing shorts in public. There are still standing in Putney village houses where the Perfectionists lived — three and four families to a house — but they are not designated by plaques or markers, and the casual tourist is not strongly urged to attempt to locate them.

Putney is the home of George D. Aiken, the present (1937) Governor of Vermont.

> On a remodeled hill farm west of Putney village is the *Putney School*, 3 *m.*, a private institution founded in 1935 along experimental lines. Its emphasis upon individual needs and aptitudes of its students, the two long vacation periods, and its consistent attempt to correlate text-book learning with extra-curricular experience make it more or less the secondary school counterpart of Bennington College (*see Education*). The members of the school and the local residents maintain an unusually close relationship. Students, for instance, who are raising animals on the school farm, as many are, are almost invariably members of the Putney 4-H Club. The autumn Harvest Festival is a community gathering in the best and fullest sense of the phrase. The tuition fee, which is rather high, provides one summer every two years in Europe, where students live in typical Austrian, German, or French homes with associates of their own age. For the accommodation of relatives and young friends of the student body, an inn and a Youth Hostel are maintained in connection with the school.

The countryside between Putney and Westminster is rolling and somewhat less open than that through which the route passes to the north.

WESTMINSTER (alt. 314, pop. township 1324), 27.3 *m.*, is a restful-looking village lying on the mile-wide plain of one of the most beautiful of the many terrace formations on the Connecticut. Its present serenity gives no hint of the violence and strife that made Vermont history here in Revolutionary and pre-Revolutionary days. Westminster was granted, probably in 1735, as Number One. The land was divided into 63 allotments; a sawmill and at least one house were built; and roads were laid out. Most important among the latter was the die-straight two-mile stretch known from the earliest days as *The King's Highway*, which runs through Westminster village northward to Westminster Station. Its unusual width (originally ten rods, now six), which contributes so much to the charm of Westminster, was due to its being designed as a training ground for the early military companies of this section. The first settlement was abandoned in 1740, when the decision on the northern boundary line of Massachusetts excluded Number One, or New Taunton, as it had come to be called, from that province. The town was regranted by Governor Wentworth of New Hampshire in 1752, and within fifteen years more than fifty families had located here. In 1772 was built the courthouse in which the then Cumberland County (New York) Court held its sessions. Loyalty to New York had never been universal, however, even in this section, and that province's refusal to adopt the resolves of the Continental Congress increased the dissatisfaction. On March 13, 1775, an armed party of local men took possession of the courthouse, refusing admittance to the court officials. The latter procured a sheriff and an armed force, and that night fired into the building, killing one William French (*see below*) and wounding several others, at least one of whom died of his wounds. This was the 'Westminster Massacre.' Since the British were at most only indirectly responsible for it, it is not rightly to be called, as it often is, the first engagement of the Revolution. It was important, however, because of the temper it displayed and the resentment it aroused. It was at a convention held in Westminster that Vermont, on January 15, 1777, declared itself a free and independent State.

The first printing office in Vermont was established at Westminster in 1778 by Judah Paddock Spooner and Timothy Green. In 1781, they issued here the State's first newspaper, *The Vermont Gazette*, or *The Green Mountain Post Boy*. Their press was the Stephen Daye press, the first one used on this continent north of Mexico and now preserved in the museum of the Vermont Historical Society (*see MONTPELIER*).

The modern brick *Community Hall* (officially Westminster Institute) (R) dominates the center of the village. It was built in 1923, the gift of G. A. Dascomb, a local philanthropist who left $250,000 for its erection and maintenance. It contains a gymnasium-auditorium, various clubrooms, children's rooms, the Butterfield Library (public), and a *Museum* (*open daily; adm. free*). The Museum preserves many relics pertinent to Westminster's florid and vivacious past, including copies of *The Green Mountain Post Boy;* a drum used in the Revolution; a door panel with a bullet hole made, it is stoutly maintained, by one of the bullets that killed William French; a Revolutionary cannon ball embedded in a tree; a large number of letters and original documents; and a sizable collection of rocks and minerals.

William French is buried in the old *Cemetery* (L) at the north end of the village. His headstone, with a long inscription telling how he was shot 'by the hands of cruel ministerial tools of George ye 3rd,' is an exact copy of the original one, which was destroyed when the old church here in which it had been placed burned many years ago. Here is buried also Judge Thomas Chandler, except for whose duplicity the Westminster Massacre would probably never have taken place. Chandler died in a debtor's cell in the very courthouse he caused to be fired upon. Because of a legal technicality regarding burial, it was several days after his death before his body, in a rough wooden box, was dragged to the jail wall and thrown into a hole that had been dug in a slanting direction into the cemetery. Beside the road (R) across from the cemetery is a curious white stone *Monument*, in the form of a wide chair, to the memory of William French and the old courthouse (razed in 1806) in which he inadvertently became, if not a hero, at least a remembered name to the posterity of this State.

West from the center of Westminster village, on a hill overlooking the broad plain, is *Kurn Hattin Home* (boys' section) (*visitors welcome*), 1.3 m. This home school for needy children, founded in 1894, is named for Kurn Hattin Hill, in Palestine. The plant, which can accommodate 100 boys, includes a school building, administration building, three dormitory cottages, a manual arts building, and a farm of 300 acres. The Home has a press and prints its own monthly and yearly bulletins. In this well-administered, debt-free institution, in a beautiful natural setting, boys between the ages of 7 and 14 can complete their elementary schooling and receive, in addition, extensive training in manual arts and crafts.

WESTMINSTER STATION, 29.2 *m.*, consists of a railroad depot and a few dwellings. It is the northern terminus of the King's Highway.

North of Westminster, the countryside is fertile agricultural land. For several miles there is a noticeable number of large orchards, this being one of the leading apple-growing districts in the State. The view to the north and east on the southern approach to Bellows Falls is striking, if not entirely beautiful, with denuded Mt. Kilburn, in New Hampshire, brooding over the busy, smoke-hung town in somewhat sinister protectiveness.

> BELLOWS FALLS (alt. 309, pop. 3930) (*see BELLOWS FALLS*), 33.3 *m.* Industrial center, with large paper mills and other factories; Bellows Falls Hydro-Electric Corp.; Rockingham Free Public Library; Immanuel Episcopal Church; home of Hetty Green; and other points of interest.

> Left from the south end of Bellows Falls, State 121 leads through the shallow Saxtons River Valley to SAXTONS RIVER (alt. 920), 4.5 *m.*, the seat of Vermont Academy. The village lies at a broadening of the valley rimmed with hills. The white *Baptist Church* (L.) is gray-trimmed, with a slate roof. The *Congregational Church*, of white-painted wood, lifts its needle spire from a square base over the head of Main St. *Vermont Academy*, a preparatory school for boys with an enrollment of about 100, is situated on a wide level plateau overlooking the northern side of town. Three red-brick buildings stand above the maples and elms that shade the green sward of the campus: Jones Hall (R), the original academy building, and Alumni Hall (L), the dormitories, flank Fuller Hall, the administration and recitation building. To the rear are Proctor Dining Hall, the small stone Wilbur Library, and the gymnasium, with the athletic field and Bowl Pond in the background. The setting is pleasant, and the atmosphere of the school is friendly and homelike. There are 11 instructors for the 100 students; classes are small and informal. Vermont Academy was founded in 1876 as a co-educational institution and reorganized in 1931 as a boarding school for boys only. The majority of students come from outside the State, and in 1936 Vermont Academy graduates enrolled in 18 different colleges. Extra-curricular activities of a diversified nature are strongly encouraged, with stress on both athletic and cultural interests. Emphasis is placed on friendliness and a family-like environment. A pioneer in the field of winter sports, Vermont Academy was instrumental in the development and spreading fame of the Dartmouth Winter Carnival.

At 36.6 *m.* is the junction with State 103 (*see Tour* 3). From this point the route bears eastward through lightly populated country, crossing the Williams River, 37.1 *m.*, near its junction with the Connecticut. North of this junction, the large level tracts lying in the elbows of the two sharp bends in the Connecticut are the Lower Meadow, on the New Hampshire side, and the Upper Meadows, on the Vermont side. The jurisdiction of the Connecticut between Vermont and New Hampshire has presented several knotty problems in the past that have not yet been solved to the entire satisfaction of all concerned; but the manner in which the Connecticut itself has allotted its rich valley lands is, in a long view, remarkably equitable.

Northward the country grows more heavily wooded. There is little arable valley land in this section, and the Connecticut itself is lost to view. This is the wildest and most scenic part of the route between Bellows Falls and the crossing of the Black River. The road is known as the Missing Link Road, because it was for a time, before the stretch north

of Norwich deteriorated, the only part of US 5 that was not hard-surfaced. The Missing Link Road was partially black-topped during 1936
and will be completed, or nearly completed, during 1937.

Turning right across the turbid Black River, the route makes a junction
with State 11 at 44.2 m. (*see Tour 2 and SPRINGFIELD*). Turning
right again at the junction, it continues eastward to the *Cheshire Toll
Bridge* (*toll* 15¢), 45.1 m., which crosses the Connecticut into New Hampshire (Charlestown).

The *Granite Marker* (L), at 45.9 m., designates the site of the eastern
terminus of the Old Crown Point Road (*see Transportation*). When the
road was built, and for long afterward, the Wentworth Ferry was in
operation across the Connecticut at this point.

The *General Lewis Morris House* (L), 47.5 m., one of the oldest and finest
houses in the township of Springfield, was built in 1795 on a beautiful
site overlooking the Connecticut. The square, white-painted house, with
two large square chimneys rising from its almost flat roof, has a sturdy
severity relieved by only a few touches — such as the modillioned cornice
— of a purely ornamental purpose. Except for the front porch, itself
less objectionable than most architectural afterthoughts, this is a typical
northern New England country 'mansion' of its period.

The route continues past level valley farms, with the Connecticut close
to the highway.

WEATHERSFIELD BOW (alt. 362), 54.2 m., is a small settlement that
gets its name from the ox-bow bends in the Connecticut at this point.
It was here that William Jarvis purchased 2000 acres of land when he
returned to this country in 1810 from Lisbon, where he had been U.S.
Consul in Portugal for nine years. In 1811 he brought here the 400
merino sheep that he had purchased, by special dispensation, from the
Escurial royal flock of Spain — almost the very first, and the first considerable number, of that jealously guarded breed to be brought to this
country. For 48 years Mr. Jarvis bred merinos at Weathersfield Bow,
while the community basked in the distinction of having been the point
of introduction into this State of the animal that was to dominate its
agriculture for half a century.

The *Wilgus State Forest Park*, 56.3 m., consists of 129 acres of park and
forest land given to the State by Colonel William J. Wilgus. The park
lies on both sides of the highway, with a lodge and picnic areas in the
eastern part. Tent camping is not permitted here.

ASCUTNEYVILLE (alt. 412), 57.4 m., was named for the mountain in
whose shadow it lies — a quiet, shady four-corner village relatively untouched by the streams of traffic that flow through it. Ascutneyville is the
chief trading center in the eastern part of the township of Weathersfield
(pop. 1156). This town had as many inhabitants in 1791 as it has today and
was commercially thriving during the greater part of the 19th century,
chiefly in connection with the lime and soapstone deposits in the western
section of the town. Among the earliest settlers were several Revolution-

ary soldiers who showed a spirit of individual independence amounting almost to a disregard for all authority. William Dean, son of Captain William Dean of Windsor, moved here before the Revolution. In 1769, he and his brother and their father were arrested and taken to New York City for violating the charter restrictions against cutting the tall white pines that were reserved for masting the King's navy. The Deans were convicted and spent several months in the New York jail. The affair of the 'Dean boys' became something of a Colonial *cause célèbre* and was actually of significance in the contest between New Hampshire and New York for the jurisdiction over what is now Vermont. Jonathan Allen, who came here from Connecticut, took part in the battle of Bunker Hill — too eager a part: a portion of one of his ears was cut off with a saber by his own commander for shooting a British officer before the order to fire was given.

In Weathersfield was born Isaac Eddy, the first Vermont engraver, whose life the most diligent research by scholarly collectors has left shrouded in mystery and contradictory evidence. It is known that he was in Weathersfield in 1812 from an engraving in a book of that date signed 'Isaac Eddy sc. Weathersfield, Vt.' In 1814 he took over the Stephen Daye press, at Windsor. Judging from an oration he delivered in Weathersfield in 1805, when he was only 26 years old, Eddy was a man of considerable learning. His engravings, however, though eagerly sought after today, are admittedly crude. Typical of his work are the plates he did for the first Vermont Bible, published in Windsor in 1812, in which all of the characters are depicted with extravagantly Hebraic features.

Between Ascutneyville and Windsor the road is double-lane cement.

At 58.2 *m.* is a junction with a dirt road.

> Left on this road is *Mt. Ascutney* (alt. 3320), 2.7 *m.*, the terrain of which constitutes *Ascutney State Forest Park*. A surfaced three-mile parkway winds up the mountain to the Saddle, which is about 500 feet lower than the summit. There are three picnic areas and several winter ski runs. The parkway is the realization of a more-than-century-old dream. When it became known that Lafayette was to visit Vermont in 1825, a carriage road to the top of Ascutney was projected, that from that coign of vantage the Marquis might see as much as possible in one panorama of a State that, like the rest of the country, was searching for new ways of doing the old soldier affectionate honor. But Lafayette came too soon. The road was not completed at that time, though there is some evidence that it was actually begun. Because of the variety of its rock composition and because it is the most important mountain of eruptive origin in the State, Ascutney has been accorded special study by the U.S. Geological Survey. 'The Geology of Ascutney Mountain, Vermont,' by Reginald Aldworth Daly (Washington, Government Printing Office, 1903; 122 pp.), is recommended to those who seek a scientific understanding of this isolated and far-dominating peak.
>
> WINDSOR (alt. 354, pop. 3689) (*see WINDSOR*), 62.1 *m.* Scene of the adoption of the Vermont Constitution; State Prison and House of Correction; Cone Automatic Machine Company; Old South Church; Old Constitution House; Evarts House; Masonic House; and other points of interest.

The *Hour Glass Country Club and Golf Course* (9 *holes, greens fee* $1 *a day*), (R), 63.4 *m.*, is a beautifully landscaped course on two main levels, with tall pines and shrubs that give it an almost parklike appearance. Directly across the road is the former summer home of the late Marie Dressler. The view across the Connecticut in this section is unobstructed, with the New Hampshire hills rising beyond. The countryside between this point and Hartland is particularly pleasing and prosperous-looking. Several of the large dairy farms have fine old farmhouses where tourists are accommodated.

HARTLAND (alt. 416, pop. township 1266), 66.6 *m.*, is the central village in Hartland Township. Originally chartered as Hertford, the name was changed to Hartland by act of legislature in 1782 to avoid confusion with Hartford to the north — a change that strangers sometimes find insufficient still. Hartland village radiates from a highway four-corners. At the junction is a *Soldiers' Monument* (L) that economically commemorates the veterans of three wars. The *Sumner-Steele House* on the knoll (R) around which the highway curves in the village is a dignified expression of the American Georgian style of architecture. The Palladian window is very fine, and the white lawn balustrade that stretches in front of the house, though not the original one, is a rare and authentic feature. The house was built in 1804 by David Sumner, a wealthy merchant and mill-owner. It descended to his daughter, the wife of Benjamin Steele, who in 1856 was appointed to the bench of the Vermont Supreme Court when he was 28 years of age, the youngest man ever to hold that position. About a quarter-mile northeast of the village are the grounds of the annual *Hartland Community Fair Horse Show*, where each August the finest horses in this part of the State, as well as the out-of-State strings of several summer residents, compete in more than a score of classes, with special emphasis on jumping.

Hartland was settled by Timothy Lull, who in the spring of 1763 paddled his family up the Connecticut River from Dummerston in a hollowed-out-log canoe. Lull's Brook, in the southern part of town, he christened by breaking a junk bottle of liquor and spilling the contents in the presence of his family, no trivial gesture to make at that distance from any source of further supply. The settlement grew so rapidly that by 1791 it was the most populous town in the county, having, in fact, about 400 more inhabitants within its borders than it has today. Perhaps it was the friction of over-congestion, by pioneer standards, that caused the men of Hartland to act so 'unlawfully, riotously, and routously' as they did on several occasions. In 1786 about thirty of them, with a few additions from Barnard, assembled fully armed at Windsor to prevent the sitting of the county court there. The leader was fined and imprisoned, and the Hartland insurgents assembled again, in greater numbers this time, to rescue him. High Sheriff Benjamin Wait captured twenty-seven of them in an early morning surprise attack on Lull's house, and lodged them in the jail at Windsor. Thereupon more than a hundred sympathizers gathered at Captain Lull's house, and only the hurried assembling of 600 men under arms at Windsor kept this miniature Shays' Rebellion from assuming tragic proportions.

North of Hartland the valley broadens, and there are many fine vistas to the east.

NORTH HARTLAND (alt. 383), (R.R. station Evarts), 72.3 *m.*, is a small rustic residential village, formerly the seat of large woolen mills. The falls here at the junction of the Ottaquechee with the Connecticut were the scene of one of the climaxes in the retreat of Rogers' Rangers, 1759 (*see NEWPORT*). The four raftsmen headed by Major Rogers were drifting downstream on the rude unwieldy float they had made at the foot of the White River Falls, where they had nearly been swept to death. They landed above the Ottaquechee rapids, faced with the problem of getting past the falls and retaining their raft for the remainder of the voyage, knowing that if this raft was lost it meant the end for them and their comrades waiting upstream for rescue. They were too weary and weak from hunger to endure the labor of building another. While the Rangers held the raft at the head of the rapids, Rogers walked to the foot of the falls and prepared to swim out and board the raft when it came down. The bound timbers hurtled over the falls, and Rogers plunged out and clambered aboard, to fight the current and bring the log craft ashore by paddling with the strength of desperation. He made the river bank, and the four men camped there overnight, spent and exhausted. In the morning they put out again and rode the current down to a point near Fort Number Four, at Charlestown, New Hampshire. Rogers himself, tireless and indomitable, led the party back upstream with supplies, and most of his men were saved. On the entire expedition, through the most terrible perils and hardships, Rogers lost 50 of the 200 men who started with him from Crown Point.

At 75.7 *m.* are the former Vermont State Fair Grounds. The Fair was discontinued several years ago after a succession of years when rainy weather during the exhibition week left it financially unstable. During its heyday, in the first two decades of this century, there were larger exhibits of Morgan horses of the best modern type assembled here for show-ring competition than have ever been brought together anywhere else. In recent years the grounds have served as a municipal airport, and the daily passenger transport line of the Central Vermont Airways (Boston & Maine Transportation Company) made here one of its three scheduled stops within the State. This stop has been discontinued, however, because the field does not meet the minimum safety requirements established by the National Government.

WHITE RIVER JUNCTION (alt. 340), 76.9 *m.*, where rivers, roads, and railways converge, is an appropriately named town that has been commercially enterprising since the early days of locks and canals on the Connecticut. The bleakness inseparable from a railroad center distinguishes White River Junction from other Connecticut Valley villages. Its crowded business center gives no hint of the pleasantly terraced residential districts, but is overshadowed by the proximity of soot-stained railroad sheds and a network of tracks. Not uncommon in more industrialized sections of the country, this aspect is an unusual one in Vermont, creating something of a shock in contrast with the clean, shady villages characteristic of the valley.

The murky atmosphere of Depot Square has been somewhat alleviated by a new post-office building, the modern bulk of which looks rather out of place, and accentuates the narrowness of the street. The diners along Main Street are usually crowded with red-faced railroad men in blue overalls and husky truck-drivers in leather jackets, while just across the way, the hotel and restaurants are frequently thronged with Dartmouth undergraduates wearing casually their tailored sports clothes. The transient business of White River is extremely heavy, and the resultant pattern of life complex and changing.

The village is a wholesale business center as well as a railroad junction. As a majority of travelers bound for Hanover get off the train at White River, the town is closely linked with Dartmouth College, and is enlivened and brightened periodically throughout the year by this association. On football weekends and other special occasions, White River is invaded by crowds in the holiday spirit, becoming a dull background for colorful scenes of merriment and revelry. Between these high points, the unceasing ebb and flow of transient life saves White River from monotony and inertia. The depot here also serves the summer and winter resort town of Woodstock (*see WOODSTOCK*).

*Sec. b, White River Junction to St. Johnsbury, 66.2 m.*

This section of the route closely follows the Connecticut River, the pathway that led the first settlers northward into an unbroken wilderness. The river, winding calmly along its rich green valley, once knew the thrust of Indian and pioneer paddles, and reflected the campfires of red man and white. Major Rogers and three starving Rangers floated downstream on a raft to reach the fort at Charlestown, New Hampshire. The pleasant villages along the valley have pre-Revolutionary backgrounds.

WHITE RIVER JUNCTION, 0 *m.*

Just north of White River Junction across the White River, the residential section lies along the north bank, in agreeable contrast to the unrelieved industrial and commercial aspect of the village center.

The rapids at the confluence of the White and Connecticut Rivers nearly took the lives of Rogers and his three scouts. Battling the tug of swift water, they barely made shore above the falls. There they had to abandon the raft, walk to the foot of the falls, and build another. Rogers accomplished this by burning down trees, and burning the trunks off at the proper length. Meanwhile Captain Ogden had the good fortune to shoot a partridge, which provided sustenance for the last lap of their terrible journey.

WILDER (alt. 430), 1.9 *m.*, was originally known as Olcott Falls, from the falls in the Connecticut here, by which large paper mills were established. Since the mills closed, the water-power is utilized by the New England Power Association, and Wilder is little more than a residential suburb of White River Junction. Its modernity is indicated in the regular pattern of planned streets and close-set houses.

Between Wilder and Norwich, US 5 follows a section of what has been known since earliest settlement days as Christian Street.

NORWICH (alt. 536, pop. township 1371), 7 m., was chartered (New Hampshire) as Norwhich, but the *h* was dropped. Resting cool-shaded under the dense foliage of maples, the village has a venerable charm. Old frame houses sit back on picket-fenced lawns, and the scene is pervaded with the atmosphere of Old New England. *Norwich University* was founded here in 1820, but removed to Northfield in 1867 (see *Tour 2, NORTHFIELD, and Education*). The original Norwich Military Academy Building once occupied the broad Common (R) where the public school now stands. With Hanover just across the river, a strong natural feud was carried on between Dartmouth and Norwich students, and there were many roistering expeditions back and forth across the Connecticut. In the *Old Cemetery* (left from Main St.) there are stones dated as early as 1770, with the usual curious inscriptions. Three rear admirals were born in Norwich: Stephen Rand, George Converse, and George Colvocoresses. The Boston musical and dramatic critic, Philip Hale, was also born here.

Between Norwich and Pompanoosuc, highway and railroad swing eastward to closely parallel the river in its narrow valley.

POMPANOOSUC (alt. 392), 14.7 m., lying near the junction of the Ompompanoosuc with the Connecticut, consists, along US 5, of pastureland and cornfields with a few straggling homes, a lattice-type covered bridge, and a railroad depot. The main part of the settlement is west of the highway, built around an old sawmill on the Ompompanoosuc and marked by lumber piles and heaps of yellow sawdust.

Left from Pompanoosuc on a country road is UNION VILLAGE (alt. 440), 3 m., a settlement in Thetford Township. Once an active little mill village, it is now a sleepy hamlet stretched under mighty elms in the lee of a bare ridge that shelters the Ompompanoosuc Valley. The brick-built *Methodist Church* was dedicated in 1837.

Between Pompanoosuc and East Thetford is one of the finest river scenes of the route, with the smooth Connecticut coursing deep and strong between gently curving banks.

EAST THETFORD (alt. 408), 17.1 m., is simply a scattering of wooden homesteads about the fertile tillage of the valley, and the railway depot at Thetford.

Left from East Thetford on an uphill country road is the *Coombs House*, 2 m., a simple white farmhouse with green blinds, a story-and-a-half with a long pitch roof and low-hung eaves. This unpretentious structure achieved fame through a photograph of it, taken by New York artist Clara Sipprell, that won first prize in the International Gold Medal Contest.

Straight beyond on the uphill road is THETFORD HILL (alt. 939, pop. township 1052), 2.3 *m.*, an attractive and secluded upland village, with an air of quiet refinement in the white houses, church, and school surrounding the irregular elm-shaded green. The atmosphere is enlightened by a kind of intellectual awareness, not usual to such a small rural village in the hills. The *Old Congregational Church*, erected in 1787, is the oldest church in the State in continuous use since construction. The tower and bell were added in 1830, and further remodeling was done in 1858. Rev. Asa Burton (1752–1836), prominent among the ministers of his time, served this church for 57 years. As a boy Burton helped clear the Dartmouth campus of trees, and was later graduated from that institution. *Thetford Academy* (L), established in 1819, is housed in a white church-like building with an adjacent dormitory. The Academy, one of the few in the State to remain a private institution, also serves as a high school for local students, through tuitional arrangements with the town. *Latham Memorial Library* (L) was founded in 1877, another evidence of the spirit prevailing in this picturesque hill town.

Richard Wallace was Thetford's Revolutionary hero; in 1777 with Ephraim Webster of Newbury, Wallace volunteered for the hazardous mission of swimming across Lake Champlain from Ticonderoga to Mt. Independence, to deliver important dispatches. The British fleet lay in the middle of the lake. It was late in the fall and swimmers had to follow a zigzag course in order to avoid the blockade. The men passed so close to the enemy boats that they clearly heard the lookout's call, 'All's well.' They swam naked with their clothes bound behind their necks by cords across the forehead. It was a night swim of two miles in ice-cold water past the British fleet, but the dispatches were delivered. Wallace's health was permanently impaired by the chill and strain of the effort. His wife, a true pioneer woman, worked the farm single-handed while Wallace was away in the army.

Straight beyond Thetford Hill is THETFORD CENTER (alt. 668), 3.3 *m.*, a little hamlet near *Lake Abenaki* (alt. 840), which is an elongated body of water enclosed by hills. A girls' camp is situated on the lake. Thetford Center was once a milling village, but now the deserted mills have crumbled and fallen into decay, leaving nothing but a general store, town hall, and a handful of wooden houses.

*Childs Pond* (L), 17.8 *m.*, a small nearly round pond with no inlet or outlet, is on a plateau 143 feet above the level of the Connecticut, and resembles a great mirror lying face-up on the level earth. The fact that the water is almost flush with the flat banks gives it this strange artificial appearance. The pond is 60 feet deep and contains carp and hornpout. Across from the pond is an *Old Graveyard* (R), where forgotten tombstones overlook the Connecticut River. The level tract just north of Childs Pond once served as a race-track, and also as a drill-field for the Thetford militia.

NORTH THETFORD (alt. 399), 19.5 *m.*, is typical of the small clean Connecticut Valley villages, with US 5 passing through on the Main St. between the elm-shaded hedges, lawns, and flower-beds that front the dwellings. White frame houses with green trim are predominant, while several handsome stone structures lend a diversifying touch. The neat white *Congregational Church* harmonizes with the general scene. During the 1936 flood the village was completely inundated, but escaped permanent damage and quickly regained its immaculate appearance.

Between North Thetford and Ely, the highway runs close to the broad deep-flowing Connecticut.

ELY (alt. 464), 22.5 *m.*, is the railroad station and turning-off place for Lake Fairlee. The depot, water-tank, and general store look out of place

in the broad valley with its hayfields and scattered farmsteads. Formerly
this was the railway station for the Ely Copper Mines (*see Tour 2B,
VERSHIRE*) and here, early one July morning in 1883, five National
Guard companies detrained to put down the insurrection of the miners,
that was called the 'Ely War.'

> Left from Ely on a country road is *Lake Fairlee* (alt. 678), 2.6 *m.*, a long, narrow
> body of water with an irregular, pine-clothed shoreline, lying in a basin of low,
> gently ascending hills. Less highly developed as a summer resort than Lake
> Morey (*see below*), Fairlee has a more simple and natural charm, and is almost en-
> tirely devoted to girls' and boys' camps.

Between Ely and Fairlee, US 5 leaves the valley floor for a stretch and
rolls over a more uneven surface.

FAIRLEE (alt. 430, pop. township 456), 27.7 *m.*, lies in the shelter of a
great rock barrier, the 600-foot *Palisades* towering like a fortress wall
over the tranquil river valley. The long wide village street is lined with
century-old houses, and interspersed with them are modern shops serving
the summer visitors to Lake Morey; the village is now commercially dependent upon summer tourist traffic and guests from the near-by lakes.

It has been advanced, not without some grounds, that the world's first
steamboat was invented and operated here on the Connecticut by
Samuel Morey, Fairlee lumberman and inventive genius. As early as
1793, or 14 years before Fulton launched the 'Clermont,' Morey was
plying up and down the river in an absurd little craft barely large enough
to hold himself, the rude machinery connected with his steam boiler, and
an armful of firewood. This was unquestionably one of the earliest steamboats. The next scene is in New York with Morey exhibiting his model
to Fulton and Livingston, and it is said that Fulton later visited Morey
in Fairlee. The details of the affair are clouded and vague. Fulton lives
in history as the creator of the steamboat. Samuel Morey was long since
relegated to obscurity, in spite of the fact that he invented many other
things, including an internal-combustion engine (pat. 1826) that was an
actual prototype of the modern gasoline engine.

> Left from Fairlee on a country road is *Lake Morey* (alt. 416), 0.5 *m.*, a charming
> little body of water set in an amphitheater of wooded hills. It is a well-developed
> summer resort of the fashionable type. There are facilities for all summer and
> water sports in this delightful natural setting. Samuel Morey operated his last
> steamboat here, and a tragic glamour is added to the scene by the story that, dis-
> couraged and embittered by lack of recognition, Captain Morey finally sunk his
> beloved boat in this lake. Many attempts to locate it have failed, but it may be
> deeply imbedded in the muddy bottom today. It is legendary that, on certain
> nights of misty moonlight when stillness is on the water, a tiny ghost steamboat
> slips through the fog. As if the hand on the wheel were restless and distraught, the
> little boat keeps turning this way and that, endlessly seeking a channel of passage
> from the secluded lake to the great outer world.

Between Fairlee and Bradford, the course of the river is straight and the
valley narrow, with rock ledges (L) rearing above the highway in places.

BRADFORD (alt. 405, pop. 598), 32.2 *m.*, originally called Waitstown,
is situated at the junction of Waits River with the Connecticut. Waits
River received its name from an incident in the retreat of Rogers' Rang-

ers. Captain Joseph Waite was leading a small foraging squad down the valley, a group of gaunt emaciated men on the verge of starvation. They started a deer on the banks of this stream, just above its union with the Connecticut, and Waite brought the deer down with the timeliest shot of his life. The venison gave them strength enough to continue the journey and reach the stronghold at Number Four.

Bradford today has some of the virility, induced by the advantages of abundant waterpower, that marks the more active villages of the valley. The culture of strawberries has become significant here, reaching a high degree of perfection on the lowlands of the Connecticut. The Main St. extends between well-shaded lawns, brightened by the presence of many red-brick houses. The narrow central green holds the *Admiral Charles E. Clark Statue;* the *birthplace* of this Spanish-American War hero is a simple shabby house on South Main St. The *Low House* (L), overlooking the Green, is the outstanding structure in the village, built about 1796. The large white mansion is one of late eighteenth-century elegance; its spacious portico is reminiscent of the southern plantation houses. *Wood's Library,* facing the Common and Main St., is an ugly structure of brick and granite in a style resembling 'Cattle Baron' Gothic. The *Craft House,* South Main St., with columned portico, was once a stage tavern.

The old stocks and whipping post once stood on the east side of Main St.; here Colonel Mike Barron, hard-boiled sheriff for 23 years, used personally to lock, and flog with a cat-o'-nine-tails, the transgressors of the law. Captain William Trotter, seaman, soldier-of-fortune, and contrabander, came to live in Bradford in 1804, after a story-book career that made him fairly rich. The first U.S. flag ever seen in the harbor of Buenos Ayres was raised by Trotter, whose commercial voyages took him often to South America. The first geographical globes made in the country were produced by James Wilson, of Bradford, in 1812.

Between Bradford and South Newbury, the Connecticut flows in wide sweeping bends, first swinging close to the road, then looping sharply eastward. Here and there palisades of stone wall the highway (L).

SOUTH NEWBURY (Conicut) (alt. 409), 39.3 *m.*, consists of a group of clapboarded houses on the highway, and a railway station that also serves West Newbury. Maple products are manufactured here.

The *Ox-Bow Cemetery* (R), at the northern edge of Newbury, one of the oldest and most beautiful in the State, contains slate headstones dating from 1761. Old Joe, the Indian guide, who, with his squaw Molly, befriended so many white settlers in various sections of Vermont, is buried here. Joe was a peaceful Indian and a favorite among Newbury pioneers; he received a magnanimous $70-a-year pension from the State for his services to the early settlers.

Captain John, another Newbury Indian, was quite the opposite of Joe. A fierce and bloody warrior of the St. Francis tribe, John had fought against Braddock, and boasted that he tried to shoot young Washington during the engagement. Later John had fought with the Americans against Burgoyne. When a young Newbury savage named Toomalek attempted to kill the Indian who had taken the squaw he loved, his bullet killed the squaw instead. Captain John, presiding as judge at the trial, decreed that Toomalek was no murderer, inasmuch as he had not intended to slay the woman. Toomalek then tomahawked the man whom his bullet had missed, and again John acquitted him. But the third victim of Toomalek was John's own son. In this case there was no question raised as to the killer's guilt, and Captain John acted as executioner with grim satisfaction.

NEWBURY (alt. 418, pop. township 1745), 40.5 *m.*, the first settlement north of Charlestown, New Hampshire, on the Connecticut River, lies in the heart of the *Coos Country*, where great double bends in the river leave broad expanses of lush meadowland — the *Ox-Bow Meadows*, that were once loved by the Abnaki Indians as they since have been by the whites. Coos Country was variously translated by the Indians, as meaning Crooked River, Wide Valley, Place of Tall Pines, Great Fishing Place, and so on. Here the Abnakis had a permanent settlement, and to this day Newbury plows occasionally turn up tomahawk blades and flint arrow-heads. For a long time Newbury was the northern outpost of pioneer settlements on the eastern side of the State. The grave composure of age, with a beautiful Connecticut Valley setting, gives Newbury a gracious charm.

In the long rectangular common surrounded by dignified old buildings at the village center is the *Jacob Bayley Monument*, dedicated to the founder of Newbury, who was a leader in the settlement and development of the whole eastern side of Vermont. The Bayley family, in fact, played in this region a rôle similar to that performed by the Allens on the other side of the Green Mountains. The rear wooden section of the *Ox-Bow Antique Shop* (R), at the south end of the village, was Jacob Bayley's residence. Bayley was plowing on the day that the British lieutenant, Pritchard, and his Tory followers came to capture him. Thomas Johnson, on parole from the British, was aware of the plot but unable to warn his friend personally, because the Tory ambuscade overlooked the Bayley meadow. Johnson contrived the warning by sending another man to the field, not to speak to Bayley, but to drop a slip of paper bearing the following message: 'The Philistines be upon thee, Samson.' Bayley escaped across the river to Haverhill, but that evening Pritchard took four prisoners from the Bayley home, including one of Jacob's sons. But for the courage of a defiant housemaid who barred their entrance, the British would have seized more captives.

The *Congregational Church* (R) (1794) is of white wood, with a double entrance under its pillared portico, and a spire rising to a point from a square base — one of the most satisfying examples of early Vermont church architecture.

The northern and oldest section of the village is known as the Ox-Bow. The *Isaac Bayley House* (left, just off US 5), a white-painted frame structure with a flat balustraded roof, was built (1790) by Jacob Bayley for his son. Since it has always remained in the family, the interior has been excellently preserved. Necessary renovations have been carefully harmonized, and in woodwork, furniture, wallpaper, and other details the house consistently retains the charm of the period in which it was built. The parlor is distinguished by recesses on either side of the fireplace, one known as the 'courting alcove,' the other as the 'marriage arch.' That this design had a truly functional value is attested by the marriage record rapidly accomplished by the eight lovely daughters of Isaac Bayley. The *Colonel Thomas Johnson House* (R), a square tan building of severe lines, was built in 1775 by the man whose leadership was on a par with that of Jacob Bayley. There is a brave gesture toward refinement in the quoins, modillioned cornice, and paneled entrance of this house.

Between Newbury and Wells River, US 5 swings along the western side of the valley, with rock ledges rising here and there like somber sentinels watching the serene flow of the river against a curtain of mountains raised to the eastern skyline.

WELLS RIVER (alt. 395, pop. 554), 45.3 *m.*, lying at the junction of the Wells River with the Connecticut, is the industrial village of Newbury Township, and an important gateway between the White Mountains and the Green Mountains. At the southern end of the brisk little community an attractive white frame *Congregational Church* (R) lifts its graceful spire above the treetops. The modern business section is rather bare and crowded, but the residential streets are shady and pleasant. Wells River enjoys a great deal of activity for a village of its size, owing to a strategic position for mill sites and on transportation lanes.

The village was once the head of navigation on the Connecticut River, New England's principal artery of commerce before the railroads. In 1830 a steamboat made the run from Hartford, Conn., to Wells River, and the following year a steamer, the 'Adam Duncan,' was launched here. With the coming of the railroads, the village became a busy junction of the Boston & Maine and Montpelier & Wells River roads. The B. & M. station remains here, but the offices and bulk of business have been transferred to Woodsville, New Hampshire, just across the river. Wells River was the starting-point of the Hazen Military Road, 1779, which was intended to open the way for an invasion of Canada, but in reality served as a path for early settlers to follow northward in extending the frontier. A celebrated criminal-chaser of the middle 19th century, John Bailey (descendant of Jacob Bayley of Newbury), made his home here.

Between Wells River and East Ryegate, tiers of White Mountain peaks edge the southeastern skyline.

EAST RYEGATE, 49.1 *m.*, is built around the Ryegate Paper Company Mill and a creamery, and is stamped with the drab uniformity of company-built houses, painted a grayish-green and set in even rows along the river flat east of the highway. This typical mill settlement is a comparatively modern development in Ryegate township.

Left from East Ryegate on an uphill country road is RYEGATE (Corner) (alt. 464, pop. township 1216), 2.4 m., a farming community on an upland plateau commanding a wide view of the White Mountains to the east. Ryegate was founded in 1773 by a colony of Scots from Glasgow, led by James Whitelaw and David Allen, who purchased the territory from Dr. Witherspoon, president of Princeton. When they arrived on the tract, they found one of their countrymen already engaged in building a house there. An excerpt from Whitelaw's journal says: 'So we helped him up with it both for the conveniences of lodging with him till we built one of our own, and also that he might assist us in building ours.' The following April they made 60 pounds of maple sugar. The next year other families from Scotland came to increase the little wilderness outpost, and to begin the making of oatmeal. Later, dairying was developed until Ryegate butter became well known in the dairy markets. James Whitelaw, six feet ten inches tall, was the founder of the town, the first surveyor in the State, and rated one of the best surveyors and mapmakers in early New England. His surveying spyglass is now in the St. Johnsbury museum. A recent novel, 'Safe Bridge,' by Frances Parkinson Keyes, deals with the Ryegate setting and characters. *Blue Mountain* (alt. 2370), rising northwest of the village, is nearly solid granite in structure, with quarries on the southern slopes. South of the village is a pretty little lake named *Ticklenaked Pond*.

McINDOE FALLS (alt. 441), 53.6 m., a little village in the center of a dairying district, has a well-kept street running between shaded lawns and flower-beds. The angular brown-painted *House* (L), with its tall wooden columns, is a landmark of hybrid architecture.

Between McIndoe Falls and Barnet, the broad Connecticut bends closer to the highway.

BARNET (alt. 425, pop. township 2604), 56.5 m., was settled in 1770, the first house in town, and in Caledonia County, being built by Elijah Hall at the foot of picturesque *Stevens Falls*. Caledonia, the ancient Roman name for Scotland, was given to the county in honor of Harvey and Whitelaw, leaders of the Scottish settlers here. Barnet and Ryegate share the distinction of being the only towns in Vermont founded by colonists from across the Atlantic. Most of the pioneer settlers of Barnet have descendants living here today.

Barnet is a sidehill village, spread from low river flats to a slanting plateau. Attractive yards and flower gardens add color to the homely wooden houses, and a sense of well-being is merged with Scottish thrift and security. In 1771, Colonel Hurd, as agent of the Stevens brothers, built a mill at the falls here. Two sturdy Scots, Stevenson and Cross, clubbed a bear to death in a hand-to-hand battle in 1776. Henry Stevens, founder of the Vermont Historical Society and head of the department of Americana in the British Museum, was born here. Another native son was Horace Fairbanks (Governor of Vermont, 1876–78).

1. Left from Barnet on an improved road is WEST BARNET, 4.9 m., a straggling little village with an air of rustic languor, which is enlivened a part of each year by the summer activity around Harvey Pond. South of West Barnet is the *Old Covenanter Church*, only meeting-house in the State where the Covenanter faith is still preserved. This plain weather-beaten structure marks the last survival in Vermont of that severe and uncompromising form of church service and church government which the first settlers of this region transplanted intact from Scot-

land (*see Tour* 2, *EAST CRAFTSBURY*). To this day instrumental music is forbidden in the service, and only psalms may be sung, hymns being of profane origin. Since the Constitution of the United States does not specifically acknowledge the power of the Almighty, members of this faith are forbidden to vote or otherwise participate in public affairs. Disenfranchisement, rather than the rigid moral code, proved the chief cause of the decline of the Covenanter Church.

2. Left from West Barnet is HARVEY POND, 0.5 *m.*, a popular summer spot named for Colonel Alexander Harvey, who was sent from Dundee, Scotland, to locate a site for settlement, and chose Barnet as the New World home of his countrymen. In a picturesque framework of notched or rolling woodland hills, this little lake has something of the character and charm of the Lochs that grace the homeland of Harvey and his fellow emigrants.

3. Right from West Barnet on a country road is SOUTH PEACHAM (alt. 1000), 1.6 *m.*, a typical small rural corner village in an atmosphere of stolid unchanging comfort and seclusion. The houses are scattered haphazardly around a bridged stream and general store. The abandoned *Mill* (R) employed three stones in grinding its grist. The first millstones were brought to Peacham by Colonel Thomas Johnson of Newbury, who hauled them in on an ox-sled, March 6, 1781. Johnson stayed that night with Jonathan Elkins. At midnight both men were surprised by Pritchard's Tories, taken prisoners, and marched off to Canada. Johnson was paroled, but Elkins was taken to England to await an exchange of prisoners.

4. Right from South Peacham on an uphill road is PEACHAM (alt. 1908, pop. township 620), 1 *m.*, in the shaded serenity of its fertile highland setting, with fenced-in orchards and venerable homes straggling along the uneven terrain of the hillcrest. Smooth-flowing hills darkened by woodland patches surround the village with pleasant seclusion, which increases its favor as a summer home for college professors and others seeking rest, quiet, and comfort. The *Congregational Church*, dating from the 1790's, is clean-cut and white, with a high tapering spire; crumbling horse-sheds flank the clapboard structure. *Peacham Academy* was founded in 1795 as the Caledonia County Grammar School. The first newspaper in the county, *The Green Mountain Patriot*, was published here in 1798. Peacham was influential in early Vermont history and intellectual life.

Deacon Jonathan Elkins was the father of the town, coming with a few followers in 1775, and making a permanent settlement the next year. The *Elkins Tavern* (1787) still stands halfway between Peacham and South Peacham on a branch road, weathered and time-blackened. The Hazen Military Road went through Peacham, and was a great convenience and main thoroughfare for the pioneer settlers. The caliber of the Peacham pioneers is suggested by the following story: A band of Tories and Indians hovered in the woods preparing to attack a crew of wood-choppers. When the wood-cutters left their axes and went to lunch, the raiders descended, but they halted in awe at the sight of the great axes. 'No, no,' said an Indian. 'We no fight men who use such big axes. We no fight.' And the raiders withdrew. Thaddeus Stevens, violent Abolitionist and foeman of the Confederacy during the Civil War and Reconstruction, spent his boyhood on a farm at East Hill, east of the village. George Harvey, editor of *Harper's Weekly* and Ambassador to England under Harding, was born in Peacham. He was a leader in the fight against Wilson's peace plans, and was influential in the nomination of Harding.

An historical flask turned out in the early 60's celebrated Flora Temple, foaled in Peacham, and the first horse in the world to trot a mile under 2.20 — time, 2.19 ¾.

From US 5, south of East Barnet, there is a fine view through the broad Connecticut Valley to the Fifteen-Mile Falls Dam.

EAST BARNET (Inwood) (alt. 504), 58.9 *m.*, is guarded on the north by a gaunt rock cliff close above the highway, and barricaded along the river with the lumber stacks of a mill, where wood products, including croquet sets, are manufactured.

East Barnet is near the junction of the Passumpsic with the Connecticut. A tragic episode in the flight of Rogers' Rangers took place at the mouth of the Passumpsic. Lord Amherst dispatched a small party from Charlestown, New Hampshire, with provision-laden canoes to meet Rogers' force returning from Canada after their amazing expedition against the St. Francis Indians. The rescue party camped at the mouth of the Passumpsic. In the morning they heard rifle-fire up the river, and fearing the approach of savages, they fled back downstream. Rogers and some of his starving men were encamped but a few miles upstream at this time, counting on the supplies they felt sure would be awaiting them. Reaching the river mouth about noon, the half-dead Rangers found the campfire abandoned by the rescue party, its ashes still warm; but not a crumb of food was left behind. Already reduced to a state of famished despair, several of the men died before the next day. Major Rogers, a man of great resourcefulness and indomitable spirit, built a raft and selected three men to accompany him. Before leaving, Rogers showed the rest of the party how to eke a subsistence from groundnuts and lily roots until he should send help and supplies. The four raftsmen then pushed off on the start of their long perilous float down the Connecticut. The men watching from the shore stood in silence, like skeletons in tattered green buckskin, bent in the middle by the pangs of hunger. The voyage was successful, and somehow or other, after the most frightful hardships and suffering, most of the men finally reached Charlestown.

Right from East Barnet on a country road is the mammoth *Fifteen-Mile Falls Dam* (*open to inspection; free guide service furnished*), 2.6 *m.*, known as Comerford Station in honor of the president of the Connecticut River Power Company. This 216,000 horsepower hydro-electric plant, constructed 1928–30, is the largest in New England. Stretching 1600 feet across the Connecticut, the 175-foot high concrete dam creates a lake seven miles long. The 850-foot spillway is on the Vermont side. A village of about 15 families has grown up in connection with the dam, but the actual operation of the great plant is handled by four men.

Between East Barnet and Passumpsic, the highway swings along the graceful bends of the Passumpsic, one of Vermont's most beautiful rivers. Here in this peaceful valley some of Rogers' Rangers gave up the unequal struggle against the wilds, and died on the march from privation and exposure.

PASSUMPSIC (alt. 531), 63.4 *m.*, a small village in Barnet Township on the banks of the river for which it was named, is shaded by elms and maples and hemmed in by uneven hills. The trim wooden homes of this dairying community wear an agreeable suburban aspect.

Between Passumpsic and St. Johnsbury, the road continues to parallel the Passumpsic River, flowing between shaded banks.

ST. JOHNSBURY (alt. 655, pop. 7920) (*see ST. JOHNSBURY*), 66.2 *m.* Home of Fairbanks Scales and Cary Maple Sugar Company; Museum of Natural Science; Athenæum; Paddock Mansion; Octagon House; Century House; South Congregational Church; and other points of interest.

*Sec. c.   St. Johnsbury to Derby Line, 55.2 m.*

This section of the route is through the heart of the lake-and-woods country of northeastern Vermont, a rugged, broken region with many rivers and mountain-guarded lakes. Traffic from New York, southern New England, and the White Mountains, follows this route toward Montreal and Quebec.

ST. JOHNSBURY, 0 *m.*

North of St. Johnsbury, US 5 runs along the Passumpsic Valley.

ST. JOHNSBURY CENTER (Centervale), 2.8 *m.* In this small, quiet residential suburb on the banks of the Passumpsic, a *Monument* in front of the Grange Hall (R) commemorates the first Grange in New England, which was founded here.

At 5.7 *m.* is the *St. Johnsbury Country Club* (9 *holes, greens fee* $1), standing above the highway (L.) Just north on the same side of the road is the entrance (L) to the *St. Johnsbury Airport.*

LYNDON (or Lyndon Corner), 7.2 *m.,* centers about a sloping bend in the highway. The old stone watering-trough that used to mark the corner was removed after a speeding automobile crashed into it. The northern end of the community dips to a level intervale of the Passumpsic.

Between Lyndon Corner and Lyndonville, there are two blind railway crossings, where the motorist should exercise caution.

> Right on a dirt road just beyond the first of these crossings is the *General William Cahoon House* (L), 0.5 *m.,* a sturdy clapboarded dwelling built in 1800–05. The first two-story house in town, the Cahoon House is now the oldest building here of any sort.

LYNDONVILLE (alt. 727, pop. 1556), 8.8 *m.,* presents its less attractive side on the southern entrance. The business district is concentrated along Depot St., bare and unshaded, but *Powers' Park* (L) gives a cool freshness to the picture, stretching from the village center to the wooded banks of the Passumpsic River. The long wide level Main St. is residential, running northward between elm trees and comfortable homes. The general impression at the northern end of town is one of rich verdure and heavy foliage. Lyndon was chartered in 1780 to Jonathan Arnold, and named after his son, Josias Lyndon Arnold. Daniel Cahoon, Jr., settled the town in 1788. For a long time Lyndonville was headquarters and terminal for the Passumpsic Division of the Boston & Maine R.R., extended here in 1866. It was as a railroad town that Lyndonville reached its peak of prosperity. The imprint left by the many public benefactors whom Lyndonville has been fortunate to have, is clearly discernible in the community.

Flanking the entrance to the Lyndonville National Bank (L), Elm St., are bronze reproductions of Donatello's *Il Marzocco* (Lion of the Republic), cast in the original mold. *St. Peter's Episcopal Church,* Elm St., is the architectural work of Henry Vaughan of Boston, with a stained glass chancel window designed by J. & R. Lamb of ·New York. *People's*

*Methodist Church*, Church St., has 'The Children's Window,' designed by Miss Jessie Van Brunt.

*Cobleigh Public Library* (L), Depot St., a square structure of red brick, contains about 9000 volumes, as well as cabinets of New England birds, Mexican curios, and American and foreign coins and bills. The volumes on art, contributed by Theodore Vail, telephone magnate, constitute the most valuable book collection. Here also is an ancient grandfather's clock, brought to Lyndon in 1798 by Jude Kimball, pioneer settler.

Left from Lyndonville on an improved road is LYNDON CENTER (pop. 207), 0.7 *m.*, the seat of *Lyndon Institute*, a secondary school for both boarding and day students, and a *Normal School*. The *Wild Boar Fountain* in the triangle (L) is a copy of the piece by Pietro Tacca, that stands in the New Market, Florence. The situation here, on a green shelf over the Passumpsic, is a pleasing one. In the central part of the beautiful cemetery here can be read curious provocative inscriptions in the Ethan Allen tradition, carved by G. P. Spencer (1825–1908), atheist stone-cutter. The verses on one side of the stone were so strongly blasphemous that churchly citizens had them obliterated. The old section of the cemetery contains many early tombstones. North of the graveyard are rolling sand dunes, forming a miniature desert unique in Vermont. Reforestation has been undertaken to combat soil erosion here.

At 9.7 *m.* on the northern outskirts of Lyndonville is the junction with State 114 (*see Tour 1E*).

Between Lyndonville and West Burke, US 5 runs in swinging loops over a hilly picturesque countryside.

WEST BURKE (pop. 359), 17 *m.*, is a small trading and milling village in the township of Burke, which was probably named for Edmund Burke, the British statesman. The settlement is haphazard and straggling, its chief appeal lying in a kind of rustic carelessness.

West Burke is at the junction with State 5A (*see Tour 1D*).

Right from West Burke on a country road is BURKE HOLLOW, 2 *m.*, pervaded with century-old quietude and as charmingly rustic as an etching from rural folk tales. A narrow stream splashes over its rocky bed at the center of the village. The *Old House* (L), white, high, and constructed with wide clapboards, is said to have been the first tavern. The *Old House* (R), painted in two shades of brown, was also an early inn. The *Old Union Meeting-House* stands white, prim, and delicately spired above the village street, beautiful in its pure simplicity. Built in 1825, the church seats 300 people and remains unaltered; the interior has the old box pews, or 'slips,' each with an individual door; and behind the high barrel pulpit is a long choir gallery.

Right from Burke Hollow on an uphill road is BURKE GREEN, 0.8 *m.*, the site of the first settlement in the township, marked by a few cellar-holes and an old cemetery on the shady hill, where early settlers sleep under the somber serenity of tall pines. On the eastern skyline Burke Mt. bulks nobly, and to the north is the striking profile presented by the guardian mountains of Lake Willoughby.

North of West Burke, US 5 wends through a wild forested country, away from the peaceful valley.

At 19.4 *m.* is the junction with a country road.

Left on this uphill road is SUTTON (alt. 1050, pop. township 605), 1.9 *m.*, a secluded little hill village on the watershed between the Connecticut and St. Lawrence River systems. The village is touched with an old world quiet and serenity, an air of peaceful decadence. Here is an old cemetery where Revolutionary soldiers are buried. One inscription reads:

> Death like an overflowing stream
> Sweeps all away; our life's a dream,
> An empty tale, a morning flower
> Cut down and with'd in an hour.

Sutton was granted to Colonel Jonathan Arnold in 1782, and originally called Billymead after Arnold's son, Billy, who came here to live. The name was changed by resentful townsmen when Billy Arnold turned out to be a bullying drunkard, who constantly abused his neighbors and disrupted the life of the community.

*Willoughby State Forest Park* (R), 21.9 *m.*, is a reforestation and conservation project developed by the Civilian Conservation Corps, with dense stands of spruce and fir in sight of the road. The CCC camp was abandoned in 1937.

*U.S. Bobbin and Shuttle Company Mill* (R), 24 *m.*, is a brick mill standing over a large wood-rimmed millpond, with a railroad spur crossing the highway to join the main line.

WILLOUGHBY, 25.4 *m.*, formerly South Barton, is a little mill village with faded wooden houses irregularly grouped on the uneven terrain.

Between Willoughby and Barton, the highway skirts the western shore of *Crystal Lake*, which lies in the ridged shelter of *Brooks Mountain* (alt. 1400) at the southern end of Barton village. This charming little body of water has an excellent bathing beach across the north end, and facilities for boating and water sports. One detachment of Rogers' Rangers, ragged, starving, and harried by Indian pursuers, camped here on their flight from Canada. The quiet shores were a haven of rest after their hardships in the wilderness, and the fish taken from the lake eased the pain of their hunger. The fine fishing still exists, with bass, lake trout, and salmon being caught. At the northeast corner of the lake is *Pageant Park*, a picturesque site for picnics and camping; the name commemorates an historical pageant of the founding and settling of Barton, which was presented at this spot in 1921. Trails wind through the woods near the park, climbing to the white rush of *May Falls* near by, and up the mountainside. An auto road leads over Brooks Mountain to the summer cottages along the eastern shore. The Barton Winter Circus, an annual event with all winter sports and an air meet, features horse-racing on the ice of the lake.

BARTON (alt. 931, pop. 1362), 30.2 *m.*, occupies the valley north of Crystal Lake, spreading from eastern hill slopes across the broad valley floor to the west. A good part of the village lies at a lower level than that of the lake. The long unshaded Main St., which US 5 follows, winds in gradual descent northward between a railway embankment (R) and dwellings and scattered stores (L). At the foot of Main St., the north end of the village clusters about a triangular Common surrounded by stores, the red-brick post-office building, and a modern municipal building with a false façade. Much more attractive are the outlying residential sections on hillside and plain, shaded by maples and tall elms. Once a lively industrial village, Barton has lapsed into relative inactivity, with

Crystal Lake its main attraction as a summer playground. With many community activities, Barton keeps up a brave front, but the industrial backbone is gone.

Ranged along Church St. are the Barton Library, the brick Methodist Church, Barton Academy in red brick, and the gray wooden Congregational Church. When the hill behind the Academy was levelled an Indian burial ground was uncovered. On High St. are two worn plain frame houses over 100 years old. *Roaring Brook Park*, an attractive fairgrounds at the western edge of town, is the site of Orleans County Fair (August); it has one of the best half-mile racetracks in the State. An unusual annual event in Barton (Wednesday following the fair) is a summertime sugaring-off party, with snow carefully preserved for the occasion.

The town was named for Colonel William Barton, grantee and first settler, although the charter was granted in the name of Providence. Among the other early settlers was a feeling of jealousy and resentment toward Colonel Barton, and he was jailed for some minor debt. The Revolutionary veteran remained in jail, so the story goes, until Lafayette's visit in 1825. Lafayette remembered Barton as a good soldier, and on hearing of his plight, the Marquis immediately had him set free. At the Common in Barton is the junction with State 12 (*see Tour 2C*).

Between Barton and Orleans, the two-lane cement highway follows the meandering Barton River through a pleasant valley banked by blunt ridges. Hops were grown along the river banks by early settlers.

At 34.9 *m.* on the southern outskirts of Orleans is a junction: US 5 (L), continues uphill on a new by-pass; the road (R), formerly US 5, leads into the center of the village, and loops back to rejoin US 5 on a higher level.

ORLEANS (alt. 740, pop. 1301), 35.4 *m.*, lies low in the valley where the Barton and Willoughby Rivers unite on their way to Memphremagog, and is sheltered by ridged slopes. Springing from the sound sub-structure of the wood-working industry here is a progressive alertness and community spirit seldom found in villages of like size. A broad level green (R) flanks the four-lane cement Main St., with the railroad depot, tracks, and a furniture factory forming an incongruous background. Large wooden business blocks face the park and depot, and the railroad bisects Main St. The village center is huddled about a small oval green with a cement base and iron fountain; the *Municipal Building* (L), a modern brick structure with tapestried front, houses village offices, a banquet hall, theater, Masonic lodge, and National Guard barracks. The outlying residential districts are more pleasant, spreading from the valley bottom to terraced hill slopes. Along with civic consciousness, Orleans has achieved State-wide fame for her championship high school basketball teams. Samuel Read Hall, pioneer educator and founder of the first normal school, is buried here (*see Tour 5, CONCORD, and Education*).

Settled as Barton Landing about 1821, the village adopted the name Orleans in 1909, not wishing to appear in any way subsidiary to Barton.

The rivalry between these neighboring villages has been intense, and many an athletic contest between the two has been marked by fist fights and riots. Orleans grew up quickly around the furniture factory; veneer and wooden heels are also turned out by Orleans mills. For many years the village has been the industrial nucleus of the section. The southern end of the village is bordered by the uniform yellow frame houses, company-built to house the mill workers.

> Left from the eastern outskirts of Orleans an uphill dirt road runs past Willoughby Falls (R), the early-spring goal of fishermen, and climbs to BROWNINGTON, (alt. 1200, pop. township 697), 2.8 *m.*, named for two Browns who were among the grantees. The village is scattered along the easy slant of a plateau surrounded by sloping farmlands and farmsteads, with mountain panoramas in the distance. At the crest of the slope above the village center stands the *Congregational Church* (L) and graveyard, the frame building painted white with green-blinded windows. The *Old Stone House* (R) at the crest, a three-storied structure of mortared granite blocks, has a grim military aspect. In 1822, the Orleans County Grammar School was established in this sturdy stone building, which now serves as the *Museum of the Orleans County Historical Society (adm.* 50¢). The museum contains old furniture, tools, weapons, documents, pictures, and the like.
>
> A leader in the early days, Brownington fell into lethargy with the shift of population from the hills to the river valleys. Now the venerable weatherbeaten houses sleep along the gentle slope in their beautiful upland setting.

Between Orleans and Coventry, US 5 rises and falls across a broken highland country, with woodlands and clearings making a patchwork design of the slopes.

At 40.1 *m.*, on the southern outskirts of Coventry, is the junction with State 12B (*see Tour 2*).

COVENTRY (alt. 718, pop. township 610), 40.6 *m.*, named after Coventry, Connecticut, lies in a green bowl of the valley. The brown clapboarded *Congregational Church* (L), with cupola and clock faces the narrow Common. The long narrow green contains a *Civil War Monument* and a cannon once owned by the Coventry militia. The bench in front of the typical country store (R) is usually lined with villagers and farmers, talking, smoking, and watching the flow of traffic on US 5.

> Left from the church in Coventry on a dirt road over the hill is the *Old Heerman Mill* (R), 0.5 *m.*, at its dam on the Black River where it has been operated by the Heerman family since 1803. Sportsmen come to this old sawmill late in April to watch steel-head trout jump the dam, a leap of six feet or more.

Between Coventry and Newport, US 5 runs through the Black River Valley of the north. This northern Black River is a trout stream, in contrast to the Black River in southern Vermont, which supplies waterpower for some of the State's largest industrial plants. From a pleasant and fertile valley scene, the highway enters a low swampy region, as the marshlands of Lake Memphremagog are approached.

> NEWPORT (alt. 723, pop. 5094) (*see NEWPORT*), 46.8 *m.* Popular as a summer resort and gateway between eastern Canada and New England. Lake Memphremagog; Federal Building; Orleans County Court House; Goodrich Memorial Library; Catholic Ave Maris Stella Church.

Between Newport and Derby Center, US 5 climbs and dips in long swooping curves, gradually attaining higher altitude. The western mountain ramparts of Memphremagog loom (L) against the horizon.

At 51.2 *m.*, on the outskirts of Derby Center, is the junction with State 105 (*see Tour 1D*). From the traffic light here, US 5 swings (L) northward toward the Canadian border.

Just north of the junction, *Derby Pond* (R), the reservoir for Newport City, lies on the high, level plain.

Between this point and Derby Line, the highway rolls and winds in long, graded curves over the uneven highlands.

DERBY LINE (alt. 1028, pop. 681), 55.2 *m.*, is on the border between Vermont and Canada. Lying on a high plain above the sharp-cleft valley that approximates the boundary line, there is a gracious quality in this gateway village, induced by the level breadth of the plateau, the abundant shade of old maples, and the dignity of homesteads with lawns and shrubbery. The long, straight, maple-shaded street is a pleasant avenue of departure from, or entry to, Vermont. The *U.S. Customhouse* (L) recorded in 1935 the entrance of 139,575 cars and 333,657 people through this station. The international boundary at this point is characterized by friendly and close-merging interests, for two Canadian villages run together with Derby Line, forming what seems to be one community. Exemplifying this close association is an *International Rotary Club* representing the three villages, and said to be the only one of its kind in existence. European visitors are often surprised to find such a friendly frontier situation, and look about in vain for armed sentries and fortifications.

These border towns of the Province of Quebec and Vermont are proud of their international status. Derby Line's *Haskell Opera House*, Caswell Ave., has its entrance in the United States and its stage in Canada. There are many stories in this connection, such as the one about the American officers who sat writhing helplessly in the audience, while the fugitive they sought performed nonchalantly on the stage, saved from their clutches by the inviolable border-line. *Legion Park* (L), near the railway station, is an international World War Memorial, the boundary post in the park bearing the flags of both countries. In prohibition times the Canadian town of Rock Island, just across the line, attracted ale-drinkers from all over northeastern Vermont, and thousands of thirsting tourists sampled their first Frontenac or Molson's or Black Horse there. During that era the back roads of the region witnessed many thrilling races between booze-laden machines driven by reckless bootleggers and the Customs Patrol cars which guarded the border.

TOUR 1A : *From* BRATTLEBORO *to* JUNCTION WITH STATE 11, 42.3 *m.*, State 30.

Via West Dummerston, Newfane, Townshend, Jamaica, Bondville.
Road is hard-surfaced between Brattleboro and Townshend; dirt for the remainder.

THIS route, a diagonal cut-over between Brattleboro, the southeastern entryway to Vermont, and the resort district of Manchester, parallels the West River a major part of the way. At its northwestern extremity the route crosses a section of the great mountain wilderness area of the State, from which point southward to the Massachusetts line lie dense highland forests, unbroken and primitive. The villages passed are remote upland valley settlements — some crude and picturesque, others, like Newfane, well cared for and immaculate. The heart of Windham County is traversed, a region noted for hunting and fishing, and particularly for deer-hunting, in which it tops the State. For more than half the way the road is paralleled and interminably crossed and recrossed by the West River R.R., now defunct, whose tiny stations (like tool boxes with chimneys) punctuate the route.

> BRATTLEBORO (alt. 260, pop. 8700) (*see BRATTLEBORO*), 0 *m.* Site of Fort Dummer, first permanent white settlement in the State; Home of Estey Organs; Estey Estate and Summer Theater; Center Congregational Church; All Souls Church; Public Library; Brattleboro Retreat; Austine School for Deaf; Brattleboro Outing Club and Ski Jump.

Northwest of Brattleboro, State 30 runs along low flats made by the confluence of the West and Connecticut Rivers, with the rugged hogback of *Wantastiquet* (alt. 1364) bolstering the east side of the latter stream. Progressing north the road follows a shelf above the West River, wide-flowing in gravelly pebbled banks. The West River R.R. along the opposite shore is now used only to transport Presbrey-Leland granite from the Black Mountain quarries to the finishing-sheds in Brattleboro.

At 4.5 *m.*, rounded foothills begin to loom closer, their slopes clothed in thick greenery.

At 5.5 *m.*, the bridge (R) leads across the river to the *Presbrey-Leland Quarries* at the base of *Black Mountain* (alt. 1269), a solid formation of granite that is said to be one of the world's largest deposits. The granite, while present in tremendous quantity, is of a rather inferior quality with a great deal of waste.

North of the bridge is the best view across-stream to the quarries, where green buildings and derrick-booms stand against the raw gray of the stone, a giant bite into the mountainside.

WEST DUMMERSTON (alt. 400, pop. township 604), 6.2 *m.*, scattered along a slight rise in the valley, has a street marked by two small white churches (Baptist, Catholic) and a large white *Grange Hall*. Broken steel rails beside the tiny depot indicate that the West River R.R. is no longer active north of the granite quarries.

The township of Dummerston was chartered as Fullam. First settler John Kathan (1752) cleared 120 acres and built a house, barn, sawmill, and potash works. His daughter was taken into Indian captivity for two-and-one-half years, after which she was ransomed.

North of West Dummerston the road continues along the side of the watercourse, in which gray, brown, and black rocks thrust above the current. At 8.4 *m.*, the stream bends close to the highway embankment, flowing deep and green.

*Williamsville Station*, 9.1 *m.*, was formerly the depot for Williamsville village in Newfane Township. Now the small station forlornly faces the unused railroad bridge that hangs futilely above the West River.

1837 *Covered Bridge*, 9.4 *m.*, of the latticed type, is one of many such structures prevalent in this region. It spans the Marlboro Branch (Baker Brook) close above its junction with the West.

At 11.9 *m.* is the junction with a country road.

> Left on this uphill road is *Newfane Hill* (alt. 1630), site of the original settlement of the township. On this cone-like hill near the township center, the pioneer village founded by Park, Stedman, and Dyer, grew up. Today there is a *Marker* to the Old Courthouse (1787), and few other vestiges of the settlement. As was the case throughout the State, people moved from the hills to the river valleys in order to utilize the water-power for their mills. The final transition occurred here around 1825, when the public buildings were transferred to the valley (*see below*).

The southern entrance to Newfane is through another covered bridge (1840). Sawmills and lumber stacks flank the stream, and a homemade wooden sign faces the bridgeway, advertising '*Palmistry*.'

NEWFANE (alt. 560, pop. 159), 12.4 *m.*, was originally chartered (New Hampshire) as Fane, for Thomas Fane, according to tradition, who was a follower of Sir Thomas Wyatt in 1553 in the movement to place Lady Jane Grey on the British throne in place of Queen Mary. The village proper was first called Park's Flats, for pioneer Jonathan Park, and then Fayetteville, in honor of Lafayette. Situated on a level valley floor banked by soft-sloping terraces, its handsome greens distinguished by town hall, church, courthouse, and old inns, Newfane stands with Woodstock as one of the most charming villages in southern Vermont. Newfane remains the shire town of Windham County, in spite of the greater size and affluence of Brattleboro and Bellows Falls. This is a rare instance in the State in which the county seat is retained in a small village instead of being transferred to a larger center. It is also a gratifying instance, for the Newfane setting is a lovely one.

Among the early settlers was lawyer Martin Field, graduate of Williams College, and having an M.A. degree from Dartmouth, who came to Newfane in 1800. One of his grandsons was Eugene Field, the poet, who spent many boyhood summers here, and based several of his poems on recollections of sunny young days in Newfane.

The broad open *Common* (R), outlined in elms, has the *Jonathan Park Memorial*, honoring the first settler who gave the land that is now the village nucleus. Park, with Stedman and Dyer, came here in 1776, to begin the original settlement on Newfane Hill (*see above*). Lieutenant Park led a detachment of Newfane volunteers to fight in the battle of Bennington. The smooth square now forms a pleasant plaza for the summer inns.

Across the street is another shaded green (L), dignified by the presence of three fine white structures. *Union* (Town) *Hall* was built as a Union Church in 1832. The *Congregational Church* (1839), set back between town hall and courthouse, is white and pure of line with a high, graceful spire. The *County Courthouse* was erected in 1825 when the center of town shifted from Newfane Hill to the valley flats, and is one of the most beautiful in Vermont. In white wood with a four-pillared portico, handsome windows, and a red-capped tower, the building shows the Greek Revival trend.

The *Newfane Inn*, a plain white building built in 1793, is said to be the second oldest hotel in the State, and with the other inns, serves a summer clientèle. The *Bank Building* (L) is a small red-brick box with narrow windows. 'Bank' is carved in granite over the door. A similar procedure has been followed in other West River Valley villages, the full name of the institution not being given, as a protection against possible costly alteration; possibly a like prudence determined the financial policies of the banks. A stone wall (L) lines the northern end of the main street.

Northwest of Newfane, the highway curves along the broad, low intervales of the West River Valley. At 15.5 *m.*, is the long green-painted *Holland Bridge*, another latticed covered bridge over the West River.

HARMONYVILLE (alt. 461), 16.4 *m.*, lies along Mill Brook above its junction with the mother stream, a string of large, rambling wooden houses and a sawmill in the township of Townshend. About 1830 Townshend village allegedly grew jealous of the progress made by its little southern neighbor, and fastened on it the name of 'Tin Pot.' In retaliation the then busy hamlet gave Townshend the title of 'Flyburg,' and nailed bold signs on its own bridge, proclaiming itself to the world as Harmonyville. Brash invaders from Townshend promptly tore down the signs, but the name has been retained.

Between Harmonyville and Townshend, the road is through the narrow valley of Mill Brook, with the sharp rocky spire of *Peaked Mountain* (alt. 1400) rising on the east.

TOWNSHEND (alt. 574, pop. township 633), 17.2 *m.*, is close-girded by abrupt, rocky hills, that on the north rise from the very back yards of the houses. The handsome stucco *Town Hall* (R) is modern and impressive for a tiny village, with its columned portico, clock-tower and belfry surmounted by an American Eagle weathervane (this concession to Federalism being suggested by the presence of the post office in the building). The *Dutton Gymnasium* (R), a neat brick structure, is another improvement that was made after a fire razed the eastern side of the street. *Leland and Gray Seminary* (R), founded in 1834 as 'The Leland Classical and English School of Townshend,' is now a high school housed in a towered building of slate-colored wood, that dates from 1894. The first president of the board of trustees was the Hon. Peter R. Taft, the grandfather of William Howard Taft, President of the United States.

The maple-shaded Common at the village center, with a brown wooden glassed-in World War Honor Roll and a fountain, is pleasantly surrounded by white houses. It is difficult to realize that this fine level Green was once so rough and rocky that 'an ox cart could not be drawn across it without being capsized.' The *Congregational Church* (1790), white with green blinds, enhances the attractiveness of the Common; from a square tower and belfry, the conical spire lifts its weathervane above the treetops.

Joseph Tyler started the settlement in 1764, dragging his possessions on a hand-sled through the wilderness from Brattleboro. Prominent among the early settlers was Samuel Fletcher, soldier and blacksmith, who served in the French and Indian War, faced the British redcoats from the earthworks on Bunker Hill, and fought under Arnold at Saratoga. For 18 years after the war, this seasoned veteran was high sheriff of Windham County.

West of Townshend the road swings back into the West River Valley, continuing its northwesterly course under the great bulging upthrust (R) of rocky-spurred *Rattlesnake Mountain* (alt. 1400).

At 19 *m.* is the junction with a country road.

> Left, this road leads across a long unpainted covered bridge over West River to the *Townshend State Forest Park*, 780 acres of woodland. Left from the end of bridge the road leads to mis-named *Bald Mountain* (alt. 2000), whose forest-clad slopes constitute the major part of the park. The northern and western slopes of Bald Mountain have been developed by the Brattleboro Outing Club into one of the finest winter sports terrains in the eastern United States. Here are excellent long ski trails and runs, ski jumps and a toboggan slide, electrically lighted. A foot-path leads to the top of the mountain, on which is a 60-foot lookout tower commanding a widespread view.

WEST TOWNSHEND (alt. 606), 22.4 *m.*, situated mainly on a low plateau above a wide ox-bow bend in the West River, stretches L-shaped from the lowland flats to its raised shelf. The southern entrance is along a stone-walled street marked by the trim tan stucco of the *Seventh Day Adventist Church* (R), neat and new in contrast to its neighbors. Rude old sheds give a rustic air to the bridge, which is at the elbow of the L. The road curves sharply from the bridge, climbing to the village center where old wooden houses are set on the tilted slope. The white *Congregational Church* (L) is less attractive than its brothers to the south.

West of West Townshend the roadside and hillsides are laced with stone-walls, and gnarled apple trees are seen on the slopes.

EAST JAMAICA (alt. 556), 23.8 *m.*, consists of a few houses and a little railway depot, no longer used. Outcroppings of rock (R) thrust in on the valley floor.

Between East Jamaica and Jamaica, immaculate summer homes are seen here and there along the edges of the valley, contrasting with the rough farmsteads.

JAMAICA (alt. 700, pop. 570), 27.2 *m.*, lies on Ball Mountain Brook at the eastern point of a triangular valley opening toward the plains of the West River. Hills wedge the village in on three sides. Aloof on the eastern outskirts stands the *Baptist Church*, with a plain front and square belfry. The white *Congregational Church* (1808) in the village is equally undistinguished architecturally. According to persistent legend, the first minister of the latter church, John Stoddard, was dismissed from the pastorate in 1799 for selling his wife to another man. Mrs. Stoddard, the scandalous and antique rumor relates, was well pleased with the transaction and raised a family for her purchaser. The Congregational Church Record Book is, naturally enough, not explicit regarding the affair, though it mentions 'matters of difficulty existing between the church and the Rev. John Stoddard' at the time when it granted his alleged request for 'a dismission from his pastoral relation to the Congregational Church and Society in Jamaica.' The chief other public buildings are the church-like *Town Hall* (L) and the tiny white *Jamaica Memorial Library* (L). Most of the houses are set close to the street, and the community is irregularly laid out. Lumbering and the manufacture of wood products, including tennis rackets, are the chief industry.

*Ball Mountain* (alt. 1745), a solid granite formation, rising north of Jamaica, is more than half enclosed by a great coil of the West River. In 1748, Captain Eleazer Melvin and 18 scouts were retreating from Lake Champlain by way of Otter Creek and the West River, followed by a band of Abnaki Indians. The scouts followed the West River in its great eastward bend around the bulk of Ball Mountain, and stopped to shoot salmon and replenish their supplies south of the heights. The Indians cut straight through the gap west of the mountain and overtook the little scouting party. The Abnakis opened fire from ambush, and four buckskin-clad scouts went down under the first volley. Stunned by the suddenness of this blow, the other soldiers dived for cover and returned the fire, advancing on the enemy through the tangled brush. Several painted warriors fell before the accurate rifle-fire, but after the Indians picked off two more victims, Melvin and his men scattered and fled through the forest toward Fort Dummer. The burial party sent out from the fort found Hayward, Taylor, Dod, and Mann where they had fallen on the bank of the river. The riddled bodies of Petty and Severance were sprawled some distance away in the thicket.

North of Jamaica, State 30 leaves the West River Valley to climb over a wild, hilly section, known as excellent hunting and fishing grounds. More deer are shot in Windham County than in any other county of Vermont.

At 31.8 *m.*, the broad blue head of *Mt. Bromley* (alt. 3260) is seen on the northern horizon.

RAWSONVILLE (alt. 1070), 32.7 *m.*, a little mountain settlement, is scattered on the uneven plain of the Winhall River surrounded by rough, forested hills. In the heart of a fine fish and game region, this hamlet was one of the last settled in Windham County. The *Rawson Monument* (L), a stone slab ringed by an iron fence, is dedicated to eccentric Bailey Rawson, who founded the settlement, 1810-12. During the Revolutionary War, 16-year-old Rawson played the fife for a Massachusetts company. Before settling here and building a sawmill, he was a traveling farrier, riding horseback from town to town to follow his trade. On one occasion Rawson gathered several bags of sorrel seed, which he sold to innocent down-countrymen as 'not clover seed.' Some of the people who used the seed in expectance of raising a special variety of clover, became irate and carried the matter to court. When confronted by the law, the bland Rawson replied: 'I sold the stuff for "not clover seed." If you can prove that they *are* clover seed, I will pay the damage.'

Between Rawsonville and Bondville, the road follows the narrow upland valley of the Winhall River.

BONDVILLE (alt. 1220, pop. township 229), 34.5 *m.*, is the only village in sparsely settled, mountainous Winhall Township, strung along narrow Winhall River Valley in the hills. The pioneers first penetrated these dense mountain wilds about 1780. The simple *Methodist Episcopal Church* was erected in 1850. The Bondville Fair, held each autumn when the ridges are burning with the flame-red of maples and the golden haze of birches, is a picturesque back-country pageant.

Between Bondville and the junction with State 11, the highway traverses the mountain wilderness of Winhall Township, with views sweeping over forests so dense that they resemble thick green mosses carpeting the earth. The mountain scenes are dominated by the broad-capped dome of Bromley on the north. To the south stretches a vast area of forest-shrouded mountains, broken only by the passage of the *Long Trail* (*see LONG TRAIL*), which crosses the highway at 41.8 *m.*

At 42.3 *m.*, is the junction with State 11 (*see Tour 4E*), 6 miles east of Manchester Center.

T O U R   1 B :   *From* ENOSBURG FALLS *to* JEFFERSON-VILLE, 21.7 *m.*, State 108.

Via Bakersfield.    The road is mainly gravel.

THIS route, somewhat removed from the main lanes of travel and not notably rich in historic interest, has still the varied inland charm of fertile farmlands alternating with clean, peaceful villages. The southern end of the route affords constant views of Mount Mansfield and its company of lesser giants bulking directly ahead.

ENOSBURG FALLS, 0 *m.*, is at the junction with State 105 (*see Tour 1C*).

Between Enosburg Falls and West Enosburg occurs the only stretch of hard-surfaced paving on this route. The country here illustrates the great unevenness of this State's surface, of which the mountains are but major manifestations. The road rises and dips through broken valley terrain and over small hills for three miles to gain an added elevation of just 18 feet between the two villages.

WEST ENOSBURG (alt. 440), 2.9 *m.*, is a small four-corner village of frame houses and one church. Snug and domestic, it is neither attractive nor unattractive; it is like a hundred other similar Vermont hamlets that constitute brief pauses in the panorama of the countryside, like marks of human punctuation in the long poem of the landscape.

South of West Enosburg the country is pleasantly diversified, wooded hillsides alternating with bare ridged pasturelands, rock-strewn and covered with a network of cow-paths. At 7.8 *m.* a sawmill stands beside the dammed stream ('The Branch') whose overflow makes white-sheeted spray on the rocks below.

BAKERSFIELD (alt. 762, pop. township 889), 10.2 *m.*, is a village of one unusually long street lying along a broad plateau. Toward the southern end is a rectangular white-fenced Common (L). Behind the Common is a neat cemetery, and bordering it on the southern side are two red-brick churches and the town hall. Bakersfield has long been an educational center for this region. Bakersfield Academy was founded in 1840, the first building being the brick structure that now serves as a Catholic church. Union Institute was founded in 1854. Neither of these schools is now in existence. *Brigham Academy*, just north of the Common, was established in 1878 by Peter Bent Brigham, a native of Bakersfield and founder of the well-known Boston hospital that bears his name. This school is still active and draws boarding pupils from a considerable area in this section of the State.

Bakersfield was named for Joseph Baker, the first settler, who purchased the township in 1791 for slightly more than one hundred times as much as Manhattan Island is alleged to have cost the Dutch. The graph of the town's industrial activity follows what constitutes the norm for countless small Vermont towns: a sharp rise during the first half of the nineteenth century to indicate a gristmill, a sawmill, a potash factory, a carding mill, and a tannery; a steady decline since, to indicate the passing of these localized ventures to larger industrial centers. Today dairying and lumbering are the basic industries. Bakersfield is now a typical northern New England residential village, pervaded with quietude.

> Right from Bakersfield a winding dirt road leads over a broken and uneven valley bottom where the farms are somewhat less fertile and prosperous than those to the east.
>
> EAST FAIRFIELD (alt. 424), 3.3 *m.*, is a small village in a hollow of the valley, a plain and unpretentious settlement lying off the main route. The industries are a

gristmill, a creamery, and lumber mills. The dark, sluggish waters of Black Creek, a tributary of the Missisquoi, flow northward through the village.

Northwest of East Fairfield are several large turkey farms. At any time between June and Thanksgiving great flocks of these birds are visible from the highway, like massed, living shadows.

FAIRFIELD (alt. 500, pop. township 1541), 8.9 m., has a peaceful air of seclusion. Though not of high altitude for this State, the view is remarkably unrestricted in three directions because of the strategic situation. Fairfield is one of the outstanding centers of maple-sugar production in the State, and evaporating equipment is manufactured here.

Right from Fairfield on a rough country road is the *Site of the Birthplace of Chester A. Arthur*, 5.7 m. Here stood the small cottage, long since fallen to ruin, in which, on October 5, 1830, the twenty-first President of the United States was born. Marking the spot is a massive single block of granite, on a cement base and encircled by an iron railing, which the State of Vermont erected in 1903. Simple as this memorial stone is, it is startling in the contrast it presents to the complete isolation of its surroundings.

South of Bakersfield, at 11.4 m., the mountains to the south, including Mansfield, fill the valley and seem to block the highway with an insurmountable barrier. The countryside along the route also grows more hilly, though the road follows the valley.

FLETCHER STATION, 16.2 m., consists of a depot of the St. Johnsbury and Lake Champlain Railroad and a few houses.

At 17.5 m. the mass of Mount Mansfield literally fills the valley ahead.

The countryside becomes more open, gradually broadening to the flat meadowlands of the Lamoille River Valley in which Jeffersonville is built. JEFFERSONVILLE, 21.7 m. (*see Tour 5A*), is at the junction with State 15 (*see Tour 5A*).

T O U R   1 C :  *From* BLOOMFIELD *to* JUNCTION WITH US 7, 108.9 *m.*, State 105.

Via Island Pond, Derby, Newport, North Troy, Richford, Enosburg Falls, Sheldon.

The railroads paralleling this route are the Canadian National (between Bloomfield and Island Pond); the Canadian Pacific (between Newport and Richford); the Central Vermont (between Richford and St. Albans).

The road is intermittently cement, blacktop, and gravel.

THIS northernmost cross-State route offers good roads, uncongested by heavy traffic. The wide scenic vistas are of a sort not generally associated with Vermont, for the route skirts the Canadian border through the major part of its course and at one point actually traverses Canadian soil for several miles. The road follows river valleys, those in the eastern part being heavily timbered and sparsely settled and, therefore, good fish and game territory. The western end of the route lies through the rich, fertile farmlands of the Champlain Valley.

BLOOMFIELD, 0 *m.* (*see Tour 1F*), is at the junction with State 102 (*see Tour 1F*).

Between Bloomfield and Island Pond, a gravel road traverses a wild and sparsely populated region. Running parallel to the highway are the dark, murky waters of the Nulhegan River, flowing swiftly toward the Connecticut. It was the Nulhegan which a party of Rogers' Rangers followed from Island Pond to the Connecticut, in 1759, on their southward flight from Canada after devastating the Indian village of St. Francis. The Rangers reached Lake Memphremagog intact, but pursued by superior Indian forces, they decided to split up into smaller foraging parties, thus bettering their chances of shooting game. Suffering from wounds, hunger, and long exposure, one small band of scouts pushed eastward toward the Connecticut. The shooting of a moose in this vicinity brought the Indians upon them, but after a fierce skirmish, most of Rogers' Rangers again escaped to continue along the Nulhegan to its junction with the Connecticut, which they grimly followed south toward Number Four, the fortified settlement at Charlestown, New Hampshire.

Small, dingy farmhouses occur at rare intervals separated by large timbered areas, some of which have been ravaged by fire. At 5.2 *m.* the road becomes hard-surfaced and passes through large groves of white birch and evergreen trees.

At 15.3 *m.* is *Spectacle Pond* (L.), its cool dark depths inviting the angler to try his skill, its quiet shores unmarred by cottages.

ISLAND POND, 17.6 *m.* (*see Tour 1E*). Here is a junction with State 114 (*see Tour 1E*).

Southwest of Island Pond the surface of the land is very uneven, high wooded hills and ridges alternating with more gentle slopes under cultivation. At 18.8 *m.* is a view to the northwest of the northernmost range of the Green Mountains.

At 19.9 *m.* is a junction with State 114 (*see Tour 1E*).

West of this junction the route leads through a wider valley, the lower slopes of which are covered with fine maple groves. At 21.5 *m.* hard surface is replaced by gravel.

EAST CHARLESTON, 25.7 *m.*, is a small village lying at a bend in the highway above the banks of the Clyde River, its sawmills and lumber stacks remaining as vestiges of a once thriving industry.

> Right from East Charleston, a winding road climbs to a highland plateau. A left turn at the first fork leads to *Echo Lake*, 1.2 *m.*, charming in its pastoral setting amid these cultivated uplands. There is good fishing here.

North of East Charleston the country becomes more open and flat, with small wooded areas and pleasant streams. The dark, heavy soil of this immediate section makes for fertile and productive farms.

At 29.9 *m.* is the junction with State 5*A* (*see Tour 1D*), which unites with State 105 for a few miles.

Between this junction and Derby, State 105 passes through West Charleston village and along the shores of Little Salem and Big Salem Ponds (*see Tour 1D*).

DERBY, 38.7 *m.* (*see Tour 1D*), is at the junction with US 5 (*see Tour 1*). Here also is a junction with State 111 (*see Tour 1D*).

Between Derby and Newport, State 105, in conjunction with US 5, descends in long curving sweeps toward the southern end of beautiful *Lake Memphremagog.*

> NEWPORT (alt. 723, pop. 5094) (*see NEWPORT*), 42.7 *m.* Popular summer resort and gateway between eastern Canada and New England; Federal Building; Orleans Country Courthouse; Goodrich Memorial Library; Catholic Ave Maris Stella Church.

West of Newport, State 100 rises and falls in long, swinging bends, with a majestic view (R) over the southern end of island-dotted Lake Memphremagog buttressed by the mountains of southern Quebec in the distant background. The road continues to climb to an elevation whence the view lies to the southeast, where the twin peaks of Pisgah and Hor, the guardians of Lake Willoughby, rear their stark profiles. As the route traverses the height of land to which it has gradually attained, the kaleidoscope turns once more as the ramparts of the Green Mountain Range loom into view to the west, dominated by the sharp, clean symmetry of *Jay Peak* (alt. 3861), one of the highest mountains in Vermont. On a cool fall morning, the sharp cone of its summit is luminous with snow, while the hills and wooded valleys below still flame in the fullness of their autumn foliage.

At 47.5 *m.* is the junction of State 105 with State 100 (*see Tour 3*).

Between this junction and Newport Center, State 105 is hard-surfaced, rolling along a shallow broken valley.

NEWPORT CENTER (alt. 723), 54.2 *m.*, is a small village bisected by the highway. A sawmill constitutes the only industry. The high school here serves a considerable area to the southwest including the townships of Westfield and Lowell.

Between Newport Center and North Troy the highway is rolling, paralleled by broad meadows and wooded hillsides. Sweeping stretches of Canadian territory to the north add to the scenic beauty of this section. At 60.1 *m.* is the junction with the 'River Road.'

> Left on this road is *Troy Falls* (R), 1.4 *m.*, a beautiful natural cascade in the Missisquoi River. The falls are seen best from the high rocky promontory that rises precipitously above the boiling white waters of the deep gorge below. A favorite spot locally for summer picnics and autumn corn roasts is the small adjacent grove, out of sight from the falls, but still within sound of their cool music.

Beyond Troy Falls is a farmstead (R) 3.9 *m.*, and (R) on foot from this point over hilly pastureland is the *Site of the Boston and Troy Iron Mine*, its old stone blast furnace still standing on the bank of the Missisquoi. Though it is beginning to crumble now, this furnace, 24 feet square and 30 feet high, is still suggestive of the magnitude of the iron industry that once existed here. Despite the excellent quality of the products of this mine and blast, it was finally abandoned as being too far from the markets for profitable operation. The iron markers set on the international boundary line between Vermont and Canada were cast here.

NORTH TROY (alt. 764, pop. 1045), 60.9 *m.*, is an industrious community with well-shaded streets bordered by clapboarded residences. Being a gateway between the United States and Canada, it has had a turbulent border history. The early settlers were a high-spirited, reckless lot with a strong love for excitement. They lacked the more staid and regular habits of some of their neighbors to the south. In May, 1812, when an invasion from Canada seemed imminent, a special town meeting was held at which the selectmen were authorized to purchase muskets, bayonets, powder, and a hundredweight of lead for the town's defense. The men of Troy were ready for a fight, whatever the odds, but the British never came. The Blair Veneer Company manufactures plywood and veneer products, and employs about 180; it is one of the largest industrial plants in this section.

North of North Troy, at 62 *m.*, is the *U.S. Customhouse* (L), four white modern structures, recently completed.

At 62.1 *m.* is the international boundary line and the *Canadian Customhouse* (R), a small, green-painted building in striking contrast with the American Customs.

For thirteen miles beyond this point the route lies in Canada, winding on a dirt road through a broken hilly terrain and passing through three small villages before arriving again at the *Canadian Customs* (L). The boundary line here is formed by the sluggish waters of the Missisquoi River (Indian: *missi* — much; *kiscoo* — water-fowl), with the *U.S. Customhouse*, in modern red brick, lying on the opposite banks on the northern edge of East Richford.

EAST RICHFORD, 75.4 *m.*, is a small cluster of houses to the left of the highway, all but hidden by a railroad embankment.

The route becomes hard-surfaced at this point and roughly parallels the Canadian Pacific Railroad to Richford.

STEVENS MILLS, 77.2 *m.*, consists of a railroad depot and a few scattered dwellings. The village derived its name from the owner of a sawmill around which it grew up. On the southern outskirts stands a brick powerhouse, inoperative since the flood of 1927, when it was severely damaged.

RICHFORD (alt. 504, pop. 1783), 81 *m.*, is approximately in the center of the northern end of the Green Mountain Range and is consequently extremely hilly, the main thoroughfare rising in sharp ascent from both banks of the Missisquoi River, which divides the village north and south. The connecting bridge, which seems much larger than necessary to span a stream usually so small and placid, was designed to resist the terrific forces of the Missisquoi at high flood: forces which have time and again swept away the bridge at this point, leaving the two parts of the village without means of communication. Richford's Main St. is dominated by the new *Federal Building*, containing the post office, and the *Town Hall*, which was remodeled from the Advent Church (1871). In addition to the usual town offices, the Town Hall houses the *A. A. Brown Public Library*, an endowed institution, opened in 1895 (4000 volumes). Facing the central three-corner intersection is the *Roman Catholic Church*, over-looking from a slight eminence a small triangular Common with an ornate iron fountain. Formerly on the site of the church, the *Union House* now stands across the street and is used as a rectory, an architectural hybrid built in 1820, but interesting for the unrelieved slope of its roof and the wide front verandas on both stories.

Because of the abundance and good quality of the timber near Richford, woodworking in its various branches is the town's main industry, nearly 500 persons being employed in the furniture, plywood, and veneer mills. The largest of these mills is in the center of the village adjacent to the falls that supplied the power for the necessary gristmill of the early settlers. Power for the present mills, however, is transmitted electrically from Newport, 30 miles away. From the upper reaches of the village the view is unusually impressive, with Jay Peak to the east, its slender, clean-cut cone commanding this part of the Green Mountain Range, and the wide-spreading Champlain Valley to the west. Especially scenic is the location of the Richford Country Club, 1.2 *m.*, northeast of the village, whose 9-hole course has one of the most magnificent settings in the State. Richford has suffered many adversities. Fires and floods have greatly retarded its growth. But the steady persistence and tenacious spirit of its inhabitants have prevailed over all disasters to achieve the present status of commercial prosperity.

At 82.7 *m.* are the *Rearing Pools* of the Franklin Rod and Gun Club. This region, which is flat and open, is one of the finest farming sections of the State.

EAST BERKSHIRE, 86 *m.*, is a T-shaped village, the stem lying across the Missisquoi at right angles to the highway. In 1866, this village was swept by a fire which destroyed 36 buildings including the church. The present stone and brick *Church* (R) is a handsome adaptation of English Gothic style. One of the early leading citizens of East Berkshire was Stephen Royce, Governor of Vermont (1854–56). His son, Homer Royce, born here, was Congressman from Vermont (1857–63) and subsequently Chief Justice of the Vermont Supreme Court for 25 years. When the village was in its infancy, supplies were obtained from Boston through a local teamster. Pollard, the local poet, with another tippler, heard that some rum they had ordered had arrived, and promptly went after it. Finding the door unlocked, but no one at home, Pollard scratched the following doggerel on a piece of bark with a nail, and pinned it to the door:

'Sir, we've come
And got our rum;

Home we've gone
Through brush and wood
And hope the rum
Will do us good.'

The village, with two creameries, is the center of the fresh milk industry in this territory. Farm machinery is also manufactured.

Between East Berkshire and Enosburg Falls the countryside is dotted with large, well-kept farms. The placid waters of the ever-winding Missisquoi River add scenic charm to this fertile valley. It is easy to understand why Franklin County, despite its large area of rough wooded land, leads the State in milk production.

ENOSBURG FALLS (alt. 426, pop. 1195), 91.7 *m.*, is a distinctive village with an attractive park in its center that strikes a keynote of planned neatness, echoed by the residential sections. The village and the township in which it was located were named for Ira Allen's father-in-law, General Rogers Enos, to whom the township was chartered in 1780 by the independent State of Vermont. Isaac Farrar, an early settler, instituted the use of wooden spouts for tapping maple trees. They were soon universally adopted and retained until replaced in recent times by metal ones; Farrar, nevertheless, was accused by his neighbors of 'scientific farming,' which was not well regarded in those days.

In the latter part of the nineteenth century, Enosburg Falls was known throughout the land as the home of panaceas and patent medicines that were 'guaranteed' to cure the ills of both man and beast. At least four major fortunes were amassed by local sons in this business. On a smaller scale, descendants of the original manufacturers are still carrying on.

Susan Mills, founder of Mills College for women in California, was born here.

Here is the junction with State 108 (*see Tour 1B*).

West of Enosburg Falls the road winds past wooded slopes and smooth fertile meadowlands.

NORTH SHELDON, 97.5 *m.*, is a small hamlet centering a dairy community.

Right from North Sheldon on State 120, the road climbs gradually to an elevation from which there are sweeping views to the north and east. At 2.1 *m.* the blue waters of Lake Carmi are visible.

FRANKLIN (alt. 426, pop. 1001), 3.8 *m.* was settled in 1789 as Huntsburg, the name being changed by the Legislature in 1817. This is a clean and pleasant village, with a modern brick library at the southern end and two white churches, a town hall, and a Civil War Memorial at the northern end. The early settlers of this region did most of their trading in Canada. With the War of 1812 came the embargo, ending their normal state of commercial and social relationship. Smuggling was rife.

This area was the scene of an event of unusual interest and significance: the major Fenian battle with the Canadians in the Irish attempt to conquer Canada and set up an independent Irish Republic. The Fenians were the American branch of the Irish Revolutionary Brotherhood, dedicated to the freeing of Ireland from England by force of arms. The odds being too great against the Irish for open warfare in the

British Isles, the conquest of Canada was decided upon as a preliminary step. In 1866, some 35,000 Fenian troops entered Canada from several points, including Franklin, and engaged in skirmishes. The movement was frustrated by the intervention of the United States authorities, who seized the Fenian arms and arrested the leaders of the movement for violation of the neutrality laws. In 1870, a second attempt was made, the major force of over 2000 men being concentrated between Franklin and Cook's Corner, just across the border. The purpose of both these attacks was to divert the attention from a main attack launched from Ogdensburg, New York, which also failed. The leaders were again captured by the U.S. Government, but most of them were soon given their freedom by General Grant in recognition of their services during the Civil War.

Before its settlement by white men, Franklin was a favorite summer hunting ground of the St. Francis Indians of Canada. The meat of the deer and moose killed in the marshes here was dried before being taken back to the Canadian settlements to be consumed during the winter months. Among the prominent native sons of Franklin are Orville E. Babcock, Brigadier General in the Civil War and later secretary to President Grant, and Charles W. Gates, Governor of Vermont (1915–17).

Right from the northern end of Franklin on a rolling dirt road is *Lake Carmi*, 2.5 *m.*, a sizable and beautiful body of water surrounded by shore farms and summer camps.

West of North Sheldon at 97.7 *m.* is the site of the Sheldon Fair (L), an agricultural exhibition long popular in this region but now discontinued.

SHELDON JUNCTION, 101.2 *m.*, consists of a few plain wooden dwellings and a creamery.

Left from Sheldon Junction on a winding dirt road is SHELDON (alt. 374, pop. 1563 township), 1.3 *m.* This village was chartered as Hungerford and settled in 1790 by a son of Colonel Sheldon and a Scotchman named MacNamera. Colonel Sheldon was of the Light Horse Dragoons and a close friend of Washington The first birth in town was a colored child born to a servant of Colonel Sheldon. The village is built on two parallel ridges. In the valley between flows the narrow, swift waters of the Black Creek. By the bridge connecting the two parts of the village stands an *Old Mill* with a stone base. As early as 1798 iron kettles were manufactured at Sheldon, the ore being mined and smelted here. This industry attained a high state of production, people placing their orders far in advance and coming from miles around to procure them. Iron was referred to as 'Sheldon Currency.' Dairying was also of major importance in the township with herds ranging from 25 to 100 head. During this period Sheldon was one of the leading centers of cheese production in the State.

SHELDON SPRINGS, 102 *m.*, lies on a sloping hillside by a bend in the Missisquoi. The town is economically dependent upon the large *Mill of the Missisquoi Pulp and Paper Company* (R) at the foot of the hill. Most of the houses in the village are owned by the company. Though built in a uniform style, of brown stained shingle, these houses do not give the village the drab appearance that mill houses usually impart because they are well spaced and landscaped. In the pine grove (L), at the foot of the hill, flows the *Mineral Spring* for which the village was named and noted. In this now deserted glade, the Missisquoi, a hotel of 100 rooms, with $35,000 invested in the furnishings alone, once accommodated the hundreds of visitors who came here annually to drink the Spring waters. Now the quiet is broken only by the villagers who come down over the hill in the cool of the evening to fill their jugs.

West of Sheldon Springs the route lies over gently rolling country, the fertile meadows on both sides of the road sloping away to distant foot-hills. At 106.5 *m.* the view of Lake Champlain with the northern Adirondacks in the background startles the traveler from the east with a beauty that is in sharp contrast to the quiet rustic charm of the region from which he has come.

GREENS CORNERS (alt. 405), 107.1 *m.*, is a small hamlet in the township of Swanton. The only industry is a creamery, as in several other settlements in this county.

At 108.9 *m.* is the junction with US 7 (*see Tour* 4), 3.3 *m.*, north of St. Albans.

---

T O U R   1 D :   *From* DERBY *to* WEST BURKE, 26.1 *m.*, State 105, 5A.

---

Via Morgan, West Charleston, Westmore.
The road is gravel except for a short stretch of blacktop at the northern end.

This route covers a wild country of woods and lakes, and is worthwhile for the sheer beauty of Lake Willoughby alone. On the north there are simpler bodies of water and the broad farmlands of the Clyde River Valley. South of West Charleston the highway leaves the valley to rise and fall through a region where areas of rocky unfertility and stump-blackened pastures give evidence of the struggle some of the farmers here are faced with. The vision of Willoughby comes with sudden and breath-taking wonder, an unforgettable picture marked with a grandeur that is rare in the usually serene landscape of Vermont. Here the mighty plow of glacial ice sheared through a barrier of granite mountains, and, goug-ing deep into the earth, left a cold and lovely lake lying between the stark cliffs of Pisgah and Hor. The inevitable comparison of Willoughby to the lakes of Switzerland gave rise to the title, 'The Lucerne of America,' which is not needed, however, to stamp Willoughby apart from the other lakes of Vermont and New England.

DERBY (alt. 1011, pop. 300), 0 *m.*, lies along the high broad level of a plateau that once served as a favorite hunting ground for the St. Francis Indians. The houses flanking the long cement main street are wood-clapboarded, constructed in the neat plainness of common domestic building, set back from the street and well-spaced. The plateau setting and the freshness of a high altitude give Derby a bright cleanness that is appealing, and make it easy to understand why the Indians loved this place. The village seems little affected by its closeness to the Canadian border.

Left from the center of Derby, State 111 crosses the level plateau eastward, climbs a gradual ascent, then rises and falls through a hilly woods country, a wild valley (R) opening a southward vista to the broad well-shaped cone of Burke Mountain; Lake Seymour is first seen (R) at 6.7 m.

MORGAN (alt. 1384, pop. township 363), 7.2 m., sprawls in barren rusticity around a simple white *Methodist Church* and a general store on the easy sloping hillside above Lake Seymour. Originally called Caldersburgh, this sparsely settled village was founded around 1800 in an outlying wilderness region of good fishing and hunting. The frontier aspect is still much in evidence.

*Lake Seymour* lies enclosed by an irregular wooded shoreline against a back-drop of forested hills, dominated by a sharp wooded knob on the immediate southern shore. A long beach stretches across the northern end of the lake beside the high-way. Seymour is noted for its fishing, but has been developed very little as a resort.

MORGAN CENTER, 9.3 m., forms a ragged crescent of crude wooden houses and primitive stores at the northeastern corner of the lake shore. This rude outlying frontier settlement seems far removed from the modern world, and some of its inhabitants show a tendency to regard all 'outsiders' with distrust. The setting of the lake, in a broken wooded terrain against mountain horizons, has a wild, barren type of beauty, but the little village itself is interesting only as an example of hinterland settlements that still exist in rural Vermont.

South of Derby, State 105 drops sharply downhill to cross a bridge over the Clyde River, past a ramshackle, dilapidated sawmill (L), and then winds upward and out of town.

*Big Salem Pond* (L), 1.8 m., lies calmly in flat wood-fringed shores near the highway. *Balm of Gilead Beach* (L), 3 m., is the name given to the unusually narrow neck of land that separates Big Salem from *Little Salem Pond* (L), 3.3 m. There are camping grounds available here, and the fishing is very good. The two ponds are sometimes collectively called Salem Pond, but locally the differentiation of Big and Little is always applied.

Between Little Salem and West Charleston the highway follows the Clyde River Valley.

WEST CHARLESTON (alt. 1028, pop. township 895), 5.8 m., is a small mill village in the township of Charleston, which was originally called Navy by Commodore Whipple, Revolutionary naval officer and grantee of the township. The highway curves into the village and winds uphill between abandoned mills, general stores, and unkempt houses, an air of crumbling decadence prevailing in the side-hill settlement. An odd stone *Community Church* (R) has an outside brick chimney and wooden belfry. The collapse of the lumber-milling industry left West Charleston dead and empty. and the community has lain dormant since that time. The dammed pond (L) at the northern end of the village is locally known as *Electric Light Pond*; a public utilities power plant generates electricity for many Orleans County communities.

At 7.1 m is the junction of State 5A and 105 (*see Tour 1C*). Here the route leaves 105 to follow 5A (R).

*Pensioner's Pond* (or *Plunkett Pond*) (L), 7.5 *m.*, lies in quiet simplicity against a distant mountain background. It was called Pensioner's Pond because a Revolutionary soldier used his pension to build a mill here.

State 5A swings right, climbing between rocky fields and barren farms, through bleak stumpage areas with ragged stone walls dividing the boulder-strewn slopes. A long, straight stretch of rising road reaches the summit and winds in descent toward Lake Willoughby. A mountain horizon is presented to the south, the distinctive heads of Mt. Pisgah and Mt. Hor coming into view at 13.2 *m.*

At 13.7 *m.* is the junction with a dirt road.

> Right on this road is EVANSVILLE, 3.9 *m.*, a small settlement centered in a narrow valley, its homesteads scattered erratically over the broken terrain. The *Whetstone Factory* (left, below the highway at the entrance to the village) is a long, yellow building below the millpond, utilizing the water-power of the dam in the Willoughby River, outlet of Willoughby Lake. The stone is quarried in Westmore. The factory is a branch of the Pike Whetstone Manufacturing Company in Pike, N.H. The millpond makes a fine swimming place during the summer months.

The grandeur of Lake Willoughby is first revealed by a bend in the descending highway at 14.1 *m.*

LAKE WILLOUGHBY (R), 14.7 *m.* The pure, shining waters of Willoughby stretch six miles south between woodland shores and rolling hills, with *Mt. Pisgah* (L) (alt. 2654) and *Mt. Hor* (R) (alt. 1592) standing stern guard over the southern end, their sheer, granite-faced heights rising with stark grandeur that is unusual in Vermont scenery. Willoughby has been ranked, by many world travelers, among the world's most beautiful lakes. It has been marred somewhat by the inevitable upgrowth of summer cottages and tourist camps, but from many angles of view these are not obtrusive, and even when they are most obvious the majesty of Willoughby relegates them to obscurity. There are fine sand beaches at either end of the lake, and excellent Crescent Beach lies in a secluded cove on the western shore.

The remarkably clear, clean, spring-fed water is delightfully refreshing to the swimmer, cold and bracing. Lake trout and salmon are caught here, and back in the surrounding hills are many fishable ponds and streams. A girl's camp (R) occupies an ideal site overlooking the north end of the lake from the west. *Westmore Mountain* (L) looms with broad heights in dominance over the northeastern horizon, and from the fire lookout tower on its summit a rare and sweeping vista is presented.

At 15.7 *m.* (L), a white *Congregational Church*, rural school, and community house stand, a plain, simple wooden triumvirate forming a social center for the natives of Westmore, who gather here for box parties, church suppers, old-fashioned dances, and community plays. During the summer months these affairs take on a more cosmopolitan and sophisticated aspect, owing to the presence of a distinguished summer colony. (Left from here uphill is the approach to the Westmore Mountain climb.)

# ILLUSTRATIONS

*to accompany*

Tours 4, 4A, 4B, 4C

GRAND ISLE COUNTY SCENE NEAR STARKSBORO

CHAMPLAIN VALLEY NEAR ST. ALBANS

TOWN HALL ORIGINALLY BUILT AS A CHURCH

VIEW FROM BATTERY PARK, BURLINGTON

GRASSEMOUNT, UNIVERSITY OF VERMONT DORMITORY  BURLINGTON

OTTER CREEK

STUMP FENCE, NEAR VERGENNES

HARVEST TIME IN ADDISON COUNTY

FIRST CONGREGATIONAL CHURCH, MIDDLEBURY

OLD COLLEGE ROW, MIDDLEBURY

LAKE DUNMORE

VERMONT'S DEEPEST MARBLE QUARRY, NEAR PITTSFORD

WESTMORE (alt. 1200, pop. township 224), 16.1 *m*. This scattered settlement, basically rural and agricultural under its resort superstructure, is centered here at a combination general store and town clerk's office (L) on the eastern shore of the lake, a few dwellings clustered about it. The native population lives mainly on farms back in the hills. A local expression states that the community is 'Willoughby Lake in the summer, and Westmore in the winter.'

> Left from Westmore on a climbing woodland road is *Long Pond* (alt. 1835), 2.5 *m.*, cupped in a pocket of wooded mountains at the foot of *Bald Mountain*, a rounded helmet-like dome. This is a favorite rendezvous of fishermen and hunters, and a few camps lie around the shores, built by sportsmen who prefer the wild seclusion offered here. A forested island rises in the middle of the pond, and the whole scene is one of wilderness beauty.

At 17.4 *m.* is the north end of *Pisgah Trail* (L), a well-defined path leading over the heights of Pisgah, a good stiff hike but not difficult, with many accessible lookouts from the cliff-tops, where the climber may stand on jutting crags and look almost straight down 1400 feet into deep blue lake waters, or across the way to the scarred, seamed granite walls of Hor. From these lookouts Willoughby appears narrow as a river flowing calmly between the mountains. The views are spectacular and thrilling, with rock ledges dropping straight down into steep, forested slopes that descend sharply to the water's edge. Rare ferns are found on the mountain-side, and botanists come from great distances to search for them.

*Stone Water Tub* (L), 18.2 *m.*, is fed by a stream running down the mountain-side from a lofty spring, and offers pure cold drinking water. By climbing a short distance above the water tub, a view may be had of the white-laced falls in their cool, precipitous rush down the mountain.

State 5A runs close beside the eastern shore in the immediate shadow of steep-rearing Pisgah, the slide-scarred cliffs of Hor visible across the glimmering water. From many places along the lake shore it is possible to dive directly from the roadside into clean deep water.

At 19.8 *m.* is the southern end of the lake with its sand beach, and one of the most magnificent views of Willoughby between its rugged, rock-faced sentinel mountains. From here State 5A climbs away from the lake.

*Site of Old Willoughby Lake House* (L), 20.2 *m.* The foundation walls now enclose a growth of birches. This was a large stage-line hostelry, and even at that early date something of a resort for a discriminating clientèle. Old prints show the hotel standing in the gap between the mountains, stage-coaches bringing new guests, and fashionably dressed men and women watching the wrestling bout of two chained bears. The coach-house stood in a hollow behind the hotel, and from it Henry Ford took an ancient coach for his Sudbury Farm. The south end of Pisgah Trail is found near the site of the coach-house.

At 21.4 *m.* a foot trail branches (L) from the highway.

> Left on foot up this grass-grown roadway along the mountain flank is the *Site of Arcadia Retreat*, 2 *m.* At the turn of the century Arcadia Retreat was an exclusive and fashionable resort, but was suddenly and mysteriously abandoned, everything

being left behind, furnishings and trappings complete. Curious and acquisitive visitors gradually dismantled the hotel, which was an unusual point of interest until it burned in the early 1920's. Many theories and legends grew around the deserted Arcadia Retreat, mostly imaginative. No one ever returned to claim the property or furniture. People still take this hike to see the ruins and wonder about the hurried, mysterious abandonment.

Between Lake Willoughby and West Burke, State 5A swings over a pleasant upland country where lovely woodland glades are interspersed with smooth undulating meadows.

WEST BURKE, 26.1 m. (see Tour 1). Here is a junction with US 5 (see Tour 1).

---

T O U R   1 E :   From CANADIAN LINE (Sherbrooke) to JUNC-TION WITH US 5, 42.8 m., State 114.

---

Via Norton Mills, Island Pond, East Haven, East Burke, Lyndonville.
Canadian National R.R. parallels the route between Norton Mills and Island Pond.
Road mainly dirt and gravel, with short stretches of hard surface.

THIS route traverses the most sparsely populated section of Vermont and some of the State's best fish and game territory. The scenery is generally wild and wooded, and the charm of the section lies chiefly in the setting, not in the historical associations, which are negligible. There are few accommodations for tourists in the northern section except those provided in season for sportsmen. It is conceivable, however, that the trip might possess a certain appeal to many tourists from the very fact that so little definite and conscious appeal is made to them.

The *Canadian Boundary*, 0 m., is crossed between Stanhope, P.Q., and Norton Mills, Vt.

NORTON MILLS (alt. 1252, pop. township 339) is a scattered village with three churches, a hotel, and a modern (1933) *Customhouse*, 0.5 m. from the line. As its name suggests, the settlement was originally the center of large lumber mills, which no longer operate. Norton Township was one of the latest to be settled in the State (1860), and the northern section of this route dates from the present century, as there was no highway communication between Norton and the rest of Vermont for 50 years, except by way of Canada.

Left from the Norton Mills customhouse a good gravel road ascends gradually to a higher level, from which. at 1 m., there is a fine view of massed mountains to the south. The route cont·nues through mediocre farming country to *Great Averill Lake*, 4.4 m., all but the northwestern tip of which lies in the unorganized township of Averill. This two-mile lake, which lies north and south and is larger than it looks to be from the road, affords some of the best still-water fishing in the State, salmon, native, lake, and golden trout being caught here in great numbers. The wild, wooded shores stretch back to hill forests that are excellent deer-hunting territory. A hotel and several camps and cottages at the northern end of the lake accommodate sportsmen in season.

South from here, through the heart of Essex County, stretch the three 'unorganized' towns of Averill, Lewis, and Ferdinand — over one hundred square miles of wilderness with a total population of only 27.

Turning sharply right at 5.1 *m.*, the road leads to *Forest Lake*, 6.9 *m.*, smaller than Great Averill but even more beautiful in its wooded seclusion. This too is good trout water, and the *Cold Spring Camps* on the west shore are open from May to mid-October.

South of Norton Mills, State 114 is gravel to 2.9 *m.*, where hard surface begins. The road grows more winding at this point, and there are few farms here. On both sides of the highway lie large forests which include more cedars than are found in any other section of the State.

LAKE, 5.9 *m.*, is a railroad station standing alone in the wilderness. It was built for the convenience of the many sportsmen who come to fish *Norton Lake*, 6.3 *m.* (R), which the road skirts for two miles.

At 6.4 *m.* the hard surface ends and the famous *Roller Coaster Road* begins. This eight-mile stretch of gravel highway is a continuous series of sharp rises and dips of varying height and degree that give the motorist a sensation similar to that derived from the amusement-park device for which the road was named. This road, however, was not constructed to that end, but merely follows the natural contours of the land. Heavy cars may take this exhilarating ride at 45 miles an hour, lighter cars at 40 miles an hour, with perfect safety, *if drivers keep to the right when approaching the tops of the steep knolls that shut out the view ahead.* A parking lookout at 8.2 *m.* affords a good view of the southern end of Norton Lake, with its fantastic jigsaw shoreline, a rarity among the lakes of Vermont. At 8.3 *m.* the mountains to the south and east fill the horizon, their profiles overlapping one another, all apparently equidistant from the traveler. One of the scenic delights of this route lies in watching these mountains grow more distinct and assume perspective as the road continues southward. The Roller Coaster Road ends at 14.4 *m.*

The view near the highway at 15.5 *m.* is enhanced by the pleasant contrast between bare precipitate cliffs (R) and gently rounded, birch-covered hills (L).

ISLAND POND (alt. 1191, pop. 1638), 18.2 *m.*, originally called Random, derives its name from a pond at the southern end of the village which has a 22-acre island in its center, quite similar to Ellen's Isle in the Trossachs. The pond itself strengthens this Scottish impression, its closely wooded shores and grave, secluded beauty rendering the comparison inevitable. There are seven other ponds in the township of Brighton, in which the village is located. Island Pond was settled late, and like most of the towns and villages in Essex County is entirely lacking in examples of interesting early architecture.  As the chief commercial importance of the village is due to the fact that it is a division headquarters of the Canadian National R.R. and a port of entry from Canada, it is fitting that its business district should be dominated by a large brick and granite railway station.  A skeleton-like elevated footbridge north of the station and an overhead highway bridge on State 105 just south of it are necessary to convey traffic in safety across the intricate network of tracks and switches spread out to the east, but this does not keep them from aggravating the gaunt bleakness of the scene. Island Pond's proximity to fine lumber country and its railroad facilities have led to the establishment of large furniture and woodworking factories here, though they are for the most part inactive at present.

From the town-planning point of view, Island Pond is a conspicuous example of unrealized opportunity.  The setting has a Trossachs charm still, but the possibility of planning what might have been one of New England's loveliest towns was precluded by the accident of its strategic situation on the main line of the railroad.

In Island Pond is a junction of State 114 and State 105, which continue coincident, westward, to 20.5 *m.*, where State 114 turns due south (L) and continues on gravel.  From this point south for about ten miles the road is winding and runs through poorly developed territory where small farms, with shabby buildings, have been wrested in Pyrrhic victory from the forests.

EAST HAVEN (pop. township 99), 31.5 *m.*, is a small hamlet of a few houses and a post office.  A neatly kept modern cemetery (R) suggests the more highly cultivated sections to the immediate south.

Continuing through a narrow valley, the road is bordered by the Passumpsic River, which even in these upper reaches, before it is broadened by confluence with other streams, exhibits the meandering placidity and pastoral quietude which invite the vanity of elms and willows and make it the most often photographed of Vermont rivers.

EAST BURKE (alt. 830, pop. township 1016), 37.5 *m.*, is a pretty village with an air of sophistication usually found only in larger towns. The *Burke Mountain Club* (L), the center of the town's social life, was donated in 1919 by the late Elmer A. Darling, a native son of Burke whose benefactions to his birthplace were many.  The graceful white wood building houses a varied library, reading and game rooms, and numerous mementoes of its donor and his family.  Among the latter the most notable is what was probably the last pass issued by Abraham Lincoln.  It reads: 'Allow the bearer, A. B. Darling, to pass to, and visit Mobile, if, and when that city shall be in our possession. A. Lincoln. April 13, 1865.'  A. B. Darling, owner and proprietor of the old Fifth Avenue Hotel in New York City, was the uncle of E. A. Darling. Lincoln, it will be remembered, was assassinated the next evening.

Immediately south of the club building stands the *White Schoolhouse*, a small, unpainted structure named for the White family, who were prominent in early Burke history. Built about two miles north of the village in 1817, this building was acquired by the Burke Historical Society in 1895 and moved to its present site and merged with the Burke Mountain Club in 1922–23. It is now a small but widely representative museum of local antiquities, including furniture, china, glassware, costumes, books, and manuscripts. A curator is in charge at the Burke Mountain Club all day (*admission free*).

1. Left from East Burke on a dirt road is *Burke Mountain* (alt. 3500), 4.9 *m.*, the central and dominant part of 1700 acres of woodland donated for public recreation in 1933 by L. A. and Henry Darling and now comprising the Darling State Forest Park. A winding macadam road from the base to the summit was completed in 1935 by workers of the Civilian Conservation Corps camp located at the foot of the mountain, 3.1 *m.*, where the macadam begins (*toll 50¢ per car*). The top of the mountain has been landscaped to provide adequate parking space for automobiles. There are picnic areas, campgrounds, foot and bridle trails, and three ski-runs to attract tourists and sport-lovers. A 36-foot glass-enclosed observation tower aids in the unobstructed enjoyment of the panoramic view that embraces the Green and the White Mountains, Willoughby Lake, southern Quebec, and Maine. Those wishing to spend the night on the mountain can secure tent floors for 50¢ per party. Firewood costs 10¢.

2. Right from the Burke Mountain Club in East Burke a dirt road ascends through scattered cedar groves to *Mountain View Farm*, 0.9 *m.*, on the 1500-acre estate developed by the late Mr. E. A. Darling and recently (1936) purchased by Mr. Earl Brown of Minnesota. Here are still raised the beautiful Morgan horses that were the pride of Mr. Darling, who was one of the leaders in the movement to revive interest in the pure breeding of this native strain. The large brick building that directly faces the road is a *Creamery*, where the milk from the farm's great herd is daily turned into 150 pounds of American cheese. Turning left at the farm, the road climbs to the magnificently situated mansion, *Burklyn Hall*, 1.2 *m.*, so called because it stands on the town line between Burke and Lyndon.

The route continues south of East Burke, bearing somewhat westward through fertile and open farming country.

At 42.8 *m.* on the northern outskirts of Lyndonville is the junction with US 5 (*see Tour 1*).

---

T O U R   1 F :   *From* CANADIAN LINE (*Sherbrooke*) *to* JUNCTION WITH US 2, 49.3 *m.*, State 114 and 102.

---

Via Canaan, Bloomfield, Guildhall.

Maine Central R.R. parallels the southern end of the route.

The road is four-fifths gravel, one-fifth hard surface.

THIS route parallels the northern part of the Connecticut River Valley. The valley is broader here than it is farther south, and the mountain walls that hem it in are loftier. For the major part of the route the great White Mountain Range to the east, though in New Hampshire, is scenically an important part of the trip.

*Canadian Boundary*, 0 *m.* The route enters the United States on State 114 at the modern *Customhouse* in the township of Canaan, the most easterly point in Vermont.

CANAAN (alt. 1042, pop. township 906), 1.6 *m.*, is a small village across the Connecticut from West Stewartstown, New Hampshire. All of these river valley towns are dual settlements built up on both sides of the river which in actuality constitute single towns or villages except in matters of government. The Maine Central R.R. follows the northern Connecticut on the New Hampshire bank, but serves the towns on the Vermont side as well. Canaan is centered about a green Common with a fountain and the inevitable war memorial. A fire in the spring of 1936 destroyed the only hotel and several other buildings, leaving the little town scarred and somewhat unsightly.

Left from Canaan on State 102 is BEECHER FALLS, 2.2 *m.*, another port of entry into Vermont from Canada. The village is supported mainly by thriving furniture mills.

South of Canaan the fine view across the Connecticut is typical of the myriad vistas to the east throughout this route.

At 2.9 *m.* is a *State Fish Hatchery* (R), a white wooden building with a system of cement raceways in front where the young fish, hatched indoors in winter, can be seen during the summer months. Like most Vermont State Hatcheries (five in number), this one, since its establishment in 1914, has been devoted almost solely to maintaining and increasing the stock of lake and brook trout in Vermont waters. On the inside walls of the hatchery, what at first appear to be actual mounted fish are in reality wooden models realistically carved from cedar by a former employee.

Between 7.5 *m.* and 8.5 *m.* the countryside is so closely settled as to constitute a kind of nameless straggling farmhouse village. Just south of this point the distant mountains of eastern Vermont seem to block the route to the south.

The hard surface ends at 10.1 *m.* The road, closely following the river, becomes more winding at this point. Now the larger part of the fertile farmlands lie on the Vermont side of the dividing Connecticut, now on the New Hampshire side. These level meadows contain countless small depressions which after a heavy rain become a patchwork of glinting pools.

BLOOMFIELD (alt. 912, pop. township, 418), 24.1 *m.*, is a small village across from North Stratford, New Hampshire, a junction of the Maine Central and the Canadian National R.R.'s. Its only products are lumber and pulpwood. Here the Nulhegan River empties into the Connecticut. One party of Rogers' Rangers, starving and harassed by Indians, followed the Nulhegan from Island Pond and were heartened at this point by

reaching the Connecticut, the waterway that would lead them south to
Charlestown, New Hampshire.

Here is the junction with State 105 (*see Tour 1C*).

At 25.5 *m.* is a junction with a dirt road.

> Left on this road is lovely, birch-bordered *Mineral Pond*, 0.6 *m.*, lying on top of
> the high river-bank plateau 80 feet above the Connecticut. Just over the brow of
> the bank toward the river flow the six *Brunswick Mineral Springs* for which the
> sparsely populated township of Brunswick has long been chiefly noted. These
> springs are said to differ from one another not only in mineral content, in which
> sulphur predominates, but also — to a proper connoisseur — in taste as well.
> The springs and the river bank ridge are well landscaped, as a result of their
> having been the leading attractions of a succession of resort hotels on this site, the
> last of which burned several years ago.

Between 25.7 *m.* and 26.2 *m.* is a real woodland drive, thick groves of
tall pines bordering the level road on both sides.

At 30.2 *m.* the view is one of unusually varied splendor, with palisades
on both sides of the highway, which hugs the elm-fringed river in its
winding course toward mountains that seem to be suspended across the
valley like a huge natural back-drop. The road at this point is not only
winding but somewhat narrow as well and is unsafe for traveling at
high speed.

At 32.7 *m.* is a junction with a dirt road.

> Right on this road lies *Maidstone Lake*, 3.1 *m.* (right through wooden gate at 2.3 *m.*).
> This beautiful three-mile lake is entirely surrounded by forests. Only a few cot-
> tages have been built here. The secluded waters are a favorite habitat of loons,
> whose mournful tremolos can usually be heard echoing between wilderness and
> wilderness. Maidstone Lake is a rare haven for those who like excellent trout and
> lunge fishing and care little for the accommodations and trappings of developed
> resorts.

At 33.1 *m.* the Connecticut makes an unusual double horseshoe bend,
the most notable of its many arabesque windings in this immediate
region, which are said to spell the word U-N-I-O-N when viewed from
the summit of a near-by mountain. The river valley here resembles the
section farther south, around Newbury, which is known as the Coos
Country, from its Indian name. Roughly speaking, the townships of
Maidstone, Guildhall, and Lunenburg, with the corresponding New
Hampshire towns across the Connecticut, constitute the *Upper Coos
Country*. This district, like its southern counterpart, was a favorite
summer camping and planting ground of the Indians long before it was
seen by any white man.

MAIDSTONE STATION, 34 *m.*, is merely a railroad stop in this thinly
populated township.

GUILDHALL (pronounced Gil-hall) (alt. 874, pop. township 351),
41.3 *m.*, is the shire town of Essex County and one of the earliest settled
towns (1764) in this part of the State. There is no other place in the
world named Guildhall, and research cannot discover why this town was
so called.

The early settlers in Guildhall were harassed by both Indians and Tories, and were apparently of a somewhat aggressive nature themselves. The New Hampshire Town Papers preserve a petition dated June 22, 1780, to the Council and Representatives in which one Enoch Bartlett of Northumberland, just across the river from Guildhall, begs redress because in the previous September 'a Sort of Banditti' entered his grist- and sawmill, cut and destroyed the wheels and shafts, and 'took away all the Iron Works of Said Mills, Mill Stones and other Gear and a Quantity of Boards and Carried them A Cross Connecticut River into the State Called Vermont And improved them for other Mills.' Guildhall's claim of having had the first mill in northeastern Vermont is perhaps a clouded distinction.

The village centers about a grass quadrangle bordered by houses and public buildings, the most interesting of which are the *Essex County Courthouse* and the *Guild Hall*, now the Town Hall, dating from 1795. Smallest of Vermont's shire towns, Guildhall is not only dominated by, but almost composed of, the physical appurtenances of local self-government. Its tiny square has not only the charm but the essence of one of New England's most excellent traditions. In summer twilight it is a stage set.

At 43 *m.* (L), lying a few rods off the road but plainly visible from it, is the *North Burying Ground*, which was laid out by the selectmen in 1797 and contains stones dating two years earlier. The verse epitaphs in this cemetery are unusually varied and interesting.

At 43.9 *m.* is the junction with a dirt road.

Right on this road lies GRANBY (pop. township 70), 8.5 *m.*, a hamlet consisting of a few houses and a church, the sole settlement in this forest township, which is rightly famous as fish and game territory.

GALLUP MILLS, 10.2 *m.*, is a small deserted-looking hamlet in the northeastern part of the township of Victory (pop. 80). Gallup Mills was formerly the site of important sawmills, which were built when this great timber region was cut for the first time. The St. Johnsbury and Lake Champlain R.R. (Victory Branch) once went through this settlement and two and a half miles north to other mills. The sturdy second growth that covers this region, which is still owned by the large lumber companies that first cut it, makes it certain that some day this silent wilderness will again be the scene of buzzing industry, when men shall have come a second time to destroy it.

At 44.9 *m.* the outstanding peak to the right is *Cow Mountain*, so called not from any semblance of bovine outline, but because an early Negro inhabitant of Guildhall who decided to break up housekeeping and retire to the fastnesses of this mountain stole a neighbor's cow and took it with him. He was finally caught by an armed posse and died in prison soon afterward. The name of this man who gave up his freedom for an assured supply of fresh milk was — Bacchus.

As the route nears its southern end, it runs along a shelf above the tracks of the Maine Central R.R., which lie between the highway and the river. At 49.3 *m.* is the junction with US 2 (*see Tour 5*).

T O U R   2 :  *From* CONNECTICUT RIVER *to* JUNCTION
WITH US 5, 144 *m.* State 11, 10, 106, 12, 12A, and 12B.

Via (*sec. a*) Springfield, Reading, Woodstock; (*sec. b*) Barnard, Bethel, Randolph, Roxbury, Northfield, Montpelier; (*sec. c*) East Montpelier, Calais, Woodbury, Hardwick, Craftsbury, Albany, Irasburg.

Between Bethel and Montpelier the Central Vermont Ry. parallels this route.

Road conditions vary from dirt to hard surface, the latter occurring chiefly on the southern end of *sec. a* and on *sec. b*.

*Sec. a.  Connecticut River to Woodstock, 33.3 m.* State 11, 10, *and* 106.

MUCH of this route runs through territory that a notably large number of out-of-State people have chosen for summer homes. The varied terrain and tree-shaded dirt and gravel roads have also made it one of the most popular districts in the State for horseback riding. In not unpleasant contrast, Springfield, at the southern end of the route, shows by its concentrated industrial vitality that Vermont is a workshop as well as a playground.

*Connecticut River* and *New Hampshire State Line,* 0 *m.*

The *Cheshire Toll Bridge* (15¢ *toll*) crosses the Connecticut River.

Between the boundary and Springfield, State 11 parallels the winding course of the Black River and the tracks of the Springfield Terminal Railway Company, the only electric line in the State.

> SPRINGFIELD (alt. 410, pop. 4943) (*see SPRINGFIELD*), 4.4 *m.* The Machine Tool Center; Congregational Church; St. Trinity Greek Orthodox Church; and other points of interest.

On the northern outskirts of Springfield, the route passes one of the large machine shops (L) that support the town industrially.

NORTH SPRINGFIELD, 7.8 *m.*, is a residential village lying mainly west of the highway on the long central street crossed by the latter at right angles. North Springfield, less than four miles from Springfield itself, is typical of several small villages near the larger industrial centers in Vermont today in that many persons who work in the latter prefer to live in the former and commute to the shops and factories.

North of North Springfield the Route follows State 106.

KENDALL'S CORNERS, 8.8 *m.*, is a small settlement distinguished chiefly by the *Hartness Municipal Airport* (R), a fine three-way flying field (with storage hangar), at which courses in aviation are given by experienced pilots.

PERKINSVILLE, 11.1 *m.*, is a typical rural trading and postal center, with a small central Common surrounded by comfortable houses and a somewhat grim church (1832), which is steepleless. Grimness is perhaps the keynote of Perkinsville, for one of the near-by rural districts is known far and wide as Murderer's Gulch.

The four-corners intersection at 14.2 *m.* is the site of the old 18th-century *Downer's Tavern*, a hostelry so widely known in the past that it is still to be found simply as 'Downer's' on many recent Vermont maps.

GREENBUSH, 14.8 *m.*, is a tiny cluster of dwellings, chiefly memorable for its pleasant name.

*Little Ascutney Mountain* (alt. 1740) (R), 15.2 *m.*, rises in rocky sheerness from its meadow floor only a short distance from the road. Much smaller and less lofty than the dominating peak for which it was named, Little Ascutney is at this point more easily comprehended in its complete and dramatic outline than Ascutney itself is from any one highway vantage-point.

At 17.3 *m.* stand (R) two *Indian Stones*, as they are called, commemorating the spot of the first night's encampment of the hostile Indians that raided Charlestown, New Hampshire, on August 30, 1754, and their captives from that place. The next morning, about half a mile from this spot, Mrs. Johnson, one of the two women captives, was delivered of a daughter, Elizabeth Captive Johnson, the third white child to be born on what is now Vermont soil. Mrs. Johnson's written story of her hardships and the wanderings leading to her ultimate safe return was one of the most popular of the early captivity narratives. She herself returned as a very old woman to erect these slate-stone slabs, more than a century and a quarter ago.

FELCHVILLE (P. O. Reading), 18 *m.*, a pleasant, uncommercial village consisting mainly of one long maple-shaded street, is the chief settlement in Reading Township. There is an unusually fine *Library* here and a commodious but rather bleak-looking *Town Hall* with an auditorium and stage equipment, both the gifts of native sons. Reading has always been theatrical-minded. For 25 years after the Civil War the Whitmore and Clark Minstrels of Reading traveled all over New England, eastern New York, and the Provinces with perennial success. Azro ('Hank') White, the leading comic, was regarded by scattered thousands as the finest natural comedian of his time. In Reading also was born, in 1853, Henri Wilkins, whose extravagant melodramas, written as a very young man, were widely successful. His 'Three Glasses a Day,' 'The Reward of Crime,' and others seem crude today, but they delighted the audiences of the '80's.

> Left from Felchville a dirt road leads through wooded wilderness to SOUTH READING, 3.3 *m.*, a small village built roughly in the shape of a triangle. The *Schoolhouse* (1835) and the one *Church*, of approximately the same date, are excellent and well-preserved examples of early building in native gray stone. This little settlement once supported a map-making industry that had branch offices in New York, Cleveland, and Montreal.

The *Budd D. Hawkins Seed Shop*, 19.1 *m.*, houses the leading business of this town. The rambling, unpainted storage sheds surrounding and attached to it cannot obscure the dignity and classic proportions of the large red-brick central part, which was built as a Masonic Hall in 1815.

HAMMONDSVILLE, 21.2 *m.*, is a tiny hamlet stretched along one side of the highway. *Graystone Inn* (L), built about 1820, is another good example of the sturdy native stone houses that are found in considerable numbers in Reading, Cavendish, and Chester. Preserved records show that the man who quarried all the stone used in building this house — from the hill facing it across the narrow valley — received as his total payment one heavy winter overcoat. The *Grange Hall* (L) just north of the inn is well over a century old. That it is not more interesting architecturally is doubtless due to the fact that it was built in haste and discouragement to replace a much finer structure, a tavern, that burned soon after its completion. In this building lived for many years the woman known as Sleeping Lucy, who later, in Boston and other cities, became one of the best-known spiritualistic mediums in New England.

> Left from the Grange Hall a dirt road winds up the little valley of Mill Brook to what was long known — and still occurs on maps — as *Bailey's Mills*, 1.2 *m.*, now called 'Dhumilburn' by its private owners. Built in 1824, this massive edifice once housed a carding mill, a blacksmith shop, a general store, six large family apartments, and, on the third floor, a dance-hall.
>
> Extending the whole length of the brow of the hill (R) above Bailey's Mills is *Fairview Farm*, a popular rural resort and one of the three or four outstanding examples of Vermont's 'continuous architecture' (*see Architecture*).

North of Hammondsville the road soon begins the ascent of *Reading Hill*, typical of the high elevations of this township, into which no water flows. The two-and-a-half-mile drive up Reading Hill and down the other side is one of great beauty, but one in which drivers should exercise more than ordinary caution.

At 25.2 *m.* the route enters the township of Woodstock.

At 27.4 *m.* are the *Upwey Farms*, which have been the leading agency in the introduction into Vermont of the Suffolk Punch draft horse, an English breed whose hardiness and tractability make it ideally suited to the needs of this State, where the horse can never be supplanted by machinery to the extent possible in less hilly regions. The Upwey Farms are a part of the estate of Owen Moon, Jr., the main mansion of which can be seen (R) on a higher elevation set in the midst of elaborately landscaped grounds that include an open-air amphitheater.

SOUTH WOODSTOCK (alt. 1055), 28 *m.*, is a drowsy little village with a Colonial air, a fitting transition between the rustic vigor of Reading and the urbane reserve of Woodstock itself. The white church-like building on the knoll across the brook (R) was the seat of the *Green Mountain Liberal Institute* (1848), which has been closed for many years, but was once the leading preparatory school of this section. The countryside around South Woodstock is largely given over to summer homes where artists, writers, and other out-of-State people spend a part of each year. Anne Bosworth Greene, author of essays and travel books, is, however, a year-round resident on one of these hill farms, as those who have read her brave and charming book 'The Lone Winter' (1923) will remember. North of South Woodstock the route follows a winding brook through countryside that is, for the most part, sparsely populated. The numerous narrow dirt roads that branch off from the main highway at intervals lead to view-commanding hill farms, many of which have been converted into summer homes.

At 32.6 *m.* is the *Woodstock Inn Golf Course* (R) (*greens fee* $1). Not one of the sportiest courses in the State, this is undoubtedly one of the most beautifully landscaped and most carefully conditioned. On the hill over-looking the golf course the *Woodstock Ski Jump* (R) is visible, a gaunt reminder in summer of the winter sports for which Woodstock is one of the leading New England resorts; the recent trend, however, is definitely away from jumping and toward downhill running on the fine open slopes which abound in this vicinity and on several of which ski-tows have been built.

> WOODSTOCK (alt. 705, pop. 1305) (*see WOODSTOCK*), 33.3 *m.* Popular summer and winter resort; site of first ski-tow in the United States; unusually fine golf course; four churches with bells cast by Paul Revere; Colonial Courthouse; collection of Japanese Art (Norman Williams Public Library); D.A.R. House and Museum.

Woodstock is at the junction with US 4 (*see Tour 6*).

*Sec. b.    Woodstock to Montpelier, 53.2 m.* State 12 *and* 12A.

This is primarily a valley route. The section of the State through which it runs is not so well known or so frequently visited by tourists as are the Lake Champlain and Connecticut River valleys. The vistas are less broad in this central valley than they are to the east and the west, and there are fewer towns here of commercial importance. But the almost cloistered intimacy of much of the route has its own special beauty and will appeal to certain travelers — or to certain moods — more strongly than the more open and more populous routes.

WOODSTOCK, 0 *m.* (*see WOODSTOCK*).

At 0.4 *m.* is the former site of the Windsor County Fair (R), which at the time of its discontinuance a few years ago was the oldest county fair in New England.

The countryside near Woodstock is more highly cultivated than it is somewhat farther north, and a few of the large estates and summer homes for which Woodstock is noted are visible from the highway.

At 1.9 *m.* is the *Woodstock Ski Hill* (R), upon which, in 1933–34, the White Cupboard Inn erected *the first ski-tow in the United States*. It was driven by an old Buick motor. Today the 2200-foot electric-powered tow on the same slope is one of several that accommodate the throngs of skiers who flock to Woodstock every winter.

PROSPER, 2.9 *m.*, in the township of Woodstock, is a small three-corner settlement of a few houses and an old mill.

North of Prosper, the countryside grows gradually wilder and the route soon begins the ascent of *Barnard Gulf*, a winding, densely wooded stretch of great scenic beauty. The Gulf ends at about 8.2 *m.*, and from the height of land the road descends a long sharp slope into Barnard village.

BARNARD (alt. 1334, pop. township 584), 10.3 *m.*, is a drowsy village located at the outlet of beautiful Silver Lake, upon the shores of which, slightly removed from the village, are a growing number of summer cottages. Once a commercially thriving community, Barnard is now chiefly noted as a haven of seclusion. Among its residents are Sinclair Lewis, novelist and Nobel Prize winner, and his wife, Dorothy Thompson, student and critic of world affairs. The last panther killed in Vermont was shot in Barnard in 1881 and is preserved at the State House in Montpelier. Unfortunately no such tangible proof remains to authenticate the legend that on June 17, 1775, when Barnard was settled, the pioneers distinctly heard the cannons of Bunker Hill, more than 100 miles away.

At 13.1 *m.* is a bronze marker commemorating the *Site of Fort Defiance* (L), which was maintained as a garrisoned stronghold during a part of the turbulent period of Barnard's early history.

Northward the road runs through a narrow valley. At 16.6 *m.* the road becomes hard surface and continues through a landscape thickly wooded with maples, birches, and evergreens.

BETHEL (alt. 600, pop. township 1650), 18.8 *m.*, lies in a natural basin in the southeastern part of Bethel Township at the junction of the Third Branch and the White River. For many years the village thrived as the cutting and shipping center for the extensive granite quarries in the eastern part of the township. These quarries were closed, however, in 1925, and the village is now primarily a trading and dairying center.

Bethel's early years were dangerous ones, as were those of its neighboring towns, for the White River Valley was a favorite raiding route with the hostile Canadian Indians. One of the first acts of the early settlers was the erection, in 1780, of Fort Fortitude, on the site of the present railroad station. Alarmed by an Indian raid upon Barnard in August of that year, the settlers of Bethel called upon the garrison at Royalton, which in response was moved to the Bethel fort. Two months later Royalton was raided and burned by a party of about 300 Indians, and Bethel was undoubtedly spared a similar fate only because of its garrisoned fort.

Bethel was formerly the home of Mary Waller, the novelist, and the scene of her best-loved book, 'The Wood-Carver of 'Lympus' (1914), is laid in the southwestern section of the township that is Olympus on all maps and Lympus on all tongues. The country road from Bethel village to the Lympus section is one of the favorite trails of the Green Mountain Horse Club, but it is not recommended to motorists.

Bethel was the first town to be chartered by the newly formed State of

Vermont, in 1778, and in that respect bears the same relation to the State that the latter bears to the Union.

At 21.8 *m.* stands the old *McKinstry House* (L), the main front part dating from about 1810, the rear ell from the 18th century. From its brick-paved butter-cellar (a small part of the cellars that underlie the whole house) to its ten-inch-square hand-hewn timbers, this structure is a fine example of the sturdiness and thoroughness with which early builders wrought. The front of the house has a simple but well-designed Palladian window.

At 22.4 *m.* stands the '*Old Church*' (R), built about 1820, with a small cemetery behind it, both enclosed by a white wood fence. This building is of excellently balanced proportions except for the turret-like tower, which is unpleasantly squat and over-ornate for the rest of the structure. Each of the large windows contains 50 separate panes of glass.

Here is a junction with a dirt road.

> Left on this road is the site of the *Birthplace of General Stephen Thomas* (1809–1903), the hero of Cedar Creek, 3.3 *m.* The road, gradual in its ascent at first, finally becomes so steep and rough that it is advisable to make the last three-quarters of a mile on foot. The commemorative stone that marks this spot is a modest granite marker, in itself probably not worth the trip except to persons with a special interest; but the hill on which it stands commands a view to the south and east of true magnificence. This northern section of Bethel township is known as Bethel Gilead.

North of this point are a considerable number of large farms with sizable brick farmhouses that give the community an air of solidity and well-being.

RANDOLPH (alt. 694, pop. 1957), 25.9 *m.*, is a trim and prosperous-looking village. It is unusually well provided with public buildings to meet all civic and social needs, though they are for the most part uninteresting architecturally. The village is divided almost equally in two by the Central Vermont Ry., the main business section lying north of the tracks. Farm implements of several types, rubber stamps, furniture, and sheet gelatin are manufactured in Randolph, and its location in one of the leading dairy districts of the State has led to the establishment of three creameries here. In the high, quiet residential section at the southern end of the village are a modern *Hospital* that serves a wide radius and the *Old Ladies' Home* maintained by the Vermont chapters of the Order of the Eastern Star.

At 26.4 *m.*, on the northern outskirts of Randolph village, is a junction with a hard-surfaced road.

> Right up this gradually climbing road lies RANDOLPH CENTER, 3.3 *m.* This quiet hilltop village, one of the highest in the State (alt. 1384), was the earliest settled part of Randolph Township, once its business as well as its geographical center, and was seriously considered in the opening years of the 19th century for the State capital. Montpelier was the final choice instead (in 1805), and in the succeeding decades the population and trade of Randolph Center — as in so many Vermont hill communities — were drawn to the valley, where there were streams to turn the wheels of the mills and, after 1850, railroads to carry their products away.

At present Randolph Center is best known as the seat of the *Vermont State School of Agriculture*, established by act of legislature in 1910 on the site of the Orange County Grammar School (1806), the original building of the latter school being still in use as a recitation hall. The curriculum is designed to include courses in scientific farming and practical farm management for young Vermonters who have not had a high-school training as well as for those who have. The neat yellow-and-white recitation halls and dormitories dominate the east side of the one wide shady street. Behind them lies the large modern farm that is operated chiefly by student labor — a great outdoor laboratory. Records show that more than 80 per cent of the alumni of this school have remained in Vermont and that the greater part of them are engaged in agricultural work. The value of such an institution to a predominantly agricultural State is self-evident.

Of the several century-old houses set back from the broad street, the most noteworthy is the Chase, or Parrish, House, *Maple Grove* (1804), one of the finest remaining examples of Adamesque adornment in Vermont. The delicate white grace of its door, fanlights, pilasters, and cornice carvings, shining through the shade and between the trunks of some dozen large maple trees planted soon after the house was built, is a sight not soon forgotten. If Randolph Center had been selected as the Capital site, as many hoped it would be, Maple Grove was to have been the Governor's Mansion. The house was sufficiently honored, however, by sheltering for a time Salmon P. Chase, Chief Justice of the United States (1864–73), who lived here and studied law with his uncle, Judge Dudley Chase, until the latter advised him to abandon it, as it was foreign to his talents.

In 1795, Justin Morgan of Randolph Center brought here from West Springfield, Massachusetts, as part payment of a debt, the two-year-old colt that was later to be known as Justin Morgan also and that founded the first pure breed of American horses (*see Tour 4, WEYBRIDGE*). The already famous animal was taken elsewhere soon after the death, in 1798, of its owner, who is buried in the cemetery by the Congregational Church at the south end of the village.

The view from Randolph Center is panoramic in all directions, but especially sweeping to the north and west. This side-trip is especially recommended to the many travelers who visit Vermont during the period when the autumn foliage is most colorful.

Also at the northern end of Randolph village is the junction with State 12A, an alternate route between this junction and Northfield.

Left on State 12A the road soon passes from open terrain into a narrow valley where there is little arable land. The farms look unyielding, the buildings drab.

BRAINTREE (alt. 777, pop. 635), 5.7 *m.*, is a small village whose business activity is centered in two sawmills.

EAST GRANVILLE (alt. 850), 8.8 *m.*, is a small rural settlement, the only industry being the manufacture of novelties. North of this point the country grows increasingly wild and sparsely populated. This is one of the localities in the State where bears are still found. The high ridge on the right, beginning about 3 miles north of East Granville, is wooded almost exclusively with white birches, which grow in greater density here than in any other section of Vermont. Only in early spring or in late autumn, when the other trees, having lost their bright foliage, seem gaunt and bare, do these birches reveal the full beauty of their white arabesques against the dark hills.

At 12.5 *m.* is a *State Fish Hatchery*, to which visitors are welcome. The general region around the hatchery is known locally as 'The Flat.' Considerable lumbering operations are carried on here.

At 13.5 *m.* a *Quarry* (L) of the Vermont Marble Company is actively operated. The product quarried here, though of limited use, is of a very lovely green color.

ROXBURY (alt. 1007, pop. township 504), 14.7 *m.*, is a quiet country village of one street, the main settlement in the township of the same name. There are no alarums and excursions in Roxbury today (except possibly in camping season), yet one of its earliest settlers was Captain Benjamin Sampson, the boy who rang the Lexington church bell to call out the Minutemen on April 19, 1775. Part of Roxbury Township lies on a height of land from which water flows to both the St. Lawrence Bay and Long Island Sound. The Central Vermont Ry. here reaches the highest point on its line.

On a ridge (R) at 14.9 *m.*, half hidden by the pines sit the many cottages of *Teela-Wooket*, a summer camp for girls. Adjacent are the tennis courts and golf links and the stables for the fine saddle horses for which this camp is noted.

From this point State 12A winds to the junction with State 12 at 20.6 *m.*

The large brick house known as *Manchester*, at 27.2 *m.*, is more than a century old. The bricks for its construction were brought here from East Middlebury. Behind its spindly porches, added later, the house itself is of excellent lines and is noteworthy in having its adjoining ell, a shed, built of brick, as is the main part, instead of the usual wood.

Northward the road traverses the eastern side of the valley. The hills to the west are gently sloping, and many of them are under cultivation. Here, as in many other places in Vermont, the high-lying fields of corn and grain and the painted farm buildings shining white on the distant uplands are comforting evidence that an austere challenge has been met successfully.

EAST BRAINTREE (alt. 720), 31.5 *m.*, is an undistinguished village built in an S-shape. Its sole product is lumber.

The road continues past pleasant valley farms, with a background of hilly pasturelands rising from the meadow floors.

At 32.9 *m.* is a junction with a dirt road, a white-fenced cemetery with early 19th-century slate stones lying in the elbow of the junction curve.

Left up this steep, brook-bordered road is WEST BROOKFIELD (alt. 1036), .8 *m.*, an open, scattering village centered loosely around a country four-corners.

At about 33.3 *m.* is the southern entrance to *Northfield Gulf*, the steepest of the three highway gulfs in central Vermont. It is nature untouched except for the excellent bituminous road and an occasional picnic area turnout, which makes the enjoyment of it more accessible to the traveler without marring its beauty. The three-mile stretch, which, despite its name, lies mainly in the township of Brookfield, is through a narrow valley with thickly wooded slopes on both sides. Maples, elms, and dense clumps of coniferous trees all but shut out the day from the arboreal tunnel through which the road winds and climbs, a small brook (L) tumbling along beside it. North of the Gulf, the valley widens somewhat, but there are few cultivated farms along the winding road.

SOUTH NORTHFIELD (alt. 839), 40.8 *m.*, is a small straggling village with one store and a gristmill.

At 42.1 *m.* is the junction of State 12 and State 12A, the latter an alternate route between Randolph and this junction (*see above*).

On the southern outskirts of Northfield village, the *Mount Hope Cemetery* (L), 42.2 *m.*, rises gradually in uniform terraces to a mausoleum-crowned summit.

NORTHFIELD (alt. 760, pop. 2075), 43.1 *m.*, is the geographical center of the State and an incorporated village of varied importance. As the home of Governor Charles Paine, one of the projectors and financial backers of the Central Vermont Ry., Northfield became an important railroad center (*see Transportation*). The railroad shops that gave the town its main business impetus were removed to St. Albans after Governor Paine's death. The large red-brick depot, now occupied in part by one of the three local banks, is on the west side of the small central square, which is dominated by a Civil War memorial monument. Today the numerous granite and monument shops are the most important of the several industries in the town, which include also two textile mills, a hosiery mill, a handkerchief mill, and several sawmills and wood-working shops.

It is as the seat of *Norwich University* (enrollment about 300), however, that Northfield is most widely known. Founded in 1819 as the American Literary, Scientific, and Military Academy, this famous school was originally located at Norwich (Vermont). Taking its name from that town, it was chartered by the State in 1843 as the Norwich University, the first scientific and classical as well as military-collegiate institution after West Point in the United States. A disastrous fire razed the old buildings at Norwich in 1866, and the following year the school was moved to its present site. The offer of grounds was a major inducement, and it was furthermore felt that Vermonters had recently suffered enough from the Civil War between the States without being longer subjected to the one between Norwich and Dartmouth College, situated less than two miles distant from Norwich across the Connecticut River.

The life at Norwich is a rugged one, but the success of its graduates for a hundred years has more than justified the vigorous routine of their training. Many of the most famous civil engineers of the country are Norwich men, and the large percentage of its graduates who have risen to high offices in the army and navy includes Admirals Dewey, Converse, and Calvocoresses, Brigadier-Generals Rice and Williston, and Major-General Dodge. Seventy-four per cent of Norwich graduates of military age were in service during the World War, 86 per cent of whom were commissioned officers.

The University buildings lie south and west of the business section of the town. Roads wind up the park-like campus hill and around the level quadrangle at the top. At almost any hour of the day during the academic year, trimly uniformed cadets can be seen hurrying across this crowning plateau in response to the calls, not of a bell, but of a bugler, who repeats his notes to the four points of the compass: a military muezzin.

On the campus hill, but not officially connected with the University, is a *U.S. Weather Bureau*, one of two in the State. The brick building, built in 1910, with its collection of wind- and weather-gauging instruments on the central roof-peak, is easily recognizable. The chief purposes of this bureau are the gathering of statistics to furnish bases for long-time predictions, and the forecast of immediate conditions, especially frosts, cold waves, and heavy snows. The widespread belief that Northfield itself is the coldest spot in the State is baseless and rests largely on the fact that this bureau's official readings are usually somewhat lower than those of the Burlington bureau. But the winter temperature of the high central and eastern parts of the State are everywhere lower than those of the Champlain Valley. The lowest temperature ever recorded in Vermont on a Government-furnished thermometer, — 50°, occurred in the extreme northeastern section of the State and was reported by one of the Northfield bureau's numerous allied observers.

NORTHFIELD FALLS (alt. 680), 44.8 *m.*, is a small residential village, the houses of which are set unusually close to the street, resulting in a noticeable absence of the green, shaded lawns that often constitute the chief charm of settlements of this size and type. On the southern outskirts of the village, however, a neat modern cemetery has received the landscaping that the private homes lack. A dirt road (L) leads from the center of the village to outlying farms across a covered bridge that is visible from the main highway.

RIVERTON, 46.5 *m.*, is an undistinguished hamlet consisting of a church, two stores, a post office, and a small scattering of plain wooden houses. On the bluffs above, several summer homes have been built, one of them being the residence of Herbert Welch, former President of the Indian Rights Association in this country. The only industry is carried on in the granite-cutting sheds (R) by the station.

For a mile north of Riverton, the highway runs close to the Dog River, passing through rock cuts, with man-made cliffs on the left, and then swings (L) away from the river through valley country. The fine maple groves on a majority of the farms in this section make it an important maple-sugar district in the spring and a vale of flaming color in the fall.

At 52.7 *m.* State 12 climbs to higher levels, but makes an almost immediate winding descent into Montpelier.

> MONTPELIER (alt. 523, pop. 7837) (*see MONTPELIER*), 53.2 *m.* State Capital; Washington County Seat; home of National Life Insurance Co.; State House; Supreme Court Bldg., with Historical Society Museum; National Life Bldg.; Wood Art Gallery; Hubbard Park; Vermont Junior College; Bethany Congregational Church; Kellogg-Hubbard Library; Colonel Jacob Davis House; and other points of interest.

*Sec. c.　Montpelier to Coventry, 58.8 m.* State 12 *and* 12B.

Between Montpelier and Hardwick the country becomes more wild and barren, less prosperous-looking, with one of the most crooked highways in the State endlessly curving and twisting through irregular narrow valleys. Utmost caution should be used through this section, as the sharp blind curves make high speed out of the question. Between Hardwick and Coventry, State 12B follows the pleasant valley of the Black River of the North, the scrolled course of the little stream wending erratically through the mellow soils of an attractive farming region. In general, this route runs through the variable scenery of the typical lake-and-woods country of northeastern Vermont.

MONTPELIER, 0 *m.* (*see MONTPELIER*).

Between Montpelier and East Montpelier, State 12, in conjunction with US 2, follows a curving cement roadway along the tortuous bends of the Winooski River in the narrow valley.

At 2.4 *m.* is the junction with US 302 (*see Tour 5B*).

At 4.1 *m.* is an extremely dangerous railroad underpass, with right-angle curves at both ends of the narrow pass.

EAST MONTPELIER (alt. 728, pop. 965), 7.3 *m.*, set apart from Montpelier as a separate township in 1848, lies along an irregular shelf over the Winooski River. Perley Davis, brother of Jacob Davis, who founded Montpelier, was the pioneer father of East Montpelier. The brick *Universalist Church* stands eminently over the highway junction at the north end of the settlement. A creamery represents the sole industry.

Here is the junction with US 2 (*see Tour 5*).

Left from the north end of East Montpelier on an uphill country road is the *Old Quaker Burial Ground* (L), 0.7 *m.* Across the fields and beyond an old unfenced graveyard on the open meadow, the Quaker Burial Ground lies in a tree-grown, fenced-in plot, with chipped and crumbling stones, many of which lean grassward or lie flat on the earth. The oldest legible slate is dated 1797.

State 12 continues uphill and down over a pleasant upland country to a junction with a hill road at 9.4 *m.*

Left on this climbing dirt road is the old *Perley Davis House* (R), 0.5 *m.*, once the show-place of this section, but now fallen into decay. Of the once-great mansion there remains only a ruined shell standing in the tangled neglect of its yard, the walls and roof partially intact, but the interior gutted and littered with débris and rubble. This house was built, sometime before 1800, by General Perley Davis, of the pioneer Davises so prominent in early Montpelier and East Montpelier history.

From the hill crest at 9.7 *m.* a fine view (R) unfolds over the undulating roll of smooth hills, cleared land alternating with patches of forest, to the tiers of mountain domes and peaks sculptured against the distant skyline.

NORTH MONTPELIER (alt. 670), 10.3 *m.*, lies in a narrow valley at the foot of a long hill descending from the south, with a millpond at its northern extremity. The square-lined *Rich House* (R), standing eminent near the top of the hill, bears the date of its erection, 1805. The *Little Woolen Company Mill* lies on both sides of the highway at the village center, its two sections connected by an overhead wooden passageway arching the road. The mill employs about fifty workmen and is the basic industry of this immediate vicinity. The *Driftwind Press* (L) is the home of Vermont's 'little poetry magazine,' *Driftwind*, edited, printed, and published by Walter J. Coates, storekeeper and poet.

A *Brick House* (R), 11.7 *m.*, stands below the main thoroughfare in the strong handsome dignity characteristic of well-built 19th-century brick homesteads.

**At 12.5** *m.* is a junction with a country road.

Left on this dirt road is PEKIN, 1 *m.*, a little hamlet curiously bearing an Oriental name, the origin of which is unknown.

At 2 *m.* is a junction with a side road; near the intersection stands the Gospel Hollow Church, now used as a Town Hall.

Left 0.8 *m.* on the side road is KENTS' CORNER.

1 *m.* South from Kents' Corner stands the *Old West Church,* exactly as it was when erected in 1824, epitomizing the stalwart severity of plain rural meeting-houses of that period. The church is the oldest landmark in Calais Township, and has been the meeting-house at different times of various sects, including the Millerites. Calais had more than its share of these fanatics, of whom it was estimated that there were about 50,000 in the country. They were followers of William Miller, who demonstrated from Scripture, to their satisfaction, that the world would end on December 31, 1843, with the earth and sea giving up their dead and those who had achieved salvation entering immediately into eternal bliss. On the last evening of 1843, the Old West Church was packed, with both Millerites and those who came to see the show. A large clock was set up near the pulpit. As midnight began to strike, women screamed, and several fainted; that was all. In ten minutes the church was empty, and the brief history of the Millerites was at an end.

CALAIS (alt. 1080, pop. township 811), 2.9 *m.*, on the main side road, is located on high fertile plateau-land with many near-by lakes and ponds, some of which remain in their primitive and unspoiled state. The first settlement was made by Francis West, and the town was named by Colonel Jacob Davis, founder of Montpelier, who here again revealed his fondness for French names. In 1838, Wareham Chase invented an electric motor here, two years after Davenport's invention (*see Tour 2A, WILLIAMSTOWN*).

Chase was born in Calais and lived to be nearly a hundred without ever going thirty miles from home. The sheer ingenuity of such an obscure, unlearned man is almost incredible. In 1922, the president of General Electric came to examine Chase's motor in the Historical Society Museum, at Montpelier, and declared it to be more nearly perfect than the Davenport motor. Dorman B. Eaton, the founder of Civil Service reform, grew from childhood to early manhood in Calais. In Calais lived for many years one of the most extreme of Vermont eccentrics, Pardon Janes (1788–1870). Janes came here from Connecticut as a child and showed unusual intelligence and promise as a young man. He was a gifted speaker and represented Calais in the legislature, 1828–31. But the latter part of his long life was clouded by a disillusionment, the source of which is not generally known, that verged upon madness. He wore for many years a short pitchfork strapped to his hand, so that he need not touch with his flesh any object touched by another human being. The very few things he bought at store — unbleached cotton, salt — he paid for with money that he carried in a tin pail on the end of his pitchfork, the clerks making the change for him. The title poem of 'The Devil is a Woman' (1929), by Alice Mary Kimball, treats of Pardon Janes by name, but is a highly colored and almost complete deviation from the facts.

Between this point and East Calais the valley dips lower and broadens, becoming richer and more beautiful.

EAST CALAIS, 15.1 *m.*, situated on a rise in the valley with gently ascending hills on either side, is built around the millpond and sawmill (L) at the north end. The calm pond and stacks of raw lumber climax a little village having the appearance of a stage setting for an old-time rustic scene, the atmosphere of backwoods New England of the past. Horses and wagons are often seen along the Main St., with villagers and farmers idly gossiping on the wooden porches. It is unusual for a village on a main thoroughfare to retain such an air of rural lethargy.

Between East Calais and Woodbury Lake, State 12 continues curving and bending through the wild narrow valley enclosed by low forested ridges.

*Woodbury Lake* (L), 18.4 *m.*, is an attractive body of water, stretching in irregular outline between wooded shores, with jutting points and shady islands diversifying the scenery with wild beauty. Affording fine boating and canoeing, this has become a popular summer resort.

SOUTH WOODBURY, 19.1 *m.* A high-façaded brown wooden *Congregational Church* (R) dominates the small cluster of buildings on the highway, facing the plateau (L) across the valley where the weather-beaten backs of houses constitute an oddly arranged pattern. Under drooping shade trees on the low plateau, faded homes and overgrown lawns lie quietly remote, a scene untouched by modern times.

Between South Woodbury and Woodbury, the highway twists and turns in endless sharp curves through a wild wooded country of rugged barrenness.

WOODBURY (pop. township 529), 21.2 *m.*, straggles sleepily along the valley, a small collection of nondescript wooden houses with a ragged central grass plot (L) before a country store. Several rather dilapidated structures here, now serving various purposes, resemble rude churches. Lumber milling on a small scale is now the main means of subsistence of a hamlet that flourished in the days when its granite industry was at its height. The *Antique Shop* (R), plain and commodious, is the oldest building in the village, constructed about 1815. The shop is upstairs in the old ballroom, which still has the original bandstand. Woodbury claims to have furnished more Civil War soldiers per capita of population than any other Vermont town. William C. Wheeler, said to be the only living son of a Revolutionary soldier, resides here at present (1937). There are 28 lakes and ponds in the township, and a peculiar feature is that no water flows into the township, all the streams flowing outward.

> Right from the Antique Shop on a narrow steep hill road are *Woodbury Mountain* and *Granite Quarries*, 1.9 *m.* This mountain is believed to be the largest deposit of building granite in the world. Mammoth quarries are here, with great gray piles of waste granite massed everywhere. The deposit is so uniformly good, and in such deep veins, that the quarrying is done horizontally, cutting into the mountain side rather than penetrating vertically down. The nine-mile railroad that connected these quarries with Hardwick ran high along the mountain flank, one of the highest railways in New England. The president of this line, seeking an exchange of passes with the president of the New York Central, admitted that his line was shorter than the Central, but insisted 'It's just as wide.' Woodbury Mountain was the source of building stone that lifted Hardwick to eminence in the granite world. The view from this height is superbly far-reaching.

*Greenwood Lake* (L), 22.3 *m.*, thickly screened by woods, is seen from the highway only in brief glimpses. With wild irregular shores, the forests marching down to the water's edge, this lake is a haven for sportsmen and lovers of solitude.

A *Private Fish Pond* (L), 23.1 *m.*, lies below the highway, which here winds downward in a long gradual climb. On clear sunny days the fish are sometimes visible from the road as they swim about in the shallow pool.

At 25.3 *m.* are typical cow-terraced pasture knolls (R). The road curves through a low narrow valley that in places becomes little more than a steep wooded ravine before ascending to the higher levels of Hardwick.

HARDWICK (alt. 861, pop. 1667), 26.7 *m.*, named after Hardwick, Massachusetts, from which the first settlers came, is an unshaded granite and industrial village, with a sloping thoroughfare winding down between the crowded wooden buildings of the business section. Growing up hurriedly under the impetus of the granite industry and its resultant prosperity, no attempt was made to beautify the village; appearance was sacrificed almost entirely to intensive industrialism. Although granite has suffered a marked decline, Hardwick is still somewhat imbued with the Barre spirit of modern aggressiveness, and is therefore unlike the usual Vermont village of its size. Laid out in a haphazard manner, Hardwick conveys the impression of unplanned disorder, resulting from too much haste in upgrowth and industrial progress rather than from lack of prosperity and civic ideals.

The first settler here in what was formerly known as South Hardwick was Captain John Bridgam, 1797. The community was mainly agricultural until the discovery of granite, and the inception of that industry by Henry R. Mack in 1868. Development was rapid, and Hardwick rose incredibly to become one of the granite centers of the United States. Stone-workers flocked in from all over the country, the foreign elements swelled, high wages meant free spending, and Hardwick, like a raw booming mining town, rode the crest of prosperity over its mushroom growth. Under the late George H. Bickford, the Woodbury Granite Company became the largest building-granite firm in the world, furnishing stone for the Pennsylvania State Capitol, the Cook County Courthouse in Chicago, and many public buildings in Washington and throughout the country. Other activities in Hardwick include the manufacture of furnaces, woodworking mills, and creameries.

The *Memorial Building*, Main and Church Sts., is a modern structure of Woodbury granite with a Memorial Room of Proctor marble, the walls of which are inscribed with the names of Hardwick soldiers from the Revolutionary to the Civil War. Here is also an especially fine and valuable collection of old coins and paper money. In the main corridor stands a World War Memorial of local granite, and on the second floor is a plaster-of-paris copy of the famous 'Last Supper' made by Frederick A. Purdy, a sculptor who was associated with the Woodbury Granite Company.

The *Jeudevine Memorial Library*, Main St., is a handsome building of sandstone containing 10,000 volumes. The *Bickford Buildings*, Main St., contain woodwork and paneling from the pews of the first church in town, the French Meeting-House. This French Meeting-House was named for an early settler, Samuel French, who built it in 1820, after sectarian variances in the town had delayed the erection of a house of worship. He put the inscription 'Liberty of Conscience' over the door and allowed all sects the use of the building, which he firmly refused, however, to sell. At one time the French Meeting-House was even used by the New Lights, a band of Hardwick fanatics whose short-lived sect, distinguished chiefly by extravagant outward manifestations of inner spiritual light, came into being in 1837. The *Old Sawmill* on the Lamoille River at the northern edge of the village has been in operation on the same site for nearly a century.

Hardwick is at the junction with State 15 (*see Tour 5A*).

Northwest of Hardwick, the route continues on State 12B, skirting artificial *Hardwick Pond* (R), 29.2 *m.*, backed up in a hilly basin by a dam at the southern end.

*Elligo Pond* (R), 35.7 *m.*, a long, narrow body of water with little wooded islands, is closely confined by a forested ridge rising sharply along the eastern shore. The highway runs close beside the western shore, with a lower ridge sheltering it, so that Elligo lies in a long narrow trough — wild in aspect and scenically charming.

North of Elligo, the valley gradually becomes broader and less heavily wooded.

At 36.9 *m.* is a junction with a country road.

> Right on this road, climbing steeply at first, then continuing in gradual ascent through rolling forested uplands, is EAST CRAFTSBURY, 2.2 *m.*, on a gently rolling elevated plain. The *Presbyterian Church* (L) stands on the site of the Old Covenanter Church (now removed to Craftsbury Common), where, until recent years, the forms of this austere faith were explicitly preserved. For several generations the almost undiluted Calvinism of the Covenanter service and discipline held together those Scotch families of the region who had come up over the Hazen Road from the original settlements on the Connecticut River. The *John Woodruff Simpson Memorial Library* (R), a pleasing little white wooden structure, was originally the community store. The interior has been retained; counters, shelves, and drawers are now lined with books instead of groceries and spices. The library, endowed and managed by a niece of the Scotch storekeeper, contains a diversified collection of books chosen with discrimination. The Simpson family has always been eminent in East Craftsbury.

CRAFTSBURY (pop. township 977), 37.6 *m.*, named for grantee Ebenezer Crafts, lies low in the river valley, built around a lumber mill and dam (R). This village, though crudely rustic in contrast with Craftsbury Common to the near north, is typical of the small mill villages found in Vermont valleys and is industrially the heart of the township. Colonel Ebenezer Crafts opened a road from Cabot to this area and founded the settlement in 1788, becoming veritably the patriarchal head of the little community that grew up in the wilderness. Samuel Crafts, Ebenezer's son, carried on the leadership of Craftsbury and became Governor of the State (1828-31). Among the pioneer families were many sturdy Scotch people who left their imprint of clean, thrifty living and sound-minded reliability on the town.

North of Craftsbury, the route climbs a sharply pitched hill, at the crest of which is the *Graham Homestead* (L), the home of Horace F. Graham, Governor of Vermont (1917–19).

CRAFTSBURY COMMON, 39.2 *m.*, crowns the broad summit of a high plateau. Everything in the place is white, gleaming in clean paint: the trim-lined houses and churches, the academy buildings, the single-railed wood fence surrounding the smooth broad green of the Common. Here is a quality of airy cleanness and light, a happy blending of tasteful architecture with the charm of natural setting, that combine to make Craftsbury Common memorable among the villages of northern Vermont. The Colonial ideals of simple purity in line and color are emphasized in this spotless village, arranged with orderly spacing about the large level green. Craftsbury Common is the center of the intellectual and social life of the township and locality.

At the south end of the village the *Old Cemetery* (R) lies iron-fenced beside the highway, with stones dating from the 1790's. Across the street a charming trio of white houses in the Colonial tradition stand behind a white picket fence shaded by giant elms. These three structures strike the keynote of Craftsbury Common's appeal and balance the scene about the Common at the north end of the village. The *Congregational Church* (L) (1820) faces the street from across the north end of the Common in attractive white wood and clear-lined simplicity. *Craftsbury Academy* (R), housed in an ungainly white wooden structure, was established in 1829; among the former headmasters of this reputable little institution was the Reverend Samuel Read Hall (*see Tour 5, CONCORD*). The *Craftsbury Public Library* (R), a tiny and unusual stone oblong, resembles a granite vault. The *Old Covenanter Church* (R), now used as the Academy gymnasium, stands well back from the street in severe white dignity. The vista west from the high plain of the Common that centers these buildings reveals the march of rugged mountains against the distant skyline.

North of Craftsbury Common, State 12B descends steeply to run along the floor of a broad shallow valley with the Black River winding in calm graceful loops through the green meadows.

At 44.2 *m.* the *Hayden Farmhouse* (L) stands in the sturdy impressiveness of structural red brick. Purchased at a low figure some years ago, it was found to be full of valuable antiques.

ALBANY (alt. 900, pop. township 910), 45.9 *m.*, was chartered as Lutterloh, the present name being adopted in 1815. The village is set on a long sloping plain with a wooded ridge (L) offering shelter on the west. The *Town Hall* and *Library* (L) are housed in an old white church building, with a belfry and ugly built-on entry hall. Beside the line of gasoline pumps fronting the village stores (R), a row of Lombardy poplars serves to relieve the drabness of the street. The atmosphere is a solid hinterland one. An annual event that gives vivid expression to this back-country air is the Albany Fair held here each September in the heart of the village, with Main St. serving as midway and race-track combined. Extensive potato-raising and a soda-bottling business are carried on here.

Between Albany and Irasburg, the highway overlooks the meandering bends of the Black River weaving an intricate pattern through a valley supporting good farm-sites. Two tiny ponds lie (L) below the highway at 50.4 *m.* and 50.9 *m.*, and the lowlands in this section are widely known duck-hunting grounds.

IRASBURG (alt. 947, pop. township 924), 53.6 *m.*, named for Ira Allen, is ranged around a large open square on a level plateau above the Black River Valley. The buildings along the north side of the square, which were razed by a fire, have been replaced by smaller and more modern structures that still retain an appearance of drabness. The community depends on lumbering and dairying for its livelihood. Once the shire town of Orleans County, this centrally located village was the active nucleus about which the political and business life of the county revolved, and the spacious square, that today seems so emptily quiet, was generally a busy scene. The *Leach Public Library* (*open Mon., Wed., Sat., evenings and Sat. afternoon*) (R), is a small, neat structure in tapestry brick. A white high-spired *Federated Protestant Church* (R) graces the southeast corner of the square. A few uncommon mansard roofs are seen on the dwelling-houses, but the stores and homes ranked around the open square are unattractive on the whole.

Just north of Irasburg, across the valley (R) on the bank of the Black River, log piles around a sawmill indicate the town's principal industry. Between Irasburg and the junction with US 5, the route runs smoothly along the gently rolling valley floor of the Black River, with dense evergreen groves standing on the east, and low mountain ridges and foothills stacked on the west.

At 58.8 *m.* is the JUNCTION WITH US 5 (*see Tour* 1), just south of Coventry village (*see Tour* 1).

---

T O U R   2 A : *From* BARRE *to* WHITE RIVER JUNCTION, 50.3 *m.*, State 14.

---

Via Websterville, Graniteville, Williamstown, Royalton, Sharon, Hartford.

Between N. Royalton and White River Junction, the Central Vermont Ry. parallels the route.

The highway is excellent hard surface, variably macadam, concrete, and blacktop.

THIS route, commonly known as 'The Williamstown Gulf Road,' proceeds from the deep, narrow defile of Williamstown Gulf enclosed sharply by steep forested mountain-sides to a broad, shallow valley bordered with rolling hills, following the Second Branch to the White River, and then wending in a southeasterly direction along the curving White River Valley. There are many farms along the fertile valley, and quiet little villages diversify the scene with homely glimpses of life in rural comfort. The mountain-pass beauty of Williamstown Gulf may be the scenic high point of the route, but the gentle placidity of river valleys aligned with mild, rolling hillsides has a soothing, chastening effect that is pleasurable.

> BARRE (alt. 609, pop. 11,307) (*see BARRE*), 0 *m.* The 'Granite Center of the World' with many finishing plants and adjacent quarries; Robert Burns Statue; Goddard Junior College; Twing House; Paddock House; Wheelock House; and other points of interest.

State 14 branches south from US 302 at Barre.
On the southern outskirts of the city at 0.9 *m.* is the junction with an improved road.

> Left on this steep, winding uphill road is WEBSTERVILLE (alt. 1400), 3 *m.*, a quarry town on the heights overlooking Barre and the distant panoramic grandeur of mountain chains. The road winds into Websterville past great gray mounds of waste rock, high walls of granite-block, and a deep abandoned quarry hole. The wooden homes are scattered about on the slope, and the *Quarries* now being worked lie at the summit above the village. Here, under mighty boom derricks and a complex overhead pattern of guy-wires, vast open pits have been cut more than 200 feet deep in solid rock, the great blocks of granite drilled out and hoisted to the surface to be loaded on flatcars and taken down the steep looping railroad to the Barre finishing plants. The view southward from this lofty hilltop overlooks the Gargantuan pits of the Graniteville quarries. Everywhere on the upland stretches are the rearing gray piles of waste granite that barricade the countless abandoned quarries. Some of these deserted quarry holes fill with spring water and make good swimming places.

Between this junction and South Barre there are farms and dwellings along the shallow valley, which broadens to the southward in its enclosure of gracefully undulant hills.

SOUTH BARRE (alt. 740) 1.5 *m.*, is a small residential suburb of Barre.

The *Denison Smith House*, built in 1805, is of white wood with an over-ornate façade. The Palladian window above the fine arched entrance is the only one in the vicinity. The windows, slightly recessed in arched panels, are harmonious with the details of the doorway. Four plain pilasters, the Doric frieze with triglyph motif, and the modillion cornice produce a richness of design. The *South Barre Recreation Field* (R) lies across the Stevens Branch of the Winooski River, containing a baseball field, tennis courts, playground, and swimming pool.

At 1.8 *m.* is the junction with a dirt road.

> Left on this road is GRANITEVILLE (alt. 1137), 2 *m.*, another quarrying community very similar to Websterville, with great gaping chasms cut deep and wide in the rock deposits that have made Barre world-famous. The village, based on a common foundation, is closely unified and compact, as an isolated encampment might be in wartime.

South of this junction the meadowland vistas on either side are typical of those seen at intervals throughout the major part of the route.

At 5.8 *m.* is the junction with a gravel road.

Left on this road is FOXVILLE, 3 *m.*, a settlement which serves neighboring quarries in Williamstown township and bears the stamp of a granite community.

WILLIAMSTOWN (alt. 872, pop. township 1606), 6.2 *m.*, sits along the broad floor of a pleasant valley with smooth-sloped hills rising on each side. The major part of the village lies compactly (L) beside the attractive Main St. The *Thomas Davenport Monument* (R), a large granite boulder with bronze tablet, rests on the front lawn of the *Ainsworth Public Library*. Davenport, the blacksmith who invented the world's first electric motor, was born here in 1802, into a large poverty stricken family. After serving his apprenticeship at a smithy in Williamstown, Davenport went to Forestdale (Brandon Township) and set up his own shop. It was there that he created the first electric motor, and the first model of an electrically driven car. His initial step was the making of a horseshoe magnet, which he wound with the silk of his wife's wedding dress. Thomas Davenport devoted his life to science and died a poor and unrecognized man.

Main St. is brightened by beautiful landscaped flower gardens (R) on the slope of a hill. The *Congregational Church* (R) is spired with unusual grace, and the huge *Civil War Monument* (R), erected in 1869, is surmounted by a stone eagle. The *Town Hall* (R) is a good example of the New England town halls of the middle nineteenth century.

At 7.6 *m.* is the junction with a short dirt road.

Right on this road is *Limehurst Pond, 500 yards*, a long, narrow pond in the shape of a dog's leg, rimmed on the west by the gentle ascendancy of hills. Privately owned, this is a popular swimming place in the summer months, with diving boards, and boats for rent at moderate rates. There are facilities for camping near-by. About 1830 a sawmill owner tried to steal the water from this pond by digging a channel to the north, so that the flow might increase the waterpower turning his mill wheels. As a result of this attempt at marine larceny, part of the pond escaped its banks, but fortunately the entire body of water did not rush out of its bed in the manner of Runaway Pond (*see Tour 2C*).

South of Limehurst Pond the valley narrows as the hill slopes encroach.

At 8.2 *m.* privately owned *Lotus Lake* (L) is barely visible from the highway. The owners have stocked it with perch and pickerel.

At 8.4 *m.* is the junction with a country road.

Left on this road is *Roods Pond* (alt. 1400), 2 *m.*, a very attractive little body of water lying at a high altitude in the hills, placid in its seclusion and quiet.

South of this junction, the massive rounded bulk of a mountain looming ahead seems to completely block the highway, which veers right to skirt the mountain base. This vicinity is a watershed, from which the Stevens Branch of the Winooski flows northward, and the Second Branch of the White River flows to the south.

At 9 *m. Ainsworth State Forest Park* (L) stretches from new growths of evergreens along the highway up the densely forested slopes of the mountains that tower on the eastern side of Williamstown Gulf.

*Williamstown Gulf* is entered at 9.4 *m.*, where State 14 swings to the left in a sharp down-grade, and the mountain walls converge to form a deep, narrow pass, cool-shaded under the sheer wooded barriers that rise skyward on either side. Behind the Gulf House (R) is a waterfall in the brook coming from Roods Pond to empty into the Second Branch, which follows the highway from this point to the White River. A cool, deep peace pervades the somber beauty of this cut through the mountains, where a silver brook tinkles beside the twisting highway, and steep, thick-wooded heights nearly shut out the sky. The southern end of the Gulf is at 11.1 *m.* and just south of here is a fine *Cold Spring* (R) in the bank beside the roadway, an agreeable place for a picnic lunch or simply for a pause in the journey and a drink of cold water.

South of Williamstown Gulf the valley broadens greatly with State 14 running in the shelter of the mountains on the west and overlooking the wide, fertile valley floor (L) to the low forested ridges at the east. Pleasant, comfortable-looking farms are seen along the route.

EAST BROOKFIELD (alt. 741), 13.4 *m.*, situated in a low point of the valley, is a village with plain residences and stores strung along the highway for some distance.

Right from East Brookfield on an uphill gravel road is the junction with another climbing road at 1.5 *m.* Left on this steadily rising road is BROOKFIELD (alt. 1481, pop. township 761), 2.3 *m.*, a mountain village in a sprawling, irregular setting with a certain cobwebby atmosphere and off-trail charm. The *Brookfield Library*, established in 1791 and the oldest continuously existent library in the State, is located in the old Town Hall. Several old-time taverns in the settlement are now used as private homes. The rustic *Tea Shop* (L) at the village center was originally a pitchfork factory, utilizing water-power from the outlet of the lake.

At the western edge of the village is *Sunset Lake*, sometimes called Colts Pond or Mirror Lake, and spanning this little body of water from east to west is the *Brookfield Floating Bridge*, the only bridge of its type in Vermont: 320 feet in length, the bridge is buoyed by 380 tarred wooden barrels which act as pontoons, and has hinged ramps at either end to allow for the seasonal rise and fall of the water level. The water is about 30 feet deep near the bridge center. The original edition of this bridge was constructed about 1812, after a man had drowned in trying to short-cut across thin pond ice during the winter of 1810. The present edition, thought to be the seventh, was formally dedicated in August, 1936.

When the State offered to build a modern overhead bridge here, the citizens of Brookfield rejected the proposal in a characteristic Vermont manner, saying that they had used a floating bridge for 124 years; it had been good enough, and they figured it would continue to be good enough. But in this case their attitude was not so backward as it might seem, for the Brookfield Floating Bridge attracts many tourists to this little community in the hills. The present bridge, its wood thoroughly soaked in a tar preparation, is expected to last for at least 50 years.

Left from Brookfield across the Floating Bridge is the junction with a country road at 0.6 *m.* Left on this road curving through an upland farming region and passing White Pond (L) is another junction at 1.2 *m.* Right on this dirt road, and left at the next junction on a graded gravel road is *Bear Hill* (alt. 2000), 2.7 *m.*, in *Allis State Forest Park*. The parking lot at the summit is large, circular, and level, bisected by a huge log fence. The *Lookout Tower*, south of the parking space, is 50 feet high and affords a truly magnificent view, a sweeping panorama over forest and mountain grandeur. White Pond lies directly below on the east, cupped in gently sloping farmlands, with villages beyond, and in the distance the noble White Mountains of New Hampshire. North, south, and west the mighty mountain ranges loom on the horizon. Here and there villages are seen nestling in the greenery of mountainsides. The park also contains a Guest House, picnic groves with outdoor fireplaces and tables, a children's playground, and camping sites. A native of Brookfield, Wallace S. Allis, presented this park to the State in 1932, and it is one of the most beautiful and highly developed parks in Vermont. Labor for the improvements made here was furnished by the Civilian Conservation Corps.

Between East Brookfield and North Randolph the highway continues through the placid charm of the Second Branch Valley.

NORTH RANDOLPH (alt. 671), 17.3 m., similar in general appearance and background to East Brookfield, is an agreeable village in a meadowland setting.

Between North Randolph and East Randolph the road runs along the splendid broad valley in a gradual descent, the valley floor blocked in on east and west by the forest-clad shoulders of hills.

EAST RANDOLPH (alt. 606), 19.8 m., is another attractive little hamlet at rest in the serenity of the valley.

Between East Randolph and South Randolph, the highway continues to descend gradually.

SOUTH RANDOLPH (alt. 563), 23.3 m., is simply the center of a scattered rural settlement with a general store, gasoline pumps, and antique shop on the main thoroughfare. The *Antique Shop* (R) is located in a low brown frame house, which was built in 1781 by Experience Davis; it was the first house put up in Randolph township and the oldest structure encountered on this route. Randolph suffered from Indian raids soon after that time, but Experience Davis's house escaped the torch, and has since withstood all the vicissitudes of nature and time. The Duke of Kent (who became father of Queen Victoria) stayed overnight in this house on his trip through Vermont about 1791. For some time the building was used as a tavern, and around 1830 it served as toll house for the old toll road, the route of which State 14 approximately follows today. The original clapboards, handmade nails, beams, and sills of Experience Davis's construction remain, and the house is substantially as it was when built, quite properly housing what collectors consider one of the best antique collections in the State, including one of the two best privately owned collections of historic china in New England.

South of South Randolph, State 14 crosses the Second Branch of the White River. At 24.3 m. an old *Covered Bridge* is seen (R) on a side road.

EAST BETHEL (alt. 570), 24.8 m., sits snugly in a small cut-out (R) beside the highway. The *Hexagonal Schoolhouse* (R) was constructed about 1830 and still serves its original purpose. The exact reason for the peculiar construction remains a mystery. One theory is that the early settlers thought its hexagonal shape would better resist the elements, especially the winter winds that roar down the valley with power and fury. The brick *Baptist Church* was erected in 1824.

Between East Bethel and North Royalton the valley narrows abruptly as hillsides converge on the curving road.

NORTH ROYALTON (alt. 520), 28.8 m., is a neat little settlement enclosed in the narrow valley, where the Second Branch flows into the White River.

At the southern end of the village is the old brick *Fox Stand* (L), where Lafayette stopped overnight on his visit in 1825. From here State 14 follows the White River in a southwesterly direction. Outside of Royalton the highway makes an S-turn through a railroad underpass.

ROYALTON (alt. 513, pop. township 1491), 30.2 *m.*, is peculiarly situated along a curve in the highway, hemmed in closely by the gaunt encroachment of a high bluff (L) and the smooth-flowing sweep of the White River (R). *Cascadnac Inn* (R), built in 1792 and remodeled in 1810, has such architectural oddities as Holy Lord hinges on the doors, witch crosses built into the door-frame to keep evil spirits away, handmade shutters, and strange archways. Lafayette and President Monroe were one-time guests here. The *Old Lyman House* (R) is of the same period as the inn.

The *Granite Monument* in the small parkway commemorates the burning of Royalton by Indian raiders in 1780, the most calamitous raid in the history of the State. From Tunbridge (*see Tour 2B*) to Royalton, 300 red marauders under an English lieutenant attacked home after isolated home and settlement after settlement, plundering and burning, taking white prisoners and slaughtering cattle, desolating the valley with torch, tomahawk, and gun. It was no massacre, although a few of the white men were killed. In many cases women and children were let go free. The object of the raid seemed to be the taking of prisoners and the terrorizing of the settlers with wanton destruction of homes and property Zadock Steele, one of the men taken prisoner to Canada, wrote a long and detailed account of the raid and his captivity, after he was released. The *Whiting House* (L) dates from about 1800; the *Congregational Church* (L) and the *Episcopal Church* (R) belong to a somewhat later period. The *Academy Building* (L) was formerly a Methodist Meeting-House, and now houses a grammar school. From the old Royalton Academy many famous men were graduated, including Salmon P. Chase, Senator, Secretary of Treasury during the Civil War, and Chief Justice of the United States; Truman Henry Safford, mental marvel who accomplished unbelievable feats of memory and lightning calculation; Albert M. Billings, co-builder of New York's first elevated railway; and the eminent lawyer family of Denisons. The *Denison House* (L), built around 1800, is a large handsome white structure surrounded by a white fence.

At the eastern outskirts of Royalton is a sharp-angled railroad underpass. East of the village the river flows wider with great white rocks projecting above the surface. The Indians called this stream Cascadnac, which meant Clear Water. Steep mountainsides shut in the river and highway on either side.

At 32.3 *m.* is the junction with State 110 (*see Tour 2B*). Near here the First Branch joins its mother stream, the White River.

Right across the bridge is SOUTH ROYALTON (alt. 502), 0.3 *m.*, the chief village in Royalton Township, pleasantly situated on the broad river flats. The nicely landscaped village green has a fountain, cannon, Civil War Memorial, and the *Handy Memorial Arch*, a marble archway at the entrance to the green that pays tribute to the memory of Hannah Hunter Handy, who faced the Indian raiders of 1780 with courage and succeeded in rescuing nine children from the red warriors, whose amazement was equalled only by their respect for this white woman's dauntless manner. A real saga of pioneer spirit is the story of Hannah Handy, snatched out of her home by Indians and knocked down by a gun butt, only to rise and persist in snatching children from the invaders' hands until they yielded to her with the savage's admiration for sheer courage. The memorial also bears an inscription in honor of Phineas Parkhurst, who was shot during the attack, but escaped to fling himself on to a horse and ride madly down the White River Valley with a bullet in his side, warning settlers along the way as far as Lebanon, New Hampshire.

Industrial activity here revolves mainly around the woodworking shops and a milk-receiving station. The village also serves as a trading center for outlying farms and smaller communities.

At 33.2 *m.* is the junction with a steep uphill road.

Left on this gravel road is the *Joseph Smith Monument*, 2.2 *m.*, at the site of the prophet's birthplace on the town line between Royalton and Sharon. The *Guest House (free admission)* an attractive little bungalow sitting on a green-lawned knoll, contains pictures, books and documents relating to the Mormon Church, and the original hearthstone from the birthplace of Joseph Smith. The *Monument* honoring the founder of the Mormon faith stands behind the cottage, nearly 60 feet in total height. The shaft proper is a granite monolith from the Barre quarries, 38½ feet in height and 39 tons in weight. Each foot represents a year of the prophet's life. The briefer of the two inscriptions is as follows:

SACRED

TO THE MEMORY OF

JOSEPH SMITH,

THE PROPHET.

BORN HERE

23d DECEMBER, 1805;

MARTYRED,

CARTHAGE, ILLINOIS,

27TH JUNE, 1844.

In a mellow June twilight, tall, fearless Joseph Smith and his brother, Hyrum, were shot to death against the well curb at the Carthage Jail in Carthage, Illinois, by an enraged mob, which had risen from the storm of hatred against Smith's Nauvoo Legion and the Mormon faith.

Born here on an isolated farm, Joseph Smith spent the first ten years of his life in these hills. It was as a farmer boy of 14 that he had his first visitation while wandering in the forest near Palmyra, New York. From there he moved to the Middle West, and, in Nauvoo, Illinois, founded the Mormon Church. More than any other Vermonter, Joseph Smith spread far-reaching influences, whose impact affected the lives of many thousands.

Between this junction and Sharon, State 14 follows closely the looping bends of the White River in its course toward the Connecticut.

SHARON (alt. 500, pop. township 569), 37.1 *m.*, lies in a little valley walled in on three sides by mountains and situated on the outside curve of a wide bend in the White River. The white *Congregational Church* (L) and the brick *Town Hall* (L) are both well over a century old. The

*Baxter Memorial Library* (L) is a modern structure, and an expensive one for such a small village.

> Left from the village center on a country road is *Downer State Forest Park*, 4 *m.*, improved recently by a Civilian Conservation Corps unit which built tree-shaded drives and picnic and camping areas. In the vicinity are fine fishing ponds, such as Lake Mitchell, Standing Pond, and Lake Crescent.

At the eastern edge of Sharon, State 14 climbs curving up Sharon Hill and swings southward along the water course. At 39.2 *m.* is a sharp dangerous curve through a railroad underpass.

WEST HARTFORD (alt. 420), 43 *m.*, is a small and rather faded hamlet, with all of its business section lying north of the highway.

> Right from the southern end of West Hartford on a gravel road through tree-shaded hill country is NORTH POMFRET (alt. 880), 4 *m.*, sprawled along the curving roadway in a narrow valley, rural in aspect.
>
> Beyond North Pomfret on an uphill road through a region of smooth-rolling hills, sparsely shaded and curiously lawn-like, is POMFRET CENTER (alt. 1220, pop. township 728), 6.8 *m.*, named after Pomfret, Connecticut, from where the settlers came in 1770. Scarcely any evidence of a settlement is left here at the central village buried high in the hills. The first pioneers to penetrate these mountain wilds found evidences of a terrific hurricane which had ravaged the slopes long before the coming of the white man.
>
> Beyond Pomfret on a downhill road is SOUTH POMFRET, 9.8 *m.*, the chief village of the township, a sleepy but pleasant little community resting in a small valley. One of the finest *Taxidermy Exhibits* in the State is displayed at the Potter Garage. The *Abbott Memorial Library* (R), a neat little building of unusual style, contains a museum collection including interesting relics from early times.

South of West Hartford, the highway continues to swing along between river and railway. At 43.7 *m.* is a trestle (L) supporting a branch road over the railway to a farmhouse.

Between the Narrows and Hartford, State 14 passes through CENTER-VILLE, a community of farmsteads strung along both sides of the road in the valley that has widened to fertile beauty.

HARTFORD (alt. 400, pop. township 4888), 48.7 *m.*, is a residential suburb of White River Junction, with attractive homes, shrubs and lawns offering a pleasing contrast to the unrelieved industrial and commercial aspect of the Junction. The trees that shade the community spread from the business district to a background of low rounded hills. Uncrowded and undeveloped, Hartford is a model residential section. The township was settled in 1761 by a few families from Lebanon, Conn., and one of the earliest comers was Joseph Marsh, later the first Lieutenant Governor of the State. Horace Wells, the discoverer of laughing gas, was born here.

At 50.1 *m.* is the junction with US 5 (*see Tour* 1), and US 4 (*see Tour* 6).

From this point, State 14, in conjunction with US 5 and US 4, swings (R) across a green steel bridge over the White River.

WHITE RIVER JUNCTION, 50.3 *m.* (*see Tour* 1).

TOUR 2 B : *From* EAST BARRE *to* JUNCTION WITH STATE 14, 26.9 *m.*, State 110.

Via Washington, Chelsea, Tunbridge.
The road is hard-surfaced almost the entire distance.

THIS valley route may lack the grandeur and beauty of mountain and lake scenery, but it is simple and tranquil, which makes it difficult for present-day travelers to visualize the pioneer days when this pleasant valley was a favorite warpath for raiding Indians, and a trail of horror for the white captives that were taken back to Canada. Now the peace is rarely broken more than once a year, and that is at the time of Tunbridge Fair when streams of autos converge from north and south upon that little hamlet in the spirit of carnival and revelry. A greater part of the way the road follows the First Branch of the White River, and the calm of ridge-walled green meadows is on everything.

EAST BARRE, 0 *m.* (*see Tour 5B*), is at the junction of State 110 and US 302 (*see Tour 5B*).

Between East Barre and Washington, State 110 rolls in a southeasterly direction, overlooking a narrow fertile valley (L), where trim farmhouses stand pleasingly against the green of meadowlands.

WASHINGTON (pop. 695), 4 *m.*, was originally called Kingsland under a New York grant, being the shire town of Gloucester County, which included the entire northeast section of the State, but the Yorker jurisdiction was short-lived, and the Vermont legislature regranted the territory in 1780, the first settlers coming five years later. The little village is neat and charming with clean-painted houses and two white churches, all having a well-kept appearance. A granite *Civil War Monument* stands at the village center. Stanley C. Wilson, Governor of Vermont (1931–35), was born here. The community subsists mainly on dairying and lumbering.

South of Washington the highway ascends sharply, with a fine view (R) of *Washington Peak* (alt. 2500), and then drops steeply winding through a wooded ravine beside a picturesque tumbling brook. This descent is rather dangerous, and fast driving should be avoided. At the foot of the hill, State 110 emerges to a valley bottom banked by forested slopes.

CHELSEA (alt. 840, pop. township 1004), 13.6 *m.*, the shire town of Orange County, sits in the valley of the First Branch of the White River sheltered by green mountain walls. An attractive village park (L), shaded by spreading elms and old maples, makes a pleasing front for the County Courthouse and Congregational Church. The Chelsea Shop (R) was at one time occupied by Charles I. Hood, capitalist and manufacturer of Hood's Sarsaparilla. Beyond the shop is an old type *Gristmill*, one of the few still in operation. Many years ago this gristmill supplied power to the Tinker Chair Shop, which was directly across the street, by means of a leather belt suspended over the roadway. The flapping of the belt frightened passing horses, and that method of transmitting power had to be abandoned. The *National Bank of Chelsea* (L) is one of the oldest in the State. Among the prominent sons Chelsea has sent out to the world are William F. Vilas, Postmaster-General (1885-88) and Secretary of the Interior (1888-89), and Brigadier-General Napoleon B. McLaughlin (Civil War). While the general exodus of population from the rural to urban centers has impaired the growth of Chelsea, the village remains active as a trading center for the surrounding farm district.

The town was first chartered as Turnersburgh and settled in 1784. The earliest comers packed furniture and provisions on their backs from Tunbridge, approximately eight miles away, exemplifying the pioneer spirit of ever pushing on to new frontiers.

> Left from Chelsea on State 113 over a series of rolling hills is VERSHIRE (alt. 1200, pop. township 368), 6.8 *m.*, settled in 1780 and originally called Ely. Here in the Vershire Hills are the headwaters of the Ompompanoosuc River, which flows to the Connecticut. Looking at this mountain settlement with its few old frame and brick dwellings resting in an air of tranquillity, it is difficult to realize that around 1880 the great Ely Copper Mines here supported a 2000 population, and in one year produced and shipped three million pounds of copper, then worth more than 20 cents per pound. At the peak of production, the Ely Mines turned out three-fifths of the entire copper output of the United States.

> In July, 1883, the 'Ely War' occurred, with 300 unpaid miners rising in insurrection to attempt collection, by force of arms if necessary, of the $25,000 back wages owed them by the company. The rioting miners seized arms and ammunition, stopped the water pumps to flood the workings, tore down a few buildings, and threatened to dynamite the works and destroy the villages of Ely and West Fairlee unless they were paid by the following afternoon. Governor Barstow called out five companies of the National Guard to go to Ely by special train in answer to the appeal of civil authorities. The troops arrived in the early morning, and were conveyed from the station to the mining villages in coke wagons while the unsuspecting miners were still sleeping. Rudely wakened in the wan gray morning light, twelve of the leading strikers opened their eyes to face bayoneted rifles, and when the other miners awoke, their leaders were under guard and the streets were full of uniformed militiamen with fixed bayonets. This procedure was followed at both Ely and West Fairlee, the strike was broken, and the Ely War was ended. The mine manager paid the men all the money he had left, about $4000, but the industrial tragedy was complete, for the mines never again operated, and three townships in the vicinity were desolated.

> Right from Vershire on a rough narrow uphill road is VERSHIRE CENTER (alt. 1700), 2 *m.* on the remote upland slopes of 'The Highlands,' from which the eastern range of the Green Mountains stands out in sharp perspective. A few old farmhouses, some of them long since abandoned, are scattered on the gusty hillsides.

Between Chelsea and Tunbridge along the gradually descending valley, dark groves of coniferous trees are interspersed with slim white birches and graceful maples, extending from the roadside to the slopes of ridges that march along either side. Through this quiet valley in 1780 a raiding party of Indians led by a British lieutenant made their stealthy way toward Tunbridge and Royalton.

NORTH TUNBRIDGE (alt. 640), 19.7 *m.*, consists of a few brick and frame houses and a plain white *Baptist Church* bordering the highway. The sole industry here is lumbering.

TUNBRIDGE (alt. 640, pop. township 903), 21.3 *m.*, lies along the highway in the valley of the First Branch, above the deep level bowl which, as the annual (October) scene of the Tunbridge World's Fair, has imbued the little rustic community with a picturesque aura of interest, color, and significance as a living monument to the rural life of the past. The setting and atmosphere are reminiscent of frontier times. When dusk descends from the stern wild mountains into the deep valley, pictures are conjured of lonely log cabins, open campfires, prowling Indian scouts, and bearded men with long rifles. In October, 1780, 300 Indians under the command of English Lieutenant Horton proceeded down the valley of the First Branch and fell upon Tunbridge, killing two settlers and taking many prisoners, before heading south to continue their depredations in Royalton (*see Tour 2A*).

The *Fairgrounds* (R), low-lying green meadowlands in a wide bend of the First Branch shadowed by rugged mountains, form an ideal setting for a true country fair, the fame of which has circulated so widely that more than 15,000 paid admissions have been recorded for a single day. With other fairs throughout the State discontinued in the face of depression, Tunbridge's little World's Fair persisted in maintaining the traditions of its origin, until it became the seasonal objective of people from all over the State as well as of autumn tourists from many parts of the country. It grew to be a fashionable fad, quite the thing to visit, and in 1936 the highway was clogged for miles either side of Tunbridge, while the green bowl on the banks of the First Branch was jammed solid-full with surging humanity. In former years it is said that at three o'clock in the afternoon all sober persons were rounded up and herded off the grounds, as undesirable. The tradition of insobriety is still carefully preserved. The carnival spirit runs rampant, but in all good-will and friendliness, with Government-labeled bottles being passed about in place of the pewter jugs of old. The elaborate antique department is of particular interest and sets the keynote for the fair. Housed in a low pine-slab building are extensive and curious exhibits from pioneer days; an early combination store and post office; a loom and full equipment for carding, spinning, weaving; a blacksmith shop with a bellows-forge; etc. The yard outside is filled with ancient agricultural implements and vehicles of transportation. At intervals during the day, old-fashioned square dances are given by local people in costume. Horse racing and livestock exhibits attract many, and the long midway is constantly packed with merry milling throngs. People from all walks of life are jostled together in the gay riotous turmoil that is Tunbridge Fair — back-country folk of the soil mingle with people from the metropolitan districts; world travelers eat hotdogs at the same booth with natives who

have never been 50 miles away from their farm; school-teachers from
Iowa, lumbermen, truck drivers, State officials, country storekeepers,
college boys, schoolgirls, bankers, and laborers are caught alike in the
hilarious whirl.

> Left from the covered bridge at the north end of Tunbridge on an uphill dirt road
> is the junction with the Old Turnpike at 4 *m.* Right on the Old Turnpike and left
> on the first side road are *Brocklebank Hill and Quarries* (alt. 2120), 5.2 *m.* The
> quarries have not been worked for years, but the view from the heights here is
> superb, ranging over the grandeur of the major Green Mountain peaks from
> Mansfield south to Killington.

Between Tunbridge and South Tunbridge State 110 runs undulating
through a beautiful wooded section.

SOUTH TUNBRIDGE (alt. 542), 24.1 *m.*, is a small farming community,
with a red-brick *Methodist Church* sitting in the midst of the well-stocked
farmsteads.

At 26.9 *m.* is the junction with State 14 (*see Tour 2A*). Just west of here
is the union of the First Branch with the White River, which flows parallel
to State 14. Across the river from the highway junction is South Royalton (*see Tour 2A*).

---

T O U R   2 C :  *From* BARTON *to* HARDWICK, 23.7 *m.*, State
12.

---

Via Glover, Sheffield, Wheelock, Greensboro.
Between Greensboro Bend and Hardwick, the St. Johnsbury & Lake Champlain R.R. parallels this route.
The road is gravel, except between Barton and Glover where it is surfaced
(blacktop).

THIS route is one of the main connections between the lake-and-woods
country of northeastern Vermont and the central part of the State and
State Capital. The road winds erratically through wild, narrow valleys
that twist between forested ridges. Woodland ponds and lakes lie in
proximity to the highway, which is so sharply curving that utmost caution is in order for motorists. Interesting components of the trip are the
site of Runaway Pond, the wilds of Sheffield Heights, and the summer
resort district of Caspian Lake in Greensboro.

BARTON, 0 *m.* (*see Tour 1*). Here is the junction with US 5 (*see Tour 1*).
State 12 branches (R) from US 5 at the common in Barton, and follows

a pleasant valley road of blacktop southward between farmlands and the cleared slopes of blunt ridges.

GLOVER (pop. 246), 3.1 *m.*, a peaceful little village surrounded by low hills, has a long Main St. with wooden houses set irregularly along either side. The town was settled in 1797 and named for General John Glover, to whom it was presented in return for military services. Many of the original settlers have descendants living here today, which is indicative of the stolid unchanging life of the rural community. A convenient bench in front of the combination general store and post office (R) is the fair-weather scene of many profound debates and discussions punctuated with expert streams of tobacco juice. An interesting *Taxidermy Shop* (L) may be visited, and there is a small *Zoo* (L) at the village center.

The *Old House* (left, above the zoo), a plain white wooden structure, was built sometime before 1800, and was the only house in the valley left standing after Runaway Pond (*see below*) swept through in 1810. Still in excellent condition, this sturdy house contains a loft unchanged from its original state with hand-hewn rafters joined by wooden pegs, as solid and strong as ever. In the basement is a huge square foundation of field stone, built for the fireplaces which no longer exist. This house still serves as a private residence. The trim white *Federated Church* (R), with green blinds, is the most attractive structure in the village. The *Union House* (R), a large roomy building with a green-and-white porched front, was built in 1846 for a stagecoach hostelry. It is now an antique-furnished inn, with the old bar and liquor-cabinet, seven fireplaces, an old door containing 20 panes of glass, many curious pieces of ancient furniture, and the characteristic third-floor ballroom.

1. Left from Glover on a steeply climbing dirt road is KEENE'S CORNER, 1 *m.*, the site of the original settlement made by pioneers from Keene, New Hampshire. This land was sold at a sheriff's sale in Danville, and the records show that one Silas Clark bought 80 acres for $3.59. The *Old Cemetery* (R) is fenced and some-what cared for, but the oldest stones are illegible. This graveyard and a scattering of poor farms are all that remain to mark the site of the first settlement in Glover Township.

2. Right from Glover on a hilly dirt road is WEST GLOVER (pop. 59), 2.4 *m.*, an upland farming community centered at a rural corner and store. The only attraction is near-by *Parker Pond*, which affords fishing and a summer camping site for the local people.

South of Glover at 4 *m.* is the junction with State 122.

Left on State 122, after a long climb through wooded hill-lanes, flattening on up-lands and then climbing again on a gradual curving slant over a wild highland country with broken plateaulands stretching to mountain borders, is SHEFFIELD (pop. township 543), 7.9 *m.* Named for Sheffield, England, this old mountain village well off the main thoroughfares of travel has time-mellowed houses, many over a century old and still serving sturdily as homesteads in the highland com-munity. The manufacture of pot- and pearl-ash was an important early industry, but at the present time dairying and lumbering on a small scale are the means of livelihood. The general aspect in Sheffield is one of quiet antiquity in a wild upland setting, remote from the rush of modern times. The *Old Church on the Hill* (L), standing above the village, in simple white wood, is opened once a year for 'Old Home Day Service.' The first blacksmith in town was a Bunker Hill veteran,

Captain Joseph Staples. Another Sheffield pioneer, Alexander Berry, sent six sons to the Union Army in the Civil War.

Beyond Sheffield and past the sawdust piles of a rude sawmill (L) on State 122 as it gradually descends southward is WHEELOCK (Hollow) (pop. township 412), 9.6 *m.*, named after President John Wheelock of Dartmouth College. This mountain hamlet, similar in general to Sheffield, lies low in an upland valley with broad-sloping sides, and is interesting for its connection with Dartmouth. The General Assembly of Vermont granted the township to Dartmouth College and Moor's Charity School at Hanover, New Hampshire, an unusual instance of a State granting territory for the support of a college in another State. As late as 1815 the rental paid by Wheelock settlers comprised at least one-half of the permanent funds of both the college and the school. The township still pays a small sum to the college, and in 1930 the trustees of Dartmouth voted full tuition scholarships to sons of Wheelock, by birth or residence, who present adequate preparation and suitable recommendation.

The *Revolutionary Soldiers' Monument* (L) is a simple plaque on a millstone taken from the first gristmill in Wheelock. The 1793 *Gristmill* (R) still stands beside its dammed river, and across the stream in early times was a sawmill employing the old up-and-down type saws. as well as a tannery. The *Sulphur Spring* (L) is strongly mineral. It is housed under a wood canopy, and its waters are free. The *Colonel Chase Inn* (L), a small plain white house with wide clapboards, was the first tavern in town, established in 1812. It is no longer an inn. The *Old Caledonia Spring House* (L), a large red-brick structure with a double porch, was once a popular resort and watering place, but is now abandoned. The mineral water from Caledonia Springs is said to be of exceptionally high quality. At one time a venture was made to bottle and sell the water, but it failed. Over a century old, the hotel remains in good condition even though deserted. The Town Hall, church and school (L) are at the southern end of the village, fronted by a grove of tall pines. The *Old Cemetery* (R) contains the graves of Revolutionary soldiers. Wheelock has an unusual military record: early settlers included 31 Revolutionary veterans; 13 men enlisted for the War of 1812; 96 citizens served in the Civil War, and 12 in the World War. Erastus Fairbanks (Governor of Vermont, 1852–53, 1860–61) was the first postmaster here in Wheelock Hollow. From 1810 to 1930, the township population dropped from 964 to 412.

South of Glover, State 12 winds in gradual ascent, now in the open and again through the cool shadows of wooded ravines.

At 6.6 *m.* is the junction with a country road.

Right on this road is *Shadow Lake*, 1 *m.*, a pleasant, secluded little body of water, calm and reposed in a setting of woods and farmlands. The plain little summer cottages along the shore are owned mainly by people from near-by villages. Cleared farmlands break the woods here and there.

*Clark's Tavern* (L), 7.7 *m.*, was built in 1827 by Silas Clark, prominent Glover pioneer, who was among the first to break the wilderness at Keene's Corner. The once-handsome stage-coach inn now stands an empty, weatherbeaten shell and broken hulk. In the interior the stairways and some of the floors and partitions stand intact amid the debris. Occasionally poor drifting families make their abode here, a pathetic picture of homeless wanderers striving to establish a home in the face of impossible difficulties.

*Mud Pond* (or *Clark Pond*) (R) lies just south of the abandoned tavern, a little body of water that was lowered and almost swept away by the action of Runaway Pond rushing through it in northward flood. State 12 closely skirts the eastern shore of this pond.

South of Mud Pond, the highway climbs along a densely forested gully, having the somber stillness of wilderness depths. It was through here that Runaway Pond burst with torrential fury, gouging a broad deep path in the woods.

*Runaway Pond* (R), 8.7 *m.* This shallow grassy valley beside the highway, locally known as Dry Pond, marks the site of a phenomenon in which an entire body of water ran away from its bed in 1810. The monument was erected in 1910 on the centennial anniversary of the event. Previous to this strange occurrence the body of water was called Long Pond, and its outlet normally ran south. The residents of Glover wished to divert the water into a northern outlet, so it would flow down into Mud Pond, raising the water level there and furnishing more power for their mills along Barton River. Long Pond was 150 feet above the level of Mud Pond, with a very sharp drop between the two. On June 6, 1810, about 60 men assembled to celebrate 'June Training Day' by cutting a channel to form a northern outlet from Long Pond into the lower body of water. The barrier holding the north end of Long Pond was a solid bar that resembled frozen gravel, through which they proceeded to cut. Unknown to the workers there was a species of quicksand deposit underneath the bar of hardpan, and once the bar was pierced this sand started washing away rapidly, undermining the whole north shore of the pond. Alarmed at the sudden great rush of water, the workmen scrambled to the safety of higher land and were treated to the amazing sight of an entire lake emptying before their eyes. Riders pounded down the valley warning settlers to flee from the path of the torrent. Rushing down upon Mud Pond, the flood ripped away those barriers and swept on down the Barton River. The great wall of unleashed water tore a path 30 to 40 rods wide and 30 to 60 feet deep, demolishing gristmills, uprooting large trees and boulders, carrying everything before it.

Eye-witnesses declared that the earth trembled and shook as the water broke loose with a tremendous deafening roar. At the start there was a rush of water toward the center and the whole pond boiled like a cauldron. Two loons, caught on the surface, were unable to rise from the water, so great was the suction. Long Pond was emptied of water in one hour and fifteen minutes. After the water had drained out, mud ran for several hours. In six hours' time the flood surged into Lake Memphremagog at Newport, a distance of more than 25 miles. The following summer thousands of coltsfoot sprang up in the channel left by the water, and Balm of Gilead trees appeared for the first time in the vicinity. At the time people regarded Runaway Pond as a warning to men against rashly tampering with the work of Nature and God.

South of Runaway Pond, State 12 climbs sharply and then continues in more gradual ascent through a forested region.

*Horse Pond* (R), 10.4 *m.*, is a small body of water with wood-fringed shores.

Between this pond and Greensboro Bend, the Lamoille River flows alongside of the twisting, curving highway in a wild irregular valley flanked by gaunt ridges and hills.

GREENSBORO BEND (alt. 1248), 16.3 *m.*, lies rather bleakly on unshaded flats where the Lamoille River, the highway and railroad make wide sweeping bends. Crude lumberstacks (R) at the north end of the village indicate one of the main industries, and piles of milk-cans on the station platform reveal the other. Railroad tracks cut across the village center and freight-cars habitually rest on a siding parallel to the Main St. The village is a trading center for the farmers of the section.

1. Right from Greensboro Bend on an uphill dirt road is GREENSBORO (alt. 1463, pop. township 831), 3 *m.*, named for the Greens, a family of early printers, an upland settlement straggling along an uneven terrain with a background of pines. This sequestered village is distinguished chiefly by its closeness to *Caspian Lake* (alt. 1404) which lies at the edge of the hamlet in wood-rimmed shores surrounded by low hills. The high elevation of this lake assures refreshing coolness in summer, and the mountain breezes that blow over the water are keenly exhilarating. The entire setting is a combination of beauty and peacefulness, and it is easily understandable why Caspian has become a haven for the many prominent educators, authors, and professional men who compose the large summer colony here. Bliss Perry, Harvard professor, scholar, essayist, and one-time editor of the *Atlantic Monthly*, is a regular summer resident of Greensboro, and Dean Christian Gauss of Princeton is another habitual vacationist here. The *Ingalls House* (*private*), center of the village, contains many interesting relics including portraits over 200 years old, the first post-office cabinet used in the county (Orleans), a 150-year-old clock with wooden works, ancient furniture, and the safe used by Martin Van Buren in Washington.

The Hazen Military Road passed through Greensboro, and in 1779 a blockhouse was built on the western shore of Caspian Lake. In 1781 four scouts in the blockhouse were surprised by Indians, two of them being slain by the raiders.

2. Left from the south end of Greensboro Bend on a narrow dirt road winding beside a rocky stream and climbing through a wild wooded country is STANNARD (alt. 1700, pop. township 154), 3.3 *m.*, named in honor of Civil War General George Stannard, who turned the tide at Gettysburg (*see Tour 4, HIGHGATE*). In this scattered rural settlement buried in a mountain wilderness farmers struggle to wrest a living from agricultural pursuits under adverse conditions. A white schoolhouse (L), the tan-and-red *Methodist Church* (R), and a farmstead are all that mark the center of this farming community. The region is wild and primitive in the extreme, vast forested uplands stretching away on all sides. Many of the farmhouses are unacquainted with electric lights and other conveniences, and life here is in a crude stage.

South of Greensboro Bend, State 12 takes wide, sweeping curves, encountering a series of dangerous railway crossings and following the meanderings of the Lamoille along its narrow wild valley.

EAST HARDWICK, 19.5 *m.*, is a side-hill village, spilling from the level of a plateau down a sharp incline into the valley of the Lamoille. In passing through, State 12 makes two right-angle turns, right and down the hill, then left from the middle of the hill. The settlement is marked only by its peculiar hillside location.

Right from the foot of the hill in East Hardwick on a gravel road is HARDWICK STREET, 2.3 *m.*, the original settlement of the township, made in 1795 by Colonel Alpha Warner and others from Hardwick, Massachusetts. The long straight street, broad and maple-shaded, is lined with old homes set well back on spacious lawns, many of which are picket-fenced. The scene on this secluded level plain is one of serenity. The *Hazen Road Monument* (R) commemorates the military road which passed through on Hardwick St. and ran northward two miles to Caspian Lake. The *Stage House* (L) *(private)* was built in 1799 by Alpha Warner, and the original tavern sign still hangs in front of the fine old structure, which now serves as a summer home for descendants of the founder of Hardwick. This is the oldest house left in town, and in back of the great fireplace has a 'Chimney Room' once used as a secret chamber.

South of East Hardwick, at 21.3 *m.*, is the junction with State 15 (*see Tour 5A*).

Between this junction and Hardwick, State 12 twists tortuously along beside the winding Lamoille River, through a rough broken valley, which reveals some of the ravages wrought by the Lamoille in floodtime.

HARDWICK, 23.7 *m.* (*see Tour* 2). Here is the junction with State 12B (*see Tour* 2).

---

T O U R  3 : *From* JUNCTION OF STATE 105 *and* STATE 100 *to* JUNCTION *with* US 5, 176 *m.*, State 100, US 2, State 100B, 107, 103.

---

Via (*sec. a*) Troy, Westfield, Lowell, Eden, Hyde Park, Morrisville, Stowe, Waterbury, Middlesex; (*sec. b*) Moretown, Waitsfield, Warren, Granville, Hancock, Rochester, Stockbridge, Pittsfield, West Bridgewater, Plymouth, Ludlow, Cavendish, Chester, Rockingham.

Between Ludlow and Bellows Falls the Rutland R.R. parallels this route.

The road is mainly hard-surfaced, with short stretches of gravel.

*Sec. a. NEWPORT to MIDDLESEX, 67.8 m.*

THIS valley route runs through the center of the State with mountain ranges paralleling it on either side for a greater part of the distance. Not a main route of travel, it nevertheless pierces the heart of Vermont and reveals a wealth of mountain and hinterland scenery. The northern section swings through a somewhat wild region varying from broad, fertile plains to narrow mountain passes, with mountains always in evidence, now ranged about the horizon in contours of grace and strength, now thrusting their forested ridges close above the highway. Small industrial centers are represented by Morrisville, and Stowe is one of the outstanding winter sports resorts of northern New England.

The junction 0 *m.*, of State 100 and 105 (*see Tour* 1C), is west of Newport (*see NEWPORT*).

Between this junction and South Troy, State 100 rises and falls in long, gradual planes, with wide, open fields stretching unevenly away from the road and the patchwork of clearings visible on distant slopes. Directly ahead the massed mountains lift their crested tiers against the skyline, which is dominated by the sharp thrust of Jay Peak.

TROY (South) (alt. 764, pop. township 1899), 7.4 *m.*, lies on a slight elevation of an open plain in the eastern Missisquoi Valley, its drab houses radiating from a small triangular common. The red-fronted ga- . rage that faces the green on the west was originally a church, as its lines reveal. A creamery (R) indicates the town's sole industry. The Grange Fair held annually in this village is an event of local importance. Since there are no special grounds, the straight, level Main St. serves as both midway and race track. Lacking in major or distinctive attractions of sophisticated appeal, this fair is truly festive in a kitchen junket way, a real community celebration.

Between Troy and Westfield, the broad valley floor constitutes some of the best farm land in the State. The river terraces (L) add grace to the valley landscape carved by the Missisquoi water system which irrigates this region. At 7.8 *m.* (R) a fine farmstead exemplifies the prosperity that can be wrought from the soil in this vicinity.

WESTFIELD (alt. 825, pop. township 448), 9.1 *m.*, is spread on the gentle slant of the plain with a small, maple-shaded green in its center. The former *Church* (R), erected in 1818 but now in a poor state of preservation, no longer serves a religious purpose. The *Hitchcock Memorial* (R), a square white building with a clock tower, combines the local library with a museum of natural history that is quite unusual in a village of this size. During the War of 1812 the inhabitants of Westfield, like those of most of the towns in northern Vermont, were rightly apprehensive of a British invasion from Canada. The barn of Captain Medad Hitchcock was converted into a blockhouse refuge, but fortunately never had to be defended. Today the village is largely made up of people who, having led a rugged, strenuous life on the near-by hill farms, have sought the well-earned comfort and sociability of village life in their declining years. In the houses along Westfield street of a winter's evening are heard tall tales of the exploits with plough, pitchfork, and axe of a whole race of agricultural Paul Bunyans who are no more.

Right from Westfield on a country road is JAY (alt. 922, pop. township 274) 4.9 *m.*, named for the grantee and statesman John Jay, when the first grant, as Carthage, reverted to the State through lack of settlement. This remote little village lies almost in the shadow of Jay Peak, close to the Canadian border.

Left from Jay on a climbing dirt road is the base of *Jay Peak* (alt. 3861), 7.5 *m.*, the commanding summit of the Vermont-Canada borderline and northern terminus of the Long Trail. Footpaths twist up the mountainside, a stiff hike, but well-marked, to the crest, from which panoramic views sweep over 100 miles in all directions.

On clear days the streets of Montreal are visible from Jay to the north. the Presidential Range of the White Mountains to the east, and Champlain and the Adirondacks to the West in what is one of the most extensive and varied views in eastern America.

Between Westfield and Lowell, State 100 continues along the broad valley of the watercourse, rich farmlands spreading on either side in smooth undulant waves to fir-clad ridges and mountains in the background.

At 15.8 *m.* is a striking view (R) of *Montgomery Notch,* the profiled pass showing distinctly in the rugged barrier of mountains. Sunsets viewed through this natural opening are notably beautiful.

LOWELL (alt. 996, pop. township 624), 16.2 *m.*, was originally granted as Kellyvale, an indication of Irish predominance among the early settlers, of which an element remains, though the French-Canadian immigrants, of whom there has been a steady influx since the turn of the century, now outnumber them. The section of Lowell village that borders the highway is called Lowell Plain, a pleasant plateau upon which are the plain but dignified white *Federated Church* (R) and the Catholic and Protestant cemeteries (L). The main part of the village lies (R) in the narrow gully-like valley of the stream which once supported busy sawmills and was alive with the droning buzz of steel cutting through wood. This central settlement of one of the largest townships in area in the State now sleeps in a commercial inactivity that seems unlikely to be broken unless the long-projected development of the large asbestos deposits here should become a reality. The French-Canadian families have brought in their own standards and customs, in many ways not unlike those of the earliest settlers, and Lowell's three-sided barrier of mountains helps to preserve them unchanged. Evening gatherings in the general stores are suggestive of the ones in Uncle Lisha's shop, pictured in the writings of Rowland Robinson (see *Literature*), but there is more than one Antoine.

Here is the junction with State 58, the Hazen's Notch Road (*see Tour 3A*).

South of Lowell, State 100 runs through an open valley the sides of which at intervals are terraced palisades. An excellent trout brook follows the road. This section is one in which the cutting of Christmas trees has been carried on intensively and on a large scale during recent years. During November and December great bundled piles of these green trees lie all along the way, ready for shipment to the city markets.

The *Shortsleeve Mink Farm,* 18.7 *m.*, is a successful venture in the breeding of fine-furred minks in captivity. About 150 of these animals are usually kept here, from which shipments of breeding stock are made to smaller breeding establishments.

South of this point the valley is enclosed by a series of rolling humps between which the highway climbs in sharp curves.

At 20.7 *m.* is a real 'Fiddler's Elbow' bend in the ascending road. Then State 100 twists through a narrow, steep-sided mountain pass shadowed by forested slopes and rocky ridges and dominated by the abrupt bulging knob of *Mt. Norris* (R) (alt. 2050), 28.1 *m.*, a watershed for this immediate section.

*Lake Eden* (alt. 1230), 23.5 *m.* (L), lies wood-hemmed in the upland wilds, with two long peninsulas almost bisecting the narrow irregular lake. Three mountains are reflected in the clear water of Eden, and its scenic attractions are augmented by the presence of sandy shores forming excellent beaches.

Between Lake Eden and Eden Mills, the road descends a narrow gully.

EDEN MILLS (alt. 1198), 25.4 *m.*, lies desolately in a narrow ravine below the picturesque ruins of an *Old Mill* (R), crumbled on the banks of the mountain stream. The white *Congregational Church* (R), which centers the tiny settlement, is open only for summer services when the wild charms of Lake Eden make the district more populous.

Between Eden Mills and Eden, the highway continues to follow a narrow descending passage, with the rocky stream threading its whited way (R) along the roadside and wooded ridges pressing in to shelter the sharp valley. Near Eden, to the south, the country opens out and becomes more level.

EDEN CORNERS (alt. 1111, pop. township 568), 26.8 *m.*, resembles the name locally given it, a rural corner settlement lying rather barren and isolated on the open plain. The horizon to the northwest is marked by the bulk of *Belvidere Mountain* (alt. 3360) with the large asbestos mines whitening an area of its shoulder. Eden was granted to Colonel Seth Warner and associates from his Revolutionary regiment, none of whom ever settled here.

> Right from Eden on State 118 and right again on the first side road is the *Asbestos Mine*, 5 *m.*, which makes a white blotch on the mountain-side visible for miles around. The view from the mines is magnificent, sweeping southward over valleys and tiers of mountains. About 150 men are regularly employed in working these mines. Formerly workers were housed in barracks on the mountain-side, but now they commute from their homes. At dusk the lighted mining works look weird and out-of-place, shining on the slope of the wild mountain-side.

South of Eden, State 100 runs through a shallow valley scooped out of the rolling hills, with river waters coursing (L) below the highway.

At 30.5 *m.* the red *Brick House* (R) bears the date of its erection, 1823, and the compact squareness of line and stability which stamp the brick structures of that period.

NORTH HYDE PARK (alt. 770), 31.1 *m.*, trails along its single street in the narrow valley, a village of plain clapboarded houses and a few stores. The lumber stacks (R) indicate the industrial trend of the community. A calm, pleasant *Millpond* (L) at the north end of the village gives a serene tone to the scene, and diving-boards projecting over the placid water show that the pond is popular as a swimming place during the hot months. Golf tees, as well as other novelty products, are turned out at the woodworking mills here in great quantity.

Between North Hyde Park and Hyde Park, mountains (R) loom in a serrated wall on the west, while wooded knobs (L) protrude to the east. A ragged patchwork of clearings breaks the distant forest slopes, which are dark and somber with fir trees.

HYDE PARK (alt. 660, pop. 313), 37.5 *m.*, named after Jedediah Hyde, who made out the charter, is the shire town of Lamoille County. The village is one of simple neatness unmarred by shops or factories. The *Lanpher Memorial Library* (R), at the junction in the center of the village, is of tan tapestry brick. Directly facing State 100 at its junction with the Main St. is the red-brick *Courthouse*, ugly and severe. The *Carroll S. Page House* on North Main St. sits well back from the road behind spacious lawns. This house is copied closely from the Henry Wadsworth Longfellow House in Cambridge, Massachusetts. Carroll S. Page, Governor of Vermont (1890–92) and U.S. Senator (1909–23), was the largest dealer in calfskins in the world, amassing wealth for himself and bringing Hyde Park commercial prominence. The pioneers of Hyde Park broke the wilderness here in 1787 to make one of the earliest settlements in this region, and here began the white settlers' long friendship with Indian Joe and his squaw Molly, who preceded the white men in choosing this spot for their home (*see Tour 1, NEWBURY*).

Here is the junction with State 15 (*see Tour 5A*).

Between Hyde Park and Morrisville, there is a view (R) of rugged mountain stretches as State 100, in conjunction with State 15, swings along a broader valley, the floor of which is rolling and broken.

At 39.9 *m.* the *Lamoille County Fairgrounds* (R) lie behind a board fence that partly conceals them from view. This fair, held annually in August, is one of the earliest in Vermont and is locally considered the herald of autumn.

MORRISVILLE (alt. 681, pop. 1822), 41 *m.*, is sprawled along a terrace above the Lamoille River and clouded with the smoke of industry, its business enterprises being concentrated in lumber and dairy products. The river flats (L) at the northern end of the village, hold long, drab, factory sheds overhung with smoke from the tall stacks of Plant 4 of the Atlas Plywood Corporation. Across the river is located the central plant of the United Farmers' Creamery Association. This association is composed of approximately 2000 farmers and owns country plants, together with a distributing plant in Boston. The largest percentage of the products go direct to the retailer, hence the slogan 'From Farmer to Consumer.' The long Main St. with its brick business section is distinguished only by the handsome and imposing *People's Academy* building (L) which faces the street from a commanding rise at the head. This is a long, rectangular, flat-roofed, two-storied structure of red brick, with granite facings and portico, fronted by a circular cement drive. It is excellently equipped, including an observatory.

The first academy in the town was incorporated in 1847, and was for several years called 'Poor People's Academy,' the reason for this being that the wealthier families had been sending their children to schools even as distant as Burlington that they might receive more adequate instruction. The present building was given to the town by Alexander H. Copley (1929), a native son who was financially successful in real estate and chain drug store ventures. To his philanthropy Morrisville is also indebted for the *Copley Hospital*, located on a plateau southeast of the village. This is a rambling white structure of two buildings connected by a passageway, with a porch at the front, surmounted by a balcony. The location is ideal for an institution of this kind.

Morrisville is nationally known as one of the half-dozen best examples of municipal ownership of public utilities. Wise management has preserved for the citizens the advantages of a plentiful local power supply, and the municipal electric light and power company (which operates two plants) has been an outstanding success for the past twenty years. Not only have the rates been kept at a consistently low level, but the profits have paid all village taxes since 1934. Morrisville's fine display of cement streets and many other civic improvements were financed by these profits derived from selling electricity at reasonable rates on a cooperative basis.

> Left from Morrisville on an improved road is *Elmore State Forest Park*, 4.5 *m.*, where an excellent half-mile bathing beach on Elmore Pond has recently been improved by the addition of a bath-house, constructed with Civilian Conservation Corps labor. Camping and picnic facilities are also available on the slope of near-by Elmore Mountain.

> Right from Morrisville on a dirt road at 1.5 *m.* is *Lake Lamoille*, an artificial body of water formed by the power dam at Cady's Falls, its wood-fringed shores casually following a horseshoe pattern. On a high plateau overlooking the western shores is a summer resort.

South of Morrisville, State 100 winds downward to a smoother valley floor edged with dark fir trees. An irregular mountain wall forms the western background, which is higher than the range that parallels the route on the east.

At 49.5 *m.* is a large white *House* (R) built in simple Colonial lines which combine beauty with practicability as later trends in the building art seldom do.

STOWE (alt. 723, pop. 531), 50.7 *m.*, named for Stowe in England, is the southern terminus of the Smugglers' Notch Road, State 108 (*See Tour 3B*). Stowe has taken advantage of its precipitous terrain and heavy snowfall to become one of the leading winter sports centers in northern New England. In season this little village in the shadow of Mt. Mansfield is alive and colorful with skiers come to test the fast, thrilling runs on the slopes of Mansfield or to try the ski-jump north of Stowe Village, one of the two largest in the State. Interscholastic ski meets are held, and frequent week-end snow trains bring crowds of eager sportsmen north from New York City and Boston. Unlike most Vermont towns, Stowe is the scene of its liveliest and most vigorous activity during the months of ice and snow. The village itself, though plain and domestic in its architecture, is uncommonly neat in appearance. The *Community Church* (R) has a four-pillared portico, and perhaps the most beautiful spire in Vermont. The *Akley Memorial Building* (R), of red brick with white Corinthian columns, houses nearly all the public institutions of the town: post office, library, museum, and a savings bank. The *Green Mountain Inn* (L) was built as a tavern in 1833, and stands in the firm security of sturdy brick, with green and white wood trimmings. Instead

# ILLUSTRATIONS
*to accompany*

Tours 4, 4C, 4D, 4E

PROCTOR MARBLE SHEDS

VILLAGE STREET, PAWLET

THE OLD STONE SHOP, WALLINGFORD

HOYT HOUSE, MANCHESTER

GARDENS IN DORSET

COUNTRY STORE, DORSET

ST. JAMES' CHURCH AND CEMETERY, ARLINGTON

CONGREGATIONAL CHURCH, OLD BENNINGTON

BENNINGTON COLLEGE, NORTH BENNINGTON

BENNINGTON BATTLE MONUMENT, OLD BENNINGTON

of the stagecoach travelers who stopped here a century ago, the inn now serves colorfully garbed tourists in summer and winter.

The *Stoware Manufacturing Company* (R) is on the river bank at the south end of the village; it produces all sorts of wooden household utensils, such as bread boards, rolling pins, and bowls.

Between Stowe and Waterbury, small brick farmhouses predominate along the road which climbs between ridges alternately bare and wooded. The noble skyline of the continuous mountain range (R) which includes the rough human profile of Mansfield itself makes the view from the highway here one of the most impressive in the State.

WATERBURY CENTER (alt. 655), 57.8 *m.*, lies mainly to the east of the highway on a small plateau. The *Federated Church* (L), red brick with wood trim, stands close to the roadside at the northern end of the little settlement. The radio tower of WDEV, one of the leading broadcasting stations in Vermont, rises from *Blush Hill* (R) above the highway, in slender skeleton outline. The hill also holds the scenic 9-hole course of the Waterbury Country Club.

Between Waterbury Center and Colbyville, State 100 twists along a narrow valley whose downward slant is diversified by small ridges and hummocks.

COLBYVILLE, 60.5 *m.*, is a scattering of wooden dwellings dotting a crest in the highway.

At 61.2 *m.* a picturesque *Gristmill*, dated 1840, stands with an air of melancholy idleness beside the dam whose waters once turned its stones — waters that now dash over the face of the dam in purposeless beauty.

WATERBURY, 61.8 *m.* (*see Tour 5*). Here is the junction with US 2 (*see Tour 5*).

Between Waterbury and Middlesex, US 2 and State 100 are united.

MIDDLESEX, 67.8 *m.* (*see Tour 5*), is at the junction of State 100B.

*Sec. b.   MIDDLESEX to JUNCTION WITH US 5, 108.2 m.*

The northern part of this section runs through Granville Gulf, the wildest and narrowest of the three 'Gulf Roads' in the central part of the State (*see Tour 2A, WILLIAMSTOWN, and Tour 2, NORTHFIELD*). The term gulf is here used to mean something comparable to gulch or gully, a narrow cut, or pass, through the mountains. In these three instances the gulfs are also watersheds from which streams rise and flow in opposite directions. This route, through a remote region devoted to lumbering and woodworking, is enclosed by wooded foothills and ridges that shut out the world and give an air of hemmed-in isolation. The sameness of the country traversed, the dearth of scenic views and historical backgrounds, tend to make this trip rather a monotonous one, at least between Middlesex and West Bridgewater. Plymouth is of interest as the birthplace of Coolidge, and south of Plymouth is a series of charming little woodland lakes. Ludlow and Proctorsville display an industrial vitality engendered by the Black River, Chester is an attractive town, and Rockingham is known for its Old Meeting House.

MIDDLESEX, 0 *m.* (*see Tour* 5), is at the junction with US 2 (*see Tour* 5).

South of Middlesex, State 100B crosses a steel bridge over the Winooski River and swings westward to parallel the stream briefly, overlooking Middlesex Gorge with rock walls and grotesquely carved ledges rising from the swift-coursing water.

At 1 *m.* the highway veers southwest into the narrow valley of the Mad River, a wild picturesque stream dashing along a rocky bed. At 2.2 *m.* is an old lattice type *Covered Bridge* (L), no longer in use but a fitting component of the general scene.

At 2.4 *m.* is the *Power Plant No.* 8 *Dam* (L) of the Green Mountain Power Corporation. South of the dam the highway winds along the bank of the river, broader and calmer now where it is backed-up from the dam.

MORETOWN (alt. 620, pop. township 888), 7.2 *m.*, is well barricaded by the lumber stacks and log piles that loom along the Mad River. Vibrant with the whine of saws and flavored by the smell of raw lumber, Moretown is a fitting introduction to a section dominated by the lumber industry. A neat high-school building of white-painted wood is the most attractive structure on Main St. The first 'pitches' here were probably made by Haseltine and Munson around 1790. The early settlers were frequently molested by bears and wolves, many of which were shot in the vicinity. In 1830 the terrific general flood that swept the State, tore through this valley destroying lives and property.

At 8 *m.* on the southern edge of Moretown is small fenced-in *Cemetery* (L) with old headstones, against a backdrop of lumber piles.

South of Moretown the upland valley widens as the hills spread out in flatter slopes, and the farms wear a more prosperous aspect. At 12.5 *m.* on the northern outskirts of Waitsfield the farmsteads (R) sit back on river terraces over areas of fertile tillage.

WAITSFIELD (alt. 698, pop. township 723), 12.8 *m.*, received its name from General Benjamin Wait who founded the settlement in 1789. Eleven of the 13 pioneers who followed Wait were veterans of the French & Indian War and the Revolution, and it is traditional that six of these 11 soldiers were among the Minutemen at Concord Bridge and Lexington Green. Wait had a long career as a soldier, starting under Amherst at the age of 18, and fighting in 40 battles before he was 25. In the Revolution he served as a captain under Washington, being raised to the rank of colonel by the close of the war, and then becoming a general of militia. After coming to Waitsfield this hardened campaigner devoted himself to religion and led an exemplary life. An amusing story is told of Deacon Moses Fisk's barn-raising in 1821, at which the deacon declared that, contrary to the usual custom, no liquor was to be drunk at his raising bee. When the time came to raise the ridge-pole, or 'rum pole' as it was called, the workers went on a strike, informing the deacon that they could not lift the ridge pole until they were strengthened by rum. But the stubborn old deacon refused to yield, and after a time the men, grumbling or joking as was their nature, completed the task without the aid of stimulants.

The village lies along the river flats walled in by hills. Dairying and lumbering are the industries. The *Federated Church* (L), a nice white structure with a tall clean spire, adds attractiveness to the village street. *Joslin Memorial Library* (R) is built of brick painted yellow. At the south end of the settlement a rock ledge (R) rears close above the highway as the western ridge encroaches on the valley.

IRASVILLE (alt. 789), 13.9 *m.*, is a small hamlet on a plateau banked by high hills.

South of Irasville the Mad River runs smaller and narrower between tree-lined banks, and the foothills roll along on either side, now bare and now wooded. The region, relatively remote from railroads and bus lines, reveals an excellent example of the decline in back-country sections not traversed by railways. At 17.1 *m.* the foothills begin to grow up to low forested mountains.

WARREN (alt. 893, pop. township 486), 19.6 *m.*, is another little lumber-milling settlement occupying an uneven terrain in the mountains between *Warren Pinnacle* (alt. 1700) (L), and *Sugarloaf Mountain* (alt. 2120) (R). Woodworking mills lie along the Mad River below the village street with puffs of white steam blowing from the pipes and fading against stacks of fresh timber. From early times lumbering has been the primary activity, and the inevitable accidents that accompany the trade took the lives of many pioneer lumberjacks, killing them under falling trees and in log jams. The *United Church* (L), on a knoll with a stonewall base, commands the unpainted homes of the street.

Here is the junction with an unnumbered road (Lincoln Pass Rd.) (*see Tour 3C*).

South of Warren the river (R) twists and turns through a rocky gorge, grim, jagged and picturesque. The *Natural Bridge of Stone* here has a 12-foot arch, and has been much photographed. The ruins of abandoned mills are seen along the way, and higher ridges overshadow the narrowing valley.

*Granville Gulf* is entered at 23.9 *m.* announced by the orange signboard of the State Forest Service, as the 'Granville Gulf Reservation — 2635 acres of woodland, six miles of natural beauty to be preserved forever.' Granville is the wildest and most intimate of Vermont's three central north-and-south gulfs; thick-wooded slopes shut in the highway, then give way to a rock-walled defile where great ragged upthrusts of stone loom over the road. In the Gulf, the Mad River on nearing its source is diminished to a slender thread along the roadside. At 27.4 *m.* the highway pitches sharply downward through a narrow rock-ledged cut, densely shaded and veritably buried in the mountains. At 28.7 *m.* is *Moss Glen Falls* (R), conceded to be one of the most beautiful waterfalls in the State. On this long winding shut-in descent, the road continually disappears ahead as it turns this way and that into the close-shouldering mountainsides. In Granville Gulf the Mad River rises and flows northward; a branch of the White River, called Alder Meadow Brook, rises to wend its way south. At 29.8 *m.* is the southern end of the Gulf.

GRANVILLE (Upper) (alt. 1013, pop. township 280), 31 *m.*, stretched on the open flat where the White River, Alder Meadow Brook and Kendall Brook unite, is a settlement built around the red mill-buildings of the *Granville Manufacturing Company* (R), makers of wooden bowls and other wood products. Originally called Kingston for grantee Reuben King, the present name was adopted in 1834.

South of Granville the valley broadens, seeming very open and wide after the close confines of Granville Gulf.

LOWER GRANVILLE (alt. 960), 32.2 *m.*, scattered along the valley floor, is centered by a general store and white wooden *Methodist Church* (R) with a high blank façade. The setting has a calm serenity in sharp contrast to the wild mountain fastnesses on the north. The White River, increased in size by its two tributaries, bends pleasantly along the valley.

HANCOCK (alt. 912, pop. township 303), 35.4 *m.*, consists of a T-shaped collection of unpainted old houses, a white-fenced cemetery and an ugly church, but there is beauty in the mountain slopes surrounding the little community. The *Vermont Plywood Corporation* (R) at the southern end of the village, is an unusually large plant for such a sparsely settled section; about 150 workers are employed here, coming from Granville, Hancock and Rochester.

Here is the junction with State 125 (*see Tour 3D*).

South of Hancock is a *Ski Jump* (R), the wooden trestle and steep runway high on a ridge that parallels the road. Jumps of 180 feet have been registered here. The valley in general is sheltered by somber pinewooded foothills, rock protrusions showing gauntly here and there.

ROCHESTER (alt. 837, pop. township 1285), 40 *m.*, was awarded the prize at the Jamestown Exhibition (1907) as the Model Town of the United States. The highway curves in on the northern end past close-set wooden dwellings to the large broad level green (L), evenly shaded and attractive at the village center. The white wooden *Congregational Church* (R), gracefully spired, faces the square across Main St. Rochester's industrial virility in no way mars its gracious and orderly appearance.

Industries, diversified to turn out bobbins, talc, marble, grist and dairy produce, are along the banks of the White River (R), separated from the residential sections which sit back in quiet dignity on the natural terraces east of the watercourse. The mountain horizon to the west is commanded by *Mount Horrid* (alt. 3120). Rochester's setting and general character appeal to an increasing number of summer visitors and winter sports followers.

South of Rochester the White River Valley is rimmed by hill stretches.

TALCVILLE (alt. 825), 42.1 *m.*, was once a vigorous mining community, built around the talc mine (L). Its deserted buildings now rest in idle disrepair on the hillside, unsightly shells of a dead industry.

South of Talcville the valley widens to become more serene and pleasant as the White River curves in wide swinging loops.

STOCKBRIDGE (alt. 734, pop. township 460), 47.8 *m.*, is a simple crossroads settlement on a little hummock in the valley with a pine-wooded ridge standing sober guard on the east.

South of Stockbridge, State 100 swings sharply right over the White River and leaves that stream behind to follow the Tweed River directly west for an interval.

PITTSFIELD (alt. 892, pop. township 256), 51.8 *m.*, named for Pittsfield, Massachusetts, from which the first settlers came, lies pleasantly deep in the hills at another junction of rivers. The north end of the little village is marred by burnt-out cellar holes, but the center is pleasing with its long narrow strip of tree-studded green and old town waterpump.

South of Pittsfield, State 100 continues in a southern trend again, along a shallow and rather monotonous valley ranged in by domed hills. At 57.2 *m.* the road climbs a bit and the forests close in to march along the highway.

GIFFORD WOODS (State Forest Park) (R), 59.4 *m.*, has an attractive stone shelter on the wooded hillside.

At 60 *m.* is a junction with US 4 (*see Tour 6*).

Between this junction and West Bridgewater, US 4 in conjunction with State 100 follows a southeasterly course in the Ottaquechee Valley.

WEST BRIDGEWATER, 66.7 *m.* (*see Tour 6*), is at the junction of State 100 and US 4 (*see Tour 6*).

South of West Bridgewater, State 100 winds southward on a steeply walled-in road.

At 68.8 *m.* is the *Dam* backing up the *Woodward Reservoir* (Plymouth Pond), which stretches along the crooked highway through a section rural in flavor, made weird by the great boulders tumbled here and there. A scattering of summer cottages overlook the water.

At 70.2 *m.* the *Northam State Picnic Area* (R) occupies wild hilly woodlands (*see Tour 4D, NORTH SHREWSBURY*).

PLYMOUTH UNION (alt. 1217), 71.9 *m.*, is strung along a narrow, irregular valley in the mountains. A patriotic wooden dwelling-house at the north end of the hamlet wears red, white, and blue paint in garish fashion.

At 72.5 *m.* at the southern outskirts of Plymouth Union is the junction with State 100A.

Left on State 100A is PLYMOUTH (alt. 1420, pop. township 331). 1 *m.* and the *Birthplace of Calvin Coolidge* (L), a country store at the crossroads in this tiny hamlet buried in the mountains. On Independence Day, 1872, Calvin Coolidge was born in the cottage attached to the rear of the combination store-and-post office. He was educated at Black River Academy (*see LUDLOW, below*) and Amherst. As mayor of Northampton, Massachusetts, he started his political career, becoming Governor of that State, and then Vice-President of the United States under Harding. Coolidge was at home with his folks in Plymouth on August 3, 1923, when he was awakened at 2 A.M. by the news of Harding's death, and sworn in as President by his father, Colonel John Coolidge, on the worn family Bible under the yellow flicker of a kerosene lamp. Calvin Coolidge finished that term and served another full term. Known as 'Silent Cal,' he was looked upon by the world as a typical Vermonter, taciturn, unsmiling, penurious — a solemn man, thin and sharp as a scythe, without humor, without emotions. He never lost the harsh farmer's twang in his voice. It was as a simple homespun person that he appealed to people. The fact that a peak of prosperity was attained in the Coolidge régime lifted him to almost legendary heights for a brief stay. 'Keep Cool with Coolidge' was the slogan, and the country looked upon him as a safe, sane balance-wheel. Coolidge died in 1933, and now sleeps in the sidehill cemetery at Plymouth beneath a severely simple stone.

The store has been turned into a sort of museum, and thousands of annual visitors have made remote little Plymouth a shrine in the Vermont hills.

Beyond Plymouth on State 100A is *Calvin Coolidge State Forest*, 3 *m.*, 5489 acres of woodland, equipped with picnic areas, tent platforms, Green Mountain lean-tos, etc. Foot trails wend to scenic vantage points.

South of Plymouth Union, State 100 follows the rocky course of the Black River (R), with stone walls along the river bank and thick-forested slopes on each side, *Mount Tom* (alt. 2040) rearing on the east.

At 76.1 *m.* is a *Crown Point Military Road Marker* (L), a high stone slab indicating the course followed by the historic trail between Charlestown, New Hampshire, and Crown Point, New York, and stating that the site of the 26-mile encampment is one-quarter mile west of the monument.

*Lake Amherst*, 76.3 *m.*, is a beautiful natural memorial to Lord Jeffrey Amherst, the military commander under whose direction the Crown Point Road was laid through the wilderness. Wooded shores rise sharply from the clear water, and the highway skirts the western edge of the wood-ringed little lake. It is likely that the builders of the old road camped by this quiet body of water, rough brawny axemen and lean, sharp-eyed riflemen resting from their labors on the shore of the peaceful lake.

*Echo Lake*, 77.3 *m.*, less closely confined by forested slopes, is similar to Lake Amherst in unspoiled quiet beauty of natural setting.

TYSON, 78.2 *m.*, is a small summer settlement at the southern end of Echo Lake, built around a large white-porched summer inn (R). A neat concrete bridge (L) with built-in lamp-posts conducts a road over the Black River to the summer homes along the eastern shores of Echo and Amherst.

*Rescue Lake* (L), 79.4 *m.*, is the southernmost and largest of this chain of pretty lakes through which the Black River flows. Its shoreline is much more broken and irregular.

South of Rescue Lake the highway runs between a pine-wooded ridge and the broad strong-flowing Black River.

At 82 *m.* is the junction with State 103 (*see Tour 4E*).

*Okemo Mountain State Forest Park* (R), 83.4 *m.*, stretches over the wild uplands to the west, 4400 acres of mountain wilderness. A park road climbs the mountain to a commanding panorama of the Adirondacks, Green Mountains, and White Mountains. The park facilities embrace picnic areas, ski trails, and foot paths.

LUDLOW (alt. 1064, pop. 1641), 84.1 *m.*, on the Rutland R.R. and lying Y-shaped in the divergent valleys of the Black River and its tributary Jewell Brook, is characterized by an industrial virility springing from the woolen mills, most of which produce shoddy, or reworked wool. The manufacturing of shoddy was introduced after the Civil War to combat the shortage of cloth that existed, and two Black River Valley towns, Ludlow and Springfield (*see SPRINGFIELD*), were among the pioneers in the field. From the huddled wood and brick structures of the business center to the long factory buildings on the river flats, Ludlow has an air of activity that marks it apart from the usual village of 1000 population. The streets are colored by houses of bright red brick, and *Fletcher Memorial Library* (R) is of red brick facing the small shaded triangle of the green. *Black River Academy* (left on hill), founded in 1834, is the high school where Calvin Coolidge received his secondary education. The building, in towered red brick, stands on a low hill immediately over the village center. The *Brick House* (L), prominent at the eastern edge of town, is the home of John Garibaldi Sargent, the boyhood friend whom Coolidge appointed Attorney-General in his Cabinet. The very large, homelike, six-chimneyed structure is the only type of house that big 'Gary' Sargent could be happy in: solid, spacious, and unpretentious. Ludlow was the home of Abby Maria Hemenway, the prodigious historian who compiled town histories covering the entire State, now available in five volumes totaling 6000 pages.

East of Ludlow, State 103 follows the Black River in its strong easterly course, through a valley that is richer in aspect.

*Fletcher Farms* (*open May 31 to Sept 8*) (L), 86.1 *m.*, house an unusual and informal sort of summer school, and is the meeting-place of various educational, economic, and social-service groups. The fine old farm buildings, the main house of which was built in 1783 by Jesse Fletcher, have been renovated to furnish pleasant quarters, in a serenely agreeable, natural setting, where the valley is folded in green slopes. The Arts and Crafts Workshop (*June 14–Aug. 16*) offers courses in sketching and painting, clay work, bookmaking, woodcarving, dyeing, etc. Drama is studied at the Fletcher Farm Theater, and the Music Institute provides a program for music lovers. Here in a leisurely and friendly atmosphere, cultural interests are pursued by people from many parts of the country and various walks of life.

PROCTORSVILLE (alt. 928), 87.6 *m.*, is named after the Proctor family, a busy village in Cavendish Township, utilizing Black River water-power to support the Black River Valley theme of industrial vigor founded on woolen and woodworking mills. Houses and stores are set close to the street. and a large brick-built woolen manufacturing plant (R) dominates the junction of roads at the village center. The *World War Memorial* (L), in the simple dignity of marble, is welcome after the gaucherie of so many war monuments. Redfield Proctor, the marble magnate, was born in a brick farmhouse here (*see Tour 4, PROCTOR*).

Left from Proctorsville on an improved road is CAVENDISH (alt. 929, pop. township 1418), 1.8 *m.*, settled in 1769 by Captain John Coffin, who built a house, and later a tavern, on the Crown Point Military Road, and whose hospitality was known to thousands of American troops stopping here on their way from Number Four (Charlestown, New Hampshire) to the military posts on Lake Champlain. In August, 1754, the Indians burst into the Johnson house at Number Four and seized the seven inmates, carrying them back to Canada. The first time they camped was in what is now Cavendish, and here Mrs Johnson gave birth to a child, whom she named Captive. Northeast of Cavendish is the *Site of Twenty-Mile Encampment*, the camping ground used by the soldiers marching on the Crown Point Road. Twenty-Mile Stream, a tributary of the Black River, was named after the encampment, which was about 20 miles from Number Four. The community is supported largely by the manufacturing of woolens, and dairying; formerly cider and apple jelly were produced in quantity. The 1927 flood tore a tremendous gorge through the township, in places revealing the fantastic carvings made by the erosion of years ago. Prominent families here are the Proctors and the Fletchers  Three Vermont governors were born in Cavendish township: Redfield Proctor (1878–80); Fletcher Proctor (1906–08); Ryland Fletcher (1856–58).

South of Proctorsville at 88.8 *m.* is the northern end of *Proctorsville Gulf*, with the sharply curved highway dropping through a narrow defile. *Proctor-Piper State Forest* (R), 1500 acres of mountain forests, has well-laid-out park roads leading to the picnic and tenting areas, and to high scenic points; and bridle trails thread the woodlands. A winter feature is the mile bobsled run, which has proved thrilling and popular. At 90 *m.* the pass widens to a placid little valley, and then narrows immediately into another hemmed-in cut.

GASSETTS (alt. 715), 92.3 *m.*, is scattered along the open plain of the Williams River south of Proctorsville Gulf, a small settlement in Chester township, uninteresting but for its odd name. A little railroad depot and watertank mark the north end of the village.

South of Gassetts the valley broadens as the Williams River winds southward paralleling highway and railroad.

*Site of First Log House in Chester* (R), 95.7 *m.* A marble tablet at the roadside above the wide meadows along the stream indicates that these river flats were the site of the first settlement in Chester, when Jabez Sargeant and Thomas Chandler hewed a home out of logs here.

CHESTER DEPOT (alt. 597), 97 *m.*, is an attractive residential suburb and the railroad station of Chester. The single street is lined with stone houses, forming clean patterns in gray and brown. The *Universalist Church* was built of stone in 1845, and harmonizes with the picturesque dwelling-houses. Visitors coming to Chester for summertime beauty or to enjoy outdoor winter sports, leave the train at the little *Depot* (R).

CHESTER (alt. 599, pop. 684), 97.7 *m.*, beautifully situated at a junction of valleys, wears an air of charming gentility over broad streets shaded by great elms and old maples. A long slender green splits the Main St., and gracious homes of wood, brick, and stone are set back on smooth lawns. The *First Baptist Church* (R) (1835), a large structure in cherry-red brick, looms over the stone-walled graveyard which flanks the street with a somber mien. A pale green *Colonial House* (L) adds a distinguished touch, and the western end of the village street is colored by homes of red brick and patterned stone. The big white *Congregational Church* (R) (1829) carries a tower of Bulfinch adaptation, suggesting the Wren traditions in architecture. While not striving to become a major winter sports center, Chester, lying in the heavy snow belt of Vermont, provides fine ski trails and runs, a ski tow, toboggan slide, ski jump, and skating rink, and welcomes small parties of skiers. An annual winter carnival is held here.

Parson Flagg of Chester made of his house a Yankee Gretna Green for the convenience of eloping couples from New Hampshire, in the old days. The practice developed to such an extent that New Hampshire elopements came to be known as 'Flagg Marriages.' Another, and much less desirable character, was Clarence Brown, a scholarly man who had been a respected citizen and legislator in the late nineteenth century, until it was discovered that he had actually been for years robbing and terrorizing fellow-citizens. Belated justice cast Brown into prison, but he escaped, it is told, by going into a trance, and playing dead so realistically that he was given burial in a cemetery vault, where he was rescued from the casket by a confederate and escaped to Canada.

Between Chester and Bartonsville, the route runs along a broad shallow valley between stone-walled fields and patches of woodland.

BARTONSVILLE (alt. 487), 101.7 *m.*, is a simple little rural corners settlement in the township of Rockingham, with faded brick homes flanking the road. The main part of the village lies on the eastern bank of the river, off the highway.

Between Bartonsville and Rockingham, State 103 curves along the bends of the Williams River.

ROCKINGHAM (alt. 480, pop. township 5302), 106.3 *m.*, a quiet little settlement drowsing in the gentle roll of hills, gave its name to a township whose population is swollen by the inclusion of Bellows Falls and Saxtons River. The tiny hill-cloistered village lies under the dominance of the *Rockingham Meeting-House* (L) on the knoll, a severely plain white structure erected in 1787, one of Vermont's earliest churches. The Puritan simplicity of this building, without steeple or decoration, gives it a distinctive charm. It was recently renovated, painted, and landscaped with FERA funds. In the shadow of the meeting-house are the tombstones of the old burying ground, adding to the reverent dignity of the picture. The interior of the church, retaining the straight-backed solemnity of old box pews, complements the Colonial restraint so evident in the clean lines of the exterior. Rockingham, but a few miles from the clamoring activity of Bellows Falls, rests in complete rural peace.

Between Rockingham and the junction with US 5, the road winds and dips along the Williams River Valley, shaded by great old trees.

In 1704, near the mouth of the Williams River, 240 Indians returning from a raid on Greenfield, Massachusetts, with 112 prisoners, stopped to camp. It was Sunday and among the prisoners was Rev. John Williams, who preached a sermon to his fellow captives. His text was Lamentations I: 18: 'The Lord is righteous; for I have rebelled against his commandments. Hear, I pray you, all people, and behold my sorrow; my virgins and my young men are gone into captivity.'

At 108.2 *m.* is the junction with US 5 (*see Tour* 1), 3.8 miles north of Bellows Falls.

---

T O U R   3 A :   *From* LOWELL *to* EAST BERKSHIRE, 18.4 *m.*, State 58, 118.

---

Via Montgomery Center, Montgomery.

THIS route affords an unusual variety of terrain and scenery within a short distance. The first part of it lies through sparsely settled country and crosses the main range of the Green Mountains through a lofty forest notch. The region west of the mountains is relatively level, and the northwestern end of the route reaches the fertile Missisquoi Valley and the heart of the leading dairying section in the State.

LOWELL, 0 *m.* (*see Tour* 3), is at the junction with State 100 (*see Tour* 3).

State 58 runs northwest of Lowell through heavily wooded country, much of the timber being original growth. There are some foothill farms. Between Lowell village and Hazen's Notch the present highway follows quite closely, it is believed, the old Hazen Military Road.

*Hazen's Notch* (alt. 1700), 5.3 *m.*, is a natural cut in the Green Mountain Range, with sheer rock cliffs rising (R) above the highway in a framework of trees. Here is a marker (L) designating this point as the northern terminus of the uncompleted road that General Hazen built in 1779 for a proposed invasion of Canada. It is believed locally, however, that the road extended a few miles farther, into the township of Montgomery, where traces of an old corduroy road were uncovered many years ago.

The *Long Trail* crosses the highway at the Notch, losing itself at once in the forests on both sides of the road which have been set aside as the

*Hazen's Notch State Forest Park.* Though it has been little developed as yet, a natural shaded glade with a cold spring, at 5.8 *m.*, has been provided with picnic tables.

The western descent from the Notch is one of extreme precipitousness and should be made under compression. Between the foot of the mountain and Montgomery Center, the country is under cultivation, but the farms are far inferior to the ones just a few miles to the west. *Jay Peak* (alt. 3861) (R), about five miles north of the highway, is visible from this section, the dominating pinnacle of the northern stretch of the Green Mountain Range from whichever side it is viewed. The descent into Montgomery Center, one of the steepest highway pitches in the State, should be made under compression.

MONTGOMERY CENTER (alt. 533, pop. township 1386), 10.4 *m.*, is a quiet residential village and trading center, one of two in this fine agricultural township. Trout River, which, as its name implies, is a fine fishing stream, is seen here.

Here is a junction of State 58 and State 118.

West of Montgomery Center, State 118 runs over a rolling terrain in contrast with the mountainous region to the east. Trout River follows the highway closely in its westward course to join the Missisquoi at East Berkshire.

MONTGOMERY (alt. 492, pop. township 1386), 13.2 *m.*, is a postal and trading center, its well-shaded streets radiating from a highway three-corners. The first settler was Captain Joshua Clapp, a Revolutionary soldier who came here in 1793. William B. Clapp, born in Montgomery, was the first man to can meat successfully in this country. At one time the town specialized in the growing of fine timothy grass seed for exportation, but its agriculture now, as in most Franklin County townships, is centered around the dairying industry.

West of Montgomery village the land becomes even more level, the farms larger and more prosperous-looking, with well-kept, modern buildings. The most interesting architectural features of this immediate section, however, are the numerous covered bridges that span Trout River as it interlaces the road between Montgomery and East Berkshire.

EAST BERKSHIRE, 18.4 *m.* (*see Tour* 1C), is at the junction with State 105 (*see Tour* 1C).

T O U R   3 B :   STOWE *to* ST. ALBANS, 43.5 *m.*, State 108, 15, 104.

Via Jeffersonville, Cambridge, Fairfax.

The Central Vermont Ry. parallels the route between Jeffersonville and a point two miles west of Cambridge.

The road is dirt and gravel except between Fairfax and North Fairfax, where it is hard surface. The Notch Road between Smugglers' Notch and Jeffersonville is not kept open in the winter.

THIS route, lying off the congested main arteries, includes some of the finest and most completely unspoiled scenery in the State. The southern part crosses Smuggler's Notch, one of the most impressive highway passes in the East. The northern section traverses a fertile upland valley with a series of magnificent views of the mountains to the south; the northern end reaches to the Champlain Valley.

STOWE, 0 *m.* (*see Tour* 3), is at the junction with State 100 (*see Tour* 3).

From Stowe village, State 108 leads northwest across a covered bridge over the Waterbury River. The view (R) of Stowe village is dominated by the slender thrust of the spire of the white Community Church. At 0.6 *m.* is a reforested hillside (L), thick with baby evergreens. The view to the north (R) is one of fine rolling farmlands as the valley broadens.

At 0.9 *m.* is a privately maintained *Ski-Tow* (L) on the northwest slope of Cady Hill. A second covered bridge spans West Branch Brook at 1.4 *m.*

WEST BRANCH, 1.8 *m.*, is a rural cluster of houses in a good farming area. The century-old white *Church* (R) is now used only occasionally for community gatherings. At 2 *m.* is a well-kept *Cemetery* (R), dotted at intervals with large hydrangea bushes. The church bell on view in front of the red barn (R) at 2.1 *m.* is a relic from the old Stowe Meeting-House of an earlier day. North of this point the valley narrows considerably, with low hills on both sides of the winding route.

The *Winter Rearing Pool* (L) at 4.6 *m.* is maintained by the Waterbury Fish and Game Club. The young fish may be inspected here in the spring.

At 4.9 *m.* is a junction with a rustic woods road.

Left up this road are the *Mt. Mansfield Ski Club's Ski Runs*, 0.5 *m.*, a major part of the developed natural facilities that have made Stowe one of the leading winter sports centers in the East. The tree-fringed road is not improved for motor travel.

The short steep climb between 4.9 *m.* and 5.2 *m.* is called Harlow Hill.

At 5.7 *m.* is a junction with the privately owned *Mt. Mansfield Toll Road* (*toll $3 per round trip for automobile and passengers to the number of six; 25¢ for each additional passenger*), with the pleasantly landscaped toll house set in a clearing (L).

Left up this Toll Road is the summit of Mt. Mansfield, with its several points of interest. At 3.4 m. is a fine view of Smuggler's Notch, on the main route to the north. At 3.8 m. is the start of the long downhill mountain ski trail (L), a part of the 40 miles of ski trails that cover the mountain. Right from this point a short uphill footpath leads to a *Stone Cabin* (*free to hiking or skiing parties*) built by the Civilian Conservation Corps under supervision of the State Forestry Department.

The *Mt. Mansfield Hotel* (alt. 3849), 4.3 m., is a gray two-story building at the base of the Nose. It marks the end of the motor road.

Mt. Mansfield is about five miles long and from many points in the valley below roughly resembles an upturned human face. The various peaks are for this reason designated, from south to north, as the Forehead, the Nose, the Lips, the Chin, and the Adam's Apple. The Chin (alt. 4393) is the highest point of the mountain and of the State. The greater portion of Mansfield is now included in the *Mt. Mansfield Forest Park* (5084 acres). A strip on the summit three miles long and 28 rods wide is owned by the University of Vermont. Various botanical rarities, including at least four varieties of ferns which were discovered in the Mansfield area, occur here. The *Long Trail*, plainly marked, follows the ridge of the mountain north and south. About 1 m. north of the hotel and a short distance down the east side is the *Rock of Terror*, a large rough boulder balanced on a ledge. The geological composition of the rock, different from that of any other near-by, as well as its precarious position, indicates that it was deposited here ages ago by glacial movement.

The *Cave of the Winds* is reached by a steep side trail, plainly indicated, down the east face of the mountain from a point just north of the Upper Lip. This cave is a peculiar cleft in the mountain which has, in its farther end, a small perpendicular channel that can be descended by rope ladder for a distance of about 75 feet. There is a layer of ice at the bottom the year round. This descent is recommended only to experienced mountaineers with strong hearts.

The *Lake of the Clouds* is a shallow, forest-circled pond lying under the Chin, past the Adam's Apple. Its outlet, Hell Brook, paralleled by a scenic foot trail, flows down the mountain-side to the east.

The best view from Mt. Mansfield is from the Chin, though that from the Nose is almost as good. To the north can be seen Mt. Royal, overlooking Montreal. To the east, across the Notch, are the Sterling Mountains and, beyond the Connecticut Valley, Mt. Washington and lesser peaks of the White Mountains. The view to the south includes the other great Vermont peaks: Camel's Hump, Mt. Killington, Mt. Lincoln, and isolated Ascutney, with villages dotting the valleys on both sides of the range. To the west lies Lake Champlain, and beyond it the irregular crest of the Adirondacks. The scope of this view — more than 100 miles in all directions with average visibility — is greater than that of any other in the State.

A score of foot trails lead down both sides of the mountain: on the east side, the Long Trail, the trail following Hell Brook, and the continuation of the trail to the Cave of the Winds; on the west, the Sunset Trail (*see Tour 5A, UNDERHILL*).

*Smuggler's Notch*, the exact limits of which are not definitely established, is entered at about 6 m. This is a deep, fairly broad cleft between Mt. Mansfield and the Sterling Mountains. The Notch acquired its name from the fact that smugglers, in the Embargo period and during the War of 1812, brought contraband goods from Canada to Boston through this pass, which was off the main routes watched by the revenue officers, and frequently used the large caves in the Notch for storage purposes.

At 6.2 m. is a junction with a woodland lane, impassable for automobiles.

Right down this lane is *Bingham Falls*, about 0.3 m. These falls, among the most beautiful in Vermont, flow from Big Spring (*see below*). In a series of varied cascades the water tumbles down from high ledges through a narrow gorge, over large water-worn boulders. The total height of the drop is about 80 feet. Below the last falls, at the end of a natural rock flume, is a placid rock pool, above which as the sunlight glints brokenly through the overhanging trees, delicately tinted mists seem to arise, from water that a few moments before was all a raging white.

At 6.8 *m.* the road enters for a short space the Mansfield State Forest (*see above*), which lies mainly to the west of the route.

The *Nose-Dive Trail* (L), 7.5 *m.*, is a sporty ski-run that swoops down Mansfield from the Nose and is temporarily combined with the Long Trail, which crosses the road at this point. The downhill race of the championship meet of the Eastern Ski Association of America was held on this run in 1937, a distinction that could not be added to unless it should be chosen for the downhill run of the next international Olympics to be held in this country.

A *Picnic Area* (R), 8.1 *m.*, is equipped with numerous rustic rock fireplaces and tables by a natural cold spring.

The route beyond this point steadily climbs to the narrower part of the Notch, where the walls rise precipitously a thousand feet above the highway.

*Big Spring* (R), 8.7 *m.*, is at the foot of the last ascent. It is one of the largest springs in the East, its cold waters gushing from the mountainside at the rate of about 1000 gallons per minute. Its source is not definitely known, though it is reputed to be the outlet of Sterling Pond, the highest sizable body of water in Vermont. The waters of this spring are so pure that they are often used in storage batteries in place of distilled water. Big Spring is the source of Bingham Falls (*see above*).

At 9.3 *m.* is a parking turnout (L). From here are visible two strange natural rock figures: the *Hunter and His Dog* (or Guardians of the Notch), across the road to the northeast, and the *Singing Bird*, high up on the cliff to the northwest. Both of these natural sculptures are remarkably close images and require less stretching of the imagination than do most such formations. Just beyond, at 9.4 *m.*, another parking turnout (L) affords a view of the *Smuggler's Face*, a gigantic rock countenance of an Egyptian cast, high up on the cliff (L) slightly south of west. *Smuggler's Cave*, a few yards west of the turnout, is a large irregular cavity several feet wide formed by the accidental juxtaposition of huge rocks. The *Natural Refrigerator* is a chasm in the rocks on the northwest side of the turnout. Cold air rising from the chasm maintains an even summer temperature of 48°. It is believed that the air is cooled in subterranean passages before it escapes through this rift.

North of this point the route slopes steeply downward, winding through the forested cleft and crossing numerous mountain brooks. At 9.6 *m.* a fine view opens to the north. The north end of the Notch is at about 12 *m.*

MORSE'S MILL, 12.3 *m.*, is almost the first human habitation north of the Notch. It consists of a few dwellings and an old mill (R) on a small dam in Brewster River.

SOUTH CAMBRIDGE, 14.4 *m.*, is a tiny hamlet built at a zigzag in the road. The double-cupolaed white *Community House* (1858) is typical of countless others in small communities throughout the State which serve their respective localities in many of the capacities in which the church, as a building, formerly served them, as well as in others in which the church, as an organization, made no attempt to serve.

JEFFERSONVILLE, 17.2 *m.* (*see Tour 5A*), is at the junction with State 15 (*see Tour 5A*).

CAMBRIDGE, 20.1 *m.* (*see Tour 5A*), is at the junction with State 15 (*see Tour 5A*) and State 104.

Right from the western end of Cambridge village (at R.R. crossing), State 104 leads west through the rich Lamoille River Valley. The valley lands lie right of the road, which parallels the tracks of the Central Vermont Ry. for about 1.5 miles. After passing for a short distance between low bordering ridges, the route becomes more open again at 24.9 *m.*, and large rounded hills are visible to the west. At 25.2 *m.* the Lamoille River (R) winds close to the road, with large crop-sown meadows outlined by the bends. At about 25.9 *m.*, the highway itself becomes very winding and should be traveled at a moderate speed.

At 26.2 *m.* is a typical *Vermont Sugar House* (L) of the type prevailing today, with small windows, steam ventilators on the roof, and a lean-to at one end where the wood for the evaporator is stored. Though of simple construction, this is an advance on the primitive sugar houses that predominated until recently, in which both light and ventilation were supplied by chinks between the boards, with perhaps a board or two knocked out altogether. During a heavy boiling, with steam issuing from every crack, these crude structures were often thought by unknowing observers to be on fire within. The northern half of this route lies through the heart of one of the most productive maple-sugar districts in the State, and several of the sugar houses are visible from the highway.

At 26.6 *m.* is a large modern example of the gambrel-roofed barn (L), of which there are several in this section. It is notable that this type of roof, popular on the earliest Colonial houses, has now, by the same exigencies of space that influenced the early builders, been transferred to the barns, where it allows for roomier mows than can be achieved with a single-slant roof.

At 27.8 *m.* one of several thick growths of evergreen trees (L) in this section and the evergreen-covered hills beyond the meadow valley (R) constitute a somber frame for the pleasing picture of agricultural prosperity that lies between them.

The route turns sharply right at 29.2 *m.* across an iron bridge spanning the Lamoille River.

At FAIRFAX FALLS (Great Falls) (L), 29.3 *m.*, is the hydro-electric plant of the Public Electric Light Company, which furnishes electricity for St. Albans, Burlington, and the surrounding countryside, utilizing the natural forces that formerly powered large flour and woolen mills. The river plunges in a series of cascades to the jagged rocks below, attaining a fall of 88 feet in a distance of 30 rds. But the turbulent thundering fury of the waters, fearsome at first glance, seems like a tempest in a teapot when the serene immutability of Mansfield, more noble than ever from this distance, is viewed to the southeast.

North of Fairfax Falls, the valley is narrower, the farms, consequently, smaller, and at 30.2 *m.* the valley is all but filled by the winding road and the river, leaving no meadowland at all.

FAIRFAX (alt. 349, pop. township 1249), 31.1 *m.*, lies partly in a hollow, at the southern end, rising to a long open plain on the north. Formerly a manufacturing town of some commercial importance, its industries today are chiefly lumbering and dairying. Here is *Bellows Free Academy* (1903), housed in a large brick building set on low ground about a quarter-mile west of the central street. At the southern end of the plain is the last building occupied by New Hampton Institute (R), a secondary school moved here from New Hampton, New Hampshire, in 1853 that functioned until the opening years of the present century. This decaying structure is given an aspect of melancholy gauntness by its unusually tall and narrow windows. Across the street (L) is the *Baptist Church*, brick on a stone foundation, with latticed towers and an uneven placement of doors. On the northern outskirts of the village, at 31.9 *m.*, the squat *Stone House* (L) is at least a century old, though the exact date is uncertain. It is an example of pure native building, of mortared stone, with solid irregular stone lintels over the door and windows, and an asymmetrical arrangement of the windows themselves, boldly proportioned to interior needs rather than exterior patterns.

Fairfax's greatest claim to distinction is its view of Mt. Mansfield to the southeast. No other village in Vermont lives in the continuous presence of its equal in grandeur. Beautiful in the greenery of summer, but even more irresistibly arresting in late fall or winter, when the barren summit is white with snow above the sullen blue of the lower slopes, Mt. Mansfield from Fairfax presents at any time a spectacle too impressive to be interpreted in terms of anything but itself. Fairfax has already been chosen as a summer home by several out-of-State people.

The road is hard-surfaced between Fairfax and North Fairfax.

North of Fairfax the country is open, with large farms, many of them with brick farmhouses, that give the locality a look of prosperous comfort. Some of the houses are more solid than beautiful, like the one (L) at 32.5 *m.*, a time-defying example of what the Georgian ideal could decline to. The number of ensilage silos throughout this region — sometimes three to a farm — is indicative of the emphasis it places on dairying.

Despite the general fertility, there are sections here where outcroppings of rock all but pre-empt the soil. At 33.6 *m.*, for instance, is a scrubby stretch of rocky terrain (R) over which a cow could scarcely pick her way; yet the remains of a stone wall show that it was once enclosed for pastureland. Sections such as this explain the origin of the ancient

Vermont saw about Nature's having made the noses of sheep pointed so that they could reach in between the rocks for small wisps of grass.

At 38.2 *m.* is a glimpse of Lake Champlain (L), a mere flash of blue or of reflected sunlight that gives no hint of the lake's magnitude and is soon lost to view.

NORTH FAIRFAX, 38.5 *m.*, is a handful of houses built on an S-curve Here is the *St. Albans City Reservoir* (R), the waters hidden from the road by the grassed embankment of the dam face. The hard surface ends here.

For about 2 miles north of North Fairfax, State 104 runs through a shallow valley between rocky and semi-wooded hill ridges. The slopes of the ridges are frequently covered with maple groves, at the open edges of which unpainted sugar houses are dimly discernible.

West of 40.3 *m.* St. Albans and Lake Champlain are intermittently visible. At 42.6 *m.* is a junction with a dirt road.

> Right on this road and right again at 0.6 *m.* is *Bellevue Hill State Forest Park*, 1.7 *m.*, 70 acres of woodland reservation on Bellevue Hill with picnic and camping facilities. The view to the north and west from this height of land is the finest in this immediate section.

At 42.8 *m.* are the city limits of St. Albans.

> ST. ALBANS (alt. 409, pop. 8020) (*see ST. ALBANS*), 43.5 *m.* The Railroad City, with headquarters and shops of the Central Vermont Ry.; Railroad Station, Elizabeth Fisk Looms; Bellows Free Academy; Hoyt House; Campbell House, Scoffield House, St. Albans Free Library; and other points of interest.

---

T O U R   3 C :  *From* WARREN *to* LAKE CHAMPLAIN BRIDGE (*Chimney Point*), 35.1 *m.*, State 17.

---

Via Lincoln, Bristol, New Haven, Addison.

The road is gravel on the east; hard-surfaced between Bristol and Chimney Point.

THIS mountain-pass route, the highest in the State, crosses the principal range of the Green Mountains, traversing a wild highland country on the east and the level plains of Addison County on the west, thus combining the rugged beauty of forested heights with the pleasing serenity of broad meadows that sweep toward the waters of Lake Champlain. Of the passes through the central portion of the Green Mountain Range this Lincoln Pass is easily the most scenic. The others have individual merits, but, to the tourist desirous of crossing the mountains in this general region, the present route is recommended for grandeur and scope of outlook. On the Champlain Valley side, the region is rich in connotations of the past from the time of Champlain's visit, the French and Indian Wars, and the Revolution.

WARREN, 0 *m.* (*see Tour* 3), is at the junction with State 100 (*see Tour* 3).

West of Warren the route follows an unnumbered highway across an old covered bridge over the Mad River and through a farming territory toward the massive mountain barrier that blockades the western horizon. *Lincoln Gap,* 2.9 *m.,* is a steep narrow pass cutting through the mountainous wilds with forested slopes towering on all sides. *Lincoln Mountain* (R) is composed of several peaks, one of which, *Mount Ellen* (alt. 4135), is the third highest in the State. Mount Abraham, another of its peaks, was known as 'Potato Hill' among early settlers, and as such appears in the stories of this region written by Rowland Robinson (*see Literature*). Scenes from Robinson are brought to mind by these wild forest-clad slopes, where his characters roved with long hunting rifles, and gathered about campfires at night for their inimitable discussions and the telling of tall tales. Rearing high on the left side of the mountain-walled defile are *Mount Grant* (alt. 3661) and *Bread Loaf Mountain* (alt. 3825). The overshadowing mountain-sides are generally wooded with here and there somber gray outcroppings of rock breaking the thick greenery.

At 4.4 *m.* is the top of the pass (alt. 2424), where the celebrated *Long Trail* crosses the highway.

> By stopping at this point and walking a short way to either side on the Long Trail, vantage-points are attained which reveal views as fine as any in the entire Green Mountain Range — vistas that sweep from the mighty thrust of mountains shouldering the sky over vast forested reaches to open lowland valleys, scenes marked with a grandeur solemn and ponderous. The Champlain Valley in all its picturesque beauty stretches north and south, the lake with its irregular shore-lines lying before the Adirondacks.

West of the Long Trail the highway drops in sharp winding descent, compelling the motorist to drive with care. A magnificent mountain panorama (R) stretches broken green-clothed lines against the horizon, and through a break in the ridge is a glimpse of the Adirondacks, hazily blue in the distance.

LINCOLN (alt. 971, pop. township 800), 9 *m.,* was settled in 1795 by Quakers. The former industrial activity of this community is indicated by the ruins of two old milldams (R); a bobbin factory and creamery are the only remaining industries. *Burnham Memorial Building* (L), an attractive brick community house, is supported by an endowment of approximately $100,000 left to the town by Walter Burnham, who was born here in 1852. The inevitable *Soldiers' Memorial* stands at a highway junction.

WEST LINCOLN (alt. 890), 10.7 *m.,* is a tiny hill settlement.

West of Lincoln the road swings along the little New Haven River (L) which is considered one of the best trout streams in the State.

*Bartlett's Falls,* 12.3 *m.,* pour with the cool musical rush of white water into a basin that forms a natural swimming pool. Accommodations are provided for picnic parties and general recreation.

ACKWORTH (alt. 630), 12.4 *m.,* is simply a group of homes lying at the junction of roads in the shadow of a forested ridge. On the west the abrupt rock-ledged knob of Hogback Mountain rears above the narrow valley.

Here is the junction with State 116 (*see Tour 5C*).

Between Ackworth and Bristol, State 116 runs alongside of the New Haven River, racing in the swift white spray of rapids over its stony course.

*Lord's Prayer Rock* (L), 13.5 *m.* Here on the bank of this fast-running stream at the outskirts of Bristol, travelers are mildly surprised to find the Lord's Prayer confronting them suddenly from the face of a huge boulder close by the roadside, where it was plainly carved to satisfy the whim of one Joseph Greene, Buffalo physician. Greene spent his boyhood in this vicinity, and always remembered the cursing, roaring teamsters who lashed their sweaty horses up the grade at this point, where the road in those days was always muddy. On returning in 1891 to the scene of his childhood disillusionment, Dr. Greene had the prayer cut deeply into the face of this prominent rock as a warning to later-day blasphemers against the evil of their ways. Greene's name is also graven on the stone. It is highly probable that his act, and private bid for immortality, provided the tough old teamsters with a great deal more ribald amusement than fear.

BRISTOL (alt. 575, pop. 1190), 13.6 *m.,* situated on a broad terrace in the shelter of bluff mountains, is a clean pleasant village with well-kept homes and grounds indicating the home-loving character of its people. In orderly arrangement wide maple-lined streets bound the square central Green with its cool-splashing fountain, park benches, old cannon, war memorials, and playground. *Hogback Mountain* (alt. 1850) forms a picturesque high-ridged background on the east, especially beautiful in autumn when the turning leaves transform it into a blazing wall of color. *Lawrence Memorial Library* (*open weekdays except Fri.,* 2 *to* 5.30; 7 *to* 9), North St., contains 6000 volumes. The *Bristol School Buildings,* School St., are annually devoted to the German Summer School Courses of Middlebury College in July and August. The *Town Hall* (Holley Hall), West St., an attractive brick structure, was erected in 1884. The *Bristol Inn,* East St., remodeled and fitted with modern improvements, has served as a hostelry for well over a century. In spite of its comparative seclusion, Bristol is active industrially, manufacturing caskets, wood novelties, and lock-corner mailing boxes, with power generated from the New Haven River.

When a party of surveyors came to this section in 1785, they found living here a lone man, a German named John Broadt, who thought himself a fugitive from justice for the killing of a neighbor near Unadilla, New York. For 12 years Broadt had lived like a hermit in the wilderness depths. It developed that the man he had fought with, and supposedly killed, was alive and well, and Broadt was able to return to his home after his years of self-imposed exile. The first permanent settlers here were Samuel Stewart and Eden Johnson, in 1786.

> 1. Left from Bristol on a country road is *Hell's Half Acre* (L), 2 *m.*, the weird gloomy site of the 'Treasure Diggings,' where overhanging trees shut out the sun and the solitude is heavy with an air of mystery. Here the quiet is broken only by the tinkle of tiny brooks over rocky beds. The wall of huge tumbled boulders surrounding the area is fantastically broken by cracks, crevices, and dim caverns, and stony clutters underfoot emphasize the atmosphere of dreary desolation. Legend tells of a mysterious stranger called DeGrau, a Spaniard, who was discovered prowling about Hell's Half Acre by the early settlers, and who told a strange tale of lost treasure. DeGrau said that his father, a Spanish miner, discovered a rich vein of silver here, which yielded an immense fortune. Unable to transport their hoard to civilization, the men hid it in a cave, planning to return the coming year. At that time DeGrau was a small boy. For one reason or other none of the men ever returned, and DeGrau had grown to manhood before he was able to come back and search for the hidden wealth. DeGrau continued the hunt for some time before giving up and leaving the vicinity. Another version of the tale is that the original DeGrau party was on its way to Canada with a fabulous treasure when they were attacked by Indians and forced to abandon their cargo. At any rate, many treasure-seekers have dug and searched for the legendary silver, until the area is literally honeycombed with futile holes and trenches. In 1840, a dozen men from Canada appeared on the scene and made a systematic and elaborate search for the lost fortune, under the direction of Simeon Coreser, who was known as 'Uncle Sim.' For over a decade this crew labored incessantly, but the buried wealth was never uncovered. The fact that many local people worked side by side with these fortune-hunters refutes the rumor that Uncle Sim's outfit was a gang of counterfeiters and their digging operations were merely a blind. Many other hopefuls have come here to toil and sweat with spade and pick, but the treasure was never unearthed.

> 2. Right from Bristol on a country road is *Bristol Pond* (alt. 460), 3.5 *m.*, a small low-lying body of water almost completely surrounded by marshlands. The pond has a muddy bottom and offers excellent fishing, being especially well stocked with pickerel. The finding of many Indian relics, arrow-heads, and spear-heads in this vicinity indicates that the Bristol Pond region was once a rendezvous for Indian tribes, and the discovery of many unfinished arrow-heads revealed that the implements were made in the locality. Near the north end of the pond early investigators uncovered the skeletons of several Indians buried in sitting positions in a sand bank.

Between Bristol and New Haven, State 17 rolls westward over a more open countryside. From the hilltop at 17.8 *m.* is a view (L) of Middlebury College in its valley setting to the south.

NEW HAVEN (alt. 454, pop. township 964), 18.1 *m.*, is known as New Haven Street, the principal village of the township consisting almost entirely of a single street running north and south across State 17. One of the early New Haven settlers, Solomon Brown, is said to have been the first man to shoot down a Britisher at the battle of Lexington. Among the prominent sons of this little town is Curtis M. Lampson, who was knighted by Queen Victoria for his services as vice-president of the company that laid the Atlantic cable.

NEW HAVEN JUNCTION, 19.5 *m.*, is at the junction with US 8 (*see Tour* 4).

West of New Haven Junction, State 17 runs along the northern base of *Snake Mountain* (alt. 1271) (L), sometimes called Grand View Mountain. The lookout tower at its summit commands a view described by Bayard Taylor, writer and traveler, as unexcelled by anything in Europe. From that elevation the long sweep of Lake Champlain is seen lying before its background of Adirondacks on the west, while to the east stand the Green Mountains in superb array.

ADDISON, 26.9 *m.* (*see Tour* 4*B*), is at the junction with State 30A (*see Tour* 4*B*).

West of Addison, State 17 traverses a level open countryside of sweeping plains and broad meadows typical of western Addison County. The air is imbued with a fresh new quality; the nearness of Lake Champlain is felt in the atmosphere. The many interesting old stone houses throughout this region are testimonials of the labor and craft of past generations.

At 32.8 *m.* the highway swings southward on a cement roadbed for the last stretch to the lake shore.

The *John Strong Mansion* (*open to inspection*) (R), 33.6 *m.*, a fine brick structure, was built in 1796-98 of bricks made on the farm of John Strong, who was a prominent figure in the early affairs of town and State. The handsome brick house stands on the site of an earlier home of John Strong, a wooden house built before the Revolution and burned by the British on their big drive down the lake in 1777. The present mansion has an entrance hall of beautiful design, and the interior contains many points of interest: corkscrew hinges on some of the doors; skillfully built-in shutters; old fireplaces with iron back walls; stenciled floors; and an artfully concealed hiding-place in the massive chimney, entered by a secret panel in the kitchen, and large enough to conceal six or seven people. The house is now cared for by the D.A.R.

The *Old Brick House*, 33.8 *m.*, antedates the Strong Mansion by several years, but was of inferior workmanship, and because of its lesser historical value has been allowed to fall into a regrettable state of disrepair.

An *Old Gravestone* (L), 34.8 *m.*, serves as a triple memorial to the three young Payne sisters who died in the summer of 1819, the curved top of the large slab dividing it into three sections.

*Crown Point Military Road Marker* (L), 34.9 *m.*, indicates the northern limit of that important trail through the wilderness which was followed by scouts, soldiers, and pioneer settlers and extended from Charlestown, New Hampshire (Old Number Four), to this point. The road was built in 1759 under General Amherst to connect the waterways of the Connecticut and Lake Champlain. The country road that branches left from this junction follows the course of the historic old Crown Point Road to Bridport, and here can be conjured pictures of the strange lonely people who tramped along it in those eighteenth-century days — lean, wiry frontier scouts in buckskin; grim, plodding settlers bearing all their earthly possessions; smart, red-coated Britishers and ragged, starving soldiers with powder-stains on their gaunt cheeks; Indians in war paint moving silently as shadows; Rogers Rangers in greenish buckskin, lithe, bronzed men who were themselves almost like Indians in their woodcraft, tireless endurance, and ruthless methods of fighting.

*Chimney Point* (alt. 120), 35.1 *m.*, is a promontory in Lake Champlain where now the modern Lake Champlain Bridge spans the narrowed waters to connect Vermont with New York State. Chimney Point is generally accepted as the spot where Samuel de Champlain stood on July 30, 1609, and gave his name to the beautiful inland sea stretching before him. Champlain crossed the lake to Chimney Point, after defeating the Iroquois Indians in a battle fought on the western shore, a battle of far-reaching consequences as proved in later warfare, for the powerful Iroquois were ever afterward hostile to the French. As early as 1690, Jacobus de Warm, heading a French expedition from Albany, built a small fort here. The first lasting settlement was made in 1730 by a little band of French colonists who came up the lake and repaired the old De Warm fort. Around their fortress, which they called Fort de Pieux, a settlement grew up to become one of the important early French possessions in the New World. The French deserted the village in 1759 before the threat of an Indian invasion, and in 1760 raiding Mohawks devastated the settlement completely. The grim picture of chimneys rising from blackened ruins resulted in the present name, Chimney Point. Many cellar-holes of the ancient French town are still visible. Where Champlain landed after blasting the Iroquois and where French trappers and hunters built up a stronghold that was ultimately destroyed by painted Mohawks, there is today a concrete highway curving toward a handsome steel bridge over the peaceful lake.

The *Barnes House* (*visitors welcome*) (L) stands on the site of the old De Warm fort and contains one wall of stone, two and one-half feet thick, which is thought to be a wall of the original fortress. In the construction of this house, by the grandfather of the present owner, bricks were brought across the lake from the ruins of Fort St. Frederic to build a wall enclosing the shell of the ancient stone blockhouse on Chimney Point. For nearly 100 years this structure served as an inn, and as the 'Old Captain Hendee House' figures prominently in 'The Green Mountain Boys,' written by Judge Daniel P. Thompson. Here in the taproom, according to the story, Ethan Allen and Seth Warner were surprised by the British and narrowly escaped capture.

The house is now a veritable treasure vault of historical relics. In the taproom, where the Green Mountain Boys once lounged to talk and plan over their rum, is the old bar and liquor cabinet with Waterford decanters; old Normandy inn chairs; collections of Indian, French, and English relics, such as arrow-heads, cannon-balls, parts of firearms, silver shoe buckles, buttons, insignia, etc. The keel and ribs of Arnold's flagship 'Congress,' salvaged from Buttonmould Bay, Panton (*see Tour 4B*), are kept here, along with small articles recovered from the wreckage, including an early hand-grenade with wooden fuse-plug. In another part of the house is one of the most beautiful and best-equipped ancient fireplaces to be found in America, and a great oven believed to be from Fort de Pieux. There are old kitchen utensils of all sorts, oil lamps, sconces of Waterford and Sandwich glass, and a heating stove long enough to take four-foot sticks and extended through a partition to heat two rooms. Among the Indian implements are serrated points, peculiar to the Oregon Indians, and obsidian points which are identified with far western tribes, making it a matter of conjecture as to how such arrow-heads reached the shores of Champlain.

The opening of the *Lake Champlain Bridge*, August 27, 1929, created a new and important route for interstate traffic, providing the first roadway across the lake, and supplementing the many existing ferries. This handsome steel structure has proved a vital gateway for traffic entering New England. The largest engineering feat ever undertaken by Vermont, its original cost of more than a million dollars, shared with New York State, the latter assuming sixty per cent of the burden, is being annually amortized by receipts from tolls ($1 *per car, including occupants up to 6*).

Just across the bridge, in New York, are the *Crown Point Fort Ruins*, remnants of the second most important fortification on the lake. Here in 1731 the French built Fort St. Frederic, which for 24 years remained their most extreme outpost in the Colonies, until in 1755 they established Fort Carillon twelve miles south on the lakeshore at Ticonderoga.

In 1759, the French evacuated before the advance of General Amherst's superior forces, blowing up part of the fortifications as they left. Amherst took possession, made repairs, and left a small garrison there, calling it Fort Amherst.

The British held the fort until 1775 when Colonel Seth Warner of the Green Mountain Boys captured it without bloodshed. An important vantage-point on the Champlain waterway, this stronghold changed hands several times, apparently without a gun being fired in its defense.

---

T O U R   3 D :   *From* HANCOCK *to* EAST MIDDLEBURY, 16.1 *m.*, State 125.

---

Via Ripton. The road is dirt and gravel.

THE eastern part of this overland route lies through a somewhat undistinguished mountain valley. The Middlebury Gap Pass is less scenic than Lincoln Pass (*see Tour 3C*), but a more gradual climb. Bread Loaf, about midway, is not typical of the State as a whole, but a fascinating variation on the general theme. The western end of the route lies through the more open and populous districts near Middlebury.

HANCOCK, 0 *m.* (*see Tour* 3), is a junction of State 100 and State 125 (*see Tour* 3).

From Hancock, State 125 leads due west toward the mountains, following closely the Hancock Branch, one of the foundation streams of the White River. The road lies in the narrow, pleasant valley of the stream and crosses it and its tributary brooks several times on small bridges.

BRANCH SCHOOL, 2.2 *m.*, is a country settlement of a few dwellings and a schoolhouse.

At 3 *m.* is a junction with a country road.

> Right on this road are *Texas Falls*, 0.4 *m.*, a beautiful natural cascade of Texas Brook.

At this point the highway begins to rise to a higher level. At 3.2 *m.* is an excellent prospect of the mountains ahead, to which the nearer range of foothills serves as a foil. The immediate scenic background is given a rugged character by the rocky cliffs (L).

At 3.7 *m.* the last human habitation is left behind, and the highway begins its steady climb toward the top of the pass through a closely wooded section. At 4 *m.* is a plainly marked cold spring (R). The highway rises rapidly and at 4.8 *m.* leaves far below the accompanying stream (L), the bed of which soon rises to the road level again, the water tumbling and splashing over the rocks in numberless foaming cascades. The stones along the brook are velveted with thick vivid green moss.

Nearing the top of the pass, the road is bordered on both sides by *Battell Park*, a forest preserve of 10,000 acres bequeathed to Middlebury College by the Hon. Joseph Battell upon his death in 1915. About 20,000 additional acres from the same bequest have been sold by the college to the Government for a national forest.

At 6.2 *m.* the top of the gap (alt. 2149) is reached, where the *Long Trail* crosses the highway.

> 1. Left on the Long Trail and (R) on a short side trail is *Pleiad Lake* (alt. 2128), 0.5 *m.*, a small, deep pond lying in a natural cup of the hills, with a Long Trail shelter on the western shore.

> 2. Right on the Long Trail, curving to a fork near the top of a hill; right on the side trail is *Silent Cliff* (alt 2450), 1 *m.*, a pine-shaded rocky ledge that hangs over the highway. This provides a favorite picnicking ground for the students of Middlebury College, and a fine view down the valley to the west. The spot is a singularly delightful one.

The western approach to the gap is bordered by Norway spruces, a part of the several plantings made by the college in 1916–17. The road drops rapidly for a mile. After crossing well-named Crystal Brook, 7.4 *m.*, the descent becomes more gradual, the countryside more open. In this immediate section are a few summer homes of out-of-State people.

BREAD LOAF, 8.9 *m.*, is a unique upland settlement centered around

Bread Loaf Inn, established in 1866 by Joseph Battell. Mr. Battell left the imprint of his dictatorial but generous personality upon this whole section. His farm at Bread Loaf was a pioneer headquarters for the development of pure-blooded Morgan horses. His love of horses and of mountain peace made him the most aggressive opponent of automotive transportation that this State has ever known. For years before his death, Mr. Battell devoted one page of each issue of his weekly newspaper, the Middlebury *Register*, to gruesome accounts of motor accidents all over the country, hoping that such reprints might at least restrain the local citizens from purchasing those infernal contraptions which seemed destined to supplant his beloved Morgans. Those of his many guests who owned automobiles were met by his men, with horses, at Ripton Hollow, three miles from the undefiled environs of Bread Loaf. Mr. Battell's two-volume 'Morgan Horse and Register' is, as might be expected, a thoroughly authoritative labor of love. His 800-page pseudo-novel, 'Ellen, or the Whisperings of an Old Pine,' is an incredible hodge-podge, consisting chiefly of discussions of theology, philosophy, and all the sciences between Ellen, a sprite-like Vermont girl, and the Old Pine, who vaguely represents Mr. Battell himself. Published at his own expense, the book did not, of course, sell, and copies of it can still be found scattered about Bread Loaf Inn, where they serve as casters and door-stops.

Bread Loaf has few rooms for transients because it is the seat of the Bread Loaf Summer School of English, conducted by Middlebury College. Here each year distinguished teachers, writers, and critics serve as guest faculty, offering courses in the creation and the appreciation of literature that draw students from all parts of the country. No laboratory of the fine arts could have a more suitable setting than this pastoral haven in the foothills of the Green Mountains. The physical plant includes not only the Inn proper, but several adjacent cottages and dormitories, a library building, and a little theater.

Started in 1920, the School of English has drawn students from 35 States and 62 colleges. The regular six-weeks session of the school is supplemented by a Writers' Conference (last two weeks in August), when a selected group of prospective writers are brought into contact with leading figures in the professional writing world, including critics, editors, and literary agents.

From Bread Loaf Inn there are a number of short, marked foot trails that wend pleasantly through the woodlands. All are worth while, but particularly so is the one to the Widow's Clearing, from which is a superb view of Bread Loaf Mountain. From the Widow's Clearing in summer the picture is one of sharply contrasting color and beauty — on clear days the sky is intensely blue, lightly bannered with fragile white clouds; the deep green blanket of treetops stretches away almost interminably; the open fields around the Inn are yellow with grain, and beyond is the blue-purple bulk of the mountains. By late August there are

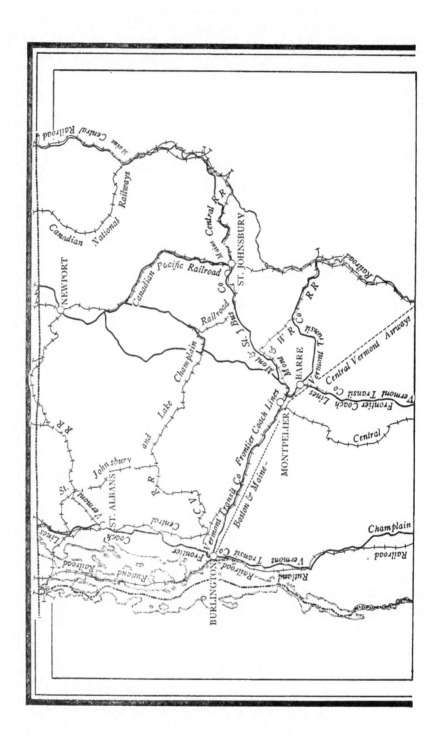

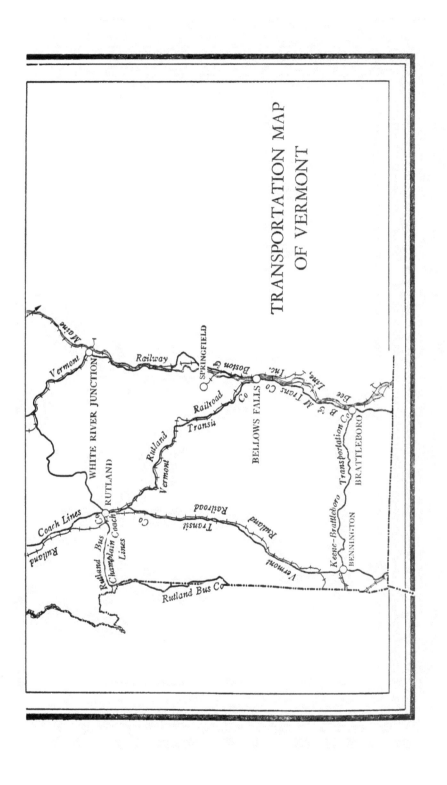

TRANSPORTATION MAP
OF VERMONT

scattered patches of brilliant red and yellow and brown, from the frosted leaves of birches and maples.

A short distance west of Bread Loaf Inn, at 9.2 *m.*, is the summer home (R) of William Hazlett Upson, best known as the creator of Alexander Botts, the Earthworm Tractor salesman.

The highway continues to drop gradually to a lower level, paralleled by the headwaters of the Middlebury River (L).

RIPTON (alt. 1017, pop. township 212), 11.6 *m.*, is a small hill village of old frame houses, a church, and a community house. Somewhat decrepit in outward appearance, it is in noticeable contrast to the sophistication against a rural background that Bread Loaf embodies. On the western edge of the village, at 11.8 *m.*, is the old home of Daniel Chipman, one of the fathers of Middlebury College, professor of Law there, and Congressman from Vermont (1815–17). This house was built in 1833, after Chipman had retired from public life and disposed of his more pretentious estate in Middlebury village. Ripton is of interest to geologists because of the large number of glacial boulders that were deposited here. Just east of the highway bridge in the village are junctions with two dirt roads.

> Right on the dirt road farther from the bridge to a fork, 1 *m.*, and left a short distance from the fork is a small country *Graveyard*. Here is buried Frederick Deattrich (1709–1864), who was, as his simple marble slab announces, a bugler in the English Army at the battle of Waterloo.

The highway clings close to the Middlebury River until, at 12.8 *m.*, it rises sharply to conform to the contour of a hill, leaving the bed of the river (R) in a deep cool rocky gorge far below. At 14.4 *m.* is an everflowing cold spring (L) where more than a century ago the drivers of the overland stage were wont to stop and let their horses drink after the first stiff climb of the mountain route.

EAST MIDDLEBURY, 15.1 *m.*, is a village of one long street, quiet and unassuming. In a white house (L) near the east end of the village is one of the most famous of all privately owned American antiques, a secretary which combines certain unique details with great beauty. The subject of one monograph and numerous articles, it is valued at $35,000. The brick community house (L) is well equipped to accommodate social gatherings and is a favorite rendezvous of Middlebury students for chicken-pie suppers.

At 16.1 *m.* is the junction with US 7 (*see Tour 4*).

T O U R   4 :   *From* CANADIAN LINE (*Montreal*) *to* MASSA-
CHUSETTS LINE (*Williamstown*), 178.9 *m.*, US 7.

Via (*sec. a*) Highgate Springs, Swanton, St. Albans, Georgia Center, Milton,
Colchester, Winooski, Burlington; (*sec. b*) Shelburne, Charlotte, Ferrisburg,
Vergennes, New Haven Junction, Middlebury, Salisbury, Leicester, Brandon,
Pittsford, Proctor, Rutland; (*sec. c*) Clarendon, Wallingford, Tinmouth, Danby,
Manchester, Arlington, Shaftsbury, Glastenbury, Bennington, Pownal.

Central Vermont R.R. parallels the route between the Canadian boundary and
Burlington; Rutland R.R. parallels the route between Burlington and Bennington.

Road is hard-surfaced throughout, and kept in good repair, as US 7 is the most
heavily trafficked highway in the State.

ONE of the main arteries of travel in Vermont, this route runs along the
western side of the State between Lake Champlain, glimmering against
its background of Adirondacks on the west, and the major range of the
Green Mountains, piled in rugged beauty on the east. The country is
rich in diversified scenery and historical tradition. US 7 is without doubt
the most cosmopolitan highway in the State, with speed the custom, and
license tags from all over the land flashing vari-colored along the winding
dipping ribbon of concrete.

*Sec. a.   Canadian boundary to Burlington, 44.6 m.*

This northern section traverses a rather wild and intermittently wooded
country, where smooth plains slant westward to the shining lake-and-
island beauty of Champlain, and fine pasturelands for large dairy herds
are interspersed with the forests. Near the border a strong similarity to
Canadian landscapes is apparent, the topography being more open and
level than is common in Vermont. The delicate, lovely tracery of elms
against the sky is a recurrent feature of this section.

*Canadian Boundary, 0 m.* This is one of the most pleasant border crossings, where the customhouses of both nations stand close together in the
peace of the open countryside, its serenity unmarred by any barriers,
fortifications, or bayoneted rifles. The entrance to Vermont is made at
the township of HIGHGATE, which was settled in 1787 by a body of
Hessian troops, professional soldiers brought here by the British, who
decided to remain in the New World. Under the impression that they
were settling in Canada, the Hessians continued to believe so until the
establishment of the permanent international boundary proved their
mistake. The iron boundary post at this gateway between the Province
of Quebec and New England is 52 *m.*, south of Victoria Bridge in Montreal. LAFAYETTE MANOIR, just over the line in Canada, is an
elaborate resort, which, during Prohibition, was a highly popular haven

for ale-lovers over a 50-mile radius, and the first Canadian objective of thousands of Volstead-ridden tourists from the States.

*U.S. Customhouse* (R) is a trim modern structure, built in 1934–35. During the latter year, 82,309 cars cleared at this point, and as many as 2300 have entered here in one day.

South of the border the highway swings over a rolling wooded country with gray rock ledges protruding.

At 1.6 *m.* is the junction with a country road.

> Left on this road is *Saxe's Monument*, 0.8 *m.*, marking the site of the birthplace of John Godfrey Saxe (1816–87), one of Vermont's outstanding poets, whose verse was in the Longfellow spirit. Lawyer, politician, lecturer, and editor, as well as poet, Saxe's significance in the latter field is supported by the fact that 13 Saxe pieces are reprinted in Burton E. Stevenson's standard 'Home Book of Verse,' a larger number than is given to many other American poets of higher acknowledged standing.

At 2.1 *m.* *Lake Champlain* is seen (R), Missisquoi Bay shimmering wide to far wooded shores across the blue water, and white crafts riding gracefully at anchor in the shelter of the Bay. Here at the mouth of Rock River are generally seen many fishermen in their flat-bottomed boats. The air blowing in from the watery stretches has a clean tang compatible with the freshness of the scene. The low roadway at this point is often inundated at flood seasons.

South of Rock River Bridge the country opens to plains, flat and gently undulating. more prosperous in aspect and much less wooded.

HIGHGATE SPRINGS (alt. 127, pop. township 1574), 3.2 *m.*, is popular as a resort because of its mineral springs and the excellent fishing, swimming, and boating in the near-by bay. The little summer settlement is built around a hotel and dance pavilion and makes no pretense of being other than a tourist place, relying mainly on summer guests for its existence. Lime is manufactured by the Missisquoi Lime Works, Inc. A queer white *Union Church* (L) stands with a tall narrow façade, high spire, and red roof. The pleasant and placid resort aspect of Highgate Springs gives little indication of the border controversies that once were rife here, when bullets and fists flew as smugglers mixed it with the revenue officers.

Between Highgate Springs and Swanton, the highway is separated from Champlain waters by the outthrust of a huge promontory, through which the Missisquoi flows northward to empty into the Bay.

SWANTON (alt. 155, pop. 1558), 7.3 *m.*, was named for a British captain in the French and Indian Wars, and centers pleasantly around the shaded green of Swanton Park, a long rectangular common. These village greens, almost standard equipment for Vermont towns, serve to differentiate them from their Canadian neighbors. Trim lawns, neat shrubs and colorful flower patches are enclosed by picket fences of wood and iron, shaded by old maples, elms, and willows. The well-spaced and cared-for homes, largely of wood, wear an aspect of comfortable and leisurely living, which has its financial basis in the *Marble Mills* of the Vermont Marble Company, principal industry of the village. *Walls of 1812 Barracks* are incorporated in the present Prouty Market (R), facing the head of the park. The *Taquahunga Club* (R) was once the home of Ethan Allen's widow and her daughter, Fanny Allen, who became a nun. *Swanton Library* (*open Tu., Th., Sat.*, 2.30 *to* 5.30 *and* 6.30 *to* 8.30) (L) is a brick structure with white-columned portico. Merchants' Row spreads around the head of the park, and a red stone *Episcopal Church* stands at the foot of the elm-shadowed green.

The St. Francis Indians occupied this area hundreds of years before the white men came, and prior to 1700 built a chapel under the guidance of the French Jesuits, which was the first church erected in the territory that is now Vermont. These Indians participated in many depredations against the whites, most terrible of which was the Deerfield Massacre, 1704, at which time they stole the Deerfield bell to use in their chapel at Swanton for many years. After France lost this new country to England, the Indians moved their beloved chapel stone by stone to St. Hyacinth on the Yamaska River. It was the repeated and bloody raids made by the St. Francis warriors that led in 1759 to the daring drive of Rogers' Rangers against the village of St. Francis, in which the Rangers attacked in Indian fashion, killing and burning without mercy to wipe out the entire settlement.

The French made a settlement in Swanton township about 1700, but an interesting legend places white visitors at a far earlier date. The legend grew out of the discovery of a lead tube on the banks of the Missisquoi, 1835, which held a piece of paper bearing this message: 'Nov. 29 A D 1564 — This is the solme day I must now die this is the 90th day since we lef the Ship all have Parished and on the Banks of this River I die to farewell may future Posteritye know our end — John Graye.' The theory was that a last survivor of one of Martin Frobisher's expeditions wrote this farewell message, but indications in general consign this discovery to the limbo of nineteenth-century forgeries. The lead tube has vanished but the manuscript is in the Highgate Library.

In 1765, an Englishman named Robertson established a lumber business here at the falls in the Missisquoi, but the first permanent white settler was John Hilliker, who came in 1779. In the early nineteenth century when border smuggling was at its height, soldiers were sent to Swanton to halt the activities of the contrabanders, and the vicinity was the scene of many thrilling hide-and-seek games and running gun-fights between the smugglers and border guards. Smuggling has always been a major business along the Vermont-Canada borderline, and the twentieth-century bootleggers who defied prohibition in roaring high-powered automobiles laden with liquor were the occupational and temperamental, if not the lineal, descendants of those early Vermont smugglers who drove plodding cattle across the line into Canada to sell to the starving British troops. In the War of 1812 English gunboats landed in Maquam

Bay and dispatched a force of 600 to burn the Swanton barracks, which had been built to quarter American soldiers sent to protect the border.

    1. Left from Swanton on a country road is the *Missisquoi Airport*, 1 *m.*, an International Customs and Immigration Port of Entry for planes. A training school for flyers is also conducted here.

    2. Right from Swanton on State 104 is a *Government Fish Hatchery*, 6 *m.*, an important factor in maintaining the supply of fish that attracts sportsmen to northern Vermont each season.

Between Swanton and St. Albans, US 7 crosses the broad calm Missisquoi River and runs shortly through a swampy lowland before climbing to a higher level and veering southward. The road is curving and tree-lined, with fertile farmlands stretching away on either side and neat brick farmhouses along the roadside.

*Champlain Country Club* and *Franklin County Rod and Gun Club* (L), 12.8 *m.*, are situated on a broad summit of considerable elevation and command a fine view westward over descending plains to Lake Champlain, the islands of Grand Isle County clearly visible across the deep blue expanse of water against a distant backdrop of blue-gray Adirondacks etched high on the horizon.

    ST. ALBANS (alt. 409, pop. 8020) (*see ST. ALBANS*), 15.8 *m.*, the Railroad City with headquarters and shops of the Central Vermont Ry., Railroad Station; Elizabeth Fisk Looms; Bellows Free Academy; Hoyt House; Campbell House; Scofield House; St. Albans Free Library; and other points of interest.

South of St. Albans via South Main St., US 7 drops down a rather sharp incline. The larger hill (L) is the *Johnnycake Hill* of Frances Frost's poems. To the southwest are lake and island vistas of beauty, that on hazy days take on a mystic ethereal quality.

Between St. Albans and Georgia Center, the fertile countryside becomes more rolling and uneven, more like the usual broken terrain of Vermont. *Birthplace of General Stannard* (L), 20.4 *m.* A monument marks the site of the farmhouse in which this Civil War hero was born. At Gettysburg when Pickett launched his gallant Confederate charge, Vermont troops were holding a key position in the Union lines. It was General George Stannard's well-timed counter-attack on Pickett's right flank that shattered the charging columns of gray. After Pickett was repulsed, an Alabama and a Florida Brigade advanced in another onrushing wall of steel-tipped gray, but Stannard's Sixteenth Vermont again smashed the enemy back with heavy losses. In this second counter-action, Stannard himself was painfully wounded in the leg, but refused to leave the field until his command was relieved and the wounded safely removed.

GEORGIA CENTER (alt. 385, pop. township 1090), 21.9 *m.* Sitting well back from the single street, homely old houses and a red brick *Methodist Church* are sequestered under leafy boughs, the whole picture clearly dominated by the great white *Town Hall* (L), which was erected in 1800 as a Baptist Church, and at that time considered one of the finest churches in the State. The large white wooden structure stands in its heroic proportions with a kind of miscellaneous nobility, interesting and pleasing to all but the architectural purists. Renovating and landscaping have been carried on recently as a Works Progress Administration project. Georgia was the scene of hectic strife between smugglers and customs officers in the 1812 era of contrabanding. Patriotic Georgia citizens allied with the customs forces to check the flow of beef cattle being smuggled into Canada to supply British troops, and the smugglers found it so difficult to win their way past Georgia that they called the place Hell's Gate.

Right from Georgia Center is GEORGIA PLAIN, 2.5 *m.*, a tiny farming community centered around a sawmill on the level plains near Lake Champlain. The inhabitants do their trading in Georgia Center, around which the commercial and social life of the township revolves. In the vicinity of Georgia Plain fossils and trilobites have been found, revealing that this territory was once submerged as the bed of a great prehistoric lake.

Between Georgia Center and Milton, lovely trees grace the landscape, which rapidly becomes more broken, rugged, and forested, more like Vermont as the hills and ridges climb into mountains. The Lamoille River flows (L) beside the highway, and in the southeast looms majestic Mansfield.

MILTON (alt. 320, pop. 641), 29.4 *m.*, named after the poet, John Milton, lies in the Lamoille Valley, in the heart of one of the finest dairying districts in the State. A green iron bridge over the Lamoille leads into the small business center with its brick buildings and Civil War Monument. A residential street (L) climbs to a low pleasant plateau above the valley, and here (L) is the *Milton Public Library* housed in late nineteenth-century brick. A large co-operative creamery constitutes the chief industry, drawing its members from several neighboring towns and handling great quantities of milk from the extensive dairy farms of the region. The southern end of the village street lies under a canopy of spreading elms.

South of Milton the highway climbs to a higher plain, and broad rich meadows drop away to either side in soft slopes.

*Milton Airport* (L), 31.2 *m.*, occupies a fine natural site on a long level plateau.

At 35.2 *m.* is the junction with US 2 (*see Tour 4A*).

South of this junction US 7 bends and dips as the countryside becomes rougher and more broken.

At 38.9 *m.* is a junction with State 116.

Left on State 116 is COLCHESTER (alt. 274, pop. township 2638), 1 *m.*, stretching along a shaded plain with a typical four-cornered center blocked in by little stores and conventional houses. Here again a creamery furnishes the basic industry of the community. The general atmosphere of rural lethargy is enlivened each morning by the farmers bringing in their milk and loitering to buy groceries and supplies, or to exchange stories and political opinions.

At 39 *m.* is the junction with Lake Shore Drive, an alternate and scenic route into Burlington.

Right on Lake Shore Drive is MALLETTS BAY, large and well-known Champlain summer resort, with waterfront cottages, long sand beaches, trim sailboats and motorboats in every cove, and extensive tourist accommodations. The dances at Bayside Pavilion attract people from great distances, as the music is furnished by dance bands of national prominence. The shaded drive closely skirts the lake shore with magnificent lake and island views opening constantly across the glittering blue waters, and fresh breezes blowing in from the wide stretches of historic Champlain. The gravel roadway is kept in good condition. This route is recommended as the most scenic northern entrance to Burlington, one that takes in the very essence of Lake Champlain beauty. At the northern edge of Burlington the road passes directly by Ethan Allen Park and Battery Park (*see BURLINGTON*). At 10 *m.* Burlington is reached.

Between this junction and Winooski on US 7, the eastern skyline is one of varied contours, dominated by the clear massive thrust of Mt. Mansfield and softened by glimpses of green valleys and rounded foothills.

WINOOSKI (alt. 200, pop. 5308), 42.6 *m.*, the Mill City, was founded in 1787 by Ira Allen and Remember Baker, who foresaw the advantages in utilizing the tremendous waterpower available at the lower falls of the Winooski River. Winooski was predestined from the start to become one of the few industrialized towns in Vermont. This industrial atmosphere, unrelieved and unadulterated, marks Winooski today, with the hint of factory smoke seeming always to hang over the closely built business section and the stain of soot darkening the brick buildings. Winooski resembles on a small scale the manufacturing towns of southern New England, such as Fall River, and so seems misplaced in northern Vermont. The manufacturing plants, textile and wood-working in the main, are in the sharp-cleft valley of the Winooski, and the major part of the city lies on the sidehill sloping up from the northern banks of the strongflowing stream. The bridge at the foot of Main St. was constructed to replace the one washed out in the raging flood of 1927; from the bridge is a fine view of the great power-distributing dam. The *Site of Fort Frederick* is on Main St. at the bridge; here once stood a blockhouse built by Ira Allen for protection against the Indians, and one of the earliest military structures in this region. The strictly industrial aspect of Winooski is tempered by its close proximity to Burlington and Lake Champlain, which permits Winooski people to enjoy the scenic, cultural, recreational and educational advantages of the largest and most beautifully located city in the State.

The development of the manufacturing directly responsible for the city's growth and virility began as early as 1835, when a woolen mill was established on the falls. Now the American Woolen Company, Inc., operates here one of the largest textile plants in the country. Other large and significant industries are the Vermont Furniture Manufacturing Company, and the Porter Screen Company, the latter of which was at one time the biggest producer of window-screens in the world. (*These plants not open to public.*)

*St. Stephen's Church*, Platt St., is built of Vermont marble in the Gothic tradition. *St. Francis Xavier Church*, Weaver St., is one of the oldest French-Canadian churches in Vermont. *St. Michael's College* (*see Tour 5A*) is just east of the city limits on State 15. There is a very large

French-Canadian population in Winooski and the Catholic influence is predominant, coloring the contemporary pattern of community life.

Between Winooski and Burlington, US 7 swings in long, sweeping curves over a pleasant hilly intervale to enter the latter city along North Willard St.

> BURLINGTON (alt. 208, pop. 24,789) (*see BURLINGTON*), 44.6 *m.*, The Queen City, largest in the State; seat of University of Vermont; Billings Library; Fleming Museum; Ira Allen Chapel; Battery Park; Ethan Allen Park; Memorial Auditorium; Fletcher Free Library; Unitarian Church; St. Mary's Church; St. Joseph's Church; Calvinistic Congregational Church; Church of Christ Scientist; St. Paul's Episcopal Church; and other points of interest.

*Sec. b. Burlington to Rutland.* US 7. 67.2 *m.*

This main artery of travel sees the heaviest and fastest traffic of any highway stretch in Vermont. Lake Champlain lies gleaming on the west, backed by the incredible massed peaks of the Adirondacks, while the Green Mountains lift graceful sweeping contours to the eastern skyline. The countryside is rich and well-cared-for in appearance, with a wealth of tradition going back to the time when the New Hampshire Grants were an independent State, shuttle-cocked between the neighboring Colonies and England. The villages along the way are older, more austere, and at the same time more immaculate and well-kept. The pressure of modern living is felt increasingly in the central and southern parts. Even though the small villages seem to slumber with true Vermont tranquillity, the roar of powerful machines over concrete indicates the tempo of the times.

BURLINGTON, 0 *m.* (*see BURLINGTON*).

US 7 passes south from Main St. along South Willard St. through Burlington's best residential section with fine homes ranging from palatial mansions to trim bungalows, a street typical of the Queen City's charm.

Between Burlington and Shelburne, the might of the Adirondacks is profiled across the blue sweep of Champlain to the west. Large apple orchards slant gently to the water's edge, and in the distant background those great irregular mountain barriers thrust jaggedly skyward.

At 2.6 *m.* is a junction with a dirt road.

> Right on this road is *Queen City Park*, 1 *m.*, a summer colony, at one time the principal bathing beach for Burlington. A generation ago Queen City Park was also the outstanding Spiritualist Camp Ground in this section of the country. Mediums and lecturers from all over the world appeared on the stage of the modest little *Temple* (R), and seances were held in dozens of near-by cottages. In recent years the movement has waned, and, although the Spiritualist Association still owns most of the land and much of the property, a short series of August meetings in the Temple is all that is left of the old atmosphere.

> West from Queen City Park an attractive footpath leads to *Redrocks*, 0.5 *m.*, a local name which applies equally to the red sandstone cliffs guarding the entrance to Shelburne Bay and to the parklike grounds of the former Hatch Estate which cover nearly a square mile adjacent to the promontory. Long disused and grass-

grown, the old carriage roads, sylvan delights of the nineties, are now excellent for rambles over evergreen-covered ledges; and although the rustic lookouts, posted at vantage points on the cliffs, have almost completely decayed, the views of the broad lake and across the bay to Shelburne Harbor (*see below*) are unchanged, among the loveliest from the Vermont shore of Champlain.

At 5 *m.* is a junction with a gravel road.

Right on this road is *Shelburne Harbor*, 4.9 *m.*, where Macdonough's fleet was quartered during the winter of 1812–13, preparing to defend the waters of Champlain against the British. At the present time a shipyard (*not open to the public*) is maintained here for the three lake steamers of the Champlain Transportation Company. The hull of the old 'Philadelphia,' sunk by the English off Valcour Island during the War of 1812, is in the harbor (1937).

SHELBURNE (alt. 174, pop. township 1006), 6.7 *m.*, lies in restful shade along the highway, with neat hedges bordering velvet lawns. The village center clusters about a small green oval, faced from the south by the attractive *Pierson Free Library* of yellow brick with white-pillared façade. The *Episcopal Church* (L), a miniature English abbey in local red sandstone, was given by W. Seward Webb (*see below*), the town's benefactor, who also maintains a rector in residence at the adjacent parsonage. The new brick *Town Hall* (right beyond village Green) is further evidence of Webb's generosity. Its graceful Georgian exterior, and well-appointed interior provide Shelburne with one of the best community buildings to be found in Vermont among towns of comparable size. The unadorned but modern red-brick High School (R) serves an area much larger than the township limits. Shelburne's only industry is the Cooperative Creamery (right at head of Main St.).

Shelburne was settled in 1768 by two Germans, who engaged in lumbering for the Canadian market. According to the legend they were killed for their money by soldiers sent from Montreal, supposedly to protect the lumbermen from Indians. In 1778, two Shelburne settlers were slain by raiding Indians and Tories, and the small garrison would have been burned by the attackers, if a timely hogshead of home-brewed beer had not served effectively as fire-extinguisher. John L. Barstow, Governor of Vermont (1882–84), was born here.

Right from Shelburne is the *Webb Estate* (South Gate, 1 *m.*). Mansion at lake shore (*grounds open to public except Sun. and holidays*) 2.2 *m.* This 4000-acre estate was established by W. Seward Webb, a relative of the Vanderbilt family. A winding gravel drive runs through the beautifully kept grounds, past great barns, neat cottages, fine woodlands, and a 9-hole golf course, to the mansion over the lake commanding a broad lake panorama to the north, with an Adirondack vista west across the water.

Between Shelburne and Charlotte the highway climbs to an elevation commanding Green Mountain (L) and Adirondack (R) views, and then descends winding.

CHARLOTTE (alt. 180, pop. township 1089), 11.9 *m.* Part of this small village lies at the foot of a hill on the highway, with the main section spreading (R) on the plain of the Champlain Valley toward the lake, an excellent orchard region. The *Congregational Church* (right of US 7), a handsome red-brick structure with white-columned portico, was built over a century ago, one of the few evidences of the Greek Revival in Vermont. The road (R) through Charlotte proper leads to the *Charlotte-Essex Ferry* (1790), one of the oldest in this part of the country, and to the lakeshore summer colonies of *Cedar Beach* and *Thompson's Point*. The first ferry in this vicinity was operated by John McNeil.

At 14.3 *m.* is a junction with an uphill dirt road.

> Left on this hill road is *Mount Philo*, 1.7 *m.*, an abrupt, knobby elevation of 968 feet, thickly wooded and set aside as *Mount Philo State Forest Park*, developed by Civilian Conservation Corps labor. A good gravel road leads to the mountaintop, where a 50-foot glass-enclosed observation tower affords a sweeping view across Champlain to the grandeur of the Adirondacks, and eastward to the long serene stretch of Green Mountain summits, which perfect this panorama. This is the best view obtainable of Vermont's largest area of level land — Addison County. The park has excellent facilities for camping and recreation.

At 15.8 *m.* is a junction with an unimproved road.

> Left on this road is NORTH FERRISBURG, 0.6 *m.*, a hilly, shady village with queer unpainted old wooden houses stretching eastward from US 7 into a deeper valley. *Allen's Hall* (R) is an old-fashioned opera house, and beyond this the main street passes through an old covered bridge. Trees arch the main street. The gravestones in the large cemetery far outnumber the present inhabitants.

Between this junction and Ferrisburg, apple orchards slope away toward the lake.

*Rokeby* (*open to public — May to November*) (L) 18.4 *m.*, the Rowland E. Robinson Homestead, sets back from the highway in tangled shade and rustic peace, attractive in a simple, venerable, unkempt way. This house, now occupied by the writer's son, was built prior to 1784, and in Civil War times was a station in the 'Underground Railway.' Robinson's private collection of pictures and antique furniture is here. Rowland E. Robinson (1833–1900) was probably Vermont's most representative and loved writer, and the outstanding Vermont literary figure of the nineteenth century. No other writer in the State has ever translated so accurately and warmly the personality of Vermont people and Vermont landscapes, and in so doing Robinson pictured a unique little corner of American civilization that has now vanished from even the remotest backwoods sections (*see Literature*).

FERRISBURG (alt. 218, pop. township 1285), 19.3 *m.*, sprawls along either side of the main thoroughfare, and trails off on the plain toward Champlain. The town, settled in 1785, was named after grantees by the name of Ferris. The Quaker influence was strong here for many decades. During the War of 1812, Fort Cassin was built at the mouth of Otter Creek in this township, to prevent the enemy from sailing upstream to Vergennes and destroying the vessels being built there (*see Tour 4B, BASIN HARBOR*).

VERGENNES (alt. 203, pop. 1705), 22.3 *m.*, the third oldest city in New England and one of the smallest incorporated cities in the world, one mile square, was settled in 1766 and incorporated 1788. It was named after Count de Vergennes, French minister of foreign affairs. Large dairy plants (L) at the northern entrance, with the accompanying railway water-tanks and freight cars, indicate the city's industrial foundation. The blocky wooden houses with mansard roofs are characteristic of the late nineteenth-century trend in architecture. An attractive central square (R), with a *Monument to Macdonough*, opens placid and shaded from the compact business district, its green surrounded by the red and white of pleasing homes.

From the business center, the main street slants sharply down to the level of Otter Creek and the falls where, during the War of 1812, forges and furnaces produced 177 tons of cannon balls. Here on the banks of the Creek, Macdonough's flagship, 'Saratoga,' and entire flotilla were constructed in the record time of forty days, for their attack on Plattsburg, 1814 (*see History*).

Colonel Reid of New York laid claims to land here in 1766, but was dispossessed in 1772 by the New Hampshire proprietors. Reid then engaged Scotch emigrants to settle his claims in Vergennes, but the Yorkers were driven out by Allen, Warner, and Baker at the head of 100 Green Mountain Boys, who ruthlessly burned the huts of Reid's envoys and tore down their gristmill at the falls, 1773.

*Bixby Memorial Library* (R), Main St., built of buff brick with a pillared entrance, is one of the finest small libraries in New England (15,586 vols.).

*Vermont Industrial School*, North Water St., the State reformatory for wayward boys and girls, is situated on a plateau above Otter Creek. *U.S. Arsenal* (1828) (L), a grim gray-stone structure, is now employed as one of the school buildings.

*General Strong House*, Main St., was built in 1793 by Samuel Strong, second son of John Strong of Addison, and has remained in the family since that time. It is a large handsome white structure in the clean simplicity of the best Colonial tradition, and is considered one of the finest in Vermont.

Between Vergennes and New Haven Junction, US 7 climbs to pass through a forested region, then falls and rises in long swoops, the land cleared and open now, the principal Green Mountain Range rising (L) ahead.

*New Haven Junction* (alt. 282, pop. township 964), 26.9 *m.*, is a small settlement on the Rutland Railroad and a junction of highways, scattered about the depot, a general store, and creamery, an irregular blotch on the valley floor. Here is the junction with State 17 (*see Tour 3C*).

At 29.9 *m.* is a junction with a dirt road.

> Right on this road is *Spring Grove Camp Ground*, 1.3 *m.*, which was once the scene of stirring old-time camp meetings and fanatical revival services, drawing large crowds from miles around. Wild-eyed, wild-haired speakers strove with fiery words and terrific gestures to whip their audiences into religious fervor and lash them on to salvation.

Between New Haven Junction and Brooksville, the highway swings farther away from Lake Champlain with the Green Mountains looming closer (L) and a choppy wooded country stretching to the west.

BROOKSVILLE (alt. 240), 31.1 *m.*, named for a prominent early family, is a tiny hamlet nestled in a low pocket of the valley. Once a thriving settlement, now nothing remains but a ruined dam to commemorate dead industry.

*Dog Team Tavern* (R), a Colonial-type mansion, was constructed in 1936 under the direction of Sir Wilfred Grenfell, a summer resident of Charlotte known for his humanitarian work among the fisherfolk of Labrador. The old white *Church* (R) near-by, has been renovated to house exhibits of Labrador handicrafts.

*Chipman Hill*, 33.8 *m.*, overlooks Middlebury from the north and is the scene of winter sports staged by the outing club of Middlebury College, with short, fast ski runs and a ski jump (L).

MIDDLEBURY (alt. 366, pop. 2006) (*see MIDDLEBURY*) 34.7 *m.* Addison County Seat; Middlebury College; Meade Memorial Chapel; Egbert Starr Library; Congregational Church; Sheldon Art Museum; and other points of interest.

Right from Middlebury on Seymour St. (old Middlebury-Vergennes Turnpike) is the *U.S. Morgan Horse Farm* (*visitors are welcome*), 2 *m.* (in the township of Weybridge). This experimental farm of some 1000 acres is conducted by the U.S. Department of Agriculture. Horses, cattle, and sheep are bred. The *Morgan Horse Monument* here (*see Tour 2, RANDOLPH CENTER*) is one of the few statues of a riderless horse in existence.

US 7 leaves Middlebury along Court St., a broad residential boulevard, and winds out over rolling plains between woodlands, with mountains towering on the east. The heavy traffic and high speed of US 7 in its southward trend induce a pressure of driving haste and a tension that are not felt along most Vermont highways.

At 37.8 *m.* is the intersection with State 125 (*see Tour 3D*).

At 38.4 *m.* is the intersection with a dirt road.

Right on this road at 1.1 *m.* is the junction with another dirt road.

Left on this road, across a cement bridge over the Middlebury River, is *Shard Villa* (*open to visitors*, 2–4, *Tues. and Fri.*) (R) at 3.0 *m.* Situated on a slight rise of ground, surrounded by a 20-acre landscaped estate, this mansion is externally the most outstanding Vermont example of the General Grant era in architecture, and is internally an amazingly profuse illustration of Victorian taste in decoration. It was built in 1872–74 by Columbus Smith, a native of Salisbury who had grown rich in England as a lawyer handling American inheritance claims, and was named for the estate the settlement of which was the first step in Smith's career. The building is of local stone, and the estate is partially surrounded by a wall of the same material.

The interior is a crowded stage-set of all the seventies held most admirable in painting, furnishings, and statuary. The walls and ceilings of the ground-floor rooms are completely covered with frescoes by Silvio Pezzoli. Caesar, Nero, Cicero, Romulus and Remus, and other Romans greet the visitor from the walls of the entrance hall; the drawing room, dining room, and library walls are embellished with painted columns, painted draperies, and portraits with painted frames. From every ceiling nymphs, cherubs, and graces gaze down at the marble busts, the heavy Victorian furniture, the Oriental rugs (the one in the dining room concealing an inlaid recumbent deer), and the elaborate mantels of marbleized slate. Even the fireplaces were deceptive, being designed as outlets for a hot-air heating system which never worked.

Shard Villa was left, together with the bulk of the Smith estate, 'for the purpose of founding a good and comfortable home for good old Christian women not addicted to drink.' Since 1928 the old ladies have been housed in a new brick annex.

SALISBURY (alt. 340, pop. township 632), 44.1 *m.*, was named after Salisbury, Connecticut, original home of the Allens and other prominent Vermont pioneers. The sidehill village is built along the sharp-curving highway above river banks in a narrow valley, and is best known as the southern junction of the Lake Dunmore road. Amos Story first settled the town in 1774, but was killed under a falling tree before he could bring his family here. Mrs. Story, a woman of great strength and courage, came with her brood of small children, to carry on the work of the farm. She remained in Salisbury during the Revolution, when nearly all the settlers fled. Her home was burned by Indians, but the dauntless woman soon had it rebuilt, and it became a popular stopping place for the Patriots in the stirring times when it was the Green Mountain Boys against the world. A monument to her memory was erected in 1905.

John E. Weeks, Governor of Vermont (1927-31) was born here.

Left from Salisbury is *Lake Dunmore*, 1.3 *m.*, snugly ensconced against the secondary range of the Green Mountains, which form a rugged wooded background for the sparkling lake waters. The stern ridged shoulder of *Mount Moosalamoo* (alt. 2650) closely guards the northeastern shores of this fashionable resort lake. thickwooded slopes rising directly from the water's edge and touching the picture with a scenic grandeur, a Lake George type of lake beauty. Two trails may be followed up Moosalamoo. The Cascade trail offers a view of Lana Falls cascading 670 feet above sea level, with a picnic ground above the waterfall. The Keewaydin trail (starting from Keewaydin Camp) is the better climb and leads to the vantage point of *Rattlesnake Point*, an old Indian lookout at the top of a sheer ledge 1900 feet over Lake Dunmore. *Ethan Allen's Cave* is also on this mountain, and many legends are woven around it, as the Green Mountain Boys were supposed to have held secret conclaves in this recess.

Lake Dunmore is a popular resort, with all facilities for swimming, fishing, and summer sports. Boating is a highly favored form of recreation. The air has a mountain-and-lake freshness and vigor, clean and stimulating. Dunmore Glass, much sought today by antique-lovers, was made on the northwestern shore, 1813–18 and 1832–39. Fragments of glass and slag are still found along the shoreline.

LEICESTER (pop. 486), 46.1 *m.* Known as Leicester Corners, this is a little crossroads settlement, its string of gasoline service stations making bright red-and-white splotches along US 7, the commercial bent being to thrive on travelers of this main thoroughfare. Off the highway (R) stands a brick church among wooden dwellings, softening somewhat the brazen front line of gas-pumps, and hinting at the true antiquity of the town, the simple homely houses offering mild rebuke to the commercial front.

The early settlement here, started in 1770, was retarded by conflicts between chartists of Leicester and Salisbury. At the first town meeting in Leicester, Jeremiah Parker, 75, first settler, outjumped all-comers to win five gallons of brandy. The settlement was broken up during the Revolution, and many Leicester prisoners taken to Canada. John Barker, prominent pioneer, was a veteran of the Revolution and also fought at Plattsburg.

Between Leicester and Brandon, a wild woodland country gradually opens into vast stretches of plain, with mountain crests outlined (L) ahead.

At 49.5 *m.* is the *Brandon State School* (L), Vermont's institution for the care of mentally handicapped children, nearly 300 of whom are treated here and at the adjoining *Farm Colony.*

BRANDON (alt. 421, pop. township 2891), 50.6 *m.*, was chartered 1761 as Neshobe, and local legend has it that the name Brandon was derived from 'Burnt Town,' after the 1777 Indian attack in which all homes were burned and many prisoners taken. Now fine Colonial homesteads and trim modern houses stand side by side under the ancient elms and maples that line the broad streets of Brandon, old churches calmly overlooking the business section, the whole atmosphere one of gracious charm in a blend of austere age and sharp modernity.

*Birthplace of Stephen A. Douglas* (*open*) (right at northern end of village), a small story-and-a-half cottage, white with green trim and a latticed entryway, faces Conant Square. Stephen A. Douglas, 'The Little Giant,' famous adversary of Lincoln, was born here in 1813. A marble monument before the cottage tells the story of the dynamic Douglas's life. The house is now headquarters of the D.A.R.

*Baptist Church* (right beside Douglas cottage), built of brick in 1832, has notable scrolled double doors under a beautiful fanlight, small-paned windows, and a tapering steeple.

*Pearl Street* (straight beyond Conant Square), once a military parade ground, was the forerunner of Brandon's wide streets. The *Farrington House* (1799), on Pearl St., is a large square cream-colored frame building, finished with ship-lap siding characteristic of the period, flanked on the south by a long line of neat barns. In the possession of the Farrington family since 1808, the house contains a century's accumulation of early furniture, old documents, and pictures, including one of Stephen A. Douglas, friend and neighbor of Franklin Farrington, father of the present owner. Franklin's father, Captain Daniel Farrington, commanded the Canadian border near Rouse's Point in 1808, where smuggling in defiance of the embargo laws was rampant. One smuggling vessel, the 'Black Snake,' was pursued for miles down the lake and finally captured near Burlington in a bloody skirmish in which several men were killed and Farrington himself wounded. The incident resulted in Vermont's first State public hanging, when Cyrus Dean of the 'Black Snake' was hanged in Burlington, November 11, 1808, to the edification of a crowd of 10,000 people.

Left from Conant Square is a bridge over the Neshobe River, revealing *Neshobe Falls* (R), where John Conant established his iron furnace, after the discovery of bog iron in 1810, and built up a business of manufacturing stoves. Conant's were the first stoves made in Vermont, and his industrial venture gave impetus to the growth of Brandon. Today early Conant stoves are much prized by antique collectors. The *Town Hall* (L), (1861), has an unusual massive appearance due to its heavy Roman portico.

The business district flanks a central park of pleasant aspect, which lends a cool note to the yellow and red brick and huddled wood of the commercial center, a respite from hot concrete highways and sidewalks. The *Congregational Church* (R) (1831), of brick with a white wooden tower and old fenced-in burying ground, faces the park. The *Ayrshire Breeders' Association National Headquarters* is located in the office building that spans the Neshobe River next to the bridge.

The *Soldiers' Monument* (L) is a large imposing memorial of granite, the high shaft topped by the figure of a Civil War soldier.

At 51.8 *m.* a *Marble Quarry* (L) lies close beside the highway.

*McConnell Rest Home* (L), 53.5 *m.*, is an old post-road tavern, remodeled as a home for retired Vermont school teachers. It was given for this purpose in 1921 by the McConnell family, the daughters of which were themselves pioneer teachers in California.

Between Brandon and Pittsford there is a continuous mountain view (R), green-clothed and graceful in contour, the broken line stretching against a blue sky. The grassy valley lies between US 7 and the mountains, a wavering line of trees marking the winding course of Otter Creek which was a most important Indian waterway in the early days. The highway here follows the *Old Crown Point Military Road*, which was extended from Charlestown, New Hampshire, to Crown Point, New York, by General Amherst, 1759.

*Site of Fort Vengeance* (R), 56.9 *m.*, is marked by a marble shaft beside the climbing roadway. This Revolutionary fort was built to protect the northwest wing from Canadian invasions. A soldier was killed by Indians when the fort was first occupied, 1780, and his comrades, in swearing vengeance, so named the fort.

*Colonial Stone House* (R), 58 *m.*, is a compactly built, picturesque structure with an interesting old fireplace and bake oven. The ford on Otter Creek behind this house was called Pitt's Ford, after Prime Minister William Pitt, and from this evolved the name of Pittsford Township.

*Split Rock* (L), 58.4 *m.* This huge split rock was once used as a hiding-place by a little pioneer girl, who thus escaped the Indians, and later ran to warn the garrison of Fort Vengeance in time to stave off the attack of the red men.

PITTSFORD (alt. 560, pop. township 2333), 58.6 *m.*, noted for pine-scented mountain air and pure water, is the site of two sanatoriums. The long rolling main street curves under shade trees between rows of comfortable homes. In many cases brick has been employed as the building material, coloring the cool green of the street. *Old Cemetery* (R) is a shaded sidehill graveyard at the entrance to the village, its ancient headstones dating back to 1774, striking the note of calm resignation and quiet that rules the village. The *Drake Homestead* (R), Main St., a small drab gray-green cottage over a hundred years old, is where the mother of President Millard Fillmore was born. *Walker Memorial Library* (R), facing the triangle as US 7 bends left, stands in the plain security of red brick. Nicholas M. Powers, who built lattice-type covered bridges throughout Vermont and New Hampshire, was born in Pittsford. Many of his sturdy and picturesque structures remain as useful memorials to him, and as links to the past.

> Left from Pittsford on a hilly dirt road is the *Caverly Preventorium*, 1 *m.*, in a pine grove on the heights over the northern end of the village. This institution combats tuberculosis in children who show tendencies toward the disease.

PITTSFORD MILLS, 59.7 *m.*, formerly a busy industrial section where mill wheels were turned by Furnace Brook, is now simply the southern residential section of Pittsford, a continuation of the village street. Rather more attractive than Pittsford proper, its cozy homes with vine-clad porches rest in calm shade.

> 1. Left from Pittsford Mills on an improved road is the *Vermont State Sanatorium*, 0.6 *m.*, an excellent and well-located institution for tubercular patients.
>
> 2. Right from Pittsford Mills on an improved road is PROCTOR (alt. 477, pop. 2515), 4.7 *m.*, named after Redfield Proctor (*see Tour 3, PROCTORSVILLE*), the 'Marble Center,' built around the headquarters and finishing plants of the Vermont Marble Company. Lying in the narrow Otter Creek Valley, Proctor is pervaded with the pleasing cleanness of its famous building stone, exemplified in neat homes and the marble of public buildings. In places even the sidewalks are of marble. The picture is glacial white against a green background.
>
> The business center of the trim, well-kept village is dominated by the great long marble mills and yards piled high with marble slabs, the whole scene neat and orderly. From the narrow valley floor residential streets wind up the shady hillsides with houses strewn irregularly at all levels, and mountains closing in on every side of the gap.
>
> Water-power is furnished by beautiful *Sutherland Falls* (right from bridge near center), which drop a sheer 118 feet in roaring foaming cascades. The falls were named for John Sutherland, an early settler who built a sawmill and gristmill here. Marble was first quarried in the vicinity, 1836, when it was a part of Rutland (*see RUTLAND*). In 1870 Redfield Proctor took over the Sutherland Falls Marble Company, rapidly absorbed other firms, and welded together the mighty Vermont Marble Company. Redfield Proctor as Governor of Vermont, 1878–80, instituted the nearest thing to a capitalistic dynasty that the State has ever known. Today Vermont Marble operates quarries throughout the State, as well as in Colorado, Montana, and Alaska, and the central offices make Proctor virtually the center of the marble world. An elaborate *Marble Exhibit (open to the public from May 1 to November 1, admission free, guide service furnished)* is held in the company display room.

Between Pittsford and Rutland, continuous mountain vistas (L) stand in bold sweeping outline against the eastern sky, where often beautiful cloud effects enhance the picture.

MILL VILLAGE, 65.1 *m.*, is the local name for this pleasant residential section stretching along US 7 into the outskirts of Rutland, with a profusion of flowers banking shaded verandas and an agreeable suburban aspect of enjoyable living.

> RUTLAND (alt. 600, pop. 17,315) (*see RUTLAND*) 67.2 *m.* The second largest city in Vermont; center of the world's largest marble-quarrying industry; site of Fort Rutland; Riverside Reformatory; Church of Christ the King; Trinity Church; Temple House.

*Sec. c. Rutland to Massachusetts Line*, 67. 1 *m.*

Between Rutland and the Massachusetts border, US 7 swings through the beautiful valleys of Otter Creek and Batten Kill, with mountain ranges banked against the skyline on either side. The mountain-sides are smooth and regular for the most part, green-forested and serene in contour. The southern portion of this route runs through an aristocratic resort section, the part of Vermont that is most nearly cosmopolitan. Here in Manchester and Old Bennington, as in Dorset, is a groomed quality that is more of the fashionable world than of Vermont. The estates, the land-scaped grounds, the smart hotels, the limousines and liveried chauffeurs, the artists, writers, and world-travelers: all this is curiously transplanted in the Vermont hills. Yet the unpretentious charm of little villages along the way, the grave dignity of eighteenth-century farmhouses, the fertile meadowlands and meandering rivers are intrinsically Vermont, and the historical traditions, with which the countryside is rich, are closely allied to the turbulent times associated with the birth of the State and its be-lated admission to the Union. Here patriots and Tories wrangled and plotted, and the founders of Vermont banded together in defiance of a hostile outer world.

RUTLAND, 0. *m.* (corner of Main and West) (*see Rutland*).

US 7 runs south of Rutland on a wide avenue, past the Fairgrounds and airport (R), and into a countryside opening to broad level meadowlands, known since the first habitation of the region as The Flats.

NORTH CLARENDON (North Flats) (alt. 580), 3.3 *m.*, lies on the out-skirts of Rutland, suburban and commercialized for tourist trade with filling stations and wayside cabins among the dull-colored wooden homes.

1. Left from North Clarendon on a country road is *Northam State Picnic Area*, 8 *m.* (*see Tour 4D, NORTH SHREWSBURY*).

2. Right from North Clarendon on a country road is *Wait's Monument*, 0.4 *m.* (R), in a field behind a barn at the crossroads. This old stone slab bearing the queer effigy of a Revolutionary soldier, and enclosed by an iron picket fence, marks the grave of Colonel Joseph Wait. Member of a prominent early Vermont family, Wait served with Rogers' Rangers during the French and Indian Wars (*see Tour 1, BRADFORD*) and fought in the Revolution until his death. He was buried by his comrades here where he died on the march, from a wound received at Valcour Island.

PIERCE'S CORNER, 5.2 *m.*, is named for the family that has lived over a century in the *Old Bowman Tavern* (L), a stage-house in early days. The pale brown house with its broad ell and vine-covered sides was erected prior to 1800, repaired in 1816, and has served as the Pierce homestead continuously since 1835.

At Pierce's Corner is the junction with State 103 (*see Tour 4D*).

Between Pierce's Corner and Clarendon, US 7 rolls over a hilly section in which many of the spacious, comfortable farmhouses offer tourist ac-commodations.

At 7.1 *m.* is the junction with a downhill road.

Right on this road is CLARENDON (South Flats) (alt. 600, pop. township 833), 0.2 *m.*, a low-lying village on the broad flat plains of Otter Creek, with homes scattered about the elm-sheltered valley floor where fine meadowlands merge into stony pastures and ridged mountains rise on the west. Around 1800 Clarendon was a leading town in Rutland County, and previous to that the center of bitter controversy between the patriots and Tories. Nicholas M. Powers (*see PITTS-FORD, Sec. b, above*), builder of covered bridges, lived here for a time.

Left from Clarendon, straight past the four-corners on an uphill road, is CHIP-PENHOOK (alt. 840), 2.9 *m.*, an antiquated upland village spread on a high plateau with higher hills rising above. Chippenhook retains an air of 1790, a wild mountaineer flavor reminiscent of the Tennessee hills. Seldom in New England is such raw rusticity found but a few miles from a main and cosmopolitan thoroughfare; a hillbilly settlement in close proximity to the modern and progressive city of Rutland. The *Oldest House* in the district stands eminently (R) at the left-hand entrance to the hamlet, and beyond is the empty shell of an old *Stone Mill* (R) on the Tinmouth River where grist was ground and cider pressed. The *Old Church*, built before 1800, stands in plain severe white at the entrance to the tiny village. Chippenhook was the home of Judge Theophilus Harrington, known for his trenchant reply to an irate slave-owner in a runaway slave case. Judge Harrington declared that the owner's claim to the slave was defective. The owner indignantly demanded to know what was lacking in his legally sound claim. The Judge exploded, 'A bill of sale, sir, from God Almighty!'

Right from Chippenhook on a country road is CLARENDON SPRINGS (alt. 560), 5.9 *m.*, the great brick hotel with its white wooden porches, deserted but still in good repair, looming huge and lonely and out-of-place in the forsaken resort village. There is an air of haunting melancholy about any 'ghost town,' but nothing is more desolate than a ghost resort town. Before the Civil War this was a famous and fashionable watering place, the mineral springs and natural setting attracting people from great distances. Most of the patrons were wealthy southerners, a fact which naturally caused the decline of the resort after the death of the Confederate cause. Today the big hotel stands incongruously on deserted grounds, still kept up by caretakers, which only accentuate its aspect of forlorn emptiness. People continue to visit the place to see the old Clarendon House and sample water from the mineral springs.

Between Clarendon and Wallingford great elms spread lofty boughs over US 7, and distinctive old homesteads, characteristically square-lined, strong, and venerable, stand beside the highway. Mountains hem the valley on either side.

The *Old Homestead* (L), 8 *m.*, is dated 1792 and carries the clear-cut stamp of its period.

WALLINGFORD (alt. 580, pop. township 1564), 10.2 *m.*, is typical of the more attractive New England villages, with a broad main street running under a tunnel of green boughs arched from lofty elms, fine, large houses set back on trim lawns, and a scrupulous cleanness everywhere. Shrubbery frames immaculate columned porches, and a gracious quality of peace permeates the whole scene. The *True Temper Tool Factory* (R) of the American Fork and Hoe Company, one of the 12 large plants operated by this firm, the biggest manufacturers of hand garden tools in the world, dominates the entrance on the north. Flower gardens brighten the general cleanness of the factory, in contrast to the industrial dinginess that might be expected.

The small brick house (L) bearing the date 1818 was the *Boyhood Home of Paul P. Harris*, founder of Rotary International. Though Michigan-born, Harris spent most of his early years in Vermont and attended the University of Vermont. The organization which he created has acquired possession of this, his grandfather's home, and a portrait of Harris is displayed within.

Another *Brick House* (L), built by William Fox, who was a 16-year-old soldier in the Revolution, embodies the compact security and clarity of line associated with its type and age. The *True Temper Inn* (L) centers the village street, the slender white pillars giving it a pseudo-Mt. Vernon aspect. The *Boy and Boot Fountain* (L) is an unusual landmark in front of the inn, with water flowing from the toe of a boot held by a boy. The *Gilbert Hart Library* (R), a brick and granite building, contains 5000 volumes. The *Old Stone Shop* (L) was the original mill building of the fork factory, established in 1836 by Lyman Batcheller, and stands picturesque and sturdy, beautifully remodeled and tastefully fitted with old furnishings to serve as a tea room.

> Right from Wallingford, then left from the depot through a covered bridge, and left again is *Elfin Lake*, 0.7 *m.*, hidden and cupped in sloping thick-wooded hills, a pretty and secluded little body of water ringed in a stillness of fir trees. A boys' camp is here. The public swimming place is equipped with bath-houses (*admission* 15¢).

> Right on an uphill road past Elfin Lake is TINMOUTH (alt. 1263, pop. township 340), 6 *m.*, reached after a scenic climbing drive. The first county seat of Rutland County, Tinmouth was once the home of iron furnaces and forges, but the enterprise was abandoned in 1837. Nathaniel Chipman, later one of Vermont's foremost jurists, built a forge here for the manufacture of bar iron, 1781. This hill town has long been known as a dairying community, producing excellent cheeses. During the Revolution patriotic spirit burned high in Tinmouth. John Irish was shot down by three local soldiers, who suspected him of being a Tory spy and who apparently decided to shoot first and ascertain the facts later. At the present time the town reposes in its upland setting, a simple peaceful farming community.

*Green Hill Cemetery* (L), 10.7 *m.* This attractive terraced graveyard rises from the roadside at the southern edge of Wallingford, with a fountain playing at its base, the grounds well-cared-for and colored with flowers. The landscaping is such as to impart a slightly incongruous Versailles atmosphere. The first man to be buried here was a Tory killed by Wallingford patriots.

At 11.9 *m.* is the junction with a country road.

> Left on this sharply climbing road is *White Rocks*, 2.5 *m.* (2 *m.* drive to parking place (R) and 0.5 *m.* walk along woodland path to foot of mountain). The bare, gray, bulging dome of White Rocks looms high above the wooded, rolling valley. The footpath leads to the *Ice Caves* at the base of the cliff, where even on warm summer days the breath of winter is felt. The great tumbled pile of boulders at the foot of the cliff is cold to the touch, and the tiny stream trickling out of the rocks is pure icewater. By penetrating the chill caves formed by the rocks, ice can be found at any season of the year. Overhead the great boulders heap up toward the blue skyline, crowned by the fir-studded gray dome of the mountain.

Between Wallingford and South Wallingford, US 7 runs through a pleasant green valley with mountains rearing on the east and undulating

# ILLUSTRATIONS

*to accompany*

Tours 5, 5A, 5B, 5C

MODERN SAP LINES (ST. JOHNSBURY IS THE LARGEST MAPLE-SUGAR CENTER IN THE WORLD)

PLOWING — CALEDONIA COUNTY

STATE HOUSE PORTICO, MONTPELIER

CAMEL'S HUMP (LION COUCHANT), FROM BOLTON GORGE

AUTUMN IN SMUGGLER'S NOTCH

LAMOILLE RIVER NEAR JOHNSON

OLD STONE HOUSE IN THE SHADOW OF MT. MANSFIELD, NEAR UNDERHILL

HANKSVILLE, SOUTH OF HUNTINGTON

WINOOSKI VALLEY AND CAMEL'S HUMP, FROM FRENCH HILL

DAIRY REGION, CHITTENDEN COUNTY

UNITARIAN CHURCH, BURLINGTON

ridges stretching on the west. The mountains are smooth-sloped and densely forested. The well-kept, prosperous-looking farmhouses along the route give this valley an aspect of well-being.

SOUTH WALLINGFORD (alt. 620), 14.4 *m.*, was something of a mill town and a small industrial center in the middle nineteenth century, but this activity has died out, leaving only a hamlet stretched along US 7 above the banks of the Otter Creek. The *Union Church* (R) is of white wood, with an odd crenellated tower.

*Old Cemetery* (R), 17.2 *m.*, lies on a knoll over the highway. Among the old tombstones is one marking the grave of Jerathmiel Doty, Revolutionary soldier who died at the age of 93 in 1858, the last survivor of Lafayette's escort on the Marquis' return to France.

Between South Wallingford and Danby, a continuous mountain range shuts in the valley from the east.

DANBY (alt. 700, pop. township 1070), 19.3 *m.*, is a pretty little valley village, sheltered by mountain stretches. Attractive homes with patterned lawns and shrubs flank the street, and the town has an air of prosperity, based on marble quarrying and dairying. In earlier times lumbering was the chief industry here. A better-than-ordinary *Civil War Monument* (L) stands at the center, the bronze figure of a soldier surmounting a marble shaft. The *S. L. Griffith Memorial Library* (R) is constructed of buff brick on a granite base.

Micah Vail, one of the first settlers, 1765, was a leading citizen during turbulent Revolutionary times and a prominent Green Mountain Boy. He and his wife are supposed to have been poisoned to death by a Tory doctor from Arlington. Many of the early settlers were Quakers, and the sect remained active here until about the middle of the nineteenth century. The first town clerk was Thomas Rowley, celebrated wit and 'the Poet of the Green Mountain Boys,' the first important Vermont versifier, and at one time Chairman of the Committee of Safety. Silas Griffith, the lumber king and the State's earliest millionaire, built his fortune from the forests of Danby. A curious business, the wholesaling of ferns, has been established here, the ferns being gathered in Mount Tabor and stored in a refrigerated warehouse in Danby to be sold to florists during the winter.

1. Right from Danby on an uphill dirt road is DANBY FOUR CORNERS (alt. 1440), 3.5 *m.*, a small mountain settlement surrounded by a broad plateau of fertile farmland. The churchyard of the *Corner Church* is lined with ancient marble slabs bearing rare old names and quaint spellings. Captain Micah Vail and his wife are buried here under a double tombstone dated 1777.

2. Left from Danby on a country road is *Mount Tabor* (alt. 700, pop. township 173), 0.5 *m.* This township is included in the *Green Mountain National Forest*, and is in general very wild, mountainous, and sparsely settled, excellent country for fishing and hunting. At one time large quantities of charcoal were exported from here, and now ferns are gathered from the mountain slopes on a commercial scale.

3. Right from the south end of Danby on a climbing road that winds through groves of white birches is the *Danby Marble Quarry* (*may be visited by permission*), 1.2 *m.* A cluster of wooden houses forms a small quarry-workers' community at the foot of the mountain, where piles of marble blocks whiten the wooded slopes.

From here is a fine view across the valley to the verdant range to the east, its sides darkened and scarred by frequent slides. At the quarries themselves, high on the eastern slope of Dorset Mountain, tunnels penetrate more than 400 feet, with lateral tunnels branching off from the main ones until more than an acre of quarry floor is opened to produce great marble blocks beneath a ceiling 100 feet high in places. All modern quarry machinery operates by electricity, and the tunnels are electrically lighted. The $10,000,000 Supreme Court Building in Washington is built of Danby marble.

Between Danby and North Dorset, US 7 continues along the mountain-hemmed valley, the slopes flattening and broadening to narrow the valley somewhat at this point.

*Quarry Terminal* (R), 21 *m.*, is a loading station on a spur from the Rutland R.R. that extends to meet the steep mountain-side railway from Danby Quarry. Here at the foot of the quarry line are high piles of marble blocks waiting to be loaded onto freight cars.

The *Ruined Stone House* (L), 22.3 *m.*, is picturesque. Although this house is beyond restoration, it is typical of the many old dwellings of this type that today are being eagerly bought by out-of-State people and converted into charming summer homes.

NORTH DORSET, 23.6 *m.* In this wayside hamlet ancient houses are strung along the highway in the narrow valley confined by mountain ridges. The *Old Cemetery* (R), a fenced-in burying ground on a knoll above the highway, is unusually congruous here. The use of marble for eighteenth-century headstones is a characteristic of the graveyards in southwestern Vermont.

*North Dorset Pond* (alt. 740) (R), 24.2 *m.*, is a narrow body of water with a wooded island rising from it, the water taking a deep green color from the shadow of the forested mountain on the western shore. Emerald Lake, the pond's other name, is, for once, a truthful appellation.

An *Old Cemetery* (R), 25.8 *m.*, lies in a hollow below the highway, the small group of ancient leaning headstones wearing a lost, forgotten look there in the meadow near the rush of traffic along US 7.

Between North Dorset and East Dorset, the mountains flatten out into long lower stretches, before rising (R) to the eminence of Mount Aeolus.

EAST DORSET (alt. 788), 26.8 *m.* In this small, quiet village at the base of *Mount Aeolus* (alt. 3185), or Green Peak, marble was quarried as early as 1812. On entering from the north, a white *Union Church* and graveyard are seen (L) across the valley. The drabness of the main street is brightened by flower-beds, and old stone hitching-posts stand before several of the houses. A more pleasant residential street branches left, a street of white houses sitting under old elms. The quarries on Mount Aeolus are no longer worked, but they can be visited by turning right from Main St. at the R.R. station. The New York Public Library is constructed of marble from these quarries. Among the pioneers who settled here was John Manley, husband of Benedict Arnold's half-sister. Today East Dorset slumbers undisturbed but for the traffic on US 7.

On the southern edge of the village, at 27.6 *m.*, is a junction with a dirt road.

Right on this hill road, right again, and then left, is the foot trail to *Dorset Cave*, 2 *m.* (*leave car in farmyard and follow signs up mountain-side to reach cave*). This interesting cave, situated at an elevation of 2400 feet and 1750 feet above the village, is walled with marble and penetrable for at least 40 or 50 rods. Quarrying operations were started at the mouth of the cave in 1812, but were soon abandoned. The earliest quarrying was accomplished by splitting off slabs from projecting ledges. These slabs were first used for chimney-backs, later as tombstones. Names of some of the pioneer settlers can be found chiseled on the rocks about the entrance.

The *Old Farmhouse* (R), 27.6 *m.*, just south of the turn to the cave, unpainted and uncared for now, was built before the Revolution by William Marsh, who turned Tory and fled to join Burgoyne's army.

A pleasant extension of East Dorset trails southward along US 7, more attractive than the village proper, with an unusual patterned *Stone House* (L).

Between East Dorset and Manchester Center, US 7 wends over rich, rolling valley land, tranquil with graceful trees, and Mount Equinox looms (R), clean-lined and impressive in its dominance over the rich green valley.

The *Old Homestead* (R), 30.4 *m.*, as so many of these older houses are called, stands well above the highway commanding a wide view to the south and west, a sturdy, square structure in white-painted wood with a square-pillared porch. It was built by Major General Martin Roberts, about the close of the War of 1812.

MANCHESTER CENTER (alt. 940), 32 *m.*, is a forerunner of the beautiful villages to the south. Trim white buildings, clean shady lawns, and multi-colored flower gardens ranged along the broad entrance from the north merge agreeably with the immaculate if uninteresting business center at the double-bend of the highway. Manchester Center ushers the traveler into the most worldly section of Vermont, at once the oldest and most smartly modern district in the State, a fashionable resort superstructure over a foundation of historical tradition inseparable from the birth of Vermont. Known as Factory Point until late in the nineteenth century, this village was the industrial nucleus of the township and still retains an air of activity about its business section, though the old industries are dead.

The *Old Tavern* (R), a pleasing structure built in 1790, renovated since, but changed very little from its stagecoach days, is of yellow-painted wood with a high white-columned porch. The interior is carefully furnished with old pieces and has the third-floor ballroom characteristic of early days. The *Colburn House* (R) stands on the site of the first house in the village. Across the street (L) is the first *Gristmill*, in worn and faded brown, lying below the street level on the river bank where Timothy Mead built it in 1780, to lay the groundwork of Factory Point.

Here is the junction with State 30 (*see Tour 4C*) and State 11 (*see Tour 4E*).

Between Manchester Center and Manchester, US 7 swings into a brief gradual climb.

MANCHESTER (alt. 694, pop. township 2004), 33.4 *m.*, is the foremost of Vermont summer resorts, wearing an air of rich and cultured living. Lying in the shadow of the broad noble heights of *Mount Equinox* (alt. 3816), the elm-bowered streets of Manchester align historic Colonial structures and fine modern summer homes, set far back from the pavement, their white-pillared porches fronted by smooth-shaven lawns. The sidewalks are of sawed marble slabs. The world of affairs, art, letters, and social registers has invaded Vermont and established here a stronghold, cosmopolitan and exclusive, enhanced by the beauty of the Vermont natural background, but otherwise unrelated to the State. Sarah Cleghorn, the poet, makes her home here.

The first Council of Safety met in Manchester, which was an unofficial capital, and Ira Allen here announced his plan to finance Vermont's Revolutionary activities by confiscation of Tory property. Many famous people, including Mrs. Abraham Lincoln and Mrs. U. S. Grant, were accustomed to spend summers here, and Robert Todd Lincoln, the President's favorite son, died here on the Lincoln estate. Presidents Taft and Theodore Roosevelt were also visitors in Manchester.

The *Mark Skinner Library* (R) (*open weekdays 10 to 12.30, 2 to 5, and 7 to 9*), a memorial to an outstanding early family, stands at the entrance to the village from the north, in buff brick with red tile roof, surrounded by trim lawns. The interior is beautifully finished and contains a fine collection of books.

*Burr and Burton Seminary*, right from the Library, founded in 1829, stands on a hill at the base of Mount Equinox, an old gray-stone building, austere in its simplicity. The red-brick *Gymnasium* (R) is the scene of the annual Southern Vermont Artists' Exhibition held every summer in August.

The *Soldiers' Monument* (L), on the narrow village Green, topped by the figure of a Revolutionary soldier, honors the fighting men of Vermont and heads the long, scrupulously cared-for main street. Incorporated in the *Equinox House* (R), a resort hotel, is the wall of a pre-Revolutionary building. The *Hoyt House* (L), a long, low yellow structure of one story, is dated 1769, and its simple dignity of line authenticates its age, with allowances for restoration.

The *Ekwanok Country Club* (L), at southern end of village, is a beautiful 18-hole golf course with a luxurious clubhouse which was the scene of the National Amateur Championship in 1914.

The *Site of Seth Warner's Camping Ground* (R, south of the Country Club entrance) slants gently up from the highway; here a regiment under Colonel Warner encamped for a few weeks, after the Battle of Hubbardton and before proceeding to the Battle of Bennington. Recently a soldier's hatchet was found embedded in a tree here, where it had been stuck a century and a half, the tree having grown entirely around it.

*Dellwood Cemetery* (L) is solemnly beautiful with miniature ponds, evergreens, and flowers.

South of the cemetery a private road (L) leads to the *Robert Todd Lincoln Estate*, on a knoll overlooking the river, visible from US 7.

Between Manchester and Arlington the concrete road rises and falls through a rich scenic valley between mountain ranges, grand castle-like estates perched on the slopes and spread in the valley, US 7 swooping along the countryside, now in the open valley, again in wooded aisles.

*Studio Tavern* (R), 37.9 *m.*, occupies the site where Ethan and Ira Allen lived during the hectic early days, and the office established by them here was virtually the capital of the Republic of Vermont. Here it was that Ethan's famous treatise 'Oracles of Reason' (1784) was largely composed. This volume, strongly rationalist in tone, added the title 'Anti-Christ of Vermont' to Ethan's other designations ('Robin Hood of Vermont,' etc.).

ARLINGTON (alt. 691, pop. township 1440), 41.3 *m.*, is another beautifully kept summer village, having more of the simple natural charm of Vermont towns and less of the polish that is Manchester's. The home of Vermont's pioneer leaders in the early times of strife, Arlington clings to a character and quality indigenous to Vermont, in spite of its attractiveness as a summer retreat. There is a similarity in the two towns, but the difference between them is vast. Arlington's appeal is unpretentious, inherently Vermont. Lacking the well-groomed sheen of Manchester, it is more homelike, more representative of the State.

Arlington was first settled in 1763, and the names of prominent pioneers are closely linked with the town's early history, in spite of which Arlington was known as a hotbed of Tory sympathizers in those trying times. Remember Baker was an early town clerk and miller; Thomas Chittenden lived here during the Revolution; Ethan Allen once resided here, and here his first wife and two children are buried. It is believed locally that these Green Mountain Boys were attracted to Tory Hollow, as Arlington was then called, by the very predominance of Loyalist and Church of England feeling, in order to keep an eye on the goings on. Nevertheless, the pattern of early social life in the community was shaped by Tory Anglicanism, and it was to enjoy the more gracious amenities permitted by their faith that the first families had deserted the puritanical rigors of Connecticut. Nowhere else in eighteenth-century Vermont were there Maypoles and Christmas trees. In 1777, the town clerk, a Tory named Isaac Bisco, is said to have destroyed the town records and fled to Canada, thus depriving historians of much important lore. Afterwards Bisco claimed that he had buried the records in a kettle, but they were never found. The landscape depicted on the Vermont State Seal can be seen by looking west from the *Site of the Chittenden House* (*Depot St. near R.R. Station*). The legend is that a British officer visiting Chittenden was so impressed by the western vista from his room that he engraved it on a horn drinking-cup, and his engraving, with minor changes, was later adopted for the State seal.

*St. James Church and Cemetery* (R) (1830), a somber stone building with crenellated tower, is evidence of the survival of Arlington's Episcopalianism. Its walled graveyard is one of the oldest and most interesting in the State, containing many queer old headstones with curious inscriptions. Mary Brownson, Ethan Allen's first wife, is buried here. Church and cemetery set a note of quiet reverence for the thick-shaded village street.

*Martha Canfield Library* (L) (*open weekdays from 3 to 5 and 7 to 9*) is an old structure of red brick, originally the home of the Canfield family, who were among the first settlers in Arlington. Some 4000 volumes are available here in this, one of the State's oldest libraries. Dorothy Canfield Fisher, novelist and critic, who lives in Arlington, is a descendant of the pioneer Canfield family. Rockwell Kent and Arthur Guiterman are among Arlington's summer visitors.

> 1. Right from Arlington on a country road along the shaded banks of the Batten Kill is WEST ARLINGTON (alt. 595), 3.6 *m*. Lumber yards (R), with orange mounds of sawdust and stacks of boards, introduce the straggling hamlet as a mill village, and there is little else to be remarked here.

> 2. Left from Arlington on an improved road is EAST ARLINGTON (alt. 740), 1 *m*., a sprawling rural suburb of Arlington proper, touched with a careless rusticity. The *Site of Remember Baker's Mill* (L) is that of the present Lawrence Mill. Baker built his mill, one of the earliest in the State, in 1764. *Green Mountain House*, formerly an old tavern, is now occupied by a feed store. The *Hard House*, one of the older houses in town, is supposed to have been the home for some time of Shays, the leader of Shays' Rebellion, after he fled from Massachusetts.

At 45.5 *m*. is a junction with a dirt road.

> Left on this road is *Lake Shaftsbury*, 0.3 *m*., a small pond lying in a shallow basin surrounded by ragged woodlands with a few cottages along the shore. It is a favorite spot for local outings.

Between Arlington and Shaftsbury the highway winds through a variety of woods in which pines and birches predominate. US 7 dips and twists over a beautiful broken terrain.

At 47 *m*. is a junction with a dirt road.

> Left on this road is SHAFTSBURY (alt. 883, pop. township 1630), 0.4 *m*., in the valley below the highway, a station on the Rutland R.R. Formerly on the main thoroughfare, this settlement has lost much of the activity that prevailed before the cement roadway passed it by. Shaftsbury was settled in 1763 by pioneers from Rhode Island. Some of the most determined patriot leaders in the struggle with New York over land titles lived here. There were only a few Tories, but John Munro, the most conspicuous Tory of them all, was a Shaftsbury man. It was Munro who led in the seizure of Remember Baker, only to have the Green Mountain Boys rescue Baker before the Tory party was able to get him across the Hudson. The first Baptist Church in Vermont was erected here in 1768.

> Left from Shaftsbury, on devious country roads, is the township of GLASTENBURY (pop. township 7), 3 *m*. One of Vermont's natural wonders, Glastenbury has the smallest population of all the towns in the State, its forty-odd square miles of mountain wilderness supporting but seven people. Until its disorganization in 1937, Glastenbury was allotted equal representation in the State Legislature with all the other towns, and its three voters biennially dispatched the head of the Mattison family to sit in the House of Representatives in Montpelier with the member from Burlington (pop. 24,780) and the member from Rutland (pop. 17,315). At one time a vigorous lumbering community, Glastenbury is now the clearest example of Vermont's basic problem: hill towns with declining population.

SHAFTSBURY CENTER (alt. 1480), 49.7 *m.*, locally known as Center Shaftsbury, is a scattered, undeveloped settlement strung along either side of the highway, characterized by open lots and tourist places. The chief landmark is the *Governor Galusha House* (R), a white Colonial structure notable for its beautiful entrance detail, the trinity window above the entrance, and the lunette windows in the gables. Lavius Fillmore, who built the Old Bennington and Middlebury Churches, is said to have constructed this house, and the clean true lines reveal the handiwork of a master architect. Jonas Galusha, who lived here, was a Revolutionary captain and nine times Governor of Vermont (1809-13; 1815-20).

Between Shaftsbury Center and South Shaftsbury, the descending ribbon of cement stretches between smooth-planed green fields.

The *Monroe-Hawkins House* (L), 50.2 *m.*, graces the north end of the village of South Shaftsbury, a perfect Georgian type of structure with an unusually beautiful entrance. Here again it is felt that the art of Lavius Fillmore, follower of Sir Christopher Wren, is apparent in the architectural details. The imposing white front has entrance pilasters and pediment with a trinity window over the doorway. On the interior are 24 spacious rooms, polished floors, soapstone-backed fireplaces, and a vaulted wine cellar. Here is found one of the earliest examples in Vermont of marble lintels above fireplaces. Constructionally the house approximates perfection for its period, about 1820.

SOUTH SHAFTSBURY (alt. 740), 51 *m.*, lies on a flat alongside the highway, lightly shaded by maples. Here is the home of the *Eagle Square Manufacturing Company* (R), the basic industry of the township, employing 100 in producing steel squares of a wide reputation. The *Old Stone Mill* (R), where the first steel square was made, has been renovated into a strikingly handsome residence. *Cole Hall* (L) was erected in 1834 as a Universalist Church.

The *Robert Frost Home* (R), 51.9 *m.*, is situated on the hill crest at the southern end of the village. Known as the 'half-stone house,' it was built in 1769, and was remodeled to serve as the home of Robert Frost, but the poet has since taken a more secluded home away from the main highway. The house, sturdy and compact in stone, is trimmed with red-painted wood.

Between South Shaftsbury and Bennington, US 7 winds on a down-grade between the dipping meadows and gently descending knolls, with the clean stone needle of *Bennington Monument* rising in sharp perspective against the southern skyline.

At 54.1 *m.* is the junction with State 67A.

Right on State 67A is the junction with an uphill road, 1.6 *m.*

Right this road enters the grounds of *Bennington College* and climbs to the broad level summit of Bingham Hill, where the long white wooden buildings with green blinds are set on smooth lawns. Straight walks and curved driveways mark the immaculate pattern, and the site is agreeably aloof and private. This girls' school, the youngest institution of higher learning in the State, was opened in 1932 after years of preliminary planning, and in less than half a decade has gained an admirable reputation. The aims of Bennington College are to encourage voluntary education throughout life; to stimulate permanent intellectual interests; to fit students for social life and responsibility; and to direct each student in the line of her individual talents, tastes, and needs. The girls are mainly from outside the State, and the increasing prestige of the young school attracts students from an ever-widening range.

Beyond this junction on State 67A is NORTH BENNINGTON (alt. 580, pop. 933), 3.4 *m.*, strung out along the shallow, curving valley and centered on a low slanting plateau above the factories that line the valley bottom. North Bennington is active industrially, mainly in woodworking and furniture-making. The *H. T. Cushman Manufacturing Company* products, widely known as 'Cushman Creations,' are Colonial furniture pieces, in some cases modified to meet the needs of modern comfort. The *Stone House* (*open* 9 *to* 5 *weekdays; Sundays, June–Sept., adm. free*) (L), at the southern edge of the village, is completely equipped with Cushman Colonial furniture, a handsome show-place to which visitors are cordially invited. The Cushman plant across the road is not open to inspection. The *McCullough Free Library* (*weekdays* 2 *to* 5, 7 *to* 9), at the village center, is a pale brick structure with a white-columned portico, erected in 1922 as a memorial to John G. McCullough, Governor of Vermont (1902–04). Its shelves hold 9500 volumes. North Bennington, besides being a virile industrial village, is the railroad station for Bennington.

Between this junction and Bennington, US 7 runs along the flats of the Walloomsac River.

BENNINGTON (alt. 672, pop. 7300) (*see BENNINGTON*), 56.1 *m.* Focal point in Vermont history; Bennington Battle Monument; Old First Church and Revolutionary Burial Yard; Bennington Museum; Jedediah Dewey House; Site of Catamount Tavern; Isaac Tichenor Mansion; Walloomsac Inn; David Robinson House; Old Academy Library; Statue of Seth Warner; Soldiers' Home; and other points of interest.

South of Bennington, US 7 climbs a long grade and then swings on through a pleasant valley.

At 57.9 *m.* is a junction with the Old Colonial Road.

Right on the *Old Colonial Road*, over which George Washington rode on August 30, 1790, on his way to confer with Governor Moses Robinson regarding Vermont's admittance to the Union, is the *Old Fenton Homestead* (L) 0 4 *m.*, a square, white, broad-clapboarded house standing stanchly alongside the historic roadway in a region of apple orchards and grand summer estates. Here, about 1790, the Fentons and Nortons, pioneer pottery makers of Bennington, turned out their beautiful pieces that today are seldom found except in the possession of museums or collectors.

Between this junction and Pownal Center, the concrete highway rises and dips through a broken pine-wooded country, the mountains flattening out into hills along the curving road.

POWNAL CENTER (alt. 986), 62.1 *m.*, is built on a knoll in the valley, with a shaded *Old Cemetery* (L) facing stores, garage, and gasoline pumps across the bare cement thoroughfare, an incongruous contrast. The old *Union Church* (L) was erected in 1789, but has been restored and renovated. The white, double-porched structure nearly opposite the church incorporates portions of the *First Tavern* in town.

Left from Pownal Center is *Lake Potter*, 2.1 *m.*, a small, pretty lake in a rich floral region, owned now by a boys' camp. This little pond was called Etchawog by the Indians, who used its water for medicinal purposes.

The *Old Bannister House* (R), 62.3 *m.*, is a landmark from Revolutionary days which plainly reveals ancient origin in its severe lines.

*Kreigger Rocks*, 63.6 *m.*, are seen (R) across the deep valley from the road swinging high over the eastern valley edge, an unusual rock formation rising in a perpendicular ledge and having the structural appearance of a large fortress wall. Geologists say that this was part of a natural dam that formed glacial Lake Bascom. Looking toward Kreigger Rocks from US 7, there is presented a valley-and-mountain vista of sharp grandeur, the valley floor far below stretching smoothly westward to the mountain flanks that rise beyond the ramparts of this great natural dam of a prehistoric era.

Between this point and Pownal, US 7 curves around a high steep embankment overlooking the broad deep valley of the Hoosic River. At sunset the beauty of this valley is intensified by the rare changing colors suffused over it from the western horizon. From here the route descends Mile Hill toward Pownal.

*Oak Grove Seminary* (R), 64.1 *m.*, sits well away from the descending highway, a queer, white, cupolaed structure resembling a rural schoolhouse. This little school was established in 1833, and two Presidents of the United States were, in their youth, instructors here: James A. Garfield and Chester A. Arthur.

POWNAL (alt. 594, pop. township 1425), 64.9 *m.*, spreads over the Hoosic Valley floor west of US 7, its wooden houses scattered on the plain, a white church spire lifting above the treetops, and the Boston & Maine R.R. running through the village. Pownal is supposed to have been settled as early as the 1720's by Dutch squatters who remained but a short while. Permanent settlement was made in 1766 by Rhode Island pioneers. Pownal, uniquely located in the corner of Vermont between New York and Massachusetts, is the scene of a Christopher Morley tale, 'Blythe Mountain,' which appeared first in his column and later in book form.

> Right from Pownal State 112 leads along the Hoosic Valley to NORTH POWNAL (alt. 602), 3.4 *m.*, a small village near the New York borderline. Born in this hamlet, the son of a peddler whose nine-cart caravan jolted over early New England, was Jubilee Jim Fisk, railroad magnate, Wall Street operator, and nationally known playboy. Fisk achieved ownership of the Erie R.R., staked his fortune against Jay Gould's for a corner on the gold market, bought an opera house in New York for his lady-of-the-moment to star in, and careened through a gaudy-colored career in the 80's and 90's with the sky the limit. A reckless gambler, free-spender and high-liver of the Diamond Jim Brady school, Fisk died as suddenly and violently as he had lived, shot to death by Ed Stokes in the elegance of the Broadway Central Hotel in New York, the victim of a love triangle.

Between Pownal and the Massachusetts border, the highway runs along the eastern side of the rich, mountain-guarded valley.

*Old Cemetery* (R), 65.7 *m.*, lies below the level of the road, lonely, neglected, and forgotten in aspect, rudely fenced in, its slabs leaning and tumbled in a tangle of grass.

At 66.8 *m.* (L) is an overhanging formation of lime and slate gravel known as the *Weeping Rocks*, from which there is a continual dripping of water, in even the driest summer. The legend is that an Indian tribe, secure for generations in a tradition that it would never be conquered 'until the rocks wept,' retreated to this spot before powerful enemies. Aghast at the apparent omen, they offered no resistance to their foes and were completely exterminated.

The *Vermont–Massachusetts Line*, 67.1 *m.*

The '*Line House*' (L) is now a private residence, bisected by the State boundary line. A former tavern, standing half in Vermont and half in Massachusetts, this faded brown-and-green wooden structure was once the scene of exciting liquor raids and other border controversies.

---

T O U R   4 A :   *From* WINDMILL POINT (*Lake Champlain*) *to* JUNCTION WITH US 7 (*near Burlington*), 39.5 *m.*, US 2.

---

Via Alburg, North Hero, Grand Isle, South Hero.

Rutland R.R. parallels this route.

The road varies from hard surface to dirt.

THIS 'Island Route,' a popular scenic gateway between Canada and Vermont, or northern New York and Vermont, traverses the unique and lovely island county of Grand Isle. From the broad fertile plains of the islands, vast sweeps of blue water stretch away toward the Green Mountains on the east and the Adirondacks on the west. The highway now skirts the lake shore with all the fresh beauty of a sea-coast drive, and again swerves inland to run through aisles of trees and between rich smooth farmlands and far-reaching orchards. The air blows in — cool, clean, delightfully refreshing — from Champlain waters. The route is as attractive in the spring with apple orchards in bloom, as it is in the fall with mowed brown fields piled with haystacks. There is a distinctive similarity throughout the islands, but one that never becomes monotonous. Branching from the main highway are endless side trips that wind along the irregular shores, revealing new wonders of island and water beauty at every turn, opening wide vistas across the glimmering blue of Lake Champlain to distant peaks sculptured in gray-blue against the changing sky. The widest heavens and broadest horizons of all Vermont are here on these flat low-lying islands in the northern part of Champlain, where the French established a settlement in the seventeenth century, where spreading elms and glittering Lombardy poplars alternate in shading the meadows, where flower-garnished village streets face the gentle waves, and mellow farmlands plane to the water's edge. In 1776 Benedict Arnold maneuvered his fleet about the islands in preparation for meeting the British naval forces in the Battle of Valcour Island, and in 1812 English gunboats sailed along these shores and anchored in the quiet coves.

WINDMILL POINT (Alburg Township), 0 *m.* At this Point on the large promontory of Alburg, US 2 enters Vermont across a new (1937) million-dollar bridge, replacing the Alburg–Rouses Point Ferry, which was the northernmost ferry on Lake Champlain. On September 3, 1776, prior to the battle of Valcour Island, Arnold anchored in the shelter of Windmill Bay, at which time the British occupied Isle-aux-Têtes, a few miles to the north. On September 6 a landing party was dispatched to Windmill Point, where it was attacked by Indians. The Americans fought their way back to the boat, but three were killed and six wounded in the savage skirmish. The survivors rowed furiously back to the ships, exchanging riflefire with the Indians as they went. A few cannonballs from the fleet sent the redmen scattering into the woods. From 1783 to 1796 the British kept a heavily armed gunboat stationed off the Point to control this extreme northern end of the lake.

East of the dock a dirt road leads inland between broad flat meadowlands graced with symmetrical elm trees and marred by strings of box-cars on a railroad siding.

ALBURG (alt. 123, pop. 633), 3.3 *m.*, is believed to be a name formed by the contraction of Allenburg, and it is thought that a tribe of Abnaki Indians originally occupied this territory. Now a railroad water-tank stands above the terminal yards of the Rutland R.R. at its junction with the Central Vermont, and tracks cross the Main St. at the depot. Alburg is the only town of any size on the islands. The village street is well shaded by elms, with flower-beds brightening the general dullness. Stone houses, characteristic of the islands, are seen here and there, and apple trees along the roadside hint of the extensive orchards that lie southward.

The *Stone House* (R), 4.3 *m.*, was built in 1823 and once served as a tavern known as Motte's Inn. It is representative of the century-old stone structures so prevalent throughout Grand Isle County, which are generally built of field stone with cornerstones of cut rock or granite, and differ from the slab stone buildings of southern Vermont.

At 5.5 *m.* is the junction with State 104.

Left on State 104 winding through a low swampy region beside a calm stream filled with water lilies and overhung with dense vegetation, the whole scene redolent with the mystery of Louisiana bayous, is a beautiful *House* (R), 1.2 *m.*, of gray and brown stone, shaded, secure, and trim. Beyond this house on State 104 is EAST ALBURG (alt. 116), 2.8 *m.*, its center forming a rustic circle of small wooden houses and a tiny depot around the circular plot with its old water-pump. The settlement spreads along the shores of Missisquoi Bay like a Maine seacoast village with vine-covered porches and slanting shingled roofs. A railroad bridge crosses from East Alburg to the mainland (Swanton), and the Alburg–Swanton Ferry here is being replaced (1937) by a highway bridge.

Left from the western edge of East Alburg on a country road is ALBURG

SPRINGS (alt. 130), 3 *m.*, once a popular resort, now lonely and abandoned except for a few residents living in its old wooden houses. The famous mineral spring, the waters of which have been sought for their curative qualities, has been locked up since the two resort hotels burned and all commercial enterprise died in the flames. Other factors which made this a favorite resort are an excellent sand beach, very good fishing, and a fine view across the narrow bay to the mainland, which lies against a background of Green Mountains.

ALBURG CENTER (alt. 140), 5.9 *m.*, the original settlement of the township, is a straggling hamlet with leafy boughs arching the highway, undistinguished except for a handsome *Stone House* (R), which once was used as a tavern. In early times a tannery was operated across the street from this house, where the farmers brought hides to be cured. After the process was finished a visiting cobbler went around to each home in the vicinity, outfitting every family with shoes handmade from the cured hides. Itinerant tailors also made the rounds in the spring after sheep-shearing time. Following the Embargo of 1808, smuggling was carried on in Alburg, as in other border towns of Vermont. In the wintertime contraband goods were sledded over the ice; one Alburg smuggler was plunged into the water and lost his load when the ice broke, but managed to save himself and the horses. His clothing froze so stiff that he was unable to walk or mount a horse, and of necessity threw himself down in his icy armor, clutched the whiffletree, and let his horses drag him to the settlement.

Between Alburg Center and Isle La Motte Station the varied beauty of the section is strikingly apparent, with views encompassing wooded islands lying on the blue water and a backdrop of Green Mountain contours etched against the skyline.

ISLE LA MOTTE STATION, 10.9 *m.*, sometimes known as South Alburg, is a small commercial settlement on the eastern shore, and also, as the name indicates, the railroad station for Isle La Motte. The collection of service stations and lunch-rooms here is somewhat relieved by rows of straight shiny-leafed Lombardy poplars with their close-lifted branches.

Right from Isle La Motte Station on a country road over a toll drawbridge (20¢ *one way;* 25¢ *round-trip*) is *Burying Ground Point* on charming little Isle La Motte. The *Memorial Tablet* (L) honors the Revolutionary soldiers buried here and outlines the history of this smallest and most beautiful of the islands. The island was named after Captain Sieur de La Motte of the famous Carignan Regiment, who built Fort Ste. Anne on the western shore in 1666.

Beyond Burying Ground Point is the village of ISLE LA MOTTE (alt. 210, pop. township 352), 5.5 *m.*, resting serenely in scenic beauty and historic tradition, clear-lined buildings of stone and brick standing along the gently sloping Main St., and apple orchards stretching to a woodland background. The people of Isle La Motte are mainly of English and Scottish descent, all very proud of their peaceful idyllic little island.

1. Right from Isle La Motte village on the Chazy Ferry road is *Chazy Ferry,* 1 *m.*, and right from this landing on a shoreline road is the *Shrine of St. Ann,* 2.1 *m.*, with a small chapel and statue (R) in a grove of pines, and the *Site of Fort Ste. Anne* (L), its outline marked by cedars and spaced rock-mounds at a commanding point on the lake shore facing across the water to New York. Here in the calm of shaded lakeside beauty, French soldiers under Capt. de La Motte built a fort in 1666 for protection against the Mohawks, and here in the essence of Champlain island love-

liness was the scene of Vermont's first, though impermanent, white settlement. The beauty of Ste. Anne is deepened by history — the pictures brought to mind of swashbuckling French gallants casting off uniform-coats to swing axes and ply spades; the solemn-faced Jesuits in their dark garb; and a garrison of 300 men celebrating mass on this wilderness isle in the chapel of Fort Ste. Anne, the first mass to be held in the State. Benedict Arnold, master military strategist on land and water, anchored his fleet off the western shore of Isle La Motte shortly before fighting the battle of Valcour Island in 1776. In 1814 Captain Pring landed his British vessel on this shore to protect a position abreast of Little Chazy where supplies were being unloaded; and from this anchorage off Isle La Motte the British fleet went to meet Macdonough in the battle of Plattsburg, September 11, 1814.

2. Straight from Isle La Motte village on a continuation of the Main St. is the *Isle La Motte Historical Building* (L), 1.5 *m.*, occupying a former schoolhouse of stone structure. Here is the junction with a country road. Left on this road is a *Coral Reef*, 1.9 *m.*, running through the pasture of the Gilbert Farm, plainly traceable for nearly a mile. This is said to be the oldest coral reef in the world, and indicates that the territory was once submerged in a sea. Many eminent geologists come here to study the coral formations that bulge through the surface of the pastureland, with a maximum relief of seven feet.

Straight beyond the Historical Building on a dirt road running southward through arches of trees, then bearing right to follow the western shore northward, is the *Marble Quarry*, 3.3 *m.*, unusually situated on the lake shore. Isle La Motte marble, including Champlain Black, French Gray, and Grand Isle Fleuri, has been extensively used in construction, both interior and exterior. Stone from the quarries on this tiny island has gone into the building of such structures as Rockefeller Center, Brooklyn Bridge, and Victoria Bridge.

Beyond the quarry is the home of the *Elizabeth Fisk Looms*, an outstanding Vermont handicraft project housed in a trim stone house overlooking the western shore (*see ST. ALBANS*). Here on the Fisk estate, linens are woven and dyed in original designs and unusual colors. Here also are the picturesque ruins of the *Fisk Mansion*, stone walls standing firmly, the interior gutted by fire.

East of Isle La Motte Station, at 11.1 *m.*, is the bridge connecting the large promontory of Alburg with the long narrow island of North Hero, which was originally called Isle Longue. The present name, with that of South Hero, was adopted to honor the Allens, Ethan and Ira.

Beyond the western shore of North Hero the highway swings inland between rows of trees, prosperous farms and smooth-sloped fields spreading to the water on either side. There are bright patches of flowers in every yard, and the lake-freshened air has a keen exhilarating tang. From the eastern shoreline US 2 overlooks a four-mile expanse of shining water, dotted with small wooded islands, stretching eastward against a distant curtain of Green Mountains.

At 14.3 *m.* the faraway Adirondacks raise their peaks to the western sky, and sunsets over this western vista are notably beautiful, staining sky and water with incredible changing colors.

The *Carrying Place*, 15.7 *m.*, where the island narrows to a mere strip of land, the graded highway alone separating the waters east and west, received its name from the activities of old-time smugglers, who were forever playing an exciting game of hide-and-seek with the revenue officers, in and around the countless coves and bays that indent the shores of Grand Isle. In order to baffle and elude their pursuers, some of the smugglers employed small boats that could be lifted from the water and carried speedily across this slender neck of land, leaving the officers cursing and raging on the other side, unable to portage their larger crafts. But the officers were not always unsuccessful in the chase; there were times when the smugglers ended up in irons, and days when outlaw blood reddened the Champlain water.

CITY BAY (L), 16.5 *m.* (*free swimming*), bordered by a long crescent beach of unusually fine sand and sheltered by a projecting hook of land on the northeast, is an excellent and popular swimming place.

NORTH HERO (alt. 120, pop. township 485), 16.8 *m.*, the shire town of Grand Isle County, faces Lake Champlain across a shoreline Main St., with the attractiveness of neat wooden houses enhanced by flowers and hedges, shadowed under tall elm trees. This village, sometimes rather incongruously called Island City, has a delightful location on the eastern shore, with slow waves washing almost at the base of its single street, and clean fresh breezes blowing in from the water. The sheltered bay is closed in by wooded points of land forming a natural harbor, and the *Catholic Church* (L) was originally a store standing near the old dock where the steamers landed. The *Courthouse* (R) was built in 1824 of Isle La Motte marble. North Hero was the home of the Rockwell family, which for a century furnished Lake Champlain steamers with captains.

*John Knight Inn* (R), 20.1 *m.*, stands on the home site of the first settler on North Hero Island. Enos Wood, accompanied by two other men, came in 1783 to stake a claim here at the southern end of the island, and later in the year came Mrs. Wood, the first white woman to step on this shore. John Knight subsequently acquired this land and his descendants still live here.

At 20.7 *m.* is the bridge linking the islands of North Hero and Grand Isle, with a magnificent view from the bridgeway that embraces all the manifold charms of island scenery. Between these two islands on the night of October 10, 1776, the British fleet anchored. The next morning it sailed southward along the shores of Grand Isle and South Hero, unaware that Arnold was lying in wait behind the high bulk of Valcour Island on the New York side. Arnold showed the enemy a few boats to draw them into pursuit, and the Battle of Valcour Island was on as the British tried to beat into the bay where the American fleet waited to greet them with the blasting roar of cannon (*see Tour 4B, PANTON*).

GRAND ISLE (alt. 160, pop. township 856), 23.6 *m.*, has somewhat more the summer-resort aspect than do the other island towns, and seems to wear a more modern polish. The road bends into the village past the usual gardens, lawns, and hedges that color every community on the islands and brighten the tidy wooden homes. Grand Isle is near the eastern shore with wide spreading plains under a vast dome of sky, the like of which are found in but one other section of Vermont, that of western Addison County (*see Tour 4B*). A man named Alexander Gordon was the first settler here, arriving in 1783 on the same day that Ebenezer Allen landed at the southern end of the island to claim priority on South Hero.

At 24.8 *m.* is the junction with a country road.

Right on this road after a scenic drive is the *Grand Isle–Plattsburg Ferry*, 2.1 *m.*, on the western shore where Quakers first settled. The view over sparkling Champlain water to the carved grandeur of the Adirondacks is an awe-inspiring one. Wall on wall the mountain barriers are massed high against the western skyline, shutting in the gleaming stretch of the inland sea that Champlain discovered for the Old World, but which long before that time knew the glide of birch canoes and the thrust of Indian paddles. A veritable network of beautiful drives covers the island, with its rich farmland and great apple orchards. Apple-blossom time is one of fragrant glory and delicate colors in this orchard region.

Between Grand Isle and South Hero villages, US 2 overlooks the gracious sweep of fields shaded by stately elms, and blue reaches of water broken by forested islands.

SOUTH HERO (alt. 140, pop. township 640), 29.8 *m.*, is spread on a more hilly and uneven terrain than are the northern villages, and consists of two sections, Keeler's Bay on the north, South Hero proper on the southeast. Over the northern part a high church spire rises from a red-brick *Catholic Church* (R), with a tall narrow façade. On the shores of the bay red-roofed cottages are seen among the trees, but in general the village inclines toward the dullness of scattered old wooden or brick houses. The *Old Stone Inn* (R), at the crossroads in the village center, was built in 1829 and known as the Island House, a favorite stopping place in early days for farmers en route to sell their produce in Montreal. Bunks were built around the walls of the lobby to accommodate the overflow. The rafters in the upstairs dance hall often resounded to music and laughter, as travelers reveled with the natives to break the monotony of slow journeys and rural isolation. Fossils found in the stone walls of this inn support the contention that the islands were once under water, for the stone was quarried locally.

Right from South Hero village on a country road is the *Site of the Ebenezer Allen Tavern* (R), 3.5 *m.*, now occupied by an ordinary farmhouse built over, or around, the remains of the old inn. It is thought that some portions of the inn are incorporated in the present structure. Ebenezer Allen, cousin of Ethan and the pioneer settler of South Hero, came in 1783, landing his raft at this southernmost tip of the island, which became known as *Allen's Point*. For many years Ebenezer Allen operated a ferry from the point which bears his name, and in 1787 he enlarged his original homestead to serve as a tavern, and entertained, among many travelers, Prince Edward of England, on his way from Montreal to Boston. On February 10, 1789, Ethan Allen came here from his Burlington farm after a load of hay. It is quite likely that in the course of a long conversation recounting exploits of the Green Mountain Boys, strife with the Yorkers, Revolutionary days, etc., a great many bottles of rum were opened and emptied after the custom of men of action the world over; and so it is not unlikely that Ethan, as legend tells us, was rather full when he started the tedious trip homeward late in the winter night. At any rate, it was Ethan Allen's last expedition. One version is that he was taken sick and died on the way home. Another, and usually discredited one, is that injuries received in falling from the hay-load led to the death of the fiery, arrogant chieftain of the Green Mountain Boys.

In all directions from South Hero village are branch roads that penetrate acres of apple orchards and fertile farmland, and reveal wide vistas of island scenery, Champlain water glimmering away into the distance, mountain peaks guarding the far horizons.

At 30.8 *m.* is the junction with a country road.

Left on this road is the *Phelps-Reade House,* 1.5 *m.* (*private*), built in 1819 by an Englishman named Hakings (or Hawkins), who built nearly all of the many stone houses in South Hero township. The house was built for Benejah Phelps, son of a pioneer settler, and has been remodeled, but retains interesting original features, including two chimneys, three fireplaces, a brick oven, and 24-pane windows with stone lintels. Stone quarried locally was used in building all the South Hero stone houses. Mrs. Reade, wife of the present owner, is a granddaughter of Commodore Thomas Macdonough, Champlain naval hero in the War of 1812.

*Sand Bar Bridge,* 33.1 *m.*, connecting South Hero with the mainland of Vermont, is a long causeway built up from the shallows of the lake, running between rock-guides and shade trees from the open stretches of Champlain to the low swamplands that usher US 2 in to the main shore.

*Sand Bar State Forest Park,* 34.4 *m.*, including camp grounds equipped with stone fireplaces and a State Bathing Beach with new stone bath house, extends to either side of the highway at the mainland end of Sand Bar Bridge. Excellently designed and landscaped, this development was made possible by Civilian Conservation Corps labor.

*State Game Refuge,* 35.6 *m.*, lies fenced in on either side of the road, an animal reservation centered at a farm where pheasants are bred.

On the mainland US 2 swings along the bank of the broad Lamoille River, flowing smooth and deep as it nears its mouth. The paved road wends over a rich rolling country, away from the lake and islands.

At 39.5 *m.* is the junction with US 7 (*see Tour 4, Sec. a*), 9.4 miles north of Burlington.

---

T O U R   4 B :   *From* VERGENNES *to* FAIR HAVEN, 42.6 *m.*, State 30A.

---

Via Addison, Bridport, Shoreham, Orwell.

The road is intermittently hard surface and dirt, with the dirt predominant. In spring the unimproved stretches are apt to be quite muddy, owing to their clay construction.

THIS route traverses the 'great plains' section of the State, the sweeping Champlain Valley meadows of western Addison County. Vast plains stretch flatly away toward the lake, with towering Adirondack peaks massed tier on tier against the western skyline. The smooth fields are lined out by fringes of tall trees, and narrow roads diverge from the main highways to run straight out over the lowlands. Here is the widest visibility found in the State, with farmsteads plainly seen for miles and miles across the fertile flats. On the basis of these features, so unusual to a mountainous State, Addison County might well be called the Arcadia of Vermont. Fine old Georgian houses stand in quiet distinction all along the route, and the prevalence of brick and stone in building adds a substantial beauty to the general scene  The extensive use of stump and rail fences is another characteristic of the region. Large apple orchards spread over the plains. At an earlier date this section was noted for sheep-raising, and a few flocks are still found pastured here and there. The villages are well planned, arranged in a spacious orderly manner. And always the broad slightly undulant plain stretches are dominated by the high blue barrier of Adirondacks on the western horizon.

This section also offers much in the way of historic lore and tradition, inevitable from its proximity to Lake Champlain, Ticonderoga, Mt. Independence, and Crown Point. Here the Green Mountain Boys gathered for their audacious attack on Ticonderoga; Benedict Arnold beached and burned five shot-torn vessels in the shallows of Buttonmould Bay, after Valcour Island; Ethan Allen once more eluded the 'Yorkers' by leaping from a Bridport window; Mt. Independence was garrisoned, lost, and recaptured; and the Crown Point Military Road neared its terminus.

VERGENNES, 0 *m*. (*see Tour* 4), is at the junction with US 7 (*see Tour* 4).

West of Vergennes State 30A climbs a long gradual slope.

At 0.5 *m*. is the junction with a country road.

At 1.5 *m*. on this road is a junction with another country road.

Left on this branch road is PANTON (Four Corners) (alt. 200, pop. township 306), 3.5 *m*., named after a British nobleman, Lord Panton. This low-lying sparsely settled town was burned by the English in 1777 when Burgoyne's forces swarmed triumphantly down the Champlain Valley, and the inhabitants who escaped capture fled southward, returning to start all over again after the Revolution.

Straight beyond Panton on a country road is *Arnold Bay*, 4.8 *m*  This tiny cove, in the larger Button Bay (originally Buttonmould Bay), owes its name to the final scene of a stirring and gallant chapter in Revolutionary history. Here it was that in October, 1776, Benedict Arnold ran his flagship 'Congress' and four smaller boats aground under the guns of the British fleet after the battle of Valcour Island. Arnold set fire to the ships and let them burn with colors flying  rather than yield them to the enemy. The rotted hulks and beams are still visible in low water; cannonballs and countless relics have been found here. *Valcour Island* is a high-hog-backed island off the New York shore across the lake from South Hero. An overpowering British fleet was ready to sail southward against Ticonderoga and Mt. Independence when Arnold put his fleet in anchorage on the New York side of Valcour to hide and surprise the enemy. When the British fleet hove into sight, Arnold left the main strength of his fleet in the bay, and swung four boats around before the enemy to lure them after him. Following Arnold back into the narrow-mouthed bay, the Britishers ran into the concerted fire of the American fleet, and the military genius of Benedict Arnold had completely outmaneuvered the English admiral, Carleton. The two fleets pounded away at each other until nightfall, with the Americans having the advantage. During the night Arnold pulled another coup, sailing his fleet out under cover of darkness and escaping southward. The British followed when daylight showed that their quarry had flown. Arnold, with the 'Congress' and a small flotilla of supporting vessels, fought a rear-guard action that allowed the main part of his fleet to reach Ticonderoga in safety, while the rear guard was being hammered to pieces by the overwhelming forces of the English. Hopelessly smashed and beaten, Arnold put to shore in Buttonmould Bay, carried his wounded to the land and fired the battered boats  While Valcour Island was technically a British victory, Arnold had accomplished his purpose, that of delaying the English advance another year  Before the British could recover and get another naval offensive under way, winter had set in and Lake Champlain was closed to navigation.  There is an excellent account of this battle in 'Rabble in Arms,' by Kenneth Roberts.

Beyond this junction on the right-hand road is BASIN HARBOR, 6 *m.*, a popular Lake Champlain summer resort with cottages and a hotel on the shore looking across the narrowed lake to the mighty Adirondacks of New York State.  Close by is the *Site of Old Fort Cassin*, named in honor of the young French lieutenant who led the defense of this fortress, blockading the British fleet's attempt to bottle up Macdonough's flotilla in the waters of Otter Creek.  On April 14, 1814, the English attacked Fort Cassin in hopes of gaining entrance to Otter Creek in order to sail upstream and destroy Macdonough's fleet under construction at Vergennes. The British were repulsed after a half-hour encounter, and Macdonough was saved to go on to subsequent Champlain victories.

Southwest of Vergennes, State 30A climbs past an ancient and long unused *Brick Schoolhouse* (L), 0.7 *m.*, and an attractive *Cemetery* (R), 0.8 *m.*

At 1 *m.* is the hill crest overlooking the long sweep of plains running to Lake Champlain, straight-lined trees marking off the fields, and in the background the Adirondacks thrust massively skyward.  Sunsets here are remarkably fine, as the sinking sun paints the mountain-and-plain pattern in changing hues of blue, ocher, and lavender under a flame-lit sky.

The 1827 *Brick House* (R), 1.9 *m.*, is a sturdy symbol in red brick of the many brick-built homes throughout the section.

*Old Cemetery* (R), 2.1 *m.*, fenced in white wood, contains ancient tombstones with curious inscriptions and verses.

At 2.3 *m.* a typical *Stump Fence* (L) is seen, gnarled and grotesque in appearance, made from the tree-stumps blasted out in clearing the land.

At 2.9 *m.* a straight narrow clay road branches (R) to run tree-lined and unswerving across the far-reaching lowlands toward distant farms clearly visible over the open terrain.  Extensive apple orchards reveal another phase of the Addison scene, and the old farmhouses along the roadside, white, wide-clapboarded and dignified, blend nicely with the prosperous aspect of the countryside.

ADDISON (Four Corners) (alt. 280, pop. township 684), 6.3 *m.*, is a little plains settlement built at the crossroads around a fenced green (R), which fronts the *Baptist Church* (1816), a simple white structure, and the *Grandview Grange*.  In the background are sweeping meadows, Champlain, and the serrated wall of the Adirondacks.  An incongruous note is struck here in this quiet crossroads village — a machine-gun is mounted on the *World War Memorial* in the peaceful green.

Here is the junction with State 17 (*see Tour 3C*).

South of Addison the hard-surfaced road gives place to gravel.  An orchard estate (R) with long straight rows of apple trees spread over level acres, and the twisted gray tentacles of stump fences are seen along the highway. *Snake Mountain* (L), whose elevation of 1271 feet is distinctive in this region, dominates the scene for miles, its long ridge curling against the eastern horizon. A handsome gray stone house at 7.1 *m.* (R) is typical of the many stone and brick structures throughout the section.

The *Bigelow House* (R), 10.1 *m.*, is a good example of the region's well-made brick homesteads, large and trim-lined in faded red brick, with the habitual end chimneys of its period, early nineteenth century.

*Stone House* (R), 10.7 *m.*, upholds the tradition of the section for combining practicality with beauty in building. These stone houses are testimonials of the thrift, labor, and craft of past generations.

At 12.8 *m.* is a distinctive *Brick Home* (L), its clear-lined simplicity marred by the addition of a wooden porch, illustrating the damage done to Georgian structures by later residents with a penchant for addition.

At 13.4 *m.* a small crossroads settlement at the edge of Bridport is distinguished by two more Georgian brick houses (R).

BRIDPORT (alt. 321, pop. township 703), 14 *m.*, lies on the plain surrounded by sweeping meadows and pastures, where merino sheep and Morgan horses were formerly raised extensively. The noted ram, 'Bismarck,' and the celebrated Morgan sire, 'Black Hawk,' were products of Bridport farms. Sheep are still raised in the vicinity, but on a lesser scale. This agricultural community spreads about a large open common (R), the surrounding homes well spaced. A pleasing brick house and a venerable old wooden homestead (L), are landmarks on the village street. The *Congregational Church* (R) was erected in 1852, a brick structure with a portico of white wooden columns and Corinthian capitals, topped by a wooden spire. The *Old Cemetery* beside the church is guarded by an iron picket fence and holds headstones dated as early as the 1780's. The view from this graveyard sweeps over the meadowlands to distant mountains. Bridport was settled in 1768 by 21-year old Philip Stone from Groton, Massachusetts. The Smiths, second family to arrive, came by ox-wagon and batteau from New Jersey. The settlement was disrupted by the strife with 'York State' and the Revolutionary War, but the pioneers returned after hostilities ceased. It was in 1772 that Ethan Allen and Eli Roberts visited Bridport and nearly fell captives to the Yorkers. New York State had placed a bounty on the head of 'Outlaw' Allen and his associates, and six British soldiers arrived in Bridport to capture the fiery Green Mountain Boy. Warned by their hostess, Mrs. Richards, Allen and Roberts escaped by leaping through an open window, and the six soldiers returned to Crown Point empty-handed, cursing stronger than ever the name of Allen and all his unruly band.

South of Bridport, pasturelands and meadows glide away from State 30A in long gentle waves, and occasional flocks of sheep whiten the green plain.

At 14.4 *m.* is a *House* (L), all porches and railings, reminiscent of Swiss chalets and looking out of place on this flat landscape.

At 16.7 *m.* the country becomes more wooded and broken, the terrain breaking up into woodland knobs and low hills.

*Crown Point Military Road Marker* (L), 17.4 *m.*, indicates the point where Amherst's old military road from Charlestown, New Hampshire, to Crown Point, New York, crossed the present highway. This was a highly important thoroughfare for pioneer settlers as well as soldiers, starting from that famous outpost at Charlestown, Number Four, and connecting the Connecticut River and Lake Champlain waterways.

SHOREHAM (alt. 396, pop. township 949), 20.7 *m.*, lies mainly west of the highway around a large sloping open common, on the high western edge of which stand two trim brick buildings: the *Congregational Church* (1846) and a *Masonic Temple* (1852), the latter having been built and used for many years as a Universalist Church. This village reveals the careful and spacious planning evident in its fellows of the region, which may be traced to the availability of large level tracts of land, seldom found anywhere else in Vermont. The *St. Genevieve Catholic Church* (left of State 30A at the junction of roads) was built in 1873 and stands in the clear-lined eminence of white-painted wood, facing west toward the main part of the village and the broad open green. A *War Memorial* is found in a little plot near the hotel (R).

The town was founded by Ephraim Doolittle, a captain under Amherst in the French and Indian War, 1755, and present at Amherst's capture of Ticonderoga and Crown Point, 1759. While engaged in opening the Crown Point Military Road Colonel Doolittle became impressed with the beauty and fertility of the Shoreham section, and in 1766 headed a party of some 14 men in settling the town. Nearly all the early comers were veteran fighting men from the French War. Doolittle and his followers established settlement on a 'share the profits' basis, undoubtedly one of the first co-operative ventures in America.

Right from Shoreham on a country road over rolling land and past apple orchards is the *Hands Cove Monument* (R), 4 *m.*, commemorating the pretentious daring of the Green Mountain Boys in crossing the lake to seize Fort Ticonderoga from the unwary British garrison. Northwest from this marker is *Hands Cove*, where on May 10, 1775, Ethan Allen and his lieutenants gathered their motley little back-woods army in readiness to strike at the stronghold on the York State side of Champlain. Here it was that Benedict Arnold arrived, handsomely uniformed and fully commissioned to head the attack, and here the proud Arnold and the dynamic Allen disputed as to who should take command, finally compromising to share the honor. The fact that they took Ticonderoga with such ridiculous ease does not detract from the willful courage and high purpose that motivated them. The prodigiousness of their feat is amply realized on viewing the beautiful restoration of Fort Ticonderoga, seemingly impregnable on its commanding site over the lake.

At 5.5 *m.* on this country road curving lakeward through a region of apple orchards is LARRABEE'S POINT on Lake Champlain. The *First Store* in Shoreham Township (R), stands near the water's edge, a strong solid structure of stone built in 1823 by John Larrabee and Samuel Holley, of stone carried across the lake from Fort Ticonderoga. The building was used as a store and warehouse, and resembles more the latter. A brief line of cottages along the shaded shore forms a little lakeside group. A beautiful quality of black marble is found near the Point.

Across the lake by ferry is *Fort Ticonderoga* (*ferry fare, $1 per auto one way, $1.25 round trip. The fort is open to the public, May 1 to October 31, 7 to 6, admission 50¢*), 1 *m.* Ticonderoga stands on a bold promontory commanding Lake Champlain, both north and south, as well as the outlet of Lake George. Recognized from earliest history as the key position, the gateway of Champlain Valley, Ticonderoga has served as military theater for the forces of France, Great Britain, and the United States, being captured, held, and lost by one after another, once without a shot being fired, again after furious fighting which cost over 2000 lives.

A splendid job has been done in restoring the fort, which was originally constructed with the characteristic thoroughness and finish of the French manner, incredibly elaborate for an eighteenth-century outpost in the wilderness. The grimness of gray cannon-guarded walls is relieved by the red-roofed barracks surrounding the central Place d'Armes. Properly garrisoned, the outer-works well manned, Ticonderoga was practically impregnable, as was indicated in 1758 when 3500 Frenchmen under Montcalm shattered and repulsed with heavy losses 15,000 attacking Britishers, who never even carried the outer lines of French defense. Each time the fort was taken, it was taken from a small and unprepared garrison, or else abandoned without a fight.

On May 10, 1775, Allen and Arnold landed in the early-morning darkness with 83 Green Mountain Boys, clubbed down a surprised sentry on their unopposed entry to the fort, routed out the sleeping British Commander LaPlace and informed him that Ticonderoga was taken. This easily won victory was significant in that it offered moral courage to the Colonies and exemplified the audacity of the raw Green Mountain Boys.

The restored South Barracks contains an excellent Museum collection, displaying uniforms, firearms, armor, powderhorns, celebrated paintings, etchings, drawings, valuable documents, and books. The West Barracks, restored as an Armory, holds hundreds of firearms and weapons of all description. Many war relics have been unearthed here, identified, classified, and labeled for display.

South of Shoreham a variety of old fences is seen — the stone wall, stump, rail, board, and wire. At 24.8 m. is a bad railroad crossing, although trains are infrequent (Addison Branch of the Rutland R.R.).

BEEMAN'S CORNERS, 26.9 m., marks the western extremity of Orwell village, a sort of tourist-servicing outpost of Orwell on the main highway.

1. Left from here on an improved road is ORWELL (alt. 385, pop. township 835), 0.2 m., well laid out, with an eye toward spacious planning, along the gentle slope of a plain rising to the east, the easternmost houses in the shadow of the woods at the crest. This orchard and dairy community centers with a pleasant airy quality about a large sloping green (L), with the white-and-green *Town Hall* (original Baptist Church, 1810) and the *Congregational Church* (1843), red brick with white wooden trim, overlooking the Common and Main St. The *Eagle Inn* (L), a large wooden-porched building with mansard roof, is a typical hostelry of the Civil War Period. *St. Paul's Catholic Church* (right on the hill) was erected 1860, of red brick with a crenellated white wood steeple. The first settler was an eccentric Scotchman named John Charter, who brought his family down from Montreal several years before the Revolution. Long before any settlement was made, armed men ranged this region concerned with Mt. Independence and Ticonderoga, keystones of the gateway to Champlain.

2. Right from Beeman's Corners on an unimproved road winding through rolling tree-fringed plains toward the lake and the Adirondack barrier, is an old square white *Mansion* with four chimneys (L). 1 m., and beyond on the lakeshore is MONTCALM LANDING, 6 m., a small lakeside community in the shadow of *Mt. Independence* (R). From this peaceful little cove is the best view of Fort Ticonderoga obtainable from the Vermont shore. Almost directly north from the Landing, the fort crowns its projecting promontory, gray-battlemented and red-roofed, commanding the lake. Mt. Independence, a wooded bluff over the Vermont shoreline, was early linked with Ticonderoga when that fortress placed a battery on the hill to perfect dominance of Champlain. The Americans built a fort on Independence, and after Allen took Ticonderoga, the two strongholds were connected by a floating bridge constructed across the narrow lake, 1775.

When the Americans evacuated Ticonderoga at two A.M., July 6, 1777, the side of Mt. Independence was illuminated by a blazing house, foolishly fired, which disclosed to Burgoyne the flight of the Americans, and led to his prompt pursuit and victory over the Colonials at Hubbardton (*see Tour* 4C). On October 17, 1777, Mt. Independence was retaken by the American troops. Many soldiers, killed by 'camp fever' in 1776, were buried on Mt. Independence. The picture from Montcalm Landing is one of scenic charm and historic significance.

South of Beeman's Corner the country gradually becomes more rolling, broken and wooded.

*Wilcox House* (L), 28.3 *m.*, is unusually grandiose for rural Vermont, with massive fluted columns extending two stories high on three sides of the central structure and on the wings. This excellent example of the Greek Revival closely resembles the Ransom House in Castleton (*see Tour* 6).

The *Stone House* (L), 29.1 *m.*, forms a typical clear-cut pattern of gray and brown field stone on the landscape, exemplifying the combination of practical building and a sense of beauty.

*Mt. Independence–Hubbardton Military Road Marker* (R), 29.8 *m.*, marks the course over which the American troops fled after yielding Ticonderoga to Burgoyne, ultimately making a stand at Hubbardton only to be blasted to pieces by the British Regulars.

At 33.2 *m.* is a junction with an unimproved hill road, the north entrance to Benson.

Right on this tree-lined dirt road over the hill is BENSON (alt. 420, pop. township 636), 0.8 *m.*, a side-hill village with wooden houses strung along the slope, distinguished by a few antiquated homes. The *Ark* (L), a private tan-colored house, has a square-pillared porch and turret-like roof. From the hill crest at the upper end of the village, an eastern valley panorama unfolds. Walter Durfee was the first-comer to Benson, before the Revolution. Driven away by Burgoyne's invasion in 1777, he returned in 1782 to establish permanent settlement. Benoni Gleason, another early settler, served at Yorktown and saw the surrender of Cornwallis. In Benson was born Rufus Wilmot Griswold (1815–57), one of the most influential, if not always most discriminating, of 19th-century American editors, critics, and anthologists. After editing the *Vergennes Vermonter*, 1838–39, he succeeded Edgar Allan Poe as editor of *Graham's Magazine* in 1842. He was Poe's literary executor, and his obituary notice and biographical sketch of the poet were frank almost to the point of moral denunciation, extenuating none of the weaknesses that had accompanied and corroded Poe's genius. Griswold's anthologies were an important factor in moulding mid-nineteenth-century American taste in verse. Much of his prose was of a polemical nature, and his retaliatory critique of Duyckinck's 'Cyclopaedia of American Literature' is still considered the most destructive book review ever written by an American.

At 34 *m.* is the south, and main, entrance to Benson (R).

South of Benson on State 30A, *Rattlesnake Ridge* (L) parallels the highway, so called because of the many rattlers found along the upper reaches of this bumpily notched and forested ridge.

At 36.5 *m.* the country broadens and opens again to the westward sweep of plains, with Rattlesnake Ridge still running (L) beside the road.

At 39 *m.* is the junction with an unimproved road.

Right on this country road is WEST HAVEN (alt. 380, pop. township 280), 3.5 *m.*, a little hamlet built around the *First Baptist Church* (1831), in a hilly region where the sparse population subsists on dairying and lumbering.

At 39.7 *m.* a little *Waterfall* (L) drops down the wooded hillside in a pattern of white-laced foam and spray.

At 40.1 *m.* a large *Orchard* (R) of young planted apple trees spreads from the roadside, and beyond (R) the low rich meadows offer fine pastureland for fall grazing. The transition from Addison to Rutland Counties is the sharp change from level plains to a broken, ridged, and forested terrain.

At 41.4 *m.* (L), distinctive mountain profiles loom on the eastern horizon, sharp-thrusting Green and Taconic Mountain heads carved against the skyline, featuring the angular outline of *Bird Mt.* (alt. 2210).

FAIR HAVEN, 42.6 *m.* (*see Tour* 6). Here is the junction with US 4 (*see Tour* 6).

---

TOUR 4C: *From* MIDDLEBURY *to* MANCHESTER CENTER, 70 *m.*, State 30.

---

Via Cornwall, Whiting, Sudbury, Hubbardton, Bomoseen, Castleton, Poultney, Wells, Pawlet, Rupert, Dorset.

Between Castleton and Poultney the Delaware and Hudson R.R. parallels this route.

The road is dirt except for a few stretches of hard surface.

THIS north-and-south route runs along the western side of the State, roughly parallel to the main thoroughfare, US 7, and through a back-country section merging the southern plains of Addison County and the hilly broken woodlands of Rutland County. The site of the only battle ever fought on Vermont soil is in the mountains of Hubbardton. Among the scenic attractions are two large and beautiful lakes, Bomoseen and St. Catherine, as well as smaller bodies of water. The Poultney slate district is of interest, and the exclusive resort village of Dorset gives a clean distinction to the southern end of the route, which winds through the foothills of the Taconic Mountains.

MIDDLEBURY (alt. 366, pop. 2006) (*see MIDDLEBURY*). 0 *m.* Addison County Seat; Middlebury College; Meade Memorial Chapel; Egbert Starr Library; Congregational Church; Sheldon Art Museum; and other points of interest.

South of Middlebury, State 30 follows a surfaced road over broad, uneven plains characteristic of Addison County, with the bold outline of Green Mountains marking the eastern skyline. The plains give way at times to rolling, lightly wooded areas, and farmsteads are scattered along the way.

The *Homer Cobb House* (L), 3 *m.*, an elongated house containing 19 rooms, was built in 1816 for use as a medical college by Dr. Frederick Ford. But little altered, the large clapboarded structure has Christian doors, seven fireplaces, spacious rooms and halls. Dr. Ford once stirred up considerable controversy in the medical world by advocating, and using, a hydropathic system for the cure of fevers. The school was discontinued.

CORNWALL (alt. 370, pop. township 640), 4.2 *m.*, a rural community stretched on a gently rolling terrain, was once a breeding center for merino sheep and Morgan horses. The nucleus of the scattered village is at a small Green bearing the usual Civil War Memorial. The *Congregational Church* (R), with its adjacent graveyard, dates from 1803, and has the agreeable simplicity of early houses of worship. The *Sampson Memorial Library* (R), of red brick and white wooden trim, also houses the Mary Baker Allen Chapter of the D.A R. The settlement, started in 1774, was disrupted by the Revolution, to be resumed again 10 years later by 30 Connecticut families. A pioneer named Andrus was captured by Indians, who also took his mare and colt. Andrus was freed and came back to the settlement. A few years later, the lost mare and the colt, now full grown, returned home with another colt, and instead of losing two horses, Andrus found he had gained one.

Henry Norman Hudson (1814-86), the first American Shakesperean critic to win a high reputation abroad, was born in Cornwall. His 20-volume 'Harvard Shakespeare' (1880-81), now issued with emendations made possible by recent research as the 'New Hudson Shakespeare,' is still widely studied. That Hudson's keenly sympathetic studies of Shakespeare's characters were based on an understanding of his work not merely as great literature, but also as great acting plays, is evidenced by the fact that he was avowed the favorite critic by both Edwin Booth and Sir Henry Irving.

South of Cornwall the hard surface yields to dirt, as State 30 rolls on between rail-fenced fields of smooth-sloping contours. Orchards spread on the plain, and in the fall flocks of sheep graze in the meadows.

*Old Brick House* (R), 7.3 *m.*, high and roomy with end chimneys, has a kind of heavy dignity. At 8.3 *m.* the highway drops into a thick-wooded patch of low swampland, the southern fringe of the great Cedar Swamp, which stretches along the western edge of the Otter Creek Valley.

South of the swamp, mountain views range on either side of the open road, the Green Mountains piled on the east, the notched wall of the Adirondacks against the western horizon. Gnarled stump fences outline the wide fields, as in many sections of Addison County.

WHITING (alt. 391, pop. township 358), 11.3 *m.*, named for grantee John Whiting of Wrentham, Massachusetts, is a rural crossroads village on the plain of the Otter Creek. The *Free Public Library* (L) is a plain church-like building of wood. The *Congregational Church* (R), white-painted wood, has a pleasing clarity of line. The *Town Hall* (L) is a formidable brown structure of cement blocks with a slate roof. A Sheffield

Farms Creamery constitutes the lone industry of the community. According to historian Crockett, when Ethan Allen wished to inform his scattered Green Mountain Boys of the proposed attack on Ticonderoga, he dispatched blacksmith Gershom Beach of Whiting as messenger. In 24 hours long-legged Beach hiked 64 miles through the wilderness to spread the call that gathered the backwoods clan for its bold venture across Lake Champlain.

The *Old Farmhouse* (R), 11.8 *m.*, fronted by a white picket fence, stands square and trim above the highway, embodying the balance and restraint of Colonial building.

Between Whiting and Sudbury, the countryside becomes a bit more rolling and broken, with a stern, rugged barrier of mountains on the east, and smooth plains extending westward, their boundaries outlined by rows of trees.

SUDBURY (alt. 572, pop. township 361), 16.1 *m.*, is situated on the edge, or lip, of a small plateau overlooking the valley of the Lemon Fair River on the west. The river's name is said to have grown out of an Indian massacre that occurred on the banks of the stream; the settlers referred to it as 'the lamentable affair,' and through constant usage this was shortened to Lemon Fair. A variant is the legend which traces the name to 'leman fair,' the old English phrase for 'mistress fair.' The *Congregational Church* (L), with double entrance and an imitation Gothic tower of wood, is active only during the summer when Hyde Manor and Lake Hortonia draw vacationists to the section. The *Old Stone Schoolhouse* (R) was erected in 1829, with heavy mortared blocks of stone, a wide arched doorway, and a red slate roof. The early settlers prospered in dairying and sheep-raising.

*Hyde Manor* (L), 17.3 *m.*, a huge, rambling white structure of wood, five stories high, is surrounded by other buildings and screened by a tall cedar hedge, with ancient trees shading the lawns. A tavern even before 1801, it was taken over at that time by Pitt W. Hyde, and established as a stage-line hostelry. Remaining in the Hyde family through five generations, the Manor is now a summer hotel accommodating 200, and embracing an estate of 1200 acres.

South of Hyde Manor, State 30 climbs along a bluff over the eastern side of the valley and in the shelter of a wooded spur of Government Hill.

*Lake Hortonia*, 19 *m.*, lies (R) in a wild setting of low hills, with an irregular forested shoreline and little islands contriving to give it an undefiled charm. Green meadows and brown plowed fields are interspersed with wooded areas in the background of this pure, spring-fed lake.

South of Lake Hortonia, the road runs through the cool green fragrance of coniferous groves standing in somber density.

The *Twin Lakes*, 20.5 *m.*, are set in the peace of woodland frames, one on each side of the highway, with a calm beauty similar to that of Hortonia. Camps for boys and girls are on the shores.

Between the Twin Lakes and Hubbardton, the highway pitches down a
steep narrow ravine with a stream threading beside the road.

HUBBARDTON (alt. 480, pop. township 307), 22.8 *m.*, named for
grantee Thomas Hubbard, rests in a valley at the foot of the wooded hill,
close to the northern end of Lake Bomoseen. The tiny settlement is distinguished by its proximity to Bomoseen, and to the site of the Revolutionary battle of Hubbardton. At the time of the battle there were nine
families in the township.

> Left from Hubbardton on a dirt road climbing through choppy woodlands is a
> junction at 1 *m.* Left from this junction the narrow climbing road passes a few
> scattered farms in wild upland valleys and winds to the *Site of the Battle of Hub-
> bardton*, 6.1 *m.*, marked (R) by a fenced-in monument beside an old deserted house
> on the broad open summit. Here high in the hills on July 7, 1777, Colonel Seth
> Warner's rear guard, protecting the retreat of General St. Clair from Mount In-
> dependence, made a desperate stand against pursuing British forces under Fraser
> and Riedesel. Warner's ragged army of farmers was cooking and eating breakfast
> on the heights when the British attacked early in the morning, coming in formid-
> able scarlet waves through the gray mists of dawn. Shocked by surprise, dazzled
> and awed by the glitter of the enemy, the backwoodsmen left campfires and skillets
> and grabbed their muskets, deploying to fight Indian fashion in an attempt to
> check the heavy onrush. Hale's company, the first to be set upon, fled in a body to
> the forest, but Warner's Vermonters and Francis's company made a grim and
> stubborn stand, and Colonel Francis was killed fighting at the head of his men. For
> a time it looked as if Fraser's British regulars would be beaten back, but the arrival
> of Baron von Riedesel's German troops turned the tide against the Americans.
> The booming of the German band heralded their approach and killed the rising
> hopes of Warner's woodsmen. Scattered rifle-fire seemed to make no impression on
> the advancing ranks of red and blue, and finally, before blasting British volleys, the
> Colonials wilted and broke. Driven from the broad heights, the rear guard fled
> down the valley to Castleton, and then on to encamp at Manchester, where they
> rested in preparation for joining John Stark's New Hampshire militia at the battle
> of Bennington (*see BENNINGTON*). While Hubbardton was a British victory, it
> was a dearly bought one, and big stalwart Seth Warner had accomplished his pur-
> pose, inflicting such heavy losses on the enemy that further pursuit of St. Clair and
> the main body of the Colonial army was out of the question. The battle site com-
> mands a fine Green Mountain vista of wilderness stretches, and is proposed (1937)
> for preservation as a State Park.

South of Hubbardton, State 30 swings close along the eastern shore of
*Lake Bomoseen*, one of the largest lakes and most highly developed summer areas in Vermont, only a mile and a half wide with an irregular,
cedar-fringed length of nearly eight miles. Bomoseen occupies a rocky
basin surrounded by low, forested hills and blunted mountains, a fine
setting for its cool, clear waters, overlooked by many neat cottages,
hotels, and elaborate summer homes. The western shore is overhung by
cliffs where slate deposits are quarried. Pineclad Neshobe Island lies at
the center of the lake with an area of ten acres: here dwell those summer
Green Mountain Boys — Alexander Woollcott and Harpo Marx.

BOMOSEEN, 28.7 *m.*, is the nucleus of this resort region, with large
smart hotels along the lakeside, dominating the picture of summer houses,
stores, and a church. In season the scene is marked by the ease and gaiety
of resort life. South of the colony is a 9-hole golf course.

Between Lake Bomoseen and Castleton Corners, the route follows a straight course on a level surface, with grim pine groves shadowing the roadside. The sharply distinctive outline of *Bird Mountain* (alt. 2210) stands out on the eastern skyline, its profiled gap bearing a marked resemblance to the sentinel mountains of Lake Willoughby (*see Tour 1D*).

CASTLETON CORNERS, 32.2 *m.* (*see Tour 6*), is at the junction with US 4 (*see Tour 6*).

South of Castleton Corners, State 30 dips across the low, marshy floor of the valley made by the Castleton River, and then rises and falls over a rolling countryside.

The *Sherman House* (L), 35.3 *m.*, a faded 19th-century brick farmhouse of simple boxlike design, was built of bricks made on the farm. Olcott Sherman, the builder, assisted in the construction of the second State Capitol at Montpelier (1836), and in the erection of Bunker Hill Monument. His father, Jonathan Sherman, was the winner of the fist-fight that determined the name of Barre (*see BARRE*). The brick homesteads throughout this section were built from products of the Sherman brick-yard.

At 35.7 *m.* is a dangerous railroad underpass.

South of the underpass, some of the Poultney slate quarry dumps are seen (R), with derrick riggings and booms jutting up from tumbled gray heaps of the stone that underlies the soil of the section in great quantities.

POULTNEY (alt. 430, pop. 1570), 38.9 *m.*, lies on the level plain of the Poultney River near the New York borderline, a neat clean village in the heart of the district that produces unfading green, purple, and mottled slates. The streets are orderly and well planned; the unpretentious brick and wooden houses with slate roofs, and here and there traces of Colonial dignity, are well kept. In spite of the fact that the depression caused slate to be widely replaced by cheaper materials, thus undermining the industrial foundation of the town, Poultney has maintained a brave and attractive front. The population includes a large proportion of Welsh, who left their native slate quarries in Wales for this new quarrying field. Hooker and Son opened the first quarry in Poultney.

*Green Mountain Junior College* (co-educational), at the western end of Main St., was founded in 1836 by the Methodist Episcopal Church as Troy Conference Academy, became Ripley Female College for a time, and took its present name and status in 1931. The fine red-brick buildings with white trim are set back on an elm-shaded campus, and center around Ames Memorial Hall, with its rounded, white-pillared portico. The athletic field is behind the school. This is one of the oldest and most respected secondary schools in Vermont.

The town was settled in 1771 by Thomas Ashley and Ebenezer Allen: the latter subsequently moved north to Grand Isle (*see Tour 4A*). Both of these pioneers, with other Poultney settlers, were with Ethan Allen and Benedict Arnold at the capture of Ticonderoga. The origin of the name,

Poultney, is not definitely known, but it is thought to derive from Lord Poultney, a friend of Governor Benning Wentworth.

Left from Poultney on an improved road (an eastward extension of Main St.) is EAST POULTNEY (alt. 520), 0.7 *m.*, strung along the valley of the Poultney River and centered at a triangular Green in the midst of austere old houses. On the Green (R) is the *Old Baptist Church* (1802-05), with three entrances, Palladian windows, and a large square clock-tower, in white-painted wood (restored by Poultney Historical Society). The *Eagle Tavern* (*private*), an old stage-coach inn (about 1790), is a handsome wide-clapboarded structure, painted pale yellow with tall two-story columns of white, and a deep porch. Reminiscent of southern Colonial buildings, it has marked distinction. Horace Greeley boarded here for two years. The tavern was the scene of many gay dinners and balls in post-Revolutionary times, and on one occasion Captain William Watson raised his glass in this toast: 'The enemies of our country! May they have cobweb breeches, a porcupine saddle, a hard-trotting horse, and an eternal journey.' Other houses of Colonial purity in line harmonize with the scene here at the Green triangle where the settlement of Poultney was begun. Heber Allen, brother of Ethan and Ira, was an early settler, and is buried in the *Old Cemetery* here.

Horace Greeley spent four years in East Poultney (1826-30), and learned the printing trade as a typesetter in the tiny office of the Poultney *Gazette*. Working in the same office with Greeley was another young lad, George Jones, who was later one of the founders of the New York *Times* (1851), ten years after Greeley had founded the New York *Tribune*. The house in which Greeley lived stands on the east side of the triangle, a plain white structure. At the age of 14, Greeley made his first political speech in the old Poultney schoolhouse.

At the southern edge of Poultney, a narrow covered bridge leads across the Poultney River. South of the river the landscape is molded roughly into hills, and the Taconic Range looms on the southeast like stunted Green Mountains with abrupt staggered domes. Many houses in this region (between Poultney and Dorset) wear red paint, and all of them, however mean and shabby, have handsome slate roofs.

At 42.9 *m.* (R), the *Slate Quarries* of South Poultney are seen on the ledges above the western shore of St. Catherine, like ruined forts overlooking the placid waters.

*Lake St. Catherine* (alt. 477), 43.5 *m.* The highway runs close above the eastern shoreline for some distance. The long lake, its broken shorelines clothed with cedars, pines, and birches, stretches between low, flattened hills. Many cottages and camps line the shaded shores, and gray masses of slate guard the western cliffs. The ledges of *St. Catherine Mountain* (alt. 1227) press in on highway and lake from the east, inducing a wild touch to the beauty of water and woodlands.

At 44.2 *m.*, the road swings climbing away from the lake toward the rocky bluff of *Pond Mountain* (alt. 1518), and a backdrop of roughly notched Taconics. *Little Pond*, the southern extremity of St. Catherine, lies (R) below the highway in a shallow setting.

WELLS (alt. 502, pop. township 515), 47.5 *m.*, is on the level plain of Wells Brook, sheltered by the rocky Taconics on the east. Three tiny churches about a triangle mark the north end of the village. The *Lochlea Little Theater*, founded 1932, is an attractive rustic building with an auditorium seating 250, and a well-equipped stage on which plays are presented by the Wells Little Theater Society. The Theater also serves as a community social center. The village proper straggles along diverging tree-lined streets on the flats south of Little Pond. Settled in 1768, Wells has had an uneventful history.

South of Wells, butte-like slate piles are seen ahead, resembling a miniature range of jagged mountains, or a stage set for a western scene.

NORTH PAWLET (alt. 602), 49.5 m. consists of a handful of wooden houses and a schoolhouse at a highway junction on the plain, hemmed in by stubborn Taconic hills.

South of North Pawlet, State 30 picks up the wandering course of the Mettawee River, and follows it between the slaty spurs of low rugged mountains.

At 51.2 m. (L), the rounded bulging head of *Haystack Mountain* (alt. 1919) achieves the true haystack form so many of the Taconics aspire to. The *Old Brick House* (R), *at* 53.3 m., has been marred by the addition of a porch. The valley along here is terraced by the meandering of the Mettawee River.

PAWLET (alt. 680, pop. township 1476), 55.1 m., is crowded into the narrow valley of Flower Brook near its union with the Mettawee. Mills, houses, and stores cluster indiscriminately around the tiny fenced-in Green with its cannon and Revolutionary Memorial, to form one of the most picturesque and completely rustic village centers in Vermont: a crossroads settlement straight from the movie lots. The tilted terrain of the hamlet is closely confined on three sides by hills. It is not easy to realize that sleepy little Pawlet was once a thriving mill town, and in 1830 rivaled the industrial activity of Rutland. Remember Baker, prominent pioneer and Green Mountain Boy, had a gristmill here in 1768. Herrick's Rangers were organized here in 1777, and became known as the 'Terror of the Tories.' After the Revolution many soldiers made their home in Pawlet.

An early settler, Jonas Fay, came from Bennington, where he served as clerk for the Council of Safety, in which the powers of the State were vested until it was possible to have a general election. Born here were Joshua C. Stoddard, originator (1855) of the steam calliope and the horse-drawn rake; and Dr. Lemuel Chipman, first president of the State Medical Society (1796.)

In West Pawlet, situated on the New York border, sea-green slate is quarried.

South of Pawlet, the route is along the floor of a broader valley beside the curving Mettawee. At 57.1 m. (R), a ramshackle wooden *Ice-House* is incongruously roofed with slate.

The *Leach House* (about 1785) (R), 57.6 m., just north of the Pawlet–Rupert town line, is a distinguished white farmhouse with a hipped roof. Clear-cut and square, the severity of line is relieved by the refinement of fanlight, triglyphs, and metopes.

South of the Leach House, the wide serene valley route continues in a southeasterly direction, with rock-ridged foothills elbowing the smooth floor of the bottomlands.

At 61.2 *m.*, is an attractive modern *Barn*, painted green, with silver ventilators and a silver-capped silo. Its prosperous appearance indicates the fertility of the valley.

EAST RUPERT (alt. 840), 61.6 *m.*, is a collection of wooden dwellings at a bend in the highway. Near here, in 1785, Reuben Harmon acquired the sole right of minting copper coins for the independent State of Vermont, and maintained the right for a decade. The face of his first coin depicted a sun rising over the hills, a plow in the foreground, and the legend *Vermontensium Res Publica, 1786;* the reverse was a radiated eye surrounded by 13 stars. These coins are now prized by collectors.

> Right from East Rupert a country road climbs over the mountain to RUPERT (alt. 814, pop. township 691), 6 *m.*, a placid little village on the White Creek, that retains the atmosphere of the past. Many of the scattered wooden houses are more than 100 years old, and the simple *Congregational Church* is more than a century and a half in age. The patent asthma remedy made here is sent to many parts of the world. Abandoned by the first settlers during the Revolution, Rupert became a Tory hang-out for two or three years.
>
> Left from Rupert is WEST RUPERT (alt. 760), 2 *m.*, another small community near the New York boundary, where wood novelties are produced.

Between East Rupert and Dorset, State 30 swings along a shelf overlooking (R) the pastoral calm of the flat valley floor.

DORSET (alt. 940, pop. township 1119), 63.7 *m.*, a center of art and literature, is perhaps the most distinctive of the southwestern Vermont cultural resorts, which include Manchester and Bennington. The terraced valley, serene in its enclosure of forested marble mountains, is an ideal setting for such a colony, and writers and artists have established winter, as well as summer, homes here. Clean white houses with green blinds sit on landscaped grounds under the shade of elm trees; the purity of white limned against a green background makes a striking picture. Dorset has an elegance that is not pretentious, a charm that is simple and fastidious. Descendants of early settlers share this with intellectuals from the outside world, and the pattern is harmonious.

The *Dorset Inn* (R) is at the center of the village, a gracious hostelry in white wood with a high, square-pillared porch, the interior furnished with old furniture. The *Dorset Memorial Library* (R), housed in a remodeled tavern built (about 1790) by John Gray, is a square trim structure. Captain Gray opened a marble quarry in Danby Notch after the Revolution, but gave up the venture when a landslide buried his quarry. He then came down from the hills to build the first Dorset tavern. Of five early inns here, the *Cephas Kent Tavern* (1773) was the most important historically. Its foundation stones and timbers are now incorporated in a summer residence. In 1776, the first convention of the New Hampshire Grants was held in Kent's taproom, where the Green Mountain Boys and Patriots first proclaimed the independence of the State. Among the names signed to their declaration of rights were: Thomas Chittenden, Ira Allen, Matthew Lyon, and Seth Warner. Cephas Kent, who became first representative and first treasurer of Dorset, sent four sons to the Revolution. The tiny rustic *Post Office* (R) upholds the white motif that is so pronounced here.

The *Congregational Church*, dedicated in 1911, stands on a side street west of State 30, in the clear beauty of native marble, with a square tower and stained-glass memorial windows. West of the church is *Cheney Woods*, a dense area of natural woodland preserved as a memorial to musician and author Cheney. At the edge of the woods is the *Dorset Playhouse*, built in rustic style of weather-beaten boards taken from old barns, on a framework of hand-hewn beams. The auditorium seats 225, and has a large, well-equipped stage. During the summer the Dorset Players put on new three-act plays every two weeks; the organization also sponsors the Vermont Little Theater Contest, an annual three-day event. The *Southern Vermont Artists* (*see Tour* 4, *MANCHESTER*) originated in Dorset, under the impetus of such painters as Herbert Meyer, Edwin B. Child, John Lillie, and Frank Dixon. Meyer's wife and daughter are artists in their own right. The daughter married Reginald Marsh, young painter of national prominence.

The Dorset Field Club maintains a 9-hole golf course, clubhouse, and tennis courts. Golf was played on pasturelands here as early as 1893, when cattle furnished many moving hazards, necessitating an intricate system of ground rules.

> Left from Dorset a good country road leads through a narrow, steep-walled mountain pass to DORSET HOLLOW, 3 *m.*, a scattered settlement of summer homes and upland farms, buried deep in the calm, verdant beauty of the mountain-sides, remote and tranquil.

South of Dorset the road follows the rich level valley.

The *Quarry Swimming Pool* (R), 65 *m.*, marks the site of the first commercial marble quarry in America, opened in 1758 by Isaac Underhill. In the primitive stage of the industry, when family burying grounds were common, stonecutters often started out in the spring with a wagonload of marble slabs, which they peddled from home to home, stopping off to do the required lettering for their customers. Later, Dorset marble went into the construction of many public buildings around the country. The quarry hole, now filled with pure spring water, makes an excellent swimming place, under the supervision of the Dorset Field Club.

SOUTH DORSET (alt. 940), 66 *m.*, a scattered rural community, is stretched along the highway where ridges encroach mildly to narrow the valley.

> Right from South Dorset on a country road is *Mill Hollow*, with the picturesque ruins of an old marble mill, and a millpond that is fine for swimming, fishing, and skating.

Between South Dorset and Manchester Center, State 30 curves along the valley of the West Branch, undulating as the terrain becomes more uneven and wooded. *Equinox Mountain* (alt. 3816) raises its broad-sided bulk to the southwest.

MANCHESTER CENTER, 70 *m.* (*see Tour* 4), is at the junction with US 7 (*see Tour* 4). Here also is the junction with State 11 (*see Tour* 4E).

---

T O U R    4 D :    *From* PIERCE'S CORNER (*Clarendon*) *to* JUNCTION WITH STATE 100, 19 *m.*, State 103.

---

Via Mt. Holly.

Rutland R.R. parallels this route.

Road is hard surface throughout.

A LINK in the main highway connecting Rutland and the north with Bellows Falls and southern New England, this diagonal cut-over is the highest trunk-line route in Vermont. It passes over the very top of the State, through highland country, open and summit-like, with mountain vistas opening on all sides in calm stolid beauty. The feeling of altitude and the invigorating purity of mountain atmosphere are pleasant phases of the brief trip.

PIERCE'S CORNER, 0 *m.* (*see Tour* 4), is the name given to the junction of State 103 with US 7, which occurs in Clarendon Township (*see Tour* 4).

Southeast of Pierce's Corner, State 103 swings curving over smooth-rolled hills.

EAST CLARENDON (alt. 740), 1.7 *m.*, lies along the wild secluded valley of Mill River, dashing along its boulder-strewn bed. The highway twists downhill into the little settlement of obvious antiquity, its wooden houses straggling along the forested and rocky gorge. The home of Benjamin Spencer, a leader of the Yorkers in the vicinity, this village was once the storm center of the strife between the New Hampshire Patriots and the New York Tories. In 1772 Spencer wrote a friend that, 'One Ethan Allen hath brought from Connecticut twelve or fifteen of the most blackguard fellows he can get, doubly armed, in order to protect him.' The *Spencer Homestead* (L) at the western edge of the village, was the setting for a strange scene on November 21, 1773, when the Green Mountain Boys arraigned Spencer for trial at his own doorstep, the Tory standing before a 'judgment seat' upon which were seated Ethan Allen, Remember Baker, Seth Warner, and Robert Cochran, while more than 100 of their heavily armed followers formed a raucous audience. That day Spencer was adjudged guilty, and the Green Mountain Boys literally tore the roof off his house 'with great shouting and much noise and tumult,' to replace it only after Spencer swore allegiance to the New Hampshire cause. Tory Spencer had little choice other than to yield to the roistering Patriots and watch them restore the roof of his home, with a great deal of rough jesting and merriment. Spencer's treatment was mild compared to that received by other Yorkers, many of whom saw their homes burned to ashes and felt the cutting lash of the beech seal on their bare backs.

At 2.3 *m.* the *Long Trail* crosses the highway.

Right on foot along the Trail is an old wooden bridge, 100 *yds.*, overhanging picturesque *Clarendon Gorge* (R), a deep narrow rock-ledged cut through which Mill River foams and boils over a rocky bed. The walls of the sharp craggy defile are lined with evergreen, which brightens the grim gray of the rock, and trees at the top of the gorge lean out dizzily, 200 feet above the white water.

East of the crossing of the Long Trail, State 103 overlooks (R) a deep-washed gulch in which the Mill River flashes far below the highway. The road continues to climb in long upward bends.

At 4.9 *m.* is the intersection with a dirt road.

Right on this mountain road at 2 *m.* is *Spring Lake* (Shrewsbury Pond). Lying at an altitude of 1457 feet, the icy waters of this spring-fed highland lake provide exceptional trout fishing. Summer cottages are scattered along the wooded shore. A State law forbidding private control of lakes of this size some years ago defeated the plans of a syndicate which had purchased a strip of land entirely surrounding the lake.

CUTTINGSVILLE (alt. 1040), 5.9 *m.*, named after pioneer Cutting who settled here, is the principal village and railroad station of Shrewsbury Township. A green-painted steel bridge spans Mill River at the center of the settlement, which extends from the narrow valley floor up the hillside to the south. About the middle of the 19th century copperas was mined, at *Copperas Hill* (alt. 1861) (L) rising east of the village. The section is excellent dairying country, and two Cuttingsville factories manufacture cheese. In the Laurel Green Cemetery (L) on the hilltop is the curious *Bowman Memorial*, a marble and granite mausoleum resembling a miniature Greek temple, with granite busts of the deceased wife, daughter, and small child inside the temple, and a life-sized figure of John P. Bowman, the mourner, outside the door. In the late nineteenth century Cuttingsville had a popular resort inn, the old Finney Tavern.

Left from Cuttingsville on an uphill country road is SHREWSBURY (alt. 1640, pop. township 540), 1.8 *m.*, a small agricultural community known for the production of excellent butter. Captain Lemuel White was the first settler, and became captain of the first militia, kept the earliest tavern, and was the first representative, although he could neither read nor write. When a neighbor asked to borrow White's harrow, White replied that if the man brought his land over he might use the harrow on it. Another early arrival was John Kilburn, coming from North Walpole, New Hampshire, where Kilburn and three other men, aided by their womenfolks, had made a heroic stand against attacking Indians. On August 17, 1775, Kilburn and an 18-year-old son, with Peak and his son, were going home to dinner from the field, when one of them saw the bare legs of Indians among the alders, 'as thick as grasshoppers.' The four whites raced to the Kilburn cabin and prepared to defend it. The war whoops rang and the savages started the assault, but the straight-shooting pioneers repulsed them time after time, the women loading the spare guns, and the men keeping the rifle barrels hot. From noon until sundown the siege went on, until at sunset the painted warriors withdrew, leaving the little log stronghold battered but unyielding. Peak was wounded by a ball through the hips, and died five days later from lack of surgical care. John Kilburn lived to see his fourth generation enjoy the land he had helped to free from primitive dangers.

Beyond Shrewsbury on the country road is NORTH SHREWSBURY (Northam) (alt. 1720), 5 m. North of this tiny hamlet, at the base of *Shrewsbury Peak* (alt. 3737) is the *Northam State Picnic Area*, 7.5 m. Part of the Calvin Coolidge State Forest, this region is connected with another section of the Forest in Pinney Hollow by a scenic road constructed by the Civilian Conservation Corps, which furnished the labor for all the developments here (*see Tour* 3, *PLYMOUTH*). Northam has become, owing to these improvements, a winter sports center, with a spacious shelter serving warm meals, a ski tow, and ski trails ranging from novice to expert, maintained by the Rutland Ski Club. *Ski Meisters* bring hundreds of skiers here from the city on favorable weekends, and college teams hold their meets in the area. Amherst, Williams. and Wesleyan staged their triangular meet at Northam in 1937. *Meeting-House Rock*, left from picnic area over a newly cut footpath, is a large flat-topped boulder where, in 1818, Elder Abiatha Knapp conducted divine service, weather permitting. Lack of a church building in North Shrewsbury at the time suggested this open-air method of worship. The rough stone benches reserved for the choir and the elders have lately been restored, and the site cleared of a century's débris.

South of Cuttingsville, State 103 follows the serene Mill River Valley between the unending roll of smooth hills and round wooded mountains.

EAST WALLINGFORD (alt. 1240), 8.9 m., is a comparatively recent settlement, owing its existence largely to the Rutland R.R. The village occupies a fairly wide place in the valley of Mill River, with plain domestic houses stretching from the riverside up the gradual slope to the west. A creamery and cheese factory constitute the industries. The white *Baptist Church* is neat and attractive in an ordinary way, as is the white school building. The cemetery occupies a hill with a stonewall base, on the eastern edge of the hamlet.

East of East Wallingford the route is through a pine-wooded upland country.

BOWLSVILLE (alt. 1300), 10.2 m., a little group of homes beside the highway in Mt. Holly Township, received its name from the factory which once made wooden bowls and other articles of wooden ware here.

At 11.5 m. is MT. HOLLY STATION, depot and turning-off place for the villages of Mt. Holly and Belmont.

1. Left from the station on a country road is MT. HOLLY (alt. 1540, pop. township 726), 0.7 m., a small cluster of wooden buildings on the slope of an upland plain, surrounded by stone-walled fields and outlying farmsteads. The open heights are breezy and fresh, with a 'top of the world' feeling. The surrounding mountains, heaped and piled against the horizon on all sides. seem but little higher than the sloping plateau of this settlement. The land, cleared by the ringing axes of early settlers, is fine for grazing. Comparatively little cultivation is attempted. Two faded and weather-beaten churches stand bravely by the center of the settlement, and a bridle trail (No. 6) of the Green Mountain Horse Association passes through here.

2. Right from the station on an uphill country road past scattered farms and through stubby scraggly second-growth timber is BELMONT (alt. 1840), 2.5 m., formerly called Mechanicsville, and located in a depression of the highlands at

the southwest corner of *Jackson Pond*. Belmont's traditional claim to the highest elevation of any village in the State has been proved false. For years the township's representative in the State Legislature boasted that he came from Mt. Holly, 'where the church steeple points nearest to God!' A recent survey, however, revealed that both Windham and Woodford are higher in altitude than Belmont, Woodford being the highest village in Vermont (*see Tour 7*). The mildly discredited Belmont steeple adorns the slate-gray *Federated Church* (L) on a knoll in the center of the town. A maple-guarded stone wall (L) flanks the Main St., and the whitewashed brick *Georgian House* (R), with end chimneys and recessed windows, has been marred but not wholly spoiled by a porch addition. The long plain I.O.O.F. Hall (left above the village) was originally a toy factory, contributing much to the financial stability of the little community. A remote highland air and sequestered peace pervade Belmont; these characteristics, with the quiet waters of Jackson Pond, attract a few summer folk each year.

At 14.3 *m.* the railroad station of SUMMIT is visible from the road (R). Highest point on the line of the Rutland R.R. (alt. 1415) this lonely outpost was the scene of one of the most important events in the history of transportation in Vermont. Here it was that the last spike was driven, completing the line, and winning the race between the Rutland and the Vermont Central for the first train from Boston into Burlington. On December 18, 1849, to celebrate the victory, trains from Burlington and Boston, with directors and other officials on board, met here at the summit of the pass, were united and drawn by a flag-decorated engine named Mt. Holly. With speeches and cannon salutes, water from Boston Harbor was mingled with water from Lake Champlain, and less symbolic liquid flowed freely from a barrel of New England rum. A prior incident in the construction of the line near Summit had been the uncovering by workmen of several bones, teeth, and tusks which Louis Agassiz pronounced to be those of an extinct species of elephant (doubtless buried by some prehistoric Democratic landslide). Mt. Holly's fragmentary elephant is now on display in the Vermont Historical Society Museum, Montpelier.

East of Summit, State 103 winds over broad rolling open heights, swept by clean mountain winds and seeming close to the blue dome of the sky. A long chain of mountains, blue, gray, and purple capped, barricade the low horizons. The road descends steadily through wild foothill landscapes, broken and rock-ridged, to flatten out in a narrow valley alongside of Branch Brook, a tributary of the Black River.

At 19 *m.* is the junction with State 100 (*see Tour 3*), 2 miles north of Ludlow.

TOUR 4 E : *From* MANCHESTER CENTER *to* CHESTER, 30.5 *m.*, State 11.

Via Peru, Londonderry.

THIS mountain route across the southern range of the Green Mountains climbs and winds on a stone-walled highway through a highland region rapidly emerging as one of the premier mountain resort sections of Vermont, with many handsome summer homes along the way. In early automobile days when motor tours were first in vogue, this route comprised a section of 'The Ideal Tour,' which ran from New York State to the White Mountains of New Hampshire via Manchester, Vermont, then as now a fashionable resort. Mountain and wilderness views are revealed from the road, and the air has the sparkling pure quality that makes highland atmosphere a delight. The bright music of mountain streams coursing white-sprayed and swift over bouldery beds is a pleasing accompaniment along the roadside.

MANCHESTER CENTER, 0 *m.* (*see Tour* 4).

MANCHESTER DEPOT, 0.6 *m.*, is the railroad station for Manchester Township (Rutland R.R.) and a small trading village. A long drab station and covered platform center the community. During the summer months the station yard is lined with automobiles, and the platform is piled high with expensive well-traveled luggage. Manchester Depot, pleasantly situated in the shadow of the hills, may seem rural and crude as compared to the other two Manchesters, and yet the settlement is not unattractive. The Depot bears the stamp of a summer resort trading center, but the large rambling wooden dwellings have a homelike aspect, with flowers in evidence on shaded lawns. Another service performed by the Depot for its 'brother' Manchesters is the supplying of liquors through a State liquor agency.

East of Manchester Depot, State 11 curves toward mountain barriers that seem solid and impassable. At 1.3 *m.* the hard surface ends and the road climbs a long gradual ascent of the foothills, between stone-fenced fields. Then the highway swings left to parallel the mountain walls (R), following the wild narrow valley of the Batten Kill Branch, a dashing white rocky stream. At 4.3 *m.* the road climbs again through hilly woodlands to forested mountain spurs.

At 5.8 *m.* is the junction with State 30 (*see Tour* 1*A*). From this point a great wilderness area stretches southward, densely forested and unpenetrated wilds that constitute the largest tract of wilderness in Vermont. The Long Trail is the only path that traverses this territory.

East of this junction, State 11 spirals steeply up a closed-in ravine with the mountain river (L) rushing along its stony bed beside the road. This is a typical mountain-pass, following a narrow watercourse to cool, densely wooded heights.

At 6.9 *m.* the country opens to ascending upland flats, the highway still mounting, on a more gradual climb now. Abandoned pastures line the road, exhibiting the rapid encroachment of bushes, once cleared land is left idle.

At 8 *m.* is the township boundary between Winhall and Peru, and sweeping east and south from the high bend in the road here are tremendous views over the rolling, humped stretches of thick-wooded mountains, the forest waves broken but infrequently by cleared farmlands along the slender thread of the highway, State 30 (*see Tour 1A*).

At 9.1 *m.* an appropriately rustic tourist camp (L) stands above the road. Stone walls trail raggedly through the woods of this vicinity, and a few secluded summer houses herald the many summer homes seen farther eastward.

PERU (alt. 1660, pop. township 156), 10.8 *m.*, lies high in the mountains, a serene shallow-pocketed village under the dominance of Bromley Mountain (alt. 3260). This hill village has a clean well-groomed aspect, refuting the general ideas regarding the slovenly backwardness of mountain settlements. Many of the homes and buildings are painted white, and the general scene is one of neatness and quiet pride. The *Community House* (R) contains the town library. The *General Store and Post Office* (R) is so much the neat model of such common rural arrangements that it resembles a movie-lot setup, even to the rustic sign hanging above the entrance. The *Congregational Church* (L), built in 1846, exemplifies in the plain severity of white-painted wood a simple effectiveness of church building, with double entrances, green-blinded windows, and square bell-tower. The interior contains four hanging oil-lamps, corner stoves with overhead pipes for winter heating, and a large painting of Bromley Mountain behind the pulpit. An appropriate quotation from Psalm 121 is on the wall: 'I will lift up mine eyes unto the hills.' The *Bromley House* (L) is early 19th century, a square roomy-looking structure of white-painted brick, with an outside fireplace on the porch. Peru was settled in 1773 and first took the name of Bromley. John Stark's forces cut a road through this township on their way to the battle of Bennington.

Left from Peru on a country road is *HAPGOOD POND*, 2 *m.*, which has been developed by the National Forest Service, with Civilian Conservation Corps labor, into one of the finest public bathing areas in the State.

The *Millpond* (L), 11.1 *m.*, lies in placid calm, an impassive and inevitable part of mountain scenery and the life of mountain folk.

East of Peru, State 11 rises and falls in long swooping bends over a broken highland terrain.

At 13.2 *m.* is the junction with a dirt road.

Left on this road is NORTH LANDGROVE (alt. 1300, pop. township 104), 1.9 *m.*, central hamlet of one of the smallest townships in area of the State. The town, in a fine lumbering region, was settled by William Utley and his son, Asa, in 1769. One of the early settlers, David Carpenter, served through the Revolution, and was on guard duty at the execution of Major André.

Between this junction and Londonderry, handsome summer homes are seen along the highway, secure in mountain quietude.

At 15.5 *m.* is the junction with a country road.

> Right on this road is SOUTH LONDONDERRY (alt. 1020), 3 *m.*, an active village, with industries centered about lumber, woodworking, and dairy products. Here is the northern terminus of the West River R.R., only State-owned railroad in Vermont. Now defunct, the line has never justified the $200,000 which was expended on its rehabilitation after the 1927 flood.

Just west of Londonderry the road descends, curving to cross a broad rippling stream at the western edge of the village.

LONDONDERRY (alt. 1400, pop. township 799), 15.9 *m.*, is built along the banks of the West River in a narrow, gully-like valley, hemmed in on the south by forested ridges. The village street has a rather raw unkempt appearance, where incomplete building mingles with decay. The West River was long ago dammed to provide water-power for the old red *Sawmill* (R), where piles of logs and boards at the village center bespeak plainly the community's industrial bent. Above the dam and gray steel bridge, the river flows in slow smooth retention, darkly placid and deep. The little *Universalist Chapel* (R), a fairy-story structure in dun and brown, has an old coach-lantern hanging on the tiny porch. Londonderry was chartered in 1770 by New York State as Kent, but was confiscated from the Tory proprietors in 1778, and regranted by Vermont in 1780, under the name of Londonderry.

> Left from Londonderry on a winding hilly dirt road is WESTON (alt. 1300, pop. township, 411), 5.4 *m.*, a beautifully restored hill village sitting at the north end of West River Valley, high-banked on all sides by forested mountain walls. The village center is ranged attractively around the shaded oval green of Farrar Park, which was a shallow frogpond previous to the Civil War. The modern awakening of Weston was essentially a revival of interest in the past with an understanding of present needs, and the results are highly gratifying. The restoration of old houses, the establishing of a fine museum, and the transformation of an old church into a modern little theater, are some of the steps in restoring beauty and cultural interests to an isolated little village lost in the mountain wilds. In transition, Weston is not emulating the hustle of commercialism in the 1860's nor the sterile indolence of the early 1900's, but is seeking a new and more vital life, the tangible results of which point to a better social and economic idealism for Vermont villages.
>
> The *Farrar-Mansur House*, north end of the Common, was built as a tavern in 1797 by Captain Farrar, housed the first town meeting in 1800, and served long as the nucleus of social and political life in Weston. This commodious and distinguished structure has been carefully restored to its original state and now serves as a local museum and community house, filled with antiques that express the provincial life of a century ago. Here are seven fireplaces; a kitchen full of early iron and brass utensils, pewter and chinaware; the taproom with its old grill bar; the council room with rare inside window-shutters; and a top floor ballroom containing exhibits of furniture, books, pictures, etc. The *Weston Playhouse*, east side of the Common, reconstructed from the abandoned Congregational Church by a local architect, is a handsome white-pillared structure modeled in the style of the Greek revival period in early American public architecture. It has been called the most beautiful small playhouse in New England, and there is no denying the charm in its patrician simplicity of line, as well as the blue-and-white interior

with four murals depicting high points in the history of the American theater. The brick *Wilder Memorial Library* was built in 1820 and occupied by Judge Wilder until the completion of the *Wilder Homestead*, across the street, in 1825. The latter building, still owned by the Judge's descendants, was the village post office from 1829–50.    Among the other interesting old houses is the *Ross House*, east side of the Common, built of red brick hand-made by shoemaker Emerson Ross in 1830. This gable-end structure now houses Vrest Orton's Countryman Press.

East of Londonderry, State 11 runs beside the West River, before swinging upland through scrubby timberland merging to thick woods before opening to flat country with stone walls marking the fields.

At 18.3 *m.* the broad dome of *Glebe Mountain* (alt. 2944) (R) looms close, as the highway swings northward.

At 19 *m.* is the junction with a dirt road.

Left on this road is *Lowell Lake* (alt. 1290), 1 *m.*, an attractive little body of water lying well up in the hills.

Between this junction and North Windham, the road ascends along the left side of a narrow mountain pass.

NORTH WINDHAM, 20.4 *m.*, consists of a few plain wooden farmhouses and apple orchards scattered on the plain at a highway junction.

Right from North Windham on a country road is WINDHAM (alt. 1980, pop. township 254), 3.8 *m.*, named for Windham, New Hampshire, a small community maintained by lumbering and talc-mining activities.    This is the second highest village in Vermont, most of the people living at an altitude around 2000 feet above sea level.    The white wooden *Congregational Church* sits on the mountain-side overlooking the rustic settlement, a landmark for the surrounding country. Its needle spire points 'closer to God' than that of the Belmont church, thus refuting the representative from Mt. Holly (*see Tour 4D*). But this Windham steeple is topped by the spike-tower of a little church in Woodford (*see Tour 7*).

At 21.3 *m.* is an *Old House* (L), with an outside fireplace opening on the porch.

At 21.8 *m.* is a gray *Brick House* (L) with gables and a semi-circular portico.

SIMONSVILLE (pop. township 258), 23.6 *m.*, is a tiny settlement with two bridges over the swift-running pebbly mountain stream that bends through the little village in white-rippled flow.  Trim stone walls follow the curving line of the street and mark the watercourse. The little white *Church* (L) with blunted tower is neatly built in a style similar to the Peru Church. *Rowell's Inn* (L), was built in 1820 by Simons, who gave his name to the community.  Constructed of red brick kilned on the farm, the building served as an inn and store, and retains such early features as the many fireplaces, Christian doors, and the third-floor ballroom.  A double porch now fronts the first two floors, with a third smaller porch opening from the ell.  In early automobile days, this inn was a stop-over on the 'Ideal Tour' between Manchester, Vermont, and the White Mountains of New Hampshire.

The *Little Red Schoolhouse* (R), 24.3 *m.*, would serve to illustrate the well-loved song of that name, and brings memories of all the sentimental songs and poems dealing with rural schooldays.

The *Parsonage* (L), 25 *m.*, stands in the attractive sturdiness of red brick, made locally in Simonsville, and is early nineteenth century, having been used as a parsonage since its construction.

Between Simonsville and Chester, State 11 winds along an upland river valley, crossing and recrossing the rocky branch stream of the Williams River, with forested ridges paralleling the highway. Hard surface is resumed in its bituminous form. Eastward near Chester the country opens a bit, the valley widening to the clear land of better and more prosperous farms.

CHESTER, 30.5 *m.* (*see Tour* 3). Here is the junction with State 103 (*see Tour* 3).

TOUR  5 :   *From* NEW HAMPSHIRE LINE (*Lancaster*) *to* BURLINGTON, 103.9 *m.*, US 2.

Via (*sec. a*) Lunenburg, Miles Pond, Concord, East St. Johnsbury, St. Johnsbury, Danville, West Danville, Marshfield, Plainfield, East Montpelier, Montpelier; (*sec. b*) Middlesex, Waterbury, Bolton, Richmond, Williston, South Burlington.

The Maine Central R.R. parallels the route between the New Hampshire Line and St. Johnsbury; the St. Johnsbury & Lake Champlain R.R. between St. Johnsbury and West Danville; the Montpelier & Wells River R.R. between Marshfield and Montpelier; the Central Vermont Ry. between Montpelier and Burlington.

The road is hard-surfaced throughout.

THIS cross-State route is the main highway connecting the White Mountains with the Adirondack region, and thus bears a large proportion of Vermont's through tourist traffic. Leading from a covered bridge over the Connecticut River to the Champlain ferries, it winds over the foothills of Caledonia County, where only the absence of heather dispels the illusion of the Scott country, picks up the Winooski River at its source, and follows the narrow cut through the main range of the Green Mountains all the way to the Champlain Valley, to the lake at its widest point. The thousands of tourists who annually see only this of Vermont, nevertheless receive in a few hours a fair sample of the State's variety: lowland, foothill, and mountain scenery; communities ranging from unspoiled quiet villages to the State's largest city, with the Capital maintaining a proper balance between the two. The east and west division of this route is quite as sharp historically as topographically. In the east the background is all that of the Scotch infusion, around St. Johnsbury; the western part lies in territory once owned largely by Ethan and Ira Allen and Thomas Chittenden, whose real estate ventures were carried on under the name of the Onion River Company.

*Sec. a. Connecticut River to Montpelier, 64.7 m., US 2.*

US 2 enters Vermont over a long covered bridge across the Connecticut River, which at this point flows in tranquil sweep between low banks.

At 0.1 m. is the junction with State 102 (*see Tour 1F*).

Southwest along the wide green valley for almost four miles the route traverses Vermont territory whose chief distinction is the lofty presence of the White Mountains commanding the eastern horizon.

LUNENBURG, 5.5 m. (alt. 844, pop. 1400, township), has the pleasant repose of the upper valley villages, its maple-shaded Green adorned with the almost inevitable Vermont grouping of Civil War monument, cannon, and bandstand. The community cluster of dwellings, small stores, and schoolhouse is enhanced by a simple white church which, though built in the 1850's, has an earlier excellence of line. The old cemetery (L) contains weathered slate markers, some of the inscriptions dating as far back as 1793. Only in sparsely settled Essex County could Lunenburg achieve the rank of second largest township.

> Right from the common on a climbing dirt road is *Neal Pond*, 1 m., known for its excellent speckled trout fishing. The views from the adjacent camping grounds on the heights (alt. 1600) are far-reaching.
>
> Left from the Common over a winding gravel road is SOUTH LUNENBURG, 3 m., a tiny roadside hamlet. South of South Lunenburg the road runs through barren, rolling country to GILMAN, 5.8 m. This company town created by the Gilman Paper interests lies on a hillside overlooking the Connecticut River, its terraced streets lined by identical small white houses. Paternalism has here avoided architectural drabness if not monotony. The company, which employs 500 men and women when in full operation, is the main economic support of Lunenburg township. For 30 years its mills have been busy with Essex County's great timber resources.

West of Lunenburg, US 2 passes through a wide area of second-growth forest, extensively lumbered a generation ago, but now deserted save for the occasional patches of cleared land about secluded farmhouses. North of here the almost unbroken wilderness of interior Essex County stretches 50 miles to the Canadian border.

MILES POND, 12.2 m., a village on a small body of water of the same name, lies (L) beside the road, with close-grouped summer cottages and birch trees lining the far shore of the pond.

West of Miles Pond the highway continues through a heavily wooded section, with fine views (R) of long, low mountain ridges, with clearings like checkerboards running nearly to the summit.

At 16.6 m. is a junction with a dirt road.

> Right on this road, up the narrow winding valley of the Moose River, is VICTORY, 5.5 m. (pop. 80, township). A crumbling sawmill and a few weather-ravaged frame dwellings comprise this minute mountain-hemmed community. The many deserted sawmills scattered through this area explain Victory's decline from a peak population of almost 600 in 1890 to its present status. Fine fishing and hunting,

however, remain. Deer are plentiful, even if Moose River is no longer an accurate designation.

Signs of agricultural prosperity appear for the first time as smooth meadowlands drive back the forest and large modern farm buildings accent the scene.

CONCORD, 18.4 *m.* (pop. 353), is an agreeable little village tucked into knobby hills on either side of the Moose River. Its modest houses, stores, and churches are held tightly by the narrow valley. Settled in 1788, Concord has enjoyed an uneventful and fairly prosperous history. The early settlers were bothered by bears. One of the animals, caught in a large trap, was being exhibited to the curious from miles around when he managed to shake himself loose and make for his tormentors. Unfortunately for him, he selected as his prey the child of one Rebecca Morse. Mrs. Morse promptly seized the trap and dispatched the bear with one blow on the head. Bears are still not infrequently slain in this section of Vermont, but by more modern means.

> Left from Concord on a winding, climbing dirt road is the *Site of the First Normal School in the United States*, 2.3 *m.*, marked by a stone shaft with bronze tablet dedicated to the Reverend Samuel Read Hall, who opened this school on March 11, 1823. The methods and principles introduced by Hall are today generally followed in practically all normal schools (*see Education*). Of the original building only vestiges of the foundation remain.

Between Concord and East St. Johnsbury the countryside grows steadily more fertile and attractive, with views to the south widening and deepening. For a mile or so here the highway passes through the township of KIRBY (pop. 311, township), a farming region possessing no village or trading center of its own. Although there is nothing for the tourist to visit in Kirby, Vermonters remember the town as the home of Russell Risley, in whom Yankee ingenuity as applied to domestic economy reached flood tide. Unmarried, he and his spinster sister worked the home place for many years with a minimum of physical exertion and a variety of labor-saving contrivances. A trapeze slid back and forth on wires between the house and barn transporting Risley to his daily chores; milk pails were carried on similar wires to the waiting sister who handled the emptying end of the process. A self-taught artist and sculptor, Risley created with Renaissance gusto and profusion, covering his barn with charcoal sketches of local notables and carving trees and fence posts galore.

EAST ST. JOHNSBURY, 22.7 *m.*, is a small trading center built along the river. Here at one time a group of Mormons had their headquarters, under the leadership of Erastus and William Snow, trusted advisers of Brigham Young. Erastus Snow, born here in 1818, was ordained one of the twelve apostles of the Latter Day Saints, 1849.

> ST. JOHNSBURY, 27 *m.* (alt. 655, pop. 7920), (*see ST. JOHNSBURY*). Home of Fairbanks Scales and Cary Maple Sugar Co.; Museum of Natural Science; Athenæum; Paddock Mansion; Octagon House; Century House; South Congregational Church; and other points of interest.

At the western edge of St. Johnsbury, US 2 diverges from Main St., curving down Western Ave. into the valley of Sleeper's River, and then climbing westward in a long winding ascent.

West of St. Johnsbury after the long climb, the highway emerges to the rolling terrain of the green uplands, with well-kept farms and undulant meadows stretching on either side of the road. From the summits are wide panoramas of rolling hills and mountains that are hazy blue in the distance.

DANVILLE, 34.4 *m.* (alt. 1341, pop. 1600, township), named for the French Admiral D'Anville, was settled in 1784. Danville Green, as the village is locally called, lies along the slope of a high airy plateau commanding views of the White Mountains, and is a resort for hay-fever sufferers. The tree-shaded common, with bandstand and Civil War Monument, was in early times the scene of June Training Day celebrations. Until 1855 Danville was the shire town of Caledonia County, and for the first 75 years of its existence an influential town in the State. The *North Star*, an early newspaper published here by Ebenezer Eaton, was in large measure responsible for this prominence. The remodeled *Town Hall* (R), was originally the county courthouse, and in 1805 the General Assembly of Vermont convened here. The *Elm House* (L) is over a century old, and a number of plain clapboarded dwellings antedate this hostelry. The small square brick *Caledonia Bank* (L) is now one of the best-protected in the State, modern safety devices having been added after the recent hold-up of the institution, an event so rare in Vermont as to cause Nation-wide interest.

Thaddeus Stevens, the bitter Abolitionist and opponent of Lincoln over the question of Reconstruction policy after the Civil War, was born in Danville, in 1792. He was elected to Congress from Pennsylvania as a Whig in 1849, and rose to political power in the anti-slavery cause. Returning to Congress in 1858, he led the fight for the Fourteenth Amendment, and almost succeeded in bringing about the impeachment of President Andrew Johnson. Because of his fanatical devotion to Abolitionism, and his harsh view of Reconstruction, Stevens was probably the most hated man in an era of universal animosities.

WEST DANVILLE, 37.3 *m.* (alt. 1496), lies at the eastern end of *Joe's Pond*, a wood-bordered sheet of water named for Old Joe, the Indian guide and friend of the pioneers (*see Tour 1, NEWBURY*). A colony of summer cottages has grown up on the shores of the pond, and the primary function of the tiny community of West Danville is now furnishing supplies to summer visitors.

Here is the junction with State 15 (*see Tour 5A*).

*Molly's Pond* (L), 39.6 *m.*, lies in a shallow open depression a placid little body of water that was named in honor of Indian Joe's squaw, Molly, who was also a favorite among the early settlers.

At 43 *m.* a westward vista opens through the Winooski Valley to the distinctive outline of *Camel's Hump*.

The *Artificial Lake*, 43.5 *m.*, is backed up by the earthen dam of the Green Mountain Power Co. on the Winooski River. Banked in hills and woodlands, this reservoir has the appearance of a natural lake.

At 46.2 *m.* the *Groton State Forest,* 15,000 acres of forested heights, extends densely to the south (*see Tour 5B, GROTON*).

MARSHFIELD, 47.3 *m.* (alt. 1140, pop. 207), was named for Captain Isaac Marsh, who bought the land from the Stockbridge Indians in 1789, the Indians having received the grant from the General Assembly of Vermont in 1782. The village is situated on a sharp-tilted plane above the Winooski Valley, and the main street is a long hill dipping in a southwesterly direction. The *Brick House* (R), facing the small triangle at the north end, dates from about 1820 and is shaded by century-old maples. The brown wooden *Federated Church* (R), above the triangle at the crest of the main street, bears the date, 1829. From the church, the highway pitches downward between homely clapboarded houses and stores to the level bottomlands of the Winooski.

> Right from the northern end of Marshfield on an unimproved road is LOWER CABOT, 4 *m.* (alt. 947), a small settlement by the river.
>
> Beyond Lower Cabot to the north is CABOT, 5 *m.* (pop. 232), named by Major Lyman Hitchcock in honor of his fiancée, a Miss Cabot of Connecticut. The Common at the village center is faced by pleasant old houses, by the Congregational Church, and the high school. The *Center Elm,* planted by early settlers at the geographic center of the township, rises from a rocky ledge and is marked by a painted sign. The *Site of the First Meeting House* and the *Site of the Whipping Post* are across the road from the Center Elm, and the *Old Pound* still stands in good condition, with only a few stones missing from one side.
>
> Zerah Colburn, child prodigy and mathematical genius, was born in Cabot, and here he first amazed people with his lightning-fast calculations of involved problems. His mind, one of the most remarkable for computation that the world has known, showed a sharp decline in later years.
>
> North of Cabot village is *Cabot Plain,* the site of the original settlement on the Hazen Military Road. *Fortification Hill* was once prepared for defense against an expected British advance, which never materialized. Major Whitcomb, who commanded a detachment of Hazen's scouts here, was a famous fighter, woodsman, and hunter. It was Whitcomb who, during the Revolution, made a single-handed invasion of Canada for the purpose of picking off a British general. The fearless wiry scout lay in ambush outside of Montreal until a British general rode by in glittering regalia, whereupon Whitcomb shot him dead and escaped from the very heart of the enemy's country. The British were enraged, setting a price on Whitcomb's head, and vowing vengeance for his allegedly unethical deed.

Between Marshfield and Plainfield, US 2 follows the Winooski River through a rather narrow and extremely fertile green valley, that broadens in progressing to the southwest, and becomes ridged and broken with rolling hummocks and smooth-turfed mounds. The wild unsettled region near here has been turned into a *State Game Refuge.*

PLAINFIELD, 54.3 *m.* (alt. 752, pop. 477), a public-spirited little community, spreads from lifted terraces on the north bank of the Winooski to low level bottomlands on the south bank. The highway dips and rises curving through the northern fringe of the village, where the two-lane cement road begins. Plainfield has been noted in recent years for the success of its active Little Theater group.

EAST MONTPELIER, 57.7 *m.* (*see Tour* 2), is at the junction with State 12 (*see Tour* 2).

Between East Montpelier and Montpelier the paved highway winds close beside the Winooski River along a narrow wooded valley.

> MONTPELIER, 64.7 *m.* (alt. 523, pop. 7837) (*see MONTPELIER*). State Capital; Washington County Seat; home of National Life Insurance Co.; State House; Supreme Court Bldg. with Historical Society Museum; National Life Bldg.; Wood Art Gallery; Hubbard Park; Vermont Junior College; Bethany Congregational Church; Kellogg-Hubbard Library; Col. Jacob Davis House; and other points of interest.

## Sec. b. *Montpelier to Burlington*, 39.2 *m.*

This section of the route follows the Winooski Valley to the plains of Lake Champlain, cutting through the main Green Mountain Range and commanding views of two of Vermont's outstanding mountains, Camel's Hump and Mansfield. The rocky gorges of the Winooski give picturesque emphasis, and the hills that advance and retreat irregularly about the valley are moulded in many shapes.

MONTPELIER, 0 *m.* (*see MONTPELIER*).

West of Montpelier, from State Street, US 2 curves closely along the broad bending Winooski in its deep green valley. The broad intervales across the river are occupied by the National Life Athletic Field.

*Green Mountain Cemetery* (R), 1.3 *m.*, rests on a terraced hillside, attractive and well-cared-for, one of the most beautifully landscaped of Vermont cemeteries. The monumental entrance-way contains a vault and chapel.

At 1.8 *m. Montpelier Junction* is seen (L) across the river, the railroad station for the Capital, connected with Montpelier and Barre by a gasoline-engine extension.

The Winooski Valley here is curiously broken by flanking hills of irregular outline, some bare and angular, others round and wooded. The highway for the most part clings to the hillsides, and in many places it has been cut through solid rock outcroppings. Only rarely between Montpelier and Richmond does it follow the straight and easy course across the bottom-lands by the river.

MIDDLESEX, 6.7 *m.* (alt. 560, pop. 751, township) is set on a hummock in the valley. Stone rip-rapping on the river banks by CCC workers has prevented serious erosion at the bend in the river above the village. The white *Community House* and the white *Methodist Church* with its red roof stand south of the highway. The little *Depot* (R) faces across the railroad tracks to a sidehill cemetery, beyond which is the abrupt rise of hill spurs. A *Stone Fireplace* (L) is all that remains of the CCC camp which helped to protect the little community.

First settler Thomas Mead tramped up the wilderness valley to this spot in 1783. Mead's later feat of shooting three bears in one forenoon gave him the reputation of a master-hunter.

West of Middlesex the valley is narrower and pine-forested knolls darken its edges.

The old faded *Farmhouse* (L), 72.9 *m.*, at the end of the long green-painted steel bridge over the Winooski, is the November scene of 'Turkey Shoots,' which attract marksmen from surrounding farms and towns, who wish to win their Thanksgiving dinner in competition.

At 9.4 *m.* are the *Palisades* (R), formed by a huge rock upthrust rising from the swirling current of the stream. Just west of this point, lofty mountain heads begin to loom over the valley.

At 10.2 *m.* is the talc mine (L) operated by the Eastern Magnesia Talc Co.

The abandoned *Trolley Car* (L) at 11.1 *m.* is a relic of the old Waterbury-Stowe electric line which, at the time of its discontinuance a few years ago, was one of the last of such lines in New England.

WATERBURY, 12.4 *m.* (alt. 425, pop. 1776), named for Waterbury, Conn., stretches along an intervale made by the Winooski in a southward bend, its beauty of setting intensified by the deep cleft to the north between the Worcester Mountains and the highest elevations of the main Green Mountain Range. The mile-long main street, pleasantly shaded, is broken by a small Green near the railroad station and by the intersection with State 100 (*see Tour* 3), at 12.4 *m.* Waterbury's industrial activity consists largely of dairy products and woodworking, the latter business impressing itself upon the visitor as he enters the town from the east past a factory bearing the formidable sign 'Scythe Snaths.' Architecturally Main Street is marked by several elaborate red-brick homes of the more pronounced General Grant style, in contrast to which the *Carpenter House* (R) reveals the graceful restraint of the American Georgian. Built in 1816, the house is notable for its excellent proportions, for its fanlight, and other decorative details. The *Waterbury Inn* (R), a large brown-shingled building near the Green, has been notable among northern Vermont hostelries since Civil War days.

The *Vermont State Hospital* (L), S. Main St., a group of brick buildings set back on a wide level sward of trimmed green, is the State hospital for the insane, with over 1000 inmates. The spacious grounds are well kept, shaded by spreading boughs and ornamented with shrubbery. Several farms in connection with the institution supply all the milk and vegetables, and the hospital has its own laundry, cannery, sewing room, and like departments.

The *Congregational Church* (L), N. Main St., is a white clapboarded structure erected in 1824, with arched windows of stained glass, and a needle spire rising from a square tower. The old cemetery behind the church is excellently preserved. The *Waterbury Public Library* (L) has

# ILLUSTRATIONS

*to accompany*

Tours 6 and 7

QUECHEE GORGE

MARBLE, WEST RUTLAND

PULPIT IN FEDERATED CHURCH, CASTLETON

TURKEY FARM, RUTLAND COUNTY

HISTORIC HAYES TAVERN, WEST BRATTLEBORO

VIEW NORTH FROM MOLLY STARK TRAIL, NEAR MARLBORO

HIGHEST CHURCH IN VERMONT, WOODFORD

SPRING ORCHARD ALONG MOLLY STARK TRAIL, NEAR WOODFORD

PARSON DEWEY HOUSE (1763), OLD BENNINGTON

8000 volumes, and a museum containing shell and basket collections, swords, guns, and documents.

Waterbury is the home of radio broadcasting station WDEV, with studios in the Waterbury *Record* Office Bldg. and in the Pavilion Hotel, Montpelier.

The village was hard hit by the 1927 flood, in which lives were lost, homes swept away, and great property damage done.

West of Waterbury at 14.1 *m.* is the junction with a country road.

Right on this road is *CCC Camp Charles Smith*, 2.5 *m.*, and the *Little River Dam Project.* This is the third and largest of the Government's flood-control dams designed to prevent repetition of the 1927 disaster in the Winooski Valley (*see MONTPELIER and Tour 5B, EAST BARRE*). Nearly completed now (1937) the work has been carried on for two years, employing over 3000 men. The dam has been built so that it may be utilized for power purposes, if desired.

At 14.6 *m.* is a clear view of *Camel's Hump* (alt. 4083) to the southwest, its bold outline in command of lesser mountains and forested foothills.

The *Green Mountain Power Plant No.* 1, 16.2 *m.*, has a picturesque setting (L) in a deep gorge below the highway, where a high craggy island of solid rock splits the course of the river, and ledges tower above the white-boiling water. The road has been widened to form a lookout on the brink of the gorge, and the scene is flood-lighted by night. From this lookout point is probably the most-photographed view of Camel's Hump. The old French name, *Le Lion Couchant* (couching lion), is here readily appreciated. Although the distinctive, double-crested mountain is a landmark for all northern Vermont, its massive leonine repose is especially compelling from this angle.

At 16.8 *m.* the little lumbering village of NORTH DUXBURY is seen (L) across the river, with the railroad station, and a small white church perched behind stacks of lumber. A generation ago this was one of the busiest lumbering centers in the valley.

West of this point the valley is broken, almost fantastically in places. Here and there gray obtrusions of rock are piled in crude Gothic peaks.

At 19.7 *m.* the *Long Trail* crosses the highway (*see LONG TRAIL*). Accessible from here is a long, laborious, but worth-while climb to Camel's Hump.

BOLTON, 19.9 *m.* (alt. 342, pop. 325, township), consists of a depot, general store, schoolhouse, and a few homesteads scattered along the level floor of the valley. Samuel Barnet, an early settler, served as one of Washington's guard in the Revolution, and in the War of 1812 fought at Plattsburg, being 68 years old at the time.

Between Bolton and Jonesville, the skeleton towers of the Green Mountain Power transmission lines march along the knobby hills above the valley.

JONESVILLE, 22.9 *m.* (alt. 326), a village in the township of Richmond named for the pioneer Jones family that settled here, is marked by an active lumber mill, railroad watertank and depot, and a handful of wooden houses. The eastern end of the hamlet is guarded by a rock ledge that rears close above the highway.

At 23.5 m. (R), is the *Birthplace of Senator George F. Edmunds* (1828-99). Appointed to the Senate at the age of 38, Edmunds served for 25 years until 1891, 20 years of which he was Chairman of the Judiciary Committee. He has been considered by some historians the most outstanding representative the State has sent to Washington (*see History*).

Between Jonesville and Richmond the valley broadens, and the hills are lower and flatter in contour.

RICHMOND, 26.4 m. (alt. 319, pop. 718), is a small crossroads village at the junction of US 2 and State 124 (*see Tour 5C*). Located in a good farming region, it has both a large co-operative creamery and a condensed milk factory. In 1908 fire destroyed the entire business part of the village and even today that section is bare and unshaded. Richmond's chief attraction is the *Old Round Church*, across the river about half a mile from US 2. Completed in 1813, this building has been called the first Community church in the country. It was the joint undertaking of five sects — Congregationalists, Universalists, Baptists, Christians, and Methodists. For many years all the denominations held services here, but they broke away one by one and the structure reverted to the town, eventually becoming the Town Hall. It is actually sixteen-sided, rather than round, with an octagonal belfry, and is painted light brown. The interior contains the original box pews, pulpit, and gallery. Henry Ford at one time wished to buy the Round Church, for removal to Dearborn, but the town refused to sell. Since 1918 an annual Pilgrimage has been held here each summer, with religious services revived for one Sunday in the year.

West of Richmond the valley is broad, terraced, and serene. The backbone of the Green Mountains is on the east, and the Winooski is scrolled in great swinging bends as it curves northward and flows nearer the plain of the Champlain Valley. *Chamberlain Hill* (L) was named for John Chamberlain, who, with Amos Brownson, began the settlement of Richmond in 1775. Although driven away by Indians, they returned after the close of the Revolutionary War to become permanent settlers.

At 28.3 m. is the junction with State 117.

> Right on State 117 is the *Chapin House* (L), 2.7 m., a handsome old mansion of whitewashed brick with end chimneys and a Palladian window, set on a maple-bordered lawn near the river bank. Martin Chittenden, eighth Governor of Vermont, and son of Thomas Chittenden, the first Governor, lived here in the wide level tranquillity of the Winooski intervale. His father's home was on a terrace diagonally across the valley (*see below*). The house dates from the 1790's.

Just beyond the junction with State 117 is the *Checkered House* (R), an old brick stage tavern with four chimneys, Palladian windows, and a curious checkered design on the end walls, made by a pattern of blue bricks inset among the red.

At 28.5 *m*. US 2 crosses the Winooski on a modern steel bridge. Between here and Burlington the highway aims straight for Lake Champlain, leaving the river it has paralleled for nearly 50 miles. The Winooski takes a more northerly sweep in reaching the lake.

At 29.8 *m*. is the junction with a country road.

> Right on this narrow dirt road beside the river is the *Site of Thomas Chittenden's House*, 1 *m*., beautifully situated on a natural terrace overlooking the broad sweep of the Winooski with a background that is sharply dominated by those two major summits of the Green Mountains — Mansfield on the northeast, Camel's Hump on the southeast. Here, in 1774–76, Thomas Chittenden, the first Governor of the State, established his home, and Colonel Jonathan Spafford built a house on the adjoining tract of land. The beauty of the setting would seem to indicate that rough, sincere, practical Chittenden had an eye for the charms of nature, as well as for the intricacies of government. Chittenden and his fellow settlers moved southward during the Revolution, but the Governor returned at its close, and lived here until his death. His mansion was destroyed by fire a few years ago, only the cellar hole now being visible.

West of this junction, US 2 climbs the steep curve of *French Hill*, from the crest of which is the finest obtainable view of the Winooski Valley, 30.1 *m*. The hillside, once littered with squatters' shacks, is now handsomely landscaped, and has been successfully reforested.

At 31.3 *m*. (R) is the *Old Williston Graveyard*, with the *Chittenden Monument* over the grave of Vermont's first Governor.

WILLISTON, 31.5 *m*. (alt. 501, pop. 961, township), named for grantee Samuel Willis, is stretched along the broad plain of a plateau. The long village street is distinguished by houses of clean-cut Colonial design, and sober red-brick structures. The large brick *Bingham House* (L), built by the Millers, who were among the first settlers, has entrances on front and side fashioned in the Greek Revival spirit. The *Federated Church* (R), is white clapboarded, with a tall spire. Standing side by side (L) at the western end of the street are three simple one-story redbrick buildings, almost identical in construction — a former church, a Woodmen's Hall, and the Town Hall.

In the farming region south of Williston village, Ringling Brothers Circus once bought a number of farms, on which they planned to keep their cold-weather animals during the winter months. Their plans did not materialize, and the farms passed into other hands.

West of Williston, the highway runs over open plains, the peaks of the Adirondacks gradually coming into view to the west.

At 33.6 *m*. the transition from the foothills to the Champlain Valley is definitely completed, and on the horizon the Adirondack wall rises in a blue irregular barrier, the western ramparts of Lake Champlain.

At 36.4 *m*. is the *Burlington Airport* (R). One of the best landing fields in the East, it has been developed largely with Government Relief funds. There are two hard-surfaced runways, hangers, and a modern administration building with a beacon.

The *University Farm* (R), 38.5 *m*., is maintained in connection with the

State Agricultural College and University of Vermont, and is located just east of the campus.

BURLINGTON, 39.2 *m.* (alt. 2c8, pop. 24,789) (*see BURLINGTON*). The Queen City, largest in the State; seat of University of Vermont; Billings Library; Fleming Museum; Ira Allen Chapel; Battery Park; Ethan Allen Park; Memorial Auditorium; Fletcher Free Library; Unitarian Church; St. Mary's Church; St. Joseph's Church; Calvinistic Congregational Church; Church of Christ Scientist; St. Paul's Episcopal Church; and other points of interest.

T O U R   5 A :   *From* WEST DANVILLE *to* WINOOSKI, 77.6 *m.,* State 15.

Via Walden, Hardwick, Wolcott, Morrisville, Hyde Park, Johnson, Jeffersonville, Cambridge, Underhill, Jericho, Essex Center, Essex Junction.
The road is intermittently blacktop and gravel.

THIS cross-State route is popular, offering as it does good roads uncongested by heavy traffic and the scenic revelations common to a highway that pierces a back-country region. The road follows the valley of the Lamoille River and its tributary from the east a major part of the way, along an upland valley through a section for the most part sparsely settled. The scenery holds little of the spectacular, but has the serenity of a river valley aligned with ridged woodlands and checkered with farm clearings, so integrally Vermont. On the west the valley gives way to wide upland flats, as the route reaches the plains of the Champlain Valley, where the Winooski River nears Lake Champlain.

WEST DANVILLE, 0 *m.* (*see Tour 5*), is at the junction with US 2 (*see Tour 5*).

Between West Danville and Walden, State 15 skirts the northern shore of *Joe's Pond* for a way, a thin line of birches standing along the edge of the lake. At 1.1 *m.* is a fine maple-sugar orchard (R), spreading over the hill slope. At 2 *m.* the highway swings westward from the end of the pond, running through a shallow upland valley with stands of coniferous trees along the way, and the river (L) dashing over its rocky bed on its way to join the Lamoille.

WALDEN (alt. 1656, pop. township 664), 4 *m.,* consists simply of a few wooden buildings clustered raggedly at a rural corner and bridge, and lying at the high altitude for which Walden Heights is known. The Hazen Military Road passed through the town, and the blockhouse built here was garrisoned under the command of Major Walden, whose name was given to the township. The blockhouse, which remained standing for many years, and housed early settlers and the first school, was the scene of the first religious services, the first birth, and at one time served as a homestead for Mr. and Mrs. Gideon Sabin and their 26 children. Today this is a purely agricultural community, with land under cultivation at an altitude of 1671 feet, one of the highest elevations at which agriculture is carried on in the State. Prominent among Walden citizens have been the Bell family, descendants of John Austin, the Glasgow artisan who invented the tulip-shaped bell now in common use, for which he was knighted by Queen Elizabeth and took the name of Bell.

At 4.9 *m.* is a view of *Mount Mansfield* and the main Green Mountain Range, straight ahead.

At 5.4 *m.* is *Lyford Pond* (L), named after Lieutenant Lyford of a Hazen Military Road detachment, shaped like an ox-bow and lying low in the fringe of trees that mark its shoreline.

At 5.7 *m.* is the junction with a dirt road.

> Left on this road is a *Scenic View* (R), 1.2 *m.*, which is one of the finest in northern Vermont. Not only is the main range of the Green Mountains nobly prominent, stretching almost 100 miles down the center of the State, but the Worcester Mountains rise sharp and clear in the middle distance.

Between Walden and South Walden the road passes through a barren, undistinguished farming country with many knolls and knobs rising on either side, and cleared land forming irregular patches in the wooded slopes.

SOUTH WALDEN, 8.5 *m.*, is another tiny rural corner-settlement built around a sawmill (L) on the banks of a mountain stream. The *Stage Tavern* (L), a long white double-porched building with green trim and three chimneys, was a stagecoach inn about the middle of the 19th century; the stone hitching-post stands by the roadside. On the hill (R) a white tin-roofed *Methodist Church* with belfry stands over the little mill settlement.

Between South Walden and the junction with State 12, smooth-terraced pasturelands (R) lie along the twisted course of the upland stream, which gathers force to dash white-sprayed over a boulder bed, on nearing its junction with the Lamoille.

The *Hardwick Country Club* (9 *holes, greens fee* $1), 11.2 *m.*, occupies an uneven terrain conducive to sporty play.

At 11.3 *m.* is the junction with State 12 (*see Tour 2C*).

State 15 and 12 continues into Hardwick alongside of the rocky Lamoille River, over a relocated roadbed, necessitated by the flood ravages of 1936.

HARDWICK, 13.9 *m.* (*see Tour 2*).

West of Hardwick at 15.2 *m.* is the junction with State 12B (*see Tour 2*).

West of this junction, State 15 swings beside the river with hillocks humped along the opposite side of the valley. Bulging gray outcroppings of rock break the greenery in places. At 19.7 *m.* a power plant (R) commands a picturesque rocky gorge of the Lamoille.

POTTERVILLE, 20.1 *m.*, a little sawmill settlement of rude unpainted houses in the narrow valley, owes its existence to the mill (R), surrounded by log piles and lumber stacks. In the township of Wolcott, this is really an outlying industrial part of Wolcott village.

Between Potterville and Wolcott, more rock outcroppings (R) are seen, thrusting gray ledges through the earth's surface.

WOLCOTT (alt. 720, pop. township 831), 20.8 *m.*, is the home of the '*Largest Country Store in the World*' (L), opened fifty years ago by Charles E. Haskell and now operated by Gilman and Seavey. A veritable Vermont 'Montgomery Ward,' the 165 × 110 feet main building faces the Main St. from the bank of the Lamoille, and a separate storehouse is packed rafter-high with incredible amounts of supplies, bought by the carload. Everything imaginable is sold here, and customers from a hundred-mile radius frequent the sales which offer merchandise ranging from toys to tractors, step-ins to stoves, groceries, fruit, grain, clothing, wallpaper, tools, and so on down through the list with mail-order house completeness. It is most unusual to find such a huge diversified establishment in a village of this size, and the sales held here have all the color, flavor, and pageantry of old-time country fairs.

Wolcott, settled in 1789, was named after General Oliver W. Wolcott, a signer of the Declaration of Independence. The population has remained practically stationary for over a century. The drab Main St., dominated by the big country store, is characterized by second-story wooden porches protruding from nearly every house.

West of Wolcott, State 15 rolls through the valley between forested ridges, with rock ledges and hills standing out here and there. Cleared areas alternate with woodlands, and the calm smooth Lamoille winds along the shallow valley.

The *Fox Farm* (L), 28.2 *m.*, is a collection of red buildings above the highway, where the scientific raising of foxes is carried on.

At 29.1 *m.* the road swings along a ledge above the railroad and the river.

MORRISVILLE, 29.7 *m.* (*see Tour* 3). Here is a junction with State 100 (*see Tour* 3).

Between Morrisville and Hyde Park, State 15 and 100 passes through a broader valley, the floor broken and rolling, with many peculiar knobs (R).

HYDE PARK, 33.1 *m.* (*see Tour* 3). Here is a junction with State 100 (*see Tour* 3).

West of Hyde Park, State 15 follows the uneven valley floor between low ridges. At 36.4 *m.* the valley narrows, the river courses (L) below the highway, and a forested ridge closes in on river and road. Approaching Johnson, the road pitches in a down-curving slant.

JOHNSON (alt. 531, pop. 659), 38.1 *m.*, named for grantee Samuel Johnson, is a small industrial center on the river flats of the Lamoille, where it is joined by the Gihon River from the north. A man named Brown, one of the first settlers in Jericho, originally received this grant, but the Brown family was captured by the Indians, taken to Canada and held prisoners until near the end of the Revolution (*see below*). In the meantime another grant was made to Samuel Johnson, 1782, and Samuel Eaton opened the settlement two years later. The Lamoille County Grammar School was incorporated here in 1836, and became the *State Normal School* (R) in 1866. The woolen mill (R) is one of the basic industries here; talc manufacturing and woodworking (L) on the river flats constitute the others. The *Masonic Temple* (R), built in 1855 as a Baptist Church, rests with a quiet mien behind its white-pillared portico.

West of Johnson, State 15 traverses the broken, rolling valley, shouldered by humped ridges (R) along which gaunt outcroppings of rock show through the green of fir trees.

At 40.7 *m.* the *Long Trail* crosses the highway, and unusual sand dunes (R) loom in bare brown mounds.

Between this point and Jeffersonville, the ridges along the valley climb into low, rambling mountains, forested and rock-ledged, with the curving sweep of the Lamoille River (R) beside the road. Real mountains begin to rise ahead, dwarfing the hills to the east. Several fine old brick houses in the Federal style of architecture stand by the highway.

CAMBRIDGE JUNCTION, 47 *m.*, is a small drab settlement huddled about a creamery (R).

JEFFERSONVILLE (alt. 480, pop. 305), 48.1 *m.*, named in honor of Thomas Jefferson by vote of the citizens in 1827, stretches L-shaped along a wide avenue on the broad flats of the Lamoille, with neat lawns and spacious verandas shaded by elms, inducing an aspect of pleasurable living in quiet comfort. The sawmills and lumber stacks along the river indicate that this is a lumbering center primarily. The *World War Memorial* (L) at the junction in the village center is carved from solid rock, an unusually impressive and distinctive memorial. Jeffersonville is the northern terminus of the Smuggler's Notch Road, and the central village of Cambridge township.

Here is the junction with State 108 (*see Tour 3B*).

West of Jeffersonville, the highway follows the graceful bending course of the river.

The *George Warner Place* (R), 49.7 *m.*, a group of farm buildings dominated by three red-brick houses, illustrates the better and more durable style of architecture employed by the landed gentry of a century ago.

At 50.8 *m.* the highway curves left through an *Old Double-Passage Covered Bridge* over the broad flow of the Lamoille, and almost immediately beyond crosses a smaller single-passage covered bridge.

CAMBRIDGE (alt. 454, pop. 237), 51 *m.*, an attractive village situated

on a broad intervale of the Lamoille at the northwest base of Mount
Mansfield, has one of the finest natural settings in the State. The unusually wide main thoroughfare gives an orderly, spacious, and parklike
aspect to the village. The macadam of State 15 forms the central strip
flanked by elm-shaded grassy parkways, which in turn are bordered by
unpaved streets fronting the well-spaced brick and wooden homes.
This arrangement was made in order that the militia might drill on the
Main St. without obstructing traffic; practical in origin, it also adds to
the attractiveness of the village street. The town was settled in 1783.
In the heart of the maple-sugar section, Cambridge has, for nearly 150
years, been a major producer of maple products.

The *Cambridge Inn* (L) was built as the Borough House over a century
ago, and stands in the strong security of ancient red brick, the dignity
of its old-time charm lingering in line, detail, and the delicate fanlight
of the entrance motif. The inn is completely furnished with antiques.
The *Congregational Church* (R) has attractive stained-glass windows.
The small *Catholic Church* (R) is finished in dull brown shingles.

Between Cambridge and Underhill, State 15 swings (L) southward,
climbing away from the Lamoille Valley to a broken upland region, with
rock-strewn pastures and bouldered slopes stretching up on a gentle
incline from the shallow valley scooped out of gaunt hills.

The *Humphrey Homestead* (*may be inspected with owner's permission*)
(L), 60.5 *m.*, is one of the most interesting houses on the route, having a
front brick section with the original 1808 cabin in the rear. The cabin
stands as it was built, with the hand-hewn beams and hand-made nails.
The front part of the house is a veritable museum of early 19th-century
furnishings of great variety, conjuring mellowed pictures of family life in
pioneer days. The *Old Coach House* has its original square exterior lamps,
and inside are old tools, utensils, and an ancient sleigh.

> Left from the Humphrey Homestead on a gravel road through pleasant rolling
> hill country is the *Old Underhill Burying Ground*, 4 *m.*, all that remains of the
> first settlement in the township. Here are old tombstones with strange inscriptions,
> some of which are dated prior to 1800.

UNDERHILL (Flats) (alt. 796, pop. township 781), 62.1 *m.*, lies along
a level plain, centered around a small tree-studded triangle surrounded
by stores, homes, and a small light tan church (L) with a shuttered belfry
and spire. A stone fountain plays in the triangle. Mount Mansfield
overshadows the village on the northeast, its broad heights carved high
against the skyline. Underhill was settled in 1786, and one of the first-
comers, Udny Hay, had been commissary general of a Revolutionary
division.

> Left from the triangle in Underhill on a gravel road is UNDERHILL CENTER, 3 *m.*,
> a pleasing little hamlet on the lower western slope of Mount Mansfield. The *Catholic
> Church* (R) dominates the village center, the largest church in the district, con-
> taining a number of excellent stained-glass windows.

> Right 4 *m.* from Underhill Center is the *U.S. Artillery Range*, said to be the largest
> range in the east and containing 4600 acres. When artillery maneuvers are held

here from time to time the quiet countryside is shattered and rocked by the roaring thunder of big guns.

Beyond Underhill Center on another road is a white schoolhouse at 3.4 *m.* and right from here on a climbing branch road is the exclusive *Stevensville Summer Colony*, 5.4 *m.*, a mountain resort in the shadow of Mansfield.

Beyond the white schoolhouse is the junction with a third branch road at 4.2 *m.* Right on this climbing road is a *Rustic Shelter* and *Free Camp Site*, established by the State Forestry Department. At 7.2 *m.* is the *Halfway House*, a white two-story summer inn and refreshment shop, the 'jumping-off' place for the hike up Mount Mansfield. One foot trail leads directly up the mountain-side to the hotel on the summit. The Sunset Trail runs diagonally to the Chin of Mansfield. Either trail may be taken, but the usual procedure is as follows: climb straight up the summit on the direct route; proceed north along the summit ridge on the Long Trail; and descend the Sunset Trail to the Halfway House.

Between Underhill Flats and Jericho, broad plains stretch on either side of hard-surfaced State 15 toward the foothills.

At 62.6 *m.* is the *Site of the First Settlement in Jericho* (L), marked by a monument commemorating Joseph Brown and family, who hewed a home out of this extreme frontier wilderness in 1774. The Browns were captured here in 1780 by Indian raiders sent out by the British, and taken to Montreal, where they were held until 1783.

At 63.1 *m.* is the junction with a country road.

Left on this country road through varied farming territory is JERICHO CENTER (alt. 765, pop. 80), 3 *m.*, attractively settled around a large elm-shaded square. The *Congregational Church* at the north side of the square was built in 1825, and stands firmly in durable red brick and severe lines, its high white spire rising in clean, towering thrust, visible for miles around. The *Jericho Academy Building*, southeast corner of the square, was also built in 1825, in the white frame style favored at that time for schools. It now serves as a library.

JERICHO (Corner) (alt. 560, pop. township 1091), 65.5 *m.*, is a village of well-constructed homes ranked along the level surface of a plain that dips downward at the southern end of the settlement. A few Georgian structures add a touch of dignity and charm to the Main St. The *Congregational Church* (L) is a pleasing red-brick building, severely plain and gracefully spired, with an old cemetery forming a somber background. The little white *Methodist Church* (R) is less appealing, with the blunt crenellated tower employed widely in religious structures throughout the State. The *Rawson House* (L), built in 1790, has received accurate restoration, retaining the serene balance and the clear-cut beauty of Colonial buildings expressed in gray brick, with characteristic end chimneys. The *Old Blacksmith Shop* (R), a low red-brick building, was erected in 1810, serving as a smithy since that date. The Main St. pitches downhill at the southern end of the village, to a small triangle with a war memorial at the junction of roads. A red-brick *Georgian House* (L) stands in trim-lined eminence on a knoll. State 15 veers right across a bridge over Brown's River, where stand the *Chittenden Mills* (R), a gristmill founded by Thomas Chittenden, first Governor of Vermont. The sawmill (L) rounds out Jericho's industrial ventures.

The late W. A. Bentley, known as the 'Snowflake King,' lived in this town for 45 years and here engaged in his endless photographic studies of snowflakes, which made him the world's foremost authority in that curious field of research. His 5300 microphotos of snowflakes constitute the largest collection of its kind in the world; the flakes, caught on a cold board covered with black velvet, were photographed in Bentley's refrigerated camera-room.

Between Jericho and Essex Center, State 15 follows a very straight course over a smooth level terrain, so straight a road as to be out of the ordinary in Vermont. Neat brick houses are seen along the flat landscape.

The *Essex Center Reforestation Project* (L), 68.2 *m.* The village owns 900 acres of land here, of which about 50 acres have been set with baby pine trees. The plan is to forest the entire area by degrees.

ESSEX CENTER (alt. 492, pop. township 2876), 69.3 *m.*, is a tiny cluster of buildings at a highway junction and a bend (L) in State 15. The *Federated Church* (R) is brick built with a belfry and weathervane, and faces an irregular little Common and the fenced-in cemetery across the road. An attractive little buff-brick house (L) adds a colorful touch to the small settlement on its rolling plain. That this was once a favorite Indian camping ground has been evidenced by the finding of pottery pieces and flint arrow-heads.

Between Essex Center and Essex Junction, there is a sweeping view westward over the plains of Champlain Valley to the distant blue-gray barrier of Adirondacks against the horizon.

At 71.1 *m.* is a *Brick House* (L), square and ornate in faded tomato-bisque brick.

ESSEX JUNCTION (alt. 358, pop. 1613), 72.7 *m.*, is an important junction where three lines of the Central Vermont R.R. and four highways converge, and is also a busy industrial center. In spite of these factors, Essex Junction remains cleaner and more pleasant than most junctions and industrial towns. The long sheds of the *Drury Brick and Tile Company (visitors welcome)*, (L) on the flats at the north end of the village, began operating in 1867, and have turned out some 350,000,000 bricks manufactured from the clay and sand found near-by. The *Congregational Church* (L), in the simplicity of red brick, exemplifies the local unwillingness to let industrial dominance mar the appearance of the village. From the busy *Railroad Station* (R) rows of shining steel tracks stretch on the plain, and the network of automobile highways makes a hub of the well-kept business district.

The station and the town have been immortalized in the poem, 'Lay of the Lost Traveller,' written in 1865 by the Hon. E. J. Phelps, one of Vermont's noted lawyers and Cleveland's Minister to England (1885). Frustrated by the long delays and baffled by the variety of directions, Phelps spent hours trying to leave the Junction and finally ended back in Burlington whence he had departed that morning bound for Boston.

> I hope in hell
> Their souls may dwell
> Who first invented Essex Junction.

This refrain of the long, classically inspired poem, which he contributed to a New York newspaper, has rendered articulate the despair of generations of Vermonters, and ranks, for Chittenden County people, second only to 'In the name of the Great Jehovah and the Continental Congress!' Economic conditions, diverting much of the traffic and almost suspending two of the lines, have in recent years done much to remedy the confusion traditionally associated with the name of Essex Junction.

A beautiful *White House* (R) holds a position of eminence, portraying a type of architecture which embraces more elaborate detail and elegance than is generally seen in Vermont. The homes in general are pleasing and well cared for. The *Vermont Maple Cooperative, Inc. (visitors welcome)* is a large farmers' organization for collective marketing of maple products.

> Left from Essex Junction on State 116 is the *Winooski River Gorge*, 0.5 *m.*, where the river has cut deeply through the rocks, forming a picturesque gorge that borders on the sensational. The *Green Mountain Hydro-Electric Power Plant (open to inspection)* (R) stands on the north side of this deep cut, with the *Dam* (L). The gorge is spanned by a modern bridge.

The *Champlain Valley Exposition Grounds* (R), 73.2 *m.*, occupy a broad flat expanse on the western outskirts of the village. The fair held annually the week before Labor Day attracts thousands daily.

The *Fort Ethan Allen Military Reservation (open to inspection)* (R), 75.9 *m.*, is admirably located on the wide level tracts of the Winooski River intervale, once the site of a large Indian settlement. Sitting well back from the highway on landscaped grounds, a long crescent of red-brick residences, 'Officers' Row,' faces the road with military orderliness. In barracks at the rear are quartered cavalry and field artillery units, a quartermaster department, hospital and medical corps, veterinary and signal corps, and the ordnance. Fort Ethan Allen is one of the few cavalry posts left in the country, and was at one time the largest. Summer and winter horse shows are conducted here, the winter one being held in the great riding hall, and a State pistol contest is held in May (*admission free to these events*). The National Guard, R.O.T.C. and C.M.T.C., are in training at the Fort, June 1 to September 1.

The *Fanny Allen Hospital* (L), 75.9 *m.*, a tan and brown wooden structure, is a Catholic institution named in honor of Ethan Allen's daughter by his second marriage.

*St. Michael's College* (R), 76.1 *m.*, enrollment (1937) about 150, is a small Catholic school situated at the outskirts of Winooski on a broad flat plateau overlooking the Winooski Valley, the Green Mountains piled in graceful contours on the east, the great Adirondacks forming a jagged wall on the western horizon. The college was established in 1904 by the Fathers of St. Edmund, who had previously conducted colleges in France. Having lost their French institutions through confiscation, the Fathers were without adequate funds, and the early history of St. Michael's was a struggle to survive under financial duress, and to carry on with meager equipment and buildings, small faculty and enrollment. Through this early period it was a boarding-school of the Continental type, including high school and college courses. In 1913 it was incorporated as St. Michael's College. Four main buildings of brick form the nucleus of the school, serving as dormitories, recitation halls, and so on. The college property includes 300 acres of land, and the college farm provides fresh dairy products and vegetables for dormitory dining-halls.

WINOOSKI, 77.6 *m.* (*see Tour* 4), is at the junction with US 7 (*see Tour* 4).

TOUR  5 B : *From* WELLS RIVER *to* MONTPELIER, 35.3 *m.*, US 302.

Via Groton, Orange, Barre.

The Montpelier & Wells River R.R. parallels this route.

The highway is variable hard surface throughout.

ON THE east this route winds through the rather wild scenery of the Wells River Valley, now narrow and tree-fringed, again broad and uneven. Progressing westward as the highway leaves the watercourse, the valley becomes on the whole wider and more picturesque. This route is important as a short-cut between the White Mountains of New Hampshire and the central part of Vermont, including the capital, Montpelier, and the Barre granite district.

WELLS RIVER, 0 *m.* (*see Tour* 1), is at the junction with US 5 (*see Tour* 1).

West of Wells River, US 302 climbs a curving incline.

The *Old Paper Mill* (*open to inspection during working hours*) (R), 0.4 *m.*, one of the first in the State, was established more than a century ago, and has been operating almost continually since then, manufacturing various types of paper.

Beyond the mill the climbing road overlooks a small *Canyon* (R) in the Wells River, and a wild irregular countryside is introduced.

BOLTONVILLE, 3.6 *m.*, is a little hamlet in Newbury Township, at a bend in the valley.

At 6.1 *m.* is the beautiful terraced *South Ryegate Cemetery* (L) on the south side of the deep green valley in which the village is nestled. The cemetery was terraced in 1922 as a memorial to Alexander Dunnett, popular and able lawyer and benefactor.

SOUTH RYEGATE (alt. 724), 6.4 *m.*, lies serenely in the broad bowl of the valley, a village in the southern part of Caledonia County populated largely by people of Scottish descent. The township of Ryegate (*see Tour* 1, *Sec. b*) was settled entirely by Scots from the vicinity of Glasgow, and their strong clan spirit has kept the blood strain surprisingly pure, which may account for a subtle difference in the atmosphere of this community.

Two *Presbyterian Churches* are maintained here, and granite cutting is the chief industry of the village.

West of South Ryegate the valley broadens again with pleasant meadow-land farms set against a background of gently rolling hills.

At 9 *m.* is the junction with an uphill gravel road.

> Right on this road climbing between uniform rows of maples to the *Old Gray House* and the *First Store* in Groton Township, 1.4 *m.* Behind the crumbling stone wall (R) at 1.3 *m.* are the graves of Dominicus and Sarah Gray, husband and wife who were the founders of Groton. The store building (L) has been slightly remodeled, but retains the original doors, windows, and ceiling of 1790. It now serves as the summer home of Waldo Glover, author of 'The Sleeping Sentinel' (pub. 1936), which deals with the Groton Civil War soldier, William Scott (*see below*). The Gray House (R) was built about the same time as the store and has, among many original features, an old brick oven and a great deal of hand-fashioned woodwork. It also is now used as a summer home. The *Old Barn* (L) is put together with wooden pegs instead of nails, and stands virtually as when erected.

At 9.1 *m.* is an *Old Cemetery* (L) with Scottish names predominating on the tombstones.

GROTON (alt. 773, pop. 437), 9.5 *m.*, named for Groton, Massachusetts, sprawls on a flat wide section of the valley with the erratic course of the Wells River bisecting the village. Sturdy Scottish people laid the foundation of this settlement, which now bases its subsistence mainly on the industries of lumber and granite. The surrounding country is wild and heavily forested, with Groton State Forest stretching densely for miles. The many ponds and woodland streams provide excellent fishing.

West of Groton, US 302 continues along the Wells River Valley.

At 11.2 *m.* is the junction with an uphill dirt road.

> Right on this road climbing along a deep, forested little valley is *Ricker Mills*, 1.5 *m.*, at the foot of *Lund Pond*, the source of the Wells River. Here the droning burr of a board saw cleaves the pure upland air, the screaming yet sibilant welcome of steel and hemlock. Weather-warped and time-ravaged, Ricker Mills still turns out its 150,000 feet of lumber each year — the oldest stationary sawmill in America in continuous operation and the only mill of its character still engaged in the production of soft-wood timber. At one time all the sawed lumber in three counties came from Ricker's. Now the output is dwindling, but the lumbermen expect to continue operating for a long time to come. This mellowed landmark on the shore of the forest-shrouded pond combines the flavor of active utility with genuine antiquity.
>
> The *Old Lake House*, just beyond the mill, was built in 1843 to serve as a boarding-house for the lumberjacks, at which time this section was being worked by big lumber companies and the woods resounded with the clean, ringing blows of countless axes. This old house and the vicinity was the hangout of 'Bristol Bill,' notorious bank robber and counterfeiter of the middle 19th century, and here in 1850 this sensational outlaw was finally captured. He was William Darlington of Bristol, England, but two continents knew him as Bristol Bill. It is ironic that, after evading the law in our major cities as well as those of England, Bristol Bill should have been taken prisoner here in the backwoods of Groton. And it was but natural that Bill should make one final gesture of flaming defiance and scorn — in

the St. Johnsbury courtroom where he was being sentenced, Bristol Bill stabbed the prosecuting attorney to death with a knife procured in some miraculous manner.

*Groton State Forest* extends in a northwesterly direction from behind the Lake House, and there are picnic areas and a well-equipped community house on the western shore of Lund Pond. Beyond Lund Pond on a new road built by CCC through thick woodlands, is *Groton Pond* (alt. 1094), 2.1 *m.*, a beautiful body of water shining with the patterned reflections of the forest slopes banked gently around it, deep green in summer and flaring with colors in the fall. There are summer homes on the shaded shores; camping sites, picnic areas, park shelters, etc. The fishing is very good.

Right from Groton Pond on a winding uphill road is *Owl's Head*, 3.1 *m.* The auto road extends to within several hundred yards of the summit, with foot trails climbing the last stretch to the *Lookout Tower* commanding grand panoramas over lakes and vast wilderness reaches to distant mountains thrust up against changing skies.

West of this junction, US 302 runs on through the valley bordered here and there by farmsteads.

The *William Scott Memorial* (L), a large granite marker, stands on the farm where the famous 'Sleeping Sentinel' of the Civil War was born in 1839. William Scott was the 22-year-old private caught sleeping at his sentry post in Camp Lyon on the Potomac, court-martialed and sentenced to be shot, and pardoned only by the order of Abraham Lincoln. The facts of the case were that Scott had been on duty the night before in place of a sick comrade, and a second night without sleep proved too much of a strain on the young infantryman. Lincoln, after being petitioned by the unfortunate boy's comrades, went in person to visit Scott, and the next day the President's order for a pardon was issued and Scott was freed. Lincoln was criticized severely for his act, which opponents declared would certainly undermine the morale of the Union Army and ruin military discipline irreparably. William Scott went on to serve as a good soldier and fighting man, until he died under the Confederate guns at Lee's Mill, Virginia, April 16, 1862. The incident of the court-martial and pardon made this Vermont farm lad the best-known private soldier in the Civil War, and the fact that he died gallantly in action made him a kind of legendary figure.

West of the memorial the highway wends its way through low hills and sparsely settled woodlands.

*Knox House* (L), 18.2 *m.*, is an old-time country inn, still catering to travelers. Sitting in rural peace and quiet, the inn faces the fine broad meadowlands that grace the tranquil valley floor across the road.

At 21.2 *m.* is privately owned *Riddle's Pond* (L), and west of here the highway slants down toward the vast gracious sweep of the valley where a white church steeple glistens above the little village.

ORANGE (pop. township 508), 24 *m.*, is strung pleasantly along the roadway with wide meadowlands flowing smoothly away to the south, situated at a high altitude where at one time extensive sheep-raising was carried on. The clean, white *Congregational Church*, whose spire dominates the village, is attractive and well kept.

From the hill crest at 24.6 *m.* on the western edge of Orange is a splendid view of the great *Granite Quarries* on the heights above Barre, where broken and massive ramparts of gray stone piles stand out from the wooded hillsides like ruined fortresses.

The *East Barre Dam* (L), 26.2 *m.*, was finished in 1935 as part of the Winooski Flood Control Project instituted by the Federal Government to prevent further flood damages in the Winooski Valley. The work was done by CCC under the direction of U.S. Army Engineers, and the great earthen dam was completed in time to protect Barre, Montpelier, and other towns of the valley during the flood of 1936. On the Jail Branch of the Winooski, which is normally little more than a brook, this massive dam, with its tremendous bulk of earth fill reinforced by stone rip-rapping, and its huge spillways, seems ridiculously out of proportion to the meager flow of water in the dry seasons. But in floodtime the Jail Branch, like all the other deceptive-looking little streams, rises with incredible wrath, and habitually unleashed its power to join the torrent of the Winooski in wreaking havoc and destruction. In March, 1936, the East Barre Dam proved conclusively that it can control the Jail Branch at its worst.

EAST BARRE (alt. 1128), 26.6 *m.*, is situated on an S-curve in the highway at a high elevation surrounded by higher forested hills. In the vicinity of the granite quarries, it is but natural that this village should emphasize the industrial aspects, and its general unattractiveness is common to quarry towns which spring up quickly and support a more or less floating type of population. The houses are scattered on a broken sloping terrain.

Here is the junction with State 110 (*see Tour 2B*). Between East Barre and Barre the road winds in steady descent along the narrow valley of the Jail Branch. The gouged and ravaged walls of the valley give evidence of the river's relentless fury in floodtime.

At 29.5 *m.* the highway swings clear of the hills that have been enclosing it, emerging to provide a fine view over the eastern industrial section of Barre, compact in the valley below against a setting of green foothills. From this point the road descends sharply toward the city.

> BARRE (alt. 609, pop. 11,307) (*see BARRE*), 30.3 *m.* The 'Granite Center of the World' with many finishing plants and adjacent quarries; Robert Burns Statue; Goddard Junior College; Twing House; Paddock House; Wheelock House; and other points of interest.

Between Barre and the junction with US 2 and State 12, the concrete highway curves along the shallow irregular valley.

At 35.3 *m.* is the junction with US 2 (*see Tour 5*), and State 12 (*see Tour 2*), 2.4 *m.* east of Montpelier.

TOUR 5 C : *From* RICHMOND *to* ACKWORTH, 23.9 *m.*,
State 116.

Via Huntington, Starksboro.
Road is unimproved for the most part, with only brief stretches of hard surface. A good average dirt road most of the distance.

THIS route runs through pleasant upland valleys, for a large part of the
way rather narrow and enclosed by ranges of low, bluntly rounded hills,
and time after time crosses swiftly flowing streams coursing smooth and
deep or flashing white spray over rocky beds. The northern section passes
almost under the shadow of Camel's Hump (alt. 4085). Though topped
by three other peaks in the State, Camel's Hump is distinguished by the
suggestiveness of its profile and the unusually wide areas from which it is
clearly visible. Grazing cattle are seen along the way, and the picture in
general is one of pastoral quietude. The low-ridged forested hills rise
from the valley floor in gentle slopes, sheltering upland farms and villages.
The countryside is typical of the hinterlands of rural Vermont with
smooth, cleared valleys, round, wooded hills, and the musical dash of
highland rivers.

RICHMOND, 0 *m.* (*see Tour 5*), is at the junction with US 2 (*see Tour 5*).

South of Richmond, beyond a dangerous railroad crossing, 0.1 *m.* from
Main St., an unnumbered road crosses a bridge that was built to replace
the one swept away by the flood of 1927. Extensive rip-rapping on the
banks above the bridge (L) prevented a recurrence of the accident when
the Winooski surged to new flood heights in 1936.

At 1.1 *m.* is the junction with a dirt road.

> Right on this narrow winding road, which skirts the broad plain of the Winooski
> and climbs to a high bank directly over the river, is a striking example of *Flood
> Damages*, 0.9 *m.* River-ravaged meadows (R) lie below the roadway at a bend in
> the powerful Winooski, their fertile soil undermined and cut away by erosion:
> 100 acres of rich farmland lying endangered and defenseless. The U.S. Soil Con-
> servation Service is, however, undertaking (1937) a program of soil protection in
> this area.

At 1.2 *m.* the road starts a long climb into the highlands. From the crest,
2.3 *m.*, there is to the rear an expansive view over the Winooski Valley
to the northern Green Mountain Range.

Between the hill crest and Huntington the road swings along a hill-
hemmed upland valley, crossing and recrossing the Huntington River,
which wends through fertile farmlands and green pastures. Two old-
fashioned covered bridges are encountered, still substantial and picturesque.

HUNTINGTON (alt. 623, pop. township 621), 7.2 *m.* The large and busy
sawmill (L) at the north end of the village, with its stacks of crude lumber

and piles of sawdust, indicates the advantage Huntington has taken of its water-power facilities. Along with lumbering, the dairy business serves as a support of this ordinary-looking upland-valley community. A small triangle centers the village. Old time-blackened livery stables (L) lend a curious touch of antiquity to the scene, their queer cupolas imitative of stable structures found on large estates.

An interesting native son and almost lifelong resident of Huntington was James Johns (1797–1874), a man of unflagging curiosity and tireless industry. As early as 1834 he began to pen-print a newspaper, *The Vermont Autograph and Remarker*, which he continued intermittently until three months before his death. In 1857 he purchased a small hand press which printed a page 4 by 6 inches, but he used it little, as he found that he could print faster with his quill pen. Johns wrote history, essays, verse, and fiction, and kept a diary for several years. The Vermont Historical Society (*see MONTPELIER*) preserves about 350 items of Johnsiana. A few samples from his 'Minutes' for 1823–24 and 1860 follow:

1823. 'June 15th ... the F.[reewill] B.[aptist] Qua. M. hold in Richmond, I attended, Saw & heard much noise and wildfire, together with the self contradiction in preaching. peculiar to Arminianism. His Freewill Highness Pope Ziba was present, and tried to see how much noise he could make. ... September 21d ... Trespass committed by our worse than no neighbor Roswell Stevens. in cutting down a bee tree. on. our land. and taking the honey. The measures which Stevens took to possess himself of the honey, cast. an indelible disgrace upon his name ... November 10th. Some two legged creatures. who ought to have been abed and asleep. took an old lame horse. (in the night). cut off his ears. mane. and tail. and equipt him with a Side saddle of hemlock boughs. and rope for crupper. and hitched him at Dr Nichols's door. apparently intended for his wife to ride upon. and who. justly fearing he was not sure footed, declined the offer.

> Twas in the night these subtle wights
> This pony did prepare
> By taking sheers, to crop his ears
> And regulate his hair.
> A saddle soft. to sit aloft
> Of hemlock boughs they made
> That Miss might ride in pompous pride
> And hold the horse's head,
> The beast so good already stood
> In patience at the door
> But pride somehow would not allow
> Herself on him to soar.'

1824. 'April — on the night between the 5th and 6th John Clark's shop. wherein Taylor had put his potash, was broken open and the potash carried off. Information supposed, or known to have been given the thieves concerning where the potash was given by that most abandoned of all villains. Gail Nichols. the curse and bane of society.'

1860. '[December] 21st. Almira Rood died. — It may not be amiss to mention here that the newspapers are ripe at this time with accounts of demonstrations made in South Carolina, of seceders from the Union in which they are abetted and seconded by Georgia, Alabama, Florida and one or two other states, and all this on the foolish contumerous pretext of the election of Lincoln as President!'

The first settlers, Jehiel Johns (father of James Johns) and Elisha Bradley, came to Huntington in 1786 from the southern part of the State. The town produced an outstanding soldier in General Emerson H. Liscum, who served in the Civil War and the Spanish-American War and was killed leading his troops at Tien-Tsin, China, in the Boxer Rebellion.

South of Huntington the road climbs briefly to country that flattens out along another upland valley shut in by the easy slope of wooded hills. This area has a somewhat barren look, and the farms appear rather decrepit and run-down in comparison with those to the north.

At 11.1 *m.* is a strange little *Sawmill Settlement* (L) below the highway, where rough primitive houses have grown up around the rude raw-boarded mill. Lumber piles and sawdust heaps are scattered indiscriminately about this crude community, isolated in the hills and bearing the stamp of frontier enterprise — a family sawmill, seldom seen today.

Between this mill and the junction with State 116, a steep ridge rises sharply (R) along the road, and a mountain brook (L) ripples swift and white over the smooth stones of its bed.

At 13.4 *m.* is the junction with State 116, the route continuing (L) on that highway.

An *Old Cemetery* (R), 13.8 *m.*, grass-grown and uncared-for, has head-stones dating from 1800.

Between the cemetery and Starksboro, the valley broadens to an un-usually wide sweep of plains, and many dairy herds are pastured on the hill slopes beyond or, in autumn, in the nearer meadows. The narrow river (R) winds in lazy loops through the valley.

STARKSBORO (alt. 612, pop. township 687), 18.3 *m.*, stretches along one street on a plain slightly above the river valley to the west, while the eastern terrain climbs to blunt hills. The Starksboro Dairies, Inc., Creamery (left at north end of the village) centers the principal industry of the region, the result of the large dairy herds seen along the route. Two old white houses (L), with end chimneys and projecting window lintels, add a pleasant distinction to the otherwise rather commonplace village street. Among the pioneers who broke the soil here in 1788 were several staunch members of the Society of Friends; their descendants still cling to the faith and conduct services in the Quaker meeting-house at South Starksboro.

South of Starksboro at 19.6 *m.* a curious outcropping of rock (R) is visible, a rugged upthrust bulging through the earth's surface. Beyond and across the valley are smooth, serene natural terraces.

An *Old Family Burial Ground* (L), 20.3 *m.*, rests in isolated peace on a mound high over the valley near the base of the eastern ridge, the grave-markers shining white and lonely in the little iron-fenced plot on the knoll.

The *Sylvester Hill House* (R), 20.6 *m.*, a sturdy white farmhouse, was built in 1836. Less typical of rural Vermont building is the odd *Yellow House* (L), at 20.9 *m.*, which is unusually long and culminates in a sort of cupola in the center. This section is locally known as Little Boston, from the Boston Irish who settled here.

At 22.7 *m.* the mountains ahead converge to form a seeming blockade as the valley is narrowed by encroaching hillsides.

ACKWORTH, 23.9 *m.* (*see Tour 3C*), is at the junction with an un-numbered road (*see Tour 3C*).

---

T O U R  6 : *From* NEW HAMPSHIRE LINE (*Lebanon*) *to* NEW YORK LINE (*Whitehall*), 69.8 *m.*, US 4.

---

Via White River Junction, Woodstock, Bridgewater, Plymouth, Sherburne, Mendon, Rutland, West Rutland, Castleton, Hydeville, Fair Haven.

The road is hard-surfaced throughout.

THIS major cross-State route traverses some of the wildest scenic sections of Vermont. It also passes through three of the most charming and historically interesting towns in the State and the second largest city and industrial center. It presents, therefore, in addition to its intrinsic interest, an unusually good cross-section of rural, suburban, and urban Vermont.

*Inter-State Bridge*, 0 *m.*, spans the Connecticut between New Hampshire and Hartford (*see Tour 2A*), which lies on the north bank of the White River at its junction with the Connecticut. Another bridge, this one arching the White River, connects Hartford with White River Junction. WHITE RIVER JUNCTION, 0.4 *m.* (*see Tour 1*). Here is the junction with US 5 (*see Tour 1*).

West of White River Junction, US 4, coincident with US 5, climbs at once to a height above the White River which affords a panoramic view of Hartford stretched along the opposite bank.

At 1.1 *m.* US 5 (*see Tour 1*) branches left.

West of this junction US 4 continues on cement along a wooded plateau high above the valley bottom which stretches westward toward massed mountains in the background. In general the highway between this point and Woodstock follows the bed of the discontinued *Woodstock R.R.*, an independent spur line that operated between Woodstock and White River Junction and was considered one of the most scenic railway routes in the East. Since the farmhouses of the region were built along the old highway rather than along the railroad, this new highway appears to be passing through all but uninhabited territory, for the farms, still served by the old road, lie off the present route.

The winding road continues through pleasantly wooded country to *Quechee Gorge*, 8.1 *m.*, one of the outstanding natural spectacles of the State. The highway bridge here, on the site of the former railroad bridge, once the highest one in the East, is 165 feet above the Ottauquechee River which, dwarfed to a turbulent thread, flows below at the bottom of the jagged gorge which it has cut from sheer rock in the course of the ages. Mosses and an occasional wind-sown tree grow on the sides of the canyon, but they merely emphasize the fact that here is a landscape which Nature in an extravagant and Gothic mood endowed with a grim majesty that neither growing things nor the power of man can soften or subdue.

At 8.6 *m.* the outskirts of QUECHEE (R) border the route, the main village lying below in the valley of the Ottauquechee, which powers the large woolen mills that are its chief industry.

TAFTSVILLE (alt. 668), 12.2 *m.*, is a small village on the high left bank of the Ottauquechee. The river is dammed here.

The course of the road between Taftsville and Woodstock was altered very little when the cement was laid, and the bed of the abandoned railroad is plainly distinguishable at intervals, paralleling the highway as in former times. Between these two villages also the country becomes more open and rolling, and at 14.4 *m.* large modern farms with attractive buildings cover the slopes across the valley (R).

WOODSTOCK (*see WOODSTOCK*) (alt. 705, pop. 1305), 15.8 *m.* Popular summer and winter resort; site of first ski-tow in the United States; unusually fine golf course; four churches with bells cast by Paul Revere; D.A.R. House and Museum; Collection of Japanese Art (Norman Williams Public Library).

Westward from Woodstock US 4 continues to follow the Ottauquechee River, the quiet flow of which is in places half-hidden by a bordering growth of delicate willows. Between Woodstock and West Bridgewater the river valley is invitingly open and dotted with pleasant modern farmhouses, many of which accommodate tourists and winter sportsmen in season.

WEST WOODSTOCK, 17.5 *m.*, is a small hamlet whose only industry is the manufacture of furniture. Across the Ottauquechee from West Woodstock is the summer home of Ed Payne, originator of the 'Billy the Boy Artist' cartoons, one of the oldest comic strips and one of the few that have been utterly uninfluenced by the drastically altered fashions in the 'funnies' since the time when impish Billy first appeared with his can of paint.

BRIDGEWATER (alt. 820, pop. township 741), 22.8 *m.*, is a small village that is given a distinctly industrial accent by the large woolen mills (L) of the *Vermont Native Industries* here. Across the highway from the mill itself is a large show-room where hundreds of tourists annually inspect the many samples of pure woolen fabrics and, if they wish, purchase materials for suits, overcoats, and dresses fresh from the loom.

In Bridgewater was born Zadock Thompson (1796–1856), a remarkable man. He put himself through the University of Vermont with proceeds from the sale of an almanac which he published annually for several years. One year his printer called to his attention the fact that he had made no weather prediction for July. 'Snow about this time,' Thompson replied absent-mindedly. And as it happened, it *did* snow considerably in Vermont that July, a natural phenomenon that gave Thompson a tremendous reputation based upon the least worthy of his many talents. His major claim to fame rests upon his original researches into the history and natural history of Vermont and the publication of the results. Without the numerous histories and gazetteers of Zadock Thompson, countless facts concerning the early Vermont towns and the men who settled and inhabited them would have been irrevocably lost.

BRIDGEWATER CORNERS (alt. 855), 24.8 *m.*, is a small cluster of houses with a post office.

> Left from Bridgewater Corners State 100A leads to PLYMOUTH (alt. 1420, pop. township 331), 5 *m.*, where on July 4, 1872, in a small cottage attached to the combination store and post office, Calvin Coolidge, 30th President of the United States, was born (*see Tour* 3).

From the highway just west of Bridgewater Corners *Bald Mountain* (alt. 2380) is visible (L), the highest of several eminences of the same name in the State, and the forerunner of the mountainous regions which the route is approaching.

WEST BRIDGEWATER (alt. 1056), 31.4 *m.*, is a small village dominated by two wood-working mills (L), large piles of the products of which can usually be seen weathering outdoors, between the highway and the river.

Here is the junction with State 100 (*see Tour* 3).

West of West Bridgewater the landscape becomes more wooded, the valley less open, the Ottauquechee narrower and more brooklike.

At 32.9 *m.* stands, curiously isolated, the *Church of Our Saviour* (Episcopal) (R), built of a handsome gray stone quarried in the neighboring town of Plymouth. This building was erected as a family memorial in 1895 by Elizabeth Wood Clement, mother of Governor Percival Clement, on the site of her birth. When the partially cumulative endowment fund which supports the church and the parsonage across the way reaches a certain sum, a home for destitute children is to be established in conjunction with the church.

The route continues along a deep narrow valley floor with high mountain ranges on the right.

SHERBURNE (alt. 1240, pop. township 336), 36.1 *m.*, is a small village of a church and a few undistinguished houses built on a highway three-corners. In the sparsely populated township of Sherburne, about five miles south of the highway, is *Killington Peak* (alt. 4241), the second highest mountain in Vermont. It was from the summit of Killington that the Rev. Samuel Peters, a Connecticut clergyman, claimed to have christened the State by a variant (Verd-Mont) of its present name, in 1763, when he took a horseback trip through this territory, preaching and baptizing. The ceremony, assisted in by many of the proprietors of near-by townships, included the breaking of a bottle of spirits on a rock, and the pronouncing of such sentiments as 'a new name worthy of the Athenians and ancient Spartans, which new name is Verd-Mont, in token that her mountains and hills shall be ever green, and shall never die.' Later Peters criticized the accepted form of the State's name. 'Since Verdmont became a state in union with the thirteen states of America, its general assembly have seen proper to change the spelling of *Verd-mont*, Green Mountain, to that of *Ver-mont*, Mountain of Maggots. Both words are French: and if the former spelling is to give place to the latter, it will prove that the state had rather be considered a *mountain of worms* than an evergreen mountain!' Peters did not assert his claim, however, until 1807, and it is demonstrable that he lied in print more than once, as when he assumed an LL.D. from the 'University of Cortona in Tuscany,' which never existed. Nevertheless, Samuel Peters was one of the first Protestant clergymen to enter what is now Vermont, and he was certainly elected the first Bishop of Vermont, at a convention of Episcopal clergymen at Rutland, in 1794, though the Archbishop of Canterbury refused to consecrate him.

From Sherburne village the road immediately begins the ascent of the Green Mountain Range. The particular eminence over which the route passes is called Sherburne Mountain.

At 38.2 *m.* is the junction with State 100 (*see Tour* 3), which has been coincident with US 4 between West Bridgewater and this point. The view of the mountain range to the north is remarkably fine here.

By a continual climb the road reaches the lofty cut known as *Sherburne Pass* (alt. 2190), 40 *m.* The *Long Trail* crosses the highway at this point. Set back somewhat from the road is the large, rustic-looking *Long Trail Lodge* (L), one of the most popular stopping-places on the Long Trail. Formerly maintained by the Long Trail Association itself, the Lodge is now under commercial management.

The long, winding descent from Sherburne Pass lies through wooded and uncultivated country. Beginning at 41.6 *m.* and continuing intermittently for about three miles are the great groves of the *Rutland City Forest*. This tract of 4000 acres was set out to white pines in 1916 to protect the Rutland City water supply, its present scenic charm being a fortuitous by-product.

MENDON (alt. 1000, pop. township 251), 45.9 *m.*, is a long, scattered village, overlooking from its higher level the distant city of Rutland. Here is the former home of General Edward Ripley, commander of the

Union forces that occupied Richmond during the Civil War. The view directly to the west from the western outskirts of Mendon is one of great scope and nobility, especially at sunset.

At 47.6 *m.* the country becomes more closely settled, as along the approach to any sizable city. After reaching the city limits, 48.7 *m.*, and the junction with US 7 (*see Tour* 4), 50 *m.*, US 4, plainly marked, leads westward through the business district of Rutland.

> RUTLAND (*see RUTLAND*), (alt. 600, pop. 17,315), 51.1 *m.* The second largest city in Vermont; center of the world's largest marble-quarrying industry; site of Fort Rutland; Riverside Reformatory; Church of Christ the King; Trinity Church; Temple House; and other points of interest.

At 52.2 *m.*, US 4 passes the western city limits of Rutland and enters Rutland Township and the suburban village of CENTER RUTLAND. Actually an extension of Rutland City, except in matters of local government, Center Rutland is an important marble center, many cutting and finishing shops being located here. At 52.4 *m.* is the *Site of Fort Ranger*, one of the two early Rutland forts. It was oval in shape and could accommodate between 200 and 300 men. State troops were garrisoned here until 1781. From the water below the *Falls* (L) under the railroad bridge at 52.5 *m.*, the brick pier of an earlier bridge rises like a marine ruin. The wind-blown spray from these falls frequently dampens the highway at this point.

WEST RUTLAND (alt. 500, pop. township 3421), 54.4 *m.*, lies on a level plain at the foot of guarding mountains and is visible for nearly a mile before it is reached from the east. The township was set off from Rutland proper in 1886. Here is located America's most famous marble deposit. Quarrying began here on a small scale about the year 1844. In recent times from 400,000 to 600,000 cubic feet of marble have been removed each year, and the quantity yet available appears to be unlimited. Without including the various grades of blue marble, which lie west of the white deposit at West Rutland, this vein produces 15 different grades of marble for monumental and building purposes. These range from the almost pure white to the dark greens, such as Verdoso and Olivo. Right from the center of town in an extremely marshy region is a new quarry, where caissons have been sunk to keep out the water.

The village has a relatively small business section and is composed chiefly of one long residential street, which US 4 crosses. The public buildings of West Rutland confute the saying that the shoemaker's children go without shoes: the *Memorial* on the school Common, the *Catholic Church* (1860), the *West Rutland High School*, and the really handsome *Library* are all constructed of native marble. Visible from the highway on the western outskirts of the village is a huge *Pile of Marble Blocks* (R) valued at $2,000,000. Viewing this stock, it is easy to understand why the Vermont Marble Company never has to quarry to fill even the largest or most unusual order. The quarrying, which is carried on unceasingly, merely adds to, or makes replacements in, these tremendous reserve supplies.

*Hanley Mountain,* 55.2 *m.* (R), though not one of the highest mountains in this region, is one of the steepest, its precipitous wooded sides made even more forbidding by numerous bare rock ledges. Many, many years ago an immigrant from Ireland purchased this entire mountain. In a letter to his kinsmen at home he reported, with more truth than truthfulness, that he had bought land in this country that neither man nor beast could get over in a day. The narrow, river-threaded valley immediately west of this point was a part of the site of a proposed canal connecting Rutland with Lake Champlain. The project was abandoned after the building of the Rutland R.R. (about 1850).

*Bird Mountain* (alt. 2210) (L), one of the noblest of the Taconics, is visible at 59.6 *m.* The height of this peak is accentuated by a very steep drop of 300 feet on the southern face. Bird Mountain, sometimes wrongly called Bird's-Eye, was named for Colonel Bird, the first settler in Castleton. Laboring under great handicaps, Colonel Bird built a sawmill, but died so soon after its completion that the first boards sawed were used for his own coffin.

At 61.2 *m.* a granite marker (R) designates the *Site of Fort Warren* (1777–79). This was the westernmost of a group of four forts constituting the western and northern line of defense for the State. A farmhouse now occupies a part of the elevation upon which the fort stood, and other parts of it have been demolished to make way for the highway and the railroad, but portions of its original contours and the advantageousness of its location are still discernible even to the layman's eye.

Between this point and the New York State Line the country is one of open rolling slopes and far horizons, topographically resembling eastern New York more closely than it does Vermont. This is a fine fruit-growing district, and several large apple orchards lie along the route, of which one just east of Castleton at 61.3 *m.* is typical, its 6500 trees (L) only partially visible from the road. Those passing through this region in May, somewhat ahead of the usual tourist season, are rewarded by the breathtaking beauty of whole hillsides hung with pink-and-white clouds of apple blossoms.

CASTLETON (alt. 450, pop. township 1794), 61.5 *m.*, is a town of historic importance and physical charm. It was here, at Zadock Remington's Tavern, that Ethan Allen, Seth Warner, and their associates planned the successful attack on Fort Ticonderoga, and the town was Hessian headquarters after the battle of Hubbardton.

The many well-preserved examples of early architecture in Castleton reflect the talent of Thomas Royal Dake, a natural genius in building design who came here about 1807 and whose all-too-narrow field of influence was centered here.

The brick and wood *Federated Church* (R), at the east end of the village, dates from 1833. The *Ransom House,* now the parsonage, across the street, is interesting for its huge Ionic columns, elaborate iron grillwork, and balance of masses. Built in the 1840's, it is as good an example of the

Greek Revival style of architecture as there is in the State (*see Architecture*). The brick *Higley House*, east of the parsonage, bears the date 1811 on the keystone of its doorway arch. The *Harris House*, directly across the road, is forgiven the late and ungainly addition of its porch when the intricate delicacy of its carved festoons and gable decorations is examined. The *Northrup House* (1810) has a remarkable pilastered doorway. The *Meecham-Ainsworth House* (R), near the center of the village, has a Corinthian-pillared portico in which three distinct types of arch are blended into a beautiful and unified design. The much-photographed *Cole House*, built by Dake in 1833, is the most startlingly original example of the devious means by which he attained to his sure goal of architectural grace. The contours of the façade are roughly those of an ox-bow, the top toward the road. The portico rises two stories, the outer columns supporting a projection of the roof. On the interior a double archway spans the hall at the foot of an enclosed staircase. The oldest building in Castleton is the diminutive *Brick House* (R) near the west end of the village, which dates from 1787 at the latest, a considerably earlier date being sometimes claimed for it with some justification.

The *State Normal School at Castleton* (enrollment about 100) lies off the main street (L) from the center of the village. The present institution has developed through a succession of changes from the Rutland County Grammar School, chartered in 1787. The first medical college in Vermont was established here in 1818 and functioned until 1854. The present school plant is largely modern, the older one having been destroyed by fire. The small but pleasant shaded campus and the dignified brick and wood buildings seem fittingly located in this serene and memoried village.

Just west of Castleton, at 63.8 *m.*, the Adirondacks first become visible to the west, the huge ramparts of their impressive peaks faintly suggesting the originals from which the Taconics were done in miniature.

CASTLETON CORNERS (alt. 460), 63.2 *m.*, is a scattered village at the four-corners junction of US 4 with State 30 (*see Tour 4B*). At the western end of the long central street are fine pine groves (L) and large apple orchards (R), the latter only partly visible in the distance.

HYDEVILLE (alt. 405), 64.6 *m.*, is industrially dominated by the slate works located here, as the large heaps of waste material and the use of the stone for common walls and wharfings suggest to even the casual observer. The brown *Episcopal Church* (R) near the center of the village is nominated by one who has seen them all as the ugliest ecclesiastical edifice in the State of Vermont. The bridge, just beyond, spans the rushing stream that constitutes the outlet of Lake Bomoseen.

The route continues westward over gently rolling, almost level country which accentuates the lofty bulk of the Adirondacks ahead.

FAIR HAVEN (alt. 400, pop. 2182), 66.8 *m.*, is the center of the only district in the United States that produces unfading green, purple, and mottled slates, with about 15 slate works in the village itself. The main quarries are located less than three miles north of the village, on Scotch

Hill. There is a large and closely knit group of Welsh in Fair Haven, descendants for the most part of the slate-workers who emigrated here from the quarries of Wales about the middle of the last century. Services at two of the churches in Fair Haven are still conducted in the Welsh tongue.

The extraordinarily large white-fenced Common, bordered by houses and churches, gives Fair Haven somewhat the appearance of an overgrown country village, more especially because the extent of the town's residential section is not apparent from US 4.

The early history of Fair Haven is dominated by one man to an extent equaled by that of very few towns in the State. This man was Matthew Lyon (1750–1822), a brilliant, headstrong, pugnacious Irishman, who moved here in 1783. Lyon had important political affiliations, having married first the niece of Ethan Allen and second the daughter of Thomas Chittenden. He erected the first sawmill, the first gristmill, employed the first teacher, built the first meeting-house, was the first moderator, established the first printing press, issued the first newspaper, and erected the forge, iron works, and paper mill that did much to make Fair Haven one of the early industrial centers of the State.

In 1797, after several terms in the State Legislature (to which he was elected nineteen times in all), he was sent as Vermont's Representative to Congress. Here he immediately became a center of attack by the Federalists, and was viciously lampooned, along with Jackson and Jefferson, in the Federalist press. On January 30, 1798, goaded by the repeated insults of Roger Griswold, a Congressman from Connecticut, Lyon spat in his opponent's face, the encounter taking place on the floor of the House. Two weeks later, Griswold attacked Lyon from behind with a heavy cane, in the same arena, the incidents being sensationally exploited as 'the first breach of decorum in Congress.'

Lyon was a bitter foe and outspoken critic of President Adams, and in October, 1798, he was sentenced under the Sedition Act to four months in the Vergennes jail and a fine of $1000, for allegedly treasonable remarks made in his newspaper, *The Scourge of Aristocracy and Repository of Important Political Truth*. He was re-elected to Congress by an overwhelming majority while still in jail and made a triumphant progression of his journey to Washington. In 1801, he moved to Kentucky, which he represented in Congress 1803–11. He was appointed a factor of the Indian Territory in Arkansas and moved to that State, which also elected him to Congress, but he died before he could assume his seat.

Lyon has often been called 'the man who elected Jefferson,' because in 1801, when the House of Representatives was voting to break the tie between Jefferson and Burr, he cast the decisive vote for Jefferson, on the 36th ballot. Lyon was the only man who has ever been elected to Congress by three different States, and he was the most influential Democrat whose name is associated with Vermont, unless we include in that group Stephen A. Douglas, who was born here (*see Tour 4, BRANDON*).

Prior to the Civil War, Fair Haven was an important 'junction' of the

Underground Railroad, which helped so many southern slaves escape to Canada. The *Zenas Ellis House* on South Main St., thought to have been the home of Matthew Lyon, was one of the slave depots. *Castle Inn*, Main St., is built on the site of a tavern built by Matthew Lyon. More interesting architecturally, however, is the *Major Tilly Gilbert House* (1806), across the highway (L) from the Common. This house, now an antique shop, is a splendid example of the Georgian architecture, in wood, depending entirely upon simplicity and the rightness of fundamental lines for its effects.

Its proximity to New York and the presence here of a considerable unassimilated foreign element combine to give Fair Haven a personality all its own among Vermont towns of its size.

West of Fair Haven, US 4 leads past prosperous-looking dairy and orchard farms.

The *Poultney River*, 69.8 *m.*, is the boundary line between Vermont and New York State.

---

T O U R   7 :   *From* NEW HAMPSHIRE LINE (*Keene*) *to* NEW YORK LINE (*Troy*), 48.4 *m.*, State 9.

---

Via Brattleboro, Marlboro, Jacksonville, Whitingham, Wilmington, Searsburg, Somerset, Woodford, Bennington.
Road is hard-surfaced throughout.

THIS southernmost cross-State route, known as the Molly Stark Trail (for the wife of General Stark who commanded at the battle of Bennington), traverses a wild mountainous country to connect Brattleboro, the southeastern entryway, with Bennington, the southwestern entrance of Vermont, and to link the two main north-and-south thoroughfares, US 5 and US 7. The mountain depths, that stretch for miles on either side of the slender ribbon of highway, are practically unbroken — a thick carpet of green in the summer, a tapestry in the fall. The richest beauty of the route is presented in the autumn, after the frost's cold torch has set the wilderness on fire, and the pattern of flame extends into the distance on all sides, dulled only by the somber darkness of pines.

BRATTLEBORO (alt. 260, pop. 8709), (*see BRATTLEBORO*), 0 *m.* Site of Fort Dummer, first permanent white settlement in State; Home of Estey Organs; Estey Estate and Summer Theater; Center Congregational Church; All Souls' Church; Public Library; Brattleboro Retreat; Austine School for Deaf; Brattleboro Outing Club and Ski Jump.

West of Brattleboro, State 9 proceeds through a pleasant tree-shaded residential section along the valley of Whetstone Brook.

WEST BRATTLEBORO (alt. 443), 2.7 *m.*, is a residential suburb of Brattleboro, stretched along a curve in the valley. The *Octagonal House* (L) stands out distinctly from the more conventional dwellings. The principal landmark (R) is the *Hayes Tavern* (1791), the oldest and most distinguished structure of the township, built by the grandfather of President Rutherford B. Hayes. The faded yellow building, its original austerity of line somewhat obscured by a comfortable porch, is now, appropriately, an antique shop.

West of West Brattleboro the road follows Whetstone Brook past bungalows and tourist camps to climb gradually, between wooded hills, *Round Mountain* (alt. 1508) raising its head to the south. The ascent is steady and twining.

At 10.6 *m.* is the junction with a country road.

Left on this road is MARLBORO (alt. 1736, pop. township 255), 0.7 *m.*, named for the Duke of Marlborough. Once quite a sizable settlement, it is now little more than a ghost town. The *Congregational Church* (1932), a simple wooden structure with a seating capacity of 350, has a lost and lonely aspect. It duplicates the first Congregational meeting house here, which was built in 1819 and destroyed by fire in 1931. Marlboro is an example of a hill village that has declined.

On Sunday, June 26, 1748, in the northern part of Marlboro Township, Capt. Humphrey Hobbs with 40 soldiers from Fort Number Four at Charlestown, New Hampshire, was attacked by a large band of Indians under a half-breed named Sackett. The soldiers took cover behind tree-trunks, boulders, and logs, and poured a scorching fire into the onrushing braves to halt the charge. Failing to carry by direct assault, Sackett deployed his redmen in a half-circle to make the advance from tree to tree. The fight lasted four hours. In such a snipers' duel, the superior marksmanship of the whites offset the advantage in numbers that the enemy possessed. Hobbs and Sackett, both famed on the frontier as fearless fighters, knew one another and constantly exchanged taunts and threats. Sackett shouted that if Hobbs refused to surrender, his whole outfit was doomed to torture and the tomahawk. Hobbs roared back a lusty invitation to 'Come on in and get us! If you're afraid, Sackett, send your red dogs of hell in after us!' Driven by their furious leader, the Abnaki warriors made thrust after thrust, but each was shattered and repulsed by the sharpshooting riflemen, until the forest floor was strewn with brown bodies. After suffering severe losses in the four-hour engagement, Sackett withdrew his forces, carrying off the dead and wounded. Hobbs lost but three men, Mitchell, Scott, and Green; three other scouts were wounded.

West of this junction, the highway climbs and curves through thick pines, occasionally dropping shortly downward as if to get a fresh start. *Hogback Mountain* (alt. 2347) is the stubborn obstacle over which the road is forced to climb.

At 15.5 *m.* the highway takes a wide, high bend near the summit of Hogback, past the daringly situated *Marlboro Tavern* (L), a neat white summer inn, whose rear porches overhang the steep drop of the mountainside. From this eminence endless forests stretch in solid tracts, southward to the Berkshires of Massachusetts. A sense of wilderness and remoteness is felt here, almost as tangible as the clean strength of the mountain breeze, and the smell of the pines.

Left from this point on a winding uphill foot trail is the *Mount Olga Fire Lookout*

*Tower*, 0.5 *m.*, rising above the cabin of the ranger who is stationed here throughout the forest-fire season. From the top of the tower is a magnificent panorama spreading over an undulating carpet of treetops into the hazy blue outline of distant crests and peaks. In October the carpet becomes a gorgeous blanket of many colors.

West of the summit, State 9 curves and dips down-grade.

At 17.4 *m.* is the junction with a country road.

Right on this road is *Lake Raponda* (Ray Pond) (alt. 1860). 1.5 *m.*, a lovely lake set high in the hills, with a few summer homes scattered along the shores, and excellent swimming and boating facilities. Walled in by hills, the little body of water is guarded on the east by Hogback Mountain.

At 17.9 *m.* (L), the long slate-gray barracks of a *CCC Camp* line the hillside. In such a heavily wooded section, the conservation projects and recreational developments of this organization are particularly beneficial.

At 19.5 *m.*, is the junction with State 8.

Left on State 8 is JACKSONVILLE (alt. 1400, pop. 221), 5.5 *m.*, situated in a glen at the southwestern corner of Jacksonville Pond, in Whitingham Township. The manufacturing of wood products and syrup cans is carried on here, and the near-by presence of Sadawga and Whitingham Lakes increases activity during the tourist season.

Right from Jacksonville, State 8 leads westward to *Sadawga Lake* (alt. 1660), 8.8 *m.*, named for an Indian who lived on the shore, and who was drowned in the Deerfield River. The small lake is popular for boating and swimming, and unusual for its *Floating Island*.

Beyond the lake on State 8 is WHITINGHAM (Sadawga Springs) (alt. 1400, pop. township 734), 9 *m.*, the birthplace of Brigham Young, Mormon prophet who led his people west into Utah, after Joseph Smith was killed in Illinois (*see Tour 2A, SHARON*). Young's father was a poor basket-maker in Whitingham.

The town was chartered (New York) in 1770 to Colonel Nathan Whiting, from whom it took its name. The mineral springs here are believed to have remarkable curative qualities, especially for diseases of a cutaneous nature. The Chase family of Whitingham descended from an ancient English family, and one of the forebears was sergeant-at-arms to King Henry VIII, the much-married monarch. The *Baptist Church*, built in 1850, has the bell from the first Whitingham church (1798–1806).

Beyond Whitingham at 10.5 *m.* is the junction with a dirt road.

Right on this road at 1.5 *m.* is the *Harriman Dam*, 12 *m.*, built 1921–24 by the New England Power Association at a cost of $18,000,000. This great 200-foot dam, one of the highest earthen dams in the world, backs up the waters of the Deerfield River to form *Lake Whitingham*, the largest body of water entirely within the State. The overflow is controlled by the *Glory Hole*, a vast concrete subterranean spillway, shaped like a morning-glory. The *Power Plant* in connection with the dam is on the western side in READSBORO (alt. 1180, pop. township 1043). The tracks of the Hoosac Tunnel R.R. cross over the crest of the mammoth dam. Visitors from all over the world come here, sometimes to the number of 2100 in a single day.

West of the junction with State 8, the highway climbs a ridge and descends into the valley of Wilmington.

WILMINGTON (alt. 1580, pop. 611), 22.1 *m.*, lies at a junction of valleys in the rough shape of a cross, a picturesque village of homey wooden houses in the miscellany of domestic building, with many second-story porches overhanging the streets, and four church spires rising above the shingled roofs. It is said that Clarence Budington Kelland studied here the original of his widely known character, Scattergood Baines. The center of the village is a true four-corners, and the high white *Baptist Church* (1833) stands close beside the green front of a little chain store, just north of the intersection. Along the stream at the western edge of the community are the industrial projects of Wilmington, concentrated in woodworking and veneer mills that formerly accounted for a relatively high degree of prosperity and that still make the village the only substantial settlement between Brattleboro and Bennington.

Revolutionary Major Jonathan Childs was outstanding among the pioneer settlers, and his descendants have been prominent in the later life of the town. The Rev. Zephaniah Swift was the first person born in Wilmington (1771). One stormy night, when the pastor was comfortably in bed, there came a loud and insistent pounding on his door. The Rev. Mr. Swift poked his reluctant head out into the gusty rain, and found below a young couple that wanted to be married. Calling them close beneath the window, Zephaniah made brief of the ceremony, shouting these words into the teeth of the storm-rent darkness:

'Under this window, in stormy weather,
I join a man and woman together;
Let none but Him who made the thunder,
Ever put this man and wife asunder!'

West of Wilmington at 22.9 *m.*, is the northern end of *Lake Whitingham*, the large reservoir formed by the Harriman Dam. The caved-in ruin of a railroad trestle extends part-way across the water, and the high concrete smokestack of a submerged mill thrusts strangely above the surface of the artificial lake. Here is the junction of two northern branches of the Deerfield River.

At 24 *m.* (L) is a brick *Power Plant*, the Searsburg Unit of the New England Power Association.

West of the power station, State 9 continues in a long gradual climb.

At 26.4 *m.*, the ascent steepens, and the road winds and climbs sharply through aisles of trees.

SEARSBURG (alt. 1760, pop. township 103), 28 *m.*, is a genuine mountain settlement of a half-dozen unpainted houses and tar-paper shacks along the high, narrow valley of the Deerfield River, buried in the ridged hills of a great wilderness tract. Once washboards and bedsteads were manufactured here, but all lumber-milling ventures have died out. The streams that thread the neighborhood afford fine fishing and attract many sportsmen.

At 28.3 *m.* is the junction with a country road.

Right on this road through deep pleasant woodlands is SOMERSET (alt. 2000, pop. township 20), 7.5 *m.*, the home of State Representative Katie Taylor, who was for a long time elected each term by the scant half-dozen voters of Somerset, which is the second smallest town in the State, Glastenbury being even smaller in population. The Legislature of 1937, however, voted to disfranchise Somerset and Glastenbury, both of which had long been censured as one-family towns. Most of the land in Somerset Township is owned by the New England Power Association, whose desire is to keep the land clear.

Beyond Somerset on this road is the *Somerset Reservoir*, 9 *m.*, the second largest body of water entirely within the State, and like Whitingham, an artificial lake made by the New England Power Association. The water stretches north and south between broken shorelines, a beautiful blue sheet in an unspoiled setting of green. The control gates are at the southwest corner of the reservoir.

West of this junction there are sweeping views northward from State 9 over dense wilderness areas. Each October the scarlet and gold of the maples burning along ridge and vale are softened by the brown and pale yellow of elms and birches and darkened by somber pines.

Along the gradually climbing road are scattered a few lonely homes, and in places scrubby second-growth mingles with stately old stands of timber.

At 33.8 *m.* (R), *Big Pond* (alt. 2263) lies below the highway, an attractive body of water ringed in a wild forest frame.

WOODFORD (alt. 2215, pop. township 139), 34.5 *m.*, is the highest village in Vermont, despite the tenacious claims of Belmont (alt. 1840) (*see Tour 4D*) and Windham (alt. 1980) (*see Tour 4E*). The short spiked tower of the plain white *Union Church* (L) is the one that points 'closer to God' than any other steeple in Vermont, to use the expression oft-repeated by the Mount Holly representative, who was unaware that both the Windham Congregational and the Woodford Union have spires that reach higher than that of his Belmont church.

The feeling of altitude is emphasized by the cleared summit-land that stretches in a broad, gradual rise to the thick-wooded backbones of even greater heights: *Prospect Mountain* (alt. 2740) on the south, and *Maple Hill* (alt. 2740) on the north. Large iron deposits were discovered in Woodford, and at one time several forges manufactured bar iron here. During Jefferson's administration, Woodford forges turned out anchors for use on American gunboats.

Between Woodford and the eastern outskirts of Bennington, the highway descends steadily, now in steep pitches, and again on a gradual slant, with forested mountain shoulders along either side. The route follows City Stream to its junction with the Walloomsac, and then parallels the latter through the outer fringes of Bennington.

BENNINGTON (alt. 672, pop. 7390) (*see BENNINGTON*). 42.7 *m.* Focal point in Vermont history; Bennington Battle Monument; Old First Church and Revolutionary Burial Yard; Bennington Museum; Jedediah Dewey House; Site of Catamount Tavern; Walloomsac Inn; Isaac Tichenor Mansion; David Robinson House; Old Academy Library; Statue of Seth Warner; Soldiers' Home; and other points of interest.

West of the center of Bennington, State 9 follows Main St. to its terminus at the right-angle crossing of Monument Ave., 43.7 *m.*, the distinguished street of OLD BENNINGTON, where Bennington's major points of interest are compactly grouped (*see BENNINGTON*).

West of Old Bennington, State 9 continues toward the New York border-

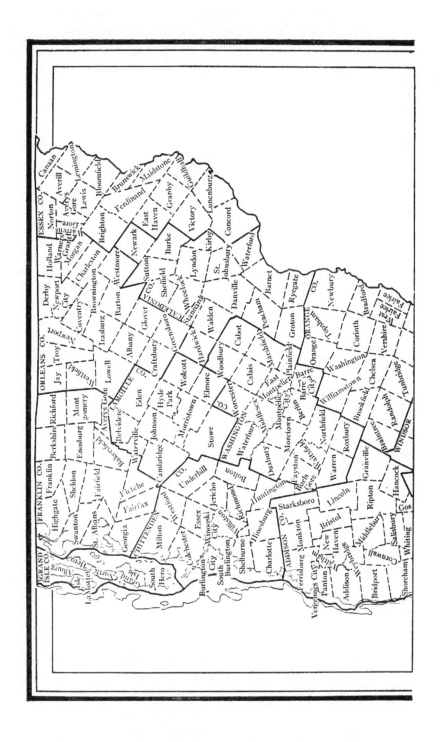

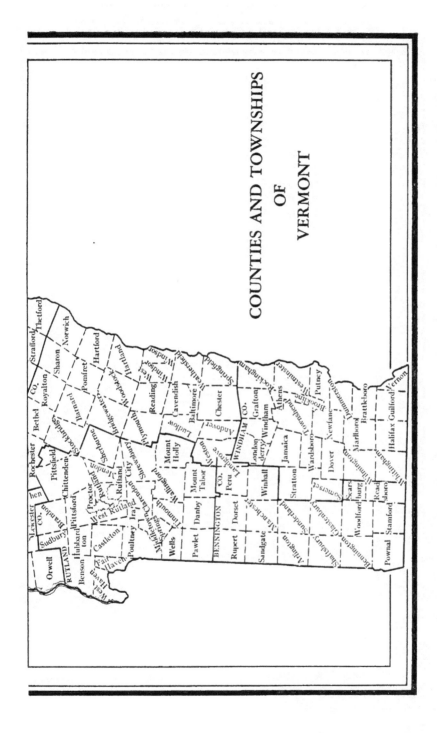

COUNTIES AND TOWNSHIPS
OF
VERMONT

line through a pleasant countryside of rich farmlands, largely owned by the *Fillmore Farms*. *Mount Anthony* (alt. 2345) rises to the south of the route.

The *Site of the Dimick Tavern* (L), 47.1 *m.*, is marked by a tablet just west of the schoolhouse. John Stark and his volunteers camped here in the valley before moving up to meet and whip the British and Hessians on Walloomsac Heights in the crucial battle of Bennington.

At 48.4 *m.* is the NEW YORK LINE.

# CHRONOLOGY

1609 Vermont discovered by Samuel Champlain.

1666 Fort and shrine to Ste. Anne built on Isle La Motte.

1690 Establishment of New York outpost at Chimney Point (Addison) under Captain Jacobus de Warm.

1704 Indian raid on Deerfield, Mass., made through Vermont.

1724 Pownal temporarily settled by the Dutch.
Fort Dummer, first permanent settlement in the State, established near present Brattleboro.

1726 First known white child born on Vermont soil at Fort Dummer (Timothy Dwight, father of President Dwight, of Yale).

1749 Grant of Bennington, which precipitated dispute between New Hampshire and New York, made by Governor Wentworth, of New Hampshire.

1752 Maple sugar first made in the State by a white settler (Captain Samuel Robinson of Bennington).

1759 Destruction of St. Francis Indian village in Canada in a raid made from Crown Point by Rogers' Rangers.

1759–60 Crown Point Military Road built.

1762 First church organized, in Bennington.

1763 France relinquished by treaty all claim to territory comprising present Vermont.

1764 King George III declared the west bank of the Connecticut to be the boundary between the provinces of New Hampshire and New York.

1770 The Green Mountain Boys organized by Ethan Allen.

1775 Armed seizure of the courthouse at Westminster, sometimes called the first engagement of the American Revolution.
Capture of Fort Ticonderoga by Ethan Allen and of Crown Point by Seth Warner.
First use of the name 'Vermont' in a letter to the people of the Grants from Dr. Thomas Young, of Philadelphia.

1777 Constitution written and adopted creating Vermont an independent republic.
The battles of Hubbardton and Bennington.

1778 Actual functioning of State government as outlined in the Constitution inaugurated.

1779 Hazen Military Road built.

1780 First secondary school incorporated (Clio Hall, at Bennington).
Raid and burning of Royalton, most savage of the several Indian raids about this time.

1781 First Vermont newspaper, *The Vermont Gazette, or Green Mountain Post Boy*, issued at Westminster.

1784–85 Toll bridge built at Bellows Falls, the first bridge of any sort across the Connecticut from its source to its mouth.

1785 First marble quarry opened, in Dorset.

1788 Vergennes incorporated, the oldest and smallest incorporated city in New England and the third oldest in the country.

1790 Thirty thousand dollars paid in complete settlement of New York claims to Vermont land.

1791 Vermont admitted to the Union as the fourteenth State.
The first library in the State, at Brookfield.

1793 First manufacture of Bennington pottery, most famous of early American ceramics.

1795 Justin Morgan, founder of the breed of Morgan horses, brought to Randolph Center.
Captain Samuel Morey of Fairlee granted patent for his invention of steamboat, at least two years after his first successful operation of one.

1805 Montpelier established as the State Capital.
Joseph Smith, founder of Mormonism, born, in Sharon.

1806 First bank in Vermont, the Vermont State Bank, chartered.

1808 The *Vermont*, second regularly operated commercial steamship in the world, launched on Lake Champlain.
First State House built at Montpelier.

1809 The State Prison established, at Windsor.

1810 Long Pond, called Runaway Pond, in Glover, broke its outlet and raced 27 miles to Lake Memphremagog — the most spectacular natural catastrophe ever to happen in this section of the country.
Introduction of merino sheep into the State, at Weathersfield.

1813 First glass factory in Vermont began operations, at Salisbury.

1823 First Normal School in America opened, at Concord Corner.
The Champlain Canal opened.

1825 Triumphant tour of the State by General Lafayette.

1830 Chester A. Arthur born, at Fairfield.
Thaddeus Fairbanks, of St. Johnsbury, invented the platform scale.

1834 Thomas Davenport invented first electric motor (patented 1837), in Brandon.

1836 The bicameral legislative system adopted.

1848 Introduction into the State of the railroad and the telegraph.

1857 Building of the present State House begun.

1864 St. Albans raided by Confederates.

1866 The Fenian Raids occurred, in Franklin and near-by towns.

1870 Legislature changed from annual to biennial sessions.

1872 Calvin Coolidge born, in Plymouth.

1893 First electric railway in State, Winooski to Burlington.

1896 First provision by law ever made anywhere for absentee voting.

1909 Champlain Tercentenary.

1910 First airplane flight in Vermont, at St. Johnsbury.

1910–30 The Long Trail built.

1927 The Great Flood.

# BIBLIOGRAPHY

THIS brief bibliography is of necessity only a selective working list. It is by no means the complete record of sources consulted in the preparation of this book. It was not prepared for the student of books as books, though a few early imprints that might interest him are included. Books mentioned in the text are not for that reason included here unless they have a pertinence beyond that which the text indicates. Cross-references are omitted entirely. Unless a book has undergone revision that makes a later issue more authoritative or informative, the date given for each entry is that of the first edition. The novels listed are those that have a Vermont background.

## HISTORY

Allen, Ira. *The Natural and Political History of the State of Vermont*, etc. London, J. W. Myers, 1798.
> Vermont's early struggles, viewed — not always impartially — from within.

Crockett, Walter H. *History of Vermont.* New York, The Century History Co., Inc., 1921. 5 v.
> Inadequate by modern standards of scholarship, but still the most complete record yet written by one person of what has happened in Vermont and who was responsible for its happening. There are literally hundreds of thumb-nail biographical sketches woven into the text.

Graham, J. A. *A Descriptive Sketch of the Present State of Vermont.* London, published by the author, 1797.
> A superficial but occasionally trenchant series of letters addressed to the Duke of Montrose.

Hall, Benjamin. *History of Eastern Vermont.* New York, D. Appleton, 1858.
> One of the best accounts, if not the best one, of what went on between the main range of the Green Mountains and the Connecticut River up to the year 1800.

Hemenway, Abby Maria, compiler and editor. *Vermont Historical Gazetteer.* Burlington, published by the editor, 1871. 5 v.
> A priceless hodge-podge of town history, biography, and anecdote preserved by the indomitable and unselfish enthusiasm of one Vermont spinster. Windsor County is lacking. Miss Hemenway deposited the manuscript as security for a debt. After her death it was destroyed by a fire, just a day or two before it was to have been redeemed by the Vermont Historical Society.

Peters, Samuel *A History of the Rev. Hugh Peters, A.M.* New York, printed for the author, 1807.
> Contains Samuel Peters' account of his christening the State Verd-Mont from the summit of Killington Peak.

Slade, William, Jr., editor. *Vermont State Papers: records and documents relative to the early history of the State.* Middlebury, J. W. Copeland, 1823.
> Source material of various sorts, including early statutes.

Thompson, Zadock. *History of Vermont, Natural, Civil, and Statistical.* Burlington, Chauncey Goodrich, 1842.
> An enlargement of an earlier work. Invaluable to research students in many fields for its careful population, livestock, and industrial statistics of every town in the State.

Walton, E. P., editor. *Records of the Governor and Council.* Montpelier, published by the State, 1873–80. 8 v.
> Covers the period from 1775–1836. Invaluable to research students.

Wardner, Henry Steele. *The Birthplace of Vermont.* New York, Charles Scribner's Sons, 1927.
> A history of Windsor, but also much more than that. It covers the whole subject of Vermont history prior to 1781. It is scholarly, even legal, in its approach, but somewhat partial to the eastern townships in emphasis.

Williams, Samuel. *The Natural and Civil History of Vermont.* Burlington, S. Mills, 1809.
> An enlargement of the first edition of 1794. Many competent critics consider this eye-witness narrative the best account of Vermont's early history that has ever been written.

A List of the Principal Civil Officers of Vermont from 1777–1918. St. Albans, published by the Secretary of State, 1918.
> The latest revision of Deming's *Vermont Officers.*

*Proceedings,* and other publications of the Vermont Historical Society. Various places and dates.
> The first of the valuable publications of the Society was issued in 1846.

*Report* of the Special Master in the Supreme Court of the U.S., October term, 1932, relative to the State of Vermont, Oratrix, *vs.* the State of New Hampshire, Defendant.
> The master's findings in the long-drawn-out case that placed the eastern boundary of Vermont at the low-water mark of the western bank of the Connecticut include several little-known but very important records relative to the struggle between New Hampshire and New York for jurisdiction over the territory of Vermont.

### SOCIAL, ECONOMIC, AND INDUSTRIAL HISTORY

Andrews, Edward Deming. *The County Grammar Schools and Academies of Vermont.* Vol. IV, no. 3 of the Proceedings of the Vermont Historical Society, 1936.
> An abridgment of a long-needed study of an important part of the educational system of the nineteenth century.

Hayes, Lyman S. *The Connecticut River Valley in Southern Vermont and New Hampshire.* Rutland, The Tuttle Co., 1929.
> A readable mingling of history and anecdote.

Horton, Guy B. *History of the Grange in Vermont.* Capital City Press, 1926.
> Not complete, but the only extended account of an organization that has exerted a very considerable influence on the social life of this State.

Lee, W. Storrs. *Father Went to College.* New York, Wilson-Erickson, Inc., 1936.
> Ostensibly an informal history of Middlebury College, but illustrative of the struggles that many similar small institutions went through during the nineteenth century and of the loyalties that sustained them.

Stilwell, Lewis D. *Migration from Vermont, 1776–1860.*
> A thesis in the possession of Professor Stilwell, of Dartmouth College,

that is soon to be published by the Vermont Historical Society. It is the most comprehensive study that has been made of an important phase of Vermont history.

Stone, Mason S. *History of Education, State of Vermont.* Montpelier, published by the author, 1934.
Poorly arranged and somewhat evangelical, this account is still fairly complete and is rich in interesting sidelights that might have been excluded by a more orderly and formal plan.

Wilson, Harold Fisher. *The Hill Country of Northern New England.* New York, Columbia University Press, 1936.
By far the best book in its field, and its field is very wide: the economic history of the three northern New England States between 1790 and 1930. The references to Vermont probably equal the sum of those to Maine and New Hampshire, for this is the State that the author knows best.

*Progress Report* of the Vermont State Planning Board. Montpelier, the State Planning Board, 1936.
Comprehensive statements of the status and recent progress in this State of population, land use, industry, transportation, recreation, welfare work, and State finances, with many charts and pictographs.

*Rural Vermont: A Program for the Future.* By Two Hundred Vermonters. Burlington, published by the Vermont Commission on Country Life, 1931.
A series of reports and recommendations regarding almost every important aspect of country life in this State, prepared by committees. Sometimes too laudatory instead of objectively critical, and, like most symposia, uneven.

### BIOGRAPHY

Beardsley, Harry M. *Joseph Smith and His Mormon Empire.* Boston and New York, Houghton Mifflin Co., 1931.
The first real biography not written by a Mormon of the man who perhaps vitally influenced the lives of a larger number of people than has any other Vermonter that ever lived. Psychoanalytical.

Davenport, Walter Rice. *Biography of Thomas Davenport.* Montpelier, The Vermont Historical Society, 1929.
A somewhat idealized account of the 'Brandon blacksmith' who gave the world the electric motor.

Evans, John Henry. *Joseph Smith, an American Prophet.* New York, The Macmillan Co., 1933.
The most recent Mormon apology. It omits mention of 26 of the prophet's 27 marriages.

Kent, Dorman B. E. *Vermonters.* Montpelier, The Vermont Historical Society, 1937.
A concise and handy reference list of about 1500 prominent men and women who were born in this State. The division is by townships. There is an index of names.

Noyes, George Wallingford, editor and compiler. *John Humphrey Noyes, the Putney Community.* Oneida, N.Y., 1931.
A reconstruction of the evolution of 'Complex Marriage' in the little village of Putney; chiefly from letters and documents.

Pell, John. *Ethan Allen.* Boston and New York, Houghton Mifflin Co., 1929.
An intensive but at times too imaginative study of a man concerning whom

no one has yet been able to write with utter impartiality. By a member of the family that owns Fort Ticonderoga.

Werner, M. R. *Brigham Young*. New York, Harcourt, Brace, 1925.
The best biography of the Whitingham boy who became the Moses of Mormonism.

### LITERATURE

Arnold, Josias Lyndon. *Poems*. Providence, Carter and Wilkinson, 1797.
The first book of verse by a Vermonter; published posthumously. The Arnold family were the most prominent early settlers in St. Johnsbury. Many of the poems are imitations or translations from Latin poets, but there are two native Odes to the Connecticut and Passumpsic Rivers.

Cleghorn, Sarah N. *A Turnpike Lady, Beartown, Vermont, 1768-1796*. New York, Henry Holt and Co., 1907.
Sarah Cleghorn is Vermont's most famous liberal spirit of recent decades, a combination of lavender and old lace and dynamite. Her lines
'The golf links lie so near the mill
That almost every day
The laboring children can look out
And see the men at play'
are the most widely quoted verses ever written by a Vermonter. Her autobiography, *Threescore*, was published in 1936.

Fisher, Dorothy Canfield. *Tourists Accommodated*. New York, Harcourt, Brace, 1932.
A pleasant play that conceals beneath its comedy Mrs. Fisher's fathomless knowledge of Vermonters and her wistful recognition of the fact that only by intimate association do outsiders come to understand them at all.

Gilman, Marcus Davis. *The Bibliography of Vermont*. Burlington, The Free Press Association, 1897.
Indispensable to scholars and interesting to bookish laymen. More than 7000 titles are listed, approximately half of which are Vermont imprints.

Greene, Anne Bosworth. *The Lone Winter*. New York, The Century Co., 1923.
Mrs. Greene spent a winter on her South Woodstock farm with only her livestock for company.

Hard, Walter. *Salt of Vermont*. Brattleboro, The Stephen Daye Press, 1931.
The second and probably the best of this writer's collections of character sketches in free verse form.

Humphrey, Zephine. *The Beloved Community*. New York, E. P. Dutton & Co., 1930.
Essays and stories about a small Vermont village. One of several similar volumes by this State's most serene interpreter and spokesman.

Lewis, Sinclair. *It Can't Happen Here*. New York, Doubleday, Doran & Co., 1935.
The protagonist is a Vermont editor.

Merrick, Elliott. *From This Hill Look Down*. Brattleboro, The Stephen Daye Press, 1934.
A fictionized but not idealized account of a young married couple's struggle to adjust themselves to the life of a rural Vermont community during the depression.

Peck, Theodora. *Hester of the Grants*. New York, Fox, Duffield & Co., 1905.
A novel laid in early Bennington.

Roberts, Kenneth. *Northwest Passage.* New York, Doubleday, Doran & Co., 1937.
> The first half of the book is a fictionized but generally accurate record of the famous retaliatory raid against the St. Francis Indians that set out from Crown Point and returned through northern Vermont.

Robinson, Rowland E. *Centennial Edition of the Works of.* Rutland, The Tuttle Co., 1934. 7 v.
> A reprint of all the important writings of the most original and autochthonous of nineteenth-century Vermont prose-writers. Each volume has a critical and appreciative introduction written especially for this edition.

Thompson, Daniel P. *The Green Mountain Boys.* Montpelier, E. P. Walton & Sons, 1839. 2 v.
> The best and most popular of Thompson's several historical tales based on early Vermont history.

Tupper, Frederick, and Brown, Helen Tyler, editors. *Grandmother Tyler's Book: The Recollections of Mary Palmer Tyler.* New York, G. P. Putnam's Sons, 1925.
> By the wife of the first really important Vermont writer, this clear-eyed and disillusioned book has an interest that transcends geographical boundaries. It is the closest thing to Jane Austen that ever came out of this State.

Tyler, Royall. *The Algerine Captive.* Walpole, N.H., David Carlisle, Jr., 1797. 2 v.
> The first American novel to be republished in England.

Tyler, Royall. *The Contrast.* Philadelphia, Prichard and Hall, 1790.
> The first play written by an American to be professionally staged.

Waller, Mary. *The Woodcarver of 'Lympus.* Boston, Little, Brown & Co., 1914.
> A novel laid in Bethel.

The Green Mountain Series. Brattleboro, The Stephen Daye Press, 1931. 4 v.
> An anthology of Vermont verse; a book of Vermont biographies; a collection of Vermont ballads; and a miscellany of Vermont prose. Sponsored by the Committee on Vermont Traditions and Ideals, of the Commission on Country Life.

### MISCELLANEOUS

Aiken, George D. *Pioneering with Wildflowers.* Putney, published for the author, 1935.
> A helpful non-technical book of instructions and suggestions about the domestication of the wildflowers of Vermont, many of which are in danger of extinction.

Allen, Ethan. *Reason the Only Oracle of Man,* etc. Bennington, Haswell and Russell. 1784.
> Most of the actual writing of this work and the Deistic doctrines contained in it are probably to be attributed to Dr. Thomas Young, the Philadelphia Deist and friend of Allen, rather than to the leader of the Green Mountain Boys. This was the first book published in America in direct opposition to the Christian religion.

Battell, Joseph. *The Morgan Horse and Register.* Middlebury, published by the author, 1894–1905. 2 v.
> An authoritative pioneer work.

Bentley, W. A., and Humphreys, W. J. *Snow Crystals.* New York, McGraw-Hill Book Co., 1931.

A magnificent book, containing hundreds of illustrations of snow crystals, to the study and micro-photographing of which Mr. Bentley, of Jericho, Vt., devoted his life.

Bullock, William Bryant. *Beautiful Waters.* Newport, The Memphremagog Press, 1926.
The anecdotal history of the region around Lake Memphremagog.

Canfield, Mary Grace. *Lafayette in Vermont.* Privately printed, 1934.
The complete story of the most famous progress ever made through this State.

Carroll, Daniel B. *The Unicameral Legislature in Vermont.* Montpelier, The Vermont Historical Society, 1932.
A careful study of the legislative system that Vermont retained until 1836. Prior to the present Nebraska experiment only two other States ever had unicameral assemblies, and both abandoned them after relatively short trials.

Chappell, George S. *Colonial Architecture in Vermont.* The White Pine Series of Architectural Monographs, vol. 6, no. 4. 1918.
A brief and superficial essay. There is no adequate study of Vermont architecture. Most of the many books on early New England houses accord this State haphazard and segmental treatment.

Crane, Charles Edward. *Let Me Show You Vermont.* New York, Alfred J. Knopf, 1937.
Probably the best essayistic interpretation ever written of this State, by one who knows Vermont, but not Vermont only.

Hard, Walter and Margaret. *This Is Vermont.* Brattleboro, The Stephen Daye Press, 1936.
The chatty record of a series of motor trips covering most of the State. Ingratiatingly written for the most part, it is not serviceable as a formal guide book.

Johnson, Luther B. *Vermont in Floodtime.* Randolph, The Roy L. Johnson Co., 1928.
An illustrated account of Vermont's worst natural catastrophe, the flood of 1927.

Lee, John Parker. *Uncommon Vermont.* Rutland, The Tuttle Co., 1926.
An ill-written miscellany containing sketches of several native eccentrics about whom little else has been written.

Marsh, George P. *The Earth as Modified by Human Action.* New York, Scribner, 1874.
A great pioneer work in pointing out the necessity of conserving and restoring depleted natural resources, by one of the greatest of Vermont's scholars.

O'Kane, Walter. *Trails and Summits of the Green Mountains.* Boston, Houghton Mifflin Co., 1926.
Rapid developments in the past decade have made this book somewhat incomplete, but it is still the best guide for climbing in Vermont.

Orton, Vrest, editor. *And So Goes Vermont.* Weston, The Countryman Press, 1937.
A book of excellent photographs showing some of the scenic beauties of the State and also some of the less idyllic aspects of country life here.

Phillips, John C., and Cabot, Thomas D. *Quick-Water and Smooth.* Brattleboro, The Stephen Daye Press, 1935.
A canoeist's guide to New England rivers, including several in Vermont.

Pixley, Aristene [Tyler, Helen Elizabeth]. *The Green Mountain Cookbook.* Brattleboro, The Stephen Daye Press, 1934.
> Only nostalgia can attribute to Vermont an indigenous cuisine, but this is a good cookbook, with many oldtime recipes.

Rice, Howard C. *Rudyard Kipling in New England.* Brattleboro, The Stephen Daye Press, 1936.
> An exposition of the quarrel with his brother-in-law that finally drove Kipling from this country. Interesting to compare with Kipling's own unhappy memories of Vermont as set forth in his autobiographical *Something of Myself* (1937).

Ripley, Thomas Emerson. *A Vermont Boyhood.* New York, D. Appleton, 1937.
> An uninhibited and entertaining account, but the author's family was too wealthy and too prominent to allow it much value as typical social history.

Spargo, John. *The Bennington Battle Monument; Its Story and Its Meaning.* Rutland, The Tuttle Co., 1925.

Spargo, John. *The Potters and Potteries of Bennington.* Boston, Houghton Mifflin Co., 1926.
> The last word on a subject of vital interest to students and collectors of early American ceramics. Richly illustrated.

Swartwout, Egerton. *Some Old-Time Churches in Vermont.* The White Pine Series of Architectural Monographs, vol. 13, no. 6.
> The text is mainly irrelevant whimsy, but the pictures are good.

Van de Water, Frederic. *A Home in the Country.* New York, John Day, 1937.
> A beautifully written account of a family that sought a refuge in Vermont and found here a home. It should be memorized by anyone contemplating taking up residence in the State.

*The Vermonter,* 1895 — . White River Junction.
> A monthly magazine containing many valuable sketches, reminiscences, and pictures. There are indices in the State Library and the library of the Vermont Historical Society.

*Walton's Vermont Register and Almanac,* 1818 to the present time. Published at Montpelier and other places.
> By no means the earliest of the various almanacs and business directories, this is the only one that has been published continuously since its inception.

# INDEX

*Abigail Adams*, the, 135
Ackworth, 267
Adams, Alvin, 153
Adams Express Company (St. Albans), 153
Adams, Deacon Martin, 125
Addison, 310
Agriculture, 38–42
    Dairy farming, 40–41, 136; United Farmers' Creamery Association (Morrisville), 247; grain and meat farming, 38–39; maple sugar production, 41–42, 136; sheep farming, 39–40
Aiken House (Rutland), 130
Airports:
    Hartness Municipal, 211; Milton, 279; Missisquoi, 278; St. Johnsbury, 180
Akley Memorial Building (Stowe), 248
Albany, 226
Alburg, 303
Alburg Bridge, 303
Alburg Center, 304
Alburg Springs, 303–04
Allen Chapel (*see* University of Vermont)
Allen, David, 177
Allen, Ebenezer, 307
Allen, Ethan, 70–71, 87, 102, 160, 277, 297, 307, 311
Allen, Fanny, 277
Allen Hospital (Essex), 349
Allen, Ira, 102, 297
Allen, Jonathan, 167
Allen, Levi, 134
Allen Tavern, site of (South Hero), 307
Allen's Cave, Ethan (Salisbury), 286
American Fidelity Building (Montpelier), 120
American Woolen Company (Winooski), 280
Appalachian Revolution, 15
Arcadia Retreat, site of (Westmore), 203–04
Architecture, 64–69
    Adam brothers, publications of, 66; Architectural influences, 64; Bailey House (Newbury), 66; building materials, 66–67; churches, 68; *Country Builder's Assistant, The*, 66; covered bridges, 68; domestic since 1850, 67; early farmhouses, 65; Grassemount (Burlington), 67; Greek Revival, 67; Hutchinson House (Woodstock), 65; Johnson House (Newbury), 65; *Maple Grove* (Randolph Center), 66; Old Constitution House (Windsor), 64; public buildings, 67–68; Ransom House (Castleton), 66; Richardson Romanesque, 140; Rockingham Meeting-House, 64; Wilcox House (Orwell), 66; Windham County Courthouse (Newfane), 68
Arlington, 297–98
Arnold, Benedict, 303
Arnold, Jonathan, 139, 180

Art, Southern Vermont artists, 323; Wood Gallery, 120
Arthur, Chester A., 34; Birthplace Site (Fairfield), 193
Artillery Range, U.S. (Underhill), 346
Ascutneyville, 166–67
Astor, John Jacob, 103
Athenwood (Montpelier), 120
Atkinson, John, 82
Austine School for the Deaf (Brattleboro), 100

Bailey House (Newbury) (*see* Architecture)
Bailey House (Woodstock), 155
Bailey's Mill (Hammondsville), 213
Baker, Joseph, 192
Baker, Remember, 87
Baker's Mill, site of (East Arlington), 298
Bakersfield, 192
Bank Building (Newfane), 188
Banner, Peter, 65
Barnard, 215
Barnard Gulf, 215
Barnes House (West Lincoln), 270
Barnet, 177
Barre, 77–81, 228
Barron, Mike, Colonel, 174
Bartlett's Fall (West Lincoln), 267
Barton, 182–83
Barton, William, Colonel, 183
Bartonville, 257
Basin Harbor, 310
Battell, Joseph, 112, 273
Battle of Bennington, 88–90
Battle of Hubbardton, site of, 318
Bayley House (Newbury), 175
Bayley, Jacob, 46, 175
Bayley Monument (Newbury), 175
Beecher Falls (Canaan), 208
Beeman's Corners, 313
Belaski, Steven, 84
Bellows, Benjamin, Colonel, 82
Bellows Falls, 81–85
Bellows Falls High School (Bellows Falls), 84
Bellows Falls Hydro-Electric Corporation (Bellows Falls), 84–85
Bellows Free Academy (Fairfax), 264
Bellows Free Academy (St. Albans), 136–37
Belmont, 326
Benjamin, Asher, 65
Bennington, 85–95, 369
Bennington Battle Monument, 94, 299
Bennington College, 299 (*see* Education)
*Bennington Mob*, 87
Benson, 314
Bentley, W. A., 347
Berry, Alexander, 240
Bethel, 215
Bickford buildings (Hardwick), 224

Bickford, George H., 224
Big Spring (West Branch), 262
Bigelow House (Addison), 311
Bill of Rights, 27
Billing Library (see University of Vermont)
Billings, Frederick, 154
Bingham Falls (West Branch), 261
Bingham House (Williston), 341
Bishop Hopkins Hall (Burlington), 110
Black River Academy (Ludlow), 255
*Black Snake*, the, 134
Blake, Bill, 83
Bloomfield, 194, 208-09
Bolton, 339
Boltonville, 350
Bomoseen, 318
Bondville, 191
Boston–Burlington Railway, 104
Bowlsville, 326
Bowman Memorial (Cuttingsville), 325
*Boy and Boot Fountain* (Wallingford), 292
Boyton, Paul, Captain, 82
Bradford, 173
Braintree, 217
Branch School, 272
Brandon lignites, 16
Brandon State School (Leicester), 287
Brattleboro, 95-100, 365-66
Brattleboro Hydropathic Establishment (Brattleboro), 99
Brattleboro Outing Club and Ski Jump (Brattleboro), 100
Brattleboro Retreat (Brattleboro), 100
Bread Loaf, 272-74
Bread Loaf Inn (Bread Loaf), 273
Bread Loaf Summer School of English (Bread Loaf), 273
Brick Home (Addison), 311
Brick House (Castleton), 363
Brick House (Essex), 348
Brick House (Ludlow), 255
Brick House (Marshfield), 336
Brick House (North Montpelier), 221
Brick House (Wallingford), 292
Bridgam, John, Captain, 224
Bridgewater, 358-59
Bridport, 311
Brigham Academy (Bakersfield), 192
Brigham House (St. Albans), 137
Brigham, Peter Bent, 192
Bristol, 267-68
*Bristol Bill*, 351-52
Bristol school buildings (Bristol), 267
Broadt, John, 267-68
Brocklebank Hill and quarries (Tunbridge), 238
Bromley House (Peru), 329
Brookfield floating bridge, 230
Brooksville, 285
Brownington, 184
Brunswick mineral springs, 209
Bryant Chucking Grinder Company (Springfield), 144
Bulfinch, Charles, 65
Burgoyne, General, 88
Burial Grounds:
　　Arlington, 298; Barre: Elmwood, 81, Hope, 81; Bennington, 91; Bridport, 311; Burlington: Greenmount, 108, Elmwood Avenue, 107; Cornwall, 316; Craftsbury, 226;

East Montpelier: Old Quaker, 221; East Poultney, 320; Groton, 351; Guildhall, 210; Lyndon Center, 181; Manchester, 297; Montpelier: Green Mountain, 337, Old, 122; Moretown, 250; North Dorset, 294; North Pownal, 301; Norwich, 171; Pownal, 300; Rutland, 132; South Newbury, 174; South Northfield, 218; South Ryegate, 350; South Wallingford, 293; Sutton, 182; Thetford, 172; Underhill, 346; Wallingford, 292; Williston, 341
Burke Green, 181
Burke Historical Society, 207
Burke Hollow, 181
Burke Mountain Club (East Burke), 206
Burklyn Hall (East Burke), 207
Burlington, 101-10, 281
Burlington City Hall, 106
Burns Memorial Statue (Barre), 78, 80
Burr and Burton Seminary (Manchester), 296

Cabot, 336
Cabot Plain (Cabot), 336
Cady, Daniel L., 72, 154
Cahoon, Daniel, Jr., 180
Cahoon House (Lyndon Center), 180
Calais, 222
Cambrian Period, 14, 15
Cambridge, 263, 345
Cambridge Inn (Cambridge), 346
Cambridge Junction, 345
Camp Elizabeth (Newport), 124
Campbell House (St. Albans), 137
Canaan, 208
Canadian Boundary, 204, 208
Capitol, the (Montpelier), 117-18
Carpenter, Benjamin, 161
Carpenter House (Middlesex), 338
Cary Maple Sugar Company (St. Johnsbury), 141
Castleton, 362-63
Catamount Tavern (Bennington), 87; site of, 92-93
Cave of the Winds (West Branch), 261
Cavendish, 256
Cedar Beach (Charlotte), 283
Cemeteries (see Burial Grounds)
Center Rutland, 361
Center Rutland Falls (Rutland), 133
Central Vermont Railway, 79, 135-36
Centrifugal separator, 41
Century House (St. Johnsbury), 141
Chamberlain Hill (Richmond), 340
Champlain Canal, 104
Champlain Country Club (Swanton), 278
Champlain, Samuel, 21
Champlain Transportation Company (Burlington), 47, 104, 106
Champlain Valley, 12, 13, 14, 16
Champlain Valley Exposition Grounds (Essex), 349
Chandler, Thomas, Judge, 164
Chapin House (Richmond), 340
Chapman, Ezekiel, 112
Charlotte, 282
Charlotte Essex Ferry, 283
Chase, Wareham, 222
Chazy Ferry, 304
Checkered House (Richmond), 340

Chelsea, 235–36
Cheshire toll bridge, 211
Chester, 257
Chester Depot, 256
Childs, Jonathan, Major, 368
Chimney Corner Tea House (Springfield), 145
Chimney Point, 270
Chipman, Daniel, 274
Chipman Hill (Brooksville), 285
Chippenhook, 291
Chittenden House, site of (Arlington), 297
Chittenden House, site of (Richmond), 341
Chittenden, Martin, Governor, 30, 134
Chittenden Mills (Jericho), 347
Chittenden, Thomas, Governor, 28
Churches: *by Denomination:*
  *Baptist:* Brandon, 287; Chester, 257; East
  Poultney, 320; Jamaica, 190; Saxtons
  River, 165. *Christian Science:* Burlington,
  109. *Congregational:* Bennington, 92; Bran-
  don, 288; Brattleboro, 99; Bridport, 311;
  Brownington, 184; Burlington, 107; Cam-
  bridge, 346; Charlotte, 282; Chester, 257;
  Cornwall, 316; Coventry, 184; Craftsbury,
  226; Dorset, 323; Essex, 348; Jamaica, 190;
  Jericho, 347; Middlebury, 114; Montpelier
  121; Newbury, 175; Newfane, 188; North
  Thetford, 172; Orange, 352–53; Peacham,
  178; Peru, 329; Rochester, 252; Rupert,
  322; Rutland, 131; Saxtons River, 165;
  South Woodbury, 223; Springfield, 145; St.
  Johnsbury, 140; Sudbury, 317; Thetford,
  172; Townshend, 189; Waterbury, 338;
  Wells River, 176; West Townshend, 189;
  Westmore, 202; Whiting, 316; Windsor,
  150. *Episcopal:* Barre, 80; Burlington, 110;
  Hydeville, 363; Lyndonville, 180; Shel-
  burne, 282. *Federated:* Castleton, 362; Es-
  sex, 348; Irasburg, 227; Marshfield, 336;
  Waitsfield, 251; Waterbury Center, 249;
  Williston, 341. *Greek Orthodox:* Springfield,
  145. *Methodist:* Bondville, 181; Jericho,
  347; Lower Granville, 252; Lyndonville,
  180–81; Pompanoosuc, 171; South Walden,
  343; St. Johnsbury, 141. *Presbyterian:*
  East Craftsbury, 225; South Ryegate, 351.
  *Roman Catholic:* Beeman's Corners, 313;
  Cambridge, 346; Newport, 126; North
  Hero, 306; Rutland, 131; Shoreham, 312;
  South Hero, 307; Springfield, 145; Under-
  hill, 346; West Rutland, 361. *Seventh Day
  Adventist:* North Townshend, 189. *Union:*
  East Dorset, 294; Pownal, 300; South Wal-
  lingford, 293. *Unitarian:* Burlington, 107.
  *United:* Warren, 251. *Universalist:* Chester
  Depot, 256; Londonderry, 330
  *By Town:*
  Arlington, 298; Bellows Falls, 84; Bethel,
  216; Brattleboro, 99; Burlington, 107;
  Clarendon, 291; Craftsbury, 226; Danby,
  293; Montpelier, 121; North Montpelier,
  222; Richmond, 340; Rutland, 131; South
  Reading, 212; Stowe, 248; West Barnet,
  177; Winooski, 280
City Bay, 306
Civil War (*see* History)
Civil War Statue (St. Johnsbury), 140
Clarendon, 291
Clarendon Gorge (East Clarendon), 325

Clarendon Springs, 291
Clark Statue (Bradford), 174
Clark's Tavern (South Glover), 240
Climate, 17
Clinton, George, Governor, 23
Clio Hall (*see* Education)
Coates, Walter J., 22
Cobb House (Cornwall), 316
Coffin, John, Captain, 256
Colburn House (Manchester), 295
Colbyville, 249
Cold Spring Camps, 205
Cole House (Castleton), 363
Collamer, Jacob, 153
College Green (Burlington), 108
College of Medicine (*see* University of Vermont)
Colonial House (Chester), 257
Colonial Stone House (Brandon), 288
Community House (Middlebury), 114
Community House (Peru), 329
Community House (Springfield), 145
Concord, 334
Confederate Raid, 33
Constitution of Vermont, First, 27
Coolidge, Calvin, 36, 253–54, 255, 359; birth-
  place of, 253–54
Coombs House (Thetford), 171
Copley Hospital (Morrisville), 247–48
Copperas Hill (Cuttingsville), 325
Coral Reef (Isle La Motte), 305
Cornwall, 316
Council of Safety, 88
*Country Builder's Assistant, The,* 114
Courser, Thomas, 78–79
Courthouse (Bennington), 91
Coventry, 184
Covered bridges:
  Jeffersonville, 345; Middlesex, 250; West
  Dummerston, 187; Windsor, 150. (*See
  Architecture*)
Craft House (Bradford), 174
Crafts, Ebenezer, Colonel, 225
Craftsbury, 225
Craftsbury Academy (Craftsbury), 226
Craftsbury Common (Craftsbury), 226
Crèvecœur, Saint-Jean de, 139
Crown Point Military Road Marker, 254, 269,
  312
Cushman Manufacturing Company (North
  Bennington), 300
Customhouses:
  Canadian, 196; Highgate, 276; Norton
  Mills, 204
Cuttingsville, 325

Dake, Thomas Royal, 66, 362
Dana, Charles L., 154
Dana Falls, 286
Dana, John Cotton, 154
Danby, 293
Danby marble quarry (Danby), 293
Danville, 335
Dartmouth College (*see* Education)
Davenport Monument (Williamstown), 229
Davenport, Thomas, 49, 229
Davis House (Montpelier), 121
Davis, Jacob, Colonel, 117, 122
Daye Press (Montpelier), 119; (St. Albans),
  152; (Westminster), 164

*Dean Boys*, 167
Deattrich, Frederick, 274
DeGrau Legend, 268
Denison Smith House (South Barre), 228
Derby, 200
Derby Line, 185
Dewey, Elijah, Captain, 92
Dewey, George, Commodore, 35, 121
Dewey House (Bennington), 92
Dewey House (Montpelier), 121
Dewey, Jedediah, Reverend, 92
Dewey, John, 106
Dewey, Julius Y., 119
Dimick Tavern, site of (Old Bennington), 370
Dog Team Tavern (Brooksville), 285
Doolittle, Ephraim, 312
Dorset, 322–23
Dorset Cave (East Dorset), 295
Dorset Hollow, 323
Dorset Inn (Dorset), 322
Dorset Playhouse (Dorset), 323
Douglas, Stephen A., birthplace of (Leicester), 287
Downer's Tavern (Perkinsville), 212
Drake Homestead (Pittsford), 288
Driftwind Press (North Montpelier), 221
Drury Brick and Tile Company (Essex), 348
Dummerston, 161
Dutton Gymnasium (Townshend), 188

Eagle Tavern (East Poultney), 320
East Alburg, 303 ·
East Arlington, 298
East Barnet, 178
East Barre, 353
East Barre Dam (East Barre), 353
East Berkshire, 197, 259
East Bethel, 231
East Braintree, 218
East Brookfield, 230
East Burke, 206–07
East Calais, 222
East Charleston, 194
East Clarendon, 324
East Craftsbury, 225
East Dorset, 294
East Fairfield, 192–93
East Granville, 217
East Hardwick, 242
East Haven, 206
East Jamaica, 189
East Middlebury, 274
East Montpelier, 221, 337
East Poultney, 320
East Randolph, 231
East Richford, 196
East Rupert, 322
East Ryegate, 176–77
East St. Johnsbury, 334
East Thetford, 171
East Wallingford, 326
Eaton, Dorman B., 222
Eaton, Ebenezer, 335
Eddy, Isaac, 167
Eden Corners, 246
Eden Mills, 246
Edgerton, Eleazer, 89
Edmunds, George F., Senator, 34; Birthplace (Jonesville), 340

Education, 53–57
    Bennington College, 56; Dartmouth College, 53; Earliest provision for, 53; First general provision for, 53; First Schools, maintenance of, 54; Middlebury College, 56; Normal School, first, 55; Norwich University, 56; Public High School, rise of, 54; School Law, first, 53; Secondary School, first, 54; St. Michael's College, 56; State School of Agriculture, 55
Ekwanok Country Club (Manchester), 296
Elkins, Jonathan, Deacon, 178
Elkins Tavern (Peacham), 178
Ellis House (Fair Haven), 365
Elm House (Danville), 335
Ely, 172
Ely Copper Mines (Vershire), 236
*Ely War, The*, 236
Enosburg Falls, 198
Equinox House (Manchester), 296
*Equivalent Lands* (Brattleboro), 96
Erie Canal (*see* Transportation)
Essex Center, 348
Essex Center Reforestation Project, 348
Essex Junction, 348
Estey, Jacob, 97
Estey Estate and Brattleboro Summer Theater (Brattleboro), 99–100
Estey Organ Company (Brattleboro), 97
Estey Organ Works (Brattleboro), 100
Evansville, 202
Evarts House (Windsor), 151
Exhibition Hall (Middlebury), 115
Eyck, Ten, Sheriff, 87

Fairbanks Family, 138–39
Fairbanks Scale Works (St. Johnsbury), 141
Fairbanks, Thaddeus, 139
Fairfax. 264
Fairfax Falls, 263–64
Fairfield, 193
Fair Haven, 363–65
Fairlee, 173
Fairview Farm (Hammondsville), 213
Falls Bridge (Springfield), 145
*Farmer's Museum, The*, 97
Farrar, Isaac, 198
Farrar-Mansur House (Weston), 330
Farrington House (Brandon), 287
Fauna (*see* Flora and Fauna)
Fay, Stephen, 87, 93
Federal Building (Newport), 125
Federal Building (Rutland), 131–32
Federal Writers' Project, vii
Felchville, 212
Fellows Gear Shaper Company (Springfield), 144
Fenians, 135
Ferrisburg, 283
Field, Eugene, 187
Field, Martin, 187
Fifteen-Mile Falls Dam (East Barnet), 179
Fillmore, Lavius, 65, 92 (*see* Architecture)
First Bridge across Connecticut River (Bellows Falls), 83
First Canal in America (Bellows Falls), 82
First Log House, site of (Chester), 256
Fish Hatchery, State. 208
Fisher, Isaac, 143

Fishery Station, Government (St. Johnsbury), 141
Fisk, James, 99, 301
Fisk Looms (St. Albans), 137; (Isle La Motte), 305
*Flagg Marriages*, 257
Fleming, Alexander, Colonel, 84
Fleming Museum (*see* University of Vermont)
Fletcher Farm, 255
Fletcher Station, 193
Flood of 1927, 36
Flora and Fauna, 18–20
Foot, Solomon, 130
Ford, Frederick, 316
Forests:
 Ainsworth State, 229; Ascutney State, 167; Battell Park, 272; Calvin Coolidge State, 254; Cheney Woods, 323; Darling State, 207; Elmore State, 248; Gifford Woods, 253; Green Mountain National, 62, 293; Groton State, 351–52; Hazen's Notch, 259; Mount Philo, 283; Okemo Mountain State, 255; Proctor-Piper State, 61, 256; Rutland City, 360; Sand Bar State, 308; Townshend State, 189; Wilgus State, 166; Willoughby State, 182; Forest Service, U.S., 61
Fortification Hills (Cabot), 336
Forts:
 Crown Point, ruins of (Addison), 271; Defiance, site of (Barnard), 215; Dummer, site of (Brattleboro), 215; Ethan Allen Military Reservation (Essex), 349; Frederick, site of (Winooski), 280; Old Cassin, site of (Basin Harbor), 310; Ranger (Rutland), 128; Ranger, site of (Rutland), 133, 361; Rutland (Rutland), 128; Ste. Ann, site of (Isle La Motte), 304; Ticonderoga, 25, 88, 313–14; Vengeance, site of (Brandon), 288; Warren, site of (Castleton), 362
Fox Farm (Wolcott), 344
Foxville, 229
Franklin, 198–99
Franklin County Rod and Gun Club (Swanton), 278
*Free Press* (Burlington), 105
French Hill (Richmond), 341
French, William, 164
Frost, Frances, 73, 136
Frost, Robert, 72; home of (South Shaftsbury), 299

Gallup Mills, 210
Galusha House (Shaftsbury), 299
Galusha, Jonas, Governor, 299
Garrison, William Lloyd, 90
Gassetts, 256
Geology, 13–17
Geography and Topography, 10–13
Georgia Center, 278
Georgia Plain (Georgia Center), 279
Georgian House (Belmont), 327
Georgian House (Jericho), 327
Gilbert House (Fair Haven), 365
Gilman, 333
Glastenbury, 298
Glover, 239
Glover, John, General, 239
Goddard Junior College (Barre), 81
Goddard, Mary, 81

Gookin House (Rutland), 132
Government, Framework of (*see* History)
Graham Homestead (Craftsbury), 226
Granby, 210
Grand Isle Bridge, 306
Grand Isle Ferry, 307
Grange Hall (Hammondsville), 213
Grange Hall (West Dummerston), 187
Grange Monument (St. Johnsbury Center), 180
Granite Monument (Royalston), 232
Granite Shed (Barre), 79
Granite Quarries (Woodbury) (*see* Industry and Commerce)
Graniteville, 228
Granville, 252
Granville Gulf, 249, 251–52
Granville Gulf Reservation, 251–52
Granville Manufacturing Company (Granville), 252
Grassemount (*see* University of Vermont; Architecture)
Gray, John, 322
Graystone Inn (Hammondsville), 213
Greeley, Horace, 320
Green, Henrietta Howland Robinson, 85; former home of (Bellows Falls), 85
Green, Henry, Captain, 84
Green House (Windsor), 151
*Green Mountain Boys*, 24, 26, 87, 297
Green Mountain House (East Arlington), 298
Green Mountain Junior College (Poultney), 319
Green Mountain Liberal Institute (South Woodstock), 213
Green Mountain Parkway, 36–37
*Green Mountain Patriot, The*, 178
Green Mountain Power Plant No. 1 (Waterbury), 339
Green Mountain Tavern (Bennington), 87
Greene, Anne Bosworth, 213
Greenleaf, Stephen, 97
Greensboro, 242
Greensboro Bend, 242
Greens Corners, 200
Griffith, Silas, 293
Gristmill (Chelsea), 236
Gristmill (Colbyville), 249
Gristmill (Manchester), 295
Groton, 351–52
Guildhall, 209–10
Guilford, 159–61

Hale, Enoch, Colonel, 83
Halfway House (Underhill), 347
Hall, Samuel Read, Reverend, 55, 183
Hammondsville, 213
Hancock, 252
Hands Cove Monument (Shoreham), 312
Hard House (East Arlington), 298
Hard, Walter, 72
Hardwick, 224, 343
Hardwick Country Club (Hardwick), 343
Hardwick Memorial Building, Hardwick, 224
Harmon, Reuben, 322
Harmonyville, 188
Harrington, Theophilus, Judge, 291
Harris House (Castleton), 363
Harris, Paul P., boyhood home of (Wallingford), 292

Hart, Emma, 112
Hartford, 234
Hartland, 168-69
Hartland Community Fair Horse Show, 168
Hartland insurgents, 168-69
Hartness, James, 143
Harvey, Alexander, Colonel, 178
Haskell, Charles E., 344
Haskell Opera House (Derby Line), 185
Hawkins Seed Shop (Felchville), 212
Hayden Farmhouse (Craftsbury), 226
Hayes Tavern (West Brattleboro), 366
Hazen Road Monument (East Hardwick), 243
Hazen's Notch (Lowell), 258
Hell's Half Acre (Bristol), 268
Hemenway, Abby Maria, 255
Henry House (North Bennington) (see Architecture)
Hexagonal Schoolhouse (East Bethel), 231
Highgate, 275
Highgate Springs, 276
Higley House (Castleton), 363
History, 21-37
    Admission to Union, 29; American Revolution, 25; Anti-Masonic Movement, 31-32; Anti-Slavery Movement, 27, 32-33; Civil War, 33; Cumberland County Convention, 24-25; earliest settlements, 21-22; Embargo Act of 1812, 30; famine of 1816, 31; government framework, 27, changes in, 34; independence, 28; Indians in Vermont, 21; land grants, 21-22; New Hampshire Grants, 23, 24, 25, 27, 128; Spanish War, 35; War of 1812, 30-31; Westminster Massacre, 24; World War, 35-36
Holland Bridge (Newfane), 188
Holstein-Friesian Breeders' Association, 99
Hoyt House (Manchester), 296
Hoyt House (St. Albans), 137
Hubbard, Ashel, 147-48
Hubbardton, 318
Hudson, Henry Norman, 316
Humphrey Homestead (Cambridge), 346
Hunt, Richard Morris, 98
Hunt, William Morris, 97
Hunter and His Dog (West Branch), 262
Huntington, 354-55
Hutchinson, Aaron, Reverend, 152
Hutchinson House (Woodstock), 155 (see Architecture)
Hyde House (St. Albans), 137
Hyde Manor (Sudbury), 317
Hyde Park, 246-47
Hydeville, 363

Ice caves (Wallingford), 292
Idiocy of rural life, The, 7
Il Marzocco, Donatello's, reproduction (Lyndonville), 180
Indian Stones (Greenbush), 212
Indians: Abnaki, 83, 84
Industry and Commerce, 43-45
    Asbestos mines, 246; Fairbanks scales (St. Johnsbury), 139; Granite: (Barre), 78-79, (Woodbury), 223 Lumbering, 43, 124; Maple sugar (St. Johnsbury), 141; Marble: (Middlebury), 112, (Rutland), 128-29, (Swanton), 277, (West Rutland), 361, Miscellaneous products, 45; Paper, 44;

Railroads (Newport), 124; Slate quarries, 320, 363-64; Textile, 44, 83
International Rotary Club (Derby Line), 185
Irasburg, 227
Irasville, 251
Irish, John, 292
Island Pond, 205-06
Island Route, 302
Isle La Motte, 304
Isle La Motte Historical Building, 305

Jacksonville, 367
Jail, site of first (Burlington), 110
Jamaica, 190
Janes, Pardon, 222
Jarvis, William, 166
Jay, 244
Jay, John, 244
Jeffersonville, 345
Jericho, 347
Jericho, site of first settlement in, 347
Johnnycake Hill, 278
Johns, James, 355
Johnson, 345
Johnson House (Newbury), 176 (see Architecture)
Johnson House (Woodstock), 155
Johnson, Thomas, Colonel, 178
Jones and Lamson Machine Company (Springfield), 144
Jonesville, 339-40
Journal of the Times, The, 90
Judd, Eben, 112

Kathan, John, 187
Kendall, Nicanor, 148
Kendall's Corners, 211
Kent Tavern (Dorset), 322
Kent's Corners, 222
Kilburn House (Rutland), 130
King, Gideon, 103
King's Highway, 163
Kipling, Rudyard, 97, 161
Kirby, 334
Knight Inn (North Hero), 306
Kreigger Rock (Pownal Center), 301
Kurn Hattin Home (Westminster), 164

La Douville, 134
Lafayette Manoir, 275
Lafayette, Marquis de, 167, 183
Lake Champlain Bridge (West Lincoln), 271
Lakes, 12-13
    Abenaki, 172; Amherst, 254; artificial, 336; Bomoseen, 12, 318; Champlain, 12, 14, 101, 103, 302; Crystal, 182; Dunmore, 286; Echo, 254; Eden, 245-46; Fairlee, 173; Forest, 205; Great Averill, 204-05; Greenwood, 223; Hortonia, 317; Lake of the Clouds, 261; Lamoille, 248; Lotus, 229; Maidstone, 209; Memphremagog, 12, 123; Morey, 173; Norton, 205; Pleiad, 272; Raponda (Ray Pond), 367; Sadawga, 367; Seymour, 201; Shaftsbury, 298; Spring, 235; St. Catherine, 320; Willoughby, 200, 202; Woodbury, 223
Lamoille County Fairgrounds, 247
Lane House (Windsor), 150

Largest country store in the world (Wolcott), 344
Larrabee's Point (Shoreham), 312
Lawrence, Richard Smith, 148
Leach House (Pawlet), 321
Leicester, 286
Leland and Gray Seminary (Townshend), 189
Lewis, Sinclair, 215
Libraries:
  *Albany*, 226; *Arlington*, Martha Canfield, 298; *Barre*, Aldrich Public, 80; *Bellows Falls*, Rockingham Free, 85; *Bennington*, Free, 91, Old Academy, 93; *Bradford*, Wood's, 174; *Brattleboro*, Public, 99; *Bristol*, Lawrence Memorial, 267; *Burlington*, Fletcher Free, 110; *Cornwall*, 316; *Craftsbury*, 226; *Danby*, Griffith Memorial, 293; *Dorset*, 322; *East Craftsbury*, Sampson Memorial, 225; *Hardwick*, Jeudevine Memorial, 224–25; *Hyde Park*, 247; *Irasburg*, Leach Public, 227; *Jamaica*, Memorial, 190; *Ludlow*, 225; *Lyndonville*, Cobleigh Public, 181; *Manchester*, Skinner, 296; *Middlebury*, Abernathy, of American Literature, 113; *Milton*, 279; *Montpelier*, Free Public, 119, Kellogg-Hubbard, 121, Vermont State, 119; *Newport*, Goodrich Memorial, 125–26; *North Bennington*, McCullough, 300; *Pittsford*, Walker Memorial, 288; *Rutland*, Free Public, 131; *Sharon*, Baxter Memorial, 234; *Shelburne*, Pierson Free, 282; *Springfield*, 145; *St. Albans*, Free, 137; *St. Johnsbury*, Athenaeum, 140; *Swanton*, 277; *Thetford*, Latham Memorial, 172; *Vergennes*, Bixby Memorial, 284; *Waitsfield*, 251; *Wallingford*, Gilbert Hart, 292; *Waterbury*, Public, 338–39; *West Rutland*, 361; *Westfield*, Hitchcock Memorial, 244; *Weston*, Wilder Memorial, 331; *Whiting*, 316; *Williamstown*, Ainsworth Public, 229; *Woodstock*, Williams Public, 154–55
Lincoln, 266
Lincoln Estate, Robert Todd (Manchester), 297
Lincoln Gap, 266
Lincoln Pass, 265
Liscum, Emerson H., General, 356
Literature, 70–73
Little Boston, 357
Little Red Schoolhouse (Simonsville), 331
Little Woolen Company Mill (North Montpelier), 221
Lochlea Little Theater (Wells), 320
Lockwood, William, 143
Londonderry, 330
Long Trail (*see* Recreation)
Lord's Prayer Rock (Bristol), 267
Lovejoy Tool Company (Springfield), 144
Low House (Bradford), 174
Lowell, 245, 258
Lower Granville, 252
Ludlow, 255
Lull, Timothy, 168
Lunenburg, 333
Lyndon Center, 180, 181
Lyndon Institute (Lyndon Center), 181
Lyndonville, 180
Lyon, Matthew, 364, 365

Macdonough Monument (Vergennes), 284
Maidstone Station, 209
Malletts Bay, 279–80
Mallett's Bay *Marble*, 11
*Man and Nature*, 153–54
Manchester, 296
*Manchester* (Randolph), 218
Manchester Center, 295
Manchester Depot, 328
Maple Grove (Randolph Center), 217 (*see* Architecture)
*Maples, The* (Rutland), 132
Marble Mills (Swanton) (*see* Industry)
Marble quarrying (West Rutland) (*see* Industry)
March, Joseph, 234
Markham, Isaac, 112
Marlboro, 366
Marlboro Tavern, 366
Marsh, George P., 153
Marsh, James, Reverend, 55
Marshfield, 336
Masonic Temple (Johnson), 345
May Falls, 182
Mayo, Henry T., Admiral, 36
McConnell Rest Home (Brandon), 288
McIndoe Falls, 177
McIntire, Samuel, 65
McKinstry House (Bethel), 216
Mead, Elinor, 99
Mead, James, 127
Mead, Larkin, 98, 140
Mead, Thomas, 337–38
Mead, William Rutherford, 98
Meecham-Ainsworth House (Castleton), 363
Meeting House Rock (North Shrewsbury), 326
Meeting-Houses:
  Burke Hollow, 181; Cabot, first, site of, 336; Hardwick, French, 224–25; Rockingham, 257–58 (*see* Architecture); Woodstock, 155
Melvin, Eleazer, Captain, 190
Mendon, 360–61
Mexican War, 32
Middlebury, 111, 115
Middlebury College, 111–12 (*see* Education); Campus, 113–14
Middlebury Female Seminary, 112
Middlebury *Register*, 273
Middlesex, 337
Middlesex Gorge, 250
Miles Pond, 333
Military Roads (*see* Transportation)
Mill Hollow, 323
Mill of the Missisquoi Pulp and Paper Company (Sheldon Springs), 199
Mill Village, 289
Miller, William, 222
Millet, Jean François, 97
Mills, Susan, 198
Milton, 279
Mineral Spring (Sheldon Springs), 199
Missisquoi Bay, 276
Monroe-Hawkins House (Shaftsbury), 299
Montcalm Landing, 313
Montgomery, 259
Montgomery Center, 259
Montgomery Notch, 245
Montpelier, 115–23, 337

Moor, Fairbank, Captain, 97
Moretown, 250
Morey, Samuel, Captain, 47, 173
Morgan, 201
Morgan Center, 201
Morgan horse, the, 42
Morrill Act, 34
Morrill Hall (see University of Vermont)
Morrill, Justin S., Senator, 34
Morris House (Springfield), 166
Morrisville, 247–48, 344
Morse, Rebecca, 334
Morse House (Rutland), 130–31
Morse's Mill, 262
Morton, Levi P., 35
Moss Glen Falls, 251–52
Motte, Sieur de La, 304
Mount Holly, 326
Mount Olga Fire Lookout Tower (Marlboro), 366–67
Mount St. Mary's Academy (Burlington), 108
Mountains, 10–11
  Aeolus, 294; Allen, 266; Ascutney, 84, 167; Bald, 189, 203; Ball, 190; Belvidere, 246; Bird, 362; Black, 186; Blue, 177; Bread Loaf, 266; Bromley, 190; Brooks, 182; Burke, 181, 207; Camel's Hump, 339; Cow, 210; Equinox, 296; Glebe, 331; Governor's, 160; Granite Hills, 11; Grant, 266; Green, 10–11; Hanley, 362; Hogback, 366; Horrid, 252; Jay Peak, 59, 195, 244; Kilburn, 81, 83; Killington Peak, 360; Lincoln, 266; Little Ascutney, 212; Mansfield, 59, 191, 193, 248, 343; Moosalamoo, 286; Peaked, 187; Prospect, 369; Rattlesnake, 189; Red Sandrack Hills, 11; Snake, 269, 310; Stratton, 60; Sugarloaf, 251; Tabor, 293; Taconic, 11, 14; Tom, 254; Wantastiquet, 84, 186; Warren Pinnacle, 251; Westmore, 202; Wood, 223; Worcester Range, 10
Mountain View Farm (East Burke), 207
Municipal Building (Orleans), 183
Museums:
  Bennington, Historical, 91; Brownington, Orleans County Historical Society, 184; East Burke, White Schoolhouse, 206–07; St. Johnsbury, Natural Science, 140; Westminster, 164; Woodstock, Williams Collection of Japanese Art, 155

National Life Building (Montpelier), 119
Natural Bridge (Warren), 251
Natural Refrigerator (West Branch), 262
Natural Setting, 10–17
Neshobe Falls (Brandon), 287
New Hampshire Grants (see History)
New Haven, 268
New Haven Junction (Vergennes), 284
New Lights, 225
Newbury, 175
Newfane, 187
Newfane Hill (Newfane), 187
Newfane Inn (Newfane), 188
Newport, 123–26, 195
Newport Center, 195
Nichols, Josiah, 112
Normal School (Lyndon Center), 181
North Bennington, 300
North Clarendon, 290

North Dorset, 294
North Fairfax, 265
North Ferrisburg (Charlotte), 283
North Hartland, 169
North Hero, 306
North Hero Courthouse, 306
North Hyde Park, 246
North Montpelier, 221
North Pawlet, 321
North Pomfret, 234
North Pownal, 301
North Randolph, 231
North Royalton, 231–32
North Sandgrove, 329–30
North Sheldon, 198
North Shrewsbury (Northam), 326
North Springfield, 211
North Thetford, 172
North Troy, 196
North Tunbridge, 237
North Windham, 331
Northam State Picnic Area (North Shrewsbury), 326
Northfield, 219
Northfield Falls, 220
Northfield Gulf (East Braintree), 218
Northrup House (Castleton), 363
Norton, John, Captain, 91
Norton, Luman, Judge, 91
Norton Mills, 204
Norton-Fenton House (Bennington), 91
Norwich, 171
Norwich University, 171, 219 (see Education)
Nose-Dive Trail (West Branch), 261
Nott, John, 142
Novelli, Samuel, 80
Noyes, John Humphrey, 162

Oak Grove Seminary (Pownal), 301
Octagon House (St. Johnsbury), 141
Octagonal House (West Brattleboro), 366
Old Bannister House (Pownal), 301
Old Bennington, 369–70
Old Blacksmith Shop (Jericho), 347
Old Bowman Tavern (North Clarendon), 290
Old Brick House (Addison), 269
Old Coach House (Cambridge), 346
Old Constitution House (Windsor), 149 (see Architecture)
Old Farmhouse (East Dorset), 295
Old Fenton Homestead (North Bennington), 300
Old Gravestone (Addison), 269
Old Gray House (Groton), 351
Old Heerman Mill (Coventry), 184
Old Homestead (Clarendon), 291
Old Homestead (East Dorset), 295
Old House (Burke Hollow), 181
Old House (Glover), 239
Old House (Springfield), 145
Old Jail (Middlebury), 115
Old Ladies' Home (Randolph), 216
Old Lake House (Groton), 351
Old Paper Mill (Wells River), 350
Old Sawmill (Hardwick), 225
Old Stone House (Brownington), 184
Old Stone Inn (South Hero), 307
Old Stone Mill (South Shaftsbury), 299
Old Stone School (Sudbury), 317

Old Stone Shop (Wallingford), 292
Old Tavern (Manchester), 295
Old Willoughby Lake House, site of (Westmore), 203
Oldest House (Clarendon), 291
One-room schools, 8
Orange, 352–53
Ordovician Period, 14–15
Orleans, 183
Orleans County Courthouse (Newport), 125
Otter Creek (see Rivers)
Owl's Head (Newport), 124
Ox-Bow Antique Shop (Newbury), 175
Ox-Bow Meadows (Newbury), 175

Paddock House (Barre), 80
Paddock Mansion (St. Johnsbury), 139–40
Paddock, Robert, 80
Page, Carroll S., 247
Page House (Hyde Park), 247
Painter, Gamaliel, 111
Paleozic Period, 14, 15
Palisades (Fairlee), 173
Palisades (Middlesex), 338
Panton, 309
Paper Industry (Bellows Falls), 83
Papineau War, 135
Park, Jonathan Memorial (Newfane), 188
Parker, Robert, 78
Parks:
    Arnold (St. Johnsbury), 139; Battell (Ripton), 61; Battery (Burlington), 104, 106; City Hall (Burlington), 103; Ethan Allen (Burlington), 110; Green Mountain National, 63; Hubbard, 122; Legion (Derby Line), 185; Maine Street (Rutland), 127, 130; Pageant, 182; Powers' (Lyndonville), 180–81; Queen City (Burlington), 281; Roaring Brook (Barton), 183; Taylor (St. Albans), 136
Parks and Woolson Machine Company (Springfield), 144
Parsonage, the (Simonsville), 332
Passumpsic, 179
Pavilion Hotel (Montpelier), 120
Pawlet, 321–22
Payne, Ed, 358
Peacham, 178
Peacham Academy (Peacham), 178
Peirce, Arthur W., 81
Pekin, 222
People's Academy (Morrisville), 247
Perfectionists, 162–63
Perkinsville, 211
Perley Davis House (East Montpelier), 221
Peru, 329
Peters, Samuel, 360
Pettibone, Daniel, 112
Phelps, Edward J., 112, 348
Phelps-Reade House (South Hero), 308
Pierce's Corner (North Clarendon), 290
Pioneer Home (Rutland), 131
Pisgah Trail, 203
Pittsfield, 253
Pittsford, 288
Pittsford Mills, 289
Plainfield, 336–37
Plattsburgh, battle of, 134
Pleistocene Glacial Age, 16

Plymouth, 253–54, 359
Plymouth Union, 253
Poland, Luke, Judge, 34
Pomfret, Center, 234
Pompanoosuc, 171
Pond House (Rutland), 130
Ponds:
    Big Salem, 201; Bristol, 268; Childs, 172; Derby, 185; Electric Light, 201; Elfin, 292; Elligo, 225; Groton, 352; Hapgood, 63, 329; Hardwick, 225; Harvey, 178; Island, 194, 205; Jackson, 327; Joe's, 335; Limehurst, 229; Little Salem, 201; Long, 203; Lyford, 343; Millpond, 329; Mineral, 209; Molly's, 335; Neal, 333; North Dorset, 294; Pensioner's, 202; Roads, 229; Runaway, 241; Sterling, 12; Ticklenaked, 177
Porter, Russell W., 143
Post office (Bennington), 90
Potash smuggling, 134
Potterville, 344
Poultney, 319–20
Power Plant (Wilmington), 368
Powers, Hiram, 154
Pownal, 301
Pownal Center, 300
Presbrey-Leland Quarries (Brattleboro), 186
Proctor, 129
Proctor, Redfield, 35, 128–29
Proctorsville, 255–56
Prosper, 214
Purdy, Frederick A., 223
Putney, 161–63
Putney School (Putney), 163

Quakers, 356
Quarry Terminal (Danby), 294
Quechee Gorge, 358

Racial Elements, 51–52
Radio stations:
    Springfield: WNBX, 145; Waterbury Center: WDEV, 249
Randolph, 216
Randolph Center, 216
Ransom House (Castleton), 362 (see Architecture)
Rattlesnake Point, 286
Rattlesnake Ridge (Benson), 314
Rawson House (Jericho), 347
Rawson Monument (Rawsonville), 190
Rawsonville, 190
Recreation, 58–63
    Footpath in the Wilderness, 59; Green Mountain Club, 59; Green Mountain Horse Association Bridle Paths, 60; Long Trail, 59, 258, 266, 325, 339, 345, 360; Long Trail Lodge, 60; Monroe Skyline Trail, 60; Mount Mansfield region, 59; Publicity Service (Montpelier), 58; Vermont Horse and Bridle Trail Bulletin, 60; Youth Hostel Movement, 62
Redstone Hall (see University of Vermont)
Rhind, J. Massey, 80
Rich House (North Montpelier), 221
Richardson House (Woodstock) (see Architecture)
Richford, 196
Richmond, 340

Ripley Mill (Rutland), 132
Ripton, 274
Rivers, 11–12
  Antecedent, defined, 12; Barton, 183; Battenkill, 12; Black, 184; Connecticut, 11–12, 165, 209; Mad, 250, 251; Missisquoi, 196; Moose, 333, 334; Nulhegan, 194, 208–09; Otter Creek, 12, 127, 133; Passumpsic, 206; Sleeper's, 141; Twenty-Mile Stream, 256; Walloomsac, 12
Riverside State Reformatory for Women (Rutland), 132
Riverton, 220
Robert, Eli, 311
Robin Hood of Vermont, 88
Robinson, Charlotte, home of, 283
Robinson, David, 94; house of, 93–94
Robinson Hall (see University of Vermont)
Robinson, Moses, Governor, 94
Robinson, Rowland E., 71, 245, 283
Robinson, Samuel, Captain, 87, 93; site of cabin (Bennington), 93
Robinson's Tomb, Betsy (Bennington), 94
Rochester, 252
Rock, types of, 13–14
Rockingham, 257–58
Rockingham Meeting House (see Architecture)
Rockingham Public Hospital (Bellows Falls), 84
Rogers' Rangers, 159, 169, 178, 194, 208–09
Rogers, Robert, Major, 124
Roller Coaster Road, 205
Ross House (Weston), 331
Rowell's Inn (Simonsville), 331
Rowley, Thomas, 70, 128, 293
Roxbury, 217
Royalton, 232
Royce, Homer, 197
Royce, Stephen, 197
Ruined Stone House (Danby), 294
Rupert, 322
Russell, William A., 83
Rustic Shelter (Underhill), 347
Rutland, 126–33, 289, 290
Rutland Herald, 128
Rutland Railroad, 128
Ryegate, 177

Salisbury, 286
Sancoick Mills, 89
Sand Bar Bridge, 308
Sargent, John Garibaldi, 255
Saxtons River, 165
Scarsburg, 368
Scoffield House (St. Albans), 137
Scott, William, 352
Shaftsbury, 298
Shaftsbury Center, 299
Shard Villa (Middlebury), 285
Sharon, 233
Sheffield, 239
Shelburne, 282
Shelburne Harbor (Burlington), 282
Sheldon Art Museum (Middlebury), 114
Sheldon Junction, 199
Sheldon Springs, 199
Sherburne, 359–60
Sherman, Alcott, 319
Sherman House (Windsor), 151
Sherman of Barre, 77

Shipman, William R., 81
Shoreham, 312
Shortsleeve Mink Farm (Lowell), 245
Shrewsbury, 325
Silent Cliff (Branch School), 272
Simonsville, 331
Singing Bird (West Branch), 262
Ski Jump (Hancock), 252
Ski Meisters (North Shrewsbury), 326
Slack Corporation (Springfield), 144
Slade Hall (see University of Vermont)
Slade, James S., 113
Slate quarrying (see Industry and Commerce)
Slavery abolished (see Bill of Rights)
Smalley, Benjamin, 111
Smith Monument (South Royalston), 233
Smuggler's Cave (West Branch), 262
Smuggler's Face (West Branch), 262
Smuggler's Notch (West Branch), 261
Snowflake King (see Bentley, W. A.)
Soldiers' Monument (Manchester), 296
Somerset, 368–69
South Barre, 228
South Barre Recreation Field, 228
South Cambridge, 262
South Dorset, 323
South Hero, 307
South Londonderry, 330
South Lunenburg, 333
South Newbury, 174
South Northfield, 218
South Peacham, 178
South Pomfret, 234
South Randolph, 231
South Reading, 212
South Royalston, 232
South Ryegate, 350–51
South Shaftsbury, 299
South Tunbridge, 238
South Walden, 343
South Wallingford, 293
South Woodbury, 223
South Woodstock, 213
Southern Vermont Artists (see Art)
Southwick Memorial Building (see University of Vermont)
Spanish War (see History)
Spencer, G. P., 181
Split Rock (Brandon), 288
Spring Camp Ground (New Haven Junction), 284
Springfield, 142–46
Springfield Terminal Railway Company, 143
St. Albans, 133–37
St. Albans Raid, 135
St. Albans Railroad Station, 136
St. Ann, Shrine of (Isle La Motte), 304
St. Johnsbury, 138–41, 179, 334–35
St. Johnsbury Academy (St. Johnsbury), 141
St. Johnsbury Center, 180
St. Johnsbury Vocational School (St. Johnsbury), 141
St. Michael's College (Essex), 349 (see Education)
Stage Tavern (South Walden), 343
Stannard, General, birthplace of (St. Albans), 278
Staples, Joseph, Captain, 240
Stark, John, Colonel, 88

Starksboro, 356
State Capitol (Montpelier) (*see* Architecture)
State Fish Hatchery (East Granville), 217
State Normal School (Castleton), 363
State Normal School (Johnson), 345
State School of Agriculture (*see* Education)
*Statue of the Green Mountain Boy* (Rutland), 130
Steele, Benjamin, 168
*Stellafane* (Springfield), 143
Stephen Daye Press (*see* Daye Press)
Stevens Mills, 196
Stevens, Thaddeus, 335
Stevensville Summer Colony (Underhill), 347
Stewart, John W., 112
Stockbridge, 253
Stone House (Addison), 311
Stone House (Alburg), 303
Stone House (Alburg Center), 304
Stone House (Beeman's Corner), 314
Stone House (North Bennington), 300
Stone Mill (Clarendon), 291
Stone, Nathan, Colonel, 146
Stone, Philip, 311
Stone water tub (Westmore), 203
Stoware Manufacturing Company (Stowe), 249
Stowe, 248–49, 260
Strong House (Vergennes), 284
Strong Mansion (Addison), 269
Studio Tavern (Manchester), 297
Sudbury, 317
Summit, 327
Sumner-Steele House (Hartland), 168
Supreme Court Building (Montpelier), 118
Sutton, 181–82
Swan House (Woodstock) (*see* Architecture)
Swanton, 216
Sycamore Lodge (Rutland), 130
*Synagogue*, the (Rutland), 132

Taftsville, 358
Talcville, 253
Taquahunga Club (Swanton), 277
Teela-Wooket (Roxbury), 218
Temple House (Rutland), 130
Tertiary Period, 16
Thetford Academy (Thetford), 172
Thetford Hill (Thetford), 172
Thomas, Stephen, General, birthplace of (Bethel), 216
Thompson, Daniel P., 71
Thompson of Holden, 77
Thompson, Zadock, 359
Thompson's Point (Charlotte), 283
Tichenor Mansion, Isaac (Bennington), 93
Tiffany Estate (Windsor), 168
Tinmouth, 292
Tosi, Gino, 80
Town Hall (Albany), 226
Town Hall (Felchville), 212
Town Hall (Townshend), 188
Townshend, 188
Twing Foundry (Barre), 80
Twing House (Barre), 80
Twing, Joshua, 78, 80
Transportation, 46–50
    *Air:* 49–50. *Highway:* 46–47, 49, Military Roads, 46–47, Turnpikes, 47. *Marine:* 47, 48, Erie Canal, 48. *Railroad:* 48–49, Electric, 49

Trotter, William, Captain, 174
Troy, 244
Troy Falls, 195–96
True Temper Inn (Wallingford), 292
Tunbridge, 237–38
Tunbridge Fair (Tunbridge), 235–38; Fairgrounds, 237–38
Tunbridge Raid, 237
Tupper, Norman, 112
Turnpikes (*see* Transportation)
Twenty-Mile Encampment, site of, 256
Tyler, Royall, 70, 97, 161
Tyson, 254

U.S. Bobbin and Shuttle Company Mill (Willoughby), 182
Underhill, 346
Underhill Center, 346
Union Hall (Newlane), 188
Union House (Richford), 197
Union Village, 171
United Farmers' Creamery Association (*see* Agriculture)
University Farm (Williston), 341–42
University of Vermont, 102, 105, 108–09, 128
Upson, William Hazlitt, 274
Upwey Farms (Hammondsville), 213

Vail, Micah, 293
Vail, Theodore, 181
Valcour Island, 309
Van Ness Hotel (Burlington), 106
Vergennes, 283, 309
Vermont Academy (Saxtons River), 165
*Vermont Autograph and Remarker, The*, 355
*Vermont Gazette, The*, 164
Vermont Historical Society (Montpelier), 119, 355; Museum of, 119
Vermont Industrial School (Vergennes), 284
*Vermont Journal and Advertiser*, 148
Vermont Junior College (Montpelier), 122
Vermont Little Theater, 323
Vermont Maple Cooperative (Essex), 349
Vermont Marble Company (Rutland), 129, 132 (*see* Industry and Commerce)
Vermont Native Industries (Bridgewater), 359
Vermont Plywood Corporation (Hancock), 252
Vermont Soldiers' Home (Bennington), 91
Vermont State Fair Grounds (North Hartland), 169
Vermont State Prison and House of Correction (Windsor), 149
Vermont State Sanatorium (Pittsford Mills), 289
Vermont State School of Agriculture (Randolph), 217
Vermont Sugar House (Cambridge), 263
*Vermont, The*, 47
Vermonters, 3–9
Vershire, 236
Vershire Center, 236
Victory, 333

Wainwright House (Middlebury), 114
Wait, Benjamin, 250
Wait, Joseph, Colonel, 290
Waite, Joseph, Captain, 174
Wait's Monument (North Clarendon), 290
Waitsfield, 250–51

Walden, 342
Warner Place (Jeffersonville), 345
Wallace, Richard, 172
Waller, Mary, 215
Wallingford, 291
Walloomsac Inn (Bennington), 92
Warner, Seth, 87, 90, 318
Warner Statue (Bennington), 94
Warner's Camping Ground, site of (Manchester), 296
Warren, 251, 266
Washington, 235
Washington County Courthouse (Montpelier), 121
Waterbury, 338
Waterbury Center, 249
Weather Bureau, U.S. (Northfield), 219
Weathersfield Bow, 166
Webb Estate (Shelburne), 282
Websterville, 228
Weeping Rock (North Pownal), 302
Welden, Jesse, 134
Wells, 320–21
Wells, Horace, 234
Wells River, 176
Wells River Valley, 350
Wentworth, Bennington, Governor, 22–23
West Arlington, 298
West Barnet, 177
West Branch, 260
West Brattleboro, 366
West Bridgewater, 359
West Brookfield, 218
West Burke, 181
West Charleston, 201–02
West Danville, 335, 342
West Dummerston, 186
West Enosburg, 192
West Hartford, 234
West Haven, 314
West Lincoln, 266
West Rupert, 322
West Rutland, 129, 361–62
West Townshend, 189
West Woodstock, 358
Westfield, 244
Westminster, 163
Westminster Massacre, 163–64 (see History)
Westminster Station, 165
Westmore, 203–04
Weston, 330
Weston Playhouse (Weston), 330
Wheeler, William C., 223
Wheelock, 240
Wheelock House (Barre), 80
Wheelock, John, 240
Whetstone factory (Evansville), 202
Whipping post, site of (Cabot), 336

White House (Essex), 349
White River Junction, 169–70
White Rocks (Wallingford), 292
Whitelaw, James, 177
Whiting, 316–17
Whitingham, 367
Widow's Clearing (Bread Loaf), 273–74
Wilcox House (Orwell), 314 (see Architecture)
Wild Boar Fountain (Lyndon Center), 181
William Hall, the, 82
Williams, John, Reverend, 84, 258
Williams, Samuel, Reverend, 128
Williams Science Hall (see University of Vermont)
Williamstown, 229
Williamstown Gulf, 229
Williamstown Gulf Road, 227–28
Williston, 341
Willoughby, 182
Willoughby Falls, 184
Wilmington, 367
Wilson, Stanley C., 235
Winchester, Oliver, Governor, 148
Windham County Courthouse (Newfane) (see Architecture)
Windmill Point, 303
Windsor, 146–51
Windsor County Courthouse (Woodstock), 155
Windsor County Fair, 153
Winooski, 280
Winooski River Gorge (Essex), 349
Winooski Valley (Montpelier), 337
Winter Rearing Pool (West Branch), 260
Wolcott, 344
Wood Gallery of Art (see Art)
Wood, Enos, 306
Wood, Thomas Waterman, 120
Woodbury, 223
Woodbury Antique Shop (Woodbury), 223
Woodford, 369
Woodstock, 151–55, 214
Woodstock Green, 152
Woodstock Inn Golf Course (South Woodstock), 214
Woodstock Railroad, 357–58
Woodstock Ski Hill, 214
Woodstock Ski Jump, 214
Woodward Reservoir Dam, 253
World War (see History)
Wright House (Montpelier), 122
Wrightsville Dam (Montpelier), 121
Writers' Summer School and Conference (Breadloaf), 73

Young, Thomas, Dr., 26
Youth Hostel Movement (see Recreation)
Youth Victorious (Barre), 80

Lightning Source UK Ltd.
Milton Keynes UK
UKHW011129260420
362298UK00002B/260